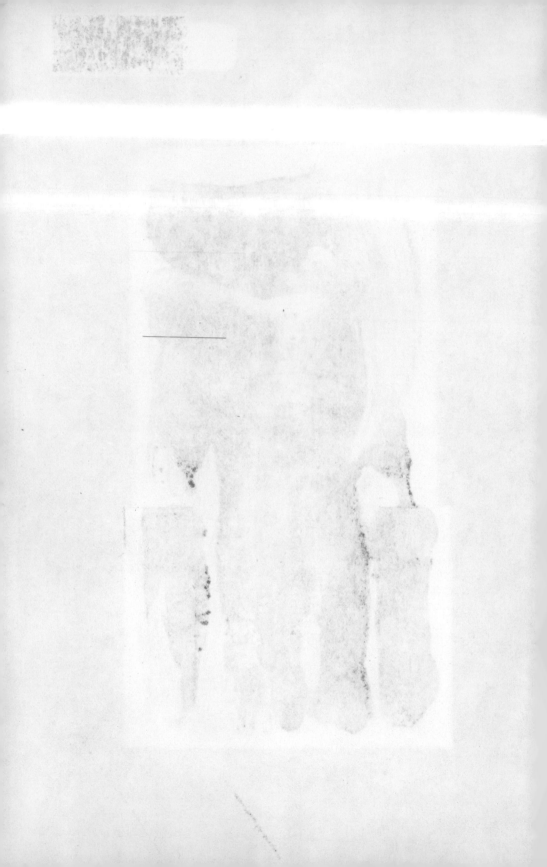

THE BIOLOGY OF ALCOHOLISM

Volume 2: Physiology and Behavior

THE BIOLOGY OF ALCOHOLISM

THE BIOLOGY OF ALCOHOLISM

Volume 2: Physiology and Behavior

Edited by

Benjamin Kissin and Henri Begleiter

Division of Alcoholism and Drug Dependence
Department of Psychiatry
State University of New York
Downstate Medical Center
Brooklyn, New York

Ⴒ PLENUM PRESS • NEW YORK–LONDON • 1972

First Printing — February 1972
Second Printing — August 1973

Library of Congress Catalog Card Number 74-131883

ISBN 0-306-37112-X

© 1972 Plenum Press, New York
A Division of Plenum Publishing Corporation
227 West 17th Street, New York, N.Y. 10011

United Kingdom edition published by Plenum Press, London
A Division of Plenum Publishing Company, Ltd.
Davis House (4th Floor), 8 Scrubs Lane, Harlesden, NW10 6SE, London, England

Contributors to This Volume

Nicholas P. Armenti, *The Center of Alcohol Studies and Department of Psychology, Rutgers University, The State University of New Jersey, New Brunswick, New Jersey*

James D. Beard, *Alcohol Research Center, Tennessee Psychiatric Hospital and Institute, Department of Physiology and Biophysics, University of Tennessee College of Basic Medical Sciences, Memphis, Tennessee*

Henri Begleiter, *Department of Psychiatry, State University of New York, Downstate Medical Center, Brooklyn, New York*

David A. Callison, *Thudichum Psychiatric Research Laboratory, Galesburg State Research Hospital, Galesburg, Illinois*

John A. Carpenter, *The Center of Alcohol Studies and Department of Psychology, Rutgers University, The State University of New Jersey, New Brunswick, New Jersey*

F. L. Fitz-Gerald, *Miama, Florida*

Ricardo Garcia-Mullin, *Department of Neurology, University of Maryland School of Medicine, Baltimore, Maryland*

Robert G. Grenell, *Professor and Director, Division of Neurobiology, Psychiatric Institute, University of Maryland, Baltimore, Maryland*

Harold E. Himwich, *Thudichum Psychiatric Research Laboratory, Galesburg State Research Hospital, Galesburg, Illinois*

David H. Knott, *Alcoholism Treatment Center, Tennessee Psychiatric Hospital and Institute, Departments of Physiology and Biophysics and of Psychiatry, University of Tennessee College of Medicine, Memphis, Tennessee*

Richard F. Mayer, *Department of Neurology, University of Maryland School of Medicine, Baltimore, Maryland*

Nancy K. Mello, *Chief, Section on Comparative Neurobehavior, National Center for the Prevention and Control of Alcoholism, National Institute of Mental Health, Chevy Chase, Maryland*

R. D. Myers, *Laboratory of Neuropsychology, Purdue University, Lafayette, Indiana*

Paul Naitoh, *Navy Medical Neuropsychiatric Research Unit, San Diego, California*

Donald A. Overton, *Department of Psychiatry, Temple Medical Center, and Eastern Pennsylvania Psychiatric Institute, Philadelphia, Pennsylvania*

Arthur Platz, *Department of Psychiatry, State University of New York, Downstate Medical Center, Brooklyn, New York*

David A. Rodgers, *Department of Psychiatry, Cleveland Clinic, Cleveland, Ohio*

A. Salamy, *Department of Psychiatry and Behavioral Sciences, University of Oklahoma Medical Center, Oklahoma City, Oklahoma*

J. St.-Laurent, *Associate Professor of Psychiatry, School of Medicine, University of Sherbrooke, Canada*

W. L. Veale, *Laboratory of Neuropsychology, Purdue University, Lafayette, Indiana*

M. Vogel-Sprott, *University of Waterloo, Waterloo, Ontario, Canada*

H. L. Williams, *Department of Psychiatry and Behavioral Sciences, University of Oklahoma Medical Center, Oklahoma City, Oklahoma*

Preface

Alcoholism is a uniquely human condition. Although some forms of alcohol dependence can be induced experimentally in a variety of laboratory animals, the complete spectrum of alcoholism with all of its physical, psychological, and social implications occurs only in man. The special quality of this relationship becomes more significant when one considers that the manifestations of most physical disease syndromes in animals and man are more similar than they are different. The uniqueness of alcoholism lies in the fact that it is one of the few physical diseases which reflects at all levels the problems of individuals coping with the complexities of human society.

In order to present a more coherent picture of these complex relationships, we have attempted to impose a logical sequence upon the material. This sequence lies along a dual parameter—from the physical to the social and from the theoretical to the empirical. Consequently, it was natural for the first volume in this series to deal with biochemistry, the most basic and physical aspect of the interaction of alcohol and man. It is equally natural for this, the second volume, to deal with physiology and behavior, for these levels of phenomenology—particularly the latter—are already more empirical and psychological in their manifestations. Finally, the third volume, clinical pathology, describes the disease itself, with all of the medical and social implications carried in the word "alcoholism."

However, when we had completed the tables of contents for the first three volumes, we realized that we had omitted entirely a description of the impact of the disease alcoholism on society as a whole. This lack became so apparent that we have felt obliged to try to remedy it. Toward that end we have undertaken a fourth volume on social biology, to deal with the broad social consequences of alcoholism. The term "social biology" as it is used here does not, perhaps, connote the usual meaning, but it does signify the relationship of the social phenomenology of alcohol abuse to the fundamental underlying biological mechanism described in the earlier volumes. To this extent, it helps to complete the cycle. The addition of this fourth and last volume will contribute, we hope, to the accomplishment of our original goal—to present a comprehensive and definitive description of the complex interactions of the chemical substance alcohol with man and with human society.

The present volume is of special interest in that it relates physiology to behavior. It deals with the interaction of mechanisms at two different levels so that the sequence is sometimes less regular than in the earlier volume. However, we trust that the advantages of the interactional approach will compensate for the somewhat less rigorous logic in the presentation of the material.

Benjamin Kissin

New York City, November 1971   Henri Begleiter

Contents of Volume 2
Physiology and Behavior

Chapter 1

Effects of Alcohol on the Neuron
by Robert G. Grenell

Chapter 2

Peripheral Nerve and Muscle Disorders Associated with Alcoholism
by Richard F. Mayer and Ricardo Garcia-Mullin

Chapter 3

The Effects of Alcohol on Evoked Potentials of Various Parts of the Central Nervous System of the Cat

by Harold E. Himwich and David A. Callison

Chapter 4

Brain Centers of Reinforcement and Effects of Alcohol

by J. St.-Laurent

Chapter 5

Factors Underlying Differences in Alcohol Preference of Inbred Strains of Mice

by David A. Rogers

Chapter 6

The Determinants of Alcohol Preference in Animals

by R. D. Myers and W. L. Veale

Chapter 7

Voluntary Alcohol Consumption in Apes

by F. L. Fitz-Gerald

Chapter 8

**State-Dependent Learning Produced by Alcohol and Its
    Relevance to Alcoholism**

by Donald A. Overton

Chapter 11

Changes in Cardiovascular Activity as a Function of Alcohol Intake

by David H. Knott and James D. Beard

Chapter 12

The Effect of Alcohol on the Autonomic Nervous System of Humans: Psychophysiological Approach

by Paul Naitoh

Chapter 13

Alcohol and Sleep

by Harold L. Williams and A. Salamy

Chapter 14

Alcoholism and Learning

by M. Vogel-Sprott

Chapter 15

Some Behavioral Effects of Alcohol on Man

by J. A. Carpenter and N. P. Armenti

Contents of Volume 1
Biochemistry

Chapter 6

The Effect of Alcohol on Carbohydrate Metabolism: Carbohydrate Metabolism in Alcoholics
by Ronald A. Arky

Chapter 7

Protein, Nucleotide, and Porphyrin Metabolism
by James M. Orten and Vishwanath M. Sardesai

Chapter 8
Effects of Ethanol on Lipid, Uric Acid, Intermediary, and Drug Metabolism, Including the Pathogenesis of the Alcoholic Fatty Liver 263
by Charles S. Lieber, Emanuel Rubin, and Leonore M. DeCarli

Chapter 9
Biochemistry of Gastrointestinal and Liver Diseases in Alcoholism 307
by Carroll M. Leevy, Abdul Kerim Tanribilir, and Francis Smith

Chapter 14
Acute and Chronic Toxicity of Alcohol 437
by Samuel W. French

Chapter 15
Biochemical Mechanisms of Alcohol Addiction 513
by Jack H. Mendelson

Chapter 16
Methods for the Determination of Ethanol and Acetaldehyde 545
by Irving Sunshine and Nicholas Hodnett

Chapter 17
The Chemistry of Alcoholic Beverages 575
by Chauncey D. Leake and Milton Silverman

Contents of Volume 3
Clinical Pathology

Contents of Volume 4
Social Biology

THE BIOLOGY OF ALCOHOLISM

Volume 2: Physiology and Behavior

CHAPTER 1

Effects of Alcohol on the Neuron*

Robert G. Grenell

Professor and Director, Division of Neurobiology
Psychiatric Institute, University of Maryland
Baltimore, Maryland

INTRODUCTION

It should be made clear at once that the nature of the ensuing discussion is deliberately limited. Consideration of the effects of alcohols on cerebral neurons (or stated another way, cerebral effects of alcohols at the cellular and subcellular levels) necessitates taking a quite specific point of view. The latter is based on certain assumptions, some of which can be stated, as well as on the setting up of arbitrary limits or boundaries with regard to both data and theory (or, depending on the degree of libidinal investment, with regard to both fact and fancy). The limits are particularly obvious if the concept of "behavior" is involved; this is certainly the primary interest of psychiatrists and psychologists dealing with the use of alcohol consumed either occasionally or chronically. For present purposes, i.e., in the neurophysiologic or neurobiologic frame of reference, behavior is also a central issue, but in more than the usual sense. The neurophysiologist, in other words, hopes, in time, to understand the effects of alcohol

---

*This chapter was written in the spring of 1970.

1

on the total organism (alone and in its relationships to others), but focuses his investigative efforts on at least three suborders of behaviors:

1. Effects of alcohols on the integrated activity of the nervous system
2. Effects of alcohols on behavior of specific areas of the central nervous system
3. Effects of alcohols on behavior of the neuron (the functional unit of the nervous system) and its junctions with other neurons.

Thus, the ensuing discussion will largely be concerned with the effects of alcohols on the "behavior" of the neuron; to some extent as a theoretically isolated cell and to some extent in relation to a population of neurons.

It is assumed, of course, that this sort of consideration is rational and therefore has biological meaning. In any case, whether there is general agreement or not, it is stipulated for the present that examination of the structural and functional effects induced in neurons by alcohols is relevant to the more complex and broader problems of the organism's need, consumption, and addiction.

It will be assumed further that the general metabolic effects of alcohol in the organism, as described by classical biochemistry, are of no real significance insofar as the brain is concerned. This assumption is based on several points. Although Raskin and Sokoloff (1968) have demonstrated an alcohol dehydrogenase (of low activity) in brain, there appears to be no real evidence that alcohol is metabolized in the brain. Some question might relate to a primary cerebral effect of metabolically produced aldehydes. However, other than the specific effect of formaldehyde on retinal cells, the rapid breakdown of acetaldehyde would suggest that any primary effect on excitable tissue is unlikely. It is, of course, well established that the concentration of acetaldehyde necessary to produce mild pharmacological effects is many times higher than that found in the blood during severe alcoholic intoxication.

The effects on oxygen consumption do not explain the mechanism of action to any more satisfactory degree. There is no question but that high enough concentrations can severely depress oxygen consumption (e.g., Battey and Heyman reported a reduction in Q_{O_2} of 30% in human brain *in vivo* with a concentration of about 300 mg%). It is also apparent that these concentrations are much higher than those necessary to alter excitability (as well as those in the blood of individuals who are unquestionably "under the influence" of alcohol). Some confusion can be eliminated by careful consideration of the preparations on which various measurements have been carried out. Not only is there a fundamental difference between *in vivo* and *in vitro* studies, but in addition, the *in vitro* preparations vary from brain slices to brain homogenates to isolated particulate structures such as mitochondria. The inadequacy of data obtained in these ways may be reflected by the fact that numerous investigators have seen no significant decrease in oxygen uptake below a concentration of about 1 M ethyl alcohol (e.g., Levy, Levy, and Olszycka, 1940; Fuhrman and Field, 1948). It has been pointed out, moreover (Grenell, 1957), that more accurate measurements with the Warburg technique can be obtained if care is taken to prevent loss of alcohol by evaporation. When this is done, an approximately linear decline in Q_{O_2} with increasing concentrations of ethanol begins at about 0.5 M.

Wallgren and Kulonen (1960) state that Q_{O_2} of rat brain cortex slices is not only inhibited by 0.4% ethanol, but is increased by about 10%. The fact that inhibition is not seen in so many instances *in vitro* may also relate to the difference in activity between *in vivo* and *in vitro* preparations. It is not surprising that cut (as in slices) or broken (as in homogenate) cells, removed from normal connection with the rest of the brain, are not in a functional state which can reasonably be compared with the intact system. It has been demonstrated, however, that if neurons in slices are depolarized, so that in part they approach more nearly some of the conditions of active neurons *in vivo*, inhibition of oxygen consumption can be produced by ethanol in a concentration as low as 0.2% (Beer and Quastel, 1958; Lindholm and Wallgren, 1962). Larrabee *et al.* (1950) found that ethanol inhibits the extra ("stimulated") Q_{O_2} in the isolated superior cervical sympathetic ganglion in concentrations which have no effect on the resting rate.

Thus far, then, several important points have arisen:

1. The basic question, apparently, is *not* generalized inhibition of respiration. Unphysiologically high concentrations may inhibit Q_{O_2} both *in vivo* and *in vitro*. On the other hand, physiological concentrations applied under technically sound conditions may even stimulate. It will be seen that it becomes necessary to deal with the concept of thermodynamic activity.

2. Even if cell respiration is involved, the rate of oxygen consumption is *not* the primary factor to be dealt with. Oxidative processes may be involved in many ways without being reflected by a change in rate of oxygen consumption. This will be discussed further below, but it should be noted that some years ago Lee and McElroy observed that ethyl, butyl, and amyl alcohols exert a dissociating effect on the processes of oxidation and phosphorylation. The potency of inhibition of phosphate uptake by the alcohol series is parallel to the carbon chain length.

3. The increased Q_{O_2} produced in depolarized preparations by low concentrations of alcohol, and the relationship of increased Q_{O_2} to "activity" make it obvious that the role of the neuronal and synaptic membranes must be considered. In fact, there is sufficient evidence to warrant the suggestion that the primary action of the alcohols is on these membranes, and consequently on their molecular structure, the fluxes across them, the biochemical processes within them, and ultimately, through these to difficulty in the maintenance of normal cell structure and function. Although a complete and final explanation

of the detailed mechanism cannot yet be given, an impressive amount of data now available not only support the rationality of this approach, but make clear a surprisingly significant part of the basic process involved in axon, neuron, and synapse. Irresponsible statements must be disregarded, such as that by Mendelson (1968), who states, "A general consensus among many neurophysiologists and neurochemists is that ethanol acts upon membrane structure and function, a statement which at times reflects an evasive position for not being able to define a specific mechanism of action or effect."

It has been apparent that neither decreased absorption nor increased oxidation of alcohol seem to be the answer to the production of tolerance to it. The altered response of the individual can be explained thus far only by the suggestion of physicochemical changes in neurons, associated with their excitability cycle. Action currents develop subsequent to changes in structural orientation at the neuron surface. The electrochemical processes involved are self-limiting and cyclic, being completed by cellular processes that restore the original excitable state. The molecular arrangements in the resting cell that are capable of such a transition from one state to another have been referred to as a metastable structure (Brink, 1951) in contrast to the excitable structure. The metastable structure responds to certain stimuli and controls ionic fluxes which give rise to potential changes. The stability of the membrane would depend on the molecular organization of this structure, and consequently, one would propose that the initial, fundamental effects of alcohols would be at this locus.

It will be seen that this type of mechanism is not entirely specific for alcohols, but appears to hold true for general depressants, anesthetics, sedatives, and narcotics. As a result, the discussion will begin with some consideration of general factors relevant to the activity of such molecules.

THE PHENOMENOLOGY OF PHYSIOLOGICAL DEPRESSION

Basic Theory of Depressant Molecular Action

It is to be considered then, that all narcotics, among which alcohols are included, act primarily on a membrane phase. The simplest general definition of narcosis (as stated by Mullins, 1954) depicts it as any reversible decrease in physiological function induced by physical or chemical agents. The definition might be improved by including the inevitable shift to the decreased functional state from a prior induced stimulatory phase. It is highly improbable, for example, particularly in relation to molecules such as the alcohols, that all areas of the brain are depressed simultaneously. Many of the effects observed could be associated with activation of cell groups with or without simultaneous depression of others. An example of such a situation is presented by the comparison of the activation of inhibition with the activated release of inhibition in a synaptic network, and direct neuronal hyperpolarization consequent to a specific ionic or molecular effect. This, of course, raises the issue of differences in action on axon, soma, and synapse. Despite the fact that these present certain differences in sensitivity and reaction to various molecules, presumably related to their individual complexity of structure and function, there are a number of physico-chemical factors common to the fundamental relationship between the potentially active molecule and these neural elements. A highly illuminating, critical review of such physical factors can be found in the classical presentation of Mullins (1954). The following part of the discussion is largely quoted from his work.

Narcosis can be produced with or without depolarization. The latter can be produced in any of three ways: first, by interfering in some way with the oxidative metabolism of the synthetic center producing new membrane; second, by removing membrane faster than it can be replaced; and third, by abolishing the potassium ion gradient across the membrane and hence the potential. Cyanide or anoxia work in the first way; ether (>0.5 M) and alcohols depolarize in the second way.

Earlier in this discussion the problem of concentration arose. The concentration of relevance, namely the thermodynamic measure of concentration, is one at which an equal number of molecules are "effective" at any given time. Thus 1 mM butanol and 14.3 mM ethanol have the same "effective" concentration. The cause for this difference in aqueous concentrations is merely that the solvent water has interacted with so many more of the ethanol molecules that they are no longer "effective." This concentration, the thermodynamic activity, is estimated as P_{nar}/p^0, where P_{nar} is the partial pressure of the narcotic in a solution that just causes narcosis and p^0 is the vapor pressure of the pure liquid. If a substance similar to the narcotic is used as a solvent, their interaction will be minimal and Raoult's law will hold, so that $P_{nar}/p^0 \cong A_{nar} \cong X_{nar}$; the activity of the narcotic will equal its mole fraction, where X is the number of moles of narcotic divided by the total number of moles of narcotic plus solvent. In the case of water, this substance is so different physically from all common narcotics that marked deviations from Raoult's law are the rule. These deviations are expressed as an activity coefficient $\gamma = A/X$; the more positive the deviation the greater the value of the coefficient γ. For dilute solutions (low mole fractions) the limiting slope of the curve is taken to obtain the activity coefficient at infinite dilution (γ_∞). Since studies in narcosis usually involve mole fractions <0.1, γ_∞ is usually the more useful value.

If narcosis can be demonstrated to take place at constant thermodynamic activity of the narcotizing molecules, this means that since

$$A_{nar} = f_{nar}/f^0 \cong P_{nar}/P^0$$

(where A_{nar} is the thermodynamic activity for narcosis; f_{nar} is the fugacity ($\cong$ vapor pressure) for narcosis; f^0 is the fugacity of narcotic in some standard state; and the p values are respective partial pressures for narcosis and for the pure narcotic), any substance ought to be narcotizing at some constant fraction of its own vapor pressure.

The introduction of the idea of thermodynamic activity gives, as a first approximation, a constancy of the data from substance to substance.

In the present instance the major interest lies in the application of such principles to the action of molecules in neuron membranes, the latter being considered to some degree as a lipid solvent. Diamond and Wright (1969) have calculated the changes which the principal substituent groups produce in the partial molar free energies (and, where possible, enthalpies and entropies separately) of interaction between nonelectrolytes and either water or lipids. These incremental thermodynamic quantities indicate to what extent the nonelectrolyte selectivity of a membrane is due to differences between various solutes relative to their solute–water forces or solute–membrane forces. They derived the following expression relating lipid–water partition coefficients (K's) to thermodynamic properties:

$$K = e^{-\Delta F_{w \to l}/RT} = e^{-(\Delta H_{w \to l} - T\Delta S_{w \to l})/RT}$$

where $\Delta F_{w \to l}$ is the free energy change in transferring one mole of solute from water to lipid solvent (or cell membrane); $\Delta H_{w \to l}$ and $\Delta S_{w \to l}$ are the corresponding partial molar enthalpy and entropy changes, R is the gas constant, and T the absolute temperature ($RT = 592$ cal/mole at 25°C). Fitting this equation into several systems and making some additional assumptions and calculations resulted in the following conclusions:

Solute–water forces are much stronger than solute–lipid solvent (or solute–membrane) forces for nonelectrolyte substituent groups. In this sense the common tendency to view permeability as controlled by "lipid solubility" represents a basic misinterpretation of the observed fact that permeability correlates with lipid–water partition coefficients. Most substituents decrease permeating power because they increase the energy required to tear the solute loose from water and despite the fact that they also increase solute–lipid attraction. Thus, explanations for qualitative selectivity patterns of biological membranes must be sought largely in terms of the physical chemistry of aqueous solutions.

Branched molecules are less permeant. Further, small polar solutes permeate more rapidly than they would through a bulk lipid phase; the interpretation supported by several lines of evidence is that some predominantly polar regions in the membrane provide a parallel permeation pathway that bypasses membrane lipids. Analysis of incremental free energies of solution in water, bulk lipids, or membranes associated with specific functional groups shows that the main pattern of selectivity is largely due to differences in water-solute intermolecular forces; the stronger these forces, the lower the solute's permeating power. The most important contributing forces are hydrogen bonds, modification of hydrogen bonding by inductive effects and intramolecular bonds, van der Waals forces in membrane lipids, and entropy effects in hydrocarbon-water interactions. Main-pattern permeability differences between different biological membranes are principally determined by the ratio of hydrogen-bonding groups to $-CH_2-$ groups in the membrane interior, and by whether these hydrogen-bonding groups are proton donors or proton acceptors. Such considerations relate interestingly to alcohol molecules in several ways. $-OH$ acts both as a proton donor and as a proton acceptor. Oxygen in most alcohols can probably accept no more than one proton, so that the total number of H bonds formed by the alcoholic $-OH$ group is estimated as two. Studies on K's of bulk lipid solvents suggest that the molecular parameter governing quantitative differences in ranges of selectivity of different cell types is the ratio of hydrogen-bonding groups to $-CH_2-$ groups in the membrane interior; the lower this ratio, the lower are the values of ΔF_l, the larger is $(-\Delta F_w + \Delta F_l)$, and hence the higher are the magnitudes of selectivity. The reason is that hydrogen-bond energies are considerably stronger than van der Waals attractions to hydrocarbons, so that solvent hydrogen-bonding groups in a predominantly lipid phase markedly increase solute–lipid forces and ΔF_l's. Analysis of Collander's studies of monohydroxy alcohols of varying chain length as solvents shows that the $-OH$ group decreases K's on the average by 5.2 times in C_4H_9OH, 7.2 times in $C_5H_{11}OH$, 8.5 times in $C_8H_{17}OH$ and 14.7 times in $C_{10}H_{35}OH$. The magnitude of selectivity increases with increasing chain length of solvent, if the solvent is an aliphatic alcohol.

Pharmacological evidence shows that the molecular volume and solubility parameter are important in predicting the action of depressant molecules. These are involved in calculating the activity coefficients to be shown by narcotics as we ascend a homologous series. The expression used by Mullins to estimate activity coefficients for narcotic molecules in the membrane is:

$$l_n\gamma_{nar} = V_m(\delta_{nar} - \delta_{mem})^2/RT$$

where δ_{mem} is the membrane solubility parameter, or cohesive energy density, and V_{mem} is the molal volume. Figure 1 shows the results of calculations of the activity coefficients of molecules in the membrane, made on the basis of assigning an arbitrary, but constant, value for the solubility parameter of the membrane and taking the values of δ and V_m for the various alcohols. The curve for activity coefficient vs. chain length rises steeply as the homologous series is ascended. Although the mole fraction of narcotic in the membrane (X_{nar}) can be calculated, Mullins suggests it would seem more likely that the volume fraction would cause narcosis. The membrane acceptance for a molecule depends upon its

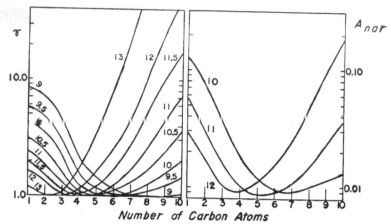

FIGURE 1. On the left the activity coefficients for the homologous series of normal alcohols are plotted *vs.* the number of carbon atoms in the chain. The numbers on the various curves designate various values of the solubility parameter of the solvent (membrane). On the right the activity threshold for narcosis to be expected in a homologous series of normal alcohols is plotted *vs.* chain length. The curves are calculated on the basis that the mole fraction for narcosis is 0.01 for the lowest member of a homologous series where $\gamma = 1.0$. For $\delta = 12$ this was at 1-propanol; for $\delta = 11$, at 1-butanol; etc. [Taken from Mullins (1954).]

having a δ and V appropriate to the space in the membrane to be occupied. The cessation of physiological activity above a certain chain length in a homologous series of compounds presumably occurs as a result of large difference in δ between membrane and narcotic, and of increases in V_m. In the case of the alcohols, the mole fraction required in the membrane for narcosis (X_{nar}) appears to be about 0.01 for both synaptic and nonsynaptic membranes, when V_m for the narcotic is 100 ml/mole. Hence $X_{nar}V_m$ is 1 ml/mole, or approximately the magnitude of the "free" volume in hydrogen-bonded liquids. If the V_m of the membrane is taken arbitrarily as 300 ml/mole, then the volume fraction for narcosis $\phi_{nar} = 0.003$. Alcohols can occlude free space in the membrane very efficiently. Effects of this will be discussed below.

It is of interest that concerning the mechanism of action of narcotics, Mullins has concluded:

> In the case of excitable structures ... it becomes less and less likely that a proposal of enzymatic inhibition can be supported by experimental data if by enzyme one means a protein structure made up solely of amino acids. Such an enzyme will have a structure totally unlike the phase to which narcotics can be shown to be partitioned. If the enzyme is modified by its being encased in a lipoidal envelope, it is conceivable that access of substrate to enzyme could be impeded by a narcotic. In this case the problem of whether narcosis is "physical" or "chemical" becomes one mainly of semantics.

In general then, it appears that the Ferguson principle of equal degrees of anesthesia at equal thermodynamic activities of the narcotic (or in Mullins' terms, equal degrees of anesthesia when the volume fraction of anesthetic in the phase where it acts is a constant) is a reasonable rule for judging the effectiveness of a substance as an anesthetic at a particular concentration. We have seen that the concentration rises as the molecules of an anesthetic become larger than about four carbon atoms. It can be stated then that narcotic molecules associate reversibly with some cell site; that large molecules are kept out because of size limitations (and so are not effective). The latter consideration makes it unlikely (and so the evidence shows) that oil is a reasonable model for the membrane site. In fact, the Meyer-Overton hypothesis does not hold up and lipid solubility becomes an inadequate explanation for the basic mechanism involved in anesthetic action. This has been pointed out most recently by Mullins (1968) and Kwan and Trevor (1969). The latter, studying the association of xenon with subcellular components of rat cerebral cortex, observed that the affinity of xenon for such particulate fractions exceeds that predicted from estimations of solubility in aqueous and lipid constituents. Such inert gases are of particular interest because of their inability to enter into ionic, covalent, or hydrogen bonding under physiological conditions (Featherstone and Muehlbaecher, 1966). There is good evidence that London interactions are the major source of energy for their binding to protein (Schoenborn and Nobbs, 1966). Xenon association with certain proteins is clear (Schoenborn and Featherstone, 1967). In fact, whether or not Pauling's (1961) suggestion of clathrate formation is valid, there appears to be slowly accumulating support for the concept of binding of narcotic molecules to membrane protein, possibly by the displacement of bound water. Initial evidence of this nature is to be inferred from microwave studies (McCulloch and Grenell, to be published). As pointed out by Kwan and Trevor, "It is reasonable to conclude that considerations of anesthetic action purely in terms of solubility in lipid materials of neural tissue are unnecessarily restrictive." Mullins (1968) also states that, "the protein crystal is a satisfactory model of anesthetic action, excluding, as it does, molecules of large size while accepting readily molecules of small size."

Alcohols as Depressant Molecules

The alcohols have been most widely used for the study of narcosis, despite their complex behavior in solution. Studies of solubility for the pure liquid narcotic in water (a highly polar solvent) have shown no apparent difference in the water solubility of the ketones, acids, alcohols, and ethers. If comparison is made at unit vapor pressure, however, the compounds fall in the order of their polarity: acids most soluble, followed by alcohols, ketones, and ethers in that order.

TABLE 1. Thermodynamic Activity Coefficients for Solutions of Alcohols in Water and in Benzene at 25°C[a]

Substance	γH_2O	γC_6H_6	Partition coefficients	
			$\gamma H_2O/\gamma C_6H_6$	$\gamma C_6H_6/\gamma H_2O$
Methanol	1.51	21.4	0.07	14.3
Ethanol	3.60	16.4	0.22	1.1
1-Propanol	14.4	15.1	0.96	1.0
1-Butanol	52.9	14.2	3.73	0.3

[a] Taken from Mullins (1954).

The change of activity of ethanol with mole fraction in a hydrocarbon demonstrates the behavior of polar–nonpolar mixtures. Activity coefficients for dilute solutions of alcohols in benzene show (Table 1) that if paraffins are used as a model of the phase to which narcotics are to be partitioned (Mullins, 1954), the alcohols will require about ten times as much mole fraction in the aqueous phase for a given mole fraction in the nonaqueous phase, when compared with nonassociated liquids.

When the lower alcohols are delivered to the intact organism as vapors, a nonequilibrium condition may be obtained, because of their very low vapor pressures relative to their molecular volume, and the relatively high aqueous mole fractions that must be reached in the blood in order for narcosis to ensue. Since the blood alcohol is being metabolized, vapors can be supplied with an A_{nar} much higher than the values obtained in the tissues. Methanol and ethanol are depolarizing agents which can interact with proteins, and in relatively high concentrations dehydrate and denature them. Mullins has suggested that the special toxicity of methanol to the retina might relate to its being a strong depolarizer at concentrations far below the narcotic level.

It should be pointed out that all considerations of the action and effects of beverage alcohols are complicated by the presence of a variety of so-called congeners. Among these are numerous aldehydes, ketones, fusel oils, etc.; little is known about the toxicity of these congeners.

It is to be presumed that some biochemical factors are involved in the neuronal effects of alcohol, once the latter has entered the membranes. It is not unlikely that the phospholipid and protein substances of the membrane which enter into the reaction with alcohol molecules are ATP and ATPase. Local concentrations of aliphatic alcohols equivalent to those inducing narcosis in the whole organism do not block oxidative phosphorylation in brain slices (Truitt et al., 1956). However, ethanol does block the incorporation of glycine —^{14}C by brain slices of rats, suggesting that ATP formation or utilization is inhibited (Quastel, 1959). Wallgren (1963) reported that 0.4% ethanol reduced by 50%

the rate of CrP (creatine phosphate) breakdown induced by electrical stimulation in rat brain cortex slices, and almost completely abolished the "stimulated" turnover of the terminal phosphate of ATP. In the absence of stimulation ethanol did not alter the steady-state level of CrP, ATP, ADP, or AMP. This sort of data strongly indicate that the alcohol does not interfere with the general metabolism of the brain, but inhibits activity localized in the membrane; activity which, it will be seen, is concerned with maintenance of ion concentration, conductance and transport, and thus with the production of the action potential. The alcohol (or other anesthetic) interference appears to be with the utilization rather than the synthesis of ATP (Mendelson and Grenell, 1954; Grenell *et al.*, 1955; Wiener, 1961; Williams *et al.*, 1968).

If consideration is given to the model proposed by Abood (1966, 1969) some interesting interrelationships appear. The functional unit of the excitatory membrane he considers is comprised of a Ca^{2+} complex with a phospholipid, ATP, and a protein, possibly ATPase, as follows:

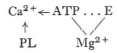

where PL is phospholipid, E a Mg^{2+}-activated enzyme (ATPase), and the arrows symbolize chelation with the respective divalent metals. According to his theory, depolarization, by promoting cleavage of the Ca^{2+}-ligand bonds, results in dissociation of the complex with release and hydrolysis of ATP. Abood discusses some of the relevant problems in detail. For present purposes, however, it is of particular interest in dealing with effects of alcohol to note the possible relationship of the membrane energy system to the presence of Ca^{2+} as a regulating ion. The reason for this will become more apparent further on, but it is important to note that the role of Ca^{2+} is tied directly to that of Na^{+}, and thus to K^{+}. Baker *et al.* (1969) report that both ethanol (1%, v/v) and isobutanol (60 mM) decreased Na^{+} efflux from squid giant axon into 10 K (Na^{+})-ASW (an artificial sea water in which the major cation is Na^{+}, the major anion is chloride, and the potassium concentration is 10 mM). The effect due to ethanol was small and isobutanol was used for investigation. Isobutanol reversibly reduced the Na^{+} efflux into 10 K (Na^{+})-ASW both before and after addition of 10^{-5} M ouabain, indicating reduction of both the ouabain-sensitive and ouabain-insensitive components of the Na^{+} efflux. It was shown earlier that there is a calcium-sensitive sodium efflux that is ouabain-insensitive. As stated by Baker *et al.* (1969), "Since the calcium influx seems to be linked to part of the sodium efflux, it is natural to suppose that part of the sodium influx might be coupled with calcium efflux." Alcohols are also known to exert an inhibitory action on both potassium transport and the isolated ($Na^{+} + K^{+}$)-activated ATPase (Israel *et al.*, 1966).

Numerous studies have dealt with these problems of effects of alcohol and anesthetics on Na^+ and K^+ stimulated ATPase.

Concentrations of 0.4–0.5% ethanol (high enough to inhibit about 40% of the extra oxygen consumption of electrical stimulation in brain slices) have been shown to inhibit to a significant degree the active K^+ transport in brain slices, red cells, and kidney slices, as well as that of Na^+ in isolated frog skin. Israel, Kalant, and Laufer (1965) have shown that K^+ in vivo counteracts the depressant effects of alcohol. A similar effect of low Ca^{2+} (Grenell, unpublished) will be discussed below.

Inhibitory effects of ethanol, diethyl ether, and halothane have also been shown on brain $(Na^+ + K^+)$-ATPase (Israel and Salazar, 1967; Ueda and Mietani, 1967). As Israel has pointed out, "the inhibitory effects of alcohol on the active transport of $(Na^+ + K^+)$-ATPase seem adequate to explain the inhibitory effect of ethanol on stimulated respiration, creatine phosphate breakdown and ATP turnover in stimulated brain cortex slices." It is important to note that reference was made to the *extra* Q_{O_2} of activity. This says nothing relative to any effect in the "resting" (i.e., nonstimulated) state. In a study of the effects of phenobarbital, however, McIlwain (1953) showed that concentrations equal to the anesthetic level inhibit the extra Q_{O_2} of activity of brain slices without any effect on the resting rate. Indeed, Larrabee *et al.* (1952) reported that ganglionic transmission is depressed markedly by narcotic concentrations which do not affect the Q_{O_2} at all. [For a discussion of this problem see Grenell, Mendelson, and McElroy (1955).] It may be added further that such effects obviously must result in abnormal brain function, and presumably in behavior. A measure of this, of course, would be reflected by the alterations of observable cerebral electrical activity and its correlates. Several interesting studies relate to this problem.

Two investigations of primary interest are those of Moore *et al.* (1964) and Armstrong and Binstock (1964). Using the voltage clamp technique in the squid giant axon, both groups demonstrated inhibition by alcohol of the maximum Na^+ and K^+ conductances basic to the production of the action potential. Although there appear to be some differences between the two studies, there is no doubt that the alcohol (as do many anesthetics) interferes markedly with the normal events going on within and across the membrane. Other reports substantiate this basic point. Grenell (1957) briefly discussed the evidence for the fact that alcohol and other "narcotics" in concentrations lower than that necessary to induce narcosis act to produce stimulation of neural structures. Data of this nature were reported previously for narcotics by Graham (1929), Arvanitaki and Chalazonitis (1951), and Hensel and Zotterman (1951). Excitation of evoked cortical responses is evident in cats after i.v. injection of low concentrations of methyl, ethyl, propyl, and butyl alcohols, as shown in Table 2 (Grenell, 1959). In each case, excitation is produced by low concentration, while high

TABLE 2. Effects of Intravenously Administered Alcohols on Cortical Responses[a]

	Solution (%)	Dosage (mg/100 g)	Effect on cortical response
Methyl	0.5	3.8	—
	1.0	7.6	Excitation
	2.0	15.2	Excitation
	5.0	38	—
	10.0	76	Transitory depression
	20.0	152	Depression
Ethyl	0.5	3.9	Excitation
	1.0	7.8	Excitation
	2.0	15.6	—
	5.0	39	—
	10.0	78	Transitory depression
	20.0	146	Depression
	50.0	390	Depression
Propyl	0.5	4.0	—
	1.0	8.0	—
	2.5	20	Excitation
	5.0	40	Excitation
	10.0	80	Depression
	20.0	160	Depression
	40.0	320	Death
Butyl	0.5	4.05	—
	1.0	8.1	Excitation
	2.5	20.2	Excitation
	5.0	40.5	Depression
	10.0	81	Depression
	20.0	162	Death

[a] Taken from Grenell (1959).

concentration is followed by depression. It is of interest that Masserman (1940) and Masserman and Jacobson (1940) noted that the reactivity of the hypothalamus may be facilitated by ethyl alcohol after injection of small quantities, while larger amounts induce depressant effects. The excitability of the motor cortex could also be increased by the intraperitoneal injection of 1 ml of ethanol per kilogram of body weight.

Some data have shown that ethanol depolarizes sciatic nerve (Gallego, 1948). When a portion of frog nerve was exposed to ethanol solutions, the membrane potential decreased in proportion to the concentration. From analysis of the rate of depolarization in frog nerve as a function of the concentration of the depolarizing agent, Mullins and Gaffey (1954) suggested that such agents act by altering the interfacial tension between the fiber and its environment. Mullins (1954) points out that "such an alteration might facilitate the removal of material from the membrane, and depolarization would occur when this rate exceeded the synthetic capacity of the fiber to replace the lost material."

A good deal of evidence, therefore, supports the notion that alcohol can produce its neuronal effects by specific physical action in the membrane, associated with alterations in ion conductances and fluxes. Although most of the work has been concerned with Na^+ and K^+, there is good reason to believe that effects involving Ca^{2+} must be taken into account. Several things call Ca^{2+} to one's attention, not the least of which is the report of Frankenhaeuser and Hodgkin (1957), that the external calcium influences the movements of sodium and potassium through the membrane of squid axons; a reduction in the external calcium concentration increases the sodium and potassium currents associated with moderate depolarizations. There is a good deal of additional evidence to show that changes in external Ca^{2+} affect the membrane permeability to Na^+ and K^+. In general, decrease in the external $Ca^{2+} \rightarrow \uparrow P_{Na^+}$ (and to a lesser extent P_{K^+}), resulted in increased membrane conductance. The studies of Moore et al. (1964) and of Armstrong and Binstock (1964) both have demonstrated the production of a marked decrease in conductance by ethanol.

These data suggest the possibility that altering the external Ca^{2+} could alter the effects of ethanol. Such experiments have been carried out by Grenell (unpublished) using the local perfusion technique (Davies and Grenell, 1962). Perfusing a small area of the suprasylvian gyrus of the cat cortex and recording the SCR (superficial cortical response), it was shown that 0.5 mM EDTA (a chelating agent which binds Ca^{2+}) added to the perfusate completely blocked the depressant effects of 10 mM ethanol. With 2.5 mM ethanol, enhancement of the SCR is marked. If, however, the concentration of the ethanol is raised to 25 mM or higher, the effect of the Ca^{2+} binding (i.e., the effective reduction of external free Ca^{2+}) is overcome and marked depression of the evoked response occurs.

A general concept underlying such processes proposes the idea that Ca^{2+} controls membrane permeability by interacting with membrane structure. This is based on the proposition that Ca^{2+} can bind with a membrane component, and that the membrane permeability which determines the membrane potential is regulated by the concentration of the bound calcium. Thus, in the resting state, Ca^{2+} is assumed to be bound to an anionic site in the membrane, thereby controlling the movement of Na^+ and K^+ across the membrane. When the membrane is depolarized by a stimulating cathodal current, the bound Ca^{2+} is assumed to be removed, thereby increasing membrane permeability to monovalent cations. There is some experimental evidence supporting a dual action for calcium:

1. Regulation of the membrane potential by changing membrane permeability in resting and active states (the role of Ca^{2+} bound in the membrane)

2. Action as a charge carrier during the active state—the role of free Ca^{2+} in the external solution. An inward Ca^{2+} current during the active state is a function of the external Ca^{2+} concentration.

To relate such mechanisms to membrane structure in a broader sense, Abood, as mentioned above, has suggested that the functional component of such an excitable membrane is formed of a Ca^{2+} complex with a phospholipid, ATP, and a protein, possibly ATPase.

$$Ca^{2+} \leftarrow ATP \ldots E$$
$$\uparrow \qquad \diagdown \diagup$$
$$PL \qquad Mg^{2+}$$

where E stands for the Mg^{2+}-activated enzyme, PL for phospholipid, and arrows symbolize chelation.

On electrical depolarization, there would result,

$$[Ca^{2+} \leftarrow PL] + [Mg^{2+} \leftarrow E] + ADP + P_i$$

Reentry of an ATP molecule, or rephosphorylation of ADP by an intermediate form of E would lead to reconstruction of the complex and repolarization. There is evidence that Ca^{2+} binds to protein.

It appears, then, that it is not only reasonable, but in agreement with numerous theoretical considerations and experimental observations to hold that alcohol exerts its primary action in the brain at the cellular level, and in particular on the excitable membrane, its permeability and the ion fluxes across it. It is possible, moreover, to go a step further by way of proposing a mechanism through which alcohol can influence information processing. In other words, there is a good deal of support for the notion that synaptic transmission can be interfered with, and the "balance" between central excitation and inhibition shifted. These changes presumably are effected by a relationship between the membrane events discussed above and the release of neurohumors such as acetylcholine at the synapses.

Many relevant observations have been made involving alcohol effects on neuromuscular transmission and muscle contraction. Although ethanol does affect acetylcholine release, in what are considered to be low concentrations (e.g., around 1%) for muscle, it has no effect on cholinesterase activity (Kalant et al., 1967). In even lower concentrations, release of an increased number of packets of ACh occurs at the neuromuscular junction without modification of the M.e.p.p. amplitude. Higher concentrations induce both pre- and postsynaptic effects. It has, however, been observed in brain slices that 0.5% ethanol depressed spontaneous liberation of acetylcholine. This is of great interest in the light of the fact that decreasing external Ca^{2+} in the brain overcomes the depressant effect of alcohol, and also causes the release of acetyl choline (Grenell and Romero, to be published). In fact, it would appear that under circumstances where there is an influx of Ca^{2+} into the cell, so that internal Ca^{2+} is higher than external, such a release of acetylcholine occurs.

The fundamental importance of calcium to the release of ACh is well established. Katz (1962) has discussed this relative to the general problem of activation in excitable cells. He states: "The importance of calcium ions in the process of transmitter release is not an isolated instance: it is to some extent analogous to the role which calcium ions appear to play in the initiation of a nerve impulse, and in the activation of muscular contraction. In all these cases depolarization of the cell membrane is a necessary, but not a sufficient condition for its subsequent effect. The presence of calcium ions or of some calcium compound within the membrane seems to be required for a membrane depolarization to produce its effect, whether the specific result is an increase of sodium permeability, the release of transmitter, or the activation of contraction. It may be that in all these cases the primary action of the electric potential change is to displace calcium ions, or a charged calcium compound within the membrane."

Birks (1963) suggests that the presence of sodium in high concentration at the inner surface of the terminal membrane may also displace calcium, and that depolarization and sodium act at the same site. "This is possible to envisage if one considers the site from which calcium is displaced as anionic. In these terms depolarization might liberate calcium by changing the charge distribution on the anion, and sodium by competing with calcium for combination with it." He goes on to imply that a sodium-calcium relationship may be involved in ACh synthesis, promoting action of Na^+. "It is interesting that evidence has been obtained recently to suggest that the transport of amino acids into nerve cells involves a calcium-dependent process. Perhaps it is not unreasonable to imagine that sodium may activate ACh synthesis, as well as ACh release, by displacing calcium from within the membrane."

Although unequivocal data relative to the effect of alcohol on ACh release in the brain still remain to be demonstrated, and much more work must be done to make clear not only this relationship, but that of alcohol to catecholamine release and uptake, a number of points are more than suggestive at the present time. These can be summarized briefly.

SUMMARY

Present evidence indicates that the primary action of alcohol in the brain is on the neuronal and synaptic membranes.

It is indicated further that the only primary biochemical events of a "classical" nature relative to alcohol action in the brain occur within neuronal membranes. Ultimately, of course, associated intracellular biochemical changes are effected.

Neuronal activity is stimulated by low concentrations, and depressed by high concentrations of alcohols.

On the basis of thermodynamic and other biophysical considerations, it is suggested that the presence of alcohol in the membranes in effective concentration decreases membrane permeability and decreases ion conductances.

Calcium levels appear to exert an important regulatory effect on biophysical events in the membranes, and have been shown to affect the action of alcohol. Decrease of the external Ca^{2+} concentration has been demonstrated to prevent the depression of evoked potentials by alcohol; such a Ca^{2+} decrease also increases Na^+ and K^+ conductance. Calcium regulation is also involved in the release of acetylcholine at certain synapses. There is some evidence that alcohol acts to decrease acetylcholine release, an action, therefore, that may be reversed by controlling the relationship of the concentrations of internal and external calcium.

Effects of alcohol on the neuron membrane, ion fluxes across it, and molecular events within it, as well as effects on neurohumoral release, affecting synaptic transduction can be the fundamental events resulting in abnormal behavior.

REFERENCES

Abood, L. G., 1966. *Intern. Rev. Neurobiol.* **9**: 223.

Abood, L. G., 1969. Calcium–ATP–lipid interactions and their significance in the excitatory membrane, in *Neurosciences Research*, S. Ehrenpreis and O. C. Solnitzky, eds. Vol. 2, pp. 41–70, Academic Press, New York.

Armstrong, C. M. and Binstock, K., 1964. The effects of several alcohols on the properties of the squid giant axon, *J. Gen. Physiol.* **48**: 265–277.

Arvanitaki, A. and Chalazonitis, N. 1951. Effets narcotiques sur les bipotentiels neuroniques et sur la cataluse respiratorie, in *Mécanismes de la Narcose*, CNRS, Paris, France.

Baker, P. F., Blaustein, M. P., Keynes, R. D., Manil, J., Shaw, I. I., and Steinhardt, R. A., 1969. The ouabain-sensitive fluxes of sodium and potassium in squid giant axons, *J. Physiol.* **200**: 459–496.

Battey, L. L. and Heyman, H. 1953. Effects of ethyl alcohol on cerebral blood flow and metabolism, *JAMA* **152**: 6–10.

Beer, C. T. and Quastel, J. H., 1958. The effects of aliphatic alcohols on the respiration of rat brain cortex slices and rat mitochondria, *Canad. J. Biochem. Physiol.* **36**: 543–556.

Birks, R. I. 1963. The role of sodium ions in the metabolism of acetylcholine, *Canad. J. Biochem. Physiol.* **41**: 2573–2597.

Brink, F., 1951. in *Handbook of Experimental Psychology* (S. S. Stevens, ed.), Chapter 2. John Wiley and Sons, New York.

Davies, P. W. and Grenell, R. G., 1962. Metabolism and function in the cerebral cortex under local perfusion, with the aid of an oxygen cathode for measuring surface Q_{O_2}., *J. Neurophysiol.* **25**: 651.

Diamond, J. M. and Wright, E. M., 1969. Biological membranes: The physical basis of ion and nonelectrolyte selectivity, *Am. Rev. Physiol.* **31**: 581–646.

Featherstone, R. M. and Muehlbaecher, C. A., 1966. *Mol. Pharmacol.* **2**: 495.

Frankenhaeuser, B. and Hodgkin, A. L., 1957. The action of calcium on the electrical properties of squid axons, *J. Physiol.* (*London*) **137**: 218–244.

Gallego, A., 1948. On the effect of ethyl alcohol upon frog nerve, *J. Cell. Comp. Physiol.* **31**: 97–106.

Graham, H. T., 1929. The narcosis of muscle by gases, *J. Pharmacol. Exptl. Therap.* **37**: 9.

Grenell, R. G., Mendelson, J., and McElroy, W. D., 1955. Neuronal metabolism and ATP synthesis in narcosis, *J. Cell. Comp. Physiol.* **46**: 143–162.

Grenell, R. G., 1957. Some effects of alcohols on the central nervous system, in *Alcoholism* (H. Himwich, ed.) pp. 7–17 Pub. No. 47, Washington, D.C.

Grenell, R. G., 1959. Alcohols and activity of cerebral neurons, *Quart. J. Stud. Alc.* **20**: 421–427.

Grenell, R. G., unpublished.

Grenell, R. G. and Romero, E. G., to be published.

Hensel, H. and Zotterman, Y., 1951. Effect of menthol on the thermoreceptors, *Acta Physiol. Scand.* **24**: 27.

Israel, Y., Kalant, H., and Laufer, I., 1965. Effects of ethanol on Na^+–K^+–Mg^{++} stimulated microsonal ATPase activity, *Biochem. Pharmacol.* **14**: 1803–1814.

Israel, Y., Kalant, H., and LeBlanc, A. E., 1966. Effects of lower alcohols on potassium transport and microsomal ATPase activity of rat cerebral cortex, *Biochem. J.* **100**: 27–33.

Israel, Y. and Salazar, I., 1967. Inhibition of brain microsomal ATPases by general depressants, *Arch. Biochem. Biophys.* **122**: 310–316.

Kalant, H., Israel, Y., and Mahon, M. A., 1967. The effect of ethanol on acetylcholine synthesis released and degradation in the brain, *Canad. J. Physiol. Pharmacol.* **45**: 172–176.

Katz, B., 1962. *Proc. Roy. Soc. B.* **155**: 455.

Kwan, E. and Trevor, A., 1969. The association of xenon with subcellular components of rat cerebral cortex, *Mol. Pharmacol.* **5**: 236–243.

Larrabee, M. G., Garcia Ramos, J., and Bulbring, E., 1950. Do anesthetics depress nerve cells by depressing oxygen consumption? *Fed. Proc.* **9**: 75.

Larrabee, M. G., Garcia Ramos, J., and Bulbring, E., 1952. Effects of anesthetics on oxygen consumption and on synaptic transmission in sympathetic ganglia, *J. Cell. Comp. Physiol.* **40**: 461–494.

Lindholm, R. and Wallgren, H., 1962. Changes in respiration of rat brain cortex slices induced by some aliphatic alcohols, *Acta Pharm. Tox. Kbh.* **19**: 53–58.

Masserman, J. H. and Jacobson, L., 1940. Effects of ethyl alcohol on the cerebral cortex and the hypothalamus of the cat, *Arch. Neurol. Psychiat. Chic.* **43**: 334–340.

Masserman, J. H., 1940. Stimulant effects of ethyl alcohol in corticohypothalamic functions, *J. Pharmac.* **70**: 450–453.

Mendelson, J., 1968. Biochemical pharmacology of alcohol, *in Psychopharmacology* (D. H. Efron, ed.) pp. 769–786, Public Health Serv. Publication No. 1836, Washington, D.C.

Mendelson, J. and Grenell, R. G., 1954. Effects of narcotics on direct acetylation of sulfanilamide, *Science* **120**: 802–803.

Moore, J. W., Ulbricht, W., and Takata, M., 1964. Effect of ethanol on the sodium and potassium conductances of the squid axon membrane, *J. Gen. Physiol.* **48**: 279–295.

Mullins, L. J., 1954. Some physical mechanics in narcosis, *Chem. Rev.* **54**: 289–323.

Mullins, L. J., 1968. From molecules to membranes, *Fed. Proc.* **27**: 898–901.

Mullins, L. J. and Gaffey, C. T., 1954. *Proc. Soc. Exp. Biol. Med.* **85**: 44.

McCulloch, D. and Grenell, R. G., to be published; NASA reports, 1967–1969, Grant No. NGR 21-002-040, Office of Biosciences.

McIlwain, H., 1953. The effect of depressants on the metabolism of stimulated cerebral tissues, *Biochem. J.* **53**: 403–411.

Pauling, L., 1961. A molecular theory of general anesthesia, *Science* **134**: 15–21.

Quastel, J. H., 1959. Effect of aliphatic alcohols on the metabolism of brain and liver, *Quart J. Studies Alc.* **20**: 428.

Raskin, N. H. and Sokoloff, L., 1968. Brain alcohol dehydrogenase, *Science* **162**: 131

Schoenborn, B. P. and Nobbs, C. L. 1966. *Mol. Pharmacol.* **2**: 495.

Schoenborn, B. P. and Featherstone, R. M., 1967. *Advan. Pharmacol.* **5**: 1.

Truitt, E. B., Jr., Ball, F. K., and Krantz, J. C., Jr., 1956. Anesthesia L III. Effects of alcohols and aldehydes on oxidative phosphorylation in brain, *Quart. J. Studies Alc.* **17**: 594.

Ueda, I. and Mietani, U., 1967. Microsomal ATPase of rabbit brain and effects of general anesthetics., *Biochem. Pharmacol.* **16**: 1370–1374.

Wallgren, H. and Kulonen, E., 1960. Effect of ethanol on respiration of rat brain cortex slices, *Biochem. J.* **75**: 150–158.

Wallgren, H., 1963. Rapid changes in creatine and adenosine phosphates of cerebral cortex slices on electrical stimulation with special reference to the effect of ethanol, *J. Neurochem.* **10**: 349–358.

Wiener, N., 1961. The content of adenine nucleotides and creatine phosphate in brain of normal and anesthetized rats: a critical study of some factors influencing their assay, *J. Neurochem.* **7**: 241–250.

Williams, S., Paterson, R. A., and Health, H., 1968. The effects of B-B'-iminod: propionitrile and anesthesia on some adenine nucleotides of rat brain and retina, *J. Neurochem.* **15**: 227.

CHAPTER 2

Peripheral Nerve and Muscle Disorders Associated with Alcoholism

Richard F. Mayer* and Ricardo Garcia-Mullin†

Department of Neurology
University of Maryland School of Medicine
Baltimore, Maryland

INTRODUCTION

The occurrence of peripheral neuropathy is common in patients with chronic alcoholism (ethyl alcohol) and has been observed for many years (Lettsom, 1780; Jackson, 1822). Initially it was most frequently described in women (Jackson, 1822; Gowers, 1899), but subsequent reports indicate that it is as common (Victor and Adams, 1953) or even more common in men (Merritt, 1955; Mawdsley and Mayer, 1965). In the early reports, several clinical types were described,

---

*Professor, Department of Neurology. Supported in part by a grant from the Bressler Foundation.
†Special Fellow, National Institute of Neurological Diseases and Stroke, United States Public Health Service (2 F11 NB 1940-02 NSRA).

depending on which peripheral nerves were most involved (sensory or motor) and the disorder was related directly to the toxic effect of alcohol (Jackson, 1822; Dreschfeld, 1886). Subsequent observers related "alcoholic neuritis" to beriberi. With the knowledge that beriberi was a nutritional disorder, Shattuck (1928) related the polyneuropathy to vitamin B deficiency. Strauss (1935) provided additional information that the neuropathy in chronic alcoholism was not due to a neurotoxic effect of alcohol since ten such patients who consumed their daily supply of whiskey improved in the hospital on treatment consisting of a balanced diet and vitamins. Since then most authors have considered alcoholic polyneuropathy to be a nutritional deficiency disease (Victor and Adams, 1961). These patients invariably have a history of poor dietary intake and frequently show systemic evidence of nutritional deficiency. Many of these patients have other signs associated with chronic alcoholism and nutritional deficiency such as cirrhosis of the liver, anemia, Wernicke's encephalopathy (Phillips et al., 1952), and amblyopia (Victor et al., 1960). However, the exact mechanism by which nutritional-vitamin deficiency produces the neuropathy in chronic alcoholism has not been determined.

Although there has been considerable debate concerning the possibility that thiamine (vitamin B_1) is the antineuritic vitamin (Meiklejohn, 1940), thiamine deficiency has been reported to produce polyneuropathy in man (Williams et al., 1943). Deficiencies of other B vitamins such as pyridoxine (Vilter et al., 1953) or pantothenic acid (Bean et al., 1955) can also produce neuropathy in man. In chronic alcoholism, there most likely is a generalized nutritional deficiency and in some of these patients with neuropathy, there are deficiencies of many of the B vitamins, especially thiamine, pantothenic acid, nicotinic acid, and pyridoxine (Fennelly et al., 1964).

Although it has been known for many years that patients with chronic alcoholism can develop muscular weakness (Huss, 1849), the association of a myopathy with alcoholism has been a recent observation. Reports have described both acute and chronic weakness occurring in chronic alcoholism as a result of primary involvement of skeletal muscle (Hed et al., 1962; Ekbom et al., 1964; and Perkoff et al., 1966). These observers utilized clinical, electrophysiological, biochemical, and histological data to demonstrate that skeletal muscle dysfunction does occur in patients with chronic alcoholism. However, the exact cause of the myopathy is unknown, although both a toxic effect of ethanol and nutritional deficiency have been incriminated (Hed et al., 1962).

In the above introduction, it is apparent that clinicians have attempted to separate diseases of the peripheral nervous system (neuropathy) from those of skeletal muscle (myopathy). This appears necessary since the structure, metabolism, and function of these two tissues are quite different and, hence, the pathogenesis and treatment of diseases which affect these tissues should also be different.

Considerable information is now available concerning the ultrastructure, function, and biochemistry of peripheral nerve and muscle tissue, but it is not the purpose of this chapter to discuss these well-established observations. However, at this point, it does appear worthwhile to consider the relationship between peripheral nerve and muscle. In man as well as other mammals, the motor nerve fibers are part of the lower motor neuron and with the muscles are part of the motor unit (Sherrington, 1929), which consists of the motor nerve cell body (perikaryon or soma) in the spinal cord or brain stem, its peripheral axon (nerve fiber), the neuromuscular junctions at the nerve terminals, and a number of muscle fibers.

It has been known for some time that the soma of the neuron is the major source of macromolecular (especially protein) synthesis (Hydén, 1943) for the whole cell and that there is axoplasmic flow from the cell body to the periphery at the rate of approximately 1 mm per day (Weiss and Hiscoe, 1948). That the motor neuron has an effect ("trophic" function) on its muscle fibers has been well demonstrated in mammals both physiologically (Buller et al., 1960) and enzymatically (Romanul and Van der Meulen, 1967). Although the nature of the "trophic" function of the neuron is not completely known (Guth, 1969), the function and metabolism of the muscle fiber can be altered by changing its nerve supply. The muscle fibers in one motor unit have been demonstrated in rat (Edstrom and Kugelberg, 1968) and cat (Doyle and Mayer, 1969) to be histochemically of the same type, I, II, or intermediate. The fibers are not collected in one small area but scattered over a wide area, interdigitating with fibers of other units. Therefore, dysfunction in a few motor neurons can produce dysfunction over a diffuse area in a muscle. These relationships, although requiring additional study and definition, are important in understanding the pathophysiology of disease processes which affect peripheral nerve and muscle.

PERIPHERAL NERVE

Clinical Description

Alcoholic-nutritional polyneuropathy has been reported to be the most common type of polyneuropathy in large municipal hospitals (Merritt, 1955). It occurs most frequently in the fourth through seventh decades of life. The onset is usually insidious, with slow progression over months, but may progress rapidly over a few weeks. Involvement of peripheral nerve is generally bilateral, beginning in the lower extremities and progressing to involve the upper extremities. Although sensory symptoms may occur initially, both motor and sensory symptoms and signs occur in most patients. Occasionally only sensory or motor symptoms and/or signs occur.

The sensory symptoms are usually described as tingling, pricking, burning, or numb sensations and usually involve feet before fingers. Occasionally there are dull or sharp pains in foot and calf muscles, especially on walking. Tenderness in calf muscles on palpation is a common finding in alcoholic-nutritional polyneuropathy. The sensory symptoms are usually uncomfortable and frequently comprise the patient's chief complaint. Although the patient's skin over the feet and tibial areas may be atrophic and very sensitive to light touch or pinprick, a decrease in superficial sensation, pain, temperature, and light touch can usually be demonstrated with minimal stimuli. The sensory changes are usually present distal to the knees and wrists. It is unusual in these patients to demonstrate complete absence of superficial sensation.

As the sensory symptoms progress, motor signs usually occur and progress slowly over many weeks. These most frequently consist of weakness and atrophy involving the small foot, anterior tibial, peroneal, and calf muscles. Weakness of all these muscle groups produces a high steppage gait, while some patients develop a bilateral foot drop due to weakness of the anterior tibial and peroneal muscles. Although severe weakness has been reported to occur in some patients over several days, these cases most likely represent primary myopathy and will be discussed in the section on muscle disease. The tendon jerks (muscle stretch reflexes) are usually depressed. In the mixed sensorimotor neuropathy, the ankle and knee jerks are usually absent but the tendon jerks are usually present in the upper extremities. Some of the patients with mild signs may be asymptomatic.

In some patients who have relatively normal superficial sensation and motor power, there is a decrease in proprioceptive sensation so that the patients have difficulty with fine coordinated movements and walking. This "ataxic" form of polyneuropathy (Dreschfeld, 1886) does occur in chronic alcoholism but is more frequently seen in association with other diseases such as diabetes mellitus, hereditary sensory neuropathy, and carcinoma.

Since the nutritional deficiency which occurs in chronic alcoholism is generalized, the neuropathy is usually bilateral and symmetrical. However, focal nerve palsies (mononeuropathy) are also common in these patients. These most frequently consist of localized involvement of the common peroneal nerve at the head of the fibula, the radial nerve in the spiral groove in the arm, and the ulnar nerve at the elbow. Subclinical involvement of the segment of the ulnar nerve at the elbow has been reported by Mawdsley and Mayer (1965) utilizing electrophysiological techniques. These focal palsies are most likely related to pressure and ischemia (Mayer and Denny-Brown, 1964) and not related to the nutritional deficiency. However, since focal neuropathies occur quite frequently in patients with chronic alcoholism as well as in patients with other systemic diseases such as diabetes mellitus (Mulder et al., 1961; Mayer, 1963), it is possible that a generalized metabolic dysfunction, which involves peripheral nerves, makes the nerves more vulnerable to ischemia where they are superficial and readily compressed.

The diagnosis of alcoholic-nutritional polyneuropathy can usually be made from the history and physical findings. Most patients have been consuming alcohol for many years. Other signs of nutritional deficiency such as cheilosis, glossitis, hepatomegaly, dermatitis, and anemia are helpful in the diagnosis. Since the signs of the polyneuropathy are similar to those of other causes, further studies may be necessary in some patients to rule out diabetes mellitus, carcinoma, amyloidosis, toxic exposure, and biochemical abnormalities such as lipoprotein deficiencies. The spinal fluid examination is usually normal in alcoholic patients.

Electrophysiological studies are helpful in establishing that a polyneuropathy is present. These studies include the determination of nerve conduction velocities, repetitive and paired stimulation of nerve and muscle, electromyography, and reflex studies. Conduction velocities are usually decreased in peripheral nerves of patients with polyneuropathy while they are normal in patients with disease of either anterior horn cells or muscle (Lambert, 1960). The studies of nerve conduction velocities in alcoholic patients will be discussed in the next section. In patients with polyneuropathy there is no primary disorder of neuromuscular transmission, but in some, rapid repetitive (50 per second) stimulation of nerve with supramaximal stimuli may either enlarge or decrease the evoked compound muscle action potential. This reflects a dysfunction of the transmitter which may result secondary to degeneration of the nerve terminals. Electromyography (EMG) reveals evidence of denervation in the involved muscles in polyneuropathy. This is characterized by the presence of fibrillation potentials, positive sharp waves, and random fasciculations. The motor unit potentials (MUP) are frequently larger than normal (5 to 10 mV) and polyphasic in shape. These giant potentials result from reinnervation of muscle fibers secondary to peripheral sprouting of axons (Hoffman, 1950; Edds, 1950). Studies of the H reflex, which is the electrically induced monosynaptic reflex recorded in calf muscles, have shown that in polyneuropathy the response is either absent or the latency increased (Mayer and Mawdsley, 1965).

Nerve and muscle biopsies also provide evidence that a polyneuropathy exists and these studies may supply evidence of specific disease processes such as vasculitis, infection, tumor, or amyloidosis. However, in many types of neuropathy, including alcoholic-nutritional polyneuropathy, the histological changes in nerve do not indicate a specific etiology. The pathological description of nerve fibers in chronic alcoholics with polyneuropathy will be discussed below. Biopsies of involved muscle in patients with chronic alcoholism and polyneuropathy reveal the changes of neural atrophy. In the early (acute or subacute) stages of the neuropathy the muscle may show evidence of single fiber atrophy, while in the chronic stage group atrophy and grouping of muscle fibers of similar histochemical type (Karpati and Engel, 1968) is usually found. These changes can be distinguished from those occurring in primary disease of skeletal muscle.

Assays of B vitamins can be done in man and provide the crucial information as to whether the patient has specific vitamin deficiencies. However, these tests are difficult to perform and, at present, are not available in most laboratories for routine studies.

Studies of Nerve Conduction Velocities

With the development of electrophysiological techniques to measure conduction velocities in motor (Hodes et al., 1948) and sensory (Dawson, 1956) nerves in man, it has become possible to more accurately assess peripheral nerve function. Mayer (1966), utilizing these techniques, measured the conduction velocities in the median and peroneal nerves of two groups of patients with chronic alcoholism.

Group I consisted of 12 males who were admitted to the hospital because of acute alcoholic intoxication. All patients had consumed large quantities of alcohol for at least 4 years and admitted to poor dietary habits during the periods of heaviest drinking. None of these patients had either any evidence of nutritional deficiency or signs or symptoms of peripheral neuropathy. These patients were subdivided into two groups: 1A consisted of five patients who had not had previous episodes by history of the alcoholic withdrawal syndrome and 1B contained seven patients who had known abstinence syndromes such as delirium tremens and "rum fits."

The nerve conduction velocities in group 1A were within normal limits utilizing standardized techniques (Mayer, 1963) (Table 1). However, the velocities in group 1B patients revealed a significant decrease ($p < 0.005$) in the distal segments of the median nerve compared with normal (Table 1). These patients had been drinking for a longer period of time (a mean of 16.6 years compared with 9.4 years) and were older (a mean age of 40 years compared with 29 years) than those in group 1A.

Group II consisted of three male volunteers who were chronic alcoholics (8 to 20 years' duration) and were without alcohol for a 2–3-month period prior to the study. All had had delirium tremens in the past. At the time of the study, all were in good physical condition and there was no evidence of nutritional deficiency. One of the patients had a normal neurological examination but the other two patients demonstrated signs of a mild distal polyneuropathy.

Conduction velocities were determined in the fastest motor and sensory nerve fibers in the median, peroneal, and posterior tibial nerves prior to the study using the same techniques as in group I. These values served as controls for each of the patients. During the study, the patients were given 120 to 180 ml

TABLE 1.   Nerve Conduction Velocities[a]

Nerve	Nerve potential (sensory)	Motor
Group 1A		
Median nerve		
Wrist–digit	65.0 ± 3.6	
Wrist–elbow	65.3 ± 3.3	58.3 ± 2.3
Elbow–axilla	66.3 ± 3.9	64.8 ± 2.8
Peroneal nerve		
Ankle–knee	49.5 ± 3.3	46.0 ± 2.5
Group 1B		
Median nerve		
Wrist–digit	60.3 ± 8.8	
Wrist–elbow	64.1 ± 2.4	53.8 ± 2.9
Elbow–axilla	67.7 ± 5.0	65.2 ± 4.6
Peroneal nerve		
Ankle–knee	49.9 ± 3.3	48.4 ± 5.8
Normals		
Median nerve		
Wrist–digit	67.5 ± 4.7	
Wrist–elbow	67.7 ± 4.4	59.3 ± 3.5
Elbow–axilla	70.4 ± 4.8	65.9 ± 5.0
Peroneal nerve		
Ankle–knee	53.0 ± 5.9	49.5 ± 5.6

[a] Mean velocities in meters per second ± 1 S.D. (Mayer, 1966).

of 43% ethyl alcohol in orange juice every 4 hr. During this period, the patients also consumed a regular hospital diet fortified with multiple vitamins. One patient was maintained on alcohol for 13 days and the other two patients for 27 days. Conduction velocities were determined at 5–8-day intervals during the period of alcohol ingestion and following its cessation. Neurological examination during the study revealed no new signs or symptoms of peripheral nerve dysfunction.

The one patient who had no signs of a peripheral neuropathy had normal conduction velocities prior to the study. In the other two patients with neuropathy, the velocity in the tibial nerves was decreased. During the period of alcohol consumption, the conduction velocities remained unchanged in all three volunteers. There was also no change in the terminal motor latency or the residual latency in these three chronic alcoholics.

A previous study by Low *et al.* (1962) reported no change in nerve conduction velocities but a decrease in the residual latency in the ulnar nerve during acute (a 3-hr period) ethanol consumption in normal volunteers. This study suggests that acute ethanol ingestion alters neuromuscular transmission in man. It has been reported in the frog that ethanol potentiates neuromuscular transmission by both a presynaptic and a postsynaptic effect (Inoue and Frank, 1967).

Additional studies of conduction velocities in patients with chronic alcoholism have revealed a subclinical form of the neuropathy (Jurko *et al.*, 1964; Mawdsley and Mayer, 1965). In 20 alcoholic patients without signs or symptoms of peripheral neuropathy, velocities in distal sensory fibers in median and ulnar nerves were reduced to a greater degree than the segments in the forearm, and velocities were normal in proximal segments (Mawdsley and Mayer, 1965) (Fig. 1). Velocities were also reduced in motor and sensory fibers in the peroneal and tibial nerves (Fig. 2). In patients with neuropathy, conduction velocities were further reduced, as low as 22 m/sec in one patient. In patients with marked clinical signs, conduction was also reduced in proximal nerve segments. Similar findings of reduced conduction velocities in alcoholic-nutritional polyneuropathy

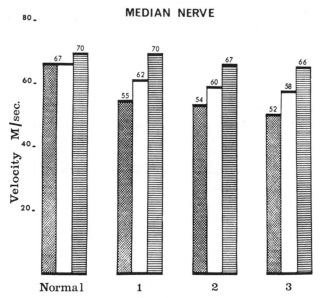

FIGURE 1.   Histograms of mean conduction velocities in the fastest afferent fibers. Results from normal group and alcoholic groups 1 (without clinical neuropathy), 2 (sensory neuropathy), and 3 (sensorimotor neuropathy), age range 20 to 50 years. Crosshatched columns on left show velocities (meters per second) from digit to wrist, white columns represent wrist to elbow segments, and horizontal bars show rates in elbow-axilla segments. [From Mawdsley and Mayer (1965).]

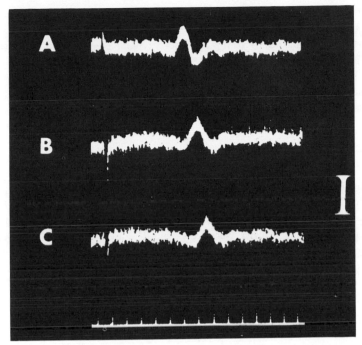

FIGURE 2. Recordings of nerve action potentials (NAP) from the peroneal nerve at the knee following stimulation at the ankle, A, normal subject, B, patient with subclinical neuropathy, and C, patient with clinical neuropathy. Note the increase in conduction times from A to C. Calibration: time, 1 msec, amplitude 20 μV.

have been reported by other investigators (Hudson and Dow, 1963; Coërs and Hildebrand, 1965).

The techniques utilized in the above studies measure the conduction velocity in the fastest (large) fibers of whole peripheral nerves. Low velocities in these nerves may indicate either reduced conduction in abnormal fibers or normal conduction in slow (small) conducting fibers following complete block of large fibers. The range of conduction velocities (due to the variation in diameter and internodal distance of fibers) in large alpha motor nerve fibers to skeletal muscle in man has been reported by several investigators (Lambert, 1960; Thomas et al., 1959; Hopf, 1963) but it is different in each report. This most likely resulted because of the differences and limitations of the techniques used. Juul-Jensen and Mayer (1966), who utilized the technique of threshold stimulation and bipolar needle electrode recording of single motor unit potentials in man, established a range of 46 to 83 m/sec in 50 fibers in the elbow-wrist segment of the ulnar nerve in normal adults between the ages of 20 and 50 years. The same technique was utilized in studying patients with chronic alcoholism and signs of polyneuropathy. A velocity range of 23 to 68 m/sec in 50 fibers was obtained in the alcoholic group and 50% of the fibers had velocities less than the lowest velocity found in normals. These results suggest that in patients with alcoholic-nutritional polyneuropathy, the conduction velocity is slowed in normally fast-conducting peripheral nerve fibers. This study supports the previous reports that conduction velocities in alcoholic polyneuropathy are reduced to a greater degree than those reported in primary nerve cell degeneration.

Pathological Description of Nerve Fibers in Chronic Alcoholics with Polyneuropathy

Following the early clinical observations of alcoholic-nutritional polyneuropathy, pathological studies of peripheral nerve revealed abnormality in the nerves (Dreschfeld, 1886; Gudden, 1896) to account for the clinical signs. Changes in the myelin sheath were reported, but in long-standing cases of polyneuropathy, changes in the axis cylinder and anterior horn cells were observed (Courville, 1955). In several histological studies of peripheral nerve in nutritional-vitamin deficiencies such as beriberi (Pekelharing and Winkler, 1893), vitamin B deficiencies (Aring et al., 1939), and vitamin B_{12} deficiency (Greenfield and Carmichael, 1935), abnormalities were found in the myelin sheaths before changes could be observed in axis cylinders. Denny-Brown (1958) described segmental thinning or loss of myelin without destruction of axis cylinders (segmental demyelination) as the initial change in alcoholic polyneuropathy. This pathological change was observed in the most peripheral parts of the longest peripheral nerves. This type of peripheral nerve change, which primarily affects the myelin sheaths, especially at the paranodal regions, was originally described by Gombault (1880). Segmental demyelination may be more difficult to see in myelin sheath stains of whole nerve trunks, but it can be readily observed in teased nerve fiber preparations stained with osmium by utilizing the technique of Vizoso and Young (1948) (Fig. 3). However, in severe alcoholic-nutritional polyneuropathy, degeneration of the myelin sheath and axis cylinder occurs (Wallerian degeneration) (Fig. 4) and does not differ from the changes observed in other types of polyneuropathy (Zimmerman, 1956). Since peripheral nerve can respond histologically to disease processes in a limited number of ways as observed by the light microscope, segmental demyelination has also been reported in a variety of different types of neuropathy in man such as hereditary (Gutrecht and Dyck, 1966; Dyck et al., 1968; Mayer and Garcia-Mullin, 1968), hypertrophic (Dyck et al., 1968), diphtheritic (Fisher and Adams, 1956), diabetic (Thomas and Lascelles, 1965), postinfectious allergic (Arnason et al., 1968; Wisniewski et al., 1969), and metachromatic leukodystrophy (Webster, 1962).

Since peripheral myelin is contained within the Schwann cell and the laminated myelin sheath is produced by rotation of individual Schwann cells (Geren, 1954; Causey, 1960), neuropathies which initially affect the myelin sheath have been interpreted as diseases of Schwann cells. Although little is known of the metabolism of Schwann cells, they are considered to be satellite cells of the axon (neuron). The relationship between neuron and Schwann cell is not completely known and further study is necessary to understand the role of the Schwann cell in maintaining the myelin sheath. The Schwann cells are separated from one another at the nodes of Ranvier. The thickness of the myelin sheath as well as the internodal distance is important in determining the conduction velocity of nerve fibers (Hursh, 1939).

Following degeneration of the neuron, as in poliomyelitis, there is degeneration of the axis cylinder, including the myelin sheath and Schwann cells, and no regeneration occurs. However, with segmental demyelination, the axon and neuron are left intact and remyelination occurs (Denny-Brown and Brenner, 1944). Hence, in the latter process, function is altered for only a short period of time and then returns, frequently to normal.

Pathogenesis of the Neuropathy Associated with Alcoholism

The clinical, physiological, and pathological studies of peripheral nerve in patients with chronic alcoholism described above all point to a primary dysfunction in nerve fibers. In the usual situation, the polyneuropathy, subclinical or clinical, does not occur in patients who are not chronic alcoholics of many years' duration (at least 5 to 10 years). In the younger patients with a shorter duration of alcoholic consumption and without abstinence syndromes, and in the three volunteer patients consuming large quantities of ethanol over periods of 13 to 27 days, no clinical or physiological evidence of polyneuropathy occurred (Mayer, 1966). These studies support all the previous evidence that the neuropathy is not related to the alcohol itself.

Recent studies have revealed ultrastructural changes in the liver of normal persons consuming moderate amounts of alcohol in the absence of deficiencies in dietary protein or vitamins (Rubin and Lieber, 1968). Although the fatty liver which occurs in chronic alcoholism has been related to nutritional deficiency in the past, the reports of this group conclude that alcohol itself is toxic to liver cells by altering mitochondrial structure and function (Lieber and Rubin, 1969). These studies have demonstrated that normal volunteers may show fat accumulation in the liver after periods of alcohol ingestion as short as 2 days and hence the authors conclude that alcohol *per se* is the cause of alcoholic fatty liver. There are no similar studies in man of the effect of alcohol ingestion on the ultrastructure of peripheral nerve. Sensitive physiological studies have not revealed any change in function during alcohol ingestion for periods up to 27 days. Liver and nerve cells are quite different in structure and function but

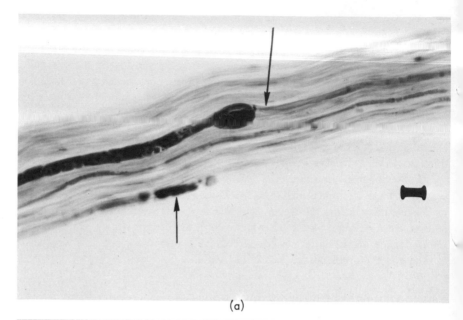

(a)

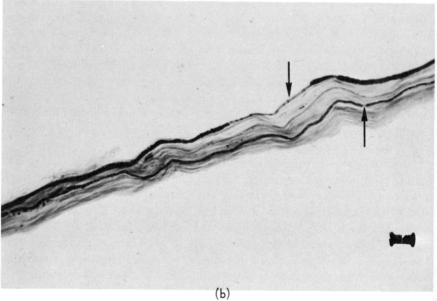

(b)

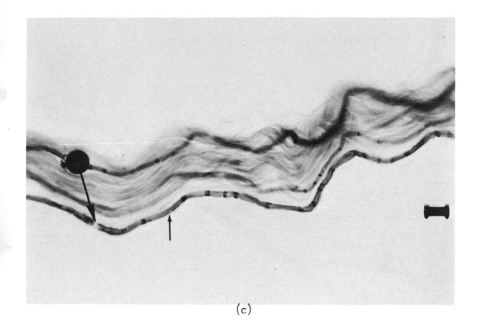

(c)

FIGURE 3. Photomicrographs of teased sural nerve fibers stained with osmium from a 50-year-old chronic alcoholic who had a moderate sensorimotor polyneuropathy and Wernicke's syndrome. No NAP could be recorded in the peroneal nerve at the knee and the motor velocity in the same segment was reduced. (a) One large fiber (upper arrow) shows segmental demyelination. This fiber could be studied for a distance of several millimeters without evidence of "ovoid" formation (Wallerian degeneration) which is present in other fibers (lower arrow). Calibration: 20 μ. (b) A short segment of demyelination with remyelination (upper arrow) in one fiber. A node of Ranvier is seen (lower arrow) in a normal fiber. Calibration: 15 μ. (c) A small fiber with an internodal segment of demyelination and remyelination (small arrow) following a node of Ranvier (large arrow). Calibration: 20 μ.

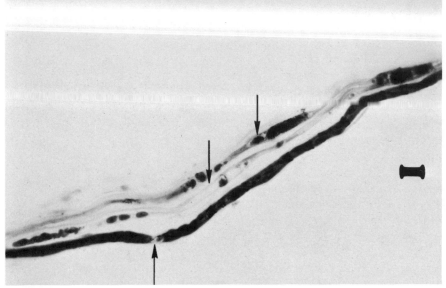

FIGURE 4.   Photomicrographs of teased sural nerve fibers stained with osmium from a 32-year-old male with a severe sensorimotor polyneuropathy. Neither NAP nor motor responses could be obtained from peroneal or posterior tibial nerves. Note the Wallerian degeneration manifested by "ovoid" formation in several fibers (upper arrows) next to one normal fiber (lower arrow). Calibration: 20 μ.

more study is necessary to definitely rule out any toxic effect of alcohol on the lower motor neuron in man.

Experimental studies on single nerve fibers of the squid (Armstrong and Binstock, 1964) have shown that ethanol does depress the sodium conductance increase associated with nerve excitation and, hence, may alter nerve transmission. However, the concentration of ethanol necessary to block impulse transmission is rather high and this suggests that the axon *per se* is rather resistant to ethanol (Moore, 1966). It has also been reported that ethanol, an organic solvent, can produce modification and extraction of the lipoprotein structure of the myelin sheath in rat peripheral nerve (Rumsby and Finean, 1966). However, it is always difficult to utilize information obtained in lower animals to interpret changes in man.

The present report deals primarily with persistent, pathological changes in nerve rather than acute readily reversible (biochemical or biophysical) ones, and the short-term experiments may not be helpful in understanding the pathogenesis of the polyneuropathy. Whether or not repeated acute "intoxication" of peripheral nerve over a period of years can produce pathological changes by interfering with the sodium conductance and membrane permeability, the lipoprotein structure of the myelin sheath, or the structure and function of mitochondria remain to be demonstrated.

In the seven patients studied by Mayer (1966) who were chronic alcoholics without evidence of nutritional deficiency at the time of testing, but who had a history of withdrawal syndromes, conduction velocities were reduced. It has been reported that patients with chronic alcoholism have low magnesium levels (Flink et al., 1954), especially those with withdrawal syndromes (Sullivan et al., 1963). It is possible that chronic episodic low magnesium levels may affect the nerve membrane or mitochondria and produce the pathological changes observed in the polyneuropathy. However, additional study is necessary before this possibility can be considered likely.

Most investigators, including the authors, prefer to classify the peripheral neuropathy occurring in chronic alcoholics as a nutritional-vitamin deficiency. This deficiency usually results from the lack of adequate intake during periods of heavy drinking. However, in some patients, chronic alcoholic gastritis and enterocolitis may contribute to this. There is also some evidence that ethanol itself may increase the excretion of B vitamins, especially thiamine, pyridoxine, and pantothenic acid (Knottinen et al., 1966). From the reports cited in the introduction, it is clear that the exact pathogenesis of the neuropathy still remains obscure.

Some authors (Greenfield, 1958; Krücke, 1959) have interpreted the polyneuropathy that occurs in beriberi and chronic alcoholism as resulting from primary neuronal degeneration. Since vitamins are necessary in the metabolic activity which occurs in the soma of the nerve cell, deficiency may alter this activity and axoplasmic flow so that the distal portion of the nerve fiber degenerates first. This type of "dying back" process due to primary nerve cell degeneration has been recognized for many years (Mott, 1896; Cavanagh, 1964) and is the explanation of why the longest nerve fibers, to feet and fingers, are first involved in the neuropathy. However, primary nerve cell degeneration will not account for the reduced conduction velocities in the peripheral nerve fibers observed in this neuropathy. Since the deficiency is a generalized one, metabolic activity is most likely affected in Schwann cells as well as many other cells in the body. Other authors (Denny-Brown, 1958; Mayer, 1966) have stressed that segmental and paranodal demyelination are the earliest lesions in alcoholic-nutritional polyneuropathy and these most likely result from metabolic dysfunction in Schwann cells. Experimental studies have reported that segmental demyelination reduces the conduction velocity at the site of the lesion (McDonald, 1963; Mayer and Denny-Brown, 1964). This pathological change would account for the reduced conduction velocity in both the subclinical and clinical forms of the neuropathy. It has been speculated that paranodal demyelination reduces the current density at the nodes of Ranvier. This in turn would delay excitation at the nodes and reduce the speed of transmission (Tasaki, 1955).

In patients with severe neuropathy, Wallerian degeneration occurs. This reflects total nerve dysfunction and degeneration which accounts for the absence of recordable action potentials in some nerves (Mawdsley and Mayer, 1965).

If the initial metabolic dysfunction occurs in Schwann cells, distal cells and myelin are affected before proximal ones. This may reflect either a dependence of the Schwann cell and myelin sheath on the body and axon of the nerve cell or differences in the metabolic activity of proximal and distal Schwann cells (Majno and Karnovsky, 1958). At present, there is little information concerning the effect of specific vitamin deficiencies on Schwann cell metabolism. Studies of rat nerve (spinal ganglia) in tissue culture suggest that thiamine deficiency produces an initial change in the myelin sheath due to a Schwann cell defect (Yonezawa and Iwanami, 1965, 1966). Deficiencies of other B vitamins, niacin, pyridoxine and pantothenic acid, produce nerve cell and Wallerian degeneration, but no segmental demyelination. These vitamin deficiencies in tissue culture were produced by antimetabolites and, therefore, may not represent the same defect as observed in human vitamin deficiencies.

It is well known that thiamine is utilized as a cofactor needed to oxidize pyruvic acid in the tricarboxylic acid cycle and also as a coenzyme of transketolase in the hexose monophosphate shunt. Transketolase activity has been reported to be highest in the heavily myelinated areas and lowest in areas of nerve cells (Dreyfus, 1965). It has been suggested that thiamine is necessary in glucose utilization in the shunt which requires thiamine pyrophosphate as a coenzyme of transketolase in myelin supporting cells such as Schwann cells (Yonezawa and Iwanami, 1966). Therefore chronic thiamine deficiency in these cells may inhibit the activity of transketolase and result in demyelination of peripheral nerve fibers. Acute or total thiamine loss may inhibit all of the oxidative processes in which thiamine is utilized as a cofactor and this may result in cell necrosis and Wallerian degeneration. Similar conclusions have been postulated concerning the effect of thiamine deficiency on the myelin supporting cells, oligodendrocytes, of the central nervous system (Dreyfus, 1965; Collins, 1967). It is also possible that Wallerian degeneration in sensory fibers reflects involvement of the capsular cells in the spinal ganglia as postulated in lead neuropathy (Schlaepfer, 1969). Thus the coexistence of segmental demyelination and Wallerian degeneration in alcoholic-nutritional polyneuropathy may result from thiamine deficiency in the supporting Schwann and capsular cells.

It has been reported that in patients with chronic alcoholism and active cirrhosis of the liver, there may be an inability to assimilate thiamine (Fennelly et al., 1967). This suggests that liver dysfunction which is so common in patients with chronic alcoholism and nutritional deficiency may play a role in the production of the polyneuropathy. A demyelinating peripheral neuropathy has been reported in patients with liver disease (Dayan and Williams, 1967). Segmental demyelination was observed in teased sural nerve fibers stained with osmium in ten patients, four of whom were alcoholics. The cause of the demyelination in these patients was related to the liver damage, but other factors such as age, nutritional status, and state of small blood vessels must also be considered in these patients.

Since multiple vitamin deficiencies do occur in chronic alcoholism (Fennelly *et al.*, 1964), it is possible that a greater deficiency of one may produce a specific clinical syndrome in some patients. From the human and experimental studies, it is possible that chronic thiamine deficiency produces the usual sensorimotor neuropathy (Williams *et al.*, 1943; Swank, 1940; Street *et al.*, 1941) while pantothenic acid deficiency may produce the "burning foot" syndrome (Bean *et al.*, 1955) and pyridoxine deficiency, the "ataxic" form (Wintrobe *et al.*, 1943). Since the clinical signs and symptoms reflect the location and type of nerve fibers involved, deficiencies of the same vitamin may produce a variety of signs and symptoms in different individuals.

Treatment and Prognosis

Since the early observations of Strauss (1935), it has been known that the primary and essential treatment of the polyneuropathy associated with chronic alcoholism is a good diet fortified with vitamins. A high caloric diet supplemented with multiple B vitamins, especially thiamine, niacin, pyridoxine, and panto-thenic acid is usually prescribed. Initially, the multiple vitamins should be given in large doses, many times the daily requirement, and injected either intra-venously or intramuscularly.

If the patient shows signs of central nervous system involvement such as Wernicke's syndrome, very large doses of thiamine (300 to 600 mg daily) should be given intravenously as soon as possible. Any delay in treatment may result in irreversible damage. Treatment of the polyneuropathy should also be started as soon as possible for the same reason.

It has been shown that following demyelination, remyelination occurs readily in peripheral nerve, and function returns (Denny-Brown and Brenner, 1944). There is an associated increase in the conduction velocity which may not return to normal in spite of normal function (Mayer and Denny-Brown, 1964). Hence, it is better to institute treatment at a time when the polyneuropathy is primarily demyelinative. However, in the usual patient who presents for diagnosis and treatment, there is degeneration of nerve fibers as well as demy-elination. In these patients recovery of function is slow, requiring months to years. Regeneration of nerve is slow; it depends on the overall distance required for the nerve fibers to grow and usually is incomplete (Berry, Grundfest, and Hinsey, 1944; Hodes, Larrabee, and German, 1948). Therefore, patients with alcoholic-nutritional polyneuropathy who show prominent Wallerian degenera-tion usually have slow recovery of function, persistent neurological signs, and reduced conduction velocities of peripheral nerves in spite of adequate diet and vitamin treatment for periods over a year. Since incomplete return of conduction and function occurs experimentally following nerve degeneration and regeneration and is related to the structure and function of the cell, incomplete recovery of the alcoholic-nutritional polyneuropathy in many patients is probably not due to inadequate or erroneous treatment.

Fennelly *et al.* (1964) reported that some patients with alcoholic-nutritional polyneuropathy were refractory to thiamine treatment but responded to either niacin, pantothenic acid, or pyridoxine. However, some of their patients with more severe neuropathy and liver disease were refractory to all vitamins. These patients most likely had prominent Wallerian degeneration of many nerve fibers.

It is recommended that the patients be followed regularly. The dietary and vitamin supplements should be continued as long as the patient has neurological signs and symptoms or until they have been stable for a period of 6 to 12 months. Most patients have a satisfactory recovery, except those who persist in consuming alcohol and remain deficient in vitamins and diet.

In the patients who also have focal mononeuropathies, no treatment is usually necessary. Since the mononeuropathy is similar to the tourniquet paralysis (Denny-Brown and Brenner, 1944), the lesion is primarily that of segmental demyelination. Recovery usually occurs over a period of weeks to months and may be complete. However, in some patients, there is a persistent foot drop which may be helped by a special spring-wire (dorsiflexor) foot brace. A persistent or progressive ulnar nerve palsy at the elbow may be helped by an operation in which the ulnar nerve is removed from the groove and transplanted anterior to the epicondyle beneath muscle.

When patients with chronic alcoholism and polyneuropathy are admitted to hospital for evaluation and treatment, they no longer are able to consume alcohol during this period. It is most important that the amount and duration of alcohol consumption be known since abrupt removal of alcohol upon admission may produce a withdrawal syndrome such as delirium tremens. This is a lethal disease in some patients and can be avoided by appropriate information and treatment.

A general medical workup is important in these patients in order to diagnose and treat other diseases associated with chronic alcoholism and nutritional deficiency such as anemia, cirrhosis, and cardiopathy. The patient is advised to abstain from alcohol, but in those with chronic alcoholism, this is a difficult problem which requires additional treatment. The nature of the treatment of chronic alcoholism will not be discussed in this chapter since it is dealt with in Chapter 19, Volume I. It may be beneficial, if possible, to maintain patients with chronic alcoholism on vitamin supplements to prevent the occurrence of nerve dysfunction.

MUSCLE

Clinical Description

Patients who are chronic alcoholics and who consume large quantities of alcohol may develop an "alcoholic" myopathy. Several clinical syndromes have been described (Table 2). These vary from acute massive necrosis of muscle fibers (acute myoglobinuria) to the asymptomatic cases.

Acute generalized myoglobinuria secondary to acute skeletal muscle necrosis (rhabdomyolysis) is a somewhat rare disorder (Farmer *et al.*, 1961) but has been reported in association with chronic alcoholism (Hed *et al.*, 1955; Fahlgren *et al.*, 1957; and Valaitis *et al.*, 1960). In one case, paroxysmal myoglobinuria occurred following episodes of ingestion of large amounts of alcohol (Erlenborn and Pilz, 1962). In some of the cases, myoglobinuric nephrosis occurred, resulting in death of the patient. However, most of the reported cases of acute myoglobinuria are either primary ("idiopathic") or secondary to crushing, severe exertion, or ischemia of muscle. Myoglobinuria has been related to the ingestion of toxic substances (Berlin, 1948; Rowland *et al.*, 1964) and may occur in chronic alcoholics who ingest "home-made" or impure alcoholic beverages (Mayer, 1965).

The clinical and laboratory features of acute myoglobinuria are well documented in the literature (Rowland *et al.*, 1964) and will not be discussed in this chapter. The mechanism of the muscle necrosis in these disorders remains unknown at the present time.

In 1962, Hed *et al.* reported 12 cases of an acute muscular syndrome in chronic alcoholism. These patients, of whom ten were men and all were over the age of 40, had acute episodes of generalized pain, aching, tenderness, or swelling of skeletal muscles. The episodes were related historically to an increase in alcohol consumption. Five of these patients had renal damage as a result of acute muscle necrosis and myoglobinuria and in three there was secondary hyperkalemia. Many patients had liver dysfunction and three had peripheral neuropathy.

This same group in Sweden (Ekbom *et al.*, 1964) reported another series of 14 patients with chronic alcoholism and muscle involvement. They divided their patients into three clinical groups. Group 1 (acute syndrome) consisted of patients with sudden aching, tenderness, or swelling in muscles occurring after periods of high-grade alcohol abuse. These patients did not have significant weakness, although muscle testing had to be limited owing to the severe pain on contraction. Electromyography revealed changes of a primary myopathy. Group 2 (chronic syndrome) consisted of five patients who developed slow progressive weakness of proximal muscles, especially those of the hips and, in some, shoulders over a period of weeks to months. The weakness in these

TABLE 2. "Alcoholic" Myopathy

Hed et al. (1962)	12 cases chronic alcoholics	Acute swelling, aching in muscles myoglobinuria (4 cases) renal damage (5 cases)	Acute mucle necrosis (7 cases)
Ekbom et al. (1964)	16 cases chronic alcoholics	1. Acute syndrome (3 cases) swelling aching, no weakness recovery in weeks 2. Chronic syndrome (5 cases) progressive proximal weakness improvement 2–4 months 3. Asymptomatic (8 cases)	1. Acute muscle necrosis, regeneration elevated SGOT, LDH, aldolase 2. Small areas, acute and chronic muscle necrosis 3. EMG, Histological evidence of myopathy
Perkoff et al. (1966, 1967)	21 cases chronic alcoholics without cirrhosis	1. Alcoholic intoxication (18, total 59 cases) muscle tenderness on palpation 2. Acute muscle cramps, (3, total 5 cases) tenderness, weakness of muscles immunologic myoglobinuria recovery 2–4 weeks	1,2. Elevated CPK levels; poor lactic acid response to ischemic exercise: Muscle phosphorylase low (3 cases) 2. Focal muscle atrophy; No necrosis; severe intracellular edema; destruction of mitochondria, myofilaments
	10 cases chronic alcoholics	3. Chronic myopathy Diffuse or proximal weakness, muscle tenderness	3. Endomysial fat rows of sarcolemmal nuclei random small fibers regenerating fibers

patients improved over a period of 2–3 months after the removal of alcohol. Group 3 (asymptomatic syndrome) consisted of eight patients who had no signs or symptoms of muscle dysfunction, but abnormalities of muscle were demonstrated by either biopsy or electromyography. All of the patients also had some abnormality of liver function. No other cause for the muscle dysfunction was apparent in these patients, and it was related directly to the effects of chronic alcoholism.

Perkoff et al. (1966) reported additional studies in 21 alcoholic patients without clinically demonstrable hepatic cirrhosis. Although only three of these patients had muscular symptoms which consisted of cramps, tenderness, or weakness, half of the other patients had muscle tenderness on physical examination. However, this symptom is also frequent in patients with alcoholic-nutritional polyneuropathy. Three patients had clinical signs of a peripheral neuropathy, but nerve conduction studies were not done to rule out a subclinical neuropathy in the remaining patients. Laboratory studies revealed that 14 of 19 patients had elevated creatine phosphokinase (CPK) activity. Nygren (1966) has also reported an increase in CPK activity during acute alcoholic intoxication. The normal rise of lactic acid during ischemic exercise (McArdle, 1951; Schmid and Mahler, 1959) was lacking in the alcoholic group within 48 hr of admission compared with normal subjects or patients with cirrhosis or debilitating disease. In two of the patients who had symptoms and who could be studied over several weeks, the production of lactic acid returned to normal. Myoglobin was determined in the urine by immunodiffusion techniques and was present in the three symptomatic patients and in five of ten urines from the other alcoholic patients. Muscle phosphorylase was definitely low in three patients and low normal in another three. The deficiency of phosphorylase activity was transient and reversible and appeared to be related to acute alcoholic intoxication.

Further studies by this group (Perkoff et al., 1967) summarized the findings in 59 chronic alcoholic patients who had either asymptomatic, acute, or chronic myopathy as described by Ekbom et al. (1964). They concluded that there was a spectrum of myopathy associated with chronic alcoholism and that an acute myopathy could progress to a chronic one. A slowly progressive myopathy has also been reported in patients with chronic alcoholism by Serratrice et al. (1966).

Recently we have studied four patients who were chronic alcoholics and who presented with acute weakness of proximal muscles not associated with significant pain or swelling (Mayer et al., 1968). These patients had dysfunction of water and electrolyte metabolism without renal failure, a finding which was not reported by the previous authors. Details of this study have not been reported previously and will be presented in this chapter.

All patients were males between the ages of 39 and 50 (Table 3). All had histories of poor nutrition. The patients had been drinking for many years and

TABLE 3. Case Reports

Patient	Alcohol history	Related diseases	Present illness	Positive signs
D.H. 50, male	10 years delirium tremens and seizures	Subtotal gastrectomy, anemia	Heavy drinking 1 month; poor nutrition; diarrhea 4 days; vomiting, weakness 1 day tremor and seizures	Weakness of face, neck proximal muscles; decreased distal sensation; depressed tendon jerks; bilateral ulnar nerve palsies
S.R. 44, male	+10 years	Anemia, folic acid deficiency	Heavy drinking for months; poor nutrition; diarrhea, vomiting 1 week progressive weakness 2 days	Weakness face, neck, proximal muscles; tetany, +Chvostek; decreased distal sensation; depressed tendon jerks
O.M. 39, male	20 years delirium tremens	Anemia, cirrhosis, previous episode of weakness	Heavy drinking for months; poor nutrition; vomiting for days; progressive weakness 2 days	Weakness neck, proximal muscles; tetany, +Chvostek; normal sensation; absent tendon jerks
L.E. 42, male	+5 years delirium tremens	Cirrhosis	Heavy drinking for months; poor nutrition; diarrhea, vomiting for days; sudden generalized paresthesias, weakness	Weakness proximal muscles; decreased distal sensation; depressed tendon jerks in legs

TABLE 4. Clinical Studies

Patient	Serum enzymes	Urine benzidine	EMG	Nerve conduction studies	Muscle biopsy	Clinical course
D.H. 1 week	SGOT > 210 SLDH 1010	Blood	Repetitive discharge on percussion; small polyphasic motor unit potentials; normal N-M refractory period repetitive stimulation normal	Nerve refractory period normal; decreased distal velocity, sensory, motor	Acute necrosis patchy, widespread	Rapid improvement, days with fluid, electrolyte replacement; weakness 4 weeks
7 weeks	SGOT 33 SLDH 460	Negative	No repetitive discharge; many small motor unit potentials	No change from above	Active regeneration chronic changes	Normal strength residual neuropathy
S.R.	CPK 81 SLDH 420		Spontaneous motor unit potentials, hand muscles, tetany; repetitive stimulation normal	Decreased distal velocity, sensory, motor	Acute necrosis	Rapid improvement, days with fluid, electrolyte replacement; weakness > 1 week
O.M.	CPK 240 SGOT 140	Negative	Small motor response to electric stimulation	Decreased distal velocity, sensory, motor		Rapid improvement, days with fluid and electrolyte replacement; weakness > 6 days
L.E.	SGOT 302 SLDH 1700	Positive myoglobin	Many small polyphasic motor unit potentials; no denervation activity in proximal muscles	Decreased distal velocity, sensory, motor	Necrosis with regeneration (3 weeks)	Rapid improvement, days with fluid and electrolyte replacement; weakness 4 weeks

heavily for at least 1 month prior to onset of symptoms. Diseases associated with chronic alcoholism such as anemia, cirrhosis of the liver, or peripheral neuropathy with reduced distal conduction velocities (Table 4) were observed in all. These patients all had vomiting, diarrhea, or both, for a few days prior to the onset of weakness. The vomiting and diarrhea were most likely due to alcoholic gastroenteritis and quickly subsided following admission to the hospital. The weakness in these patients developed over a 1–2-day period, was severe and, although initially generalized, involved proximal muscles more than distal ones. Shoulder girdle muscles were more involved than hip muscles. In two patients, there was also prominent weakness of face and neck muscles. The weakness improved rapidly over a number of days after hospitalization and appropriate treatment, but mild weakness persisted for at least a week (Table 4).

Laboratory studies revealed that three of the patients had low serum potassiums associated with hypochloremic alkalosis at the time of admission (Table 5). Two of these patients also had low serum calcium levels and transient tetany. The other patient, D.H., had normal potassium levels but evidence of overhydration and especially low serum sodium. Serum enzyme studies such as SGOT (glutamic oxalacetic transaminase), SLDH (lactic dehydrogenase), and CPK were elevated initially in all patients secondary to the muscle necrosis. Myoglobinuria was present in one patient using the benzidene test and spectrophotometric analysis (Table 4).

There was a normal rise in serum lactic acid during ischemic exercise in patient D.H. utilizing the technique of Schmid and Mahler (1959). This was performed at a time when symptoms and signs were still present (Table 6).

Electromyographic studies revealed a myopathic pattern in the proximal muscles in all patients. This was characterized by many small polyphasic motor unit potentials upon contraction without fibrillation or fasciculation potentials. There was a repetitive discharge of the MUP with percussion in the weak muscles of one patient (D.H.) (Fig. 5). This was present only during the acute phase (1–2 weeks) of the illness. In this same patient, detailed electrophysiological studies of neuromuscular (N-M) transmission, including the responses following paired or repetitive stimuli, were normal (Table 4).

Detailed serum and intramuscular cation determinations* were performed in one patient (D.H., Table 6). Muscle sodium and potassium (expressed as millimoles per kilogram of fiber water) were determined in biopsy specimens from the sternocleidomastoid muscles utilizing the techniques of Sjodin and Henderson (1964). During the acute phase of the illness when the patient demonstrated both weakness and a repetitive MUP upon percussion, there was a significant decrease in intracellular muscle potassium and an increase in muscle

---

*The intramuscular cation determinations were performed by Dr. R. A. Sjodin, Professor, Department of Biophysics, University of Maryland School of Medicine.

TABLE 5. Admission Blood Studies

Patient	BUN (mg%)	Urine specific gravity	Na (meq/liter)	K (meq/liter)	Cl (meq/liter)	CO$_2$ (meq/liter)	Ca (mg%)	Mg (meq/liter)	pH
D.H.	12	1.015	112	4.2	82	22	9.5[a]	2.0[a]	
S.R.	Normal		140	2.0	80	40	6.0	Low	7.5
O.M.	11	1.023	143	2.1	75	45	7.5		
L.E.	15–7	1.020	145	2.2	80	40	9.0		7.55

[a] Performed after 1 week.

TABLE 6. Patient D.H.

Time	Serum					Urine			Muscle		
	Na (meq/liter)	K (meq/liter)	Cl (meq/liter)	Osmolality (osmoles)	Lactic acid (mg%)	Na (meq/liter)	Osmolality (osmoles)	Specific gravity	Na (mM/kg fiber water)	K (mM/g fiber water)	Histology
Onset											
+2 Days	112	4.2	82	242		10	373	1.014			
+5 Days	140	4.3	100		5–22 1-min ischemia			1.024	45.5	74.7	Acute necrosis
+50 Days	142	4.1	106					1.019	33.0	106.0	Active regeneration

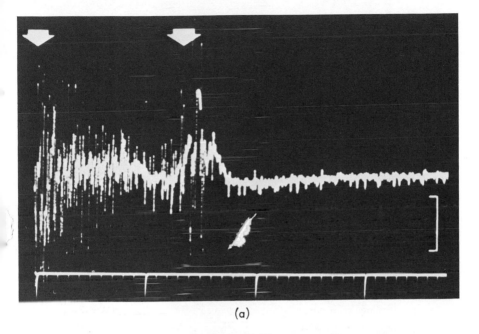

(a)

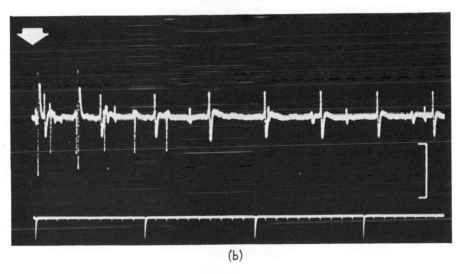

(b)

FIGURE 5. (a) Percussion (arrows) of the right sternocleidomastoid muscle of patient D.H. 2 days after admission. Note the fast repetitive discharge of MUP which were large following the first tap and small following the second one. (b) Percussion (arrow) of the right deltoid muscle as in (a). Note the slow repetitive discharge of several MUP. Recordings were made with a bipolar needle electrode in the muscles. Calibration: amplitude, 200 μV; time, 10 and 100 msec.

sodium. When the same technique was repeated on a biopsy specimen of the other sternocleidomastoid muscle at a time when the patient had no signs or symptoms, the intramuscular cations revealed a lower concentration of sodium and a higher concentration of potassium than obtained initially. These values approached those of normal muscle (Engel *et al.*, 1965).

Although these clinical syndromes of myopathy associated with chronic alcholism are relatively well defined, they must be separated from other disorders of peripheral nerve and muscle. Chronic alcoholism is a common disease and frequently there is an associated polyneuropathy, but a clinical myopathy is relatively rare. Therefore, it is most important to separate these disorders as carefully as possible. This frequently can be done with a careful history and physical examination. However, in some cases in which the symptoms and signs are mild, further studies are necessary. Serum enzyme studies such as CPK, aldolase, SLDH, and SGOT are helpful, since they are usually elevated in acute muscle necrosis but normal in polyneuropathy. However, they may not be markedly elevated in a chronic myopathy but may be elevated to a similar level in some neural atrophies in which there are degenerating muscle fibers (Heyck and Laudahn, 1967). In these cases, nerve conduction studies may be helpful. In chronic myopathies, the conduction velocities are normal, while in most polyneuropathies the velocities are reduced. Electromyography may be helpful in detecting neural atrophy and myositis, but the changes may not be specific enough in some of the milder cases. Muscle biopsies should be performed in all cases in which there is some doubt as to the exact diagnosis. Although careful histological study of muscle can usually provide the information necessary to separate a myopathy from a neuropathy, there are some cases in which this is difficult also. Therefore, it is necessary to combine all the studies, physiological, biochemical, and histological, to establish which tissue is primarily affected. However, as pointed out in the introduction, the muscle fibers are dependent in part on the nerve cell and its processes and satellite cells for normal function. Hence in some patients, both nerve and muscle cells may be affected by a generalized toxic or metabolic dysfunction. These studies, along with a complete medical workup, are necessary to rule out other causes of myopathy, which might occur coincidentally in patients with chronic alcoholism. These include such disorders as endocrinopathies, collagen-vasculitis, neoplasms, and infectious and granulomatous diseases.

Pathological Description of Muscle Fibers in Chronic Alcoholics

In the acute muscular syndrome, biopsies of muscle revealed acute necrosis of muscle fibers which was extensive in several patients (Hed *et al.*, 1962). There was a mild inflammatory response in the region of the necrotic fibers but there were no specific changes in blood vessels or connective tissue. Many

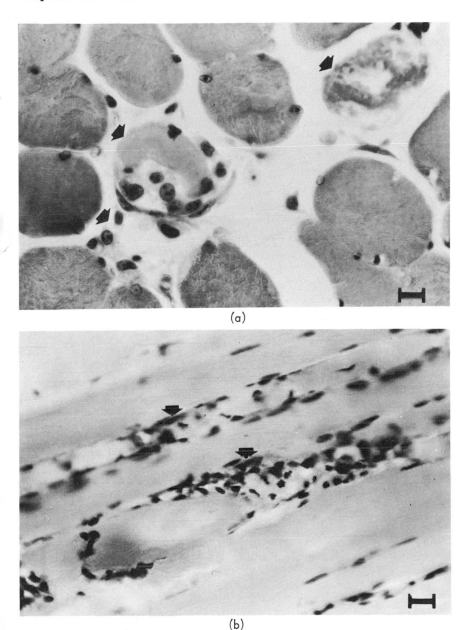

(a)

(b)

FIGURE 6. Photomicrographs of the biopsy from the right sternocleidomastoid muscle of patient D.H. 5 days after onset of weakness. Hematoxylin and eosin stain, calibration, 10 μ. (a) Cross section shows acute necrotic fibers (arrows) interspersed with normal fibers. (b) Longitudinal section shows segmental necrosis of fibers (arrows) with mild secondary inflammatory response.

muscle fibers were involved, but in a patchy distribution. Segmental necrosis of fibers was seen as well as vacuolation and hyalinization. In some cases, active regeneration was present as well as active degeneration. Regeneration was recognized by the presence of multiplication and enlargement of sarcolemmal nuclei and basophilic cytoplasm. This type of necrotizing myopathy is nonspecific and may be observed in myopathies of other etiologies (Denny-Brown, 1960).

In the less severe cases (Perkoff et al., 1966), muscle biopsies did not demonstrate necrosis of fibers. Mild focal or diffuse atrophy of muscle fibers and an increase in sarcolemmal nuclei were observed.

Detailed histologic studies, including electron microscopy of muscle fibers by Klinkerfuss et al. (1967), revealed that in the acute myopathy there was severe intracellular edema and destruction of mitochondria and myofilaments. They concluded that the initial structural change occurring in muscle fibers in chronic alcoholism was probably an alteration of cell membrane permeability.

In the four chronic alcoholic patients we have studied with acute weakness associated with water and electrolyte dysfunction, acute necrosis of muscle fibers was observed in three (the fourth patient refused muscle biopsy). Active degeneration of individual muscle fibers was observed with fragmentation and vacuolation of muscle fibers (Fig. 6). Many fibers were affected in a patchy

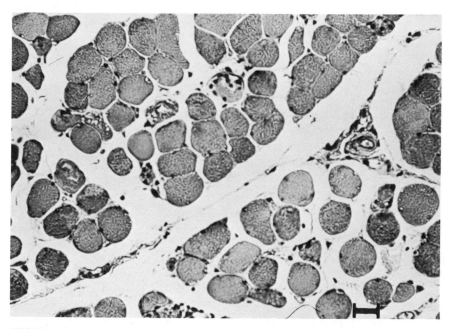

FIGURE 7. Cross section of same muscle as in Fig. 6 showing patchy distribution of necrotic fibers. Vacuolation and fragmentation of fibers and proliferation of sarcolemmal nuclei can also be seen. Hematoxylin and eosin stain; calibration, 40 μ.

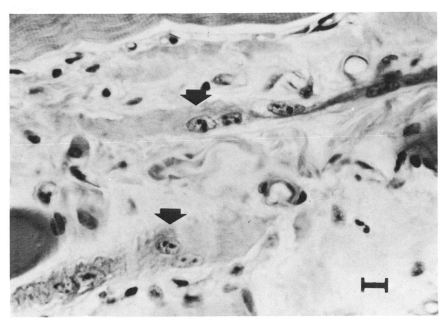

FIGURE 8.   Longitudinal section of left sternocleidomastoid muscle 7 weeks after onset of weakness (patient D.H.). Note the regenerating muscle fibers (arrows) with active division of sarcolemmal nuclei. Hematoxylin and eosin stain; calibration, 10 μ.

distribution, but many fibers appeared normal (Fig. 7). There was a localized inflammatory reaction in the area of necrotic fibers. These changes are similar to those reported previously in the acute muscular syndrome.

Repeat biopsy in one patient (D.H.) 7 weeks after onset of weakness revealed active regeneration of many fibers (Fig. 8). However, there was atrophy and hyaline degeneration of many fibers, with replacement by fat cells and connective tissue (Fig. 9). In one area, there was a group of muscle fibers which had abnormal collections of PAS-positive material (presumably glycogen) in the subsarcolemmal space (Fig. 10). This change is similar to that observed in McArdle's syndrome (Adams *et al.*, 1962). The changes in this muscle biopsy appeared similar to those of a chronic myopathy although the patient was asymptomatic.

In patients with proximal weakness and chronic myopathy studied by Ekbom *et al.* (1964), a small number of fibers could be found undergoing acute degeneration. There were regenerating fibers and moderate infiltration with fat cells. Many fibers were atrophic. There was no pattern to the distribution of the changes. Similar changes were observed by Klinkerfuss *et al.* (1967), and electron microscopy revealed that the majority of fibers had a normal internal structure. However, many of the fibers were small in size and there was an increase in sarcolemmal nuclei. The I band was frequently involved severely by the destruction,

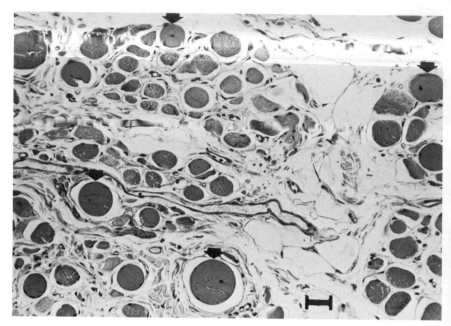

FIGURE 9. Cross section of same muscle as in Fig. 8. Note the variation in size of muscle fibers, hyalinized fibers with central nuclei (arrows), atrophic fibers and an increase in fat and connective tissue. Some regenerating fibers are present throughout the section. Hematoxylin and eosin stain; calibration, 40 μ.

while the A band and Z disk were relatively spared. Both degenerating and regenerating fibers could be found in the biopsy specimens.

In the asymptomatic cases only minor abnormalities were reported, such as rows of fat cells and degenerated or thin muscle fibers (Ekbom *et al.*, 1964).

Pathogenesis of the Myopathies Associated with Alcoholism

From the clinical, electrophysiological, biochemical, and pathological studies, it is clear that patients with chronic alcoholism can develop a myopathy. The muscle involvement can occur with or without clinical dysfunction in other organ systems (such as liver, blood, peripheral nerve, or skin). Dysfunction in these systems, which is also associated with chronic alcoholism, however, usually occurs at the same time as the myopathy. The exact relationship of the myopathy to chronic alcoholism and acute ethanol consumption is not clear at the present time. From the clinical descriptions of the myopathies, it is most likely that there are different causes for the muscle involvement (Table 7). However, an asymptomatic or acute myopathy of one cause may progress or eventually become a chronic myopathy.

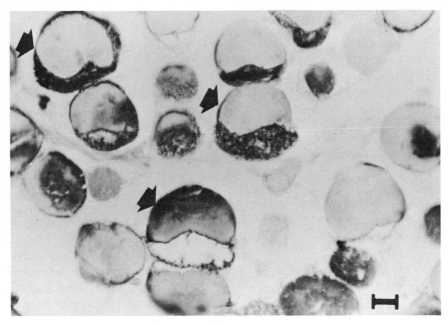

FIGURE 10.   Cross section of part of the same muscle as in Fig. 8. Note the muscle fibers with large collections of granules in the subsarcolemmal space (arrows). These stain deeply with the periodic acid-Schiff (PAS) stain; calibration, 10 μ.

TABLE 7.   Acute Muscle Necrosis

Acute-chronic alcoholism

1. Water and electrolyte abnormalities
   Secondary to gastrointestinal dysfunction
   Na, K, Cl, CO_2, pH, Ca, Mg
   (K depletion)
   (steroids, diuretics)

2. Nutritional deficiency
   Vitamins, carbohydrate, protein
   (vitamin E deficiency)

3. Toxins–drugs
   Alcohol, barbiturates

4. Exercise
   Seizures

5. Metabolic–enzymatic
   Phosphorylase deficiency, other

6. Vascular–ischemia

7. Infection–fever

It has been reported by Knutsson and Katz (1967) that in frog muscle, ethanol decreases the resting membrane potential of fibers in Na-rich solutions. They concluded that ethanol might increase the sodium permeability of the membrane. This may be related to the solvent effect of ethanol on the lipids in muscle membrane as observed on myelin sheaths (Rumsby and Finean, 1966). Inoue and Frank (1967) concluded that ethanol does not block the action potential in frog muscle by depolarization but by inhibition of the specific increase in sodium conductivity which normally follows an adequate stimulus. This may be secondary to a toxic effect of ethanol on cation transport as suggested by Israel et al. (1965). It is possible that repeated bouts of alcoholic consumption may alter the muscle membrane and its permeability (Klinkerfuss et al., 1967) which eventually may lead to necrosis of fibers. This may be the cause of one type of muscle involvement observed in chronic alcoholics.

In the initial studies of Perkoff et al. (1966), it was postulated that alcohol may interfere with intramuscular phosphorylase activity and result in a myopathy as observed in McArdle's syndrome (hereditary phosphorylase deficiency). However, the pathological changes reported in the alcoholic myopathies (except for the one patient reported in this chapter) differ from those reported in McArdle's syndrome. Experimental studies in rats have not demonstrated any change in muscle phosphorylase activity during alcohol consumption for periods up to 30 days (Laasonen and Palkama, 1967). Later studies by Klinkerfuss et al. (1967) emphasized the alteration of cell membrane permeability. However, they did observe destruction of mitochondria and myofilaments. Filaments of the I band were also fragmented and this change has been observed in McArdle's syndrome (Schotland et al., 1965). Douglas et al. (1966) concluded that injury to the mitochondria was the initial defect in a patient with recurrent rhabdomyolysis precipitated by alcohol. They postulated that alcohol, which can decrease blood flow through muscle, may injure the mitochondria as a result of ischemia. However, it is well known that skeletal muscle can withstand long periods (hours) of ischemic anoxia (Eiken et al., 1964). This period of anoxia is unlikely to occur in chronic alcoholism without affecting the central nervous system. Whether or not the myopathy results from a toxic effect of alcohol on the mitochondria of muscle cells as suggested for liver cells (Lieber and Rubin, 1969) remains to be proved in man. Christophersen (1964) has suggested that ethanol affects the mitochondrial membranes in rats.

Since the majority of patients who are chronic alcoholics are usually malnourished and have other organ systems involved as well as muscle, it is possible that some factor other than alcohol is responsible for the myopathy. Although experimental myopathies have been produced in animals with nutritional and vitamin deficiencies (especially vitamin E), it is doubtful whether these produce myopathy in human adults (Adams et al., 1962). Patients with chronic alcoholism and poor nutrition lose weight and their muscle mass decreases. In this condition, as in cachexia, muscle fibers become atrophic and degeneration of some fibers occurs (Marin and Denny-Brown, 1962). This also occurs in association with carcinoma (Henson *et al.*, 1954). The exact cause of this change is unknown at the present time but most likely reflects an enzymatic defect in muscle cell metabolism.

Patients with chronic alcoholism can develop a myopathy of cardiac muscle (Alexander, 1968) as well as skeletal muscle. In a study by Wendt *et al.* (1965), it was observed that in patients with chronic alcoholism without malnutrition or vitamin deficiencies, there was swelling of mitochondria in cardiac muscle fibers. This was related to the decreased levels of magnesium recorded in chronic alcoholism, since similar pathological changes have been observed in cardiac muscle of rats fed magnesium-deficient diets (Susin and Herdson, 1967). These authors suggested that episodes of alcoholism produce changes in cardiac muscle which eventually lead to a cardiomyopathy. It is possible that the hypomagnesemia observed in some patients with chronic alcoholism may also produce changes in skeletal muscle and eventually necrosis of fibers. Although muscular weakness has been reported to be part of the syndrome of magnesium deficiency in man (Hanna *et al.*, 1960), further studies in man are necessary to relate an acute or chronic myopathy directly to the effects of altered magnesium metabolism. In rats on adequate diets, magnesium levels in muscle of ethanol-fed animals have been reported to be not significantly different from those in control animals (Saville and Lieber, 1965).

The pathogenesis of the acute muscular syndrome we have described in chronic alcoholism in this chapter appears quite different from that previously reported. The weakness was precipitated by acute gastrointestinal dysfunction which produced fluid and electrolyte depletion, especially hypokalemia, hyponatremia, and hypomagnesemia. Although muscle weakness is a well-known symptom of potassium depletion (Welt *et al.*, 1960), severe weakness with muscle necrosis is unusual in these patients. In the reports in which marked weakness, muscle necrosis, and myoglobinuria occurred in patients with potassium depletion, other factors such as nutritional deficiency (Achor and Smith, 1955), regional enteritis, and chronic steroid therapy (Heitzman *et al.*, 1962) and kaliuretic agents such as licorice (Gross *et al.*, 1966) were associated. However, in most of the clinical studies of potassium depletion in man, little attention has been paid to the histological features of skeletal muscle.

In patients with primary periodic paralysis and hypokalemia, vacuolation of muscle fibers occurs (Shy *et al.*, 1961) but necrosis and degeneration of muscle fibers do not occur until the patient has had multiple episodes of weakness over a period of years (Pearson, 1964; Engel *et al.*, 1965). The etiology of primary hypokalemic periodic paralysis is unknown (Engel *et al.*, 1967) at the present time and dysfunction does not always correlate with serum potassium levels. Some authors have concluded that in this disorder, there is an abnormality of the muscle sarcoplasmic reticulum and that this is the primary abnormality rather than that of potassium metabolism (Shy, 1966).

In experimental animals, potassium deficiency has been reported to produce necrosis of muscle fibers in the dog but not in the rat (Smith et al., 1950). In man additional studies are necessary to prove that acute potassium depletion alone can produce muscle necrosis.

In the patients we have described with fluid and electrolyte dysfunction, chronic and acute alcoholism may play a role in the production of the acute muscle necrosis. The findings of decreased intramuscular potassium and increased sodium suggest that there is a change in the permeability of the muscle membrane. This may be secondary to the effect of ethanol on the membrane or on the enzyme systems involved in cation transport across the membrane. It is well known that muscle cells transport sodium outward and potassium inward, usually against concentration gradients. This process requires energy which may be produced by the activity of sodium-potassium-activated adenosine triphosphatase in the cells (Skou, 1965). Whether or not this enzyme system is altered in these patients is only speculative, but it is possible that its function is changed by the combined effects of ethanol and cation depletion. However, the changes in intracellular cations may be secondary to degeneration of muscle fibers as reported in patients with muscular dystrophy (Horvath et al., 1955). Therefore, at the present time, the exact cause of the acute muscle necrosis in these patients remains unknown. Other factors which are known to produce muscle necrosis may also play a role in producing the myopathy in chronic alcoholics. These are listed in Table 7. One or more of these factors may also be involved in the production of the acute or chronic myopathies in chronic alcoholism reported by previous authors.

In the one patient (D.H.) who was studied in detail, a repetitive discharge of motor unit potentials was recorded at a time when the intracellular concentrations of potassium were low and sodium high. Using the Nernst equation and, thereby, estimating the resting membrane potential of muscle, it is likely that partial depolarization of the membrane occurred initially. The partial depolarization of the muscle membrane most likely accounts for the repetitive discharge recorded during the acute stage of the myopathy. The electrical phenomenon returned to normal at the same time as regeneration of muscle occurred and the intracellular potassium increased and sodium decreased. In patients with periodic paralysis and hyperkalemia (adynamia episodica hereditaria), partial depolarization of the muscle membrane occurs during the attacks (Creutzfeldt et al., 1963) and during this period spontaneous discharges of MUP (repetitive or myotonic) occur (Buchthal et al., 1958).

The finding of PAS-positive granules in the subsarcolemmal space in the chronic (regenerative) phase of the acute myopathy in patient D.H. suggests that there may be dysfunction in the enzyme systems involved in the breakdown of glycogen. This change was not observed during the acute phase and may be non-specific. However, additional studies of glycolytic metabolism should be performed in these patients.

Treatment and Prognosis

In patients with either acute or chronic myopathy associated with chronic alcoholism and without other disease processes, recovery is relatively rapid and complete following hospitalization (Ekbom *et al.*, 1964). The treatment consists of removing alcohol and providing a well-balanced diet fortified with multiple vitamins. In a few patients who have massive muscle necrosis, death may result secondary to myoglobinuria and renal failure. However, this may be prevented by immediate renal dialysis. In the patients who also have evidence of water and electrolyte imbalance, careful replacement of fluid and electrolytes is necessary. Usually a balanced solution administered intravenously will correct the defect in a few days. Additional potassium and magnesium may be given if the patient is severely depleted of these ions. However, they must be given with care since overdosage may produce serious cardiac dysfunction. During the first week in the hospital, the patients with the acute syndrome usually show dramatic and rapid recovery. This is especially true in those patients with water and electrolyte dysfunction. The patients with the chronic syndrome may require months to recover. Since the muscle biopsies reveal degenerative changes even after clinical recovery, it is possible that some of the patients may have progression of the myopathy in the future. This is especially likely if they return to consuming large quantities of ethanol.

Since most of the patients with significant myopathy associated with chronic alcoholism have evidence of dysfunction in other organ systems, it is important that the patient be examined completely and treated for these as well. This part of the examination has been discussed in the section dealing with the treatment of alcoholic-nutritional polyneuropathy.

These patients need and require constant supervision and counseling if the myopathy as well as the polyneuropathy are to be treated properly. This is necessary for functional recovery as well as to prevent reoccurrence of the disorders.

SUMMARY AND CONCLUSIONS

There is considerable evidence now that both a generalized polyneuropathy and a myopathy do occur in patients who consume large quantities of alcohol over a protracted period of time. Although the clinical, physiological, biochemical, and structural features of these disorders are well described, the pathogenesis and

relationship of the disorders to chronic alcoholism remain incompletely understood.

The polyneuropathy may present in numerous ways clinically, but there is
usually a generalized dysfunction of the peripheral nerves tested physiologically.
The reduction of conduction velocity in involved nerve fibers is best explained by
the histological changes of segmental demyelination and remyelination. These
changes in turn suggest that the primary dysfunction lies in the Schwann cells.
However, the metabolic dysfunction is most likely ubiquitous and involves other
satellite cells such as the capsular cells as well as the axon and perikaryon of the
neuron. It is unlikely that the polyneuropathy results from the direct toxic effect
of alcohol on these cells but rather from the associated nutritional and vitamin
deficiencies. Although these deficiencies may be multiple and may vary from one
patient to the next, deficiencies of B vitamins, especially thiamine, appear to be
the underlying cause in most cases. This is the most likely explanation of why the
polyneuropathy either does not occur or improves in the chronic alcoholic who is
well nourished and ingests multiple vitamins. However, the mechanism by which
these deficiencies produce either segmental demyelination or Wallerian degeneration of nerve fibers is not completely known. Further studies of this mechanism
are necessary and may help in the overall understanding of the anatomy, function, and metabolism of the lower motor neuron in man.

The myopathy may be asymptomatic or present as an acute or chronic syndrome. The latter may result from a series of asymptomatic or acute episodes.
Although the disorder in some patients may result from the direct toxic effect of
alcohol on the muscle cell, the exact mechanism by which the myopathy occurs
is unknown at the present time. It has been suggested that alcohol may affect the
metabolism of the cell membrane and the mitochondria of muscle cells. This
type of myopathy has been reported to improve following the removal of alcohol.
However, in some of the patients with chronic alcoholism who develop a myopathy, there may be factors other than alcohol which account for the muscle disorder. An acute muscle disease occurring in chronic alcoholics of different
etiology is described in this chapter. This disorder most likely results from alterations in water and electrolyte metabolism secondary to gastrointestinal dysfunction. A necrotizing myopathy occurs in these patients and may result from a
disorder of cation transport at the muscle cell membrane. This disorder may be
augmented by alcohol, but additional studies are needed concerning the effect of
alcohol on mammalian muscle membrane. The myopathy in these patients improves following the correction of the water and electrolyte imbalance. Since
other factors may also be responsible for muscle necrosis in patients with chronic
alcoholism, continued study of these patients is necessary to delineate all the
possible pathogenic mechanisms of "alcoholic" myopathy.

REFERENCES

Achor, R. W. and Smith, L. A., 1955. Nutritional deficiency syndrome with diarrhea resulting in hypopotassemia, muscle degeneration and renal insufficiency: Report of case with recovery, *Proc. Mayo Clinic* **30**: 207.

Adams, R. D., Denny-Brown, D., and Pearson, R. M., 1962. *Disease of Muscle. A Study in Pathology.* Harper and Row, New York.

Alexander, C. S., 1968. The concept of alcoholic myocardiopathy, *Med. Clin. North Amer.* **52**: 1183.

Aring, C. D., Evans, J. P., and Spies, T. D., 1939. Some clinical neurologic aspects of vitamin B deficiencies, *J. Amer. Med. Assoc.* **113**: 2105.

Armstrong, C. M. and Binstock, L., 1964. The effects of several alcohols on the properties of the squid giant axon, *J. Gen. Physiol.* **48**: 265.

Arnason, B. G., Asbury, A. K., Astrom, K.-E., and Adams, R. D., 1968. EAN as a model for iodiopathic polyneuritis, *Trans. Amer. Neurol. Assoc.* **93**: 133.

Bean, W. B., Hodges, R. E., and Daum, K., 1955. Pantothenic acid deficiency induced in human subjects, *J. Clin. Invest.* **34**: 1073.

Berlin, R., 1948. Haff disease in Sweden, *Acta Med. Scand.* **129**: 560.

Berry, C. M., Grundfest, H., and Hinsey, J. C., 1944. The electrical activity of regenerating nerves in the cat, *J. Neurophysiol.* **7**: 103.

Buchthal, F., Engbaek, L., and Gamstorp, I., 1958. Paresis and hyperexcitability in adynamia episodica hereditaria, *Neurology (Minneap.)* **8**: 347.

Buller, A. J., Eccles, J. C., and Eccles, R. M., 1960. Differentiation of fast and slow muscles in the cat hind limb, *J. Physiol.* **150**: 399.

Causey, G., 1960. *The Cell of Schwann.* E & S Livingstone, Edinburgh.

Cavanagh, J. B., 1964. The significance of the "dying back" process in experimental and human neurological disease, *Int. Rev. Exp. Path.* **3**: 219.

Christophersen, B. O., 1964. Effects of ethanol on mitochondrial oxidations, *Biochem. Biophys. Acta* **86**: 14.

Coërs, C. and Hildebrand, J., 1965. Latent neuropathy in diabetes and alcoholism; electromyographic and histological study, *Neurology (Minneap.)* **15**: 19.

Collins, G. H., 1967. Glial cell changes in the brain stem of thiamine-deficient rats, *Amer. J. Path.* **50**: 791.

Courville, C. B., 1955. *Effects of Alcohol on the Nervous System of Man.* San Lucas Press, Los Angeles.

Creutzfeldt, O. D., Abbott, B. C., Fowler, W. M., and Pearson, C. M., 1963. Muscle membrane potentials in episodic adynamia, *Electroenceph. Clin. Neurophysiol.* **15**: 508.

Dawson, G. D., 1956. The relative excitability and conduction velocity of sensory and motor nerve fibers in man, *J. Physiol. (Lond.)* **131**: 436.

Dayan, A. D. and Williams, R., 1967. Demyelinating peripheral neuropathy and liver disease, *Lancet* (1): 133.

Denny-Brown, D., 1958. The neurologic aspects of thiamine deficiency, *Fed. Proc.* **17** Suppl 2: 35.

Denny-Brown, D., 1960. The nature of polymyositis and related muscular diseases, *Trans. Studies Coll. Phys. Phil.* **28**: 14.

Denny-Brown, D. and Brenner, C., 1944. Paralysis of nerve induced by direct pressure and by tourniquet, *Arch. Neurol. Psychiat.* **51**: 1.

Douglas, R. M., Fewings, J. D., Casley-Smith, J. R., and West, R. F., 1966. Recurrent-rhabdomyolysis precipitated by alcohol: A case report with physiological and electron microscopic studies of skeletal muscle, *Aust. Ann. Med.* **15**: 251.

Doyle, A. M. and Mayer, R. F., 1969. Studies of the motor unit in the cat. *Bull. Sch. Med. U. Md.* **54**: 11.

Dreschfeld, J., 1886. Further observations on alcoholic paralysis, *Brain* **8**: 433.

Dreyfus, P. M., 1965. The regional distribution of transketolase in the normal and the thiamine deficient nervous system, *J. Neuropath. Exp. Neurol.* **24**: 119.

Dyck, P. J., Gutrecht, J. A., Bastron, J. A., Karnes, W. E., and Dale, A. J. D., 1968. Histologic and teased-fiber measurements of sural nerve in disorders of lower motor and primary sensory neurons, *Mayo Clinic Proc.* **43**: 81.

Edds, M. V., 1950. Collateral regeneration of residual motor axons in partially denervated muscles, *J. Exp. Zool.* **113**: 517.

Edstrom, L. and Kugelberg, E., 1968. Histochemical composition, distribution of fibers and fatiguability of single motor units, *J. Neurol. Neurosurg. Psychiat.* **31**: 424.

Eiken, O., Nabseth, D. C., Mayer, R. F., and Deterling, R. A., Jr., 1964. Limb replantation. II. The pathophysiological effects, *Arch. Surg.* **88**: 54.

Ekbom, K., Hed, R., Kirstein, L., and Astrom, K.-E., 1964. Muscular affections in chronic alcoholism, *Arch. Neurol. (Chic.)*, **10**: 449.

Engel, A. G., Lambert, E. H., Rosevear, J. W., and Tauxe, W. N., 1965. Clinical and electromyographic studies in a patient with primary hypokalemic periodic paralysis, *Amer. J. Med.* **38**: 626.

Engel, A. G., Potter, C. S., and Rosevear, J. W., 1967. Studies on carbohydrate metabolism and mitochondrial respiratory activities in primary hypokalemic periodic paralysis, *Neurology (Minneap.)* **17**: 329.

Erlenborn, J. W. and Pilz, C. G., 1962. Paroxysmal myoglobinuria, *J. Amer. Med. Assoc.* **181**: 1111.

Fahlgren, H., Hed, R., and Lundmark, C., 1957. Myonecrosis and myoglobinuria in alcohol and barbiturate intoxication, *Acta Med. Scand.* **158**: 405.

Farmer, T. A., Jr., Hammack, W. J., and Frommeyer, W. B., Jr., 1961. Idiopathic recurrent rhabdomyolysis associated with myoglobinuria, *New Eng. J. Med.* **264**: 60.

Fennelly, J., Frank, O., Baker, H., and Lewy, C. M., 1964. Peripheral neuropathy of the alcoholic: I. Aetiological role of aneurin and other B-complex vitamins, *Brit. Med. J.* **2**: 1290.

Fennelly, J., Frank, O., Baker, H., and Lewy, C. M., 1967. Red blood cell-transketolase activity in malnourished alcoholics with cirrhosis, *Amer. J. Clin. Nut.* **20**: 946.

Fisher, C. M. and Adams, R. D., 1956. Diphtheritic polyneuritis. A pathological study, *J. Neuropath. Exp. Neurol.* **15**: 243.

Flink, E. B., Stutzman, F. L., Anderson, A. R., Konig, T., and Fraser, R., 1954. Magnesium deficiency after prolonged parenteral fluid administration and after chronic alcoholism complicated by delirium tremens, *J. Lab. Cl. Med.* **43**: 169.

Geren, B. B., 1954. The formation from the Schwann cell surface of myelin in the peripheral nerves of chick embryos, *Exp. Cell Res.* **7**: 558.

Gombault, A., 1880. Contribution a l'etude anatomique de la nevrite parenchymateuse subaigüe et chronique; nevrite segmentaire peri-axile, *Arch. Neurol. (Paris)* **1**: 11.

Gowers, W. R., 1899. *A Manual of Diseases of the Nervous System*, Vol. I, J. & A. Churchill, London.

Greenfield, J. G., 1958. *Neuropathology*. Edward Arnold, London.

Greenfield, J. G. and Carmichael, E. A., 1935. The peripheral nerves in cases of subacute combined degeneration of the cord, *Brain* **58**: 483.

Gross, E. G , Dexter, J. D., and Roth, R. G., 1966. Hypokalemic myopathy with myoglobinuria associated with licorice ingestion, *New Eng. J. Med.* **274**: 602.

Gudden, H., 1896. Klinische und anatomische beiträge zur kenntnis der multiplen alkoholneuritis nebst bemerkungen über die regenerationvorgänge im peripheren nervensystem, *Arch. f. Psychiat.* **28**: 643.

Guth, L., 1969. "Trophic" effects of vertebrate neurons, *Bull. Neurosci. Res. Prog.* **7** (No. 1): 5.

Gutrecht, J. A., and Dyck, P. J., 1966. Segmental demyelination: Peroneal muscular atrophy, *Mayo Clinic Proc.* **41**: 775.

Hanna, S., Harrison, M., MacIntyre, I., and Fraser, R., 1960. The syndrome of magnesium deficiency in man, *Lancet* **2**: 172.

Hed, R., Larssen, H., and Wahlgren, F., 1955. Acute myoglobinuria. Report of a case with fatal outcome, *Acta Med. Scand.* **152**: 459.

Hed, R., Lundmark, C., Fahlgren, H., and Orell, S., 1962. Acute muscular syndrome in chronic alcoholism, *Acta Med. Scand.* **171**: 585.

Heitzman, E. J., Patterson, J. F., and Stanley, M. M., 1962. Myoglobinuria and hypokalemia in regional enteritis, *Arch. Int. Med.* **110**: 117.

Henson, R. A., Russell, D. S., and Wilkinson, M., 1954. Carcinomatous neuropathy and myopathy, *Brain* **77**: 82.

Heyck, H. and Laudahn, G., 1967. Muscle and serum enzymes in muscular dystrophy and neurogenic muscular atrophy. A comparative study, *in Exploratory Concepts in Muscular Dystrophy and Related Disorders* (A. T. Milhorat, ed.) p. 232. Excerpta Med. Found. Amsterdam.

Hodes, R., Larrabee, M. G., and German, W., 1948. The human electromyogram in response to nerve stimulation and the conduction velocity of motor axons, studies in normal and in injured peripheral nerves, *Arch. Neurol. Psychiat.* **60**: 340.

Hoffman, H., 1950. Local re-innervation in partially denervated muscle: A histopathologic study, *Aust. J. Exp. Biol. Med. Sci.* **28**: 383.

Hopf, H. C., 1963. Electromyographic study on so-called mononeuritis, *Arch. Neurol.* (*Chic.*) **9**: 307.

Horvath, B., Berg, L., Cummings, D. J., and Shy, G. M., 1955. Muscular dystrophy. Cation concentration in residual muscles, *J. Appl. Physiol.* **8**: 21.

Hudson, C. H. and Dow, R. S., 1963. Motor nerve conduction velocity determination, A neurodiagnostic aid, *Neurology* (*Minneap.*) **13**: 982.

Hursh, J. B., 1939. Conduction velocity and diameter of nerve fibers, *Amer. J. Physiol.* **127**: 131.

Huss, M., 1849. *Alcoholismus Chronicus.* J. Beckman, Stockholm.

Hydén, H., 1943. Protein metabolism in the nerve cell during growth and function, *Acta Physiol. Scand.* **6** (suppl. 17): 5.

Inoue, F. and Frank, G. B., 1967. Effects of ethyl alcohol on excitability and on neuromuscular transmission in frog skeletal muscle, *Brit. J. Pharmac. Chemother.* **30**: 186.

Israel, Y., Kalant, H., and Laufer, I., 1965. Effects of ethanol on Na, K, Mg-stimulated microsomal ATPase activity, *Biochem. Pharm.* **14**: 1803.

Jackson, J., 1822. On a peculiar disease resulting from the use of ardent spirits, *New Eng. J. Med. Surg.* **11**: 351.

Jurko, M. F., Currier, R. D., and Foshee, D. P., 1964. Peripheral nerve changes in chronic alcoholics: A study of conduction velocity in motor nerves, *J. Nerv. Ment. Dis.* **139**: 488.

Juul-Jensen, P. and Mayer, R. F., 1966. Threshold stimulation for nerve conduction studies in man, *Arch. Neurol.* (*Chic.*) **15**: 410.

Karpati, G. and Engel, W. K., 1968. "Type grouping" in skeletal muscles after experimental reinnervation, *Neurology* (*Minneap.*) **18**: 447.

Klinkerfuss, G., Bleisch, V., Dioso, M. M., and Perkoff, G. T., 1967. A spectrum of myopathy associated with alcoholism. II. Light and electron microscopic observations, *Ann. Int. Med.* **67**: 493.

Knottinen, K., Oura, E., and Suomalainen, H., 1966. Influence of short-term alcohol consumption on the excretion of some components of the vitamin B group in the urine of rats, *Ann. Med. Exp. Fenn.* **45**: 63.

Knutsson, E. and Katz, S., 1967. The effect of ethanol on the membrane permeability to sodium and potassium ions in frog muscle fibers, *Acta Pharmacol et Toxicol.* **25**: 54.

Krücke, W., 1959. Histopathologie der polyneuritis und polyneuropathie, *Deutch Z. Nervenheilk.* **180**: 1.

Laasonen, L. and Palkama, A., 1967. Effect of alcohol on histochemically demonstrable liver and muscle phosphorylase activity in rats, *Ann. Med. Exp. Fenn.* **45**: 307.

Lambert, E. H., 1960. Neurophysiological techniques useful in the study of neuromuscular disorders, *Assoc. Res. Nerv. Ment. Dis. Proc.* **38**: 247.

Lettsom, J. C., 1780. Some remarks on the effects of lignum quassiae amarae, *Mem. Med. Soc. London* **1**: 128.

Lieber, C. S. and Rubin, E., 1969. Alcoholic fatty liver, *New Eng. J. Med.*, **280**: 705.

Low, M. D., Basmajian, J. V., and Lyons, G. M., 1962. Conduction velocity and residual latency in the human ulnar nerve and the effects on them of ethyl alcohol, *Amer. J. Med. Sci.* **244**: 720.

Majno, G. and Karnovsky, M. D., 1958. A biochemical and morphological study of myelination and demyelination, *J. Exp. Med.* **107**: 475.

Marin, O. S. M. and Denny-Brown, D., 1962. Changes in skeletal muscle associated with cachexia, *Amer. J. Path.* **41**: 23.

Mawdsley, C. and Mayer, R. F., 1965. Nerve conduction in alcoholic polyneuropathy, *Brain* **88**: 335.

Mayer, R. F., 1963. Nerve conduction studies in man, *Neurology (Minneap.)*, **13**: 1021.

Mayer, R. F., 1965. Personal observations.

Mayer, R. F., 1966. Peripheral nerve conduction in alcoholics. Studies of the effects of acute and chronic intoxication, *Psychosomat. Med.* **28** (Part 2): 475.

Mayer, R. F. and Denny-Brown, D., 1964. Conduction velocity in peripheral nerve during experimental demyelination in the cat, *Neurology (Minneap.)* **14**: 714.

Mayer, R. F. and Garcia-Mullin, R., 1968. Hereditary neuropathy manifested by pressure palsies—A Schwann cell disorder? *Trans. Amer. Neurol. Assoc.* **93**: 328.

Mayer, R. F. and Mawdsley, C., 1965. Parameters of the H reflex in pathological states, *Proc. 6th Int. Cong. EEG Clin. Neurophysiology*, Vienna, 635.

Mayer, R. F., Garcia-Mullin, R., and Eckholdt, J., 1968. Acute "alcoholic" myopathy, *Neurology (Minneap.)* (Abstract), **18**: 275.

McArdle, B., 1951. Myopathy due to a defect in muscle glycogen breakdown, *Clin. Sci.* **10**: 13.

McDonald, W. I., 1963. The effects of experimental demyelination on conduction in peripheral nerve: A histological and electrophysiological study. II. Electrophysiological observations, *Brain* **86**: 501.

Meiklejohn, A. P., 1940. Is thiamine the antineuritic vitamin? *New Eng. J. Med.* **223**: 265.

Merritt, H. H., 1955. *A Textbook of Neurology.* Lea and Febiger, Philadelphia.

Moore, J. W., 1966. Effects of ethanol on ionic conductances in the squid axon membrane, *Psychosomat. Med.* **28** (Part 2): 450.

Mott, F. W., 1896. Discussion of: On peripheral neuritis, S. J. Sharkey, *Brit. Med. J.* **1**: 457.

Mulder, D. W., Lambert, E. H., and Sprague, R. G., 1961. The neuropathies associated with diabetes mellitus, *Neurology (Minneap.)* **11**: 275.

Nygren, A., 1966. Serum creatine phosphokinase activity in chronic alcoholism in connection with acute alcohol intoxication, *Acta Med. Scand.* **179**: 623.

Pearson, C. M., 1964. The periodic paralyses: Differential features and pathological observations in permanent myopathic weakness, *Brain* **87**: 341.

Pekelharing, C. A. and Winkler, C., 1893. *Beriberi: Researches Concerning its Nature and Cause and the Means of its Arrest.* Pentland, Edinburgh.

Perkoff, G. T., Hardy, P., and Velez-Garcia, E., 1966. Reversible acute muscular syndrome in chronic alcoholism, *New Eng. J. Med.* **274**: 1277.

Perkoff, G. T., Dioso, M. M., Bleisch, V., and Klinkerfuss, G., 1967. A spectrum of myopathy associated with alcoholism. I. Clinical and laboratory features, *Ann. Int. Med.*, **67**: 481.

Phillips, G. B., Victor, M., Adams, R. D., and Davidson, C. S., 1952. A study of the nutritional defect in Wernicke's syndrome, *J. Clin. Invest.* **31**: 859.

Romanul, F. C. A. and Van Der Meulen, J. P., 1967. Slow and fast muscles after cross innervation: Enzymatic and physiological changes, *Arch. Neurol. (Chic.)* **17**: 387.

Rowland, L. P., Fahn, S., Hirschberg, E., and Harter, D. H., 1964. Myoglobinuria, *Arch. Neurol. (Chic.)* **10**: 537.

Rubin, E. and Lieber, C. S., 1968. Alcohol-induced hepatic injury in non-alcoholic volunteers, *New Eng. J. Med.* **278**: 869.

Rumsby, M. G. and Finean, J. B., 1966. The action of organic solvents on the myelin sheath of peripheral nerve tissue. I. Methanol, ethanol, chloroform and chloroform-methanol, *J. Neurochem.* **13**: 1501.

Saville, P. D., and Lieber, C. S., 1965. Effect of alcohol on growth, bone density and muscle magnesium in the rat, *J. Nutrition* **87**: 477.

Schlaepfer, W. W., 1969. Experimental lead neuropathy: A disease of the supporting cells in the peripheral nervous system, *J. Neuropath. Exp. Neurol.* **28**: 401.

Schmid, R. and Mahler, R., 1959. Chronic progressive myopathy with myoglobinuria: demonstration of glycogenolytic defect in muscle, *J. Clin. Invest.* **38**: 2044.

Schotland, D. L., Spiro, D., Rowland, L. P., and Carmel, P., 1965. Ultrastructural studies of muscle in McArdle's disease, *J. Neuropath. Exp. Neurol.* **24**: 629.

Serratrice, G., Toga, M., and Roux, H., 1966. Chronic proximal syndromes of alcoholic etiology, (Fr) *Presse Med.* **74**: 1721.

Shattuck, G. C., 1928. Relation of beriberi to polyneuritis from other causes, *Amer. J. Trop. Med.* **8**: 539.

Sherrington, C. S., 1929. Some functional problems attaching to convergence, *Proc. Roy. Soc. (London) Series B*, **105**: 332.

Shy, G. M., 1966. Chemical and morphological abnormalities in muscle disease, *Ann. N.Y. Acad. Sci.* **138** (1): 232.

Shy, G. M., Wanko, T., Rowley, P. T., and Engel, A. G., 1961. Studies in familial periodic paralysis, *Exp. Neurol.* **3**: 53.

Sjodin, R. A. and Henderson, E. G., 1964. Tracer and non-tracer potassium fluxes in frog sartorious muscle and the kinetics of net potassium movement, *J. Gen. Physiol.* **47**: 605.

Skou, J. C., 1965. Enzymatic basis for active transport of Na^+ and K^+ across cell membrane, *Physiol. Rev.* **45**: 596.

Smith, S. G., Black-Schaffer, B., and Lasater, T. E., 1950. Potassium deficiency syndrome in the rat and the dog, *Arch. Path.* **49**: 185.

Strauss, M. B., 1935. The etiology of "alcoholic polyneuritis," *Amer. J. Med. Sci.* **189**: 378.

Street, H. R., Zimmerman, H. M., Cowgill, G. R., II. T., II. F., and Fox J. G., Jr., 1941. Some effects produced by long-continued subminimal intakes of vitamin B₁, *Yale J. Biol. Med.* **13**: 293.

Sullivan, J. F., Lankford, H. G., Swartz, M. J., and Farrell, C., 1963. Magnesium metabolism in alcoholism, *Am. J. Clin. Nut.* **13**: 297.

Susin, M., and Herdson, P. B., 1967. Fine structural changes in rat myocardium induced by thyroxine and by magnesium deficiency, *Arch. Path.* **83**: 86.

Swank, R. L., 1940. Avian thiamine deficiency, A correlation of the pathology and clinical behavior, *J. Exp. Med.* **71**: 683.

Tasaki, I., 1955. New measurements of the capacity and the resistance of the myelin sheath and the nodal membrane of the isolated frog nerve fiber, *Amer. J. Physiol.* **181**: 639.

Thomas, P. K. and Lascelles, R. G., 1965. Schwann-cell abnormalities in diabetic neuropathy, *Lancet* **1**: 1355.

Thomas, P. K., Sears, T. A., and Gilliatt, R. W., 1959. Range of conduction velocity in normal nerve fibers to small muscles of hand and foot, *J. Neurol. Neurosurg. Psychiat.* **22**: 175.

Valaitis, J., Pilz, C. G., Oliver, H., and Chomet, B., 1960. Myoglobinuria, myoglobinuric nephrosis and alcoholism, *Arch. Path.* **70**: 195.

Victor, M. and Adams, R. D., 1953. The effect of alcohol on the nervous system, *Assoc. Res. Nerv. Ment. Dis. Proc.* **32**: 526.

Victor, M. and Adams, R. D., 1961. On the etiology of the alcoholic neurologic diseases, *Amer. J. Clin. Nut.* **9**: 379.

Victor, M., Mancall, E. L., and Dreyfus, P. M., 1960. Nutritional amblyopia in the alcoholic patient: A clinical-pathological study, *A.M.A. Arch. Ophthal.* **64**: 1.

Vilter, R. W., Mueller, J. F., Glazer, H. S., Jarrold, T., Abraham, J., Thompson, C., and Hawkins, V. R., 1953. The effect of vitamin B₆ deficiency induced by desoxypyridoxine in human beings, *J. Lab. Clin. Med.* **42**: 335.

Vizoso, A. D. and Young, J. Z., 1948. Internode length and fiber diameter in developing and regenerating nerves, *J. Anat.* **82**: 110.

Webster, H. deF., 1962. Schwann cell alterations in metachromatic leukodystrophy: Preliminary phase and electron microscopic observations, *J. Neuropath. Exp. Neurol.* **21**: 534.

Weiss, P. and Hiscoe, H. B., 1948. Experiments on the mechanism of nerve growth, *J. Exp. Zool.* **107**: 315.

Welt, L. G., Hollander, W. Jr., and Blythe, W. B., 1960. The consequences of potassium depletion, *J. Chron. Dis.* **11**: 213.

Wendt, V. E., Wu, C., Balcon, R., Doty, G., and Bing, R. J., 1965. Hemodynamic and metabolic effects of chronic alcoholism in man, *Amer. J. Cardiol.* **15**: 175.

Williams, R. D., Mason, H. L., Power, M. G., and Wilder, R. M., 1943. Induced thiamine (vitamin B₁) deficiency in man. Relation of depletion of thiamine to development of biochemical defect and of polyneuropathy, *Arch. Int. Med.* **71**: 38.

Wintrobe, M. M., Follis, R. H., Jr., Miller, M. H., Stein, H. J., Alcayoga, R., Humphreys, S., Suksta, A., and Cartwright, G. E., 1943. Pyridoxine deficiency in swine, *Bull Johns Hopkins Hosp.* **72**: 1.

Wisniewski, H., Terry, R. D., Whitaker, J. N., Cook, S. D., and Dowling, P. C., 1969. Landry–Guillain–Barré syndrome. A primary demyelinating disease, *Arch. Neurol.* (*Chic.*) **21**: 269.

Yonezawa, T. and Iwanami, H., 1965. In vitro study of vitamin B deficiency of the nervous tissue produced by antivitamins, *Proc. V Int. Cong. Neuropath., Zurich., Excerpta Med. Found.*: 868.

Yonezawa, T. and Iwanami, H., 1966. An experimental study of thiamine deficiency in nervous tissue, using tissue culture techniques, *J. Neuropath. Exp. Neurol.* 25: 362.

Zimmerman, H. M., 1956. Neuropathies due to vitamin deficiency, *J. Neuropath. Exp. Neurol.* 15: 335.

CHAPTER 3

The Effects of Alcohol on Evoked Potentials of Various Parts of the Central Nervous System of the Cat

Harold E. Himwich and David A. Callison

Thudichum Psychiatric Research Laboratory
Galesburg State Research Hospital
Galesburg, Illinois

INTRODUCTION

The actions of alcohol on the electrical activity of the cortex and deep structures of the brain in various animals have been the subject of investigations by many workers. Included in these studies are the contributions of Horsey and Akert (1953) and Caspers (1958), who worked on animals. Alcohol permeates the brain readily, and there appears to be no doubt that alcohol in adequate doses depresses the functions of the central nervous system. The effects of small doses of alcohol are less clear but evidence is in favor of a transient excitatory stage in electroencephalographic (EEG) activity (Horsey and Akert, 1953; Masserman, 1940). There is general agreement that alcohol has a synchronizing effect on the spontaneous electrical activity of the cerebral cortex and, depending on the dose, that such activity shows varying degrees of reduction in frequency and decreases in amplitude. In a comprehensive review, Kalant (1961) quotes Caspers (1958) who worked on rats and furthered the idea that alcohol exerts its earliest effect at the level of the reticular formation and that changes in electrical cortical activity are secondary to the primary reticular depression. However, this viewpoint has been questioned by several investigators (Himwich et al., 1966; DiPerri et al., 1968) and it will be discussed in detail later in the chapter. The reticular formation, as defined by Moruzzi and Magoun (1949), has been shown to play an important role in modifying sensory patterns (Hernández-Peon et al., 1956, 1957; Killam, 1962; Steriade and Demetrescu, 1962; Chin et al., 1965). Generally speaking, the observations of the latter authors suggest that blocking of afferent impulses in the lower portion of a sensory path may be a mechanism whereby sensory stimuli outside the scope of attention can be markedly reduced while they are still in their trajectory toward higher levels of the central nervous system. This central inhibitory mechanism may therefore play an important role in the selective exclusion of sensory messages along their passage toward mechanisms of perception and consciousness. It is thought that the synapse is probably the nervous structure most sensitive to alcohol. According to Larrabee and Posternak (1952), anesthetics exert a reversible depressant action at the synaptic level. This statement, however, is only a first approximation in seeking an explanation for the mechanism of action of alcohol. Though it is highly probable that this compound acts diffusely over the entire nervous system, nevertheless it does so with different intensities at various sites. We still must explain why neural transmission, the function most affected by alcohol, is more sensitive in some parts of the brain than in others. Since detailed knowledge of the subject is relatively incomplete, it is thought that the use of the technique of recording evoked potentials might disclose sensitive sites of action for alcohol in the central nervous system. In this chapter we intend to review and analyze the effects of alcohol on various sensory modalities of the cat as revealed by recording evoked potentials elicited by peripheral stimulation.

EXPERIMENTAL METHODS

It is important to remember in analyzing the results of the effects of alcohol on the central nervous system of the cat that some of the divergent opinions expressed in various studies may be due in part to differences in recording areas and techniques. Therefore, it is necessary to review a few of the techniques that various researchers have used in studying the effects of alcohol on the evoked potentials from the cat's central nervous system. The majority of studies were done acutely in curarized or spinalized cats, with only a few on chronic or unrestrained animals. All of the experiments reviewed were carried out on healthy adult cats ranging in weight from 2.0 to 4.0 kg. Alcohol was administered either intravenously or intraperitoneally in acute studies and via stomach tube in chronic studies. All of the operations were done under general or local anesthetic or a combination of both. The electrodes were implanted with the aid of a stereotaxic apparatus and in most of the studies, both acute and chronic, all electrode placements were histologically verified.

Acute Studies

Horsey and Akert (1953) recorded the effects of various doses of alcohol on the spontaneous activity of the cerebral cortex, thalamus, caudate nucleus, and striatum in cats immobilized mechanically or chemically with curare. The EEG recordings were made on a Grass III D electroencephalograph and an Offner frequency analyzer. Story et al. (1961) recorded electrical activity from cortical, limbic, and thalamic nuclei, tegmental loci (midbrain), hippocampus, and the basolateral amygdaloid nuclei. Their animals were immobilized with gallamine triethiodide (Flaxedil) and artificially respired. The effects of alcohol on evoked potentials were investigated by studying cortical and hippocampal potential changes elicited by short-pulse electrical stimuli. Dravid et al. (1963), Schweigerdt et al. (1965), Himwich et al. (1966), and DiPerri et al. (1968) recorded evoked potentials from the lateral funiculus of the spinal cord, reticular formation, nucleus ventralis posterolateralis of the thalamus (VPL), visual cortex, auditory cortex, primary somatosensory area (SI), and somatosensory association cortex (SAA) in animals immobilized with Intocostrin (d-tubocurarine) and maintained on artificial respiration. The animals were repeatedly injected with pontocaine at all wound margins and pressure points, including those caused by the ear bars of the stereotaxic instrument. These investigators used radial and sciatic nerve (electrical), photic (light), and auditory (click) stimulation to evoke the various responses they measured. Evoked potentials from SI and SAA were amplified, displayed on the face of a dual-beam oscilloscope, and were simultaneously summated by a computer of average transients (CAT). Data obtained by both methods were recorded by means of a kymographic camera. Nakai (1964), Nakai and Takaori (1965), and Nakai et al. (1965) in similar studies investigated the effects of central depressants, including ethyl alcohol, in encéphale isolé cats artificially respired. They recorded the EEG and evoked potentials from the middle ectosylvian gyrus (auditory cortex), inferior colliculus, and ipsilateral sigmoid gyrus of the cerebral cortex. These studies used auditory click stimuli and electrical stimuli of the nucleus centrum medianum of the thalamus and the reticular formation. The evoked potentials were recorded on a cathode ray oscilloscope and photographed. Nakai and Domino (1969) studied the effects of ethyl alcohol as well as those of pentobarbital and chlorpromazine on visually evoked responses elicited by electrical stimulation of the ipsilateral optic tract and on the facilitation of such evoked potentials by electrical stimulation of the mesencephalic reticular formation. The animals in this experiment were immobilized with decamethionium and maintained on artificial respiration. The evoked responses were recorded monopolarly from the primary visual cortex (left lateral gyrus). The EEG was monitored on a Grass Model III D electroencephalograph and the evoked responses were amplified and displayed on a dual-beam oscilloscope. A long-recording camera, the stimulator, and the oscilloscope used to record the evoked potentials were simultaneously triggered by a Hunter timer. Sauerland et al. (1967) studied the effects of alcohol on orbital-cortically induced reflex inhibition in the cat. They immobilized their animals with Flaxedil and used the soleus and monosynaptic masseteric reflexes as test reflexes. The stimulus parameters for reflex elicitation and orbital-gyral stimulation were kept constant in each experiment. Small silver hooks were used for recording the reflex discharges, which were registered on an oscilloscope and averaged with a computer. Hadji-Dimo et al. (1968) conducted their studies on cats immobilized with Flaxedil and maintained on artificial respiration. The electrical activity of the brain was recorded with an Offner dynograph by means of bipolar electrodes placed on the cortex. Changes in the amplitude and frequency of the EEG were revealed by histographic analyses, and the effects of alcohol on cortical blood flow were also measured.

In the majority of the above-mentioned studies, the blood pressure was monitored and the concentration of alcohol in the blood was determined. The amounts and the concentrations of the alcohol solutions were carefully controlled and measured. The administration and the concentration of alcohol used in each study will be explained more fully in the Results and Discussion sections of the chapter.

Chronic Studies

Horsey and Akert (1953), besides conducting acute studies, also recorded the EEG in 17 unrestrained cats with chronically implanted electrodes. They recorded from the frontal, parietal, and occipital cortices and from two subcortical structures, the striatum and thalamus. As in their acute studies, they used a Grass Model III D electroencephalograph and an Offner frequency analyzer to reveal alcohol-induced alterations in the electrical activity of the brain.

In addition to their acute studies, Story et al. (1961) conducted chronic alcohol studies in cats by implanting chronic electrodes in four animals. Subcortical electrodes were placed in various thalamic nuclei, midbrain tegmentum, lateral hypothalamus, basolateral amygdaloid nuclei and hippocampus, and additional cortical electrodes were placed on the post cruciate and suprasylvian gyri. Records were made with an eight-channel ink writing oscillograph.

RESULTS OF VARIOUS TYPES OF STIMULATION

Electrical Stimulation of the Radial and Sciatic Nerves

DiPerri *et al.* (1968) have done extensive work in recording the effects of alcohol on potentials evoked by stimulation of the radial and sciatic nerves. The evoked responses were recorded from electrodes placed in the lateral funiculus of the spinal cord at the level of the second cervical vertebra homolateral to the stimulated nerve. Responses were also recorded from the reticular formation at the midcollicular level and from the nucleus ventralis posterolateralis (VPL) of the thalamus contralateral to the stimulated nerve. In the first series of experiments evoked potentials following stimulation of the homolateral radial nerve

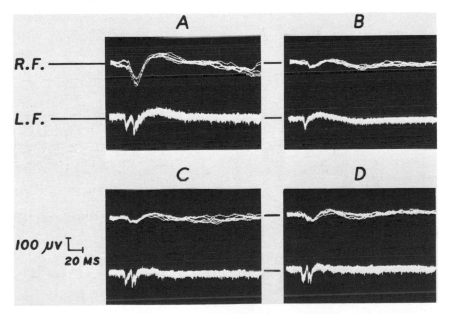

FIGURE 1. Evoked responses to electrical stimulation of the radial nerve recorded from the contralateral midbrain reticular formation (RF) and homolateral lateral funiculus (LF) of the spinal cord at C_2 level. A, control; B, C, D, 5, 15, and 60 min after intravenous injection of ethyl alcohol (1 g/kg). A depression is evident in both responses (B), the lateral funiculus is almost fully recovered 15 min after alcohol administration (C), while the reticular formation is still partially depressed at 60 min (D). Note that the first spike of the LF was not affected at all by this dosage of alcohol. In this figure and in the following ones (except Fig. 4), each trace displays five superimposed frames; upward deflection indicates negativity. [From DiPerri *et al.* (1968).]

were recorded from the lateral funiculus and the reticular formation. The funicular response in the untreated animal consisted of a double positive deflection of which the first peak had a latency of 2 msec while the second deflection began 10 msec after the presentation of the stimulus. The total duration of both deflections was 20 to 24 msec and they were followed by a low-amplitude negative wave of longer duration. Following the intravenous administration of a solution of 20% ethanol (1 g/kg) slowly injected to prevent a drop in blood pressure, a depressant action on the evoked potentials was observed to affect almost exclusively the second positive component of the funicular responses and the positive component of the reticular response, while latency was little affected (Fig. 1). Fifteen minutes after injection, recovery was more pronounced in the spinal cord than at the reticular level. It was noted that the first positive wave in the response from the lateral funiculus, in contrast to the second one, was very little affected by this dosage of alcohol. Also, this response as a whole was more resistant to alcohol than the one from the reticular formation. In three other experiments responses were recorded from the caudal

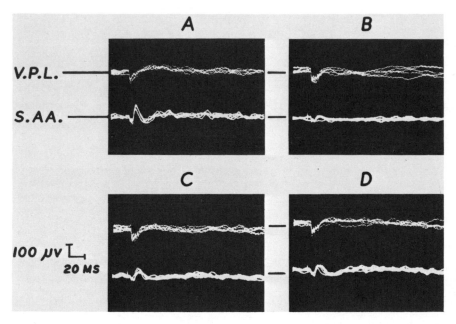

FIGURE 2. Evoked responses to electrical stimulation of radial nerve recorded from the contralateral nucleus ventralis posterolateralis (VPL) of the thalmus and from the somatosensory association area (SAA) homolateral to VPL. A, control; B, C, D, 5, 15, and 60 min after intravenous administration of ethyl alcohol (1 g/kg). The response from VPL is hardly affected while marked depression of the cortical response is evident (B) and continues though to a lesser degree 1 hr after the injection of alcohol (D). [From DiPerri et al. (1968).]

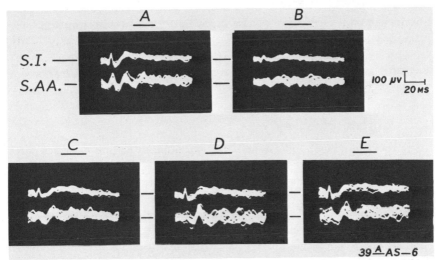

FIGURE 3. Evoked responses to electrical stimulation of the sciatic nerve recorded from the two cortical sites: (1) Primary somatosensory cortex (SI) and (2) association area (SAA). A, control; B, C, D, E, 2, 15, 30 and 60 min after intravenous injection of alcohol (1 g/kg). The evoked potentials from SAA yield rather variable responses while at SI they are of a more consistent form. The responses from both recording sites are depressed by alcohol, the effect being more severe in SAA than in SI. [From DiPerri et al. (1968).]

end of the VPL and the somatosensory association area (SAA) contralateral to the stimulated nerve. The evoked response recorded from the VPL upon stimulation of the radial nerve was a positive wave 3 msec in latency and 16 msec in duration. This response consisted of a triphasic deflection, initially positive. Figure 2 shows that both the negative and positive waves of the cortical response were depressed to approximately the same degree but that no change in latency was observed. Up to 60 min after the injection, the cortical response (SAA) was not fully restored. In contrast, the thalamic response was hardly affected at all by this dosage of alcohol.

Responses to electrical stimulation of the sciatic nerve were recorded from two cortical sites, the primary somatosensory (SI) and the somatosensory association (SAA) areas (Himwich et al., 1966). The evoked potentials recorded from SAA in three experiments exhibited a relatively deep depression throughout the entire experiment (Fig. 3), although in two other observations the comparable effects were variable. The authors concluded from these results that potentials evoked in the SAA area were more depressed by alcohol than potentials in SI (Himwich et al., 1966; DiPerri et al., 1968), and these results agree with those of Caspers (1958), although he investigated only one cortical site in rats. Control experiments using normal saline were also performed to rule out the effects of the volume of the injected alcohol solution on blood pressure and on the evoked responses. A minor drop of blood pressure occurred in the first few seconds after the initial injection of alcohol and as a rule the blood pressure values were completely recovered by the time the first record was made after injection. These minor changes in blood pressure did not seem to influence the amplitudes of the evoked potentials.

Direct Cortical Stimulation

Story *et al.* (1961) and Grenell (1959) conducted studies in which direct cortical stimulation was used to investigate the effects of alcohol on the cortical evoked response. In both series of experiments it was found that comparatively low doses of ethanol (1 to 2 ml/kg) caused mild to moderate enhancement of the initial negative deflection of the cortical response. Ethanol in higher doses was found to elicit the appearance of, or to increase markedly the amplitude of a late surface-positive component of the cortical response (Story *et al.*, 1961). Grenell (1959), however, noticed a depressant effect of alcohol in concentrations of 50 mM and above on the dendritic response. It should be pointed out that Grenell (1959) used a local perfusion technique of ethanol through a pial vessel directly onto a localized area of the cerebral cortex, while Story *et al.* (1961) administered ethanol either by the intraperitoneal or intravenous route.

Stimulation of Subcortical Structures with Special Reference to the Reticular Formation

Evoked potentials recorded from the posterior sigmoid gyrus in response to stimulation of sensory relay nonspecific thalamic nuclei (recruiting response) were not significantly changed with a 2 ml/kg dose of ethanol. However, cortical responses to stimulation of the sensory relay nuclei of the thalamus (augmenting response) were profoundly depressed or completely flattened after ethanol injection (Story *et al.*, 1961). A comparable depression of the visual cortical response to optic tract stimulation was also reported. This investigation in addition showed a mild enhancement of the initial negative deflection of the transcallosal and interhippocampal responses after 2 ml/kg doses of ethanol. The first effect on the direct cortical responses, an enhancement by ethanol, lasted less than 2 hr, while the ensuing depression of sensory responses persisted for 3 to 4 hr.

Nakai and Takaori (1965) also tested the effects of increasing doses of ethanol on the recruiting response recorded from the sigmoid gyrus. In their investigation ethanol did not change the stimulus threshold until a dose of 400 mg/kg was reached. However, with doses above 1200 mg/kg, the threshold was moderately increased and a slight change in the configuration of the response was observed.

The effects of electrical stimulation of the reticular formation on responses evoked by click stimuli in the auditory cortex and the relay nucleus were studied by Takaori et al. (1966). In most cases stimulation of the reticular formation decreased the amplitude of the responses to repetitive click stimuli. However, facilitation of the response was also observed after stimulation of certain areas of the reticular formation. In general, the inhibitory sites were diffusely distributed in the reticular formation, while the facilitatory areas were located mainly in the pontine reticular formation and rarely in its rostral and caudal parts. During reticular stimulation the amplitudes of the responses to click stimuli recorded from the auditory cortex and medial geniculate body were decreased by 30.1 and 25.6%, respectively, while the responses in the inferior colliculus were not altered by reticular stimulation. The responses from the cochlear nucleus showed a slight decrease in amplitude during reticular formation stimulation. Following the infusion of ethanol, the investigators (Takaori et al., 1966) noted a progressive dose-related decrease in the amplitudes of the cortical responses to click stimuli. Furthermore, the inhibition of the response caused by reticular stimulation was invariably observed even after the infusion of 400 to 800 mg/kg of ethanol (Fig. 4).

Nakai and Domino (1969) conducted similar experiments, only they recorded the effects of stimulation of the reticular formation on visually evoked responses elicited by electrical stimulation of the ipsilateral optic tract. The

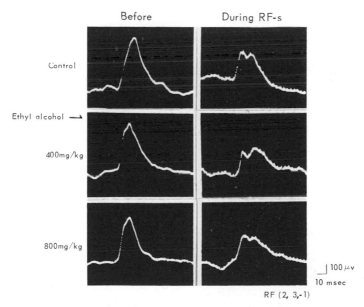

FIGURE 4. Effect of ethyl alcohol on the inhibition of cortical click responses caused by RF stimulation. [From Takaori et al. (1966).]

response to stimulation of the optic tract was found to be dramatically facilitated
by stimulation of the reticular formation. This is in contrast to the known
variability of the effects of reticular stimuli in altering evoked responses in the
auditory or somatosensory system (Nakai, 1964). The intravenous administration of a 25% solution of ethanol produced a cortical depression, but in
contrast produced no significant depression of the reticular facilitation of the
visually evoked responses. In fact, stimulation of the reticular formation restored
the visually evoked responses almost to control values.

Auditory Stimulation

In a series of experiments in cats exposed to various concentrations of
methanol, ethanol, butanol, and octanol, Grenell (1959) recorded the auditory
cortical response to repetitive (1/sec) click stimuli. He found that with each of
the alcohols used, mild excitation was produced by low concentrations while
higher concentrations were followed by depression. DiPerri et al. (1968) recorded
the auditory responses to click stimuli from the inferior colliculus and from the
homolateral primary auditory cortex. The effects of ethanol (1 g/kg) on the evoked
potentials included a degree of depression in both responses. In most instances
the negative peak of the cortical response was fully recovered 15 min after
alcohol injection, although the collicular response was still partially depressed
even after 60 min (Fig. 5). Nakai (1964) stimulated encéphale isolé cats with
binaural clicks and recorded from the middle ectosylvian gyrus. When an
hour-long injection of ethanol was intravenously infused to a total dose of
1.6 g/kg dissolved in 100 ml of Ringer's solution, the amplitudes of the evoked
potentials slowly but progressively decreased without manifesting any increase,
even early in the injection period when the dosages were lowest. Moreover, the
continued administration of the alcohol resulted in further decreases of the
already reduced amplitude. In this study the latencies of the responses were also
prolonged to a slight extent when a total dose of 0.8 g/kg of ethanol was reached.
The evoked rhythmic afterdischarge in the response to a click stimulus was
little affected during the beginning phase of the infusion; it was, however,
significantly depressed in frequency and prolonged in duration with doses of
0.4 mg/kg or more.

Nakai and Takaori (1965), in studies with an experimental design similar
to those mentioned above, investigated the effects of alcohol on the responses of
the auditory cortex to repetitive click stimuli and found a progressive decrease
in the amplitudes of the early potentials, i.e., those responses which occurred in
the first 0.5 sec of a 10-sec stimulation period, and that the depression was more
marked in the potentials elicited by high frequency stimulation than in those
evoked by low frequency stimulation. Nakai et al. (1965) studied the unitary
discharges of the inferior colliculus in response to single click stimuli. In the late

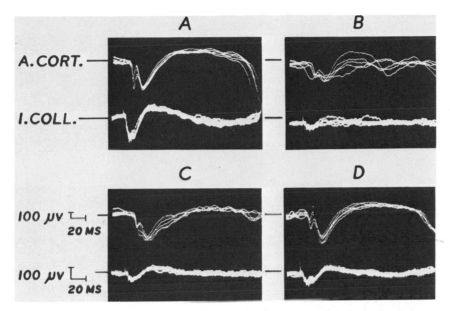

FIGURE 5. Evoked responses to auditory stimulation recorded from the primary auditory cortex (A. CORT.), and from the homolateral inferior colliculus (I. COLL.). A, control; B, C, D, 5, 15, and 60 min after the administration of ethyl alcohol (1 g/kg). The cortical response is fully recovered 60 min after alcohol treatment while the inferior colliculus still shows marked depression. [From DiPerri *et al.* (1968).]

spike group the discharges were slightly decreased in number and amplitude, but no change was ever observed in the early spike group until the dose of 400 mg/kg was attained. Even at the dose of 800 mg/kg, the early spikes might remain unaffected or might be only slightly depressed in number. On the other hand, the later spikes were variably obtunded by ethanol (above 800 mg/kg) and were reduced to the extent of less than half their earlier number. These findings suggested that the depressant effect of alcohol upon the late spike group may be related to the transmission of acoustic impulses through collateral ascending pathways or the recurrent transmission through the higher efferent pathways. The hypersensitivity of multiple synaptic transmission to central depressants is well known. The early spike group may be a manifestation of the primary reaction of the inferior colliculus to click stimuli.

Photic Stimulation

The effects of alcohol upon the evoked response elicited by photic stimulation have been examined by DiPerri *et al.* (1968) who recorded from the lateral geniculate body (LGB) and the homolateral visual cortex. The typical response from the LGB consisted of a small positive deflection, followed by a long

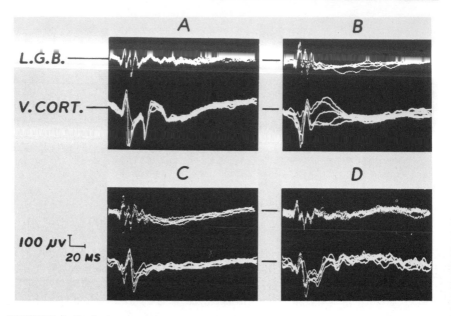

FIGURE 6. Evoked responses to photic stimulation recorded from one lateral geniculate body (LGB) and homolateral visual cortex (V. CORT.). A, control; B, C, D, 5, 15, and 30 min after intravenous injection of alcohol (1 g/kg). Depressant effect of alcohol is seen on the later waves of the cortical response which, however, are partially recovered 30 min after alcohol treatment (D). The LGB is hardly affected by this dosage of alcohol. In these traces the onset of the stimulus and the beginning of the oscilloscope record are concomitant. [From DiPerri et al. (1968).].

negative wave on which were superimposed three sharp negative-positive waves. The evoked potentials recorded from the visual cortex were similar to those described by other authors (Marshall et al., 1943, and Buser and Borenstein, 1959) and a typical example revealed a sharp triphasic positive-negative-positive pair of spikes of about 18 msec duration followed by a second series of sharp waves, usually positive in nature, although sometimes negative ones were intermixed. Figure 6 reveals the absence of any effect of alcohol on the response recorded from the LGB. At the cortical level the later components of the evoked responses were affected more readily and for a longer period while the primary ones showed only slight, if any, depression. Moreover, no effect was noted on the latency of the response, but 30 min after injection, the cortical depression had been reversed to a great degree.

DISCUSSION AND CONCLUSIONS

The above reviewed results disclose that alcohol in adequate doses depresses the functions of the central nervous system. The effects of small doses of alcohol are less clear and the evidence in favor of the stimulating action is becoming more prominent. Masserman and Jacobson (1940) found that the responses of the hypothalamus and the somatosensory cortex to rapid electrical stimulation in cats were slightly increased after local injections of alcohol at concentrations of about 0.02%, but were definitely decreased after the injection of concentrations higher than 0.06%. Larrabee and Posternak (1952) similarly noted that a 1% solution of alcohol facilitated the transmission of the nerve impulse across the stellate ganglion of cats while a 3% solution produced the usual inhibition. Along the same lines, with high levels of alcohol in the blood, above 70 mg%, a general depressant action and a narcotic effect were observed in the EEG as well as in the behavior of cats (Horsey and Akert, 1953). But with lower concentrations, 20 to 40 mg%, transient excitatory changes appeared in the EEG. Similarly, Grenell (1959) showed that the cortical evoked response to auditory stimulation was enhanced by the intravenous injection of alcohol in low dosages, but was depressed by amounts higher than 146 mg/100 g. Again, the infusion of small doses of several depressant drugs, including ethanol, was found to accelerate the manifestation of the rhythmic afterdischarge of the response to a click stimulus (Nakai, 1964). However, further infusion of the depressants resulted in a slowing of the background activity of the EEG recorded from the auditory cortex, which was accompanied by a depression of the corresponding manifestation of the evoked rhythmic afterdischarge. In addition, the evoked rhythmic afterdischarge was decreased in frequency and prolonged in duration (Nakai, 1964). Thus it may be concluded that minute doses of alcohol tend to be stimulating.

In the experiments concerned with stimulation of the radial nerve, the comparative responses in the primary somatosensory cortex were less susceptible to alcohol than those in the reticular formation, but more susceptible than the evoked potentials in the lateral funiculus (DiPerri et al., 1968).

It has been widely accepted that central nervous system depressants markedly affect polysynaptic structures, such as the brainstem reticular formation. This is especially true of general anesthetics and other coma-producing agents like pentobarbital and ethanol (Arduini and Arduini, 1954; French et al., 1953; Killam, 1962). In evaluating the results obtained by DiPerri et al. (1968) at the two different cortical sites, we must take into consideration their anatomical and neurophysiological characteristics. Amassian (1954) in his studies with cats under chloralose, noted that the association cortex is at least partly dependent on relays of afferent volleys from the sensorimotor cortex. Analysis of the association response following electrical stimulation of somatosensory areas suggests that the primary areas transmit impulses to the association area both directly and indirectly through a deep relay. Thus in regard to evoked potentials, the association area presents a greater polysynaptic development than the primary somatosensory cortex and for that reason it may be more readily depressed by alcohol. Perhaps polysynaptic development in the midbrain reticular formation is intermediate between that in the primary somatosensory cortex and that in the association area. If the greater degree of depression depends upon the greater extent of polysynaptic development, it is not surprising that the reticular formation is depressed to a greater extent than the primary somatosensory cortex. Such an action on the part of alcohol may also account for the greater sensitivity of the association area, not only as compared to the primary somatosensory cortex, but to the reticular formation as well. Of all the brain regions studied by DiPerri *et al.* (1968), the accessory somatosensory area was the one most sensitive to alcohol. A similar explanation seems to apply to transmission to the association area via the lateral funiculus and the VPL nucleus. The failure of alcohol to obtund the first spike of the response in the lateral funiculus while markedly depressing the second may also be accounted for by more complex synaptic neural pathways being involved in the production of the second spike.

Sauerland *et al.* (1970) in studying the effects of ethyl alcohol on the trigeminal sensory neurons of the cat, found that a blood alcohol concentration above 0.05% induced primary afferent depolarization. They demonstrated that this depolarizing effect was limited to the central (presynaptic) terminals within the spinal nucleus of the fifth cranial nerve. This process of presynaptic depolarization has been closely linked to Eccles (1964) concept of "presynaptic inhibition." Thus, it appears that signals in the trigeminal cutaneous afferents are partially suppressed before they reach secondary neurons. Sauerland *et al.* (1970) conclude that at least part of the depressant action of alcohol on the central nervous system is due to enhancement of presynaptic inhibition.

Sauerland and Harper (1970) found an excitatory effect of ethyl alcohol on the central cortex of the cat (power spectra analysis). This augmenting effect of alcohol on the synaptically driven activity of the sensorimotor cortex might possibly be explained by a depression of the ascending reticular activating system (Caspers, 1958; Himwich *et al.*, 1966). Sauerland and Harper (1970) concluded that both the reticular formation and forebrain are influenced by alcohol since alcohol depolarizes the central process of the first neuron and has no effect on the peripheral processes or cell bodies. In other words, alcohol produces presynaptic inhibition of incoming information and the phenomenon is enhanced by influences descending from the forebrain down to the level of the central processes.

In contrast to Himwich *et al.* (1966), Nakai and Domino (1969) observed in their experiments no effect of ethyl alcohol on the facilitation of the visual evoked response by stimulation of the reticular formation. Their analysis of the last group of results depends in part on the anatomical concept that single axon cells originate in the brainstem and send fibers to the diencephalon. A large number of neurons of the reticular formation belong to this type of cell. Therefore, according to their results, it may be expected that the central nervous system depressants, including ethyl alcohol, have relatively little effect on these monosynaptic neurons. It may well be that reticular facilitation of sensory input at the thalamic level is mediated by long axon cells as opposed to shorter ones, which is shown by the relative resistance of the system to depression by pentobarbital and ethyl alcohol (Nakai and Domino, 1969).

However, from what is known about the effects of anesthetics (French *et al.*, 1953) on the reticular formation, and alcohol may be regarded as an anesthetic, it could be expected that the reticular formation would be more sensitive than the somatosensory cortex. The impulses emanating from the reticular level may cease earlier than those from a cortical area which is not immediately dependent upon this subcortical structure. But the data of DiPerri *et al.* (1968) from the comparative study of two cortical sites, the SI and SAA areas, revealed a complex situation in which some aspects of the cortical contribution are more susceptible to alcohol than those of the reticular formation. Similarly, the auditory evoked potentials recorded from the inferior colliculus are as susceptible, if not more so, than those of the primary auditory cortex (DiPerri *et al.*, 1968). Therefore in this case the hearing and the understanding of sound would be lost simultaneously. But for vision, the differences between the responses of the lateral geniculate body and the visual cortex support the concept of greater cortical sensitivity to alcohol, so that the discrete awareness of what is seen might disappear before the function of seeing as such (DiPerri *et al.*, 1968). A study concerning the effects of alcohol on the auditory response in humans tends to confirm the idea that there is a reduction of input of auditory information into the perceptual and cognitive systems owing to the depressant effect of alcohol (Gross *et al.*, 1966). If we refer to the concept of reverberating circuits and positive and negative feedback mechanism, we see that for some sensory modalities, but not for others, some circuits with cortical components cease functioning before those which are represented chiefly by subcortical elements.

It is also important to point out that overall behavioral response to alcohol reveals effects which appear to be most marked in the so-called higher functions of the brain: learning, judgment, and self-criticism. Only with increasing dosages do we see the depression extending down the brainstem to lower areas and finally enveloping the vital centers of the medulla oblongata, resulting in the productions of shock (Himwich, 1956). That the earlier more profound and more enduring effect is exerted on cortical rather than on subcortical structures is in accordance with the clinical viewpoint that depression extends along the neuraxis from above downward.

In addition to the electrophysiological explanations of the effects of alcohol on the central nervous system, there are several important biochemical theories concerning the central depressant action of alcohol (Kalant and Israel, 1966; Kalant *et al.*, 1967, and Wallgren, 1967). Wallgren (1967) in an investigation of neuronal activity, respiration, and utilization of energy-rich phosphates, has suggested that the metabolic depression caused by alcohol is probably secondary to the interference with nerve cell activity. Its primary action seems to be on excitable membranes, where alcohol may induce membrane depolarization which may block impulse conduction. Kalant and Israel (1966) propose the idea that interference with active transport of cations across nerve cell and muscle cell membranes contributes to the effects of alcohol intoxication. Kalant *et al.* (1967) also concluded that the effect *in vivo* of alcohol may be due in part to an inhibition of acetylcholine release at the central cholinergic synapse.

The foregoing review indicates that alcohol hits hardest some parts of the brain required for the most highly integrated actions. Alcohol affects to some degree all the functions of the brain, but the experimental data indicate that the functions with largest cortical components seem to be most susceptible. Kraepelin (1927) compares alcohol with other narcotic drugs and stresses, for example, that auditory perception seems to be strong although the content is no longer recognized. A loss of the efficiency of the most complex movements possessing cortical components is apparent. There are, however, no hallucinations or loss of memory. Only in the deeper stages does amnesia supervene, and this occurs after functional paralysis has enveloped the cortex. The second stage of excitement is therefore marked by release from cortical control and loss of environmental contact. When depression is pushed beyond that stage, its predominant effects spread further down the neuraxis. Succeeding areas become involved in time until the medullary centers may undergo a dangerous depression and if the anesthesia is not circumvented, respiratory failure and shock may be expected. Thus a path seems to be established starting from cephalad areas of the brain and extending in the caudal direction. It is interesting that the neurological signs of recovery show in general the reverse direction, and that the first stage of alcohol depression is the last one to return, revealing a recapitulation of the evolutionary path. The primary influence of alcohol is therefore exerted on central mechanisms which suffer the greatest depression.

REFERENCES

Amassian, V. E., 1954. Studies on organization of a somesthetic association area, including a single unit analysis, *J. Neurophysiol.* **17**: 39.

Arduini, A. and Arduini, M. G., 1954. Effect of drugs and metabolic alterations on brain stem arousal mechanism, *J. Pharmacol. Exp. Therap.* **110**: 76.

Buser, P. and Borenstein, P., 1959. Responses somesthesiques, visuelles et auditives, recueillies au niveau du cortex "associatif" supersylvien chez le chat curarise non anesthesie, *Electroencephalog. Clin. Neurophysiol.* **11**: 285.

Caspers, H., 1958. Die Beeinflussung der corticalen Krampferregbackeit durch das aufsteigende Reticular-system des Hirnitammes. II. Narkosewirkungen, *Z. Ges. Exp. Med.* **129**: 582.

Chin, J. H., Killam, E. K., and Killam, K. F., 1965. Factors affecting sensory input in the cat: Modification of evoked auditory potentials by reticular formation, *Electroencephalog. Clin. Neurophysiol.* **18**: 567.

DiPerri, R., Dravid, A., Schweigerdt, A., and Himwich, H. E., 1968. Effects of alcohol on evoked potentials of various parts of the central nervous system of cat, *Quart. J. Studies Alc.* **29**: 20.

Dravid, A. R., DiPerri, R., Morillo, A., and Himwich, H. E., 1963. Alcohol and evoked potentials in the cat, *Nature* **200**: 1328.

Eccles, J. C., 1964. Presynaptic inhibition in the spinal cord, in *Physiology of Spinal Neurons, Progress in Brain Research*, (J. C. Eccles and J. P. Schadé, eds.) Vol. 12, pp. 65–91, Elsevier, Amsterdam.

French, J. D., Verzeano, M., and Magoun, H. W., 1953. A neural basis of the anesthetic state, *Arch. Neurol. Psychiat.* **69**: 519.

Grenell, R. G., 1959. Alcohols and activity of cerebral neurons, *Quart. J. Studies Alc.* **20**: 421.

Gross, M. M., Begleiter, H., Tobin, M., and Kissin, B., 1966. Changes in auditory evoked response induced by alcohol, *J. Nerv. Ment. Dis.* **143**: 152.

Hadji-Dimo, A. A., Ekberg, R., and Ingvar, D. H., 1968. Effects of ethanol on EEG and cortical blood flow in the cat, *Quart. J. Studies A c.* **29**: 828.

Hernández-Peon, R., Scherrer, H., and Velascu, M., 1956. Central influences on afferent conduction in the somatic and visual pathways, *Acta Neurol. Latinoam.* **2**: 8.

Hernández-Peon, R., Guzmin-Flores, C., Alcuraz, M., and Fernandez-Guardiola, A., 1957. Sensory transmission in visual pathway during "attention" in unanesthetized cats, *Acta Neurol. Latinoam.* **3**: 1.

Himwich, H. E., 1956. Alcohol and brain physiology, in *Alcoholism* (G. N. Thompson, ed.) pp. 291–408, Charles C Thomas, Springfield, Ill.

Himwich, H. E., DiPerri, R., Dravid, A., and Schweigerdt, A., 1966. Comparative susceptibility to alcohol of the cortical area and midbrain reticular formation of the cat, *Psychosomat. Med.* **28**: 458.

Horsey, W. J. and Akert, K., 1953. The influence of ethyl alcohol on the spontaneous electrical activity of the cerebral cortex and subcortical structures of the cat, *Quart. J. Studies Alc.* **14**: 363.

Kalant, H., 1961. The pharmacology of alcohol intoxication, *Quart. J. Studies Alc.* **22**: (Suppl. 1) 1.

Kalant, H. and Israel, Y., 1966. Effects of ethanol on active transport of cations, in *Biochemical Factors in Alcoholism*, pp. 25–37, Pergamon Press, New York

Kalant, H., Israel, Y., and Mahon, M. A., 1967. The effect of ethanol on acetylcholine synthesis, release, and degradation in brain, *Can. J. Physiol. Pharmacol.* **45**: 172.

Killam, E. K., 1962. Drug action on the brain-stem reticular formation, *Pharmacol. Rev.* **14**: 175.

Kraepelin, E., 1927. *Psychiatrie.* J. A. Barth, Leipzig.

Larrabee, M. and Posternak, J. M., 1952. Selective action of anesthetics on synapses and axons in mammalian sympathetic ganglia, *J. Neurophysiol.* **15**: 91.

Marshall, W. H., Talbot, S. A., and Ades, H. W., 1943. Cortical response of the anesthetised cat to gross photic and electrical afferent stimulation, *J. Neurophysiol.* **6**: 1.

Masserman, J. H., 1940. Stimulant effects of ethyl alcohol in cortico-hypothalamic functions, *J. Pharmacol. Exp. Therap.* **70**: 450.

Masserman, J. H. and Jacobson, L., 1940. Effects of ethyl alcohol on the cerebral cortex and the hypothalamus of the cat, *Arch. Neurol. Psychiat.* **43**: 334.

Moruzzi, G. and Magoun, H. W., 1949. Brain stem reticular formation and activation of the EEG, *Electroencephalog. Clin. Neurophysiol.* **1**: 455.

Nakai, Y., 1964. Effects of intravenous infusion of central depressants on the evoked potentials of the auditory cortex in the cats, *Japan. J. Pharmacol.* **14**: 235.

Nakai, Y. and Domino, E. F., 1969. Differential effects of pentobarbital, ethyl alcohol, and chlorpromazine in modifying reticular facilitation of visually evoked responses in the cat, *Inutni ni nIn pharmacol* 9: 61

Nakai, Y. and Takaori, S., 1965. Effects of central depressants on the cortical auditory responses evoked by repetitive click stimuli in the cat, *Japan. J. Pharmacol.* **15**: 165.

Nakai, Y., Matsuoka, I., and Takaori, S., 1965. Pharmacological analysis of unitary discharges recorded from the inferior colliculus caused by click stimuli in cats, *Japan. J. Pharmacol.* **15**: 378.

Sauerland, E. K. and Harper, R. M., 1970. Effects of ethanol on EEG spectra of the intact brain and isolated forebrain, *Exp. Neurol.* **27**: 490.

Sauerland, E. K., Mizuno, N., and Harper, R. M., 1970. Presynaptic depolarization of trigeminal cutaneous afferent fibers induced by ethanol, *Exp. Neurol.* **27**: 476.

Sauerland, E. K., Knauss, T., and Clemente, C. D., 1967. Effect of ethyl alcohol on orbital-cortically induced reflex inhibition in the cat, *Brain Res.* **6**: 181.

Schweigerdt, A. K., Dravid, A. R., Stewart, A. H., and Himwich, H. E., 1965. Alcohol and evoked potentials in the cat, *Nature* **208**: 688.

Steriade, M. and Demetrescu, M., 1962. Reticular facilitation of responses to acoustic stimuli, *Electroencephalog. Clin. Neurophysiol.* **14**: 21.

Story, J. L., Eidelberg, E., and French, J. D., 1961. Electrographic changes induced in cats by ethanol intoxication, *Arch. Neurol.* **5**: 565.

Takaori, S., Nakai, Y., Sasa, M., and Shimamoto, K., 1966. Central depressants and evoked click responses with special reference to the reticular formation in the cat, *Japan. J. Pharmacol.* **16**: 264.

Wallgren, H., 1967. Biochemical aspects of the effects of alcohol on the central nervous system, in XXXVIe Congrès International de Chimie Industrielle, Bruxelles, 1966, *Compte Rend.* **3**: 812.

CHAPTER 4

Brain Centers of Reinforcement and the Effects of Alcohol

J. St.-Laurent

Associate Professor of Psychiatry
School of Medicine, University of Sherbrooke
Canada

INTRODUCTION

This chapter will report briefly on findings that preceded the observation that brain stimulation could have positive reinforcement properties, and on the questions raised by this observation. We will report as well on further investigations carried out to learn more precisely the nature of this phenomenon. Finally, we will discuss the effects of ethanol and other drugs on the brain centers.

HISTORY

Present understanding of brain centers in which positive reinforcement of behavior is produced by direct electric stimulation had its roots in two nearly simultaneous methodological advances. In the 1930's, W. R. Hess began chronic implantation of electrodes in brain. By passing electrical current, he could elicit different types of behavior. At about the same time, B. F. Skinner (1938) introduced response-reward conditioning.

The next major step was taken in the early 1950's when Miller (1957), Delgado (1955), Hebb (1955) and others began to bring together the chronic implantation methodology and psychological experimentation.

The self-stimulation studies started with an accidental observation made late in 1953 by Olds and Milner. A chronically implanted rat was free to move around relatively unimpeded in a field of approximately 5 ft by 5 ft. The animal was free to explore all parts of the field. By pressing a button, they applied a sine wave stimulus of 60 cycles/sec and about 100 μA root-mean-square each time the animal reached a particular corner area in the field. They more or less expected to see some negative reinforcing effects of electric stimulation, as had been observed earlier that year by Miller and Delgado. The surprising observation was that the rat returned to that corner over and over again, much more often than one would have expected either with a negative reinforcement or on a chance basis.

At first it appeared as if the rat showed "interest" or "curiosity" in the electric stimulus. Further testing, however, indicated that the electrical stimulus acted as a positive reinforcement, i.e., a brain stimulus with all the characteristics of a primary reward.

It was undoubtedly Skinner's method that put the experiments on a quantitative basis. A circuit was arranged so that a particular response of the animal produced a brief train of electric stimulation in the part of the brain to be studied (Fig. 1). With this method, the rate at which the animal stimulated its brain seems to be a relatively satisfactory method of measuring the reinforcing properties of the stimulus (Olds and Milner, 1954). It was found that the stimulus causing more rapid self-stimulation rates also causes more positive reinforcement in other tests applied: for example, connecting passage and obstacle tests.

A number of questions about this positive reinforcement phenomenon have been responsible for the series of further investigations (Olds, 1962).

TOPOGRAPHIC ORGANIZATION

Positive reinforcement produced by electric stimulation of the brain was first thought to be mainly related to the olfactory cortex; this cortex is called the rhinencephalon. Later studies showed that the focus of the phenomenon, if maximum response for a minimum of stimulation could be taken to indicate a focus, was not in the anterior olfactory cortex but rather posteriorly in other olfactory projections directed toward the spinal cord through the hypothalamus and ventromedial area of the midbrain tegmentum. In experiments where each response was followed by one stimulus reward, response rates were far higher

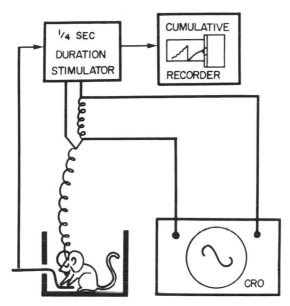

FIGURE 1. Animal is placed in a Skinner box and is connected to an electrical circuit so that every time the rat presses on the lever he gets a quarter-second pulse (60 cycles/sec) delivered to his brain. The number of presses per unit of time are recorded on a graph paper fixed to a drum which rotates at a fixed speed. As the drum turns, the pen records each press in an upward movement which is added to the previous mark until a total of 500 presses is reached. At this point the pen automatically returns to its original position at the bottom of the scale and proceeds to record the next series of presses.

with hypothalamic than with rhinencephalic stimulation (Olds and Olds, 1964). The ventromedial tegmentum and the lateral hypothalamus were considered to be part of "the focus" area; whereas some anterior areas yielding lower rates of self-stimulation (S.S.) were conceptualized as "the field."

INTENSITY OF EFFECT

As shown by Olds *et al.* (1960), when the electrodes were placed in the ventromedial tegmentum or lateral hypothalamic area of the rat and an optimal current was used, it was possible to generate more "motive force" with a brain stimulus reward than with any other reward ordinarily used in animal experimentation. If the electrodes were placed in a more anterior area, such as the septum, far milder effects were achieved (Bower and Miller, 1958; Olds and Milner, 1954; Olds and Olds, 1963). These effects were comparable to conventional rewards.

With electrodes in the focus, in order to get at a lever delivering current to this area, animals will cross a grid carrying a current seven times as strong as that normally tolerated to get at ordinary rewards (food, female, or stimulation in a field area) (Olds and Sinclair, 1957). In another test, an animal ran a connecting passage faster for obtainment of the electrical stimulation of the brain than for obtainment of food (Fig. 2) (Olds, 1956).

This same excess of motivation to the brain stimulus reward has been shown by Routtenberg and Olds (1964) in a choice situation where animals had just enough time in the box to maintain body weight by pressing on the food pedal and eating at the magazine. Animals gave up food when the brain shock was made available, thereby starving themselves to get the brain shock. Body weight steadily declined on this schedule, even to point of death.

Appetite for stimulation at the focus often seemed relatively insatiable, whereas a definite satiation point was usually reached in experiments with field stimulation (Olds, 1958b). Animals stimulated themselves several thousand times in the field area, and then stopped for the day. Animals stimulated themselves hour after hour in the focus, maintaining a rate of several thousand responses per hour and stopping only when a state of physical exhaustion appeared.

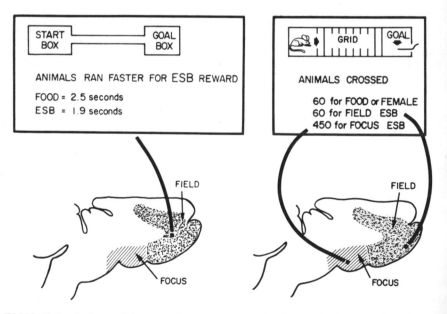

FIGURE 2. It is possible to produce stronger motivations with the brain stimulation than with any of the ordinary rewards. (1) In connecting passage experiments, animals ran faster to obtain the electrical stimulation of the brain (E.S.B.) than to obtain food. (2) In grid-crossing experiments, animals crossed a 60 μA foot shock for food or for E.S.B. via probes in the mild field; for E.S.B. via probes in the hypothalamic focus they crossed a 450 μA foot shock.

DRIVE RELATIONS

The hypothalamus and the rhinencephalon have for long been known to house a series of drive centers. Not only was positive reinforcement regularly provoked by stimulating approximately the same areas as those previously implicated in studies of basic drives, but also the positive reinforcement behavior provoked by stimulating any given brain point was usually sensitive to manipulation of at least one of the basic drives; and with stimulating probes at different brain points, different basic drives were affected (Olds, 1958a).

With probes in the olfactory-tegmental focus, the differences were small and difficult to demonstrate, possibly because the many drive systems are funneled through a very small area in this region and cannot be separated by the relatively gross electrical stimulation methods. With probes in the olfactory-cortical boundary regions, however, it was clearly demonstrated that medial points were sensitive to hunger and lateral points sensitive to the levels of male sex hormone.

In other experiments, it has regularly been demonstrated that in addition to positive reinforcement, the same brain probes often yielded the consummatory response appropriate to one of the basic drives (Miller, 1957).

This brings to mind earlier experiments by Anand and Brobeck, Stellar (1951; 1954), Teitelbaum (1955), Kluver and Bucy (1939) in which these same areas are shown to have drive relevance because lesions here regularly caused disorganization and drive behaviors. "Hyperphagia" and "aphagia", and aberrations in sexual and aversive behavior were observed consecutive to lesions in the lower focus and in the upper rhinencephalic field. However, another interesting difference between focus and field is worth mentioning: Studies on effects of limbic systems S.S. showed that while there were some apparent pain or anxiety-reducing effects of the rewarding stimulus in the olfactory cortex (Brady and Conrad, 1960), there were places in the hypothalamus where the reward stimulus did not have these effects (Olds and Olds, 1962). In studies on humans by Higgins et al. (1956), Delgado and Hamlin (1960), Heath (1960), and Sem-Jacobsen and Torkildsen (1960), euphoria was apparently elicited by stimulation in the hypothalamus while stimulation in the septal area would have inhibited pain and induced feelings of relaxation.

AUTONOMIC RELATIONS

Moving on to discussion of further anatomical overlaps, this reinforcement system is also the system of structures which has been shown to hold the higher control centers of automatic function (Fig. 3). The sympathetic and parasympathetic centers were studied by W. R. Hess in the earliest work utilizing chronically implanted depth probes. The autonomic responses obtained are

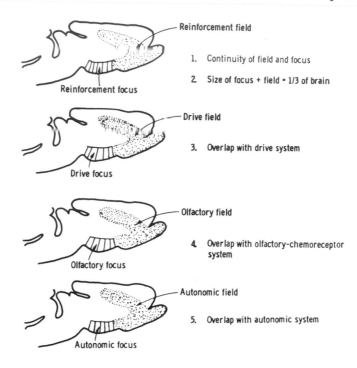

FIGURE 3.   Anatomical relations of brain centers of positive reinforcement.

usually mixed. This is not surprising considering the widely variable nature of the instrumental and subsequent consummatory behavior encountered following stimulation of a drive-reward system.

POSITIVE AND NEGATIVE REINFORCEMENT

Anatomical Relations

There is besides the overlaps mentioned above, a heavy overlap of brain structures yielding positive reinforcement and brain structures yielding negative reinforcement. Roberts (1958) and Bower and Miller (1958) have demonstrated that in many places, electric stimulation causes both positive reinforcement behavior and negative reinforcement behavior simultaneously. When a large number of brain areas were mapped by Olds (1963) (all points being tested for both electrically stimulated positive and negative behavior), it was found that some yielded only positive reinforcement, others only negative reinforcement, and a third extensive set of structures yielded mixed effects.

Interaction Experiment

The next question, therefore, was whether inhibitory relations might be demonstrated by simultaneous stimulation of the aversive and approach brain areas. We can best describe this work rapidly if we divide the reinforcement systems into three parts. First is the penultimate, positive reinforcement field which we spoke of earlier as residing in olfactory cortical anterior regions. Second, there is the aversive or negative reinforcement mechanisms which we spoke of as being related to the reticular activating system. Third, there is the positive reinforcement focus which was described as residing posteriorly in hypothalamic and tegmental areas.

In the first case Routtenberg and Olds (1964) found that stimulation of the penultimate positive reinforcement field in the olfactory cortex depressed the negative reinforcement behavior caused by stimulation in hypothalamo-reticular fibers. In the second case, Olds and Olds (1962) found that stimulation of this hypothalamic-reticular negative reinforcement mechanism regularly brought about cessation of the positive reinforcement behavior caused by stimulating the lateral hypothalamic olfactory mechanism. From these studies it appeared that a chain of inhibitory connections may exist with the olfactory areas of cortex, inhibiting the hypothalamo-reticular fibers, and the hypothalamo-reticular fibers inhibiting some final common mechanism in the lateral focus. Such a view has been fostered by the fact that stimulation in the lateral focus did not in its turn inhibit anything but, instead, stimulation of this supposed focus of positive reinforcement has a generally facilitatory effect not only on the positive reinforcement behavior drive from the olfactory cortex, but also on the negative reinforcement behavior drive from the hypothalamo-reticular fibers (Olds and Olds, 1962). This has led to the supposition that even the negative reinforcement behavior might in some way depend on excitement in this region previously called the positive reinforcement focus and which is now considered as a possible general reinforcement focus.

Lesion Experiments

In the laboratory of Ward (1960, 1961) and Miller (1963), lesions were made in the olfactory-cortical parts of the positive reinforcement system, that is, lesions were made in the penultimate positive reinforcement field (amygdala and septum). They consistently failed to eliminate positive reinforcement behavior obtained by stimulation of the focus. More recently, lesions were made by Olds and Olds (1964) at the tegmento-hypothalamic end of the olfactory-hypothalamic tegmental system, and it was clear that these posterior lesions substantially reduced or completely abolished positive reinforcement behavior produced by electric stimulation in the penultimate rhinencephalic field (Fig. 4).

In a second set of experiments, the same workers tested for effects of lesions at the escape point on positive reinforcement behavior, and lesions at the positive reinforcement focus on escape behavior. This gave the strongest confirmation to date to the view that the focus is something of a common denominator in operant behavior, being involved in aversive as well as rewarded operants. The lesions in the lateral focus often abolished more or less completely the negative reinforcement behavior caused by stimulating the hypothalamo-reticular aversive area. However lesions in the hypothalamo-reticular aversive area not only failed to antagonize positive reinforcement behavior, but in some circumstances even augmented it (Olds and Olds, 1964). Recent studies by Lorens (1965) and Valenstein (1966) report that large lesions in the anterior and posterior areas failed to abolish S.S. These results imply that there is no focal or essential area of S.S.

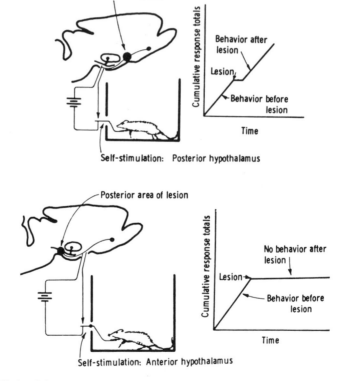

FIGURE 4. Schematic picture of field and focus lesion experiments, showing effects of anterior and posterior lesions in the olfacto-tegmental system. Anterior lesions (in the rhinencephalic field) did not counter self-stimulation via probes at the focus. Posterior lesions (in the hypothalamic focus) did counter self-stimulation via some anterior probes.

It is, of course, not clear from these experiments that the lateral hypothalamus is a final common path in control of operant behavior. Most of these do seem to suggest, however, that aversive mechanisms might act by inhibiting a focus. It is clear that no simple pleasure center exists here, but rather in one way or another a complex integrating mechanism. For here is an area where electric stimulation produces a maximally intense form of positive reinforcement; and yet lesions produce distinct depressions in both positive and negative reinforcement behavior.

SELF-STIMULATION, EPILEPTIFORM ACTIVITY AND NEURONAL ACTIVITY

Despite the results of the motivational tests given earlier, some workers did not share the view that the rat was pressing the lever just because it was pleasurable. It was pointed out that through electrical stimulation of the brain, one may induce an epileptic discharge, and self-stimulation might be correlated with epileptiform activity (Porter et al., 1959; Newman and Feldman, 1964). However, Reid et al. (1964) observed that anticonvulsant drugs facilitated S.S. behavior. It was suggested that seizures are not necessary for maintenance of S.S.

In order to find out whether or not the two phenomena, that is, the self-stimulation and epileptiform activity, were the same, we implanted electrodes in various areas yielding S.S. (1965). As S.S. was elicited from one area, the electrical activity at other sites of the brain was concomitantly recorded. We started to look for the threshold of current which would yield S.S. Then we would progressively increase the current until we reached the seizure threshold.

At the point which yielded the fastest rates of self-stimulation, that is, the ventromedial tegmentum, the threshold of S.S. was very low at 15 μA. Even with current as high as 140 μA, it was impossible to induce a seizure. At the posterior lateral hypothalamus, random sharp activity was observed at high current intensity, but no electrical afterdischarge was seen. At the level of the anterior lateral hypothalamus and septal area, there was no seizure at threshold of S.S., but both localized and generalized seizures were observed at high current intensity.

In conclusion, the arguments for the existence of a dissociation between the S.S. phenomenon and the epileptiform activity are:

1. No epileptiform activity could be recorded at the posterior areas; that is, the ventromedial tegmentum and posterior lateral hypothalamus, the areas where we obtained the maximum rates of S.S.

2. In the anterior areas of the field where the seizure thresholds are low, the S.S. threshold is even lower.

It is more than plausible, however, that there is a change in the excitability of the cells during S.S., but it is not of an epileptiform nature. The question of change of excitability of brain cells by seizures, drugs, or pathological processes in the various areas of brain is, of course, of great interest to the psychiatrist.

Previous studies on the ongoing electrical activity of the brain in psychiatric patients have been disappointing (Gastaut et al., 1959; Gottlieb et al., 1947; Heath and Mickle, 1960; Hill, 1952; St.-Laurent et al., 1966). The evoked potential studies appear more promising (Shagass and Schwartz, 1964): their initial results indicate that it may be possible to find patterns of state excitability characteristic of some pathological functional states. With recovery, independent of the therapeutic methods used (drugs, electroshock), these patterns would come back to normal. At present, no definite conclusions can be drawn from the evoked potential studies (Begleiter et al., 1967). However, it is possibly through studies aimed at finding out what the factors are which modulate the excitability of neurons during the states of wakefulness and sleep, that some insight may be gained in the pathophysiology of some mental diseases, and on how electroshock therapy and psychotropic drugs act.

Rebound in rapid eye movement sleep (REMS) time after REMS deprivation as well as a refractory period for a repeated electrical induction of REMS has suggested a neurohumoral substrate (Peyrethon-Duzan et al., 1967). Other evidence of changes in brain chemistry is derived from studies of the deprivation of REMS in rats that brought about increases in excitability of the central nervous sytem, including lower seizure threshold (Cohen and Dement, 1965). The numerous studies on sleep, involving various psychiatric syndromes, will have to consider the question of changes in the neurochemical substrate and neuronal excitability by various factors (Dement, 1967).

Various causes appear to be involved in the pathophysiology of numerous emotional disorders such as premenstrual dypsomania, premenstrual tension, postpartum psychoses, psychoses related to endocrinopathies and endogeneous affective disorders. Among the important parameters to consider in those studies are the neurochemical correlates (Himwich and Himwich, 1967). In recent years, the use of magnesium salt in the treatment of delirium tremens and the use of lithium in the treatment of affective disorders (acute mania and prevention of depression), including some cases of premenstrual tensions, have brought new speculations on the pathophysiology of psychiatric disorders. The studies involve catecholamine metabolism (Bunney and Davis, 1965; Schildkraut, 1965) and electrolyte mechanism (Coppen, 1965). In the case of lithium, Coppen et al. (1965), have recently suggested that it decreases the exchanges of sodium across the cell membrane while Nielsen (1964), Greenspan (1968), and Bunney et al. (1968) suggest an increase of serum magnesium. Magnesium itself is critical to the function of adenosine triphosphatase which is involved in the active transport of sodium and potassium in nerve cells (Skou, 1965). In affective psychoses, neurotransmitters would become unstable at the neuronal membrane and lithium would help in reestablishing this stability (Bunney et al., 1968).

BEHAVIORAL ASPECTS

Roberts found that the reward produced by focus stimulation seemed to be accompanied by a heightened general activity level (1958), whereas the reward produced by olfactory cortex stimulation seemed often to be accompanied by more or less complete inhibition of general activity (Miller, 1957). Stimulation in the midbrain close to the central gray as well as causing negative reinforcement responses tended to cause aversive behavior: i.e., backing up, turning away, and at times freezing. We would like to report that from preliminary studies on the behavioral reaction and patterns of skeletal movements elicited during S.S., no single behavioral pattern appeared common to S.S. Although S.S. from the focal areas yielded various intensities of increased motor activity, sniffing, and exploration, the impression obtained was that different patterns were observed and these varied according to the region stimulated along the pathway. However, some of the individual features of the behavioral patterns were at times common to many brain areas. Concerning the locomotor activity, when the point of stimulation was changed from the ventromedial tegmentum, posterior and anterior lateral hypothalamus to the septal area, an orderly change from locomotor excitation to locomotor depression appeared (Fig. 5a,b). Marked exploring behavior was observed at ventromedial tegmentum and in the posterior lateral hypothalamus; none was seen at the septum or the posterior lateral thalamus. Searching was seen at anterior lateral hypothalamus and epithalamus.

In conclusion, in the case of the posterior areas, the S.S. occurs in areas which are involved in activation of motricity and high drive behavior, and in the case of the septal and anterior part of the medial forebrain bundle, S.S. occurs in regions which, according to Hernández Peón and Chávez Eberra (1963), contain elements which inhibit the arousing neurons of the posterior areas of the meso-diencephalon, and in which according to Sawyer and Kawakami (1959) sleep spindles can be observed concomitantly with orgasm following copulation or vaginal stimulation. Clemente and Sterman (1963) conceive the basal forebrain synchronizing zone as projecting in the lateral hypothalamus and in the thalamus. In the last structure both activating and inhibiting effects on motricity and vigilance have been observed by Hess (1944), Monnier et al. (1963), and Buser et al. (1966). It appears then that S.S. behavior can be elicited mainly from areas involved in the triggering and inhibition of behavior.

DRUG EXPERIMENTS

Drugs that facilitate S.S. (for example, amphetamine, Stein, 1964) release catecholamines from active sites. This facilitation by amphetamine on S.S. is

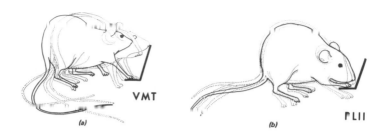

VMT

ΓLII

(a)   *(b)*

FIGURE 5. Drawings taken from the superimposition of every eight frames being taken at the speed of sixteen frames per second. The VMT drawing shows general bodily activity while the PLH one shows exploration.

increased by inhibitors of monoamine oxidase which protect catecholamine from destruction and also by drugs similar to imipramine which retard the reuptake of catecholamines. Reserpine, which depletes the brain of catecholamines, and chlorpromazine which blocks adrenergic transmission, inhibit S.S. (Olds *et al.*, 1956). Wise and Stein (1969) report reduced rates of S.S. after systemic and intraventricular administration of inhibitors of dopamine-β-hydroxylase (disulfiram and diethyldithiocarbamate) which are responsible for the final step of norepinephrine biosynthesis. The suppressed S.S. was reinstated by intraventricular injections of norepinephrine, suggesting the existence of an adrenergic excitatory system.

Recently, Domino and Olds (1968) obtained depression of S.S. in the hypothalamic area utilizing physostigmine, which suggests that depression of S.S. and other operant behaviors might be due to activation of an inhibitory cholinergic system. These findings complement the adrenergic excitatory system as suggested by Poshel and Ninteman (1963, 1966), Stein (1964), and Wise and Stein (1969). This system would overlap the distribution of the medial forebrain bundle and would contain adrenergic and serotonergic neurons (Fuxe, 1965).

The major tranquilizers and the sedative hypnotic drugs (including barbiturates, meprobamate, and alcohol) proved to have most interesting effects (Olds *et al.*, 1956; Olds and Olds, 1964). As mentioned before, chlorpromazine had a counteracting effect on S.S. This was more obvious when the electrodes were placed in the posterior focus, which would normally cause intense S.S., than when placed in the milder anterior-modulating areas of the field. One naturally wonders why small doses of chlorpromazine, which seemed to have no other effect on animal behavior, could so completely counteract the vehement electrical self-stimulation behavior.

On the other hand, the effects of alcohol, meprobamate, and pentobarbital were the reverse. When electrodes were implanted in posterior focal areas, practically no change was revealed in the rate of S.S. This was true even with increasing doses to a point where an almost completely comatose state was produced (Fig. 6). One can wonder whether or not the S.S. has a counteracting effect on alcohol.

With respect to alcohol, since this drug is known to affect other behavior systems and drugs such as chlorpromazine (Zircle, 1959) and tricyclic anti-depressants (Landauer et al., 1969), why could it not affect as well self-stimulation behavior?

It has been suggested that the effect of alcohol may be due to the alteration of amine metabolism in the brain. Alcohol ingestion would produce a shift of serotonin (5-hydroxytryptamine) from the oxidative pathway with formation of 5-hydroxyindol acetic acid to the reductive pathway with formation of 5-hydroxytryptophol (Davis et al., 1967; Tyce et al., 1968). Although it is far from definite that such changes in serotonin metabolism contribute to the toxicity of alcohol (Tyce et al., 1968), it remains possible that serotonin metabolism along

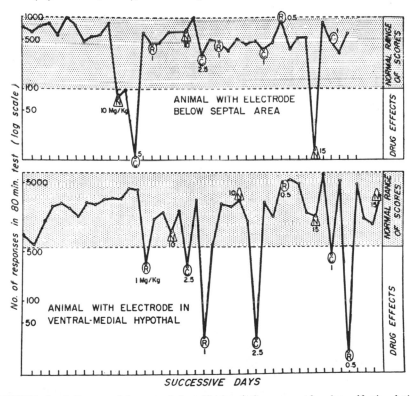

FIGURE 6.   Influence of drugs on daily self-stimulation scores, showing self-stimulation in forebrain and hypothalamus as affected by reserpine (R), chlorpromazine (C), and sodium pentobarbital (N).

with other biogenic amines is altered. Furthermore, it has been suggested (Croonborg et al, 1968) that alcohol in high concentration produces a deprivation of dreaming; again, most probably this is through changes in the chemical mediators of certain brain structures. A role of biogenic amines in the states of sleep is now accepted and Jouvet (1969) has reviewed this subject. As for the effect of electrical S.S. along the posterior medial forebrain bundle, it may be mediated by the changes which the electrical stimulation of fibers produces on the biogenic amines in specific areas of the central nervous system. Previous studies (Heller et al., 1962; Poirier and Sourkes, 1965; Goldstein et al., 1966; Poirier et al., 1966, 1967, 1969; Parent et al., 1969) have shown that lesions in the ventromedial tegmentum and medial forebrain bundle, that is, in areas which elicit intense S.S., produce changes in brain amines. Ventromedial tegmental lesions in the monkey are associated with a decreased concentration of dopamine, tyrosine hydroxylase, and serotonin in the striatum. In the cat, such lesions result in a decreased concentration of tyrosine hydroxylase in the caudate nucleus and septal areas; of dopamine in the striatum and of serotonin in the striatum and hypothalamus. Lesions in the medial forebrain bundle would bring a decreased concentration of serotonin in the whole brain of the rat. The anatomic interruption by lesions of catecholinergic and serotonergic fibers which would originate in the basomedial part of the tegmentum appear to be responsible for these changes (Poirier et al., 1964). Electrical stimulation of the same fibers during S.S. probably effects changes as well which possibly counteract the acute effect of alcohol.

During our alcohol experimentation (Figs. 7, 8, and 9), six probe electrodes were implanted in the lateral hypothalamus or in the anterior area of the medial forebrain bundle. Four consecutive tests were run daily during which all electrodes were tested in turn for 2 min, and this continued for 12 days, i.e., 4 days pre-control, 4 days under ethanol, 4 days postcontrol.

The dose of ethanol used, 2 ml/kg body weight, injected intraperitoneally, in all cases produced a marked state of intoxication which was assessed through neurological examination. In all cases, steadiness of gait, placing reaction, righting reflex, and sense of equilibrium were grossly impaired.

Figure 7 reveals that when the electrodes were placed in the positive focus (the lateral hypothalamus), ethanol did not markedly affect the scores for any of the self-stimulating electrodes. Only a slight attenuation in rate was noted which could be attributed to loss of skill. It appeared that behavior derived from direct stimulation of the posterior deep structures tended strongly to survive an excess of alcohol and indeed there might be some tendency of such stimulation to work against the effect of alcohol.

For the most part, the forward self-stimulating electrodes had their scores affected by ethanol, but the effects were diverse (Figs. 8, 9) and it would seem that the placement of the probe was a determining factor. Why some probe points caused depressed behavior under alcohol and others caused no change is not clear.

Considering the greater influence of alcohol with anterior placement of the electrodes and the variation in effect with placement, one could theorize that alcohol, influencing the cortical mechanisms, changes behavior only where environmental factors are most important. Further, it may be that paleocortical areas are points of access to deeper systems, with environmental factors either facilitating or inhibiting each access line. These, then, would be places of special influence from particular environments and neighboring cortical structures.

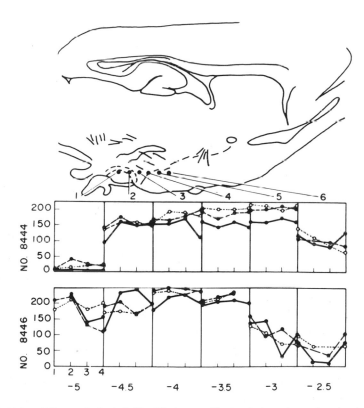

FIGURE 7.   Effects of alcohol (2 ml/kg) on self-stimulation via probes in the hypo-thalamic focus. Scores are in responses per 2-min test. There were four daily tests in each of which electrodes one through six were tested in succession for a 2-min period. After the completion of one such cycle, a second was begun and so forth until the fourth was completed. These repetitive tests were made so that each electrode would be tested at various stages after application of the drug. The 2 days of testing just prior to application of ethanol and the first day of ethanol application are shown. Intraperitoneal applications were made just prior to the start of these tests. (– – –) control 1; (· · ·) control 2; (———) ethanol, 2 cc/kg.

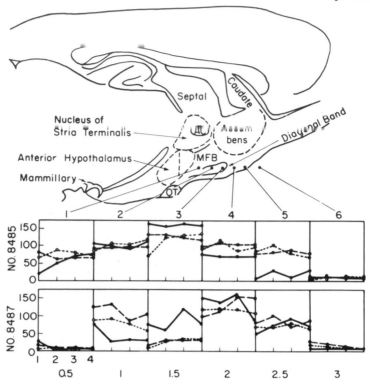

FIGURE 8. Effects of alcohol on self-stimulation via probes arrayed across the medial forebrain bundle at the junction between diencephalon and telencephalon. Details are the same as in the previous figure. (– – –) control 1; (· · ·) control 2; (———) ethanol, 2 cc/kg.

These access or "input" pathways would seem to be especially sensitive to alcohol and would be involved in the first stages of alcoholism such as psychological dependence, while the deeper behavior systems involving more posterior structures would possibly be effected only during long-term alcohol consumption. The long-term changes on the paleocortical and deeper systems would be involved in the disorders encountered in the later stages of alcoholism. Such a hypothesis would be supported by the recent report (Freund, 1970) that after long-term alcohol ingestion, mice showed impairment of shock avoidance learning, and that alcohol may affect behavior during and after ingestion of alcohol through the possible biosynthesis of tetrahydroisoquelonines and tetra-hydropapeverolines (a morphine-like alkaloid) from the condensation of acetaldehyde generated during ethanol metabolism with tissue catecholamines, epinephrine, norepinephrine, dopamine, and dopa (Davis and Walsh, 1969; Cohen and Collins, 1970). Morphine has been reported (Clouet and Ratner, 1970) to

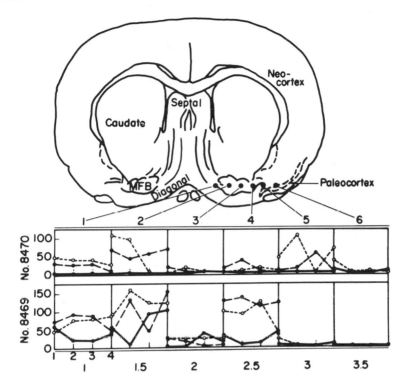

FIGURE 9.   Effects of alcohol on self-stimulation via probes arrayed along the telencephalic portion of the medial forebrain bundle. Details are as in the two preceding figures. (– – –) control 1; (· ·) control 2; (——) ethanol, 2 cc/kg.

increase the biosynthesis of dopamine and norepinephrine in the hypothalamus and striatum of naive rats. In tolerant rats, this was even more marked. Although it remains to be determined, it is felt that alkaloids may possibly be bound in the same brain tissues as the catecholamines, and cause both transient and permanent actions and/or changes (Majchrowicz and Mendelson, 1970). The brain areas along the medial forebrain bundle, which are part of the ascending midbrain circuit of Nauta, yield S.S. and are involved in motor activity, high drive behavior, motivation, primary learning phenomena, and paradoxical sleep. The actions of these alkaloids could underlie the process of physical dependence and both the acute and chronic disorders of alcoholism, e.g., hyperexcitability, tremulousness, seizures, excitation, narcosis of acute pathological intoxication, acute hallucinosis, delirium tremens, chronic mental deterioration, chronic alcoholic psychosis, and Korsakoff psychosis.

It appears that the effect of the major tranquilizers is to affect directly those deeper systems which are involved in high drives, positive reinforcement, and phenomena of low order, like the approach behavior (i.e., increase locomotor activity, exploration and searching). These deeper systems became the basis for the development and organization of systems of higher complexity, such as the ones involved in voluntary activity (Olds and Olds, 1964).

SUMMARY

A historical review of the phenomenon of self-stimulation (S.S.) is presented and the main arguments are given in support of the view that electrical stimulation in some areas of the brain has positive reinforcing properties. Concerning the intensity of the effect, with electrodes placed in the lateral hypothalamic area, it was possible to generate more highly motivated behavior with a brain stimulus than with any other reward. With electrodes placed in anterior areas such as the septum, milder effects comparable to conventional rewards were obtained. Further studies on the topographic organizations have indicated a gradient of self-stimulation along the course of an olfactory midbrain pathway with a "focus" in the posterior areas. Stimulation in other areas of the brain may also have negative reinforcing properties and the anatomical relations between the two systems are reported as well as some interaction and lesion experiments.

Finally, drug experiments show that the major tranquilizers, chlorpromazine and reserpine, abolish S.S. from the focus but do not affect the S.S. phenomenon as elicited from anterior structures. On the contrary, barbiturates and alcohol depress S.S. from anterior structures but do not affect S.S. at the focus. However, in the case of alcohol, while most probe points caused depression of the behavior, some points induced increased S.S.

The results obtained are interpreted in the light of recent studies on the pathophysiology of alcoholism involving the effect of alcohol on catecholamine and serotonin metabolism.

ACKNOWLEDGMENT

The author wishes to express his gratitude to Springer Publishing Co., Inc., New York, for permission to quote and use illustrations from the chapter "Alcohol and Brain Centers of Positive Reinforcement" in *Alcoholism, Behavioural Research, Therapeutic Approaches*, 1967. Also to Ruth Fox, editor, and James Olds, coauthor. This study is now being supported jointly by the Medical Research Council of Canada (Grant Ma 3289) and an establishment grant from the Medical Research Council of Quebec. Thanks are expressed to Mr. Jean Rossano, Mr. Clifford Sarrazin, and Madame N. Gagné for their generous collaboration on this manuscript.

REFERENCES

Anand, B. K. and Brobeck, J. R., 1951. Localization of a "feeding center" in the hypothalamus of the rat, *Proc. Soc. Expt. Biol. Med.* **77**: 323–324.

Begleiter, H., Porjesz, B., and Milton, M. M., 1967. Cortical evoked potentials and psychopathology, *Arch. Gen. Psychiat.* **17**: 755–758.

Bogacz, J., St.-Laurent, J., and Olds, J., 1965. Dissociation of self-stimulation and epileptiform activity, *Electroenceph. Clin. Neurophysiol.* **19**: 75–87.

Bower, G. H. and Miller, N. E., 1958. Rewarding and punishing effects from stimulating the same place in the rat's brain, *J. Comp. Physiol. Psychol.* **51**: 669–674.

Bunney, W. E., Jr. and Davis, J. M., 1965. Norepinephrine in depressive reactions, *Arch. Gen. Psychiat.* **13**: 483–494.

Bunney, W. E., Goodwin, K. K., Davis, J. M., and Fawcett, J. A., 1968. A behavioral biochemical study of lithium treatment, *Amer. J. Psychiat.* **125**: 499–512.

Buser, P., Rougeul, A., and Perret, C., 1966. Caudate and thalamic influences on conditioned motor responses in the cat, *Bull. Inst. Estud. Med. Biol. Mex.*, **22**: 293–307.

Brady, J. V. and Conrad, D., 1960. Some effects of limbic system self-stimulation upon conditioned emotional behavior, *J. Comp. Physiol. Psychol.* **53**: 128–137.

Clemente, C. D. and Sterman, M. B., 1963. Sleep induced by electrical or chemical stimulation of the forebrain, in *The Physiological Basis of Mental Activity* (R. Hernández Peón, ed.) *Electroenceph. Clin. Neurophysiol.* Supp. 1, **24**: 172–187.

Clouet, D. H. and Ratner, M., 1970. Catecholamine biosynthesis in brains of rats treated with morphine, *Science* **168**: 854–856.

Cohen, G. and Collins, M. A., 1970. Alkaloids from catecholamines in adrenal tissue: Possible role in alcoholism, *Science* **197**: 1749–1751.

Cohen, H. B. and Dement, W. C., 1965. Sleep: changes in threshold to electroconvulsive shock in rats after deprivation of "paradoxical" phase, **150**: 1318–1319.

Coppen, A., 1965. Mineral metabolism in affective disorders, *Brit. J. Psychiat.* **111**: 1133–1142.

Coppen, A., Malleson, A., and Shaw, D. M., 1965. Effects of lithium carbonate on electrolyte distribution in man, *Lancet* **1**. 682–683.

Davis, Virginia E., Brown, H., Huff, J. A., and Cashaw, J. L., 1967. The alteration of serotonin metabolism to 5-hydroxytryptophol by ethanol ingestion in man, *J. Lab. Clin. Med.* **69**: 132–140.

Davis, V. E. and Walsh, M. J., 1969. Alcohols, amines and alkaloids: A possible biochemical basis for alcohol addiction, *Science* **167**: 1005–1009.

Delgado, J. M. R., 1955. Cerebral structures involved in transmission and elaboration of noxious stimulation, *J. Neurophysiol.* **18**: 261–275.

Delgado, J. M. R. and Hamlin, H., 1960. Spontaneous and evoked seizures in animals and humans, in *Clinical Studies on the Anesthetized Brain* (E. R. Ramey and D. S. O'Doherty, eds.) p. 133, Paul Hoeber, Inc., New York.

Dement, W. C., 1967. Sleep and dreams, in *Comprehensive Textbook of Psychiatry* (A. M. Freedman, H. I. Kaplan, and H. S. Kaplan, eds.) p. 77. Williams & Wilkins Co., Baltimore.

Domino, E. F. and Olds, M. E., 1968. Cholinergic inhibition of self-stimulation behavior, *J. Pharmacol. Exp. Ther.* **164**: 202–211.

Freund, G., 1970. Impairment of shock avoidance learning after long-term alcohol ingestion in mice, *Science* **168**: 1599–1601.

Fuxe, K., 1965. Evidence for the existence of monoamine neurons in the central nervous system. Distribution of monoamine nerve terminals in the central nervous system, *Acta Physiol. Scand.* **64**: Suppl. 247, 37–84.

Gastaut, H., Dongier, S., and Dongier, M., 1939. Electroencephalographic of normous; *Rev. Neurol.* (Paris) **101**: 435.

Goldstein, M., Anagnoste, B., Owen, W. S., and Battista, A. F., 1966. The effects of ventromedial tegmental lesions in the biosynthesis of catecholamines on the striatum, *Life Sci.* **5**: 2171–2176.

Gottlieb, J. S., Ashby, M. C., and Knott, J. R., 1947. Studies in primary behavior disorders and psychopathic personality. The inhibitance of electroautiral activity, *Am J Psychiat.* **103**: 823–827.

Greenburg, R., Pearlman, C., Brooks, R., Mayer, R., and Hartmann, F., 1968. Dreaming and Korsakoff's psychosis, *Arch. Gen. Psychiat.* **18**: 203–209.

Greenspan, K. E., 1968. Clinical pharmacology and pending biochemical questions of lithium therapy, *Dis. Nerv. Syst.* **29**: 178–181.

Heath, R. G. and Mickle, W. A., 1960. Evaluation of seven years experience with depth electrode studies in human patients, in *Electrical Studies on the Unanesthetized Brain* (E. E. Ramey and D. S. O'Doherty, eds.) p. 214, Paul Hoeber, Inc., New York.

Hebb, D. O., 1955. Drives and the conceptual nervous system, *Psychol. Rev.*, **62**: 243–254.

Heller, A., Harvey, J., and Moore, R., 1962. A demonstration of a fall in brain serotonin following central nervous system lesions in the rat, *Biochem. Pharmacol.* **11**: 859–866.

Hernández Peón, R. and Chávez Eberra, G., 1963. Sleep induced by electrical or chemical stimulation of the forebrain, in *The Physiological Basis of Mental Activity* (R. Hernández Peón, ed.), *Electroenceph. Clin. Neurophysiol.* Suppl. **24**: 188–198.

Hess, W. R., 1944. Das Schlogsyndrom als Folge diencephaler Reizung, *Helv. Physiol. Acta.* **2**: 305–244.

Hess, W. R., 1954. *Diencephalon: Autonomic and Extrapyramidal Functions.* Grune and Stratton, Inc., New York.

Higgins, J. W., Mahl, G. F., Delgado, J. M. R., and Hamlin, H., 1956. Behavioral changes during intracerebral electrical stimulation, *A.M.A. Arch. Neurol. Psychiat.* **76**: 399–419.

Hill, D., 1952. EEG in episodic psychotic and psychopathic behavior, *Electroenceph. Clin. Neurophysiol.* **4**: 419–447.

Himwich, W. A. and Himwich, H. E., 1967. Neurochemistry, in *Comprehensive Textbook of Psychiatry* (A. M. Freedman, H. I. Kaplan, and H. S. Kaplan, eds.) p. 49, Williams & Wilkins Co., Baltimore.

Jouvet, M., 1969. Biogenic amines and the states of sleep, *Science* **163**: 32–41.

Kluver, H. and Bucy, P. C., 1939. Preliminary analysis of functions of the temporal lobes in monkeys, *A.M.A. Arch. Neurol. Psychiat.* **42**: 979–1000.

Landauer, A. A., Milner, G., and Patman, J., 1969. Alcohol and amitriptyline. Effects on skills related to driving behavior, *Science* **163**: 1467–1468.

Lorens, S. A., 1965. The effect of lesions in the central nervous system on self-stimulation in the rat, Ph.D. Dissertation. Univ. of Chicago.

Majchrowicz, E. and Mendelson, J. H., 1970. Blood concentration of acetaldehyde and ethanol in chronic alcoholics, *Science* **168**: 1100–1102.

Miller, N. E., 1957. Experiments on motivation, *Science* **126**: 1271–1278.

Miller, N. E., 1963. Some motivational effects of electrical and chemical stimulation of the brain, *Electroenceph. Clin. Neurophysiol.* Suppl. **24**: 247–259.

Monnier, M., Hosli, L., and Krupp, P., 1963. Moderating and activating systems in the medio-central thalamus and reticular formation, in *The Physiological Basis of Mental*

Activity (R. Hernández Peón, ed.), *Electroenceph. Clin. Neurophysiol.*, Suppl. **24**: 97–112.

Newman, B. L. and Feldman, S. S., 1964. Electrophysiological activity accompanying intracranial self-stimulation, *J. Comp. Physiol. Psychol.* **57**: 244–247.

Nielsen, J., 1964. Magnesium-lithium studies—I—Serum and erythrocyte magnesium in patients with manic states during lithium treatment, *Acta Psychiat. Scand.* **40**: 190–196.

Olds, J., 1956. Runway and maze behavior controlled by basomedial forebrain stimulation in the rat, *J. Comp. Physiol. Psychol.* **49**: 507–512.

Olds, J., 1958a. Effects of hunger and male sex hormones on self-stimulation of the brain, *J. Comp. Physiol. Psychol.* **51**: 320–324.

Olds, J., 1958b. Satiation effects in self-stimulation on the brain, *J. Comp. Physiol. Psychol.* **51**: 675–678.

Olds, J., 1962. Hypothalamic substrates of reward, *Physiol. Rev.* **42**: 554–604.

Olds, J., Killam, K. F., and Bach-y-Rita, P., 1956. Self-stimulation of the brain used as a screening method for tranquilizing drugs, *Science* **124**: 265–266.

Olds, J. and Milner, P., 1954. Positive reinforcement produced by electrical stimulation of septal area and other regions of rat brain, *J. Comp. Physiol. Psychol.* **47**: 419–427.

Olds, J. and Sinclair, J. C., 1957. Stimulation in the obstruction box. (Abstract) *Am. Psychologist* **12**: 464.

Olds, J., Travis, R. P., and Schwing, R., 1960. Topographic organization of hypothalamic self-stimulation functions, *J. Comp. Physiol. Psychol.* **53**: 23–32.

Olds, M. E. and Olds, J., 1962. Approach-escape interactions in rat brain, *Am. J. Physiol.* **203**: 803–810.

Olds, M. E. and Olds, J., 1963. Approach-avoidance analysis of rat diencephalon, *J. Comp. Neurol.* **120**: 259–295.

Olds, M. E. and Olds, J., 1964a. Pharmacological patterns in subcortical reinforcement behavior, *Int. J. Neuropharmacol.* **2**: 309–325.

Olds, J. and Olds, M. E., 1964b. The mechanisms of voluntary behavior, in *The Role of Pleasure in Behavior* (R. G. Heath, ed.) p. 23, Harper and Row, Inc., New York.

Parent, A., St.-Jacques, C., and Poirier, L. J., 1969. Effects on interrupting the hypothalamic nervous connections on the norepinephrine and serotonin content of the hypothalamus, *Exp. Neurol.* **23**: 67–75.

Peyrethon-Duzan, D., Peyrethon, J., and Jouvet, M., 1967. Etude quantitative des phénomènes phasiques du sommeil paradoxal pendant et après sa déprivation instrumentale, *C. R. Soc. Biol.* **161**: 2530–2537.

Poirier, L. J. and Sourkes, T. L., 1965. Influence of the substantia nigra on the catecholamine content of the striatum, *Brain* **88**: 181–192.

Poirier, L. J., Singh, P., Boucher, R., Bouvier, G., Olivier, A., and Larochelle, P., 1967. Effect of brain lesions on striatal monoamines in the cat, *Arch. Neurol. (Chic.)* **17**: 601–608.

Poirier, L. J., McGreer, L., Larochelle, L., McGreer, P. L., Bédard, P., and Boucher, R., 1969. The effects of brain stem lesions on tyrosine and tryptophan hydroxylases in various structures of the telencephalon of the cat, *Brain Res.* **14**: 147–154.

Poschel, B. P. H. and Ninteman, F. W., 1963. Norepinephrine: A possible excitatory neurohormone of the reward system, *Life Sci.* **2**: 782–788.

Poschel, B. P. H. and Ninteman, F. W., 1966. Hypothalamic self-stimulation: Its suppression by blockade of norepinephrine biosynthesis and reinstatement by methamphetamine, *Life Sci.* **5**: 11–16.

Porter, R. W., Conrad, D., and Brady, J. V., 1959. Some neural and behavioral correlates of electrical self-stimulation in the limbic system, *J. Exp. Anal. Behav.* **2**: 43–55.

Reid, L. D., Gibson, W. E., Gledhill, S. M., and Porter, P. E., 1964. Anticonvulsant drugs and self-stimulating behavior, *J. Comp. Physiol. Psychol.* **57**: 353–356.

Roberts, W. W., 1958. Both rewarding and punishing effects from stimulation of posterior hypothalamus of cat with same electrode at same intensity, *J. Comp. Physiol. Psychol.* **51**: 400–407.

Routtenberg, A. and Olds, J., 1964. The attenuation of response to an aversive brain stimulus by concurrent rewarding septal stimulation, *Fed. Proc.* **22**: 515 (Abstract).

Sawyer, C. H. and Kawakami, M., 1959. Characteristic of behavioral and after-reactions to copulations and vaginal stimulation in the female rabbit, *Endocrinol.* **65**: 622–630.

Schildkraut, J. J., 1965. The catecholamine hypothesis of affective disorders: a review of supporting evidence, *Amer. J. Psychiat.* **122**: 509–522.

Sem-Jacobsen, C. W. and Torkildsen, A., 1960. Depth recording and electrical stimulation in the human brain, in *Electrical Studies on the Unanaesthetized Brain* (E. R. Ramey and D. S. O'Doherty, ed.) p. 275, Paul B. Hoeber, Inc., New York.

Shagass, C. and Schwartz, M., 1964. Evoked potential studies in psychiatric patients, *Ann. N.Y. Acad. Sci.* **112**, Art **1**: 526–542.

Skinner, B. F., 1938. *The Behaviour of Organisms.* Appelton-Century-Crofts, New York.

Skou, J. C., 1965. Enzymatic basis for active transport of Na^+ and K^+ across cell membrane, *Physiol. Rev.* **45**: 596–617.

Stein, L., 1964. Self-stimulation of the brain and the central stimulant action of amphetamine, *Fed. Proc.* **23**: 836–850.

Stellar, E., 1954. The physiology of motivation, *Psychol. Rev.* **61**: 5–22.

St.-Laurent, J., Gastaut, H., Lanoir, J., and Naquet, R., 1966. Le rythme lent postérieur: étude électroclinique de 100 nouveaux cas, *C.M.A.J.*, **95**: 135–142.

Teitelbaum, P., 1955. Sensory control of hypothalamic hyperphagia, *J. Comp. Physiol. Psychol.* **48**: 156–163.

Tyce, G. M., Flock, E. V., and Owen, C. A., 1968. Effect of ethanol on serotonin (5-HT) metabolism in brain and in isolated perfused liver, (Abstr.) *Fed. Proc.* **27**: 400.

Tyce, G. M., Flock, E. V., and Owen, C. A., 1968. 5-Hydroxytryptamine metabolism in brains of ethanol-intoxicated rats, *Mayo Clin. Proc.* **43**: 668–673.

Valenstein, E. S., 1966. The anatomical locus of reinforcement, in *Progress in Physiological Psychology* (Elliot Stellar and James M. Sprague, eds.) pp. 149–190, Academic Press, New York.

Ward, H. P., 1960. Basal tegmental self-stimulation after septal ablation in rats, *Arch. Neurol.* **3**: 158–162.

Ward, H. P., 1961. Tegmental self-stimulation after amygdaloid ablation: Results of studies in rats, *Arch. Neurol.* **4**: 657–659.

Wise, C. D. and Stein, L., 1969. Facilitation of brain self-stimulation by central administration of norepinephrine, *Science* **163**: 299–301.

Zircle, G. A., King, P. D., McAtee, O. B., and Van Dyke, R., 1959. Effects of chlorpromazine and alcohol on coordination and judgment, *J. Amer. Med. Assoc.* **171**: 1496.

CHAPTER 5

Factors Underlying Differences in Alcohol Preference of Inbred Strains of Mice

David A. Rodgers

Department of Psychiatry
Cleveland Clinic
Cleveland, Ohio

THE INBRED MOUSE AS SUBJECT

Introduction

The use of inbred strains of animals in research has introduced to physiological work a high degree of precision and replicability. The similarity of two animals from the same inbred line closely approaches that of identical twins, and thousands of replications with this degree of similarity can be utilized in a single study or research series. One study of alcohol consumption of inbred strains of mice illustrates the degree of precision possible. In this study, the amount of alcohol voluntarily ingested in a free choice situation was related to strain differences, sex differences, age differences, and the corresponding interacting effects (Rodgers and McClearn, 1962). Although the experimental procedures were complex, the strain (genotype) variable accounted for over 97% of total variance, with error of measurement, sex differences, age differences (litter effects), and combined other effects accounting for less than 3% of total variance

Such precision in the "physiologic raw material" of the experimental study forces the investigator to be clear and precise concerning the phenomenon he is studying. The concept of "alcoholism" is a notoriously imprecise concept. One advantage, therefore, of using inbred strains in the study of alcoholism is that the investigator is forced to clarify precisely what phenomenon he is measuring. Whether or not the study of inbred strains of mice elucidates the problem of human alcoholism depends on the correspondence between the phenomena studied in the mice and the phenomenon or phenomena of human alcoholism. Some brief comments would therefore seem in order in this chapter on both the phenomena studied in the mice and a conception of human alcoholism to which these phenomena might be related.

Alcoholism as a Behavior Pathology

A more or less acceptable, if not overly precise, definition of alcoholism is the continuing habitual or repetitive voluntary ingestion of ethanol beyond the point that physiological integrity or social potential are impaired. The emphasis is on the behavior of continuing to consume alcohol voluntarily even though physical or social well-being is jeopardized thereby. Such behavior can be characterized as pathological and the resulting condition can be characterized as a behavioral pathology, in contrast to a physiologic or tissue pathology such as is produced by an invasive organism or traumatic lesion. Tissue changes secondary to alcohol abuse, such as liver cirrhosis, and physiopathologic syndromes, such as delirium tremens, lie within the alcoholism spectrum but are not the essential dimension of alcoholism *per se.*

If alcoholism is a behavioral pathology, then the parameters influencing voluntary ingestion of alcohol or the relationship between voluntary alcohol consumption and subsequent physiological or other definable pathology would seem to constitute critical variables amenable to rather precise study. Two related questions might be posed, however, concerning the choice of inbred mice as subjects for such study. First, what is the gain from stabilizing physiology very precisely when the parameter to be studied is gross behavior rather than physiological tissue change? Second, and related, if inbred strains result in precisely stabilized physiological systems and if such stabilization is useful for understanding behavioral parameters, then what is the rationale for using mouse physiology to understand a human behavioral pathology?

The Physiobehavioral Cycle

Figure 1 summarizes the physiobehavioral cycle through which both organisms and behavioral patterns are generated. From this cycle, it should be

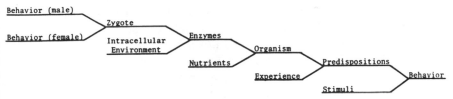

FIGURE 1.   The physiobehavioral cycle.

apparent that behavior is as essentially tied to physiology as it is to external stimuli. The "black box" nonsense in psychology that has deemphasized the role of physiology in behavior has been thoroughly discredited, as will be illustrated by subsequent data in the present chapter.

The question still remains as to whether a mouse zygote can appropriately antecede behavior that is of relevance to human alcoholism. The position has been argued elsewhere (Rodgers, 1970) that mechanism-specific behavior segments can be studied in cross-species material just as can chemical systems such as metabolic pathways. To the extent that behavior can be explicitly related to mediating mechanisms that can exist with equal validity in the mouse and the human, this argument would hold that the mouse is an appropriate organism within which to study behavior relevant to the problem of human alcoholism. An example that anticipates a later conclusion in this chapter is the finding that some mouse strains normally consume alcohol to almost metabolic capacity under nonstressful conditions and, not surprisingly therefore, do not notably increase alcohol intake under conditions of emotional stress. This finding suggests the generalization, applicable to human studies as well as other animal studies, that a causal relationship between stress and voluntary alcohol ingestion cannot be demonstrated unless baseline alcohol consumption is well below peak metabolic capacity. While this seems a trivial self-evident conclusion, many studies have nevertheless been done on animal analogues of human alcoholism in which the attempt has been made to relate stress to alcohol consumption, but in which there has been no knowledge of baseline metabolic capacity. Other conclusions that can be drawn from the mouse work may not be so trivial as they relate to the problem of human alcoholism.

The Nature of Inbred Strains

Mammalian organisms are diploid, deriving one set of chromosomes from the male parent and a paired set from the female parent. For example, humans have 23 pairs of chromosomes and mice have 20 pairs. Each chromosome is made up of numerous genes and is transmitted from parent to offspring as a unit.

Two offspring receiving an identical chromosome will therefore have a packet of identical genetic information of considerable complexity. In a normally heterozygotic parent, each chromosome will differ significantly from its paired chromosome, and these nonidentical pairs of chromosomes will be randomly assorted into the gametes that transmit the genetic complement to the offspring. Figure 2 shows schematically how the zygote of an offspring is composed. Since the particular chromosome of each pair obtained from each parent is a matter of random chance, the probability that two human offspring from normally heterozygotic parents would receive exactly the same genetic complement (unless they were identical twins, in which the process of differentiation occurs after the genetic complement has been transmitted) would be less than 1 in 70 trillion. The normal genetic process thus ensures much individuality. However, inbreeding systematically manipulates the genetic pool in such a manner that this individuality is eliminated, as is illustrated by the brother-by-sister inbreeding program in Fig. 3. In this hypothetical example, the fifth generation offspring are homozygous and identical for the first four chromosome pairs and (except for crossovers or other genetic "irregularities") will always produce offspring in brother-by-sister crosses that are identical genetically with respect to these first four chromosomes.

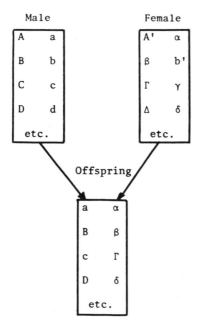

FIGURE 2. Example of random assorting of parental chromosomes in the reproductive process.

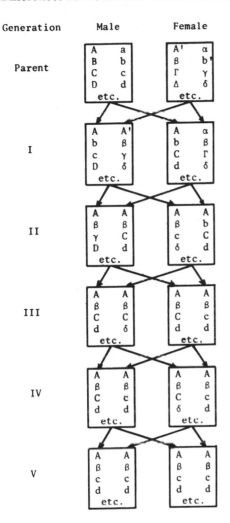

FIGURE 3. Example of development of stable replicable genetic uniformity through homozygosity by brother-by-sister inbreeding.

By extension, all chromosomes should be subject to such stabilization that all members of a given inbred line could be genetically essentially identical. This would mean that the zygote in Fig. 1 would be stabilized for all members of a given inbred line. Under conditions of essentially uniform nutrition, intracellular environment and nutrients would also be essentially stabilized, so that the resulting organisms of Fig. 1 should be essentially identical. Experience and stimuli could then be varied so that their influence on subsequent behavior could be examined against a highly uniform physiologic background.

As a physiological system, the house mouse (*Mus musculus*) lives comfortably in an essentially human environment, eating many of the same foodstuffs and sharing similar environmental conditions. This suggests the possibility of at least some physiologic similarities, which in fact are known to exist. At the same time, man and mouse are not closely related evolutionally and therefore inevitably have significant differences, some of which are important in terms of differential response to alcohol consumption. One example is that man can realize almost his entire daily caloric need from ethanol ingestion, whereas the mice that have been studied so far can obtain no more than 20% to 35% of their daily caloric need from ethanol (Rodgers *et al.*, 1967; Freund, 1969). A mouse thus must consume approximately 65% to 80% of a normal diet in addition to peak alcohol consumption, a factor which may well protect it from the liver damage that man experiences when he essentially replaces all other foodstuffs with alcohol. These and other differences should be warning enough that alcohol consumption of the mouse is not identical to alcoholism in the human. With this inevitable qualification, there has nevertheless developed a significant body of research on the mouse that may have relevant implications for the understanding of human alcoholism.

MEASUREMENT OF ALCOHOL PREFERENCE

There are many alcohols, chemically speaking, in addition to the ethyl alcohol that constitutes the primary beverage ingredient associated with human alcoholism. The present chapter explicitly focuses solely on ethyl alcohol preference of mice. Ethyl alcohol is a colorless liquid in pure form that is totally miscible with water in all proportions, that is damaging and highly irritating to esophageal, stomach and other tissues in undiluted form. It diffuses through most tissue membranes, including the blood–brain barrier, placenta, lungs, and stomach wall. As a beverage, it is nearly always consumed in concentrations equal to or less than 50% alcohol-to-water by volume. Most animals so far tested will avoid alcohol solutions that exceed 15% alcohol v/v. There are many individual differences in preference for alcohol solutions of 5% to 10% concentration, so it has been this range of concentrations that has been used in most mouse preference studies. In some instances, concentrations have differed significantly from this range, however.

Humans usually drink alcohol in a diluted water mixture ranging from about $3\frac{1}{2}\%$ alcohol (near beer) to about 50% (100-proof liquor taken neat). Most of the preference work with mice has been done with approximately 10% mixtures, a concentration that is in the general range of tablewine strength. Humans normally consume alcohol in beverages containing numerous other flavors that considerably alter the taste of the alcohol itself, and usually at cooled temperatures that further attenuate the taste of the ethanol. Human taste preference, *per se*, for alcoholic beverages is therefore considerably confused with taste preferences for a variety of other components than alcohol alone. What role such taste preference plays in human alcoholism, especially in the early stages when drinking patterns are first being established, is not known. Most of the work with the mice has been done with unflavored alcohol solutions at room temperature, a beverage that most humans would find unpalatable.

The "beverage" with which most of the mouse research has been done is therefore not one which figures to any significant degree as a factor in human alcoholism. This clearly raises the question of what kind of preference is being measured with the mice and what relevance it has to human alcohol consumption. Is the primary variable a taste factor, in which some mice do and others do not enjoy the taste of tepid 10% ethanol? Or is it a preference-for-the-alcohol-effect factor, such as probably characterizes the primary basis for most human alcohol consumption? At this stage, these are questions that are as yet unanswered. In operational terms, "preference" has consisted of the tendency of the mice to consume an alcohol solution (usually 10% volume-to-volume in tap water or distilled water at room temperature), offered ad lib as an alternative to ad lib water not containing the ethanol. The preference measure most commonly used has been the ratio of alcohol solution consumed to water consumed. If environmental temperature, diet, and other factors are essentially uniform, then this ratio is usually highly stable over time, after the first week of exposure, and relatively uninfluenced by body weight of the animals. However, fluctuating environmental temperatures and other factors such as pregnancy can markedly alter this ratio from day to day, such that its use as a preference measure is clearly dependent on the constancy of environmental factors. It is at least nominally a direct measure of "preference" for the alcohol solution as opposed to a water solution. There is some evidence, however, that, at least in the high-alcohol-consuming strains, their consumption of alcohol is essentially constant and their consumption of water will fluctuate depending on ambient temperature. The alcohol preference would thus seem probably to be somewhat independent of water preference, so that the preference ratio is at best an index and not a direct measure of preference *per se*.

Other indices of alcohol consumption and other procedures for measuring alcohol preference are of course possible and have been used in some studies. Absolute amount of alcohol consumed per kilogram body weight is sometimes reported. Consumption is sometimes measured when alcohol is available for only a limited portion of the day rather than ad lib. Multiple concentrations of alcohol are sometimes made available simultaneously, or the concentrations may be systematically varied over time. Bottle positions may be altered in a variety of ways (they are nearly always, or should be, systematically varied at least enough to demonstrate position habit effects or to prevent such effects from occurring). Sugar or other solutions are sometimes used as an alternative to the alcohol solution, and the alcohol solutions are sometimes sweetened or otherwise altered in flavor. Some unreported attempts have been made to test preference through use of bar pressing in operant conditioning equipment. Licking rate at the drinking tube and total time the animal drinks, rather than amount of fluid consumed, have also been used as indices. The particular index of alcohol consumption used and the particular procedure by which it is obtained can markedly affect results obtained, as has been especially emphasized by Fuller (1964, 1967).

It is worth comment that "10% ethanol solution" can have three distinctly different meanings in the mouse work. It can mean 10% alcohol by weight (w/v) or 10% alcohol by volume (v/v) or 10% commercial alcohol (approximately 95% alcohol) by volume. The latter solution, which is the easiest to prepare, contains approximately 75% as much alcohol as the w/v measure. When the "commercial" v/v solution is used, account is almost never taken of the slight shrinkage in total volume that occurs when water and alcohol are mixed, a shrinkage that is opposite in direction from the dilution error already introduced into this preparation. Investigators using the more precise indices may or may not take such shrinkage into account (cf. Barry and Wallgren, 1968).

Some theoreticians have questioned the use of the term "preference" to describe the alcohol consumption of the mice. Technically it should be possible to assess the strength of drive involved in the alcohol consumption, by imposing graded barriers to determine how much resistance the mice will overcome in order to obtain alcohol. Such work has not been adequately done yet, although preliminary studies suggest that the degree of interference which the mice will overcome to obtain alcohol is relatively small, such that the "preference" of the mice does not begin to approach the "craving" of the human alcoholic. Nevertheless, there seems to be little basis for operational quibbling with use of the term preference in a self-selection study in which the mice have ready access to alternative solutions and in which some mice avoid the alcohol solutions while others consume them systematically in a pattern that clearly indicates purposive rather than random selection. There is no doubt, however, that the word "preference" in this context should not be read as synonymous with the "preference" of the human alcoholic for ethanol; and the degree of correspondence or difference between these two conditions is explicitly not known and not carefully studied at this point.

GENETIC EFFECTS ON ALCOHOL PREFERENCE

Williams, Berry, and Beerstecker (1949) and Mirone (1952, 1957, and 1958) were the first investigators to report use of inbred strains of mice in studies of alcohol consumption. These various studies demonstrated probable strain differences in alcohol preference, but were not focused on the problem of strain differences *per se*. McClearn and Rodgers (1959) demonstrated significant differences in alcohol preference among five inbred strains. A variety of subsequent studies has further established strain patterns in alcohol preference. One summary of strain differences is shown in Fig. 4 (Rodgers, 1967). In general, the C57 sublines have consistently shown relatively high preference for alcohol and the DBA sublines have consistently shown very low preference for alcohol under standard conditions. Most other strains tested show relatively low preference for alcohol but consume somewhat more than do the DBA's. Preference characteristics in many inbred strains and sublines have not yet been determined.

The strain comparison data clearly establish that there is a consistent reproducible relationship between voluntary alcohol ingestion and genotype. They do not suggest the nature of this relationship and provide only limited

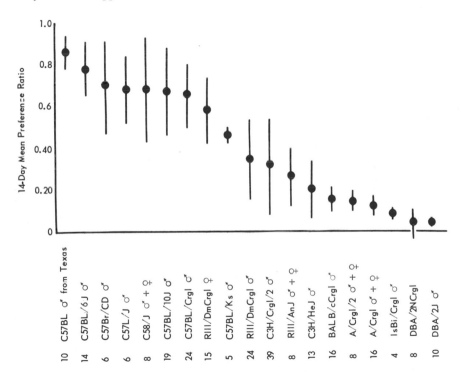

FIGURE 4. Ethanol preference of mouse sublines. Limits are shown for one raw score standard deviation. [From D. A. Rodgers, Alcohol preference in mice, in *Comparative Psychopathology—Animal and Human*, J. Zubin and H. Hunt, eds., Grune and Stratton, 1967, with copyright permission from the publishers.]

information about the genetic complexity that might be involved. The DBA strain (and to some lesser extent, many others) systematically avoids 10% alcohol solutions when water is simultaneously available, suggesting that there is something aversive about either the taste or the effect of the ethanol. The C57 strain consumes most of a normal fluid intake (3.5 to 4.5 ml per day) as 10% ethanol under the same conditions, consuming relatively little additional water per se. This rate of consumption tends to be maintained over an indefinite period (Rodgers et al., 1967). When access to water is removed, so that 10% ethanol is the only drinking fluid, then total volume of alcohol solution consumed by the C57BL strain increases somewhat, to between $5\frac{1}{2}$ and 6 ml per day of 10% v/v ethanol (Rodgers et al., 1967). These results suggest some positive attraction to the alcohol by the C57 strain and suggest but do not clearly demonstrate that the consumption is not solely a substitution of alcohol solution for normal fluid consumption.

Several studies have been done with different strains of mice in an attempt to assess the genetic complexity of the alcohol preference phenomenon manifested by the C57BL strain, as contrasted to the preference of strains that voluntarily consume less alcohol. It should be noted that the analyses at this level are focused solely on the phenotypic drinking response as defined by the standard conditions under which this response was measured. These studies explicitly have not been studies of the "genetics of alcoholism."

McClearn and Rodgers (1961) examined alcohol preference of several genetic crosses, involving C57BL, A/2, Balb/C, C3H/2, and DBA/2N strains (all CRGL sublines) and concluded that F_1 offspring of these crosses fell intermediate in preference between the parent strains, without evidence of heterosis or complete dominance, although there was possibly partial regression toward the low parent preference value. They failed to find differences in reciprocal cross offspring, which might have resulted from maternal effects or X or Y chromosome effects. In this same study, they derived F_1, F_2, and backcross offspring from crosses of the C57BL and A strains. F_1 and F_2 offsprings and all backcrosses fell intermediate between the parent strains, with mean preference of the C57BL backcross being higher than mean preference of the A backcross. The general patterning clearly demonstrated genetic effects on alcohol preference as measured. In this study, the F_1 variance was greater than the F_2 variance, which prevented further assessment of heritability, proportional contribution of additives, dominance, and epistatic components, and relative contributions of genetic and environmental factors, analyses which are sometimes possible from these kinds of data. The evidence suggested a polygenic system of inheritance but the complexity of the system was not specifically analyzable.

Fuller (1964) criticized the previous study on the basis of the kind of preference ratio used and attempted to assess genetic complexity in a similar study, using somewhat different methods of assessing alcohol preference, and using A, C3HeB/6, C57BL/6, and DBA/2 sublines from the Jackson laboratories. He also demonstrated clear genetic factors in the alcohol preference measures, utilizing a range of alcohol concentrations to assess an "indifferent point" of alcohol concentration rather than amount of 10% alcohol consumed. Again, the results of the study were not definitive in terms of genetic complexity but suggested that the physiological substrate underlying the observed preferences may vary from strain to strain and that there was some tendency toward dominance of the genetic substrate of the highest and the lowest preference strains.

Eriksson (1968a) estimated heritability and genetic determination of alcohol consumption of mice to be 75%, using CBA and C57BL strains. Rodgers and McClearn (1962) further demonstrated that postnatal maternal effects were not significant as compared to genetic effects when A/CRGL and C57/BL/CRGL were cross-fostered by the opposite strain mothers. They also demonstrated in first generation selective breeding from a 4-way cross heterogeneous population that differences in alcohol preference could be obtained from a selective breeding program. This selective breeding program was not carried sufficiently far to establish the potential of this approach or to utilize it for identifying genetic parameters.

Sex differences in alcohol consumption or preference have been reported in some strains (e.g., Eriksson and Pikkarainen, 1968; Rodgers, 1967) and suggest the possibility of localizing some influences on the X or Y chromosomes of these strains. The finding of sex differences is not uniformly consistent, however, either across strains or within the same strain.

In general, then, only preliminary genetic analyses of the complexity and specific genetic nature of the alcohol preference response of the mice have been carried out. These studies indicate considerable potential for effectively exploring this problem further and clearly demonstrate the practicality of gaining genetic control over important parameters of the alcohol consumatory response.

NUTRITIONAL EFFECTS ON ALCOHOL PREFERENCE

Both theoretical and experimental considerations have suggested that nutritional factors may be especially important in alcohol preference. Ethanol is a source of calories that are utilizable for energy purposes and that place minimal demands on physiologic reserves. The catabolic pathway is short and involves few intermediate steps. Thiamine in particular is utilized less per given calorie yield from ethanol than from either sugar or fat. Westerfeld and Lawrow (1953) compute a proportionate yield of 180 calories per thiamine utilization from glucose, 286 calories from stearic acid, and 322 from alcohol. In a vitamin B-deficient system, alcohol might thus be an attractive source of calories that places minimal demands on vitamin reserves. Since most alcoholic beverages contain almost no replacement vitamins or other nutritional components other than calories, In contrast to many other natural food sources, alcoholic beverages might thus serve the individual's calorie needs without repairing the nutritional deficiencies that give rise to those needs. This mechanism of a nutritional "need" for alcohol, which does not really correct the nutritional problem that gives rise to the need, is compatible with Williams' genetotrophic theory of alcoholism (Williams, 1947). Experimental data by Mardones and Onfrey (1942 and subsequently), by Richter and Barelare (1939), by Beerstecher *et al.* (1951), by Mirone (1957), and by Sirnes (1953), among other workers, have tended to confirm that relationships do indeed exist between nutritional variables and alcohol consumption. Of these studies, only the one by Mirone was concerned with mice, the C57BL strain. One summary of this area of work is contained in Rodgers and McClearn (1962).

Of the studies specifically focused on mice, the one by Mirone (1957) has already been briefly mentioned. Using C57BL mice, some reared on 5% ethanol as their only drinking fluid and others reared on water without access to alcohol, she demonstrated an increase in alcohol preference in a voluntary choice situation in animals placed on a high-protein diet, protein-free diet, and vitamin B complex-deficient diet. Animals showed an almost statistically significant increase in alcohol preference on a thiamine-deficient diet as well. These animals showed a significant decrease in voluntary alcohol consumption on a high-fat diet and on an iodine-deficient diet. They showed a decrease that approached statistical significance on a pyridoxine-deficient diet. Nutritional factors are thus shown to be capable of significantly influencing alcohol consumption of the mice. Mirone also concluded from this and a previous study (1952) that previous forced exposure to alcohol increases amount of alcohol consumed subsequently. Her data are quite clear in indicating that the "experienced" mice consume more alcohol initially than do the animals never exposed to alcohol. Since C57BL consumption normally does not plateau until after about a week of initial exposure to alcohol (see graphs of developmental preference in McClearn and Rodgers, 1959), her results may pertain more to a novelty response to alcohol than they do to a long-term impact of long-term exposure to ethanol. In any event, her data demonstrate that nutritional factors can significantly influence alcohol consumption in the C57BL mouse.

Rodgers and McClearn (1964) demonstrated that C57BL mice consistently prefer a sucrose solution to an equal-caloric alcohol solution. These results indicate that the normal alcohol preference of the C57BL strain is not a direct result of the thiamine-sparing action of alcohol metabolism, since sucrose makes greater thiamine demands than does alcohol for a given calorie yield. The results also indicate that the preference of the mice for alcohol is not marked as compared to their preference for a sucrose solution, in contrast to the craving of the human alcoholic. The preference of the mice for a sucrose solution is itself quite marked, sufficiently so that the normal aversion for ethanol of nine low-preference inbred strains could be overcome by adding sucrose in sufficient quantity to the alcohol solution (Rodgers and McClearn, 1964). Thus, both alcohol preference and alcohol aversion, in the range tested, constituted a less coercive appetite than did sucrose preference.

Rodgers *et al.* (1963) attempted to determine whether mice that have had experience with the caloric utility of alcohol while on a semistarvation diet would continue to utilize alcohol for its caloric yield in a voluntary choice situation. When 10% ethanol was provided as the only source of liquid, C57BL, RIII, and DBA strains of mice showed significantly less weight loss on a restricted food diet than did controls that were given water instead of 10% ethanol as a drinking solution and that were otherwise given the same restricted diet. A3, C3H/2, and Balb/c strains did not show a corresponding lower rate of weight loss, suggesting that there may be strain differences in ability to utilize alcohol calories for weight maintenance. When all animals were subsequently offered a choice between alcohol and water, while still on a semistarvation diet, the normally high-preference C57BL animals that had previously been exposed to alcohol consumed significantly more than did their water controls, whereas the normally low preference DBA/2 animals previously exposed to alcohol consumed significantly less than did their water controls, even though the consumption of the DBA water controls was itself quite low. These data were interpreted as indicating that factors other than caloric utility were involved in alcohol preference of the mice, especially of the DBA/2 strain.

Rodgers and co-workers (Rodgers, 1967) attempted to assess the effects of impaired metabolic capacity on alcohol consumption. Metabolic capacity was impaired by dietarily induced thiamine deficiency and by liver damage induced by either surgical procedures or carbon tetrachloride toxicity. None of these procedures resulted in either significant increase or significant decrease in alcohol consumption as compared to control animals, within the range of impairment that was induced, in the low to intermediate preference strains that were tested.

Eriksson (1968b), working primarily with rats, has elaborated a nutritional conception of alcohol preference and has related this to the alcohol preference of the CBA and C57BL strains as well as, speculatively, to human alcoholism. In general, the work on nutritional parameters of alcohol preference in the mice has suggested many leads that could fruitfully be explored further, but it has not definitively established clear-cut relationships that might have immediate relevance to the problem of human alcoholism. There has been some support for a genetotrophic theory of alcoholism, but the support has not been as dramatic as would be necessary to establish this as a major explanation of human alcoholism. Nutritional factors clearly play some role in alcohol consumption of mice but have not yet been demonstrated to be capable of making heavy drinkers out of normally low preference strains or to account in any significant way for the normal high consumption of the normally high preference C57BL strain. The work to date clearly demonstrates that nutritional factors in alcohol preference of inbred strains of mice is an eminently researchable topic that warrants much further investigation.

EXPERIENTIAL EFFECTS ON ALCOHOL PREFERENCE

Past exposure to alcohol, stress experiences, social facilitation, and similar variables are often posited as factors contributing to human alcoholism. Stress in particular has been emphasized as a contributor to alcohol consumption. Different authors vary in their emphasis on the degree to which stress alone could be expected to induce increased alcohol consumption or on the necessity for a learning experience in which alcohol ingestion and subsequent effects are associated with a reduction of anxiety secondary to stress. The explicit animal analogue to test a given hypothesis would of course depend on the explicit nature of the hypothesis. Work with mice has not been carefully done to test highly precise learning theories of alcoholism. Several studies have nevertheless assessed the rather nonspecific assumption of a general relationship between stress and increased alcohol intake.

Utilizing population density as a variable known to increase adrenal size in mice and therefore presumed to be stressful, Rodgers and Thiessen (1964) failed to find any significant increase in alcohol consumption of C3H/2 mice, even though they demonstrated adrenal enlargement and behavioral changes commonly associated with behavioral activation and stress. In further studies of grouping and alcohol consumption, with the added stressor of alcohol or saline injections, Thiessen and Rodgers (1965) also failed to demonstrate any increase in alcohol consumption in the C57BL or RIII substrains in response to stress, and in fact found some reduction in ethanol intake of the stressed C57BL animals. The same results were obtained in studies utilizing other injections that could be expected to be stressful (Rodgers, 1967). These studies thus strongly suggest that alcohol consumption of the C57BL in particular and of the other strains so far tested is not explainable on the basis of a response to stress. The rank-order correlation of emotionality ratings with alcohol preference ratings across six inbred strains of mice very closely approached zero in one study and offered no support for the possibility that strain differences in alcohol preference might be due to differences in general emotionality of the strains (Rodgers, 1967).

The same studies that utilized grouping as a stressor and failed to find increase in alcohol consumption secondary thereto can also be reinterpreted as failing to demonstrate any social facilitation in alcohol consumption in the strains of mice thus tested. Social parameters in the mice might be expected to be quite different from social parameters in the human, so directly relevant comparisons might not be possible. In any event, in the strains so far tested, mice living in community with other mice do not increase their alcohol consumption as compared to mice living in isolation.

Mirone (1952) has demonstrated an increase in alcohol consumption of C57BL mice previously exposed to alcohol. As already mentioned, it is not entirely clear whether this increased consumption reflected an initial period of getting used to the alcohol or whether it reflected a more significant long-term effect. C57BL/Crgl male mice failed to show much change in level of alcohol consumption over a 65-week period when measurements were begun 10 weeks after their initial exposure to alcohol (Rodgers et al., 1967). There thus is not an indefinite growth in alcohol preference of the C57BL strain, although there is certainly an initial gain in preference during the first few days. It is my impression that this preference level plateaus within the first 2 weeks, although further parametric studies of this problem might possibly be done. In general, systematic parametric studies of preference and preference development have not been adequately done in the mice. Kakihana and McClearn (1963), have done perhaps the most systematic study of one strain, the Balb/c, in examining development of preference from ages 3 weeks to 20 weeks.

Work to date suggests that there are major strain differences in response to previous exposure to alcohol. As above, the C57 strain shows some development of alcohol preference following exposure. The work on alcohol consumption during a semistarvation diet, previously discussed, appears to demonstrate a decrease in preference of the DBA strain following exposure to alcohol. Incidental data on the AKR/c strain tentatively suggested in one study that this strain might show a marked increase in preference for alcohol following previous exposure, although the data were too minimal for firm conclusions (Rodgers and McClearn, 1964). It is clear from the work to date that forced alcohol consumption does not inevitably increase alcohol preference of mice in general. This is especially true of those strains that initially show an aversive response to alcohol.

In general, relatively little highly precise work has been done on experiential antecedents, and especially on previous learning as it might relate to alcohol consumption of inbred strains of mice. This relative neglect may be due to the apparently highly coercive factor of physiologic difference that seems to overdetermine the alcohol preference across strains (e.g., compare Fuller, 1967). Related to this, it may also be due to the theoretical preoccupation of the workers in this area with physiological or other parameters rather than with some of the current learning theory models. There are no conceptual reasons that would restrict the use of the mice for studies of these parameters, however.

PHYSIOLOGIC CORRELATES OF ALCOHOL PREFERENCE

Perhaps because the inbred strain approach so precisely standardizes physiology, the most precise and seemingly insightful work on alcohol preference of the inbred mice has involved physiologic parameters. In its metabolism, alcohol is presumably first oxidized to acetaldehyde by alcohol dehydrogenase enzyme. The acetaldehyde is then presumably further oxidized to acetate by acetaldehyde dehydrogenase enzyme. Since enzymes are under close genetic control, these enzyme systems would be obvious ones to examine for physiologic correlates of the differences in alcohol preference demonstrated in the mice. Both have in fact shown relevant correlations.

Rodgers et al. (1963) found a perfect rank order correlation over six inbred strains between alcohol preference in a food-deprivation situation and liver alcohol dehydrogenase activity per unit body weight. That is, those animals with highest apparent liver capacity for metabolizing alcohol consumed more of it than did those animals with lower capacity. The alcohol consumption in this particular study was measured under conditions of relative calorie deprivation, which could be expected to enhance the relationship between alcohol consumption and metabolic capacity. However, the strain ordering is essentially the same as has been repeatedly obtained under noncalorie-deprivation conditions. In studies of mice not subjected to calorie deprivation, McClearn et al. (1964) and Sheppard, Albersheim, and McClearn (1968) demonstrated higher liver alcohol dehydrogenase activity levels in the high-preference C57BL strain than in the low-preference DBA strain. Eriksson and Pikkarainen (1968) demonstrated a similar relationship between liver alcohol dehydrogenase enzyme activity and alcohol preference, both between sexes of the C57BL strain and between the C57BL and the CBA strains. These data suggest the possible generalization that high alcohol consumption is associated with high ability to metabolize alcohol.

Several considerations call into question this simple generalization. First, the metabolic capacity of the lowest preference strain (DBA) has repeatedly been measured as more than half that of the highest preference strain (C57BL), although its voluntary consumption of alcohol is consistently a small fraction of that of the C57BL. The same general relationship also holds between the C57BL and CBA strains. Furthermore, live animal assays of rate of disappearance of radioactively tagged carbon secondary to alcohol metabolism (Rodgers and McClearn, 1962; and Schlesinger, 1964) have not substantiated the *in vitro* findings of differences in rate of metabolism between the C57BL and DBA strains. McClearn et al. (1964) and Schlesinger et al. (1966) demonstrated increase in liver alcohol dehydrogenase activity following previous ingestion of ethanol, in both C57BL and the DBA/2 strain. While the C57BL strain does indeed show an increase in consumption of alcohol following previous exposure, the DBA/2 strain does not, even though it presumably develops some increase in metabolic capacity. Thus, capacity to oxidize alcohol to acetaldehyde does not appear to be a sufficient explanation of strain differences in alcohol preference, even though it may play some role.

While it appears insufficient to account for the strain difference in alcohol preference, metabolic capacity nevertheless appears to be an important variable in determining alcohol consumption of the C57BL strain. Thiessen, Whitworth, and Rodgers (1966, 1967) demonstrated an increase in alcohol consumption of pregnant and lactating C57BL dams that closely paralleled change in liver size and presumably closely paralleled change in capacity to metabolize alcohol. Data on measured rates of alcohol metabolism have been reviewed (Rodgers, 1966) and total metabolic capacity has been shown to approach closely actual observed voluntary consumption of the C57BL strain. When the ethanol solution is sweetened with sucrose, consumption very closely approximates total estimated metabolic capacity of this strain. It is not surprising, then, if attempts to increase alcohol consumption of the C57BL strain, for example by exposure to stress or nutritional deficiencies, fail of success, if this strain normally drinks close to metabolic capacity. It can even be speculated that the apparent reduction in alcohol consumption of the C57BL strain under stress may be a result of reduced capacity to metabolize alcohol under stress (Rodgers, 1967), although definitive data do not now exist concerning the effect of stress on alcohol metabolism of this or other strains. Most studies of rate of metabolism have been done under stressful conditions, for example, following hypodermic injection of alcohol or as a result of measuring changes in blood alcohol level between two periods of rather stressful procedures of blood sampling. If stress does reduce normal capacity for metabolizing alcohol, then previously assessed rates of alcohol metabolism of the C57BL strain may be somewhat low. Further careful work in this area should help to clarify some of the present anomalies in the literature.

Although the alcohol dehydrogenase system may be a critical one in alcohol preference of the C57BL strain, it does not appear to provide much explanation of preference phenomena in the low preference strains and especially in the DBA/2 strain. For this strain, the dynamics of acetaldehyde metabolism may be critical. Schlesinger (1964, 1966) noted that the DBA/2 strain showed an atypical response to Antabuse, as compared to the C57BL strain, showing less blocking effect on alcohol metabolism of the Antabuse. Sheppard, Albersheim, and McClearn (1968) have recently found C57BL/6J mice to have 300% more acetaldehyde dehydrogenase activity than DBA/2J mice, as compared to only 30% more alcohol dehydrogenase activity. Data from Schlesinger, Kakihana, and Bennett (1966) are suggestive that acetaldehyde accumulation in DBA mice is significantly higher than in C57 mice following ethanol ingestion. Since acetaldehyde is a pharmacologically toxic substance that produces considerable subjective distress at suitable blood level concentrations, these findings suggest a "built-in disulfiram" response in the DBA strain such that alcohol ingestion results in noxious accumulation of acetaldehyde, a mechanism that would explain their low preference for alcohol. In contrast, the greater capacity of the C57BL mice to metabolize acetaldehyde would presumably prevent such accumulation. For the mouse strains, therefore, acetaldehyde metabolism in relationship to the alcohol dehydrogenase system may be a critical dimension of alcohol consumption dynamics.

The acetaldehyde metabolism findings in the mouse work suggest the possibility of similar dynamics at the human level, such that some people may be metabolically protected from significant predisposition toward alcoholism by an inborn metabolic bias toward an aversive experience following ingestion of large alcohol loads. The mouse work thus strongly suggests the desirability of looking for the "genetics of alcohol aversion" in humans as well as for the "genetics of predisposition toward alcoholism."

Other physiologic correlates with alcohol preference have been explored in some studies. Mirone found successive generations of offspring of Swiss mice reared on 10% ethanol as a sole drinking fluid to show different alcohol preference patterns (sometimes higher preference and sometimes lower preference) than controls from parents reared on water. The physiologic or possibly other mechanisms mediating these differences were not elucidated. Iida (1957) reported an increase in alcohol preference of mice subjected to an increased sodium chloride load, although the observed effect was small and the mechanism of action was not apparent. Both Fuller (1967) and Thiessen and McClearn (1965) have demonstrated that alcohol consumption can be altered under conditions of thirst, probably secondary to the animal's desire for water rather than because of any relationship to alcohol dynamics *per se*. Iida (1960) reported data suggesting a possible relationship between alcohol preference and a material tentatively identified as glucurone in the liver of Swiss albino mice. Rodgers and Lewis (1962) failed to find similar relationships in C57BL, C3H/2, and A strains. Iida's findings concerning glucose levels in alcohol preference in the Swiss albino strain were also not confirmed in these other strains.

McClearn (1962) has demonstrated significant strain differences in activity following forced alcohol ingestion, the activity differences not being associated in any systematic way with strain differences in alcohol preference and apparently not being consistent from one activity situation to another. The physiologic substrate or correlates of this response to alcohol have not been elucidated. McClearn (1962) also demonstrated marked strain differences in sleeping time following intraperitoneal injection of a heavy alcohol load. There was some consistent tendency for high-alcohol-preferring strain to have a shorter sleeping time than low-alcohol-preferring strains. In a subsequent study of the C57BL and Balb/c strains, Kakihana et al. (1966) confirmed the previously found difference in sleeping time following intraperitoneal injection of a heavy alcohol load and further demonstrated that recovery from alcohol-induced sleep occurred at a higher blood alcohol level in the C57BL strain than in the lower-preference Balb/c strain. They failed to find significant evidence of difference in rate of metabolism, as measured *in vivo*, in these strains. They concluded that brain sensitivity to alcohol was less in the C57BL than in the Balb/c strain and that this difference in sensitivity was unrelated to rate of alcohol metabolism. The mechanism of action that might be involved was not elucidated.

PATHOLOGICAL EFFECTS OF LONG-TERM ALCOHOL CONSUMPTION

The defining characteristic of a mouse analogue of human alcoholic consumption posited at the beginning of this chapter was voluntary alcohol ingestion beyond the point of physiologic or sociologic impairment. The data reported so far have concerned only the phenomenon of alcohol preference and have not touched upon the issue of consumption to the point of pathology. Rodgers *et al.* (1967) maintained C57BL males with ad lib access to 10% ethanol, under otherwise standard laboratory conditions, for a period of 75 weeks, from age 150 days onward. Animals were autopsied and examined for evidence of possible pathology at that time. This study suggested that prolonged voluntary alcohol intake might increase susceptibility to parasitic infestation and might impair coat condition somewhat (suggestive of a vitamin deficiency), but did not affect body weight, increase mortality rates, or give rise to characteristic organ pathology. Prolonged voluntary alcohol ingestion of these mice did not therefore demonstrate morbid changes commonly associated with human alcoholism.

It was determined that these animals, although routinely drinking amounts of alcohol that approach metabolic tolerance, did not reduce their normal food intake by more than approximately 20%. Since human alcoholics will reduce normal food intake by 50% to 90%, and since most physiologic pathology secondary to alcoholism is largely a result of nutritional deficiency of other foodstuffs rather than a direct result of heavy alcohol load, it seems likely that the C57BL animals were protected from negative physiologic consequences by the relatively small reduction in normal nutrition that alcohol consumption induced. These investigators therefore assessed the consequences of prolonged voluntary consumption of alcohol to which sucrose was added to increase the caloric yield. C3H, C57BL, RIII, Balb/c, and DBA/2 were maintained for approximately 1 year under standard laboratory conditions and standard laboratory diet except that half of each group was provided a choice between sweetened alcohol and water as a drinking fluid and the other half was provided a choice between water and a sucrose solution not containing alcohol. In addition, C3H mice were maintained on water without access to either alcohol or sucrose solutions. The C57BL reduced their normal food intake approximately 50% when they had access to the sweetened alcohol solution. The other strains reduced their food intake somewhat less than did the C57's, with DBA/2's making the least reduction (less than 10%). At the end of 1 year, one of the five C57BL animals on the sweetened alcohol choice condition had died and the remaining four showed significant pathology on autopsy, the most common find being pronounced vacuolar changes in the hepatic cord cells, suggestive of changes commonly associated with fatty infiltration of the liver in human alcoholics. None of the C57BL animals on a water vs. sucrose choice condition showed demonstrable pathology at autopsy after 1 year, even though their caloric intake from the sucrose solution on the average exceeded that of the other C57BL animals on sweetened alcohol choice. With the exception of one Balb/c animal that showed evidence of early fibrosis suggestive of early liver sclerosis of dietary origin, none of the other animals that survived to autopsy showed pathological changes that were particularly characteristic of human alcoholics, although a variety of inflammatory processes and other types of pathology were demonstrable in some animals in both the alcohol and the sugar groups. Susceptibility to parasitic infestation was again demonstrated in the animals on alcohol choice, but not in those on sucrose choice alone, suggesting that the alcohol consumption *per se* has some role in increasing susceptibility to the parasites.

These data suggest that under suitable experimental conditions, mice will continue to consume an alcohol solution beyond the point that physiological pathology is induced. To this degree, there would seem to be a parallel to the human alcoholic. The results clearly highlight the difference between humans and mice with regard to the proportion of daily caloric need that can be realized from ethanol alone. The parallel to the human situation could easily be exaggerated in other respects, also. The mice did not really have free access to alternative foodstuffs—merely access to a standard laboratory diet in pelletized form which allowed only the selective option of either eating it or not eating it. They did not necessarily "know" that it was the consumption of alcohol which was producing the pathology they experienced, whereas the human alcoholic presumably does have knowledge of this causal relationship. No "craving" for the alcohol was demonstrated beyond the fact that the mice would consume it if it was immediately available, and even this degree of craving may have had as much to do with the sucrose content of the beverage as with the alcohol content. When mice have been offered an alternative choice between sweetened alcohol or sucrose alone, they have tended to prefer the sucrose solution alone, so that the pathology demonstrated in the present studies from alcohol consumption might have been avoided if the mice had had the same alternative selections of beverages that the human alcoholic has. Thus, these studies are only early beginnings toward elaboration of a mouse model of human alcoholism and by no means provide a complete parallel. Whether a satisfactory model could ever be evolved remains for future work to demonstrate or fail to demonstrate. These beginnings do suggest some conditions under which some pathological changes of a type found in human alcoholics can be achieved secondary to at least limited voluntary choice of an alcoholic beverage.

PATHOLOGICAL EFFECTS OF ALCOHOL NOT VOLUNTARILY INGESTED

It was not the intent of this chapter to review toxic effects of alcohol on mice (such as the paper by Mirone, 1966). However, one recent study is of sufficient relevance to the problem of a mouse model of human alcoholism to deserve mention. Freund (1969) has recently demonstrated an alcohol withdrawal syndrome in ICR-DUB mice forced to consume a diet in which approximately 35% of caloric intake was from alcohol, after their body weight had been reduced approximately one-third by a semistarvation diet. The syndrome described sounds similar to many dimensions of the alcohol withdrawal syndrome found in human beings after a period of heavy intoxication. This clearly would not constitute a mouse analogue of human alcoholism *per se*, but it does appear to constitute a mouse analogue of an important dimension of the human alcoholic pathology syndrome. This alcohol withdrawal syndrome has not been observed following voluntary ingestion of ethanol when alternative foodstuffs were available.

SUMMARY AND IMPLICATIONS

Genetic control over some dimensions that produce marked differences in voluntary ingestion of 10% alcohol offered in addition to a standard laboratory diet has been well documented in inbred strains of mice. A substantial body of literature has developed on the mouse as an experimental animal in the study of alcohol preference, such that many of the pitfalls, relevant experimental procedures, and relevant parameters have been elucidated. The work to date suggests that relatively high capacity to metabolize alcohol, a relatively greater capacity to metabolize acetaldehyde, and perhaps a relative neurological insensitivity to alcohol constitute some of the most important parameters in the consumption of the high preference C57BL strain. A relative inability to metabolize acetaldehyde may constitute the primary deterrent from alcohol consumption of the DBA/2 strain. The high preference strain will ingest alcohol at close to metabolic capacity apparently indefinitely. Pathological effects from such ingestion seem minimal so long as the animals consume a nutritional diet for the remaining 75% or more of their daily caloric need which cannot be realized from alcohol alone. Liver pathology characteristic of early stages of human alcoholism can develop in the high-preference C57BL II no more than 60% of their caloric need is obtained from a standard laboratory chow, with the remaining portion coming from refined sucrose and ethanol. There has been some elucidation of genetic relationships, of nutritional factors involved in alcohol preference, of effects of stress and other experiences on alcohol consumption, and of other physiologic correlates of alcohol preference.

As these data have relevance to the understanding of human alcoholism, they clearly do not provide any definitive clarification of the problem of alcoholism. Perhaps the most promising implication is the possibility that some people may be protected from developing alcoholism because of physiologic processes that make the experience of a heavy alcohol load excessively aversive. Another possible implication might be drawn from the impression obtained in the mouse work that the craving for alcohol is not marked but its persistent consumption under appropriate conditions can nevertheless lead to pathological changes. Is it possible that there has been too much emphasis on the "irresistible craving" of the human alcoholic for alcohol and too little emphasis on the potential for induced pathology secondary to heavy regular alcohol consumption regardless of how much or how little craving is involved? These are obviously speculations that go well beyond the present data. One of the advantages of the inbred-strain mouse work is that flights of speculative fantasy tend to be promptly scuttled in the precision of the data obtainable and the potential for testing speculative hypotheses under conditions of minimal physiological "noise" in the investigation.

REFERENCES

Barry, H., III and Wallgren, H., 1968. A further note on preparing alcohol solutions, *Quart. J. Stud. Alc.* **29**: 176–178.

Beerstecker, E., Jr., Reed, J. G., Brown, W. D., and Berry, L. J., 1951. The effects of single vitamin deficiencies on the consumption of alcohol by white rats, *Univ. Tex. Pub.*, No. 5109, pp. 115–138.

Eriksson, K., 1968a. Periman ja ympariston osuus alkoholin nauttimista saatelevina tekijoina koe-elaimilla suoritettujen tutkimusten perusteella. *Eripainos Alkoholikysymys* **1**: 3–9.

Eriksson, K., 1968b. En biologisk utredning over alkoholismens etiologi med djurexperiment, *Sartryck ur Alkoholpolitik* **31**: 111–117.

Eriksson, K. and Pikkarainen, P. H., 1968. Differences between the sexes in voluntary alcohol consumption and liver ADH activity in inbred strains of mice, *Metabolism* **17**: 1037–1042.

Fuller, J. L., 1964. Measurement of alcohol preference in genetic experiments, *J. Comp. Physiol. Psych.* **57** (1), 85–88.

Fuller, J. L., 1967. Effect of drinking schedule upon alcohol preference in mice, *Quart. J. Stud. Alc.* **28**: 22–26.

Freund, G., 1969. Alcohol withdrawal syndrome in mice, *Arch. Neurol.* **21**: 315–320.

Iida, S., 1957. Experimental studies on the craving for alcohol: I. Alcoholic drive in mice following administration of saline, *Jap. J. Pharm.* **6**: 87–93.

Iida, S., 1958. Experimental studies on the craving for alcohol: II. Alcoholic drive in mice following administration of hepatotoxic agents, *Jap. J. Pharm.* **8**: 70–74.

Iida, S., 1960. Experimental studies on the craving for alcohol: III. The relationship between alcoholic craving and carbohydrate metabolism, *Jap. J. Pharm.* **10**: 15–20.

Kakihana, R. and McClearn, G. E., 1963. Development of alcohol preference in BALB/c mice, *Nature* **199**: 511–512.

Kakihana, R., Brown, D. R., McClearn, G. E., and Tabershaw, I. R., 1966. Brain sensitivity to alcohol in inbred mouse strains, *Science* **154**: 1574–1575.

Mardones, R. J. and Onfrey, B. E., 1942. Influencia de una substancia de la levadura (elemento del complejo vitaminico B?) sobre el consumo de alcohol en rates en experimentos de antoseliccion, *Rev. Chil. Hig. Med. Prev.* **4**: 293–297.

McClearn, G. E. and Rodgers, D. A., 1959. Differences in alcohol preference among inbred strains of mice, *Quart. J. Stud. Alc.* **20**: 691–695.

McClearn, G. E. and Rodgers, D. A., 1961. Genetic factors in alcohol preference of laboratory mice, *J. Comp. Physiol. Psych.* **54**: 116–119.

McClearn, G. E., 1963. Genetic differences in the effect of alcohol upon behavior of mice, in *Alcohol and Road Traffic.* (J. D. J. Harvard, ed.) Tavistock Square, London: British Medical Assoc.

McClearn, G. E., Bennett, E. L., Hebert, M., Kakihana, R., and Schlesinger, K., 1964. Alcohol dehydrogenase activity and previous ethanol consumption in mice, *Nature* **203**: 793–794.

Mirone, L., 1952. The effect of ethyl alcohol on growth, fecundity and voluntary consumption of alcohol by mice, *Quart. J. Stud. Alc.* **13**: 365–369.

Mirone, L., 1957. Dietary deficiency in mice in relation to voluntary alcohol consumption, *Quart. J. Stud. Alc.* **18**: 552–560.

Mirone, L., 1958. The effect of ethyl alcohol on growth and voluntary consumption of alcohol by successive generations of mice, *Quart. Stud. Alc.* **19**: 388–393.

Mirone, L., 1959. Water and alcohol consumption by mice, *Quart. Stud. Alc.* **20**: 24–27.

Mirone, L., 1966. Effect of ethanol in single dose on liver of ethanol-treated and non-treated mice, *Amer. J. Physiol.* **210**: 390–394.

Richter, C. P. and Barelare, B., 1939. Further observations on the carbohydrate, fat, and protein appetite of Vitamin B deficient rats, *Amer. J. Physiol.* **127**: 199–210.

Rodgers, D. A. and McClearn, G. E., 1962. Alcohol preference in mice, in *Roots of Behavior: Genetics, Instinct, and Socialization in Animal Behavior,* (E. L. Bliss, ed.) pp. 68–95, Paul B. Hoeber, Inc., Medical Division of Harper & Brothers.

Rodgers, D. A. and McClearn, G. E., 1962. Mouse strain differences in preference for various concentrations of alcohol, *Quart. J. Stud. Alc.* **23**: 26–33.

Rodgers, D. A. and Lewis, U. J., 1963. Relationship of liver content of glucose and glucurone and ethanol preference of inbred mice, *Jap. J. Pharm.* **13**: 125–126.

Rodgers, D. A., McClearn, G. E., Bennett, E. L., and Hebert, M., 1963. Alcohol preference as a function of its caloric utility in mice, *J. Comp. Physiol. Psych.* **56**: 666–672.

Rodgers, D. A. and McClearn, G. E., 1964. Sucrose versus ethanol appetite in inbred strains of mice, *Quart. J. Stud. Alc.* **25**: 26–35.

Rodgers, D. A. and Thiessen, D. D., 1964. Effects of population density on adrenal size, behavioral arousal, and alcohol preference of inbred mice, *Quart. J. Stud. Alc.* **25:** 240–247.

Rodgers, D. A., 1966. Factors underlying differences in alcohol preference among inbred strains of mice, *Psychosom. Med.* **28** (4, Part 2), 498–513.

Rodgers, D. A., 1967. Alcohol preference in mice, in *Comparative Psychopathology*, (J. Zubin & H. Hunt, eds.) pp. 184–201, Grune & Stratton, Inc.

Rodgers, D. A., Ward, P. A., Thiessen, D. D., and Whitworth, N. S., 1967. Pathological effects of prolonged voluntary consumption of alcohol by mice, *Quart. J. Stud. Alc.* **28:** 618–630.

Rodgers, D. A., 1970. Mechanism-specific behavior: an experimental alternative, in *Contributions to Behavior-Genetic Analysis: The Mouse as Prototype*, (G. Lindzey & D. D. Thiessen, eds.) pp. 207–218, Appleton Century Crofts, New York (in press).

Schlesinger, K., 1964. Genetic and biochemical determinants of alcohol preference and alcohol metabolism in mice. Unpublished doctoral dissertation, University of California, Berkeley.

Schlesinger, K., 1966. Genetic and biochemical correlates of alcohol preference in mice, *Amer. J. Psych.* **122:** 767–773.

Schlesinger, K., Bennett, E. L., Hebert, M., and McClearn, G. E., 1966. Effects of alcohol consumption on the activity of liver enzymes in C57BL/Crgl mice, *Nature* **209:** 488–489.

Schlesinger, K., Kakihana, R., and Bennett, E. L., 1966. Effects of tetraethylthiuramidisulfide (antabuse) on metabolism and consumption of ethanol in mice, *Psychosom. Med.* **28:** 514–520.

Sheppard, J. R., Albersheim, P., and McClearn, G. E., 1968. Enzyme activities and ethanol preference in mice, *Biochem. Genet.* **2:** 205–212.

Sirnes, T. B., 1953. Voluntary consumption of alcohol in rats with cirrhosis of the liver: a preliminary report, *Quart. J. Stud. Alc.* **14:** 3–18.

Thiessen, D. D. and McClearn, G. E., 1965. Thirst and alcohol preference of inbred strains of mice, *J. Comp. Physiol. Psych.* **59:** 436–438.

Thiessen, D. D. and Rodgers, D. A., 1965. Alcohol injection, grouping, and voluntary alcohol consumption of inbred strains of mice, *Quart. J. Stud. Alc.* **26:** 378–383.

Thiessen, D. D., Whitworth, N. S., and Rodgers, D. A., 1966. Reproductive variables and alcohol consumption of the C57BL/Crgl female mouse, *Quart. J. Stud. Alc.* **27:** 591–595.

Thiessen, D. D., Whitworth, N. S., and Rodgers, D. A., 1967. Reproductive functions and metabolic capacity as determinants of alcohol preference in C57BL female mice, *J. Comp. Physiol. Psych.* **63:** 151–154.

Westerfeld, W. W. and Lawrow, J., 1953. The effect of caloric restriction and thiamin deficiency on the voluntary consumption of alcohol by rats, *Quart. J. Stud. Alc.* **14:** 378–384.

Williams, R. J., 1967. The etiology of alcoholism: a working hypothesis involving the interplay of hereditary and environmental factors, *Quart. J. Stud. Alc.* **7:** 567–87.

Williams, R. J., Berry, L. J., and Beerstecher, E., Jr., 1969. Biochemical individuality. III. Genetotrophic factors in the etiology of alcoholism, *Arch. Biochem.* **16:** 275–290.

CHAPTER 6

The Determinants of Alcohol Preference in Animals

R. D. Myers and W. L. Veale

Laboratory of Neuropsychology
Purdue University
Lafayette, Indiana

INTRODUCTION

If an animal drinks a solution containing ethyl alcohol when another fluid is available, it is difficult to know what this selection actually means. Facing the scientist are exceedingly complex variables: those inherent in the environmental situation as well as those associated with the animal itself. We, the human observers, recording events and watching through the mesh of the cage, can only attempt to identify the factors which are responsible for the animal's choice of an alcohol solution.

Alcoholism is not an affliction of the animal kingdom, but is a unique human disease for which no animal analogue exists. One could argue that it is a fruitless endeavor for an investigator to place an animal in an experimental situation in order to simulate the human circumstance which generates and perpetuates the immoderate intake of alcoholic beverages. This pessimistic view is enhanced further by the fact that a gap wider than ever before has opened between researchers who are seeking to find the underlying mechanisms of alcohol excess, including metabolic vagaries in the brain or liver, and those who give alcohol parenterally to an animal, then test its effects in an esoteric behavioral task so remote from a human social context that the formulation of an animal model for alcoholism staggers one's imagination. What, then, can we do to improve this discouraging outlook?

Many advances have been made in the understanding of the pathways of alcohol metabolism and of the systems affected by this compound. At the same time, our knowledge of the conditions under which an animal will consume alcohol in a choice situation has increased substantially. What seems to be required for the ultimate understanding of an aberrant drinking pattern is a synthesis of information involving behavioral, physiological, and biochemical research. In essence, the scientist working in this field will, of necessity, have to comprehend or at least be aware of what is transpiring in the laboratory "next door"; he must be particularly cognizant of the pitfalls involved in conducting an investigation on alcohol consumption in which certain critical variables must be precisely controlled.

In the first part of this chapter, we have outlined criteria for evaluating the self-selection of alcohol in animals. Several hundred journal articles were reviewed; only a small fraction met the basic requirements of sound research in which (1) a careful experimental design was followed; (2) an adequate number of animals were used; (3) suitable environmental controls were exercised; (4) control groups were employed; (5) sufficient data were presented; or (6) the results were analyzed or interpreted appropriately. Unfortunately, we still have a legacy of early papers that often represented a first attempt and gave only preliminary results. Many of these have never been adequately followed up or completed using parametric experimental designs.

The Meaning of Alcohol Selection

Before the problems surrounding the measurement of alcohol preference are explored, the question should be answered as to what is meant when an animal selects alcohol rather than another fluid. In connection with the ingestion of alcohol, several anthropomorphic and clinically used terms are employed to describe the phenomena associated with volitional alcohol intake of animals. Unfortunately, certain misleading phrases have been used, such as "self-administration" rather than volitional consumption, voluntary intake, or self-selection; because it is so nonspecific this term may imply self-injection. Also, "alcoholic craving" or "drive" connote an intense anthropomorphic desire or need which cannot be inferred on the basis of the proportion or volume of alcohol consumed.

As is reviewed later, tolerance to alcohol has been demonstrated in animals, since alcohol may be consumed in ever-increasing quantities without loss of a particular function as measured in a specified behavioral task. Habituation to alcohol may also occur in animals which consume certain amounts of the fluid in preference to water or a solution of another substance. Acclimation describes in temporal terms the process of an animal's becoming familiar with or experiencing the gustatory, olfactory, and other properties of alcohol. Dependence, on the other hand, has been rather more difficult to demonstrate in animals, since the human physical symptoms related to alcohol dependence such as the withdrawal syndrome, hallucinations, or convulsions must be clearly exhibited when the fluid is removed; the symptoms likewise disappear when alcohol is made available again. Therefore, as Mendelson and Mello (1964) have indicated, a concept such as addiction to ethyl alcohol is usable only when an animal exhibits tolerance and is observed to be habituated and dependent on this fluid.

Notwithstanding the cogent criticism of Lester (1968), one ordinarily speaks of preference for alcohol if more than half of the fluid consumed consistently within a given test interval is the alcohol solution offered. The preference threshold then is defined as that concentration at which alcohol constitutes one-half of the animals' daily fluid intake when a series of concentrations are offered in an ascending or descending series (Myers, 1966). The word selection denotes or describes whether or not an animal takes or does not take a given fluid such as alcohol or water. In the two-choice situation, the animal may either select water or an alcohol solution or if not, select to die. If the animal does in fact drink, preference defines operationally which of the two fluids the animal selects and describes quite clearly the relationship between the fluids selected. Selection, then, is defined operationally by the number of milliliters ingested, and a ratio or proportional relationship is not to be inferred.

MEASURING ALCOHOL PREFERENCE IN ANIMALS

In many studies in which the intake of alcohol constitutes the principal measurement, 10% alcohol is the solution offered to the animal. The arbitrary use of this or any other single test solution can result in a serious misinterpretation of the data collected. To use one concentration for testing an animal's alcohol preference is similar to administering only one dose of a drug and then describing its biological properties. What are the alternatives?

Techniques of Self-Selection

Because of individual differences between animals, a valid measure of alcohol preference can be obtained by offering the animal a series of different test concentrations of alcohol (Fuller, 1964). Since animals of the same age, sex, and strain may exhibit vastly different drinking patterns, the presentation of multiple concentrations of alcohol over a number of days, as illustrated in Fig. 1, will yield data on alcohol intake analogous to a dose-response curve. To illustrate this, rats of several strains will usually prefer solutions of alcohol lower than 6 or 7% over water (Myers, 1966; 1968). If, let us say, only a 3% concentration of alcohol is presented together with water, then most animals would drink this solution as their preferred fluid (Fig. 1). On the other hand, if an alcohol solution of high concentration such as 26% were offered, few, if any, of the animals would ingest a significant volume. From this simple illustration, it is clear that the use of a single concentration in conjunction with a behavioral or physiological manipulation is unwise, unless a prior determination is made of the animal's drinking pattern.

The most common way of using a multiple solution method is to increase the concentration of an alcohol solution on a periodic basis and in a stepwise fashion from a low initial value to a high concentration (Richter and Campbell,

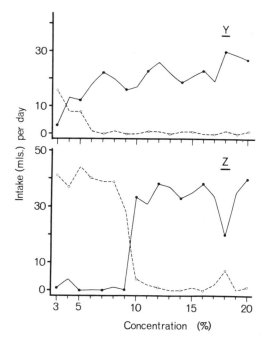

FIGURE 1. Alcohol (EtOH) and water intakes for two rats (Y and Z) of the same age, sex, and strain offered the choice between these fluids over an 18-day test period. The alcohol solution was increased in 1% steps on consecutive days as shown on the abscissa. (– – –) EtOH, (——) H_2O. [From Myers and Holman (1966).]

1940); the concentration is increased by 1 or 2% after a given interval, usually 1 day (Fig. 1). A variation in this procedure consists of decreasing the concentration in percent steps on each day (Myers and Carey, 1961). By this method, psychophysical relationships can be derived and a complete spectrum of alcohol intake ascertained. Other multiple solution procedures involve the presentation of more than one concentration of alcohol at one time (Fuller, 1964; Myers, 1966).

The principal disadvantage of the multiple solution methods is encountered in experiments in which a short-term exposure to alcohol is given in a behavioral task. Although in this case a single concentration is more expedient, an animal's preference threshold should be determined and a test solution offered which is based on its own self-selection curve (Cicero and Myers, 1968). This is accomplished by offering water and a slightly higher concentration of alcohol on each day, which is increased in 1% steps from a low to a high concentration. The test concentration of alcohol is a solution which is 3% higher than the preference threshold. By offering a concentration only 3% above the threshold, the animal is deterred from spontaneous drinking of this slightly aversive solution; however, volitional selection of the nonpreferred solution may occur during certain experimental situations such as those of shock stress (Cicero *et al.*, 1968).

When examining the effects of a given variable on alcohol preference, usually the animal is maintained in isolation. In some experiments, several animals have been housed together in one cage, but this is done only if animals of the same strain are used (Rodgers and McClearn, 1962). The danger here is that one animal with an atypical preference for or aversion to alcohol could distort considerably the mean drinking pattern of the group.

Position Habit

For years, it has been recognized that an animal often adopts a certain place or position in its cage where it always eats or drinks. There is no satisfactory explanation of this well-known phenomenon; some animals may drink from one tube until the test solution is raised to a concentration that is so noxious that the animal is forced to switch to another spout in order to survive (Myers and Holman, 1966). Even though the location of each bottle is switched every day, the set position habit is not eliminated.

In addition to a position habit, many animals prefer to drink from one bottle rather than from another. Korn (1960) reported that in a group of 30 rats, over half developed either a position habit or a bottle preference. Other investigators have found that a so-called alcohol "craving" in rats was eliminated simply by altering the position of the drinking tubes on the side of the cage (Gillespie and Lucas, 1958). In view of these findings, it is easy to understand why some investigators often find such great fluctuations in an individual animal's intake;

a 50–50 split between water and alcohol consumed is not uncommon because of
the problems of position or bottle preference.

A method has recently been developed which overcomes the position habit
yet retains the advantages of a two-choice procedure (Myers and Holman, 1966).
Three bottles are fastened on the cage and their positions varied according to a
predetermined random sequence. Only two are used for the test fluids; the
third is empty and serves as a "dummy." The bottles are removed daily from
each cage for refilling and are placed on a different cage. The use of a "dummy"
bottle apparently forces the animal to move about and explore the contents of
the other drinking tubes. With this method, reliable and stable preference-
aversion functions for different concentrations of alcohol have been obtained
with rats (Myers and Holman, 1966), mice (Lester, 1968), and monkeys (Myers
and Holman, 1966; Myers, Veale and Yaksh, unpublished observations).

Interpreting Self-Selection Data

A common way of analyzing data collected on fluid intakes is to present it
in the form of a ratio or proportion of alcohol to water consumed. Since an
adipsic animal could drink only a small amount of fluid, which would exaggerate
the ratio measure, the information on proportional intakes must be supplemented
by a comparison of the volumes ingested. In addition, the actual amount (in
grams or grams per kilogram body weight) of alcohol ingested should likewise
be given, particularly if different concentrations are offered (Veale and Myers,
1968). To illustrate the need for this, when an animal consumes a given volume
of 5% alcohol and only a fourth of that amount of a 20% solution, the amount of
absolute alcohol ingested is identical, and the pharmacological effects would be
similar in terms of the dose.

Another important consideration is the meaning of a shift in the pattern
of alcohol intake. The preference threshold, as described earlier, is a very
useful measure for examining the effects of an experimental treatment; however,
alcohol intakes over the entire range of solutions must be taken into account.
Although alcohol intake in comparison to water intake may drop below the
50–50 level, consumption of a small volume of a high concentration may reflect
the ingestion of a significant amount (grams) of ethyl alcohol. To prevent dehydration, the animal could select water as a diluent of the alcohol solution.

In conclusion, it is essential that the alcohol and water intakes are calculated
and plotted on a day-to-day basis. Measurements based on combined days of
water and alcohol intakes may be entirely invalid because of a number of factors,
including a position habit, a bottle preference rather than a fluid preference,
diurnal variations, and estrus cycles if female animals are used. By summing
up all of the intake data, the actual drinking patterns are entirely obliterated and
conclusions about the results are difficult to draw.

BIOLOGICAL MECHANISMS IN ALCOHOL SELECTION

Innate Factors

A "genetotrophic" theory of alcoholism based on animal research and clinical findings was formulated originally by Williams and his co-workers about 20 years ago (Williams et al., 1950; Williams, 1952). The theory was proposed that there is an inherited tendency that varies from individual to individual toward an abnormal imbibition of alcohol, which is caused mainly by deficiencies in nutritional factors. Williams' position and some of the interpretations of his experimental findings have been the subject of strong criticisms (Popham, 1953); nevertheless, it seems quite certain that a genetically linked preference for alcohol exists at least in mice and rats (Rodgers, 1967; Eriksson, 1968).

Mardones and his group were the first to show that in successive generations of rats, the traits for preference or rejection of 10% alcohol can be selectively bred "in" or bred "out" (Mardones et al., 1953; Mardones, 1960; Segovia-Riquelme et al., 1969). These findings have generally been confirmed (Eriksson, 1968), but the use of a single concentration of alcohol in genetic studies with rats has been criticized (Myers, 1968). McClearn, Rodgers, and their colleagues have carried out extensive research in which different strains of mice have been tested for their alcohol preference under a wide variety of experimental conditions (McClearn and Rodgers, 1959; Rodgers and McClearn, 1962; Thiessen et al., 1967). Although the commonly used methods of employing a single test concentration of alcohol and examining crosses between two strains of mice has been questioned (Fuller, 1964), various strains of animals differ widely in their selection of alcohol in relation to: (a) environmental temperature (Myers, 1962); (b) the concentration of alcohol used as the test solution (Rodgers and McClearn, 1962); (c) metabolic differences (Williams et al., 1950) particularly in ADH activity (Rodgers et al., 1963) and in the capacity to metabolize alcohol (Thiessen et al., 1965); (d) accumulation of blood acetaldehyde (Schlesinger, 1966); and (e) the conditions of pregnancy and lactation (Thiessen et al., 1967). The subject matter dealing with the genetic factors related to alcohol preference has been covered by Rodgers in another chapter.

The importance of the complex polygenetic variables in the selection of alcohol cannot be overemphasized, because the factors which regulate an animal's intake of alcohol as an organism develops may undoubtedly be modified, or in some instances, wholly determined by unique genetic factors. One of the most important findings bearing on this point was reported by Nichols and Hsiao (1967) who showed that by the process of selective breeding, two strains of rats were evolved which differed in their susceptibility to morphine addiction. When 10% alcohol and water were offered to these rats on successive presentations, a relapse to alcohol drinking occurred only in the morphine-susceptible rats. Thus, one common genetic element was passed on from generation to generation, and this could be a universal or general "addiction factor."

Endocrine Systems and Internal Factors

From our knowledge that an alcoholic often possesses endocrine imbalances (Tintera and Lovell, 1949), it would not be surprising if one or more of the hormonal systems were involved in the volitional selection of alcohol. An imbalance in steroid synthesis, release, and subsequent circulation could evoke an increase or decrease in the intake of alcohol. The experiments done with animals have been complicated by methodological problems such as the use of a single concentration and the fact that a slight preference for alcohol, which may have occurred as the result of experimental interference with a hormonal system, is abolished by offering a sweetened fluid as an alternative choice (Zarrow et al., 1960). Of the endocrine systems examined thus far, it would appear that sex steroids could contribute to the mechanims of alcohol selection, whereas other glandular systems apparently do not exert a direct influence.

The thyroid gland was perhaps the first to be implicated in alcohol self-selection, when it was found that drugs such as propyl thiouracil, which suppress thyroid function of rats, elevate alcohol intake (Rosenberg and Zarrow, 1952) just as does a deficiency in iodine (Mäenpää and Forsander, 1966); conversely, feeding of thyroxine lowers alcohol preference (Richter, 1956). A human alcoholic may often display myxedemic symptoms, but thyroidectomy does not seem to influence the intake of alcohol in rats (Rosenberg and Zarrow, 1952; Richter, 1957). In one report by Aschkenasy-Lelu (1962), it was found that thyroidectomy caused a slight decrease in alcohol intake. It must be recognized, however, that all of these studies are confounded by the uncontrolled variable of caloric utilization and recovery of normal food consumption postoperatively. The results of studies in which the adrenocortical function has been altered are somewhat perplexing, since one would expect a positive relationship between stress, adrenal activity, and alcohol consumption. This may not be the case, as Rodgers (1967) reports that an increase in the adrenal response of mice correlates negatively with an elevation in alcohol preference in this species. The implications of this are discussed more fully in the section on stress.

Following the report of Mirone (1959) that no sex differences exist in terms of the amount of 10% alcohol preferred by Swiss mice, Zarrow et al. (1960) showed in rats that gonadectomy also had no effect on the selection of an alcohol solution of the same concentration. Wallgren (1959), however, found that fasted female rats had a higher tolerance to alcohol than fasted males, and this result corresponds to the finding that the feeding of estrogen reduced the alcohol intake of rats (Aschkenasy-Lelu, 1958). Since then, Clay (1964) reported that male rats of unspecified strains drink more alcohol than females, although in that study, volumes ingested or gram intakes were not presented. In other water-alcohol choice studies, it was reported that male Wistar rats drink more of a 10% concentration of alcohol than females (Powell *et al.*, 1966); similar results were obtained with hamsters offered 10, 25, 30, or 40% alcohol (Arvola and Forsander, 1963). With respect to strain differences, BALB/c mice show no sex differences in a water versus 10% alcohol choice (Kakihana and McClearn, 1963), but C57BL female mice drank significantly more alcohol of the same concentration than male mice of the same strain (Eriksson and Pikkarainen, 1968).

The discrepancy in the results of these few scientific investigations cannot be explained as yet. At present, it is difficult to speculate about the possible sex differences in physiological systems such as liver ADH activity (Eriksson and Pikkarainen, 1968) until well-controlled studies are carried out in which preference thresholds are obtained, taste is considered, and other variables are isolated. It may then be possible to clarify the issue of the role of reproductive and other hormones in the volitional selection of alcohol.

Aging

The voluntary consumption of alcohol seems to vary with the age of the animal (Kakihana and McClearn, 1963). In a study in which different concentrations of alcohol as well as a third choice of 5% nuorooo oolutions were offered, alcohol preference was greater in young postpubertal rats of 2–3 months of age than in animals up to 2 years of age (Parisella and Pritham, 1964). These results would lead one to reject a hypothesis that early exposure to alcohol results in a greater degree of preference for alcohol. In a similar study in which concentrations of alcohol from 2 to 8% were offered together with water, Goodrick (1967) found that alcohol ingestion increased in the age range of 1 to 5 months; however, so-called senescent, 24-month-old rats drank more alcohol than 15-month-old rats at every concentration offered. It is possible, therefore, that in the older animals, taste discrimination begins to decline, although these concentrations are certainly within the range of normal preference (Myers and Carey, 1961). Also, a slight increase in alcohol intake over time can always be due to the gradual acclimation to alcohol (Veale and Myers, 1969).

ENVIRONMENTAL CHANGES AND ALCOHOL PREFERENCE

To derive a convincing animal model of the human alcoholic, one must first demonstrate clearly than an animal will drink alcohol volitionally in an amount which has a pharmacological effect. Second, symptoms of dependence such as the withdrawal syndrome should characterize the later stages of prolonged alcohol consumption. To date, there is little evidence that either condition arises in rats or other species, at least based on the results of the self-selection of alcohol following continued exposure (Mello and Mendelson, 1965; Myers, 1966).

Habituation, Acclimation, and Tolerance to Alcohol

Richter was responsible for the initial forecast of the difficulty to be encountered with animals in eliciting alcohol intake in sufficient quantities that a condition of "addiction" could be demonstrated with this drug. Except for three wild Norway rats which drank progressively more 10% alcohol, then exhibited withdrawal symptoms and died (Richter, 1957), virtually no evidence exists for the "addiction" of animals to alcohol. The validity of these data are even questionable now, since in a much larger study involving wild Arizona pack rats, Richter's results were not confirmed (Eimer and Senter, 1968).

In the 1920's, Richter (1926) reported that habituation to alcohol did not occur in laboratory rats; later, different investigators showed that forced ingestion of alcohol solutions in concentrations ranging from 8 to 24% also did not evoke a later preference (Richter, 1953; Williams et al., 1959; Mardones, 1960). In rats which would not press a lever to obtain a solution of alcohol at a concentration as low as 5%, responding for this solution was induced if the animal was restricted to that solution for 10 days (Myers, 1961a); but forced consumption of 5 or 20% alcohol for as long as 4 months caused a minimal shift in preference, since lever responses were emitted for solutions of alcohol only up to the 9% concentration (Myers and Carey, 1961). In an extension of the latter study, Rick and Wilson (1966) found that rats restricted to 2 to 16% alcohol for 6 months increased their preference for 2 to 8% alcohol only slightly in an alcohol-water choice situation, but the 16% solution was rejected consistently. One reason why forced consumption of alcohol does not lead to an increased selection in a choice situation is the dehydrating effect of alcohol and the subsequent water-electrolyte imbalance. Prieto et al. (1958) found that water intake was greater in rats immediately after forced consumption of a 10% alcohol solution, and Rick and Wilson (1966) reported that a fluid deficit apparently occurs in rats after forced drinking of 8 and 16% alcohol solutions. These general findings have been confirmed by Essig (1968).

Usually, alcoholic beverages are not used in choice experiments with animals, because the beverage may be preferred because of its taste, nutritional value, or the caloric content of an additive, rather than because of the properties of the alcohol moiety itself (Myers, 1966). The importance of the flavor of the choice fluid was demonstrated by Mendelson and Mello (1964) who offered rats diluted bourbon whiskey and an alcohol solution equal in concentration. In concentrations ranging from 5 to 25%, the whiskey solution was not preferred over water, even if the content of the congeners of the bourbon solution was reduced by one-fourth. It is interesting that whiskey and alcohol solutions were not totally rejected at any concentration, but for some inexplicable reason, a 20% alcohol solution was preferred, whereas the 15 and 25% concentrations were not.

In a study with 12 monkeys, forced consumption of bourbon, the only fluid available, in dose levels of 4 to 12 g/day for 70 days did not result in a preference for bourbon over water in a choice situation (Mello and Mendelson, 1971). Although 30–100 ml of bourbon was consumed daily during the forced-choice period, the bourbon intake dropped to the baseline level of 20 ml per day once water was again made available.

Flavoring of the alcoholic beverage also influences the intake of infrahuman primates. Chimpanzees and orangutans preferred a solution of vodka to alcohol of the same concentration, and in both species, orange, grape, or grapefruit juices were selected rather than alcohol solutions (Fitz-Gerald et al., 1968). Some chimpanzees drank a sufficient volume of alcohol so that symptoms of intoxication were displayed; the excessive intake could have been related to the amount of prior exposure of the primates to alcohol. Rhesus monkeys show a preference for a 5% solution of alcohol over a 10 or 20% solution, and this is dependent upon the number of hours of fluid deprivation to which these primates were subjected (Anderson and Smith, 1963). That the aversive properties of alcohol account for the rejection of alcohol solution in monkeys just as in rodents, has been confirmed recently (Myers, Veale and Yaksh, unpublished observations), since concentrations of alcohol only in the range of 3–6% were selected over water in a free-choice situation even after prolonged acclimation to a wide range of concentrations.

Rhesus monkeys were maintained in individual cages and had free access to three drinking spouts, one of which dispensed grape or orange-flavored alcohol, another water, and the third served as a "dummy" and was used in the rotation to eliminate the position habit. The monkeys were offered the choice between a water and a grape-alcohol solution which was increased from 3 to 30% during an 11-day sequence. Figure 2 shows the mean alcohol intakes for 13 such sequences carried out over 155 days. The alcohol intake increased to about 5 g/kg by the seventh sequence, which parallels the temporal characteristics of the acclimation effect observed in the rat (Veale and Myers, 1969). However, during the following six preference sequences, the monkey's alcohol intake declined to a point even below the initial sequence. After the thirteenth choice sequence, the monkeys were then forced to drink a 6, 8, or 12% solution of grape-flavored alcohol for periods ranging from 4 to 11 days. This period was then followed by an abstinence period of 120 days on ad lib water (Fig. 2). Then, monkeys were forced to drink an 8% solution of alcohol mixed in orange juice rather than in grape flavoring for 42 days.

During the period of forced orange-alcohol consumption, the intake of ethanol reached an all-time high. Nevertheless, when the monkeys were given a

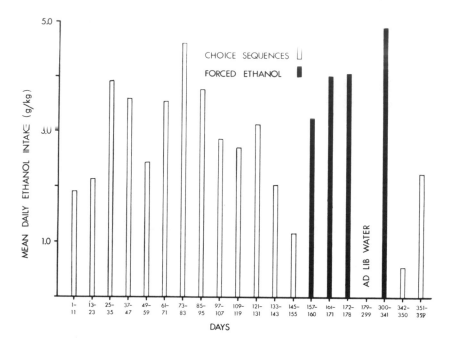

FIGURE 2. Average daily alcohol intake in grams per kilogram for five monkeys living in primate cages. Water and a grape-flavored alcohol solution, which was increased from 3 to 30% over an 11-day sequence, were available between days 1–155. Between days 157 and 178, only a grape-flavored alcohol solution was offered in concentrations of 12% (days 157–160), 6% (days 161–171) and 8% (days 172–178). Orange juice was substituted for the grape flavoring during the final three test sessions (days 300–359).

choice between water and an unflavored alcohol solution on days 342 through 350, their intake of alcohol dropped to an all-time low (Fig. 2). Moreover, when the monkeys were given a choice between water and orange-flavored alcohol during the final sequence from days 351 to 359, the alcohol solutions were not preferred even after this long period of forced and free-choice alcohol conditions.

In order to illustrate the typical patterns of alcohol intake of the monkeys, the mean ratio of alcohol to total fluid intake per day is presented in Fig. 3 for the sequence preceding the forced alcohol drinking (days 145 to 155) and the two sequences immediately following the forced alcohol period (days 342 to 350 and days 351 to 359). The persistent aversion to this fluid is remarkably well documented after 300 days of exposure to alcohol.

There appears now to be a possibility that restricting animals to non-preferred concentrations of alcohol may cause an even greater rejection of alcohol. Figure 4 shows that rats forced to drink a 15% solution, and unable therefore to obtain any water, reduce their consumption of alcohol in later

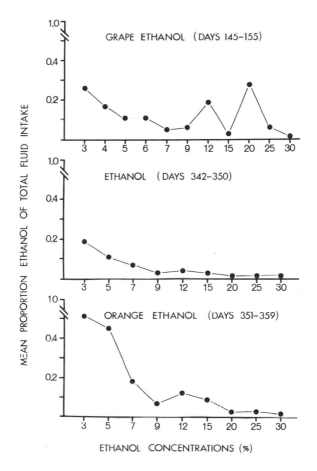

FIGURE 3. Average ratios of water intake for those monkeys offered a choice between these fluids during three sequences shown in Fig. 2: (1) days 145 155; (2) days 342–350; and (3) days 351–359. The alcohol was grape flavored during the first sequence, in an orange juice solution during the third, and not flavored during the second sequence.

preference tests (Veale and Myers, 1969). In the presence of water, however, repeated exposures over 11 days to solutions of alcohol in the 3 to 30% range will cause a two-to-three-fold increase in alcohol intake after several such exposures (Fig. 5). Mice of certain strains such as the C3H/2, show a similar week-by-week increase in preference for some alcohol solutions when a multiple concentration method is used (Rodgers and McClearn, 1962). Similarly, when rats are presented with a 6 or 7% alcohol solution in the presence of water, for a period of time ranging from several weeks to 6 months, and then deprived of the alcohol solution for 6 days, the animals will increase their intake of alcohol in concentrations even

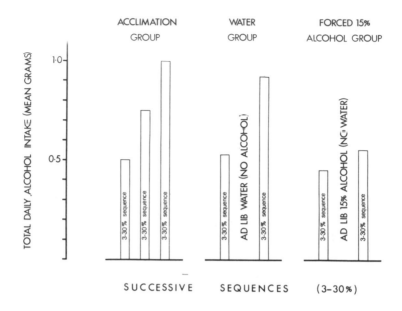

FIGURE 4. Mean daily alcohol intake expressed in grams for successive test sequences in which water and a solution of alcohol were offered. The concentration of the alcohol solution was increased systematically during the 9-day period from 3 to 30%. The acclimation group (left) was tested for three consecutive preference sequences; the water group (middle) received only water rather than the alcohol-water choice during the second sequence; and the forced-alcohol group (right) received a nonpreferred 15% solution of alcohol during the second test period. [From Veale and Myers (1969).]

as high as 20% (Sinclair and Senter, 1968; Senter and Richman, 1969). This "alcohol-deprivation effect," which seems to be a temporary phenomenon, is not related to a novel characteristic of the fluid alternative to water, since withholding a saccharin solution after it was consumed for a similar interval did not evoke a sudden preference for saccharin (Sinclair and Senter, 1968).

If rats lick one drinking tube containing 10% alcohol solution in order to obtain a milk reward in a second tube and then are given the alcohol solution instead of milk in the second tube, their selection of alcohol not only declines sharply but no evidence of addiction arises (Mello and Mendelson, 1965). A result opposite to this has been reported in a situation in which reinforcement with food pellets, contingent upon drinking a 7% alcohol solution, did evoke a subsequent increase in the preference for this concentration following the conditioning period (Senter et al., 1967); in this experiment there was no control for acclimation which could result in an increase in alcohol selection. In both studies, only one concentration was used and it is difficult, therefore, to resolve the differences in results other than on the basis of unequal taste thresholds.

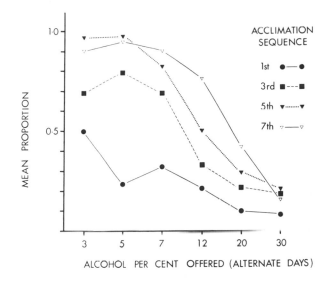

FIGURE 5. Increased intake of alcohol, expressed as the mean proportion of alcohol to total fluid intake (water plus alcohol) for the first, third, fifth, and seventh preference sequences. The solutions offered during each sequence were increased on alternate days according to the percent concentrations indicated on the abscissa. [From Veale and Myers (1969).]

The positive, rewarding value of alcohol under conditions of deprivation can be learned. Rats will "work" by depressing an operant lever to obtain an alcohol solution in a multichoice situation (Myers, 1961a; 1961b), and will respond for concentrations as high as 15% without the use of an aversive stimulus such as electric shock (Mello and Mendelson, 1964). In these experimental situations, tolerance or physical dependence have not been demonstrated. If alcohol is administered intragastrically by a stomach tube rather than by forced ingestion, then tolerance to the pharmacological actions of alcohol may be observed. Moskowitz and Wapner (1964) showed that little decrement in escaping foot shock was observed in rats which received alcohol intragastrically three times a week for 30 weeks. A similar finding with fewer alcohol stomach loads has also been reported (Chen, 1968). When alcohol in doses causing "intoxication" is given repeatedly on alternate days, tolerance to alcohol develops as measured behaviorally by the performance on a tilted platform; an equated amount of alcohol given in the drinking water to a matched group of rats, but spread out over 2 days, does not produce this tolerance effect (Wallgren *et al.*, 1967). The time course of alcohol tolerance as measured by performance on a behavioral task is most interesting, since it develops maximally within 3 weeks following daily "intoxicating" treatments with alcohol, but is significantly reduced after 1 week during which no alcohol is administered (LeBlanc *et al.*, 1969).

Severe physical dependence on alcohol occurs in dogs and mice if the alcohol is given by the oral route. Essig and Lam (1968) report that beagles given repeated intragastric loads of 40% alcohol exhibited hallucinatory behavior and convulsions when alcohol was withheld. In this study one-third of the animals died as the result of the withdrawal of alcohol, but in another experiment the more severe features of the withdrawal syndrome were ameliorated when a barbiturate was given in a nonanesthetic dose (Essig *et al.*, 1969). Force-feeding of a liquid diet containing one-third of the calories in the form of alcohol also causes similar withdrawal responses in mice, including convulsions and death (Freund, 1969).

Nutrition, Taste, Smell, and Alcohol Preference

In addition to its well-known pharmacological properties, alcohol can serve as a nutritional substitute or supplement; also, it may under certain conditions be selected or refused by an animal because of its gustatory properties. In early investigations, it was found that a deficiency in vitamin B complex causes a marked increase in alcohol consumption (Mardones and Onfray, 1942; Brady and Westerfield, 1947; Williams *et al.*, 1949). This led to the notion held for many years that the disease of alcoholism was related to some sort of nutritional deficiency. Williams (1959) describes in fact the "cures" of many alcoholics and presents personal testimonials of those who were fed "Tycopan" or "Nutricol" (vitamin and food supplements); similarly it was reported that rats reduced their alcohol consumption when given vitamin complexes and glutamine. What is the evidence for these remarkable claims?

In acute thiamine deficiency, a decline of food intake occurs as a result of the deficit, and the pronounced need for calories can evoke the abnormal intake of alcohol. Richter (1953) showed that rats reduced their food intake in proportion to the solution of ethyl alcohol consumed in the form of 8, 16, or 24% solutions or as 12% table wine or 4.4% beer. In a most convincing experiment, Westerfeld and Lawrow (1953) showed that a "pure" thiamine deficiency will not evoke a significant increase in the selection of 10% alcohol, but rather causes a profound drop in food intake. Since alcohol possesses a thiamine-sparing action, it would seem that consumption of the fluid is caused by the caloric requirement alone. If a solution of thiamine in 7% alcohol is offered to a thiamine-deficient rat, this fluid is consumed rapidly; however, after thiamine deficiency, rats prefer less alcohol than controls following the period of deficiency (Senter and Sinclair, 1968). In 1960, Mardones reviewed the experiments related to the so-called "factor N" and its effect on consumption of 10% alcohol. As reported, this nutritional factor is a mixture of thermolabile thiamine and an unknown substance found in purified yeast. Because of a number of complicated methodological problems, including the use of one concentration and "intraindividual variations" due perhaps to the lack of control of the position habit, the role of "factor N" in alcohol preference is not clear.

Whether or not dietary changes in and of themselves do alter the choice of an alcohol solution is not yet known, because rats or mice discontinue their drinking of alcohol in a water vs. 10% alcohol choice situation as soon as a third choice of sucrose, lipid, or saccharin solution is presented (Lester and Greenberg, 1952; Mardones et al., 1955; Rodgers and McClearn, 1964). Since nonnutritive saccharin has the same effect in reducing alcohol intake as a substance which is nutritionally usable in the body, it would seem that the taste of the alcohol solution is a much more important factor in self-selection experiments than its nutritional value or caloric utility. When taste sensibility is diminished by methylpentynol, rats will drink 20% alcohol (Dicker, 1958). Further, even when alcohol consumption serves as the response required for delivery of food pellets, and blood alcohol levels reach 0.2%, a nonnutritive solution sweetened by saccharin is preferred by rats (Keehn, 1969). The aversive taste of concentrations greater than 7 or 8% is enough to offset the caloric value of alcohol even during conditions of severe food deprivation (Myers and Carey, 1961). In view of this, Rodgers and McClearn (1964) have suggested that the volume of fluid taken may be the mechanism which limits the consumption of an alcoholic solution when offered simultaneously with a sucrose solution. Moreover, there may well be a metabolic limiting factor which mediates the rejection of the fluid (Forsander, 1962) and this factor could be the enzymatic activity of ADH in the liver, since a near perfect relationship exists between liver ADH activity and alcohol preference (Rodgers et al., 1963). However, this notion is complicated and possibly invalidated by the finding that rats forced to drink a mixture of 32% alcohol and 5% sucrose solution, in association with a low fat and protein diet, developed marked hepatic lesions (Porta and Gomez-Dumm, 1968). Similar structural damage occurred if the diet was similar except that the alcohol was omitted. More research is certainly required on the relationship between ADH activity and self-selection of alcohol.

In terms of an animal model for alcoholism, few, if any, human alcoholics become alcohol-dependent because the beverage tastes or smells so delectably or becomes more appealing than other foods. An overall analysis of the question of the nutritional basis of experimentally induced alcohol selection is confounded by three interacting variables: (1) the gustatory factor in which rejection or selection of alcohol occurs because its taste is either noxious or palatable to the animal; (2) olfactory factors, since rats made anosmic by extirpation of the olfactory bulbs select somewhat higher concentrations of alcohol (Kahn and Stellar, 1960); and (3) the caloric requirement which is manifested in food deprived rats by their drinking for calories rather than for the pharmacological properties of alcohol.

Stress-Induced Drinking

There have been several attempts to simulate in an animal the same sort of stress to which a person might be exposed in order that an analogy with the human alcoholic might be drawn. Experiments of this kind are based on the notion that an animal may be susceptible to the effects of alcohol in the same way as a human who drinks as the result of psychological or social pressures (Kalant, 1962). For the animal, alcohol may provide relief from a stressor and possess physiological consequences which are rewarding (Myers, 1969). Early evidence for this was provided by an experiment in which cats ultimately preferred a solution of milk and alcohol after they had been submitted to the "conflict" consisting of a blast of air presented as the cat approached its food (Masserman and Yum, 1946). Emotionality, as reflected by the proneness of a rat to audiogenic seizures, seems to be directly related to the ingestion of a 5% alcohol solution (Dember and Kristofferson, 1955); also, preference for a 3.4% alcohol solution has been ascribed to the "timidity" of the rat (Tobach, 1957).

Whether or not animals will consume an alcohol solution which from a sensory standpoint is itself equally as noxious in terms of taste as shock itself, is certainly debatable. Adamson and Black (1959) reported that a curvilinear relationship exists between the alcohol intake of rats and "tension" as measured by the acquisition of an avoidance response, but in this study the volume or grams of alcohol consumed were not presented. In a study which had no control group, Casey (1960) found that randomly delivered electric shock did not produce an increase in the intake of 16% alcohol in rats; after shock was terminated, there was a slight elevation in the selection of this concentration, but this could have been due to the acclimation to alcohol (Veale and Myers, 1969). In a more straightforward experiment, it was shown that rats stressed by intense shock given randomly around the clock for 14 days did not increase their intake of alcohol offered in concentrations varying from 3 to 20% (Myers and Holman, 1967). This lack of preference prevailed whether the rats were naive or acclimated to alcohol.

From these results, it would seem that the delivery of unavoidable electric shock to the footpads of an animal does not necessarily constitute the kind of stressor that is useful for examining the etiology of alcohol consumption. This is borne out by an experiment of Korman and Stephens (1960) who found that the intake of 10% alcohol may increase slightly when an animal is shocked, but the alcohol solution was never preferred over water and had no pharmacological effect in the amount consumed. When rats are exposed to brief periods of electric shock, the preference for 10% alcohol is not altered in male rats (Powell *et al.*, 1966). A presumed environmental stressor such as high density grouping in a single cage also does not evoke alcohol preference; when as many as 10 mice were housed together, alcohol intake remained unchanged although individual adrenal weights increased (Rodgers and Thiessen, 1964). Surprisingly, Thiessen and Rodgers (1965) have proposed that adrenal activation caused either by high density housing or intraperitoneal injections of saline is the peripheral mechanism whereby alcohol preference is reduced. In this connection, Zarrow and his co-workers (1960) concluded that adrenal stressors such as cold, injections of formaldehyde, or adrenalectomy itself are not related to the preferential consumption of alcohol.

It now appears that physical stress alone will not elicit alcohol consumption in amounts sufficient to produce pharmacological effects. There is some evidence to suggest that psychological or behavioral stressors may bring about an increase in an animal's selection of alcohol. For instance, two monkeys drank a normally nonpreferred alcohol solution (20%) for several weeks during which a lever had to be pressed continuously so that shock was avoided during a daily 10-hr period (Clark and Polish, 1960). One of the monkeys continued to drink after the shock avoidance sessions were discontinued. These results were later confirmed by Mello and Mendelson (1966), and in addition, they found that the increase in a monkey's alcohol intake may persist for as long as 75 days after avoidance conditioning was terminated.

In an extensive study carried out by Mello and Mendelson (1971), monkeys were trained to lick for a fluid in order to avoid being shocked. After the avoidance behavior was established with water, 5, 15, or 25% alcohol or bourbon solutions were substituted. As the concentrations of the fluids were increased, the lick duration became shorter and the volume of alcohol consumed declined significantly. In the monkeys exposed to alcohol for over $2\frac{1}{2}$ years, the licking behavior, which did not disperse any fluid, persisted. Thus, the monkeys had learned a dual type of avoidance response by the way in which they licked the drinking spout: one which postponed the delivery of aversive shock at the time, and the other which enabled them to avoid drinking a noxious alcohol solution (Mello and Mendelson, 1971). From these results, Mello and Mendelson have concluded that a behavioral technique to produce addictive-type drinking in the infrahuman primate has not as yet been devised.

Rats also may be induced to drink alcohol when punishment is given randomly during a shock avoidance task (Cicero *et al.*, 1968). After being trained to avoid shock in response to a warning light, rats were shocked on a random basis, and as a result their intake of alcohol rose significantly. Random shock not cued by the warning light, and hence equivalent to unavoidable shock, failed to produce a rise in alcohol consumption; this further substantiates the fact that the stress of electric shock does not elicit alcohol preference (Korman and

Stephens, 1960; Myers and Holman, 1967). In an extension of the random-punishment study, p-chlorophenylalanine (pCPA), a drug which lowers alcohol preference (Myers and Veale, 1968), reduced the alcohol intake of rats, particularly after they had consumed large amounts during the period of random unavoidable shock (Myers and Cicero, 1969). The importance of an environmental stimulus associated with alcohol, such as a warning light, has also been demonstrated by Senter and Persensky (1968) who found that alcohol preference was greater in rats which remained in a test apparatus where alcohol had to be consumed to avoid electric shock, than in animals which had been returned to their home cages. It should be mentioned that in these stress studies, a palatable, sweetened fluid was not offered as a third choice nor were blood alcohol levels determined (Lester, 1966).

There are a number of studies not reviewed in this chapter in which alcohol is given parenterally and is used in much the same way as any central depressant drug. Many interesting results have been found, particularly in those studies dealing with the action of alcohol in relieving the so-called stress of approach-avoidance conflict and also in relation to certain physiological processes (Dember et al., 1953; Conger, 1956; Weiss, 1958; Reynolds and van Sommers, 1960; Hogans et al., 1961; Zarrow et al., 1962; Wallgren and Savolainen, 1962; Leikola, 1962; Broadhurst and Wallgren, 1964; Smart, 1965; Freed, 1967; and Barry, 1968). Unfortunately, the relevance of these studies to chronic alcoholism is remote, because barbiturates, narcotic analgesics, major and minor tranquilizers, anesthetics and other compounds may exert the same effect as alcohol on a behavioral task. Even though one might be able to show that alcohol possesses some unique property as a drug, it would still be impossible to generalize from these findings to the self-selection of alcohol.

Psychogenic Polydipsia and Alcohol

One very promising hope for circumventing the noxious gustatory qualities of alcohol and inducing ingestion of large amounts of this fluid was provided by the observation of Falk (1961). A rat that is pressing a lever for food pellets on an intermittent 90-sec schedule of reward will, for some unknown reason, drink three to four times its normal daily intake of water within a 3-hr test period. This so-called "schedule-induced polydipsia" has been employed to produce excessive intakes of a 5.6% alcohol solution (Lester, 1961), so that blood levels increase significantly to a point whereby an "intoxicated" condition is maintained for over 2 days. This experiment has been repeated, but its utility questioned since alcohol preference following the polydipsia regimen does not increase above the pretraining level (Senter and Sinclair, 1967). An even more important finding which seems to limit the applicability of this method is the fact that the intake of alcohol under the condition of "schedule-induced polydipsia" is concentration dependent. As shown in Fig. 6, an increase in alcohol intake occurs only when the concentrations of alcohol are within the normal preference range of an individual rat (Holman, 1967). Furthermore, it was found that the amount of alcohol consumed during a 3-hr test period averaged only 1.0 g or less as concentrations were increased over the range of normally preferred concentrations (Fig. 6). This amount is well below that which exerts a pharmacological action (Holman and Myers, 1968). Moreover, the lever-pressing rates as well as the number of pellets consumed per test session remained constant, which would indicate that the decline in alcohol intake was not due to a pharmacological action of the drug but most likely to the noxious taste of the higher concentrations. Using two rats, Meisch and Pickens (1968) also confirmed the fact that only low concentrations of alcohol are selected under the psychogenic polydipsia paradigm.

Once again, we are faced with the issue of the drive state and the subsequent motivation of the animal to drink alcohol. Since a rat is deprived of food in order

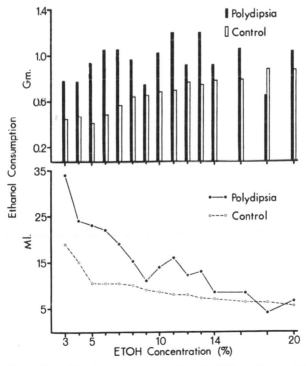

FIGURE 6.   Mean alcohol intakes in grams (top) and milliliters (bottom) for six rats at each of the concentrations given on the abscissa. The rats were tested under control conditions and in the polydipsia paradigm in which food pellets were delivered intermittently on a 90-sec interval of reinforcement during each 3–5-hr test session. [From Holman and Myers (1968).]

to evoke lever responses for pellets, and because alcohol is a particularly good source of calories, one cannot specify the reasons for the ingestion of relatively high volumes of alcohol, even at low concentrations.

BIOCHEMICAL FACTORS IN SELF-SELECTION OF ALCOHOL

Many factors which contribute to the excessive intake of alcohol appear to be biochemical in nature and may involve the central nervous system, liver, or other organs. A metabolic mechanism may even serve to sustain drinking in the absence of any grave psychiatric problem, and if the mechanism is irreversible, an individual may become incapable of ingesting small amounts of alcohol without lapsing into uncontrolled, self-regenerative drinking.

Action of Alcohol on the Brain and Other Systems

Prolonged consumption of alcohol will produce major functional or structural changes in an animal's liver (Lieber, 1967; Koch et al., 1968), pancreas (Sardesai and Orten, 1968), hypothalamus (Crossland and Ratcliffe, 1968), but not perhaps in the cerebral cortex (Mendelson and Mello, 1964). Only in two studies in which alcohol was consumed by rats for protracted periods has a deficit in learning been reported (Myers, 1961a; Denenberg et al., 1961). Further, the stress-relieving qualities of alcohol which are ostensibly recognized by an animal usually require time to be learned (Myers, 1961b). Although the liver is responsible for the degradation of circulating alcohol (Westerfeld and Schulman, 1959; von Wartburg and Papenberg, 1966), the brain does contain an alcohol dehydrogenase system and is therefore capable of metabolizing limited amounts of alcohol (Raskin and Sokoloff, 1968).

Several years ago, evidence was presented to indicate that the brain is the target organ which mediates the abnormal selection of alcohol rather than the liver, endocrine glands, or other organs (Myers, 1963). Experiments were carried out in which alcohol was infused chronically (i.e., every 15 min for 24 hr a day) into the cerebral ventricles of unrestrained rats which had never been exposed to alcohol before. The preference for alcohol in concentrations ranging from 3 to 40% increased significantly in direct proportion to the intraventricular dose of alcohol. Several animals which received up to 1000 microinfusions of alcohol drank 30% alcohol in preference to water. It was also shown that this unusual shift in preference occurred rapidly, within 12 to 24 hr, and was more pronounced in naive rats not previously exposed to a preference sequence (Myers, 1964). Lester (1966) has suggested that the hypertonicity of a solution could evoke an elevation in alcohol preference, but this possibility was ruled out in later studies (Myers and Veale, 1969). In the rat, as in other species, a single infusion lasting up to 30 min does not cause a change in preference (Myers, 1966; Koz and Mendelson, 1967). It would therefore appear that a constant elevation in the level of intracerebral alcohol, for a prolonged period of time, is the main causal factor in the development of the strong alcohol preference. Because ataxia or other signs of intoxication never appeared during the period of intraventricular infusion (Myers, 1964), alcohol probably acts directly on one or more of the structures which form the walls of the cerebral ventricles and comprise the so-called "drinking-emotional circuit" within the limbic system (Morgane, 1969).

Recently, we found that marked alcohol preference can be induced by intracerebral infusion of substances other than ethyl alcohol. In rats which ordinarily drank only low concentrations of alcohol, intraventricular infusions of $2\,\mu$l of 0.5% acetaldehyde, 0.5% paraldehyde or 0.2% methanol every 15 min for 14 days produced a significant increase in alcohol intake (Myers and Veale, 1969). The shift in preference occurred whether or not the animals were exposed to alcohol prior to the repeated infusions. Figure 7 illustrates the overall effects of

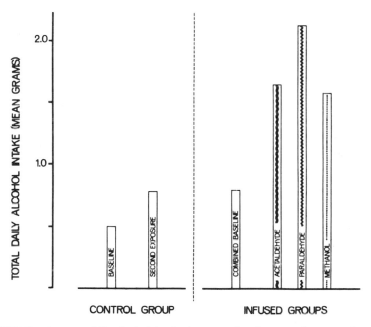

FIGURE 7.   Average daily alcohol intake in grams for the control group of rats (left), and for all rats implanted with intraventricular cannulae before infusion (combined baseline) and during infusion with acetaldehyde, paraldehyde, or methanol (right). Preference sequences lasted for 9 days during which water and a solution of alcohol were offered. The concentration of alcohol was increased on each day from 3 to 30%. [From Myers and Veale (1969).]

infusion of the three compounds on total daily intake. Generally, paraldehyde exerted the greatest effect on preference although other individual rats infused with the other compounds also exhibited a sharp rise in alcohol preference. Figure 8 illustrates the proportion of alcohol consumed by a rat infused with acetaldehyde in relation to total fluid ingested. The ratio did not shift below 0.5 until the 20% solution was offered, and at the 30% concentration, nearly one-third of the rat's fluid intake consisted of alcohol. Although the reasons for these results are unknown, it is possible that methanol and the aldehydes are mimicking the action of ethyl alcohol in eliciting a strong preference for alcohol when given by way of the intracerebral route. Also, acetaldehyde, which is a principal metabolic intermediary of alcohol, could possess a unique cellular action in mediating the selection of alcohol.

Because the rhesus monkey possesses a general aversion to alcohol, as does a normal rat, and because of its phylogenetic closeness to man, the effects of direct intracerebral infusion of alcohol, acetaldehyde, and paraldehyde have been

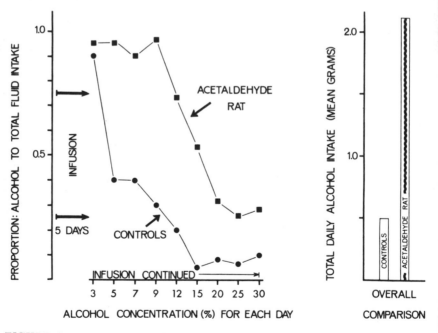

FIGURE 8. (Left): Alcohol preference of a representative rat implanted with an intraventricular cannula and infused subsequently with 2.0 μl of a 0.5% acetaldehyde solution every 15 min around the clock. The chronic infusion was begun 5 days prior to and continued throughout preference testing. The alcohol solution offered was increased in concentration on each of 9 days as shown on the abscissa. (Right): The overall daily alcohol intake in grams for the acetaldehyde infused rats in comparison with the mean intake of the infused control rats. [From Myers and Veale (1969).]

FIGURE 9. A representative monkey acclimated to a primate restraining chair and offered the choice between water and an alcohol solution increased from 3 to 30% over a 9- or 11-day sequence. Note the presence of a third "dummy" spout which prevents the development of a position habit. The polyethylene tube which connects the intraventricular cannulae to the chronic infusion pump is shown suspended above the monkey.

investigated. Infusion cannulae were permanently implanted in the skull so that their tips rested in the lateral or third cerebral ventricles of animals which had previously been acclimated to primate restraining chairs. Repeated infusions of a solution of an aldehyde or alcohol were then made every 15 min around the clock throughout the period of tests for alcohol preference. In this way, the brain levels of these substances could be chronically elevated. Figure 9 illustrates the procedure by which water or an alcohol solution can be selected in the three-tube, two-fluid choice situation as the ventricle of the monkey is infused with alcohol.

Figure 10 illustrates the alcohol intake in grams per kilogram for six representative monkeys and it is clear that the control animal presented here selected no more alcohol than unrestrained monkeys in a cage given free access to alcohol and water (see Fig. 3). However, the chronic infusion of 0.1% acetaldehyde or paraldehyde or 8% ethanol caused a substantial increase in the alcohol intake of certain monkeys, but not in others. It can be seen from Fig. 10 that infusion with 8% alcohol failed to alter the alcohol preference in one animal, but another

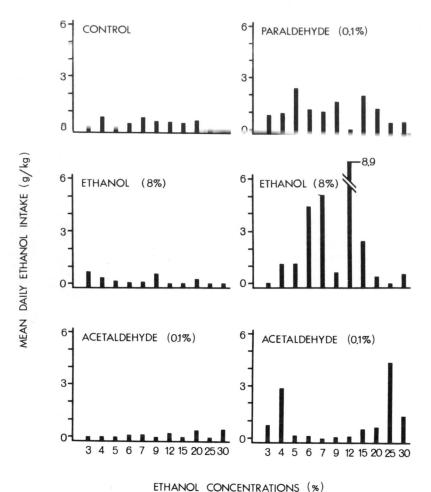

FIGURE 10. Average daily alcohol intake in grams per kilogram for six monkeys on each day of the preference sequence during which alcohol concentration was increased from 3 to 30% over an 11-day period. Solutions of paraldehyde, alcohol, or acetaldehyde were infused, in concentrations as indicated, into the central ventricles of the monkeys every 15 min around the clock for the 11 days.

monkey drank sufficient quantities at periods during the day to make him appear "intoxicated." A similar dichotomy in the preference pattern occurred for the two monkeys infused with acetaldehyde, whereas the monkey in which paraldehyde was infused intraventricularly drank to an intermediate degree.

It is difficult to explain the differences between the drinking patterns of these monkeys. The position of the cannula in the ventricle and hence the particular structures reached by each perfusate could be an important factor. In contrast to the finding of Koz and Mendelson (1967), it is apparent from these infusion experiments that the rhesus monkey can be induced to drink very large amounts of alcohol (8.1 g/kg). In future research, it will be important, therefore, to identify those limbic structures stimulated by the infusions and then examine the mechanisms of each with respect to their role in alcohol drinking.

Finally, it is interesting that stimulation with a cholinergic compound at a specific site in the brain does not elicit alcohol consumption (Cicero and Myers, 1969). Rats with cannulae implanted in the brainstem failed to drink alcohol when a cholinomimetric compound was injected into regions which mediate excessive water intake. When 4, 8, or 12% solutions of alcohol were offered, these concentrations were rejected following the microinjection of carbamylcholine or acetylcholine into the preoptic area, nucleus reuniens, or septum pellucidum.

Drugs and Other Systemic Alterations

In addition to the alterations in alcohol intake brought about by vitamin and caloric restrictions, a limited amount of research has been carried out on the self-selection of alcohol following drug injections and similar experimental manipulations. Several compounds have been found which tend to reduce alcohol intake in certain situations, whereas others do not. Common tranquilizers fail to affect preference in a free-choice situation; meprobamate, for instance, does not depress lever responding for 5% alcohol (Myers, 1961b). This mephenesin derivative as well as hydroxyphenamate also did not reduce the selection of higher concentrations in rats infused earlier with intraventricular alcohol (Myers, 1964). Tybamate, an ataractic compound with properties similar to meprobamate, also did not alter alcohol preference in animals exposed to the stress of randomly delivered shock (Myers and Cicero, 1968).

If the ability of the animal to metabolize alcohol is interfered with, then alcohol intake is reduced. In an early paper, carbon tetrachloride given subcutaneously was reported to cause rats to ingest four times the amount of 20% alcohol than controls in a water-alcohol choice situation (Sirnes, 1953); the same effect was produced by chloroform and methanol, and reversed by vitamin C (Iida, 1958). However, other hepatotoxins failed to produce an increase in alcohol selection. The finding that liver damage caused by hepatotoxic agents increases preference is in a sense paradoxical, since this kind of treatment should reduce the consumption of alcohol which would serve to cause further injury to the liver. This has now been verified since depressed hepatic function produced by disulfiram (Harkness et al., 1953) or by puromycin (Mendelson et al., 1965) results in a decline in the intake of 10% alcohol, presumably because of the inhibition of activity of liver alcohol dehydrogenase. Thus, the originally observed effects of carbon tetrachloride and other toxins could have been due to an alteration or an action on a structure within the central nervous system, perhaps the hypothalamus.

Lesions to the hypothalamus produced chemically by gold thioglucose reduce alcohol preference markedly in C57BL mice, a high preferring strain (Kakihana *et al.*, 1968). A similar type of aversion to alcohol can also be produced by whole body radiation (Peacock and Watson, 1964) although the evidence for direct central effects is not as yet available. The possible central mechanism related to the reduction of alcohol selection could be linked to the metabolism and release of the candidate neurohumoral transmitter, serotonin (Myers and Veale, 1968).

Biogenic Amines and Alcohol Preference

Because serotonin (5-HT) and norepinephrine have been related to changes in behavioral and emotional states (Schildkraut and Kety, 1967), alcohol may alter the synaptic function of one of these monoamines or another candidate transmitter. Already there is some evidence that alcohol, if given acutely, increases the activity of brainstem neurons containing catecholamines (Corrodi *et al.*, 1966). Recently, the levels of endogenous substances were altered in the brainstem of rats to determine whether an animal's preference for alcohol could be elevated or suppressed. The concentrations of monoamines were selectively reduced by two compounds: *p*CPA which lowers brain 5-HT, and α-methyl-*p*-tyrosine (aM*p*T) which lowers brain catecholamines. Following the chronic administration of *p*CPA during an 11-day self-selection sequence, the selection of alcohol in the 3 to 30% range of concentrations declined significantly (Myers and Veale, 1968). Parallel administration of aM*p*T had no significant effect on alcohol intake. Surprisingly, the reduction in alcohol preference was even greater following the discontinuation of the *p*CPA treatment. This is illustrated in Fig. 11.

In a later study it was found that *p*CPA also reduced the selection of alcohol in rats during a period of stress produced by randomly delivered electric shock (Myers and Cicero, 1969). The effect of the drug was particularly potent in an animal categorized as a "high drinker" because of the large volume of alcohol selected. Again, aM*p*T had little effect on alcohol preference during the shock-avoidance condition. These results have been further extended in other experiments in which it was found that *p*CPA caused a significant decline in alcohol intake in rats which drank because of (a) a genetic predisposition toward the fluid, (b) the gradual acclimation of alcohol, or (c) earlier stress produced by punishment in a conditioned avoidance task (Veale and Myers, 1970). The action of *p*CPA in lowering alcohol preference or alcohol intake in a forced situation has been confirmed recently (Frey *et al.*, 1970).

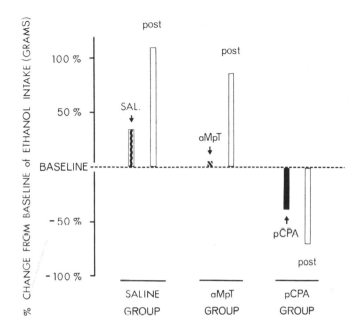

FIGURE 11. Shift in alcohol intake (grams) from the baseline intake level before, during and after the administration of the drugs. The increases in alcohol preference are shown for the control group (saline) and α-methyl-*p*-tyrosine (aM*p*T) rats, whereas the percentage decrease is likewise given for rats intubated with *p*-chlorophenylalanine (*p*CPA). Each bar represents an 11-day preference sequence during which the alcohol concentration was increased systematically from 3 to 30%. [From Myers and Veale (1968).]

These findings strongly suggest that a relationship exists between the metabolism of 5-HT or its activity as a transmitter in the mechanism of alcohol selection. Considerable evidence for the relationship between biogenic amines and alcohol selection has arisen from the results of studies of 5-HT urine analyses, particularly with regard to the route of 5-HT degradation (Olson *et al.*, 1960; Feldstein *et al.*, 1964; Davis *et al.*, 1967). It has been suggested in other reports that a connection exists between 5-HT content and systemically administered alcohol, although this is not yet firmly established (Pscheidt *et al.*, 1961; Bonnycastle *et al.*, 1962; Häggendal and Lindqvist, 1961; Efron and Gessa, 1963; Duritz and Truitt, 1966). In a direct experiment in which both brain and liver slices were examined, Eccleston *et al.* (1969) found that when alcohol was added to the incubating medium, the rate of utilization of 5-HT in the slices of brain was markedly suppressed, whereas alcohol had little effect on the utilization of 5-HT in liver tissue. Moreover, in the presence of alcohol, the 5-HT in brain slices was still metabolized *in vitro* by the normal route from 5-hydroxyacetalde-hyde to 5-hydroxyindoleacetaldehyde, and there was no substantial rise in the formation of 5-hydroxytryptophol. On the other hand, 5-HT degradation in liver slices took an alternative pathway to 5-hydroxytryptophol when alcohol was added to the incubation medium, but the rate of utilization was unchanged (Eccleston et al., 1969). A significant alcohol-induced shift in the metabolism of 5-HT to the formation of 5-HTOL rather than to 5-HIAA also does not occur in the brain of a rat (Tyce et al., 1968). Thus, the metabolism of cerebral 5-HT in the presence of alcohol does not shift to an alternate pathway, and this may be the basis of the apparent interference between 5-HT and alcohol metabolism if they do indeed use the same enzymatic system for degradation.

Therefore, in the experiments in which pCPA was administered, the ingestion of alcohol would serve to interfere with utilization of the remaining fraction of cerebral 5-HT, when the content of 5-HT is lowered in the brain by the blockade of its synthesis. That is, when pCPA and alcohol are present simultaneously, a reduction of available 5-HT by pCPA occurs together with an interference of 5-HT utilization by alcohol (Myers and Veale, 1968). Because of a disruption in the normal indoleamine metabolism, which is apparently essential for cerebral function (Davis et al., 1969), the rat of necessity would reduce its alcohol intake to avoid further deleterious effects. Further research is, of course, required before a complete picture of the role of 5-HT in alcohol selection is obtained.

CONCLUSIONS

Although the formulation of a suitable animal model for human alcoholism appears to be a dim prospect at the present time, a number of fruitful areas should be explored. It is essential that improved methods are developed for inducing an animal to consume alcohol in a choice situation. By using a permanently implanted gastric fistula (Mook, 1963) or a chronic indwelling intravenous catheter (Schuster and Thompson, 1969), the aversive oral qualities of alcohol could be temporarily circumvented. Also, a more thorough examination of the role of stress should be pursued using perhaps more relevant behavioral tasks and psychologically negative situations in addition to the traditional electric shock. Further, certain kinds of social situations could be established which may enhance alcohol preference. Finally, as emphasized already by Lester (1968), it is desirable that primates be used more widely, especially in connection with biochemical analyses and pharmacological treatments. If an alcohol syndrome is fully produced in the monkey and a successful method can be evolved for treating this infrahuman primate, then an extension to man and the eventual control of this disease would be close at hand.

One of the most important questions pertains to the localization of the effects of alcohol within the central nervous system. If alcohol acts on the cortex to produce its intoxicating effects, does the limbic system mediate the addictive process? It is already known that parts of the limbic lobe are concerned with the evocation of emotional responses and still other anatomical regions are involved in the regulation of drinking, thirst, and the maintenance of the fluid-electrolyte balance (Morgane, 1969). In this connection, there may be a general "addictive factor" in the central nervous system which revolves about the synthesis, release, or turnover of serotonin in one or more areas of the brainstem (Collier, 1968). An additional value to be gained by determining the central locus of an "addictive mechanism" rests in the possibility that lesioning a subcortical structure may abolish an abnormal intake of alcohol just as lesions alleviate the symptoms of Parkinson's and other diseases. In a preliminary study completed in our laboratory, there was a suggestion that the septum pellucidum is one of the structures involved in the preference for alcohol (Gwinn, 1967). Conversely, an area of the thalamus could mediate the cessation of drinking (Marconi et al., 1969).

In concluding this review, we would hope that it would serve to alert the new researcher to the problems existing in this field, and to remind the established investigator, who may undertake a study concerning the voluntary ingestion of alcohol, of the numerous variables involved in such an endeavor. It is essential that the scientist establish whether or not an animal prefers alcohol for its pharmacological effect, or for its taste, or because of its caloric utility. Here the important but often overlooked concept is choice. Unfortunately, forcing an animal to drink alcohol, even when contained in a palatable solution with high nutritional value (Koch et al., 1968; Freund, 1969), does not impart information about the volitional component of drinking. If one is ever to extrapolate from an animal condition to the human disease state, data must at least be provided which relate to the evocation of alcohol preference over another fluid and to the abolition of a well-established pattern of alcohol consumption.

REFERENCES

Adamson, R. and Black, R., 1959. Volitional drinking and avoidance learning in the white rat, *J. Comp. Physiol. Psychol.* **52**: 734–736.

Anderson, W. D. and Smith, O. A., Jr., 1963. Taste and volume preferences for alcohol in macaca Nemestrina, *J. Comp. Physiol. Psychol.* **56**: 144–149.

Arvola, A. and Forsander, O. A., 1963. Hamsters in experiments of free choice between alcohol and water, *Quart. J. Stud. Alc.* **24**: 591–597.

Aschkenasy-Lelu, P., 1958. Action d'un oestrogène sur la consommation spontanée d'une boisson alcoolisée chez le rat, *C. R. Acad. Sci. (Paris)* **247**: 1044–1047.

Aschkenasy-Lelu, P., 1962. L'action inhibitrice des oestrogènes sur la consommation élective d'alcool du rat; passe-t-elle par un relais thyroidien? *Arch. Sci. Physiol.* **16**: 203–211.

Barry, H., III, 1968. Prolonged measurements of discrimination between alcohol and non-drug states, *J. Comp. Physiol. Psychol.* **65**: 349–352.

Bonnycastle, D. D., Bonnycastle, M. F., and Anderson, E. G., 1962. The effect of a number of central depressant drugs upon brain 5-hydroxytryptamine levels in the rat, *J. Pharmacol. Exp. Ther.* 135. 17 20.

Brady, R. A. and Westerfeld, W. W., 1947. The effect of B-complex vitamins on the voluntary consumption of alcohol by rats, *Quart. J. Stud. Alc.* 7: 499–505.

Broadhurst, P. L. and Wallgren, H., 1964. Ethanol and the acquisition of a conditioned avoidance response in selected strains of rats, *Quart. J. Stud. Alc.* 25: 476–489.

Casey, A., 1960. The effect of stress on the consumption of alcohol and reserpine, *Quart. J. Stud. Alc.* 21: 208–216.

Chen, C. S., 1968. A study of the alcohol-tolerance effect and an introduction of a new behavioral technique, *Psychopharmacologia* 12: 433–440.

Cicero, T. J. and Myers, R. D., 1968. Selection of a single ethanol test solution in free-choice studies with animals, *Quart. J. Stud. Alc.* 29: 446–448.

Cicero, T. J. and Myers, R. D., 1969. Preference-aversion functions for alcohol after cholinergic stimulation of the brain and fluid deprivation, *Physiol. Behav.* 4: 559–562.

Cicero, T. J., Myers, R. D., and Black, W. C., 1968. Increase in volitional ethanol consumption following interference with a learned avoidance response, *Physiol. Behav.* 3: 657–660.

Clark, R. and Polish E., 1960. Avoidance conditioning and alcohol consumption in rhesus monkeys, *Science* 132: 223–224.

Clay, M. L., 1964. Conditions affecting voluntary alcohol consumption in rats, *Quart. J. Stud. Alc.*, 25: 36–55.

Collier, H. O. J., 1968. Supersensitivity and dependence, *Nature* 220: 228–231.

Conger, J. J., 1956. Reinforcement theory and the dynamics of alcoholism, *Quart. J. Stud. Alc.* 17: 296–305.

Corrodi, H., Fuxe, K., and Hökfelt, T., 1966. The effect of ethanol on the activity of central catecholamine neurones in rat brain, *J. Pharm. Pharmacol.* 18: 821–823.

Crossland, J. and Ratcliffe, F., 1968. Some effects of chronic alcohol administration in the rat, *Brit. J. Pharmacol. Chemother.* 32: 413P.

Davis, V. E., Huff, J. A., and Brown, H., 1969. Alcohol and biogenic amines, in *Biochemical and Clinical Aspects of Alcohol Metabolism* (V. M. Sardesai, ed.) pp. 95–104, Charles C Thomas, Springfield, Ill.

Davis, V. E., Brown, H., Huff, J. A., and Cashaw, J. L., 1967. The alteration of serotonin metabolism to 5-hydroxytryptophol by ethanol ingestion in man, *J. Lab. Clin. Med.* 69: 132–140.

Dember, W. N. and Kristofferson, A. B., 1955. The relation between free-choice alcohol consumption and susceptibility to audiogenic seizures, *Quart. J. Stud. Alc.* 16: 86–95.

Dember, W. N., Ellen, P., and Kristofferson, A. B., 1953. The effects of alcohol on seizure behavior in rats, *Quart. J. Stud. Alc.* 14: 390–394.

Denenberg, V. H., Pawlowski, A. A., and Zarrow, M. X., 1961. Prolonged alcohol consumption in the rat. I. Acquisition and extinction of a bar-pressing response, *Quart. J. Stud. Alc.* 22: 14–21.

Dicker, S. E., 1958. The effects of methylpentynol on ethanol drinking and on water metabolism in rats, *J. Physiol.* 144: 138–147.

Duritz, G. and Truitt, E. B., 1966. Importance of acetaldehyde in the action of ethanol on brain norepinephrine and 5-hydroxytryptamine, *Biochem. Pharmacol.* 15: 711–721.

Eccleston, D., Reading, W. H., and Ritchie, I. M., 1969. 5-Hydroxytryptamine metabolism in brain and liver slices and the effects of ethanol, *J. Neurochem.* 16: 274–276.

Efron, D. H. and Gessa, G. L., 1963. Failure of ethanol and barbiturates to alter brain monoamine content, *Arch. Int. Pharmacodyn. Ther.* **142**: 111–116.

Eimer, E. O. and Senter, R. J., 1968. Alcohol consumption in domestic and wild rats, *Psychon. Sci.* **10**: 310–320.

Eriksson, K., 1968. Genetic selection for voluntary alcohol consumption in the albino rat, *Science* **159**: 739–741.

Eriksson, K. and Pikkarainen, J., 1968. Differences between the sexes in voluntary alcohol consumption and liver ADH-activity in inbred strains of mice, *Metabolism* 1037–1042.

Essig, C. F., 1968. Increased water consumption following forced drinking of alcohol in rats, *Psychopharmacologia* **12**: 333–337.

Essig, C. F., and Lam, R. C., 1968. Convulsions and hallucinatory behavior, *Arch. Neurol.* **18**: 626–632.

Essig, C. F., Jones, B. E., and Lam, R. C., 1969. The effect of pentobarbital on alcohol withdrawal in dogs, *Arch. Neurol.* **20**: 554–558.

Falk, J. L., 1961. Production of polydipsia in normal rats by an intermittent food schedule, *Science* **133**: 195–196.

Feldstein, A., Hoagland, H., Wong, K., and Freeman, H., 1964. Biogenic amines, biogenic aldehydes, and alcohol, *Quart. J. Stud. Alc.* **25**: 218–225.

Fitz-Gerald, F. L., Barfield, M. A., and Warrington, R. J., 1968. Voluntary alcohol consumption in chimpanzees and orangutans, *Quart. J. Stud. Alc.* **29**: 330–336.

Forsander, O. A., 1962. Metabolic tolerance to alcohol as a possible limiting factor in its consumption, *Quart. J. Stud. Alc.* **23**: 480–482.

Freed, E. X., 1967. The effect of alcohol upon approach-avoidance conflict in the white rat, *Quart. J. Stud. Alc.* **28**: 236–254.

Freund, G., 1969. Alcohol withdrawal syndrome in mice, *Arch. Neurol.* **21**: 315–320.

Frey, H. H., Magnussen, M. P., and Nielsen, C. K., 1970. The effect of *p*-chloroamphetamine on the consumption of ethanol by rats, *Arch. Int. Pharmacodyn. Ther.* **183**: 165–172 (1970).

Fuller, J. L., 1964. Measurement of alcohol preference in genetic experiments, *J. Comp. Physiol. Psychol.* **57**: 85–88.

Gillespie, R. J. G., and Lucas, C. C., 1958. An unexpected factor affecting the alcohol intake of rats, *Can. J. Biochem. Physiol.* **36**: 37–44.

Goodrick, C. L., 1967. Alcohol preference of the male Sprague-Dawley albino rat as a function of age, *J. Geront.* **22**: 369–371.

Gwinn, J. F., 1967. An attempt to alter ethanol preference in rats by brain lesions, Unpublished thesis, Purdue University.

Häggendal, J. and Lindqvist, M., 1961. Ineffectiveness of ethanol on noradrenaline, dopamine, or 5-hydroxytryptamine levels in brain, *Acta Pharmacol. Toxicol.* **18**: 278–280.

Harkness, W. D., Johnston, C. D., and Woodard, G., 1953. Methods to evaluate in rats the antipathy to alcohol produced by Antabuse and related compounds, *Fed. Proc.* **12**: 328–329.

Hogans, A. F., Moreno, O. M., and Brodie, D. A., 1961. Effects of ethyl alcohol on EEG and avoidance behavior of chronic electrode monkeys, *Am. J. Physiol.* **201**: 434–436.

Holman, R. B., 1967. The effect of psychogenic polydipsia on volitional ethanol consumption in the rat, Unpublished thesis, Purdue University.

Holman, R. B. and Myers, R. D., 1968. Ethanol consumption under conditions of psychogenic polydipsia, *Physiol. Behav.* **3**: 369–371.

Iida, S., 1958. Experimental studies on the craving for alcohol. II. Alcoholic drive in mice following administration of hepatotoxic agents, *Jap. J. Pharmacol.* **8**: 70–74.

Kahn, M. and Stellar, E., 1960. Alcohol preference in normal and anosmic rats, *J. Comp. Physiol. Psychol.* **53**: 571–575.

Kakihana, R. and McClearn, G. E., 1963. Development of alcohol preference in BALB/c mice, *Nature* **199**: 511–512.

Kakihana, R., Butte, J. C., and Noble, E. P., 1968. Effects of goldthioglucose on alcohol consumption in C57BL mice, *Life Sci.* **7**: 825–832.

Kalant, H., 1962. Some recent physiological and biochemical investigations on alcohol and alcoholism, a review, *Quart. J. Stud. Alc.* **23**: 52–93.

Keehn, J. D., 1969. "Voluntary" consumption of alcohol by rats, *Quart. J. Stud. Alc.* **30**: 320–329.

Koch, O. R., Porta, E. A., and Hartroft, W. S., 1968. A new experimental approach in the study of chronic alcoholism. III. Role of alcohol versus sucrose or fat-derived calories in hepatic damage, *Lab. Invest.* **18**: 379–386.

Korman, M. and Stephens, H. D., 1960. Effects of training on the alcohol consummatory response in rats, *Psychol. Rep.* **6**: 327–331.

Korn, S. J., 1960. The relationship between individual differences in the responsivity of rats to stress and intake of alcohol, *Quart. J. Stud. Alc.* **21**: 605–617.

Koz, G. and Mendelson, J. H., 1967. Effects of intraventricular ethanol infusion on free choice alcohol consumption by monkeys, in *Biochemical Factors in Alcoholism* (R. P. Maikel, ed.) pp. 17–24, Pergamon Press, Oxford.

LeBlanc, A. E., Kalant, H., Gibbons, R. J., and Berman, N. D., 1969. Acquisition and loss of tolerance to ethanol by the rat, *J. Pharmacol. Exp. Ther.* **168**: 244–250.

Leikola, A., 1962. Influence of stress on alcohol intoxication in rats, *Quart. J. Stud. Alc.* **23**: 369–375.

Lester, D., 1961. Self-maintenance of intoxication in the rat, *Quart. J. Stud. Alc.* **22**: 223–231.

Lester, D., 1966. Self-selection of alcohol by animals, human variation, and the etiology of alcoholism, *Quart. J. Stud. Alc.* **27**: 395–438.

Lester, D., 1968. Non-human primates in research on the problems of alcohol, in *Use of Nonhuman Primates in Drug Evaluation* (H. Vagtborg, ed.) pp. 249–264, Univ. of Texas Press, Austin.

Lester, D. and Greenberg, L. A., 1952. Nutrition and the etiology of alcoholism. The effect of sucrose, saccharine and fat on the self-selection of ethyl alcohol by rats, *Quart. J. Stud. Alc.* **13**: 553–560.

Lieber, C. S., 1967. Metabolic derangement induced by alcohol, *Ann. Rev. Med.* **18**: 35–54.

Mäenpää, P. H. and Forsander, O. A., 1966. Influence of iodine deficiency on free choice between alcohol and water in rats, *Quart. J. Stud. Alc.* **27**: 596–603.

Marconi, J., Poblete, M., Palestini, M., Moya, L., and Bahamondes, A., 1969. Participacion del nucleo dorsomediano del talamo en la "incapacidad de detenerse" y "abstenerse" durante la ingestion de ethanol, *Arch. Biol. Med. Exp.*, Suppl. 3, 126–132.

Mardones, J., 1960. Experimentally induced changes in the free selection of ethanol, in *International Review of Neurobiology* (C. C. Pfeiffer and J. R. Smythies, ed.) Vol. 2, pp. 41–76, Academic Press, New York.

Mardones, J. and Onfray, B. E., 1942. Influencia de una substancia de la levadura (elemento del complejo vitamínico B?) sobre el consumo de alcohol en ratas en experimentos de autoselección, *Rev. Chil. Hig. Med. Prev.* **4**: 293–297.

Mardones, J., Segovia-Riquelme, N., and Hederra, D., 1953. Heredity of experimental alcohol preference in rats. II. Coefficient of heredity, *Quart. J. Stud. Alc.* **14**: 1–2.

Mardonnes, J., Segovia-Riquelme, N., Hederra, A., and Alcanico, F., 1955. Effect of some self-selection conditions on the voluntary alcohol intake of rats, *Quart. J. Stud. Alc.* **16**: 425–437.

Masserman, J. H. and Yum, K. S., 1946. An analysis of the influence of alcohol on experimental neuroses in cats, *Psychosom. Med.* **8**: 36–52.

McClearn, G. E. and Rodgers, D. A., 1959. Differences in alcohol preference among inbred strains of mice, *Quart. J. Stud. Alc.* **20**: 691–695.

Meisch, R. and Pickens, R., 1968. Oral self-administration of ethanol by the rat, Paper presented at Psychonomic Society Meeting, St. Louis, Missouri.

Mello, N. K. and Mendelson, J. H., 1964. Operant performance by rats for alcohol reinforcement; a comparison of alcohol-preferring and non-preferring animals, *Quart. J. Stud. Alc.* **25**: 226–234.

Mello, N. K. and Mendelson, J. H., 1965. Operant drinking of alcohol on a rate-contingent ratio schedule of reinforcement, *J. Psychiat. Res.* **3**: 145–152.

Mello, N. K. and Mendelson, J. H., 1966. Factors affecting alcohol consumption in primates, *Psychosom. Med.* **28**. 4, 529–550.

Mello, N. K. and Mendelson, J. H., 1971. The effects of drinking to avoid shock on alcohol intake in primates, in *Biological Aspects of Alcohol* (P. J. Creaven and M. K. Roach, eds.) Univ. of Texas Press, Austin.

Mendelson, J. H. and Mello, N. K., 1964. Ethanol and whisky drinking patterns in rats under free-choice and forced-choice conditions, *Quart. J. Stud. Alc.* **25**: 1–25.

Mendelson, J. H. and Mello, N. K., 1964. Potassium-stimulated respiration of rat cerebral cortex, *Quart. J. Stud. Alc.* **25**: 235–239.

Mendelson, J. H., Mello, N. K., Corbett, C., and Ballard, R., 1965. Puromycin inhibition of ethanol ingestion and liver alcohol dehydrogenase activity in the rat, *J. Psychiat. Res.* **3**: 133–143.

Mirone, L., 1959. Water and alcohol consumption by mice, *Quart. J. Stud. Alc.* **20**: 24–27.

Mook, D. G., 1963. Oral and postingestional determinants of the intake of various solutions in rats with esophageal fistulas, *J. Comp. Physiol. Psychol.* **56**: 645–659.

Morgane, P. J., 1969. The function of the limbic and rhinic forebrain-limbic midbrain systems and reticular formation in the regulation of food and water intake, *Annals N. Y. Acad. Sci.* **157**: 806–838.

Moskowitz, H. and Wapner, M., 1964. Studies on the acquisition of behavioral tolerance to alcohol, *Quart. J. Stud. Alc.* **25**: 619–626.

Myers, A. K., 1962. Alcohol choice in Wistar and G-4 rats as a function of environmental temperature and alcohol concentration, *J. Comp. Physiol. Psychol.* **55**: 606–609.

Myers, R. D., 1961a. Changes in learning, extinction, and fluid preferences as a function of chronic alcohol consumption in rats, *J. Comp. Physiol. Psychol.* **54**: 510–516.

Myers, R. D., 1961b. Effects of meprobamate on alcohol preference and on the stress of response extinction in rats, *Psychol. Rep.* **8**: 385–392.

Myers, R. D., 1963. Alcohol consumption in rats: effects of intracranial injections of ethanol, *Science* **142**: 240–241.

Myers, R. D., 1964. Modification of drinking patterns by chronic intracranial chemical infusion, in *Thirst in the Regulation of Body Water* (M. Wayner, ed.) pp. 533–551, Pergamon Press, Oxford.

Myers, R. D., 1966. Voluntary alcohol consumption in animals: peripheral and intra-cerebral factors, *Psychosom. Med.* **28**: 484–497.

Myers, R. D., 1968. Ethyl alcohol consumption: valid measurement in albino rats, *Science* 161: 76–77.

Myers, R. D., 1969. Influencia de la ..... (..........) .... ratas, *Arch. Biol. Med. Exp.*, Suppl. 3: 97–100.

Myers, R. D. and Carey, R., 1961. Preference factors in experimental alcoholism, *Science* 134: 469–470.

Myers, R. D. and Cicero, T. J., 1968. Effects of tybamate on ethanol intake in rats during psychological stress in an avoidance task, *Arch. Int. Pharmacodyn.* 175: 440–446.

Myers, R. D. and Cicero, T. J., 1969. Effects of serotonin depletion on the volitional alcohol intake of rats during a condition of psychological stress, *Psychopharmacologia* 15: 373–381.

Myers, R. D. and Holman, R. B., 1966. A procedure for eliminating position habit in preference-aversion tests for ethanol and other fluids, *Psychon. Sci.* 6: 235–236.

Myers, R. D. and Holman, R. B., 1967. Failure of stress of electric shock to increase ethanol intake in rats, *Quart. J. Stud. Alc.* 28: 132–137.

Myers, R. D. and Veale, W. L., 1968. Alcohol preference in the rat: reduction following depletion of brain serotonin, *Science* 160: 1469–1471.

Myers, R. D. and Veale, W. L., 1969. Alterations in volitional alcohol intake produced in rats by chronic intraventricular infusions of acetaldehyde, paraldehyde or methanol, *Arch. Int. Pharmacodyn.* 180: 100–113.

Nichols, J. R. and Hsiao, S., 1967. Addiction liability of albino rats: breeding for quantitative differences in morphine drinking, *Science* 157: 561–563.

Olson, R. E., Gursey, D., and Vester, J. W., 1960. Evidence for defect in tryptophan metabolism in chronic alcoholism, *New Engl. J. Med.* 263: 1169–1174.

Parisella, R. M. and Pritham, G. H., 1964. Effect of age on alcohol preference by rats, *Quart. J. Stud. Alc.* 25: 248–252.

Peacock, L. J. and Watson, J. A., 1964. Radiation-induced aversion to alcohol, *Science* 143: 1462–1463.

Popham, R. E., 1953. A critique of the genetotrophic theory of the etiology of alcoholism, *Quart. J. Stud. Alc.* 14: 228–237.

Porta, E. A. and Gomez-Dumm, C. L. A., 1968. A new experimental approach in the study of chronic alcoholism. I. Effects of high alcohol intake in rats fed a commercial laboratory diet, *Lab. Invest.* 18: 352–364.

Powell, B. J., Kamano, D. K., and Martin L. K., 1966. Multiple factors affecting volitional consumption of alcohol in the Abrams Wistar rat, *Quart. J. Stud. Alc.* 27: 7–15.

Prieto, R., Varela, A., and Mardones, J., 1958. Influence of oral administration of thyroid powder on the voluntary alcohol intake by rats, *Acta Physiol. Latinoamer.* 8: 203.

Pscheidt, G. R., Issekutz, B., and Himwich, H. E., 1961. Failure of ethanol to lower brain stem concentration of biogenic amines, *Quart. J. Stud. Alc.* 22: 550–553.

Raskin, N. H. and Sokoloff, L., 1968. Brain alcohol dehydrogenase, *Science* 162: 131–132.

Reynolds, G. S. and van Sommers, P., 1960. Effects of ethyl alcohol on avoidance behavior, *Science* 132: 42–43.

Richter, C. P., 1926. A study of the effect of moderate doses of alcohol on the growth and behavior of the rat, *J. Exp. Zool.* 44: 397–418.

Richter, C. P., 1953. Alcohol, beer and wine as foods, *Quart. J. Stud. Alc.* 14: 525–539.

Richter, C. P., 1956. Loss of appetite for alcohol and alcoholic beverages produced in rats by treatment with thyroid preparations, *Endocrin.* 59: 472–478.

Richter, C. P., 1957. Production and control of alcoholic cravings in rats, in *Neuropharmacology* (H. A. Abramson, ed.) 39–146, Madison Printing Co. Inc., N.J.

Richter, C. P. and Campbell, K. H., 1940. Alcohol taste thresholds and concentration of solutions preferred by rats, *Science* **91**: 507–508.

Rick, J. T. and Wilson, C. W. M., 1966. Alcohol preference in the rat: its relationship to total fluid consumption, *Quart. J. Stud. Alc.* **27**: 447–458.

Rodgers, D. A., 1967. Alcohol preference in mice, *Comp. Psychopath.* 184–201.

Rodgers, D. A. and McClearn, G. E., 1962. Mouse strain differences in preference for various concentrations of alcohol, *Quart. J. Stud. Alc.* **23**: 26–33.

Rodgers, D. A. and McClearn, G. E., 1964. Sucrose versus appetite in inbred strains of mice, *Quart. J. Stud. Alc.* **25**: 26–35.

Rodgers, D. A. and Thiessen, D. D., 1964. Effects of population density on adrenal size, behavioral arousal and alcohol preference of inbred mice, *Quart. J. Stud. Alc.* **25**: 240–247.

Rodgers, D. A., McClearn, G. E., Bennett, E. L., and Hebert, M., 1963. Alcohol preference as a function of its caloric utility in mice, *J. Comp. Physiol. Psychol.* **56**: 666–672.

Rosenberg, B. and Zarrow, M. X., 1952. Alcoholic drive in rats treated with propyl thiouracil, *Fed. Proc.* 11.

Sardesai, V. M. and Orten, J. M., 1968. Effect of prolonged alcohol consumption in rats on pancreatic protein synthesis, *J. Nutr.* **96**: 241–246.

Schlesinger, K., 1966. Genetic and biochemical correlates of alcohol preference in mice, *Am. J. Psychiat.* **122**: 767–773.

Schildkraut, J. J. and Kety, S. S., 1967. Biogenic amines and emotion, *Science* **156**: 21–30.

Schuster, C. R. and Thompson, T., 1969. Self administration of and behavioral dependence on drugs, *Ann. Rev. Pharmacol.* **9**: 483–502.

Segovia-Riquelme, N., Hederra, A., Anex, M., Barnier, D., Figuerola-Camps, I., Campos-Hoppe, I., Jara, N., and Mardones, J., 1969. Factores nutrimentales y geneticos que influyen sobre la apetencia de alcohol, *Arch. Biol. Med. Exp.*, Suppl. 3, 89–96.

Senter, R. J. and Persensky, J. J., 1968. Effects of environment on ethanol consumption in rats after conditioning, *Quart. J. Stud. Alc.* **29**: 856–862.

Senter, R. J. and Sinclair, J. D., 1967. Self-maintenance of intoxication in the rat: A modified replication, *Psychon. Sci.* **9**: 291–292.

Senter, R. J. and Sinclair, J. D., 1968. Thiamin-induced alcohol consumption in rats, *Quart. J. Stud. Alc.* **29**: 337–341.

Senter, R. J. and Richman, C. L., 1969. Induced consumption of high concentration ethanol solution in rats, *Quart. J. Stud. Alc.* **30**: 330–335.

Senter, R. J., Smith, F. W., and Lewin, S., 1967. Ethanol ingestion as an operant response, *Psychon. Sci.* **8**: 291–292.

Sinclair, J. D. and Senter, R. J., 1968. Development of an alcohol-deprivation effect in rats, *Quart. J. Stud. Alc.* **29**: 863–867.

Sirnes, T. B., 1953. Voluntary consumption of alcohol in rats with cirrhosis of the liver, *Quart. J. Stud. Alc.* **14**: 3–18.

Smart, R. G., 1965. Effects of alcohol on conflict and avoidance behavior, *Quart. J. Stud. Alc.* **26**: 187–205.

Thiessen, D. D. and Rodgers, D. A., 1965. Alcohol injection, grouping, and voluntary alcohol consumption of inbred strains of mice, *Quart. J. Stud. Alc.* **26**: 378–383.

Thiessen, D. D., Whitworth, N., and Rodgers, D. A., 1965. Reproductive functions and metabolic capacity as determinants of alcohol preference in C57BL female mice, *J. Comp. Physiol. Psychol.* **63**: 151–154.

Thiessen, D. D., Whitworth, N. S., and Rodgers, D. A., 1967. Reproductive variables and alcohol consumption of the C57BL/Crgl female mouse, *Quart. J. Stud. Alc.* **27**: 591–595.

Tintera, J. W. and Lovell, H. W., 1949. Endocrine treatment of alcoholism, *Geriatrics* 4: 274–280.

┆ ╷╷ ╷╷╷╷, ╷╷ ╷ ╷╷╷╷ ┆ ╷╷╷╷╷╷╷╷╷╷╷╷ ╷╷╷╷╷╷╷╷╷╷╷╷╷╷ ╷╷╷ ╷╷╷╷╷╷╷╷╷╷╷╷ ╷╷╷╷╷ ╷╷╷╷╷╷╷╷╷╷╷ ╷╷╷╷╷╷╷╷╷╷╷╷╷╷╷╷╷ ╷╷╷ ╷╷╷╷ ╷╷╷, *Quart. J. Stud. Alc.* 18: 19–29.

Tyce, G. M., Flock, E. V., and Owen, C. A., 1968. 5-Hydroxytryptamine metabolism in brains of ethanol-intoxicated rats, *Mayo Clin. Proc.* 43: 668–673.

Veale, W. L. and Myers, R. D., 1968. Tables for determining grams and caloric values of ethanol solutions, Purdue Neuropsychology Series: Report No. 1: 1–8.

Veale, W. L. and Myers, R. D., 1969. Increased alcohol preference in rats following repeated exposures to alcohol, *Psychopharmacologia* 15: 361–372.

Veale, W. L. and Myers, R. D., 1970. Decrease in ethanol intake in rats following administration of p-chlorophenylalanine, *Int. J. Neuropharmacol.* 9: 317–326.

von Wartburg, J. P. and Papenberg, J., 1966. Alcohol dehydrogenase in ethanol metabolism, *Psychosomat. Med.* 28: 405–413.

Wallgren, H., 1959. Sex difference in ethanol tolerance of rats, *Nature* 184: 726–727.

Wallgren, H. and Savolainen, S., 1962. The effect of ethyl alcohol on a conditioned avoidance response in rats, *Acta Pharmacol. Toxicol.* 19: 59–67.

Wallgren, H., Ahlqvist, J., Ahman, K., and Suomalainen, H., 1967. Repeated alcoholic intoxication compared with continued consumption of dilute ethanol in experiments with rats on a marginal diet, *Brit. J. Nutr.* 21: 643–660.

Weiss, M., 1958. Alcohol as a depressant in psychological conflict in rats, *Quart. J. Stud. Alc.* 19: 226–237.

Westerfeld, W. W. and Lawrow, J., 1953. The effect of caloric restriction and thiamin deficiency on the voluntary consumption of alcohol by rats, *Quart. J. Stud. Alc.* 14: 378–384.

Westerfeld, W. W. and Schulman, M. P., 1959. Some biochemical aspects of the alcohol problem, *Quart. J. Stud. Alc.* 20: 439–451.

Williams, R. J., 1952. Alcoholism as a nutritional problem, *J. Clin. Nutr.* 1: 32–36.

Williams, R. J., 1959. *Alcoholism—the Nutritional Approach*, Univ. Texas Press, Austin.

Williams, R. J., Berry, L. J., and Beerstecher, E., Jr., 1949. Biochemical individuality. III. Genetotrophic factors in the etiology of alcoholism, *Arch. Biochem.* 23: 275–290.

Williams, R. J., Berry, L. J., and Beerstecher, E., Jr., 1950. Genetotrophic diseases, alcoholism, *Tex. Rep. Biol. Med.* 8: 238–256.

Zarrow, M. X., Aduss, H., and Denison, M. E., 1960. Failure of the endocrine system to influence alcohol choice in rats, *Quart. J. Stud. Alc.* 21: 400–413.

Zarrow, M. X., Pawlowski, A. A., and Denenberg, V. H., 1962. Electroshock convulsion threshold and organ weights in rats after alcohol consumption, *Am. J. Physiol.* 203: 197–200.

CHAPTER 7

Voluntary Alcohol Consumption in Apes

F. L. Fitz-Gerald

Miami, Florida

USE OF NONHUMAN PRIMATES IN STUDIES OF ALCOHOL CONSUMPTION

The use of nonhuman animals in experiments investigating the etiology of addiction to alcohol and the effects of alcohol has been of unusual importance. In view of the possibility of inducing addiction, investigators have been understandably reluctant to use human subjects in procedures that require repeated exposure to alcohol over long periods of time. Consequently, data concerning experimental alcohol administration in man have been limited to two main lines of evidence: studies of the effects of alcohol upon nonaddicted individuals (Carpenter, 1962; Goldberg, 1943) and clinical observations of patients displaying previously established addictions to alcohol or other drugs. Much of the research involving addicted subjects has consisted of studies of continuing alcohol ingestion and of the effects of withdrawal from the drug (Isbell *et al.*, 1955; Mendelson, 1964). Current reviews of recent work in these areas are presented by Carpenter and Armenti, French, and Mendelson in Volumes 1 and 2 of this work.

While experimental approaches aimed at producing alcohol addiction must be carried out with nonhuman subjects, evidence from animal studies has indicated that it is extremely difficult, if not impossible, to produce an "alcoholic" animal in the sense in which the term is applied to man. It should be noted that there are some very real differences between the usual alcohol-drinking behavior observed in human beings and the reported instances of alcohol intake in other species. It is true that nonhuman animals have been induced to drink solutions containing alcohol and to become intoxicated (Lester, 1966). The inducements have, however, been rather drastic. For example, animals deprived of water for many hours develop extreme thirst which forces them to tolerate alcohol solutions. Similarly, animals deprived of food for long periods of time have been observed to consume solutions containing alcohol, presumably for caloric value (Malmo, 1965). When not in need of food or water, however, animals generally avoid alcohol. Current approaches to this problem are reviewed by Rodgers (Chapter 5), Myers and Veale (Chapter 6), and Mello (Chapter 9) in this volume.

In view of the importance of determining whether or not a nonhuman organism can become addicted to alcohol, research should be designed in which the relevant variables are manipulated as favorably as possible for the development of addiction. As previously suggested, such studies require not only carefully planned experimental procedures, but also the selection of a species whose physiological and behavioral responses to drug administration and deprivation correspond closely to those seen in man (Fitz-Gerald, 1967a). Taking into account the large number of variables which presumably interact to produce alcohol addiction in man, it would be reasonable to seek an animal model in a species as closely related to man, and as psychobiologically complex, as possible. Thus, the most appropriate species would appear to be found among the nonhuman primates. With the exception of the material presented here, the extant research in this area has been limited to monkeys and has been well reviewed recently by Lester (1968).

Numerous studies of apes have clearly established that the majority of the fundamental characteristics of the chimpanzee, *Pan troglodytes*, resemble corresponding human functions more closely than do those of any other species. Of particular relevance here is the fact that many of the chimpanzee's behavioral responses to various psychotropic drugs appear similar to those seen in man (Fitz-Gerald, 1964, 1967b). In addition, Spragg's (1940) investigations of morphine administration in chimpanzees indicated that this species is capable of acquiring a distinct physiological addiction. The subjects displayed symptoms of physical dependence, craving for morphine, and withdrawal. It seems reasonable to speculate that the chimpanzee might well acquire a comparable addiction to alcohol. The demonstration of such a syndrome in the chimpanzee, together with the comparative study of relevant physiological and behavioral variables in ape and man, could be of great value to those searching for experimental models of alcohol addiction.

It should be emphasized that the chimpanzee, *per se*, is viewed as filling a significant role, not only because of its similarities to man and its accessibility to experimental control, but also because of its dissimilarities to man. One of the primary features of comparative study is the elucidation of factors which are specific to a particular species, as well as those which are general in nature. Thus, the utilization of the chimpanzee is seen as important not just as a substitute for man, but also as a means of further defining critical differences which distinguish human and nonhuman primates.

GENERAL VARIABLES RELATED TO ALCOHOL CONSUMPTION IN APES

One aspect of the evaluation of the suitability of the chimpanzee for studies concerned with alcohol addiction lies in the consideration of such parameters as preferences for alcohols, ranges of alcohol consumption, and patterns of drinking behavior. Various dimensions of these parameters have been explored in the investigations described below. It should be noted that an important feature of those studies was to make the apes' initial experiences with alcohol as comparable as possible to those of human beings. Accordingly, the only differences in the animals' normal routine occurred when they were offered alcohol solutions.

Preferences for Alcohols

In order to draw parallels between the alcohol-drinking behavior of man and ape, it is necessary to establish what kinds of alcoholic beverages the ape ingests voluntarily. It has been found, for example, that some chimpanzees will drink beer; the amount consumed however, has not been remarkable (0–72 oz of 3.2% alcohol) nor consistent over time (Rogers, 1964). When offered wines (12–20% alcohol) chimpanzees tended to drink more of the sweeter beverages, sherry and port, than the less sweet Chianti and Rhine wines. Chimpanzees have also been exposed to scotch, bourbon, rye, gin, and rum, all mixed with water to a 14% concentration. In every instance, the solution was tasted and rejected (Fitz-Gerald and Fox, unpublished data).

In an effort to explore the palatability of ethanol solutions, a variety of flavored mixtures, all 14% alcohol, were offered to a group of chimpanzees. The animals showed the greatest preferences for solutions flavored with grape, blackberry, pineapple, or milk. The intermediate preferences included orange, strawberry, cranberry, lemon, or peach-flavored mixtures. The least preferred solutions were those flavored with yam, banana, almond, or black walnut. While the information regarding flavor preferences is useful, it also appeared that the taste of ethanol in a 14% solution is somewhat difficult to disguise, at least for chimpanzee consumption (Fitz-Gerald and Fox, unpublished data).

In another series of studies, chimpanzees and orangutans were surveyed for ~~mmmifia mrfurences~~ for three kinds of fruit juice and ethanol or vodka-fruit juice mixtures of 10% alcohol. All of the apes tested preferred plain juices to the alcohol-juice combinations. When plain juice was offered, both chimpanzees and orangutans drank more orange than grapefruit or grape juices. The animals apparently detected the presence of ethanol or vodka in the juices, and when alcohol was present, choices shifted from orange to grape juice. Presumably, grape juice masks the taste of alcohol more effectively than do the other two kinds of juice. It was also discovered that the chimpanzees and orangutans tended to ingest more vodka than ethanol. In a group of chimpanzees that was tested under both alcohol conditions, vodka consumption was significantly higher than that of ethanol (Fitz-Gerald et al., 1968).

Ranges of Alcohol Consumption

In the same investigations, consumption of plain juice ranged from 0 to 144 oz among chimpanzees and from 0 to 75 oz among orangutans. As in man, there were marked individual differences in alcohol ingestion; intake ranged from the equivalent of 0–20 oz and 0–10 oz of 40% alcohol for chimpanzees and orangutans, respectively. Unlike various chimpanzees, none of the orangutans displayed symptoms of intoxication. It is worth noting not only the large amounts of fluids that were consumed in a given session, but also the speed with which such quantities were ingested; the range was 1–60 min, with a mean of 10 min.

Patterns of Drinking Behavior

The same studies revealed that alcohol consumption was significantly related to such variables as sex, weight, age, prior exposure to alcohol, and total volume intake.

Male chimpanzees drank significantly more alcohol than did the females, as shown in Fig. 1, and the same differences occurred in plain juice consumption. Of the male chimpanzees that were tested, 54% ingested enough alcohol to become intoxicated at least once out of 12 or 24 opportunities. Only 25% of the females showed symptoms of intoxication. Among the intoxicated animals, the amount of alcohol consumed on a given occasion ranged from the equivalent of 15–20 oz of 40% alcohol, with a mean of 18 oz for the males and 16 oz for the females. It has often been assumed that the reported differences between males and females in the incidence of human drinking and addiction could be explained largely by cultural factors. These observations, together with those of others (Clay, 1964), suggest that sex differences in drinking may be more strongly related to physiological variables.

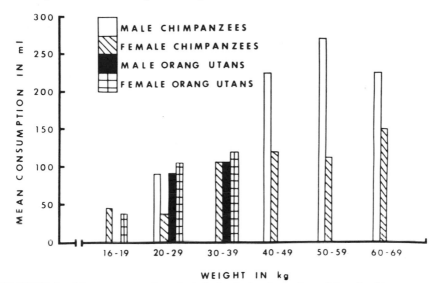

FIGURE 1. Mean consumption of alcohol solution by male and female chimpanzees and orangutans, by weight. For purposes of comparison the amounts of 10% alcohol solution consumed have been converted to 40% alcohol. [Reprinted by permission from *Quart. J. Stud. Alc.* **29**: 334, 1968. Copyright by Journal of Studies on Alcohol, Inc., New Brunswick, N.J.]

Weight appeared to be one of the most significant variables in voluntary alcohol consumption among the apes. With one exception, heavier animals ingested significantly more alcohol than did the lighter ones. Those differences, shown in Fig. 1, were consistent within species and sexes and for plain juice intake, as well. The exception, attributable to an adult male chimpanzee in the heaviest weight group who drank very little alcohol, serves to emphasize the relevance of individual differences in drinking behavior.

As in the case of weight, consumption of plain juice and alcohol-juice mixtures was significantly greater by older chimpanzees up to the fourth decade. At that point, alcohol intake decreased markedly, as shown in Fig. 2. That effect was a clear reflection of the drinking behavior of the only two animals in the oldest age group; neither ingested more than 3 oz of 40% alcohol in any session. There was a similar, but not as pronounced drop in plain juice consumption.

In agreement with reports of other investigators, it was found that alcohol ingestion was influenced by prior exposure to alcohol. Chimpanzees who were surveyed first with ethanol, and then with vodka, drank significantly more vodka than animals without previous experience with alcohol.

Alcohol intake also appeared to be related to consumption of plain juice. In general, apes who drank large quantities of plain juice also ingested large amounts of alcohol-juice combinations, and this seemed to be associated with body weight.

F. L. Fitz-Gerald

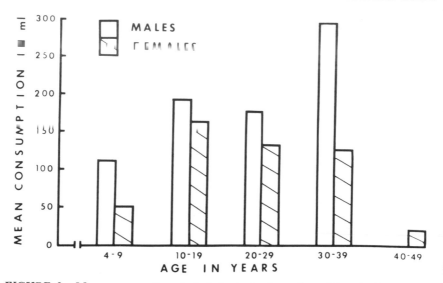

FIGURE 2. Mean consumption of alcohol solution by male and female chimpanzees, by age. For purposes of comparison the amounts of 10% alcohol solution have been converted to 40% alcohol. [Reprinted by permission from *Quart. J. Stud. Alc.* **29**: 335, 1968. Copyright by Journal of Studies on Alcohol, Inc., New Brunswick, N.J.]

The initial level of plain juice consumption was high and then dropped and became stable over time. It appeared that once the novelty of having large quantities of fruit juice available disappeared, the intake fell to a constant level. There were not, however, any significant differences in the amount of alcohol ingested over sessions. Nor, in later studies, were there any significant changes in alcohol intake over 6-month periods (Fitz-Gerald and Fox, unpublished data).

Analyses of behavioral observations in the earlier studies indicated that gross physical indices of intoxication, for example, locomotor ataxia, did not appear until the adult chimpanzee had ingested at least 15 oz of 40% alcohol and the juvenile chimpanzee, 10 oz. Such amounts are somewhat greater than those required to produce ataxia in nonhabituated human beings of comparable weight. Using Widmark's (Newman, 1941) formula with the constant factor derived for man, *theoretical* maximum blood alcohol concentrations were calculated for those chimpanzees who consumed large amounts of alcohol in short periods of time. A number of the determinations were well within the lethal range for human beings (Fitz-Gerald and Fox, unpublished data).

These observations, taken together with the fact that none of the intoxicated animals in these studies became unconscious, suggested that there might be some fundamental difference between man and the chimpanzee in the manner in which alcohol is absorbed and distributed. In reference to this point, Lester (1968) raised the question of the association of body weight and rate of alcohol metabolism. Lester proposed that in order to maintain a given level of blood alcohol in an animal smaller than man, alcohol ingestion must occur at a rate inversely proportional to the animal's weight. Thus, he concluded that the nonhuman primate requires alcohol intake at a higher level than does man. While more work must be done on the problem of alcohol metabolism in the chimpanzee, Lester's conclusion appears to have been confirmed in these experiments and in later ones.

EFFECTS OF ALCOHOL CONSUMPTION IN APES

In the investigations reviewed below, a number of parameters were studied in order to delineate similarities and differences between man and the chimpanzee with respect to physiological and behavioral responses to alcohol ingestion.

Physiological Variables

The purpose of this group of studies was to collect controlled, physiological data that could be compared with established clinical observations of human beings. The data included the results of physical examinations, biochemical investigations, and evaluations of physical symptomotology which appeared similar to syndromes accompanying high levels of alcohol consumption and subsequent withdrawal in man.

The subjects were eight adult chimpanzees, ranging in age from 12 to 40 years and in weight, from 38.6 to 71.0 kg, or 85 to 156 lb. They were selected on the basis of their consistently high alcohol intake in the studies described above (Fitz-Gerald et al., 1968). The size of the sample was too small to warrant valid conclusions concerning the influence of genetic variables, but it was noted that the subject population included a mother and son, a half-brother and half-sister, and the brother's son by the sister's mother. The data were collected before, at the same time as, and after the subjects were involved in various behavioral experiments performed under placebo and alcohol conditions (Fitz-Gerald and Fox, unpublished data). The animals were not anesthetized on the same day that they were given alcohol. The two dose levels of alcohol used were the equivalents of 2 and 3 g/kg of absolute alcohol. In the experimental procedures, vodka (40% alcohol) was mixed with fruit juice to a 10–14% solution and administered on an empty stomach. Consumption by the chimpanzees was voluntary, and over a 6-month period each subject was exposed to the placebo 12 times and to alcohol 24 times.

The data are reviewed here in some detail to acquaint the reader with clinical values of chimpanzees and to illustrate the striking similarities between ape and man in their physiological responses to alcohol ingestion.

Cardiovascular System

The ranges of temperature, pulse, respiration, and blood pressure, recorded for the same subjects before and during the time that they were involved in experiments requiring alcohol ingestion, are given in Table 1. The values of the chimpanzees were within the ranges observed in man, with the exception of the blood pressure readings which tended to be consistently higher than those normally obtained in human beings. The recordings in the chimpanzee were made under conditions of stress produced by capture, restraint, and anesthetization prior to examination, which might account for the higher blood pressure readings obtained. While the differences between the before-alcohol and during-alcohol values were not statistically significant, they do lead to speculation, not only as to the mechanisms underlying some of the changes seen in human patients after high levels of alcohol intake, but also as to the significance of these findings for the chimpanzee.

In man, the ingestion of alcohol increases gastric and cutaneous blood flow, producing vasodilation and often, sweating. Following exposure to high levels of alcohol, central temperature-regulating mechanisms become depressed, and decreases in body temperature may become more pronounced (Ritchie, 1965). In the chimpanzee, vasodilation and occasional heavy sweating occurred 30 min after alcohol ingestion and persisted for 12–14 hr. The slight increases in the animals' rectal temperatures observed during periods of alcohol consumption were consistent with these findings.

Early studies of the effects of alcohol upon the cardiovascular system reported that moderate doses of alcohol had little effect upon cardiac output and

TABLE 1. Ranges of Temperature, Pulse, Respiration, and Blood Pressure in Six Adult Chimpanzees Before and During High Levels of Alcohol Consumption

Measures	Before alcohol	During alcohol
Temperature		
Males	97.8–101.0	98.2–100.6°F
Females	96.8– 98.6	98.2– 99.2°F
Pulse		
Males	72–128	100–120
Females	100–108	72–120
Respiration		
Males	16–20	16–24
Females	16–20	20–24
Blood pressure		
Males	158/102–206/160	175/125–210/155
Females	140/ 94–148/110	110/ 64–140/115

that intoxicating dose levels tended to depress cardiac function (Ritchie, 1965). More recent reports, however, have indicated that increased pulse rate and tachycardia follow high alcohol consumption and continue during withdrawal (Isbell et al., 1955; Mendelson and La Dou, 1964). The chimpanzees displayed tachycardia as early as 30 min after ingestion of 3 g/kg of alcohol, and it continued for 10 hr during experimental conditions. Elevated pulse rates were also observed for 24–48 hr after the original administration of alcohol.

Mendelson and La Dou (1964) postulated several mechanisms to account for the increased cardiac rate observed in their subjects which would account equally well for the same phenomenon observed in the chimpanzee. First, alcohol acts directly upon central processes which influence heart rate through vagal activity. Second, alcohol produces vasodilation which might be associated with increased cardiac stroke volume, thus accelerating heart rate. Third, alcohol increases cardiac rate through peripheral stimulation of endocrine mechanisms. Fourth, an interaction of all of these factors might explain the observed increase in heart rate.

The differences between the various respiratory rates were negligible. During experimental situations, however, some changes were observed. Under placebo conditions, there were no changes in respiratory patterns. Under alcohol conditions, there were instances of heavy and irregular respirations, including sighing and hiccups, appearing with increasing frequency from 30 min after ingestion through 3 hr. These observations were comparable to those in early studies which indicated that moderate amounts of alcohol stimulate respiration in man for short periods of time (Hitchcock, 1942).

The differences between the blood pressure readings shown in Table 1 were not significant. Since it was not possible to obtain readings during the experimental procedures, it is not known what effects alcohol has upon blood pressure in the chimpanzee.

Gastrointestinal System

In man, a number of modifications of gastrointestinal function occur during alcohol ingestion. For example, intoxicating dose levels of alcohol markedly reduce motor and secretory activity of the colon (Ritchie, 1965). In accord with this report, it was found that over a 4-hr period, the observed mean frequency of defecation, also related to level of emotional excitation in the chimpanzee, varied from 5% under placebo conditions to 1% under intoxicating levels of alcohol.

Mendelson and La Dou (1964) raised the issue of lack of weight gain by their subjects and contrasted their findings with those of Isbell et al. (1955). The caloric intake in the Isbell study greatly exceeded the amount available in the other study, and Mendelson and La Dou hypothesized that the differences in body weight observed in the two studies might be due to differences between

the number of calories available to support increased metabolic activity stimulated by alcohol consumption. It was suggested that increased metabolic activity
might be inferred from the observed increase in cardiac rate.

The chimpanzees showed a mean weight gain of 5 lb over the 6-month
testing period. The gain was thought to represent the effects of added caloric
intake from the alcohol, fruit juice, and food rewards involved in the behavioral
experiments. There were, however, two sets of apparently contradictory observations which might be reconciled by Mendelson and La Dou's hypothesis.

Alcohol produced anorexia in the chimpanzee insofar as the consumption
of the total daily food ration was markedly reduced. The effect was generally
proportional to the quantity of alcohol consumed and was more pronounced
5 hr after alcohol administration than after 4 hr.

In a concomitant experiment, the effects of alcohol ingestion upon subsequent selection of orange juice, a 10% alcohol solution (vodka and grape juice),
or bananas, were studied in a free choice situation (Fitz-Gerald and Fox,
unpublished data). The 2 g/kg dose level had no influence upon orange juice
selection until 3 hr after administration; at that point, orange juice selection
increased and continued to do so through the fourth hour. Under 3 g/kg of
alcohol, orange juice selection dropped 1 hr after alcohol ingestion and then
increased until the end of the fourth hour. The increases were thought to be
related to diuresis and subsequent thirst, discussed below, and to the chimpanzee's
need for additional calories to support increased metabolic activity subsequent
to alcohol consumption. Additional support for this notion was suggested by the
observations that alcohol ingestion tended to decrease the subsequent selection
of the vodka-grape juice solution. The effects were distinguishable from those of
the placebo for a period of 2–4 hr after the original consumption of alcohol. As
in the case of orange juice selection, the effects tended to be proportional to dose
level. Exposure to alcohol also produced increased selection of bananas. The
effects appeared 30 min after alcohol intake and continued for 4 hr. The levels of
selection under both alcohol conditions followed the placebo levels in that they
peaked from 30 min to 2 hr and then began to return to original levels. Apparently,
in that situation, alcohol did not depress food selection and consumption; it
enhanced it for 2 hr. These observations might be taken as further evidence of
the postulated need for additional caloric intake to support increased metabolic
rate, subsequent to alcohol ingestion, as well as of the associated occurrence of
heightened food consumption secondary to increased gastric stimulation.

Liver

The etiology of fatty liver in human alcohol addiction is not completely
understood. It has been shown that fatty liver can be produced by the ingestion
of alcohol, even in the presence of adequate diet and before the appearance of
any decreases in hepatic lipid release or notable mobilization of peripheral fats.

Thus, Lieber *et al.* (1964) have postulated that the instances of fatty liver observed in human patients addicted to alcohol might be the result of a direct effect of alcohol upon hepatic lipid metabolism, subsequent to a rise in the NADH/NAD ratio produced by oxidation of alcohol in the liver. Thus, they concluded that the increase in this ratio could account for the hyperlipemia, involving glycerides, cholesterol, and phospholipids, demonstrated by spontaneously intoxicated human alcoholics. For a more recent review of lipid metabolism in human alcoholism, see Lieber *et al.* (1971). The rise in serum uric acid levels observed in the same studies was also thought to be due to alcohol intake and subsequent rise in the NADH/NAD ratio. While suggestive of the data reported by Lieber *et al.* (1964), the effects of alcohol ingestion upon serum uric acid levels and upon cholesterol and cholesterol fractions in the chimpanzees, given in Table 2, were not significant after the length and amount of exposure to alcohol provided in those studies.

TABLE 2. Ranges of Blood Chemistry Values of Eight Adult Chimpanzees Before and During High Levels of Alcohol Consumption (mg/100 ml, or as noted)

Constituents	Before alcohol	During alcohol
Electrolytes		
Calcium	9.0–9.9	9.4–9.8
Chloride	98–100	99–100 meq/liter
Phosphorus	1.8–4.3	4.0–4.4
Potassium	2.7–3.7	2.7–3.7 meq/liter
Sodium	140–146	140–143 meq/liter
Transaminases		
SGOT	10–20	21–32 units
SGPT	4–6	6–7 units
Proteins		
Albumin	2.5–3.3	3.3–3.9 g/100 ml
Total	5.9–8.0	7.4–8.4 g/100 ml
Others		
Amylase	38–70	44–68 units
Bilirubin, total	0.1–0.5	0.2–0.6
Cholesterol, fractions	78–193	114–174
Cholesterol, total	176–264	176–225
CO_2	22–28	24–27 meq/liter
Creatinine	0.8–1.5	1.1–1.4
Glucose	46–65	53–68
Potassium-bound iodine	4.2–6.0	4.0–5.3 μg/100 ml
Urea nitrogen	8–27	11–14
Uric acid	2.3–3.5	2.9–3.9

Hepatic function, as measured by the bromsulfalein test, was not significantly altered in the chimpanzees over the experimental period. Adequate liver
function is important for the regulation of serum glucose levels (Alky, 1971).
It has been postulated that ethanol inhibits gluconeogenesis and, when accompanied by decreased hepatic glycogen, results in pronounced hypoglycemia
(Field *et al.*, 1963; Wilson *et al.*, 1962). Mendelson *et al.* (1964b) suggested that this
process might be the result of the reduction of NAD to NADH following metabolism of alcohol by the liver. They did find, however, that in instances of
adequate diet, chronic ingestion of large quantities of alcohol did not produce
significant hypoglycemia in human alcoholics. The glucose tolerance values of
the chimpanzees did not differ significantly between the before-alcohol and
during-alcohol conditions. The during-alcohol values were slightly lower but
did not reach hypoglycemic levels.

In summarizing the evidence concerning direct hepatotoxic actions of
ethyl alcohol, Kalant (1961) mentioned that Bang *et al.* (1958, 1959) found that a
moderate dose of alcohol administered to alcoholics within a few days of hospitalization produced a pronounced increase in serum transaminases, probably
through leakage of these enzymes from hepatic cells into the blood. After two or
more weeks of good nutrition, the same patients did not manifest such increases
at the same dose level. It was concluded that moderate amounts of alcohol in
healthy, well-nourished individuals are not hepatotoxic. It is difficult, however,
to interpret transaminase activity measured during and immediately following
acute intoxication in patients known to have had repeated periods of heavy
exposure to alcohol. It has been found, for example, that SGOT values were
extremely variable in a series of patients hospitalized for detoxification. They
were evaluated at admission and 3 days later. Some patients displayed high
SGOT levels upon admission with subsequent decreases; an equal number
showed low levels with subsequent increases. A number of the same patients
were reevaluated upon subsequent readmissions under similar circumstances, and
normal or opposite values were found (Fitz-Gerald and Fox, unpublished data).

The chimpanzees were apparently well nourished, but they did show
increases in SGOT and SGPT levels following alcohol consumption, as given in
Table 2. This was taken as an indication that high dose levels of alcohol did
produce this rise along with slight, if transitory, alterations in hepatic function.
Additional evidence of this appeared in the changes in total bilirubin values.
While not pathological, it was suggested that these changes might also be taken
as indices of altered function in the chimpanzee referent to the ingestion of large
amounts of alcohol.

Kidney

It is common knowledge that alcohol consumption frequently produces
diuresis. Even though the large volume of fluids usually ingested along with

alcohol contributes to diuresis, alcohol itself has been shown to produce a marked diuretic effect, persisting for approximately 2–4 hr after administration in man (Haggard et al., 1941). Later studies have demonstrated that alcohol inhibits the release of antidiuretic hormone from the posterior pituitary or from the locus of its synthesis at the supraoptic nucleus of the hypothalamus (Beard, 1971; Kleeman et al., 1955; Rubini et al., 1955). In the chimpanzee, diuresis occurred over approximately the same time course as that observed in man, and its incidence tended to be proportional to the amount of alcohol consumed.

Patients undergoing treatment for alcohol withdrawal syndromes often display transient proteinuria, glycosuria, and ketonuria not associated with urinary tract infections, diabetes, or liver impairment. Mendelson and La Dou (1964) suggested that glomerular filtration might be affected when blood alcohol levels are high and postulated that high dose levels might have a direct nephrotoxic effect in man. Chimpanzees ingesting large quantities of alcohol also displayed proteinuria, glycosuria, and ketonuria, as shown in Table 3. Serum albumin and total protein levels were higher in the during-alcohol conditions than in the before-alcohol conditions, as shown in Table 2. Thus it is possible that alcohol may have some nephrotoxic effect in the chimpanzee as well as in man.

TABLE 3. Ranges of Urine Values in Six Adult Chimpanzees Before and During High Levels of Alcohol Consumption

Measures	Before alcohol	During alcohol
Specific gravity	1.005–1.006	1.003–1.010
pH	7.0–8.5	7.5–9.5
Sugar	0	0–1[a]
Ketones	0	0–1[b]
Protein	0–100[a]	0–200 mg[c]

[a] 33% of the subjects.
[b] 17% of the subjects.
[c] 67% of the subjects.

Mendelson and La Dou indicated that their observations of glycosuria were the first reported during experimental administrations of alcohol to human subjects. This was also seen in 33% of the chimpanzees involved in the experiments reviewed here. The ketonuria observed by Mendelson and La Dou was thought to be an effect of decreased caloric intake and/or dehydration. Since caloric intake was considered to be adequate in the chimpanzees, it is possible that the one instance of ketonuria observed among the animals might be attributed to dehydration. Taking account of the data mentioned above concerning orange juice selection, and observations of voluntary water consumption, the evidence for dehydration was not strong. Comparison of the time courses of diuresis, orange juice selection, and water consumption indicated that the chimpanzees made some attempt to compensate for diuresis through increased fluid intake. That this compensation was reasonably effective was inferred from the evidence regarding serum electrolyte values, given in Table 2; there were no significant differences between before-alcohol and during-alcohol levels. The possibility of some dehydration, however, was suggested by the slight decreases in serum urea nitrogen values after alcohol ingestion, as well as by slight increases in hematocrit and sedimentation rates, shown in Table 4, and in the MCV, MCH, MCHC, and volume indices given in Table 5.

TABLE 4. Ranges of Hematocrit, Hemoglobin, and Sedimentation Rate in Eight Adult Chimpanzees Before and During High Levels of Alcohol Consumption

Measures	Before alcohol	During alcohol
Hematocrit		
Males	46–51	46–56%
Females	38–41	41%
Hemoglobin		
Males	14–16	14–17 g%
Females	12–13	13–14 g%
Sedimentation rate		
Males	0–3	11–26 mm/hr
Females	12	18 mm/hr

Usually, acute ingestion of large amounts of alcohol in man produces an acid pH in the urine. Mendelson and La Dou (1964) reported increased alkalinity and suggested that it might be a unique consequence of chronic alcohol consumption. As shown in Table 3, this phenomenon also occurred in the chimpanzee. This might be taken as a further indication that these chimpanzees were subject to changes secondary to prolonged exposure to alcohol which are comparable to changes seen in man.

Blood

The ranges of hematocrit and hemoglobin were within the normal limits for man, and there was no evidence of anemia in the chimpanzees over the 6-month period of exposure to alcohol. The values of the blood counts of the chimpanzees were also within the normal ranges reported for human beings, with the exception of the leukocyte counts. The high leukocyte counts were thought to be the consequence of a combination of factors, including a nonspecific stress syndrome

TABLE 5. Ranges of Blood Counts in Six Adult Chimpanzees Before and During High Levels of Alcohol Consumption

Blood counts	Before alcohol	During alcohol
Erythrocytes		
Males	5.6–6.0	5.7–6.4×10^6
Females	4.7–5.3	4.5–5.0×10^6
MCV	77–83	82–90 cuμ
MCH	25–26	28–29 μmcg
MCHC	31–32	32–35%
Volume indices	0.89–0.95	0.95–1.04%
Reticulocytes	0–0.5	0.1–0.6
Leukocytes		
Total	7400–15,800	4800–16,200
Myelocytes	0	0
Juvenile neutrophils	0	0
Band neutrophils	0–200	0
Segmented neutrophils	5500–8600	4100–9000
Lymphocytes	1200–4000	800–5700
Eosinophils	0–600	0–300
Basophils	0	0
Monocytes	0–400	0–300
Platelets	202,000–258,000	202,000–312,000

related to the capture, restraint, and anesthetization of the chimpanzees prior to blood collection. The even higher leukocyte counts obtained after exposure to alcohol might be a reflection of those factors plus some aspect of an adrenocortical stress syndrome similar to that displayed by man under conditions of acute alcoholic intoxication (Smith, 1949).

There were no appreciable differences between the before-alcohol and during-alcohol levels of serum amylase, CO_2, or creatinine, as shown in Table 2. The slightly lower potassium-bound iodine values in the during-alcohol conditions were not pathological, but they were suggestive of postulated associations between hypothyroidism and high alcohol intake (Goldberg, 1962).

Central Nervous System

In man, the central nervous system (CNS) is more profoundly affected by alcohol than any other system. Alcohol acts as a primary and progressive depressant of the CNS. Electrophysiological investigations have indicated that alcohol, like other general CNS depressants, exerts its first effects upon the midbrain reticular activating system. As this system is depressed, the cerebral cortex, via the ascending and descending reticular activity systems, is selectively and progressively released from integrating control, and cognitive organization and sensory and motor processes become disrupted.

In view of the increasing experimental evidence implicating the reticular activating system in interpretations of the effects of alcohol upon physiology and behavior (Gross *et al.*, 1966; Horsey and Akert, 1953; Moskowitz, 1967; Van Laer *et al.*, 1965; Weiss *et al.*, 1964a,b), it is helpful to have a general concept of the nature of this system.

It has been established that sensory input to the cerebral cortex, from the classical sensory pathways alone, produces relatively little effect in the way of evoking appropriate responses from the organism. When, however, sensory input occurs normally, various parts of the ascending reticular activating system are also stimulated, via afferent collateral projections from the main sensory tracts, and appropriate responses are evoked. Thus, the reticular activating system functions as an arousal mechanism, selectively activating and inhibiting specific processes in the cerebral cortex and in the centers in the thalamus and hypothalamus that regulate autonomic functions and other components of physiological and psychological responses to stimuli (Brazier, 1954; Moruzzi and Magoun, 1949; Killam, 1962).

Various studies (Moruzzi, 1963) have demonstrated several anatomically and functionally distinct components of the reticular system. There are, for example, at least two mutually antagonistic structures. The first, in the mesencephalic tegmentum, produces a desynchronizing effect upon activity of higher structures and is postulated to be responsible for the high-frequency cortical activity characteristic of the waking EEG. The second, in the medulla and neurons of the solitary tract, produces a tonic, synchronizing effect upon the EEG. There is evidence that the two systems are reciprocally related, the medullary synchronizing activity being produced during arousal and operating as a negative feedback circuit to reduce the activating effects of midbrain structures (Bonvallet and Bloch, 1961; Dell *et al.*, 1960; Magni *et al.*, 1961). Sharpless (1965) used this evidence to help account for instances of high-frequency cortical activity observed during the induction of barbiturate anesthesia. He speculated that in such a feedback system, the effects of a small dose of a CNS depressant could produce either synchrony or asynchrony of the EEG relevant to the quantitative relations between the two systems.

Kalant (1962) reviewed Caspers' (1958) work which provided important data on the reticular system. Using microelectrode implantation techniques in the conscious, unanesthetized rat, the effects of alcohol in doses ranging from 0.5 to 12 g/kg were studied. It was found that alcohol produced an immediate decrease in spontaneous activity in the reticular formation which became more pronounced with increasing blood alcohol levels. The degree of inhibition of reticular activity appeared to be a function of the height of the blood alcohol peak and the rate of increase of blood alcohol level. As activity in the reticular formation was depressed, there was a corresponding increase in the amplitude of electrocortical activity, with a marked trend toward synchrony, of the convulsive seizure class. Cortical activity and hyperexcitability dropped to sub-waking levels only after very high blood alcohol levels had been reached. Similar findings in rabbits have been recently reported by Kakolewski and Himwich (1968).

In another study, McQuarrie and Fingl (1958) found that alcohol, administered in doses high enough to produce cortical depression in the rat, evoked a period of cortical hyperexcitability and seizure susceptibility when the effects of the alcohol dosage were dissipated. The degree of hyperexcitability was related to dose level and to duration of exposure to alcohol. Following single exposures, the period of hyperexcitability ranged from 4 to 8 hr. Following thrice-daily exposures for 2 weeks and abrupt withdrawal, the period of hyperexcitability was more prolonged, peaking at 2 days and reaching normal at 8 days. Kalant (1962) drew the parallel between these observations and withdrawal phenomena seen in man. He also suggested that the electrophysiological data were indicative of the physiological nature of alcohol addiction, to the extent that the magnitude of the effects was related to the level and duration of exposure to alcohol. Reviews of recent research concerning the effects of alcohol upon various aspects of the CNS and ANS and their activity are presented by Begleiter and Platz (Chapter 10), Grenell (Chapter 1), Himwich and Callison (Chapter 3), Naitoh (Chapter 12), St. Laurent (Chapter 4), and Williams and Salamy (Chapter 13) in this volume.

In summary, the primary effect of alcohol upon the CNS is progressive depression ascending from the midbrain reticular activating system through the cerebral cortex and spreading through other processes, including thalamic and hypothalamic systems. Paradoxical stimulatory effects are thought to be consequences of disinhibition of normally inhibitory processes. Physical symptomatology referent to the action of alcohol upon the human CNS includes such phenomena as pupillary dilation, lateral nystagmus, tremor, impaired coordination, locomotor ataxia, behavioral hyperexcitability and hyperactivity, stupor, and sleep. The same phenomena appeared in the chimpanzee subsequent to alcohol ingestion.

In accord with observations of human beings (Goldberg, 1961), pupillary dilation and lateral nystagmus were observed during the periods that the chimpanzees consumed large quantities of alcohol and during withdrawal; the effects appeared 2 hr after alcohol ingestion and were still present 14 hr later.

Tremor has long been considered a significant symptom of withdrawal from alcohol. Mendelson and La Dou (1964), however, found that tremor also appeared during periods of high consumption without any other signs of withdrawal. Occasionally, fine and coarse tremors appeared in the chimpanzee at intervals of 1–3 hr after alcohol ingestion, as well as during withdrawal. This occurrence might be explained in part by the disinhibitory effects of alcohol upon cortical integrating processes through its preliminary effects upon reciprocal feedback mechanisms in the reticular activating system. Increases in cortical excitability that have been observed to occur before and after maximum reticular and cortical depression by alcohol might account for the tremor, hyperexcitability, and hyperactive behavior observed in the chimpanzee during early stages of intoxication and during subsequent withdrawal.

High dose levels of alcohol produced impairments in coordination 30 min after ingestion, and these effects continued for as long as 14 hr. Comparisons of the data presented in Table 6 indicate that locomotor ataxia followed the time course of impaired coordination closely. The primary difference was that levels of ataxia dropped more quickly and lasted for shorter periods of time, usually 30 min to 10 hr, but occasionally as long as 14 hr.

TABLE 6. Mean Percent Incidence of Locomotor Ataxia, Impaired Coordination, Stupor, and Sleep in Eight Adult Chimpanzees at Various Intervals After Alcohol Ingestion

Behavior	Minutes					
	0	30	60	120	180	240
Impaired coordination						
2 g/kg	7	8	17	18	16	14
3 g/kg	10	25	32	45	36	35
Locomotor ataxia						
2 g/kg	11	11	23	18	17	5
3 g/kg	17	22	35	45	29	20
Stupor and sleep						
2 g/kg	5	3	34	25	15	2
3 g/kg	10	15	35	18	26	8

A further indication of the depressant action of alcohol upon the CNS of the chimpanzee is given in Table 6, showing the incidence of alcohol-induced stupor and sleep. As in the case of impaired coordination and ataxia, the effects were generally proportional to the amount of alcohol ingested. The pattern for the higher dose level was, however, bimodal, with peaks at 1 and 3 hr after alcohol consumption. It was suggested that this disparity was a reflection of individual differences among the animals in their responses to alcohol ingestion; some of the chimpanzees responded initially with stupor and sleep, while others responded first with restlessness, hyperexcitability, and hyperactivity, including increased play, sexual, and aggressive behavior. From periods of 5–14 hr after alcohol administration, there were occasional instances of behavioral depression, stupor, and sleep, but the subjects more consistently displayed restlessness, irritability, hyperreflexia, hyperexcitability, and hyperactivity reminiscent of clinical observations of psychomotor agitation in human patients undergoing treatment for withdrawal symptomatology.

Behavioral Variables

At the time of writing, there exists a considerable amount of research concerning the effects of alcohol upon behavioral variables in the chimpanzee; the data have been collected but not yet completely analyzed and interpreted (Fitz-Gerald and Fox, unpublished data). They are mentioned here briefly in order to give the reader some knowledge of the scope of what has already been done and to provide a referent point for further discussion and research.

The purpose of these studies was to investigate the behavioral time courses of action and the effects of different dose levels of alcohol upon performance of objective tasks designed to measure various parameters of behavior and upon individual and social responses of the chimpanzee. The behavioral parameters included attention, visual perception, coordination, and motivation, and involved studies of delayed response, visual acuity, locomotor and perceptual-motor coordination, manual dexterity, frustration tolerance, energy expenditure, and choice-preferences of reinforcement. The investigations of individual and social patterns included observations of general activity levels, stereotyped and self-directed behavior, and social and environmentally directed responses.

The effects of alcohol upon behavioral responses generally began to appear about 30 min after ingestion and usually lasted throughout the 4-hr experimental periods. It is worth noting that shorter time courses of action occurred only at the lower dose level of alcohol, 2 g/kg, which lends further support to the notion that effects upon the CNS are generally proportional to blood alcohol levels and are more pronounced when the concentration is rising than when it is stable or falling (Mellanby, 1919; Mirsky et al., 1941).

At the lower dose level, the maximum effects of alcohol upon behavior generally occurred 1 hr after ingestion. This point in time corresponds to the maximum incidence of stupor and sleep observed at this dose level, and presumably to maximum CNS depression as far as could be inferred from behavioral observations. This time course also corresponds to that seen in man where the peak of blood alcohol concentration occurred approximately 1 hr after onset of drinking (Forney et al., 1963; Pihkanen, 1957). At the higher dose level, 3 g/kg, the maximum effects upon behavior of the chimpanzee also appeared 1 hr after alcohol ingestion, except in a few instances where they occurred at the third hour. These times also correspond to the maximum incidences of stupor and sleep seen at this dose level.

Increasing dose levels of alcohol tended to increase response latencies and durations of task-performance periods. Higher levels of alcohol consumption produced marked impairments in efficiency and correctness of response as well as in locomotor and perceptual-motor coordination. Attention, perception, and motivation were disrupted by high dose levels, and general activity levels were often greatly reduced. In a number of instances, the chimpanzee spent much of the time in a passive or reclining position, and occasionally despite consciousness, refused to participate in experimental procedures.

In general, the magnitude of the depressant effects of alcohol upon stereotyped and self-directed behavior and upon social and environmentally directed responses tended to be proportionally related to the amount of alcohol ingested and to the length of time elapsed from the original administration. Thus, the results of these studies indicated that the general patterns of the chimpanzee's behavioral responses to alcohol ingestion appeared to be similar to those observed in man under comparable circumstances (Mendelson et al., 1964a; Talland et al., 1964a,b).

OVERVIEW

It is now clear that many chimpanzees do ingest alcohol voluntarily, some display symptoms of intoxication, and their responses seem comparable to those observed in man. It also appears that chimpanzees are able to handle larger quantities of alcohol more efficiently than can nonhabituated human beings of comparable size.

Lester (1968) has called attention to one serious omission in alcohol research involving nonhuman primates. That is the lack of measurement of the concentration of circulating blood alcohol, which would provide an objective pharmacological criterion for the evaluation of the animal's responses to alcohol ingestion. This was also true of the studies reviewed here; Fitz-Gerald and Fox found that it was impossible to collect blood specimens or samples of rebreathed air from unanesthetized, unrestrained adult chimpanzees. Thus, inferences regarding the effects of alcohol upon the chimpanzee must be limited to clinical judgments of overt physical symptomatology and to the results of objective physiological, biochemical, and behavioral investigations.

The results of the experiments reviewed here not only illustrated and confirmed the marked biological parallels between the chimpanzee and man, but they also demonstrated the striking similarities between the two species in their physiological and behavioral responses to alcohol ingestion. While many of the functional mechanisms underlying these responses have not been studied directly in man or in the chimpanzee, Fitz-Gerald and Fox inferred from their data that the mechanisms are highly similar, if not identical, to those postulated to be responsible for the responses seen in man.

It remains to be seen whether or not the chimpanzee is capable of acquiring an addiction to alcohol. In view of the evidence to date, it appears that the chimpanzee is the one nonhuman organism that presents a reasonable potential for acquiring such an addiction. The available evidence also indicates that studies of alcohol consumption in the chimpanzee provide the most comprehensive experimental model available for the elucidation of parameters involved in human alcoholism.

ACKNOWLEDGMENT

Work on unpublished research described in this paper was carried out at the Yerkes Laboratories of Primate Biology, Orange Park, Florida, and the Yerkes Regional Primate Research Center, Emory University, Atlanta, Georgia. The projects were supported in part through Grants FR-00165, FR-05235, II-5691, and MII-12090, from the National Institutes of Health. I wish to thank Drs. V. Fox and N. B. Guilloud and Miss P. A. Grubbs for their assistance.

REFERENCES

Arky, R. A., 1971. The effect of alcohol on glucose metabolism: Carbohydrate metabolism in alcoholics, in *The Biology of Alcoholism* (B. Kissin and H. Begleiter, eds.), Vol. 1, *Biochemistry*, Plenum Press, New York.

Bang, N. V., Iversen, K., Jagt, T., and Madsen, S., 1958. Serum glutamic oxalacetic transaminase activity in acute and chronic alcoholism, *J. Amer. Med. Assoc.* **168**: 156.

Beard, J., 1971. Water and electrolyte metabolism, in *The Biology of Alcoholism* (B. Kissin and H. Begleiter, eds.) Vol. I, *Biochemistry*, Plenum Press, New York.

Bonvallet, M. and Bloch, V., 1961. Bulbar control of cortical arousal, *Science* **133**: 1133.

Brazier, M. A. B., 1954. The action of anesthetics on the nervous system, in *C.I.O.M.S. Symposium on Brain Mechanisms and Consciousness* (E. D. Adrian, F. Bremer, and H. Jasper, eds.) pp. 163–199, Charles C. Thomas, Springfield, Ill.

Carpenter, J. A., 1962. Effects of alcohol upon some psychological processes; a critical review with special reference to automobile driving skill, *Quart. J. Stud. Alc.* **23**: 274.

Caspers, H., 1958. Die Beeinflussung der corticalen Krampferregbarkeit durch das aufsteigende Retikulärsystem des Hirnstammes. II. Narkosewirkungen, *Z. Ges. Exp. Med.* **129**: 582.

Clay, M., 1964. Conditions affecting voluntary alcohol consumption in rats, *Quart. J. Stud. Alc.* **25**: 36.

Dell, P., Bonvallet, M., and Hugelin, A., 1960. in *The Nature of Sleep* (A Ciba Foundation Symposium) (G. E. W. Wolstenholm and M. O'Connor, eds.) pp. 86–102, Little, Brown, Boston.

Field, J. B., Williams, H. E., and Mortimore, G. E., 1963. Studies on the mechanism of ethanol-induced hypoglycemia, *J. Clin. Invest.* **42**: 497.

Fitz-Gerald, F. L., 1964. Effects of drugs upon stereotyped behavior in isolation-reared chimpanzees, paper read at American Association for Advancement of Science, Montreal, Canada.

Fitz-Gerald, F. L., 1967a. Alcohol consumption in apes, paper read at International Institute on the Prevention and Treatment of Alcoholism, Zagreb, Yugoslavia.

Fitz-Gerald, F. L., 1967b. Effects of *d*-amphetamine upon behavior of young chimpanzees reared under different conditions, in *Neuropsychopharmacology* (H. Brill, J. O. Cole, P. Deniker, H. Hippius, and P. B. Bradley, eds.) pp. 1226–1227, Exerpta Medica Foundation, New York.

Fitz-Gerald, F. L. and Fox, V. unpublished data.

Fitz-Gerald, F. L., Barfield, M. A., and Warrington, R. J., 1968. Voluntary alcohol consumption in chimpanzees and orangutans, *Quart. J. Stud. Alc.* **29**: 330.

Forney, R. B., Hughes, F. W., Harger, R. N. and Richards, A. B., 1963. Alcohol distribution in the vascular system, *Quart. J. Stud. Alc.* **24**: 205.

French, S. W., 1971. Acute and chronic toxicity of alcohol, in *The Biology of Alcoholism* (B. Kissin and H. Begleiter, eds.) Vol. 1, *Biochemistry*, Plenum Press, New York.

Goldberg, L., 1943. Quantitative studies on alcohol tolerance in man; the influence of ethyl alcohol on sensory, motor and psychological functions referred to blood alcohol in normal and habituated individuals, *Acta. Physiol. Scand.*, Suppl. 16, **5**: 1–128.

Goldberg, L., 1961. Alcohol, tranquilizers and hangover, *Quart. J. Stud. Alc.*, Suppl. 1, 37–56.

Goldberg, M., 1962. Thyroid impairment in chronic alcoholics, *Amer. J. Psychiat.* **119**: 255.

Gross, M. M., Begleiter, H., Tobin, M., and Kissen, M., 1966. Changes in auditory evoked response induced by alcohol, *J. Nerv. Ment. Dis.* **143**: 152.

Haggard, H. W., Greenberg, L. A., and Carroll, R. P., 1941. Studies in the adsorption, distribution, and elimination of alcohol. VIII. The diuresis from alcohol and its influence on the elimination of alcohol in the urine, *J. Pharmac. Exp. Ther.* **71**: 348.

Hitchcock, F. A., 1942. Alteration in respiration caused by alcohol, *Quart. J. Stud. Alc.* **2**: 641.

Horsey, W. J. and Akert, K., 1953. The influence of ethyl alcohol on the spontaneous electrical activity of the cerebral cortex and subcortical structures of the cat, *Quart. J. Stud. Alc.* **14**: 363.

Isbell, H., Fraser, H. F., Wikler, A., Belleville, R. E., and Eisenman, A. J., 1955. An experimental study of the etiology of "rum fits" and delirium tremens, *Quart. J. Stud. Alc.* **16**: 1.

Kalant, H., 1961. The pharmacology of alcohol intoxication, *Quart. J. Stud. Alc.*, Suppl. 1, 1–23.

Kalant, H., 1962. Some recent physiological and biochemical investigations on alcohol and alcoholism, *Quart. J. Stud. Alc.* **23**: 52.

Kakolewski, J. W. and Himwich, H. E., 1968. Effects of ethanol on EEG and blood pressure in the rabbit, *Quart. J. Stud. Alc.* **29**: 290.

Killam, E. K., 1962. Drug action on the brain-stem reticular formation, *Pharmac. Rev.* **14**: 175.

Kleeman, C. R., Rubini, M. E., Lamdin, E., and Epstein, F. H., 1955. Studies on alcohol diuresis. II. The evaluation of ethyl alcohol as an inhibitor of the neurohypophysis, *J. Clin. Invest.* **34**: 448.

Lester, D., 1966. Self-selection of alcohol by animals, human variation, and the etiology of alcoholism, *Quart. J. Stud. Alc.* **27**: 395.

Lester, D., 1968. Nonhuman primates in research on the problem of alcohol, in *Use of Nonhuman Primates in Drug Evaluation* (H. Vagtborg, ed.) pp. 249–261, Univ. Texas Press, Austin.

Lieber, C. S., Mendelson, J. H., and Decarli, L. M., 1964. Experimentally induced chronic intoxication and withdrawal in alcoholics. Pt. 8. Serum lipids and uric acid, *Quart. J. Stud. Alc.*, Suppl. 2, 100–107.

Lieber, C., Rubin, E., and DeCarli, L. M., 1971. Effects of ethanol on lipid, uric acid, intermediary, and drug metabolism, including the pathogenesis of the alcoholic fatty liver, in *The Biology of Alcoholism* (B. Kissin and H. Begleiter, eds.) Vol. 1, *Biochemistry*, Plenum Press, New York.

Madsen, S., Bang, N., Iversen, K., and Jagt, T., 1959. The influence of diet on the serum glutamic oxalacetic transaminase in acute intoxication of chronic alcoholics, *Dan. Med. Bull.* **6:** 33.

Magni, F., Moruzzi, G., Rossi, G. F., and Zanchetti, A., 1961. EEG arousal following inactivation of the lower brain stem by selective injection of barbiturate into the vertebral circulation, *Archs. Ital. Biol.* **99:** 33.

Malmo, R. B., 1965. Personal communication.

McQuarrie, D. G. and Fingl, E., 1958. Effects of single doses and chronic administration of ethanol on experimental seizures in mice, *J. Pharmacol.* **124:** 264.

Mellanby, E., 1919. Alcohol: Its absorption into and disappearance from the blood stream under different conditions, (Gt. Brit., Medical Research Council, Special Report Series No. 31.) H. M. Stat. Off., London.

Mendelson, J. H., 1964. Experimentally induced chronic intoxication and withdrawal in alcoholics. Pt. 10. Conclusions and implications, *Quart. J. Stud. Alc.*, Suppl. 2, 117–126.

Mendelson, J. H., 1971. Biochemical mechanisms of alcohol addiction, in *The Biology of Alcoholism* (B. Kissin and H. Begleiter, eds.) Vol. 1, *Biochemistry*, Plenum Press, New York.

Mendelson, J. H. and La Dou, J., 1964. Experimentally induced chronic intoxication and withdrawal in alcoholics. Pt. 2. Psychophysiological findings, *Quart. J. Stud. Alc.*, Suppl. 2, 14–39.

Mendelson, J. H., La Dou, J., and Solomon, P., 1964a. Experimentally induced chronic intoxication and withdrawal in alcoholics. Pt. 3. Psychiatric findings, *Quart. J. Stud. Alc.*, Suppl. 2, 40–52.

Mendelson, J. H., La Dou, J., and Corbett, C., 1964b. Experimentally induced chronic intoxication and withdrawal in alcoholics. Pt. 9. Serum magnesium and glucose, *Quart. J. Stud. Alc.*, Suppl. 2, 108–116.

Mirsky, I. A., Piker, P., Rosenbaum, M., and Lederer, H., 1941. Adaptation of the central nervous system to varying concentrations of alcohol in the blood, *Quart. J. Stud. Alc.* **2:** 35.

Moruzzi, G., 1963. Active processes in the brain stem during sleep, *Harvey Lect.* **58:** 233.

Moruzzi, G. and Magoun, H. W., 1949. Brain stem reticular formation and activation of the EEG, *Electroenceph. Clin. Neurophysiol.* **1:** 455.

Moskowitz, H., 1967. The effects of alcohol upon the differential brightness threshold in rats, *Psychopharmacologia* **10:** 354.

Newman, H. W., 1941. "Acute Alcoholic Intoxication: A Critical Review", Stanford Univ. Press, Stanford, Calif.

Pihkanen, T., 1957. On static atactic functional disorders caused by alcohol. A comparative study of different beverages, *Quart. J. Stud. Alc.* **18:** 183.

Ritchie, J. M., 1965. The aliphatic alcohols, in *The Pharmacological Basis of Therapeutics* (L. S. Goodman and A. Gilman, eds.) pp. 143–158, Macmillan, New York.

Rogers, C. M., 1964. Personal communication.

Rubini, M. E., Kleeman, C. R., and Lamdin, E., 1955. Studies on alcohol diuresis. I. The effect of ethyl alcohol ingestion on water, electrolyte and acid-base metabolism, *J. Clin. Invest.* **34**: 439.

Sharpless, S. K., 1965. The barbiturates, in *The Pharmacological Basis of Therapeutics* (L. S. Goodman and A. Gilman, eds.) pp. 105–128, Macmillan, New York.

Smith, J. J., 1949. A medical approach to problem drinking. Preliminary report, Quart. *J. Stud. Alc.* **10**: 251.

Spragg, S. D. S., 1940. Morphine addiction in chimpanzees, *Comp. Psychol. Monogr.* **15**: 1–132.

Talland, G. A., Mendelson, J. H., and Ryack, P., 1964a. Experimentally induced chronic intoxication and withdrawal in alcoholics. Pt. 4. Tests of motor skills, *Quart J. Stud. Alc.*, Suppl. 2, 53–73.

Talland, G. A., Mendelson, J. H., and Ryack, P., 1964b. Experimentally induced chronic intoxication and withdrawal in alcoholics. Pt. 5. Tests of attention, *Quart. J. Stud. Alc.*, Suppl. 2, 74–86.

Van Laer, E. K., Jarvik, M. E., and Van Laer, J., 1965. Effects of ethyl alcohol on retention in a delayed-response test, *Quart. J. Stud. Alc.* **26**: 384.

Weiss, A. D., Victor, M., Mendelson, J. H., and La Dou, J., 1964a. Experimentally induced chronic intoxication and withdrawal in alcoholics. Pt. 6. Critical flicker fusion studies, *Quart. J. Stud. Alc.*, Suppl. 2, 87–95.

Weiss, A. D., Victor, M., Mendelson, J. H., and La Dou, J., 1964b. Experimentally induced chronic intoxication and withdrawal in alcoholics. Pt. 7. Electroencephalographic findings, *Quart. J. Stud. Alc.*, Suppl. 2, 96–99.

Wilson, J. E., Clark, W. C., and Hulpieu, H. R., 1962. Ethanol induced hypoglycemia in oxythiamine treated animals, *J. Pharmacol.* **137**: 179.

CHAPTER 8

State-Dependent Learning Produced by Alcohol and Its Relevance to Alcoholism

Donald A. Overton

Department of Psychiatry
Temple Medical Center and
Eastern Pennsylvania Psychiatric Institute
Philadelphia, Pennsylvania

INTRODUCTION

A behavior learned while an animal is drugged sometimes fails to appear during subsequent nondrug test trials, although it appears reliably whenever the drug is readministered. Conversely, if the same behavior is learned when the animal is not drugged, it may then be performed only as long as the animal remains undrugged. For some reason, the ability to perform appears to be conditional upon the drug conditions present during initial acquisition (Overton, 1964). Experimental workers generally refer to this surprising phenomenon as "dissociated" learning or as "state dependent" learning. Clinically trained readers may find it convenient to think of the drug as inducing a sort of temporary "fugue" state separated from the nondrug state by a partial or complete amnesic barrier.

Although no direct relationship between state-dependent learning and alcoholism has yet been demonstrated, there are two reasons for including a chapter on dissociated learning in this volume. First, alcohol apparently produces dissociation in humans, and this has at least forensic significance. Second, there is virtually a one-to-one correspondence between the drugs which produce dissociation and those which are subject to abuse. This correlation suggests that state dependency may play a causal role in the addictive process, a possibility which remains to be investigated.

AVAILABLE INFORMATION

Our current knowledge about dissociated learning is derived from both human and animal studies. The animal studies have been more thorough. A variety of drugs produce the phenomenon, and these have been compared and contrasted. Several conclusions about the parametric properties of dissociated learning can be drawn from animal experiments performed with alcohol or with closely related drugs. By inference, dissociated learning in man will probably have similar properties, although this remains to be tested.

Most human studies to date have used alcohol. They appear to demonstrate that dissociation occurs in man under some conditions. A limited variety of learning tasks has been used, and the results suggest that the degree of dissociation varies according to the nature of the learning task. However, the data are too sparse and unreliable to allow any very confident statements about the relative amount of dissociation in any specific task. No parametric data have yet been reported concerning the relative amount of dissociation produced in man by different drugs or by various doses of alcohol.

Although our main interest is in the dissociative effects of alcohol in man, they will be discussed last. A better understanding of the phenomenon can be obtained by first outlining the experimental procedures used to study dissociation. Then, we will describe the properties of the phenomenon which have been demonstrated in animals. Finally, we will summarize and discuss the significance of the results of studies in man.

EXPERIMENTAL PROCEDURES

Two basic procedures are used to study the dissociative effects of drugs. We shall call these transfer procedures and drug-discrimination procedures.

Transfer procedures directly measure the degree to which the effects of learning in one drug state (which may be the nondrug state) can affect performance in a second drug state. For example, one may train a group of subjects while they are drugged (D), and on the following day test half of them for retention in the nondrug condition (N), while testing the other half with the drug condition reestablished. If dissociation is complete, only the second group will show evidence of their previous training during the test session. The first group will behave as if they had never been trained. Note, however, that this procedure does not conclusively demonstrate dissociation, as the same results might be obtained if the drug facilitated performance of the task. Failure to perform during no-drug test trials might simply indicate that the task was not sufficiently well learned to be performed in the absence of the drug's facilitating effects.

A more adequate design for the study of dissociative effects (the 2×2 design) was proposed by Miller (1957) and is diagrammed in Table 1A. If dissociation occurs, groups N–D and D–N will show relatively poor test trial performance since the drug conditions are different during training and testing in these two groups. The degree to which the test performance of these two groups is poorer than that of groups D–D and N–N, respectively, indicates the amount of dissociation. This pattern of results can be readily distinguished from that produced by a stimulant drug effect, which would result in poor test-trial performance in group D–N but exceptionally good test performance in group N–D, and in relatively slower acquisition in groups N–N and N–D during the training session. As long as the effect of dissociation on test performance is stronger than that of other drug actions, the 2×2 design can rather conclusively differentiate dissociation from other depressant or stimulant drug effects. The main problem with the design emerges when the dissociative effect is weak and is obscured by stronger drug effects.

Table 1B shows an altered design in which each subject is tested twice and acts as its own control. This design may be less sensitive than the 2×2 design, but requires fewer subjects. Girden and Culler (1937) discovered dissociated learning over 30 years ago in a pioneering series of experiments using this design, and pointed out the similarity of state-dependent learning to dissociated states in humans. Probably their interesting findings were not followed up by other scientists because they used erythroidine, a rather uncommon curareform drug. The recent discovery that many commonly used drugs can dissociate learning has revived research on the phenomenon.

When subjects cannot be tested under extinction conditions, the design in Table 1C may be used. Here subjects are retrained (or reversal trained) during the test session. A measure is obtained of the extent to which initial training facilitates (or impairs) subsequent task relearning in either the same or in a changed drug condition. There is some evidence that this design may be more sensitive than those described above when reversal training is used to measure dissociation (Bindra and Reichert, 1967; Caul, 1967; Tarter, 1968).

The designs in Table 1 are the simplest which can be employed to differentiate dissociative effects from other drug effects. Even with these designs, a mixture of effects often leads to difficulties of interpretation, and several additional control experiments may be required to demonstrate dissociation conclusively (Overton, 1970). Whatever their shortcomings, most of the transfer experiments on dissociation presently in the literature have used some variation of the designs in Table 1.

Drug discriminations are closely related to dissociation. If learning under drugs is dissociated, then we might expect that animals could learn to perform one response when drugged, and a different response when undrugged. Girden and Culler found that conditioned right and left leg flexion responses could coexist in the drug and nondrug conditions without interference. As there was no transfer of training between the two drug conditions, the results were equivalent to those which could be obtained by training two different animals to perform the two responses. Such differential responding can be established with only one training session in each drug state if dissociation is complete (Bliss *et al.*, 1971).

TABLE 1.   Experimental Designs for the Study of Transfer of Learning Between Drug States

A. 2 × 2 design

Group	Training condition	Test condition
N–N	No drug	No drug
N–D	No drug	Drug
D–N	Drug	No drug
D–D	Drug	Drug

B. Repeated tests design

Group	Training condition	First test	Second test
N–N–D	No drug	No drug	Drug
N–D–N	No drug	Drug	No drug
D–N–D	Drug	No drug	Drug
D–D–N	Drug	Drug	No drug

C. 2 × 2 with retraining

Group	Initial training	Retraining
N–N	No drug	No drug
N–D	No drug	Drug
D–N	Drug	No drug
D–D	Drug	Drug

TABLE 2.   Experimental Designs for Drug Discrimination

A. Training procedure

Day	Drug condition	Required response
1	No drug	Left
2	Drug A	Right
3	No drug	Left
4	Drug A	Right
5	No drug	Left
6	*etc.*	

B. Test procedure

Day	Drug condition	Required response
n	No drug	Left
$n + 1$	Drug A	Right
$n + 2$	Drug X	Either (test)
$n + 3$	No drug	Left
$n + 4$	Drug A	Right
$n + 5$	No drug	Left
$n + 6$	Drug X	Either (test)
$n + 7$	Drug A	Right
$n + 8$	No drug	Left
$n + 9$	Drug Y	Either (test)
$n + 10$	*etc.*	

Drug-discrimination procedures can also be used to evaluate weak dissociative effects. The training procedure is completely analogous to that used to establish sensory discriminations (Table 2A). One response (e.g., right turn in a T-maze) is reinforced when the animal is drugged and a different response (e.g., left turn) is rewarded when no drug is injected. Rats can be trained within 10–20 sessions to differentiate reliably the presence or absence of a drug dosage as low as one-fifth that required to produce complete dissociation. Such discriminations are apparently based on the same drug effects which produce total dissociation when higher doses are used (Overton, 1964).

The primary virtue of the drug-discrimination technique is that it allows the investigator to measure weak dissociative effects. The practical importance of this fact can hardly be overstated. Only a few drugs produce total dissociation at sublethal doses, and these do so only at dose levels which are extremely debilitating to the animal. Most drugs never produce more than partial dissociation at any dose level, often too little to be noticeable in transfer experiments.

Drug-discrimination techniques allow the dissociative effects of a variety of
ˌ̶ ̶
at which the subjects are relatively intact behaviorally.

Two types of measurements can be made with drug-discrimination techniques. The amount of training required before rats differentiate a pair of drug
states (one of which may be the no-drug state) varies greatly depending upon the
drugs selected. This apparently provides a measure of the degree of dissociation
between learning in the two states, with more rapidly acquired discriminations
indicating relatively more dissociation. A test for the similarity of the dissociative
effects of various drugs is also possible. After rats have been trained to differentiate a selected pair of drug states, they may be tested under one or more additional
drug conditions (Table 2B). Essentially the rat is asked to indicate which of the
training conditions is more closely approximated by the drug state established
during the test trial.

Such tests compare drugs specifically with regard to those effects which are
responsible for dissociation. These need not be the most important pharmacological properties of the drugs, although drugs with similar pharmacological
actions have generally been judged by rats to have similar "stimulus" properties.

PROPERTIES OF DRUG DISCRIMINABILITY

Studies on the discriminability of various drugs have yielded rather
consistent results. We will review these findings here, without describing the
detailed procedures by which they were obtained:

1. If subjects are required to discriminate different doses of a drug from
the nondrug condition, the discrimination is more rapidly acquired by the
subjects given higher doses. Apparently the discriminability of a drug state is
proportional to dose. This perfectly reasonable conclusion holds for all drugs
tested so far with the exception of antimuscarinics, such as scopolamine, where
both drug state discriminability and a variety of other CNS effects appear to
asymptote at a moderately high dose level. Beyond this dose level, no further
increases in discriminability are achieved by further raising the dose of an antimuscarinic drug (Giarman and Pepeu, 1964; Overton, 1969; White et al., 1961).

2. Rats can differentiate between different doses of a single drug. For
example, the drug conditions pentobarbital 20 mg/kg vs. pentobarbital 10 mg/kg
may be differentiated about as rapidly as the conditions pentobarbital 10 mg/kg
vs. no drug (Overton, 1968a). The drug vs. no drug discrimination appears to be
a special case of this ability to distinguish different dose levels.

3. The time course of drug-state discriminability appears to parallel that of
other obvious CNS effects of alcohol, such as ataxia. Apparently the drug state
present at the time of the learning experience determines the conditions for

optimal recall. If training takes place without drug, and the drug state is induced immediately after training, learning is not dissociated and will be best recalled in the no-drug condition (John, 1967; also see time course data below).

4. Centrally acting drugs may be classified as similar or dissimilar with regard to their discriminable effects. Rats trained to differentiate a particular drug from the no-drug condition will give drug responses when tested with appropriate doses of similar drugs, but not when tested with dissimilar drugs (Harris and Balster, 1971). Also, it is difficult or impossible to train rats to differentiate between interchangeable drugs if equally effective doses of each drug are used. This is apparently a more stringent test for the equivalence of the discriminable properties of two drugs (Overton, 1966).

5. About a dozen discriminable (dissimilar) states can be produced by the administration of various types of drugs (e.g., anesthetics, antimuscarinics, nicotinics, amphetamines, etc.). Drugs of each class apparently produce states from which learning transfers only with a decrement to either the nondrug state or to the drug states induced by drugs in other classes. Rats may be trained to differentiate any two dissimilar drugs, irrespective of dose level, as long as the selected doses are not so low as to be indistinguishable from the nondrug condition. The number of classes of drugs known to be discriminable from one another and from the nondrug condition has increased considerably owing to the work of several investigators (Harris and Balster, 1971; Kubena and Barry, 1969; Overton, 1966, 1971; Stewart, 1962; and others). Further research will probably expand the list of drugs known to be discriminable. Table 3 lists most of the drugs which have thus far been tested for discriminability from the nondrug condition. Drugs within each group are approximately interchangeable with regard to their discriminable effects.* The reader will note that this categorization according to drug "stimulus" properties nicely parallels the usual pharmacological categorization of these drugs.

6. Drugs which act only outside the central nervous system usually do not provide an adequate basis for rapidly acquired differential responding (Overton, 1971). With a single exception (Harris and Balster, 1971), only centrally acting drugs have acquired good discriminative control.

7. Drug discriminations can often be established more rapidly than most sensory discriminations. This fact, along with point 6, suggests that the formal similarities between drug discriminations and sensory discriminations may be more misleading than informative. Although it is convenient to speak of the "stimulus" properties of drugs, there is little evidence to suggest that when rats learn a drug discrimination they are actually discriminating the sensory consequences of drug action. Instead, such discriminations appear to take advantage

---

*The anesthetics and minor tranquilizers have very similar dissociative effects and perhaps belong in the same group (Overton, 1966).

TABLE 3. Centrally Acting Drugs Tested for Discriminative Control[a]

Strong control		Moderate control		Weak control	
Anesthetic drugs		Antimuscarinic drugs		Phenothiazines	
Pentobarbital	10–20	Atropine	20–200	Chlorpromazine	4
Phenobarbital	60–80	Scopolamine	1–300	Acepromazine	8
Secobarbital	15–20	Benactyzine	10–50	Perphenazine	5
Sodium barbital	150	Ditran	5–60	Prothipendyl	12
Amobarbital	30	Nicotinic drugs		Dibenzazepines	
Ethyl alcohol	1000–3000	Nicotine	1–4	Imipramine	20
Paraldehyde	300	Lobeline	40	Relatively inactive drugs	
Chloral hydrate	150	Narcotics		Prylamine	50
Ethyl carbamate	750	Morphine	9–36	Phenoxybenzamine	10
Hydroxydione	25	Stimulants		Physostigmine	1
Progesterone	125	Amphetamine	0.5–5	Dilantin	175
Ether		Methylphenidate	4		
Nitrous oxide		Convulsants			
Minor tranquilizers		Metrazol	30		
Librium	30	Bemegride	7.5		
Meprobamate	200	Antinicotinics			
		Mecamylamine	10–30		
		Other drugs			
		Mescaline	10–50		
		Tetrahydrocannabinol	4		
		LSD	0.01–0.1		

[a] *Note:* Tested dose levels are given in mg/kg for i.p. injection in the rat. The ordering according to relative effectiveness is only approximate and refers to the minimally effective tested dose of each drug.
Partial references can be found in: Harris and Balster, 1971; Overton, 1966, 1968b, 1971; Kubena and Barry, 1969.

of and sharpen the preexisting generalization gradient which impairs transfer of training between the drug and no-drug conditions (Overton, 1971).

8. The ability to learn drug discriminations is not restricted to any particular species or age group. Such discriminations have been reported with mice, cats, dogs, and monkeys. Rats ranging in age from 60 to 300 days form drug discriminations with about equal rapidity.

9. Drugs that are not easily differentiated from the no-drug condition are not subject to abuse (see Table 3). Conversely, most readily discriminable drugs are subject to abuse. This is simply an observed correlation. While there is as yet no direct evidence showing that drug discriminability plays a causal role in the addictive process, the correlation is very interesting. We will discuss later one way in which drug discriminability might lead to psychological dependence.

There is no information available concerning the development of tolerance to the discriminable effects of drugs. This is most unfortunate inasmuch as alcoholics frequently show substantial tolerance to many of the effects of alcohol. However, at this time we are not able to say whether tolerance to the "stimulus" effects of alcohol parallels tolerance to other effects of that drug.

DISCRIMINATIVE CONTROL BY ALCOHOL

Conger (1951) first reported that alcohol could acquire discriminative control. The discriminable properties of alcohol are not unique (Overton, 1966). Apparently they are the same as those of the barbiturate anesthetics and of some nonbarbiturate anesthetics (see Table 3). Thus although some characteristics of alcoholism differ from barbiturate addictions, any role played by drug state discriminability in alcoholism is probably also present in barbiturate addictions. Many of the characteristics of drug state discriminability described above have been demonstrated with alcohol (specifically properties 1, 3, 4a, and 7). The others presumably apply as well.

Parametric data on the variation of alcohol's discriminability as a function of dosage and of time following injection have not previously been reported, and will be presented here.

The discriminability of the state existing at various intervals subsequent to the intraperitoneal injection of 2000 mg/kg ethyl alcohol (10% solution) is shown in Fig. 1. These data were obtained by requiring adult male hooded rats to escape from foot shock in a T-maze. Each day every rat received a 5-min training session consisting of five trials. On even-numbered sessions, the rats were injected with alcohol prior to training and were required to turn right. During odd-numbered sessions, no drugs were administered and the rats were required to turn left (Table 2A). The interval between injection and the beginning of training was different for each of the 12 groups of rats in this experiment.

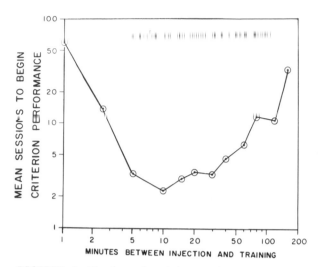

FIGURE 1. Number of training sessions required to
differentiate the no-drug state from the drug state established
at various intervals following intraperitoneal injection of
alcohol 2 g/kg. Total $N = 44$.

The number of training sessions necessary before rats were able to correctly
select their responses on the basis of the current drug state was used as an
indication of drug state discriminability. The figure shows group means for the
number of training sessions before each rat reached the beginning of a criterion
of 8 correct first-trial choices during 10 consecutive training sessions. Rats
failing to reach criterion performance within 60 sessions were assigned a score of
60; this occurred only in the group trained 1 min after injection. Except for the
use of a 5-trial training session, this procedure is identical to one previously used
and described elsewhere in more detail (Overton, 1966). The data are quite
straightforward. The time course of alcohol's dissociative effects very closely
matches that of alcohol's effect on muscular coordination as determined with a
"tilted plane" test (Kalant and Czaja, 1962; Wallgren, 1960).

The discriminability of the state existing 20 min after intraperitoneal
injection of various doses of alcohol in the rat is shown in Fig. 2. The procedures
used to obtain these data were identical to those used in the time-course
experiment, except that here each group received a different dose, and the
injection was always given 20 min prior to the training session. Drug state
discriminability increased rapidly as dose was increased. Although Fig. 2 gives
some indication of a plateau of action between 2–3 g/kg, this is probably an
artifact reflecting decreased learning ability rather than an asymptote in drug
state discriminability. Total dissociation was not produced by any of the alcohol

doses tested. The highest doses tested did produce a very substantial amount of dissociation which could probably be demonstrated directly using a 2 × 2 experimental design. With lower doses, transfer of training between the drug and nondrug conditions appeared virtually complete. Yet even with these lower doses, stable differential responding appeared after sufficient training, and thereafter the "drug" response appeared whenever drug was administered.

Storm has hypothesized that repeated exposure to the intoxicated state will increase the dissociation between the drug and the no-drug states (Storm and Smart, 1965). His hypothesis has two meanings: First, a drinker's observable behavior while drunk will increasingly differ from his behavior while sober as he develops a repertoire of dissociated drug state habits. This proposal appears to be in accord with the animal data. Second, a given dose of alcohol will dissociate a newly acquired habit more completely if the subject has a long history of drinking (Storm and Caird, 1967). As there appeared to be no animal data directly relevant to this hypothesis, I performed the following modest experimental test.

Ten male hooded rats were divided into two groups and subjected to an alcohol treatment regimen prior to training. One group received 2.4 g/kg daily for 10 days. The second group received no injections. Rats were returned to their home cages immediately after each injection. Following this alcohol treatment, both groups rested for 2 days. They were then trained to differentiate

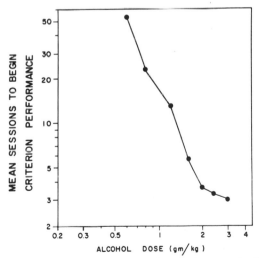

FIGURE 2. Number of training sessions required to differentiate the no-drug state from the drug state established by various doses of alcohol. $N \geq 3$ per group. Total $N = 29$.

alcohol 1.6 g/kg from no injection in the T-maze shock escape task. Training followed intraperitoneal injection by 15 min and the rats received 10 training trials per daily training session. The learning curves for the two groups were virtually identical. During the first 9 training sessions, alcohol pretreated rats made an average of 1.8 first-trial errors and nonpretreated rats averaged 1.4 errors. Thus 10 alcohol intoxications had no significant effect on the distinctiveness of the alcohol state.

This small experiment is hardly an adequate test of Storm's hypothesis, but it gives little support to the idea that repeated intoxications will increase the dissociation produced by alcohol. The effect of a larger number of intoxications should be tested. Also, Storm has predicted that the shape of the generalization gradient between the drug and no-drug conditions will change after repeated intoxications. This gradient can be directly measured with a series of intermediate test doses (Overton, 1966). Such tests could be repeated at various stages of training to detect any change in the gradient.

ANIMAL DISSOCIATION EXPERIMENTS

By inference, the properties of drug discriminability summarized above also describe properties of drug dissociation which could be demonstrated using a 2 × 2 transfer design (Overton, 1964). However, few parametric studies have been reported using such designs. Dissociation is usually less than total if any reasonable drug dose is used, and transfer procedures are less sensitive than drug discrimination procedures. Hence a large number of subjects must be used to demonstrate quantitative differences in the degree of dissociation as an independent variable is manipulated. Also, quite variable results have been obtained from transfer experiments using different drugs and different experimental tasks, probably because dissociative effects are confounded with other drug effects. Despite these difficulties, some of the "stimulus" properties of drugs demonstrated in drug discrimination experiments have also been observed in transfer experiments. Data obtained using alcohol (Crow, 1966, 1970; Barry et al., 1962; Seymore, 1967) can be considered together with that obtained using other anesthetic drugs, as there appear to be no significant differences between the dissociative effects of the various depressants. The following results have been obtained.

1. The degree to which learning under drug is dissociated from nondrug learning appears to be proportional to drug dosage. Dissociation is only observed when moderately high drug doses are used and becomes less noticeable when lower doses are employed (Barry et al., 1965; Overton, 1968b; Pusakulich and Nielson, 1970; Ryback, 1969).

2. Drugs which have been shown to be interchangeable using drug discrimination techniques also appear interchangeable when a transfer design is used, in those cases tested. Similarly, drugs which appear noninterchangeable in the drug discrimination experiments are not interchangeable in transfer experiments (Holmgren, 1965; Sachs *et al.*, 1966).

3. The drugs with which dissociation is most often reported (alcohol, barbiturates, antimuscarinics) are those which most rapidly acquire response control in drug discrimination experiments (Overton, 1968b). There is one exception, as phenothiazines have been reported to produce dissociation (Otis, 1964; Heistad and Torres, 1959) whereas these drugs are usually not found to be readily discriminable from no drug (Overton, 1966; Stewart, 1962). Replication of the dissociation studies appears desirable, however, as not all investigators report dissociation with these drugs (Doty and Doty, 1963; Iwahara *et al.*, 1968).

4. Dissociation is not reported with peripherally acting drugs as long as they have no actions within the central nervous system (Arbit, 1958; Auld, 1951).

Several investigators have reported "asymmetrical" dissociation (Barnhart, 1967; Berger and Stein, 1969a, 1969b; Overton, 1968b). In these experiments using a 2 × 2 design, good transfer of training was observed in the N–D group whereas poor transfer occurred in the D–N group. Serious methodological problems result if dissociation is asymmetrical, as the 2 × 2 experimental design will not adequately differentiate such a phenomenon from other drug effects. Also, such an asymmetry is at variance with the predictions of most theoretical models which attempt to explain dissociation (Overton, 1968b), although some models allow it (Berger and Stein, 1969b; Sachs, 1967). It is worth noting, however, that a drug-discrimination could not be based on a one-way dissociation, as on drug trials the rats would be equally prone to give drug and nondrug responses. No such tendency is seen in most drug discrimination experiments. Also, it is rather easy to see how an apparent "one-way" dissociation could result from the summation of a symmetrical state dependency effect with other drug effects (Berger and Stein, 1969a). This is a parsimonious explanation and there are no asymmetrical results which cannot be explained in this way.

STATE-DEPENDENT LEARNING IN HUMANS

The literature on state-dependent learning in humans is small, but does deal primarily with dissociation induced by alcohol. Nine papers have been found of which seven used the drug state induced by alcohol 1 to 1.6 oz per 100 lb administered orally, or in one case by 200 mg of amobarbital (Bustamante *et al.*, 1968, 1970). These seven papers report the results of 15 experiments which primarily used three types of learning tasks. As the 15 experiments appear comparable, we will discuss them together.

Simple verbal learning tasks have been used in eight experiments (Bustamante *et al.*, 1968; Goodwin *et al.*, 1969a; Madill, 1967; Storm and Caird, 1967; Storm *et al.*, 1965; Tarter, 1968). The materials learned include lists of nonsense syllables or words, and paired-associate lists involving letters, nonsense syllables, or words. Statistically significant dissociation was observed using all of these tasks. Some materials could be learned with a single presentation, whereas others required 10–20 repetitions. Simple recall provided evidence of dissociation in some cases (Goodwin *et al.*, 1969a; Bustamante *et al.*, 1968). In other experiments more significant results were obtained with relearning scores, perhaps because of the larger number of observations per subject (Storm *et al.*, 1965). In one experiment, relearning a new task with interference from the original task provided stronger evidence of dissociation than did simple relearning of the original task in an altered state (Tarter, 1968). None of these minor variations in procedure appear to make a consistent difference in the results obtained when comparison is made across the several published experiments. Apparently partially dissociated learning is not too difficult to demonstrate with simple verbal tasks. There is no consistent evidence of a difference between alcoholics and normals, except that alcoholics were typically tested with a somewhat higher dose level due to their relative insensitivity to alcohol. The literature does not allow us to specify any task parameters which influence the degree of dissociation obtained.

Operant discriminative avoidance behavior has been studied in three experiments using visual patterns as discriminative stimuli, shock or aversive loud noise as the unconditioned stimulus, and a button-press response (Goodwin *et al.*, 1969a; Madill, 1967). In two of these experiments using normal subjects, a partial symmetrical dissociation was observed. In a third, using alcoholic subjects, an unusual asymmetrical dissociation was reported (see below). Apparently we can conclude that alcohol partially dissociates discriminated operant behaviors in man.*

Dissociation has not been observed using visual recognition tasks in which the subject simply has to recognize a picture which he has previously seen and select it from among several other pictures. This result has been obtained with both "neutral" and "emotional" (nude) stimuli (Goodwin *et al.*, 1969a; Osborn

---

*One methodological question can be raised about the experiment by Goodwin *et al.* Their subjects learned the discriminative avoidance task to criterion on day 1. On day 2 the task was relearned using an altered pairing of stimuli with correct responses. The authors considered that day 1 learning would interfere with day 2 learning and that dissociation would reduce this interference. However, it seems possible that day 1 learning could also produce a learning set which would facilitate day 2 relearning despite the altered reinforcement contingencies. Such a learning set might be dissociated to a different degree than the operant response. The possibility of such an effect was not discussed by the authors, although judging from their results it was less significant as a determinant of day 2 performance than was the interference effect which they discuss.

et al., 1967). However, Bustamante *et al.* (1970) found clear evidence of dissociation with a rather different visual learning task. His subjects were requested to memorize several geometric designs and were subsequently asked to draw as many of these designs as they could remember. Obviously the learning process in this case is somewhat different from that which takes place when a subject is simply asked to look at a photograph, and this may account for the differing results obtained. The available data do not allow us to specify in any more detail what properties of visual learning tasks are likely to allow dissociated learning.

Bustamante's results appear to contain less variance than those of any other dissociation studies, and this may reflect his rather stringent subject selection procedures. Starting with a group of 700 subjects, he initially selected a subgroup of "normal" learners with equal learning ability on the task to be used. Then subjects who used drugs or reported severe emotional states were eliminated. The final experimental group contained only 10% of those screened, normal subjects matched for learning ability in the task to be used, and these subjects showed very consistent dissociative effects. However, it is unclear whether the objectives of the experiment were disclosed to these subjects, and if they were, expectancy may have played an important role in producing the results.

The failure to find dissociation reported by Osborn *et al.* (1967) deserves comment, as they worked with heavily drugged subjects. In animals, dissociation is dose-dependent, with higher doses producing more dissociation. However, if the selected dosage is high enough to have a major depressant effect on learning or performance, this often makes it difficult to see any dissociative effects which may be present. The trick is to find a dosage, or task, in which depressant effects are not too severe, so that dissociative effects can be seen if they occur. Osborn *et al.* used high dosages at which subjects required five to ten times as much training to reach criterion performance as was necessary without drugs. Only 30 min after a word association task was learned to criterion under drug, less than 50% of the associated pairs could be recalled. Thus their data show major depressant drug effects, and do not directly conflict with the results discussed above owing to the different drug conditions which they used. Perhaps some task can be found in which learning is very resistant to depressant drug effects (as is T-maze learning in the rat). Otherwise it appears that dissociated learning can be more easily demonstrated in man using moderate drug doses than with high drug doses.

Goodwin *et al.* (1969a) reported that dissociation was asymmetrical in verbal learning tasks. Training transferred readily in the direction N–D, whereas dissociation resulted from the state change D–N. A similar asymmetry appears in the data of Storm and Caird (1967), and this finding is analogous to the results of many animal studies. Madill, however, reported an opposite asymmetry in three experiments, with dissociation occurring only in the N–D group of her alcoholic subjects.* It is worth noting that all three of Madill's experiments were conducted simultaneously using a total of only 16 subjects. Hence individual variations in learning ability or in drug conditions could produce the same trends in all three experiments. As there are three studies which show dissociation only in the direction N–D and three in which the strongest dissociation appears in the direction D–N, we can parsimoniously conclude that there is no consistent evidence supporting the existence of an asymmetrical dissociation in either direction.

Several additional studies on dissociated learning have been reported, but these are not readily comparable with each other, or with those discussed above. Dissociation of finger maze learning has been studied in both normals and alcoholics (Madill, 1967). Dissociation was not observed in a mirror drawing task by Caird (unpublished). Kurland (1968) failed to find dissociation induced by chlorpromazine 50 mg/day using a visual perception task. Finally, Bustamante et al. (1968, 1969) have reported good evidence for dissociated learning induced by 20 mg amphetamine using both verbal and visual learning tasks.

In summary, then, experiments with human subjects indicate that moderate doses of alcohol produce a partial dissociation of some types of learning. It is equally clear that a total dissociation is not produced by moderate drinking. More quantitative data comparing the degree of dissociation occurring in various tasks and with various dosages are not available.

DRUG DISCRIMINATION IN HUMANS

Experiments dealing with the ability of drugs to acquire discriminative control in human subjects have not yet been reported. Introspection tempts one to conclude that drugs could certainly exert discriminative control because their effects are quite discriminable. Therefore the study of such response control would seemingly yield no very interesting results. However, extrapolation from animal experiments leads to a quite different conclusion. Peripherally acting drugs, which apparently produce obviously discriminable effects (dry mouth, paralysis, etc.) actually acquire response control very slowly, if at all, in animals. Centrally acting drugs such as alcohol rapidly acquire discriminative control by virtue of their dissociative effects, even though introspection suggests that they

---

*Madill also claims the same unusual asymmetry in her results with normal subjects, but here her analysis of the data is open to question. It seems clear to me from her data obtained with normal subjects that dissociation was symmetrical and occurred in both the D–N and N–D directions. Apparently Madill reached her interpretation of the results by comparing different experimental groups than I would consider appropriate. However, in her three experiments with alcoholics, the data do show an asymmetry opposite to that usually reported in animal studies, as she concluded.

would be no more discriminable than peripherally acting drugs. It is important to recognize the direct contradiction between the results of animal experiments and our expectations based on introspection. Since drug discrimination experiments have been so useful in providing quantitative information about dissociation in animals, and because of the possibility that after repeated intoxication alcoholics may acquire behaviors conditional on the drug state, it appears sensible to try such experiments on human subjects.

In order to be useful for the study of weak dissociative effects, an experimental paradigm for drug discrimination must have several characteristics:

1. The objective stimulus environment external to the subject should be identical for all training sessions.

2. A continuing measure of response accuracy should be obtained throughout training. In some tasks, the method of anticipation provides this by first allowing the subject to select his response and then advising him whether or not the response was correct.

3. Repeated measures should be taken to indicate whether the subject can yet respond differentially on the basis of his current drug state. In practice this means that drug states should be frequently alternated, as the subject's performance during the first few trials after a change in drug state indicates the degree to which he can select responses appropriate to the newly imposed drug state. Procedures in which subjects do not receive too much training per session are apparently preferable to those in which subjects are overtrained during each session, unless the dissociative effects under study are quite profound.

4. The level of drug action must be more or less uniform throughout the several drug sessions. In most animal experiments a fixed drug dose has been administered at a specified interval before the drug session, thus disregarding any interindividual differences in drug absorption or drug metabolism. Sessions must be kept short to stay within the period of drug action.

The most serious practical difficulties anticipated in human drug discrimination experiments would appear to result from the necessity of repeatedly administering rather large drug doses, and managing subjects throughout the period of drug action. These difficulties could be reduced by the use of a gaseous drug, such as nitrous oxide. Total dissociation would not be expected with moderate doses of nitrous oxide (Summerfield and Steinberg, 1957), but drug discrimination could probably be obtained. Rapid drug excretion might make it feasible to run several experimental sessions per day on a single subject, separated by 1 or 2-hr intervals. Animal data indicate that the dissociative effects of nitrous oxide and ether are roughly interchangeable with those of alcohol (Overton, 1966). Thus we could expect that results obtained using nitrous oxide in humans could be replicated with alcohol, albeit with more difficulty.

A promising design for a verbal learning drug discrimination experiment was proposed by Bliss (unpublished). Construct two equally difficult paired associate lists. The same stimulus words should be used in each list, but with different associated words. Train subjects using the method of anticipation in a series of short alternating drug and nondrug sessions. Within each session, minimally train the subjects with perhaps two or three repetitions of the appropriate list. Accuracy on the first few trials after a change in drug state will indicate the degree to which the subject can alter his response to match the altered drug state. Response accuracy toward the end of each session will indicate the degree to which subjects have mastered the current list. The data can be scored for "guessing" errors when the subject's response is not found in either list, and for "generalization" errors when the subject's response is found as a correct associate in the list of associates used in the other drug state. The experiment could be presented to the subject as a test of drug effects on learning ability, without mention of the number of lists used or their relationship to the drug state. Assuming that a discrimination develops, introspective reports concerning the nature and basis of the discrimination might be sought at the end of the experiment. This procedure seems to provide a fair replica of those which have proved most useful in experiments with animals.

DISSOCIATION AND THE ALCOHOLIC BLACKOUT

Recent experiments by Tamerin et al. (1971), Goodwin et al. (1970), and Ryback (1970) have greatly clarified the relationship between drug dissociation and the alcoholic "blackout." They showed that high doses of alcohol produce a dose-dependent defect in memory registration such that permanent engrams tend not to be formed. Although immediate memory is intact and the subject can answer questions and do mental arithmetic, simple memory tests show that many ongoing events are forgotten within 2–30 min. If the short-term memory defect is severe, a blackout results, covering the period of time during which the short-term memory defect was present. Recall for both significant and emotionally trivial experiences is equally affected. Such a memory defect and consequent blackout can occur with blood alcohol levels around 250 mg/100 ml. However, individual alcoholics vary considerably in susceptibility, and Tamerin et al. found that the degree of short-term memory defect provided a better predictor of memory loss after 24 hr than did blood alcohol level. There is disagreement between these three reports on only one issue. Ryback reported more blackouts during the first 2 days of drinking while blood alcohol levels were rising. Tamerin et al., using more quantitative methods, found that 24-hr recall was uniformly impaired during a 12-day drinking period during which blood alcohol levels were stable.

It has been known for some time that similar defects in memory registration could be produced by anesthetics (Artusio, 1954; Randt and Mazzia, 1965) and by other centrally acting drugs (DeVito and Frank, 1964). Probably most of the more striking alcoholic "blackouts" are caused by this type of defect in memory registration, rather than by state-dependent learning (as hypothesized by Storm and Smart, 1965). The memories are never permanently registered, and hence cannot be subsequently retrieved either while drugged or while sober. In order to be dissociated, learning must first occur and this only happens at lower dose levels.

The same investigators (Goodwin *et al.*, 1969b; Ryback, 1970) differentiate the total "*en bloc*" blackouts, produced as above, from other more evanescent dissociative effects that they attribute to state-dependent learning. Alcoholics may initially be unable to remember events which happened while they were drinking, and yet after being reminded, memory may gradually return. While inebriated, they may report emotionally important experiences which they would not discuss, and seemingly could not remember while sober (Diethelm and Barr, 1962; Mello, 1969). Some alcoholics specifically report that drinking improves their memory for events that happened during previous drinking episodes (Goodwin *et al.*, 1969b; Storm and Smart, 1965). These temporary amnesias, in which recall can be recovered under the proper circumstances, are apparently caused by deficits in memory retrieval rather than in memory registration. The difficulty with retrieval may result from drug dissociation, although this has not been demonstrated experimentally.

CAN DISSOCIATION CAUSE DRUG DEPENDENCE?

Most explanations for drug addiction attribute drug use to some intrinsic "beneficial" effect of the drug. For example, alcohol has a disinhibiting effect on behavior, and an inebriated person may be able to behave in ways which bring him more reinforcement than he would otherwise obtain. Drug intake may terminate uncomfortable withdrawal symptoms. A fear-reducing effect can be shown in animals (Barry *et al.*, 1965) and is often assumed to take place in people despite the dysphoria reported, but later forgotten, by some alcoholics when they drink (Tamerin *et al.*, 1970). The impairment of thought and memorization produced by alcohol may be reinforcing to some persons. Also, many drugs act as positive reinforcers in animals (Pickens and Thompson, 1971) and alcohol may have similar effects in man. Dissociation is apparently not relevant to an understanding of the operation of these factors in alcoholism. In all these cases the direct pharmacological effects of alcohol have some positive value to the alcoholic.

The relevance of state-dependent learning to alcoholism arises from the possibility of conditioned reactions to alcohol, as distinct from its unconditioned

pharmacological effects. Alcoholics may drink to obtain access to behavioral
patterns or emotional reactions which have become conditioned to the presence
of alcohol, rather than to obtain any of the intrinsic effects of alcohol. As a simple
example, suppose that early drinking takes place in pleasant social surroundings
which induce positive affect. We might predict that subsequent solitary drinking
would reevoke the same positive affect as a conditioned reaction, even if it would
not be evoked by the drug alone in the absence of prior conditioning.

    To put the argument in a more general form, consider a potential alcoholic
who has never before been drunk. During his early exposures to the drug state,
he may simply experience disinhibition and consequently experiment with some
new behaviors. After a year of drinking, the disinhibiting effects will still occur,
but now our subject will concurrently have selectively improved access to the
behavioral and emotional reactions learned during his previous drug experiences.
The net effect of drinking will be much greater than that experienced during
early exposures to alcohol, since various affects and behaviors are now conditioned to the drug state. As the process continues, a habitual drug user might
develop a whole set of behaviors and emotional responses peculiar to the drug
condition, and distinct from those which he displays when sober.

    This is a very speculative idea. However, we have recently discovered that
animals repeatedly experiencing drug states may develop behavior patterns
conditional upon a particular drug state for their occurrence. It appears worthwhile to consider what role this effect might have in the addictive process.
Apparently an alcoholic might be able to gain access to part of his behavioral
repertoire only by drinking. Insofar as he has developed drug state behaviors
which are more reinforcing than his sober behaviors, the drug state will have
acquired a more positive valence than it initially possessed, by virtue of its
conditioned associations.

    There is, incidentally, nothing about this argument which uniquely applies
to alcoholism. It appears equally relevant to other drugs with strong stimulus
properties, such as nicotine and tetrahydrocannabinol. However, it is not easily
applicable to people who use a variety of drugs with dissimilar dissociative
effects.

IMPLICATIONS FOR THE TREATMENT OF ALCOHOLISM

    Storm and Smart (1965) have pointed out that the treatment of alcoholism
by either aversive conditioning or conversational techniques might be more
effective if it were carried out while the subject was intoxicated. The rationale
for this proposal is quite straightforward. Therapeutic maneuvers carried out
with a sober alcoholic may be moderately effective as long as he does not drink.
However, if the subject does begin to drink, the lessons of therapy will tend to

become unavailable owing to dissociation; the more he drinks, the less influenced he will be by his previous treatment. There is general clinical agreement that therapeutic maneuvers directed against alcoholism lose their effectiveness rapidly once the alcoholic starts to drink. This is usually attributed to the disinhibiting and thought-dissolving properties of alcohol. However, it appears that dissociation may be another mechanism active in making the treated alcoholic look untreated once drinking resumes. This unfortunate state of affairs might be altered if therapy were carried out while the alcoholic was intoxicated. In this case, when the subject began to drink, he would move toward the drug state in which conditioning took place, and the habits developed during therapy should become more accessible.

The most apparent argument against such a procedure is that conditioning is more difficult to obtain with intoxicated subjects; conversational treatments may even appear to be forgotten on the following day. However, recent research provides several counterarguments which are worth noting. Cheek (1959) and Levinson (1967) have both reported that some permanent learning can take place under stage 2 anesthesia, even though recall appears to be absent on the following day when tested by standard interview techniques. Gruber (1968), in an experiment more specifically relevant to alcoholism, has reported that a conditioned GSR reaction could be established under stage 1 anesthesia. An interesting feature of this study is that the subjects, when tested on the following day for conditioned GSR's, reported no recall for the conditioning procedures, presumably because of the memory disorder induced by the anesthetic. Nonetheless, the conditioned GSR appeared, indicating that the response had been conditioned and that dissociation was less than complete. Gruber (personal communication) points out one singular advantage to carrying out aversive conditioning procedures under light anesthesia—namely, that the subjects cannot remember the conditioning procedures. Hence, more aversive conditioning procedures could be used than would otherwise be possible, and the subjects might still be willing to return for repeated treatments.

In another relevant report, Berger (1970) has studied conditioned aversions to flavored liquids in rats. Such an aversion can be induced if a rat is injected with scopolamine shortly after drinking a novelly flavored liquid, indicating that the liquid itself does not have to be poisoned, as the association will be made if a state of malaise is induced pharmacologically. The most interesting part of this report is that the conditioned aversion could be established even if the rats were made surgically anesthetic prior to scopolamine injection and were maintained in a state of anesthesia throughout the duration of action of scopolamine. This remarkable result suggests that the mechanisms which mediate such conditioned aversions are not blocked by anesthetics to anywhere near the same degree as are most of the higher mechanisms of conditioning and learning. Although the influence of conditioned aversions on beverage selection may be much weaker in man than in rats, Berger's results do suggest a treatment method. The alcoholic could be given a bottle of scopolamine pills, and told to take one after each bout of heavy drinking (" to reduce hangover"). If Berger's effect takes place in man, then we might expect such a procedure to reinstate a conditioned aversion to alcohol after each drinking session. Such a treatment, although extremely speculative, would seem to warrant a clinical trial.

Dissociation is not apparent in the results obtained by Gruber and Berger However, these reports do both indicate that viable conditioned responses can be established in very intoxicated subjects. Thus the requirement that some therapeutic maneuvers be conducted with alcoholics while they are intoxicated appears to be a realizable one. The dissociation data indicate that such treatment techniques might be more effective than those presently in use.

SUMMARY

This paper has reviewed the methodology used to study state-dependent learning, the known facts about the phenomenon, and their relevance to alcoholism. The literature on drug state discriminations in animals allows a rather orderly set of conclusions. A larger literature exists on drug-induced dissociation of learning in animals, but this material is more difficult to systematize owing to conflicts and inconsistencies between the various reports. A few experiments using human subjects allow us to conclude that learning can be partially dissociated in man by changes in drug state. However, there is no parametric information defining the amount of dissociation which will occur in man with various tasks and drug conditions. We have tried to infer how dissociation might be related to alcoholism. However, there is as yet no experimental evidence to support these hypotheses. An obvious need exists for further investigations on many aspects of this topic, particularly on the occurrence of drug discriminations in man and on the relationship of dissociation to the addictive process.

REFERENCES

Arbit, J., 1958. Shock motivated serial discrimination learning and the chemical block of autonomic impulses, *J. Comp. Physiol. Psychol.* **51**: 199–201.

Artusio, J. F., 1954. Di-ethyl ether analgesia: A detailed description of the first stage of ether anesthesia in man, *J. Pharmacol. Exp. Therap.* **111**: 343–348.

Auld, F., 1951. The effects of tetraethylammonium on a habit motivated by fear, *J. Comp. Physiol. Psychol.* **44**: 565–574.

Barnhart, S. S. and Abbott, D. W., 1967. Dissociation of learning and meprobamate, *Psychol. Rep.* **20**: 520–522.

Barry, H., Miller, N. E., and Tidd, G. E., 1962. Control for stimulus change while testing effects of amobarbital on conflict, *J. Comp. Physiol. Psychol.* **55**: 1071–1074.

Barry, H., Etheredge, E. E., and Miller, N. E., 1965. Counter-conditioning and extinction of fear fail to transfer from amobarbital to nondrug state, *Psychopharmacologia (Berl.)* **8**: 150–156.

Berger, B. D., 1970. Learning in the anesthetized rat, *Fed. Proc.* **29**: 749 (abstract).

Berger, B. D. and Stein, L., 1969a. An analysis of learning deficits produced by scopolamine, *Psychopharmacologia (Berl.)* **14**: 271–283.

Berger, B. and Stein, L., 1969b. Asymmetrical dissociation of learning between scopolamine and Wy4036, a new benzodiazepine tranquilizer, *Psychopharmacologia (Berl.)* **14**: 351–358.

Bindra, D. and Reichert, H., 1967. The nature of dissociation: Effects of transitions between normal and barbiturate-induced states on reversal learning and habituation, *Psychopharmacologia (Berl.)* **10**: 330–344.

Bliss, D. K., Sledjeski, M., and Leiman, A., 1971. State dependent choice behavior in the rhesus monkey, *Neuropsychologica*, **9**: 51–59.

Bustamante, J. A., Rosselló, A., Jordán, A., Pradere, E., and Insua, A., 1968. Learning and drugs, *Physiol. Behav.* **3**: 553–555.

Bustamante, J. A., Jordán, A., Vila, M., González, A., and Insua, A., 1970. State dependent learning in humans, *Physiol. Behav.* **5**: 793–796.

Caird, W. K. An investigation of the effects of alcohol on human learning, Unpublished progress report, Dalhousie University, Halifax, Nova Scotia.

Caul, W. F., 1967. Effects of amobarbital on discrimination acquisition and reversal, *Psychopharmacologia (Berl.)* **11**: 414–421.

Cheek, D. B., 1959. Unconscious perception of meaningful sounds during surgical anesthesia as revealed under hypnosis, *Amer. J. Clin. Hypnosis* **1**: 101–113.

Conger, J. J., 1951. The effects of alcohol on conflict behavior in the albino rat, *Quart. J. Stud. Alcohol* **12**: 29.

Crow, L. T., 1966. Effects of alcohol on conditioned avoidance responding, *Physiol. Behav.* **1**: 89–91.

Crow, L. T., 1970. Alcohol state transfer effects with performance maintained by intracranial self-stimulation, *Physiol. Behav.* **5**: 515–517.

De Vito, R. A. and Frank, I. M., 1964. Ditran—searchlights on psychosis, *J. Neuropsychiat.* **5**: 300–305.

Diethelm, O. and Barr, R. M., 1962. Psychotherapeutic interviews and alcohol intoxication, *Quart. J. Stud. Alc.* **23**: 243–251.

Doty, L. A. and Doty, B. A., 1963. Chlorpromazine-produced response decrements as a function of problem difficulty level, *J. Comp. Physiol. Psychol.* **56**: 740–745.

Giarman, N. J. and Pepeu, G., 1964. The influence of centrally-acting cholinolytic drugs on brain acetylcholine levels, *Brit. J. Pharmacol.* **23**: 123–130.

Girden, E. and Culler, E. A., 1937. Conditioned responses in curarized striate muscle in dogs, *J. Comp. Psychol.* **23**: 261–274.

Goodwin, D. W., Powell, B., Bremer, D., Hoine, H., and Stern, J., 1969a. Alcohol and recall: State dependent effects in man, *Science* **163**: 1358–1360.

Goodwin, D. W., Crane, J. B., and Guze, S. B., 1969b. Phenomenological aspects of the alcoholic "blackout," *Brit. J. Psychiat.* **115**: 1033–1038.

Goodwin, D. W., Othmer, E., Halikas, J. A., and Freemon, F., 1970. Loss of short term memory as a predictor of the alcoholic blackout, *Nature* **227**: 201–202.

Gruber, R. P., Reed, D. R., and Block, J. B., 1968. Transfer of the conditioned GSR from drug to nondrug state without awareness. *J. Psychol.* **70:** 149–155

Harris, R. and Balster, R., 1971. An analysis of the function of drugs in the stimulus control of operant behavior, in *Stimulus Properties of Drugs* (T. Thompson and R. Pickens, eds.) pp. 111–132, Appleton–Century–Croft, New York.

Heistad, G. T. and Torres, A. A., 1959. A mechanism for the effect of a tranquilizing drug on learned emotional responses, *Univ. Minn. Med. Bull.* **30:** 518–527.

Holmgren, B., 1965. Drug dependent conditioned reflexes. Paper presented at International Symposium on Cortical–Subcortical Relationships in Sensory Regulation, Havana, Cuba.

Iwahara, S., Iwasaki, T., and Hasegawa, Y., 1968. Effects of chlorpromazine and homofenazine upon a passive avoidance response in rats, *Psychopharmacologia (Berl.)* **13:** 320–331.

John, E. R., 1967. State dependent learning, in *Mechanisms of Memory* Chapter 5, Academic Press, New York.

Kalant, H. and Czaja, C., 1962. The effect of repeated alcoholic intoxication on adrenal ascorbic acid and cholesterol in the rat, *Can. J. Biochem. Physiol.* **40:** 975–981.

Kubena, R. K. and Barry, H. III, 1969. Generalization by rats of alcohol and atropine stimulus characteristics to other drugs, *Psychopharmacologia (Berl.)* **15:** 196–206.

Kurland, H. D., Cassell, S. and Goldberg, E. M., 1968. The effects of chlorpromazine on the transferability of learning in humans, Paper presented at the Society of Biological Psychiatry, Washington, D.C.

Levinson, B. W., 1967. States of awareness during general anesthesia, in *Hypnosis and Psychosomatic Medicine* (J. Lassner, ed.) pp. 200–207, Springer-Verlag, New York.

Madill, Mary-Frances, 1967. Alcohol induced dissociation in humans: A possible treatment technique for alcoholism, Ph.D. Thesis, Queens University, Kingston, Ontario, Canada.

Mello, N. K. and Mendelson, J. H., 1969. Alterations in states of consciousness associated with chronic ingestion of alcohol, in *Neurobiological Aspects of Psychopathology* (J. Zubin and C. Shagass, eds.) pp. 183–218, Grune and Stratton, New York.

Miller, N. E., 1957. Objective techniques for studying motivational effects of drugs on animals, in *Proc. International Symposium on Psychotropic Drugs* (S. Garattini and V. Ghetti, eds.) pp. 83–103, Elsevier, Amsterdam.

Osborn, A. G., Bunker, J. P., Cooper, L. F., Frank, G. S., and Hilgard, E. R., 1967. Effects of thiopental sedation on learning and memory, *Science* **157:** 574–576.

Otis, L. S., 1964. Dissociation and recovery of a response learned under the influence of chlorpromazine or saline, *Science* **143:** 1347–1348.

Overton, D. A., 1964. State-dependent or "dissociated" learning produced with pentobarbital, *J. Comp. Physiol. Psychol.* **57:** 3–12.

Overton, D. A., 1966. State dependent learning produced by depressant and atropinelike drugs, *Psychopharmacologia (Berl.)* **10:** 6–31.

Overton, D. A., 1968a. Visual cues and shock sensitivity in the control of T maze choice by drug conditions, *J. Comp. Physiol. Psychol.* **66:** 216–219.

Overton, D. A., 1968b. Dissociated learning in drug states (state-dependent learning), in *Psychopharmacology. A Review of Progress* (D. H. Efron, J. O. Cole, J. Levine, and J. R. Wittenborn, eds.) pp. 918–930, Public Health Service Publication No. 1836, U.S. Government Printing Office, Washington, D.C.

Overton, D. A., 1969. Control of T maze choice by nicotinic, antinicotinic and antimuscarinic drugs, Proceedings of the 77th American Psychological Association, pp. 869–870.

Overton, D. A., 1970. Commentary on state dependent learning, in *Behavioral Analysis of Drug Action: Research and Commentary* (J. Harvey, ed.), Scott Foresman, Chicago, in press.

Overton, D. A., 1971. Discriminative control of behavior by drug states, in *Stimulus Properties of Drugs* (T. Thompson and R. Pickens, eds.) pp. 87–110, Appleton–Century–Crofts, New York.

Pickens, R. and Thompson, T., 1971. Characteristics of stimulant drug reinforcement, in *Stimulus Properties of Drugs* (T. Thompson and R. Pickens, eds.) pp. 177–192, Appleton–Century–Crofts, New York.

Pusakulich, R. L. and Nielson, H. C., 1970. State dependent learning and brain excitability, Paper presented at Western Psychological Association, Los Angeles, California.

Randt, C. T. and Mazzia, V. D. B., 1965. Recent memory fixation in man, *Trans. Am. Neurol. Assn.*, pp. 141–144.

Ryback, R. S., 1969. State dependent or "dissociated" learning with alcohol in the goldfish, *Quart. J. Stud. Alc.* **30:** 598–608.

Ryback, R. S., 1970. Alcohol amnesia: Observations on seven drinking in-patient alcoholics, *Quart. J. Stud. Alc.* **31:** 616–632.

Sachs, E., 1967. Dissociation of learning in rats and its similarities to dissociative states in man, in *Comparative Psychopathology* (J. Zubin and H. Hunt, eds.) pp. 249–304, Grune & Stratton, New York.

Sachs, E., Weingarten, M., and Klein, N. W. Jr., 1966. Effects of chlordiazepoxide on the acquisition of avoidance learning and its transfer to the normal state and other drug conditions, *Psychopharmacologia (Berl.)* **9:** 17–30.

Seymore, J. D., 1967. The effect of ethyl alcohol in producing state dependent or "dissociated" learning in rats, Masters Thesis, Department of Psychology, University of Southern Mississippi.

Stewart, Jane, 1962. Differential responses based on the physiological consequences of pharmacological agents, *Psychopharmacologia (Berl.)* **3:** 132–138.

Storm, T. and Caird, W. K., 1967. The effects of alcohol on serial verbal learning in chronic alcoholics, *Psychon. Sci.* **9:** 43–44.

Storm, T., Caird, W. K., and Corbin, E., 1965. The effects of alcohol on rote verbal learning and retention, Paper presented at Canadian Psychological Association, Vancouver, Canada.

Storm, T. and Smart, R. G., 1965. Dissociation: A possible explanation of some features of chronic alcoholism and implications for treatment, *Quart. J. Stud. Alc.* **26:** 111–115.

Summerfield, A. and Steinberg, H., 1957. Reducing interference in forgetting, *Quart. J. Exp. Psychol.* **9:** 146–154.

Tamerin, J. S., Weiner, S., and Mendelson, J. H., 1970. Alcoholics expectancies and recall of experiences during intoxication, *Amer. J. Psychiat.* **126:** 39–46.

Tamerin, J. S., Weiner, S., Poppen, R., Steinglass, P., and Mendelson, J. H., 1971. Alcohol and memory: Amnesia and short-term memory function during experimentally induced intoxication, *Amer. J. Psychiat.* **127:** 1659-1664.

Tarter, R. E., 1968. Dissociative effects of ethyl alcohol, M.A. Thesis, Department of Psychology, Dalhousie University, Halifax, Nova Scotia.

Wallgren, H., 1960. Relative intoxicating effects on rats of ethyl, propyl, and butyl alcohols, *Acta. Pharmacol. Toxicol.* **16:** 217–222.

White, R. P., Nash, C. B., Westerbeke, E. J., and Possanza, G. J., 1961. Phylogenetic comparison of central actions produced by different doses of atropine and hyoscine, *Arch. Int. Pharmacodyn.* **132:** 349–363.

CHAPTER 9

Behavioral Studies of Alcoholism*

Nancy K. Mello

Chief, Section on Comparative Neurobehavior
National Center for the Prevention and Control of Alcoholism
National Institute of Mental Health
Chevy Chase, Maryland

INTRODUCTION

Before 1965 there was relatively little experimental attention paid to the problem of alcoholism. However, within the past 5 years there has been a dramatic increase in the number of alcoholism-related studies in many disciplines. The recent admission of alcoholism into the scientifically sanctioned circle of diseases reflects a number of interacting factors, including the increased attention of the federal government, to what has been estimated to be the third most serious health problem in this country (Nelson, 1967). The studies described in this review represent a beginning in the task of trying to formulate an adequate conceptual and empirical framework within which to study the diverse phenomena of alcohol addiction.

This review will focus upon some major findings concerning the behavioral and biological correlates of chronic intoxication and withdrawal obtained in the

---

*This review was completed in January 1970.

past 5 years. An effort will be made to trace the chronological development of ... ... illustrate ... ... of a primarily empirical, phenomenological and atheoretical approach to the study of a complex behavior disorder. In a now rapidly evolving field, an historical perspective may help to redefine the latest trends and to simplify the evaluation of past directions. I will draw heavily upon data from our laboratory* to illustrate the kinds of experimental problems that have been examined and the rationale for the behavioral techniques that have been developed.

The Concept of Addiction

Only within the last decade has there been general acceptance of the concept that alcoholism is a disease, a form of addiction. The critical determinants in the development of alcohol addiction are unknown and beyond the obvious requirement of consumption of sufficient quantities of alcohol over a long enough period of time, the nature of the addictive process remains a matter of conjecture.

The classical pharmacological criteria of addiction are tolerance for and dependence upon the addictive agent (cf. Fig. 1). The alcoholic fulfills these criteria and differs from the moderate or heavy drinker in that he must ingest progressively larger quantities of alcohol through time in order to produce a change in feelings and behavior which had previously been attained with smaller doses of alcohol (tolerance). The abrupt cessation of drinking may produce dramatic withdrawal signs and symptoms (i.e., dependence) in the alcoholic.

Dependence

The alcohol withdrawal syndrome is manifest by tremulousness, hallucinosis and, in the most severe instances, overt convulsions, confusion, and delirium. Maximal expression of symptoms usually occurs between 12 and 72 hr after cessation of drinking although the time course and severity are quite variable (Victor and Adams, 1953; Victor, 1966). At one time it was thought that the withdrawal syndrome reflected intercurrent illness or vitamin and nutritional deficiency rather than the effects of cessation of drinking. This interpretation of withdrawal phenomena was challenged by the clinical observations of Victor and Adams (1953) and the studies of Isbell et al. (1955). However, experimental demonstration that withdrawal signs and symptoms occur in healthy, well-nourished alcoholics, solely as a function of cessation of drinking appeared only as recently as 1964 (Mendelson, 1964).

---

*All studies described from our laboratory were conducted in collaboration with Dr. Jack H. Mendelson, Chief, National Center for Prevention and Control of Alcoholism, National Institute of Mental Health.

FIGURE 1.   Alcoholism as a form of addiction based on the pharmacological criteria of dependence and tolerance for alcohol.

The critical determinants of the onset of withdrawal symptoms are unclear since either a relative decrease in blood alcohol levels or abrupt cessation of drinking may precipitate the syndrome. After a rapid fall in blood alcohol levels, abstinence signs have been observed in subjects with blood alcohol levels as high as 100 mg/100 ml (Isbell *et al.*, 1955; Mello and Mendelson, 1970a). The development of withdrawal phenomena is not an invariant sequel of a drinking episode and does not appear to be consistently related to the absolute dosage or duration of the drinking period. We have observed withdrawal signs in subjects who have been drinking very small amounts of alcohol for as little as 4 days. The severity and duration of withdrawal symptoms also do not appear to be directly related either to the volume of alcohol consumed or the duration of a drinking spree. We have concluded that the pattern of drinking may be more important than the duration of drinking in accounting for the expression of the alcohol abstinence syndrome (Mello and Mendelson, 1970a).

Alcohol dependence involves the anomalous situation in which the abstinence syndrome is evoked by the removal of, rather than the administration of alcohol. Attempts to explain withdrawal phenomena have suggested that the removal of alcohol results in a release of an alcohol-induced CNS inhibition or can be attributed to a rebound hypersensitivity of the central nervous system (cf. discussion in Mello and Mendelson, 1969). The empirical relevance of these constructs remains to be demonstrated, but available data suggest that the biological bases of alcohol addiction involve complex adaptive changes in the central nervous system. These as yet unspecified changes are undoubtedly long lasting and could be thought of as a form of memory. The time course of development and the duration of such an agent-induced "addiction-memory" are not known. In this connection, it is of interest that Goldberg and Schuster (1969) have shown that 3 months after morphine addiction and withdrawal, rhesus monkeys show an increased sensitivity to a morphine antagonist, nalorphine. Previous studies have shown a comparable persistent effect of chronic addiction to morphine in man and rats over 4–6 months (Himmelsbach, 1942; Fraser and Isbell, 1952; Martin et al., 1963; Sloan and Eisenman, 1968). Even single doses of morphine have been shown to produce tolerance in rats for up to 6 months (Cochin and Kornetsky, 1964; Kornetsky and Bain, 1968).

Tolerance

The mechanisms underlying tolerance for alcohol are also unknown. Prolonged drinking may produce qualitatively as well as quantitatively different effects in the alcohol addict and the normal individual. We have found that most alcohol addicts can drink between four-fifths and one quart of bourbon per day without signs of gross inebriation (Mello and Mendelson, 1970a). In addition to behavioral tolerance for alcohol, the alcoholic shows pharmacological tolerance in that consistent consumption of a quart of bourbon per day may result in unexpectedly low levels of alcohol in blood as measured by an enzymatic method (Mendelson et al., 1971; Mello and Mendelson, 1970a). Similarly, the alcoholic may show cross tolerance for other CNS depressants such as morphine and barbiturates (cf. review by Seevers and Deneau, 1963). There are many anecdotal reports that alcohol addicts undergoing surgery require far larger doses of anesthesia than nonaddict patients (Bloomquist, 1959; Lee et al., 1964). In addition, it has been shown that alcoholics may metabolize a number of drugs more rapidly than nonalcoholics (Kater et al., 1968, 1969).

It was once thought that tolerance could be accounted for by differences in the rate of metabolism by alcohol addicts and heavy drinkers. However, the available data argue strongly against such an explanation. In studies of the metabolism of ^{14}C-labeled ethanol, it has been found that although administration of alcohol induces an increased rate of alcohol metabolism in both normal and alcoholic subjects, the overall rate of metabolism does not differentiate the two groups (Mendelson et al., 1965; Mendelson, 1968). These data are consistent with the suggestion that adaptive processes subserving tolerance may occur in the central nervous system rather than at a metabolic level (cf. Mello and Mendelson, 1969). This hypothesis is supported by the finding that alcoholics show tolerance for many toxic alcohols and are able to ingest these in quantities that would be fatal for nonalcoholics (Mendelson et al., 1957). Also alcoholics show cross tolerance to other central nervous system depressants which involve different physiochemical mechanisms of action.

A Disease Model of Alcoholism

Since alcoholism is a form of addiction, it is useful to think of the disease in terms of a model generally applied in medical science. The model assumes that the expression of the disorder is dependent upon an interaction between host, the agent of the disease, and the environment in which the disease occurs

Disease processes can rarely be explained on the basis of any specific factor within each of these three categories. An analogy can be drawn between alcoholism and infectious disease in which the presence of an agent can also be identified, but expression of the disease is perhaps more closely related to host resistance factors and to environmental variables than to the presence or even to the virulence of a given agent.

In our laboratory, the goal has been to try to determine what variables contribute to the maintenance of alcoholism rather than attempt to determine etiological factors. We have argued that reconstruction of a presumed precipitating constellation of events in the development of alcoholism is probably not an effective strategy for modifying the disease process (Mendelson and Mello, 1969a). The final end point, alcohol addiction, may derive from as many diverse factors in the individual and his environment as can be postulated to contribute to the development of any behavior disorder. However, if the spontaneous initiation, perpetuation, and cessation of a drinking spree were found to be correlated with a consistent pattern of behavioral and biological variables, then manipulation of these variables could result in the modification of drinking behavior.

Selection of Subjects

Subjects in all studies reviewed from our laboratory have fulfilled the pharmacological criteria of dependence upon and tolerance for alcohol. Usually, subjects have presented a history of alcoholism of 5 to 30 years' duration. In the selection of subjects, the distinction between a pharmacological and sociological definition of alcoholism is an extremely important one. The sociocultural approach attempts to define alcoholism in terms of its social consequences rather than in terms of objective pharmacological criteria of addiction. This approach has necessarily led to some confusion and irresolvable argument since it is impossible to apply consistent social criteria even with a single culture. Cross-cultural comparisons employing sociocultural definitions present even greater difficulty. However, if alcoholism is defined in terms of objective pharmacological criteria, it is possible to choose similar subjects and to make comparisons between data obtained in different laboratories independent of the socioeconomic characteristics of the particular region. See Mendelson and Stein (1966) for a fuller discussion of the polemics involved in defining "alcoholism."

In our studies, all subjects were volunteers and were not under any legal constraint nor awaiting judgment for pending litigation. The nature of the study was carefully explained to each volunteer and each was offered an opportunity to receive psychotherapy and social service assistance. When facilities permitted, subjects could choose to live in the hospital on a halfway house basis after termination of the study. All subjects were under 45 years of age and in good

health with no history of other drug addiction and no evidence of neurological
disease, nutritional, or metabolic disorder (cf. Mendelson, 1964 for a complete
description of selection criteria). Subjects were selected from a local correctional
institution and had been abstinent from alcohol for at least 2 weeks prior to the
initiation of baseline studies. These subjects were, for the most part, homeless
men with a history of repeated incarceration for public drunkenness.

Our alcoholic subjects were studied on a research ward for drinking periods
ranging from 7 days to 3 months. During this period subjects lived in individual
bedrooms with access to a dayroom; they ate a 2000-calorie diet with daily
vitamin supplements and their health was supervised by an internist and a
psychiatrist. Television, radio, games and books were continuously available.

Methods of Alcohol Administration

Our studies of the effects of alcohol on biochemical, physiological, and
psychological variables in the alcohol addict have used two basic paradigms of
alcohol administration: (1) a programmed administration regimen in which
alcohol was administered in divided doses once every 4 hr (shown by the solid
line), and (2) some variant of free choice administration (shown by the dotted
line) in which the subject was allowed to determine the periodicity and the
volume of his own alcohol intake constrained only by the total volume potentially
available over the defined drinking period. In each study the subject was used
as his own control and data obtained during drinking were compared with
observations during a baseline and withdrawal period. A schematic diagram of
these basic procedures is illustrated in the graphic description of the research
paradigm shown in Fig. 2.

A programmed administration regimen in which alcohol is administered in
divided doses (e.g., once every 4 hr) has been traditionally used in clinical
psychopharmacology research. One obvious advantage of the programmed mode
of alcohol administration is that precise control of amount and time of administration makes it possible to construct time–dose–response curves relevant to the
variables in question. The free choice mode of administration does not yield
dose-response relationships according to predetermined temporal intervals but
does have the advantage of more closely simulating real-life drinking behavior.
Moreover, recent results obtained in our laboratory suggest that data obtained
with a programmed alcohol administration regimen may be of limited generality
in clarifying the complex determinants of the clinical expression of alcohol
addiction (Mello and Mendelson, 1970a).

We became interested in determining the extent to which correlates of
drinking are a consequence of the pharmacological properties of alcohol *per se*
or of the pattern in which it is consumed (Mello and Mendelson, 1970a). One

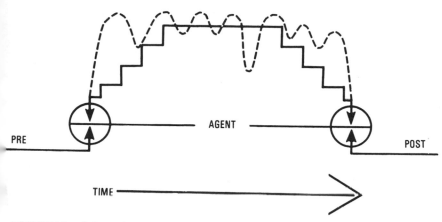

FIGURE 2.   Schematic diagram of a model research paradigm which involves the use of a subject as his own control prior to, during, and following administration of an agent, alcohol. The switches at the intersection of the preperiods and postperiods are intended to convey the fact that the agent can be abruptly turned on and off by the investigator. The middle portion of the figure indicates that the agent can be administered in programmed doses depicted by incremental steps increasing to a plateau and decreasing; or, as is shown by the dashed line, the subject can determine the volume and frequency of his own alcohol ingestion. All related behavioral physiological and biochemical factors can be examined during the pre, agent, and postperiods as a function of time. [From Mendelson and Mello (1969).]

pragmatic implication of this question is the optimal research strategy for the study of biological and biochemical correlates of alcoholism. For example, if ingestion of a quart of alcohol within a 24-hr period produced predictable and comparable effects, irrespective of the pattern of ingestion, then the many behavioral efforts to simulate real-life drinking patterns would be unnecessary and the application of traditional programmed dosage research paradigms would be justified. To study this question, we compared the effects of programmed and free choice alcohol administration in the same eight alcoholic subjects over identical periods of time. Subjects drank for 20 days in each condition and underwent a period of alcohol abstinence after each drinking episode.

All subjects showed idiosyncratic free choice drinking patterns, but all were able to drink more alcohol with less adverse reactions (e.g., gastritis) than during the initial programmed drinking period. The pattern of drinking during free choice alcohol administration consistently produced the most severe, varied, and prolonged withdrawal signs and symptoms. Pattern of drinking appears to be more important than duration of drinking in accounting for the expression of the alcohol abstinence syndrome. We concluded that the pattern of drinking produces discernible differences in physiological and behavioral correlates of intoxication and withdrawal (Mello and Mendelson, 1970a).

DRINKING PATTERNS

Most of our information about an alcoholic's drinking patterns and behavior during a drinking episode comes from his retrospective reports during sobriety. The sober alcoholic tends to be a most unreliable informant and the adequacy of his descriptions of a drinking experience may suffer from his inability to recall or his attempt to anticipate the expectancies of the interviewer. Consequently, the behavioral aspect of our research program has initially focused upon obtaining some basic phenomenological information about how an alcoholic drinks and what effects alcohol has on his behavior. In the studies to be described we have attempted to examine the kinds of variables that may contribute to the perpetuation, termination, and reinitiation of a drinking episode. In every instance, a variety of biochemical measures have been made on these subjects and these data are reported elsewhere (cf. Mendelson 1970a,b for review).

Techniques Used to Study Alcohol Acquisition and Periodicity of Drinking

Initially, we were concerned with developing a systematic method for studying drinking patterns whereby an alcoholic subject could control both the amount and the rate of his alcohol intake (Mello and Mendelson, 1965). Although we were unaware of the extent of the limitations of the programmed method of alcohol administration (cf. Mello and Mendelson, 1970a), we recognized that it bore little resemblance to the way in which an alcoholic drinks in real life.

A spontaneous drinking situation in which the subject is allowed to determine the periodicity and volume of his alcohol intake can be arranged either by providing tokens with which to buy alcohol at any time or by setting up a simple task at which he must work in order to obtain tokens to buy alcohol. Most of the studies to be reviewed in this chapter fall into the latter category. An alcoholic's ability to persist in alcohol-seeking behavior is an important aspect of his overall drinking pattern. One disadvantage of a "free token" or "alcohol spigot" procedure is that it can provide little information about motivation as inferred from the persistence of alcohol acquisition behavior. Alcohol acquisition in real life involves engaging in a variety of behaviors in order to obtain alcohol. Alcohol is never freely available to most alcoholics and therefore we thought it was realistic to require that the alcoholic subject perform a simple task to obtain his alcohol.

Operant conditioning procedures provide a systematic approach to the study of human behavior (Skinner, 1953) and we felt that a modification of operant techniques might provide a way to assess an alcoholic's preferred pattern of drinking (i.e., alcohol acquisition behavior) in a relatively free situation. The value of applying operant methods to the study of psychotic behavior and a variety of other clinical problems had already been amply demonstrated (e.g., Skinner *et al.*, 1954; Lindsley, 1956, 1960; Flannigan *et al.*, 1958; Ayllon and Michael, 1959).

Using the techniques of operant conditioning, we designed a system with the following characteristics:

1. The subject was required to make a key pressing response in the presence of appropriate visual stimuli in order to earn alcohol (or tokens).

The automatic apparatus provides an objective measure of performance on a visual-motor task at different levels of inebriation. Moreover, motivation for alcohol can be measured by varying the amount or difficulty of the task requirement.

2. Upon successful completion of the task requirement, alcohol was automatically dispensed into a receptacle.

This ensures that the drinking patterns observed would be free from the potentially confounding influence of staff interaction with the subjects, *vis-à-vis* alcohol administration.

3. The amount of alcohol earned and the frequency with which the subject removes his glass to drink can be automatically recorded, thereby providing an objective record of the volume and periodicity of a subject's drinking. This technique also permits determination of whether an alcoholic subject will drink small quantities of alcohol as soon as it is available or will allow a quantity to accumulate before drinking.

In designing our first operant paradigm, we thought it necessary to devise a task sufficiently simple that subjects could perform it and earn alcohol irrespective of their intoxication level (Mello and Mendelson, 1965). We anticipated that if alcohol reinforcement was made contingent on successful performance of a complex discrimination task, a subject would not be able to sustain his initial performance as he became increasingly inebriated. This would, of course, preclude examination of behavior to acquire alcohol and would only yield data on the effects of alcohol on some aspect of perceptual and cognitive function, which was not our primary goal. We subsequently realized that our concern about task complexity was unrealistic since our subjects have consistently shown behavioral tolerance for alcohol. Subjects have continued to perform complex operant tasks with a surprising degree of accuracy even at blood alcohol levels in excess of 250 mg/100 ml (Mello *et al.*, 1968).

A Multiple Chain Schedule of Reinforcement (Mello and Mendelson, 1965)

Two alcoholic subjects were provided with free access to individual operant conditioning booths at any time of day or night. Their entire alcohol intake over a 14-day period was dependent upon their performance of a simple operant task. Each subject had an ignition key to turn on his machine. At the beginning of each session he could select whether to work for alcohol or for money by turning a switch. The value of a single alcohol or money reinforcement was equated (10 ml of bourbon — 15 cents) based on the then current retail value of beverage alcohol in local areas with heavy endemic alcoholism. Money reinforcements were recorded on a counter in front of the subject. Alcohol was automatically dispensed into a glass directly in front of the subject. Removal of the glass shut off the machine for a period of 10 min. This procedure permitted determination of the amount of alcohol earned in a session and the session length. The response panel was a greatly simplified version of that shown in Fig. 3.

Subjects were told that the apparatus was a "gambling machine" and that they should try to learn how to beat the machine. They were instructed to press a translucent response key on which one of a series of colored lights was projected. Their task was to make the key color change as often as possible, since reinforcement occurred only when the colors changed. Each color was associated with a different schedule of reinforcement (Ferster and Skinner, 1957) as follows: Red (FR)—a fixed ratio of 360, 240, 120, 60; blue (FI)—fixed intervals of 1 min, 2 min, and 3 min; yellow (EXT)—extinction of 1 min; green (DRO)—differential reinforcement of zero response for 30 sec. These schedules of reinforcement occurred in a random sequence. After an appropriate number of responses were emitted or the necessary interval of time had elapsed, the key color changed and reinforcement occurred on an irregular basis. This situation is usually referred to as a multiple chain schedule of reinforcement. Consequently, the subject's task was simply to press the response key or to refrain from pressing the key, depending upon the particular schedule of reinforcement in effect at the given moment.

Initially, subjects were not told the appropriate pattern of responding which was associated with each of the colors on the response key. Midway through the experiment it became apparent that neither subjects' performance was coming under stimulus control as would be expected in the usual performance on a multiple chain schedule from a sophisticated pigeon* (cf. Ferster and Skinner, 1957). The main evidence of stimulus control was that subjects tended to leave the room each time the color associated with the DRO schedule came on. Since the machine advanced to another schedule once the DRO contingency of no response had been fulfilled, this superstitious escape behavior increased in frequency. After 6 days, one subject was told the best way to "beat the machine." Subsequently, this subject was able to maintain a good discrimination between ratio and interval schedules. Although the average session length decreased about 50% as the efficiency of this subject's performance increased, the number of sessions and the amount of alcohol that he earned remained essentially the same.

---

*A number of investigators have had difficulty achieving schedule control with human subjects (cf. review by Weiner, 1969).

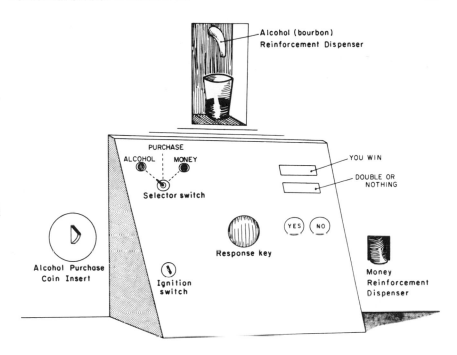

FIGURE 3. Operant response panel. Ignition switch: Each subject had a key to turn on his own machine. Selector switch: The subject could choose whether to work for alcohol or money reinforcement. The purchase position was used when the subject used money accumulated to buy alcohol. Response key: The subject's task was to press the response key whenever a stimulus light appeared on the key. You win/double or nothing: These panels were illuminated at each reinforcement opportunity and the subject had to choose whether or not to gamble within 5 sec. Yes and no keys: At each reinforcement opportunity the subject chose either to gamble by pressing the "yes" key or to take the reinforcement that he had earned by pressing the "no" key. Alcohol dispenser: Upon reinforcement, 10 ml of alcohol were directly dispensed into a glass. Removal of the glass shut off the circuit. Money dispenser: Upon reinforcement, three nickles were directly dispensed. Alcohol purchase coin insert: In order to buy alcohol, the subject placed three nickles in the purchase slot. Alcohol (10 ml) was directly dispensed into the subject's glass. [From Mello *et al.* (1968).]

Subjects continued to drink steadily for 11 and 14 days respectively, unless drinking was disrupted by gastritis. There were no intermittent periods of abstinence. Despite their inefficient performance, both subjects were able to maintain relatively stable blood alcohol levels ranging between 150 and 250 mg/100 ml with a peak at 300 to 350 mg/100 ml. Subjects were able to earn enough alcohol to sustain high blood alcohol levels by working only about 2 hr a day (1 hr 15 min to 4 hr 30 min). They tended to work in short sessions, usually between 10 and 25 min in length.

As the drinking period progressed, subjects tended to work more frequently
and in flurries, a continued to work intermittent to maintain at all hts. It was noted that
subjects were attempting to maintain a stable blood alcohol level by so adjusting
the distribution of their work behavior.

It might seem that the imposition of a 10-min time out following a glass
removal would force subjects to accumulate large quantities of alcohol before
drinking. However, these men worked for small amounts of alcohol and tended
to accumulate only 1–2 oz before removing their glass. Subsequently, they drank
the alcohol rather slowly and then returned to the operant task. Both subjects
preferred to work for alcohol directly dispensed than for money to spend in the
future.

Upon cessation of drinking, both subjects experienced severe withdrawal
symptoms of tremulousness, hallucinosis and, in one instance, delirium tremens
with disorientation, confusion, delusional ideation, and hallucinosis. This
subject's delusional system involved distorted perceptions of the operant
instrument and frightening visual imagery involving the response key and the
colored lights.

During inebriation, both subjects complained constantly about the monotony
involved in performing this task and commented that "The Machine" made
them feel "dehumanized," "like trained animals." Consequently, we became
impressed with the importance of devising a situation which had more intrinsic
interest or gamelike properties for the subjects. An unpleasant task could
confound observation of spontaneous frequency of drinking and spree duration.

A Modified Driving Machine (Mendelson and Mello, 1966)

Our first effort to design a more inviting task for alcoholics to perform to
earn alcohol was a modification of a penny-arcade driving machine similar to that
shown in Fig. 8. The two subjects were told that their task was to try to keep a
model auto on the road and to respond to the aperiodic brake and turn com-
mands as rapidly as possible. They were told that alcohol would be dispensed
into the glass only after enough points had been earned. Each subject had an
ignition key and each could work at the machine on alternate hours or a total
of 12 hr each day. Subjects were allowed to work for alcohol for an unlimited
number of days.

Twenty points were required for 0.75 ml of 84% laboratory alcohol to be
dispensed directly into a glass beside the machine. Contact points on the road
passed the auto at a rate of about one per second. Points earned as a result of
turning or stopping varied with the speed of the subject's reaction. A maximum
of eight points could be earned at each brake or turn signal. Eight points were
earned if a subject reacted within 250 msec; 7 points if he reacted within 500 msec;
and no points if the reaction time exceeded 2 sec. If a subject performed on these
tasks with maximum efficiency, it was possible to earn one reinforcement about

every 60 sec or about 5 oz of alcohol per hour. Removal of the glass from the receptacle automatically turned off the machine for a period of 10 min. Reinforcements and points earned for tracking, braking, and turning were recorded automatically.

Each subject maintained a stable blood level ranging between 150–250 mg/ 100 ml and 200–300 mg/100 ml respectively. Despite these high blood alcohol levels, subjects showed only mild intoxication, characterized by a tendency to be talkative and boisterous but without any concomitant slurring of speech, ataxia, or gross behavior disturbance. Neither subject became markedly intoxicated or showed severe ataxia, dysarthria, or stupor. Neither subject was unable to work at the operant task because of his level of intoxication. The number of tracking points earned remained relatively constant whereas braking and turning points tended to decrease through time. This evidence of behavioral tolerance at blood alcohol levels of 200–300 mg/100 ml is especially striking when compared with effects of high doses of alcohol in normals. Blood alcohol levels of 100 to 200 mg% result in mental confusion, irregularity of gait, and lack of coordination of the extremities in nonaddicts (Krantz and Carr, 1963).

These subjects also showed a temporal shift in their pattern of working and drinking. During the first few days of the drinking episode, they worked primarily during the day and then began to work increasingly more at night.

After 14 days, one subject stopped drinking because of gastritis. The second subject elected to stop after 16 days, explaining that he missed having an inebriated companion. It was of interest to find that the availability of alcohol *per se* was not sufficient to sustain his drinking behavior. He did not gradually reduce his drinking and both subjects had withdrawal signs and symptoms.

Discussion

These two exploratory studies of drinking patterns, using operant conditioning procedures, convinced us of the value of this approach for examination of behavior relating to the acquisition of, tolerance for, and motivation for alcohol. It could be objected that the reported observations were confounded to the extent that performance on an operant task forced some distribution of alcohol intake over time. However, this objection can be discounted since each of these experimental programs allowed subjects to earn between 5 and 10 oz of alcohol each hour. The estimated upper limit of alcohol metabolism is approximately 1 oz per hour (Westerfeld and Schulman, 1959; Mendelson *et al.*, 1965).

It is not possible to generalize about patterns of drinking in alcoholics on the basis of data obtained on four subjects. However, some commonalities observed in these subjects have been repeatedly observed in subsequent studies. Most important, these attempts to look at the phenomenology of drinking behavior served to focus our attention on some unexpected findings which led to a reformulation and expansion of our research interests. There follows a summary of the major findings of these studies and their implications:

1. All subjects have shown a striking behavioral tolerance for alcohol and all have been able to continue to perform operant tasks of varying complexity, despite blood alcohol levels ranging between 200 and 300 mg/100 ml. No exceptions to this finding have yet been observed (Mello et al., 1968). Consequently, these data testify to the feasibility of combining operant performance for alcohol with concurrent assessment of perceptual-cognitive function, memory, visual-motor coordination, etc. We have designed a multipurpose system for the analysis of these behaviors for the behavior laboratory of the National Center for Prevention and Control of Alcoholism at the National Institute of Mental Health.

2. A tendency to work for alcohol increasingly at night as the drinking period progresses has been consistently observed. Our preliminary impression that subjects may try to titrate drinking and maintain a constant blood alcohol level has not been confirmed since a comparable pattern of nocturnal drinking occurs in subjects with wide fluctuations in blood alcohol levels (Mello et al., 1968; Mendelson et al., 1968). The persistent development of nocturnal drinking led us to examine the effects of alcohol per se on sleep-wakefulness patterns (Mello and Mendelson, 1970b). These data are discussed in the section on sleep patterns.

3. All subjects have shown severe withdrawal signs and symptoms upon cessation of drinking. These data confirmed and extended the original observations of Mendelson (1964). The consistency of the occurrence of withdrawal signs and symptoms following spontaneous, in contrast to programmed, drinking (cf. Mendelson et al., 1966) eventually prompted the examination of the effects of different patterns of drinking in the same subjects (Mello and Mendelson, 1970a).

4. No subject allowed unlimited access to alcohol attempted to drink himself into oblivion. There was no evidence of a compulsive, uncontrollable drinking pattern following initial achievement of high blood alcohol levels. These data challenged the validity of the widely held concept of "craving" so often invoked to explain compulsive drinking (see the section on craving as an unvalidated construct).

We were surprised to find that subjects worked for and drank relatively small amounts of alcohol (1–2 oz). This suggested that the alcoholic did exercise some degree of control over his drinking behavior and prompted us to try to see if it could be brought under some greater degree of experimental control (Mello et al., 1968).

5. The potential importance of social interactional factors in determining the episodic periodicity of drinking was illustrated by the subject who terminated an unlimited period of drinking after 16 days because his companion had stopped.

Although the Skid Row alcoholic has been described as a social isolate in terms of his drinking behavior (Myerson, 1957), Rubington's (1968) intensive study of a "bottle gang" testifies to the highly structured social organization and interaction pattern that may exist among homeless alcoholics. Resolution of this complex question remains to be determined despite a series of studies of the problem (Mendelson *et al.*, 1968; Nathan *et al.*, 1970a,b, 1971; Weiner *et al.*, 1971; Steinglass *et al.*, 1971) (cf. the next section).

6. The idiosyncratic pattern of drinking exhibited by each of our subjects and the many factors (gastritis, food intake, sleeplessness, anxiety, stress, social interactions, and ward milieu) which contributed to the observed fluctuations discouraged us from further study of spontaneous drinking patterns *per se.* Rather, we became concerned with trying to identify and assess the relative contribution of these several influences on drinking periodicity within a drinking episode. We also became more interested in trying to manipulate drinking patterns in a task-specific predictable way (Mello *et al.*, 1968).

Factors Which Affect Drinking Patterns

Work Requirement and Motivation

Gambling and Motivation for Alcohol (Mello *et al.*, 1968). Motivation for alcohol can be examined by manipulating the requirements of an operant task so as to increase the amount of work, the frustration, or the risks involved in performance to obtain alcohol. In this study we were concerned with the following issues: (1) Can the volume or periodicity of drinking be consistently manipulated by systematic variation in the work requirement of the operant task? (2) Will an alcoholic be more likely to gamble for his alcohol at moderate or high levels of inebriation? (3) Given an opportunity to work either for alcohol or for money, will alcoholic subjects show a consistent preference for one or the other?

A schematic diagram of the apparatus used in this experiment is presented in Fig. 3. At the beginning of each session the subject could choose whether to work for alcohol or money. A single alcohol reinforcement (10 ml), a single money reinforcement (15 cents) and the price (15 cents) of 10 ml of alcohol were equivalent. Subjects could use the money earned to buy alcohol automatically dispensed from the machine. Consequently, accumulation of money would provide a subject with the greatest flexibility in obtaining alcohol since it could be purchased at any time. A subject was allowed to remove his glass at any time but this automatically shut off the machine. The glass had to be returned to its position and remain there for 5 min before the machine could be turned on again. This on-delay was included to encourage the subject to drink all accumulated alcohol once he removed his glass. It was hoped that this would increase the accuracy of our estimate of how much alcohol a subject earned before he drank.

The subject's task was essentially a vigilance procedure which required him to attend to the machine continuously. Subjects were instructed to press the response key in the center of the panel within $\frac{1}{2}$ sec following appearance of a stimulus light. The light onset occurred at unpredictable irregular intervals ranging between $2\frac{1}{2}$ and 10 sec. The subject was required to accumulate a specified number of consecutive correct responses in order to earn a single alcohol or money reinforcement. A failure to respond or responses when no light was present resulted in the loss of all accumulated points.

A gambling contingency was included in order to assess "risk taking" behavior. Following each series of successfully completed responses, the subject could choose whether to take the reinforcement that he had already earned or to gamble and try for double or nothing. The machine was programmed so that the subject could win on a chance basis (50–50). The following data were automatically recorded: time spent working for alcohol and for money; number of correct responses; number of omission errors and commission errors; number of reinforcement opportunities; number of responses to the *no* and the *yes* button; number of alcohol and money reinforcements; number of alcohol purchases.

The required number of consecutive correct responses was varied between the two groups of subjects. The first six subjects were required to make 32 consecutive correct responses (FR 32) for a single reinforcement. Consequently, they could earn 10 ml of bourbon about every 3 min or 200 ml per hour of perfect performance ($6\frac{2}{3}$ oz). The last three pair of subjects were required to make 16 consecutive correct responses for a single reinforcement (FR 16). These subjects could earn 10 ml of bourbon about every $1\frac{1}{2}$ min or 400 ml per hour or $13\frac{1}{3}$ oz for each hour of perfect performance, i.e. twice as much per hour as the FR 32 group. Although subjects were unable to perform perfectly on this task, their performance efficiency was not impaired by high blood alcohol levels but rather tended to improve through time. These data are evidence of behavioral tolerance for alcohol since high blood alcohol levels did not interfere with performance *or* attenuate the effects of practice at the task. The average amount of time actually spent working for alcohol each day was about 3–4 hr for each group. Time spent working was more a function of the response efficiency of an individual subject than of the ratio of correct responses required. However, there did appear to be definite limits to the length of time that an alcoholic would devote to alcohol acquisition behavior. These data suggest that alcoholics establish some compromise between the amount of alcohol ingested and the period required to procure it. A shift toward a nocturnal working pattern was also observed in these subjects.

It was found that the FR 16 group averaged blood alcohol levels that were twice as high as the FR 32 group. In other words, those subjects that were required to work half as much for their alcohol drank twice as much as a comparable group of subjects in the same situation.

The observation that the volume of alcohol consumed by an alcoholic can be manipulated by the amount of work required to obtain it argues strongly against the validity of the concept of "craving." This term refers to the circular argument that drinking is maintained by a "craving" for alcohol that is initiated by the first drink. Despite clinical evidence to the contrary, this fallacious concept has formed the basis for the goal of absolute abstinence which has characterized most therapeutic programs for alcoholics.

Further evidence of an alcoholic's capacity to control his drinking was the finding that subjects in the FR 32 and FR 16 groups tended to work for comparable amounts of alcohol in single sessions. Most subjects tended to earn between 1 and $2\frac{1}{2}$ oz before drinking and thereby terminating a session. Subjects neither hoarded alcohol nor did they consume a single reinforcement as soon as it became available.

All subjects maintained alcohol levels above 50 mg/100 ml and blood alcohol levels as high as 325 mg/100 ml were observed. In contrast to our previous subjects, most of these men showed wide variability in their blood alcohol levels. Despite the short 7-day period allowed for drinking, only 11 of the 14 subjects worked for and consumed alcohol over this entire period. One subject became depressed and agitated after 3 days and was not allowed to continue and two of the subjects developed gastritis after 6 days and elected to stop drinking at that time.

All subjects expressed considerable anxiety at the prospect of withdrawal from alcohol. However, despite their verbalized fears, only four of the 14 subjects decreased their alcohol intake during the final portion of the drinking period; three other subjects increased their alcohol consumption on the final day of the drinking period.

Subjects rarely gambled and gambling frequency did not correlate with blood alcohol level or the type of reinforcement alcohol or money selected. No subject persisted in gambling long enough to learn the probability of winning. The fact that gambling for alcohol reinforcements was a significant risk for these subjects can be inferred both from the low frequency of gambling behavior and the influence of ratio size on total alcohol earned.

Only one subject showed any sustained preference for money over alcohol reinforcements even though 12 of the 14 worked for money on at least one occasion. Working to earn money to support a sustained period of drinking dissociated from working would have been an adaptive pattern. However, the subjects studied in this experiment had histories of little or no gainful employment. It appears that their pattern of alcohol acquisition was consistent with their life style of drinking, i.e., little sustained procurement and saving of funds for the purchase of alcohol.

These data indicate that given access to alcohol, alcoholics do not drink the maximum amount available, and under the conditions of this experiment, do not drink to achieve a state of oblivion. Motivation for alcohol appears to be a complex interaction of availability and the effort required to obtain alcohol. The observation that an alcoholic's alcohol intake can be modified by the cost contingencies in an experimental situation has implications for therapeutic management. It is reasonable to suppose that an alcoholic could learn to control his drinking. The usual therapeutic goal of abstinence for the alcoholic derives from the premise that any alcohol contact will initiate an uncontrolled drinking sequence. It is curious that the somewhat trivial cost effort contingency in this experiment did affect drinking behavior since the cost consequences of alcoholism in real life fail to modify the drinking response except on a transitory basis. However, there are considerable data to demonstrate that the efficacy of a rewarding or punishing event and subsequent control of behavior is a function of temporal proximity of the consequence to the behavior. Therefore, an expenditure of 15 min as opposed to 30 min of effort for one drink may be more effective in controlling alcohol intake than repeated threats of job loss or home loss over months or years. A better clarification of this issue would require study of drinking behavior modification in a therapeutic cost economy something like the token economy for alcoholics explored by Narrol (1967).

Long-Term Drinking and Working for Alcohol (Mello and Mendelson, 1970c, 1971a). The initial focus of this study was to demonstrate if alcoholic subjects, allowed to control the volume and frequency of their alcohol intake would show consistent recurrent patterns over drinking periods of 30 to 60 days. Two groups of four men were studied. Each man earned all of his alcohol and cigarettes by working at a simple operant task. This situation differs from a previous study in which we had also observed drinking patterns of alcoholics over a 30-day period in that those subjects worked to contribute to a group reservoir rather than to support only their own drinking (Mendelson *et al.*, 1968).

In the present study, a small ($2\frac{1}{2}$ inch $\times$ 4 inch $\times$ $2\frac{1}{2}$ inch) portable box, containing a movable button and two counters was used as a manipulandum. A sliding button arrangement permitted the subject to work (i.e., button press) either for alcohol or for cigarettes, but not for both simultaneously. Each subject had a box of a distinctive color and subjects did not exchange boxes. The points registered on the counters during a 24-hr period were exchanged for poker chips once each day at 8:00 a.m. Each subject had his own color poker chips, identical to his operant box. The poker chips could be used to buy bourbon or cigarettes from an automatic dispenser located on one wall of the dayroom.

Subjects were unable to open the boxes and see the counters and they were not told how many points were required to earn a single poker chip. One thousand

(1000) responses on the portable button box earned a single poker chip which could be spent to obtain a single cigarette or a single ounce of bourbon. This reinforcement equation was made on the assumption that it required equivalent time (about 15 min) to smoke a single cigarette or to consume a single ounce of bourbon. In an experimental ward situation, time is probably a more relevant dimension on which to equate relative cost of reinforcers than actual cost in the real world. Subjects were able to earn one poker chip in about 5 min of maximally rapid performance or about 12 oz of alcohol per hour. Although this task was very simple and could be performed easily while watching television, eating or talking, subjects complained that it was tedious and tiresome. The exigencies of setting up a new laboratory at the NIMH required us to devise this task while awaiting completion of our facilities and programming equipment.

All subjects showed a dramatic dissociation between periods of working for alcohol and cigarettes and periods of consumption. Subjects rarely worked while they were drinking and all maintained a pattern of discrete working-drinking intervals over 2 months. The earning and spending pattern of one typical subject over a 62-day period is shown in Fig. 4. After an initial drinking period during which tokens accumulated during the baseline period were spent, all subjects tended to work for 1 or 2 days until they earned enough tokens to drink for 2 or 3 days. During the work-associated abstinent periods of 24 to 36 hr, subjects frequently exhibited partial withdrawal signs—mild to moderate tremor of the extremities. As is illustrated by the data shown in Fig. 4, these withdrawal signs were associated with a rapid fall in blood alcohol levels. Usually a decrease in blood alcohol levels of 100 mg/100 ml within a 24-hr period was sufficient to produce partial withdrawal signs. Partial withdrawal phenomena were observed at blood alcohol levels as high as 100 mg/100 ml as well as at zero blood alcohol levels. These data confirm and extend our previous observations that it is the rate of fall rather than the absolute blood alcohol level that initiates the expression of partial withdrawal phenomena (Mello and Mendelson, 1970a).

The cyclical pattern of drinking facilitated the development of partial withdrawal signs; however, these have also been observed in programmed drinking paradigms (Isbell et al., 1955; Mello and Mendelson, 1970a), often as a concomitant of gastritis (Mendelson et al., 1971). This cyclical pattern of drinking appears to have some generality, since it has also been observed in the self-administration patterns of intravenous ethanol in the alcohol-addicted rhesus monkey (Woods et al., 1970) and in 20 alcoholics who earned their alcohol by breaking a photocell beam (Nathan et al., 1970a,b, 1971). Nathan's subjects also showed a dissociation between earning and spending. After an initial week of drinking, paid for by points earned during the baseline period, these subjects began to work again only when they had completely exhausted their supply of alcohol points or were in imminent danger of doing so.

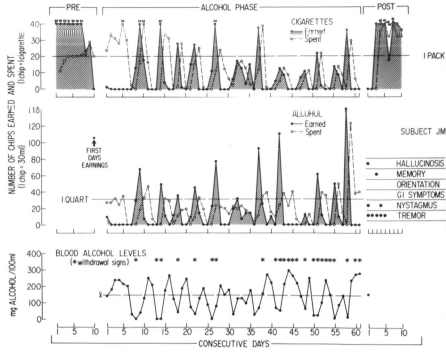

FIGURE 4. The earning and spending pattern of a single subject working for cigarettes and alcohol during a 10-day baseline period, a 62-day alcohol-available period and a 10-day withdrawal period. This subject worked to earn poker chips by pressing on a portable operant box and was paid for his previous day's earnings each morning at 8 a.m. Cigarettes and alcohol could be purchased from an automatic dispenser located on the wall of the dayroom at any time (1 chip = 1 oz of bourbon or 1 cigarette). Chips earned for alcohol were not interchangeable with chips earned for cigarettes. Chips earned for alcohol could be spent at any time during the 62-day alcohol-available period.

The pattern of earning and spending for cigarettes is shown in the top row. The pattern of earning and spending for alcohol is shown in the middle row. Subjects were allowed to work for alcohol chips during the last 24 hr of the baseline period and these chips could be spent after 8 a.m. on the first day of the drinking period. The type and duration of withdrawal signs and symptoms observed upon cessation of drinking are shown at the right of the middle row. The daily mean blood alcohol levels, based on three daily measurements, are shown in the bottom row. The occurrence of partial withdrawal signs (tremor and gastritis) are indicated as asterisks. [From Mello and Mendelson (1971a).]

Subsequently, work was usually sustained only long enough to accumulate points for a single drink. However, unlike our subjects, Nathan's subjects did work for alcohol every day, although at a lower rate than during the baseline period. After the initial drinking spree, the rate of earning and spending was usually approximately equivalent. Although the blood alcohol levels in these subjects also fell rapidly to zero on numerous occasions throughout the drinking period, Nathan does not report observation of partial withdrawal signs and symptoms (Nathan *et al.*, 1970a,b, 1971).

In an effort to clarify the extent to which the cyclical fluctuations observed in our work-contingent drinking situation were determined by the specific task requirements, we subsequently studied 18 subjects for drinking periods of 12 to 15 days during which they were given 32 poker chips each day which they could spend at any time during the drinking period (Mello and Mendelson, 1971a). These subjects also showed cyclical patterns of drinking; however, the envelope of variability of alcohol consumption and resultant blood alcohol levels was appreciably narrower. These 18 subjects did not have intervals of abstinence during which blood alcohol levels fell to zero. However, partial withdrawal signs were frequently observed in these subjects as blood alcohol levels fell or as gastritis developed. Three of these 18 subjects had been studied in the 62-day experiment and two of them maintained higher average blood alcohol levels (200 and 250 mg/100 ml compared with 180 and 140 mg/100 ml) during the free access study. From these combined data and the observations of other investigators, it would appear that the encapsulated drinking-working pattern seen over 62 days may resemble the episodic drinking patterns followed by many alcoholics in real life.

There was an approximate correlation between the drinking-working cycles and the smoking-working cycles; however, subjects worked for cigarettes less consistently than for alcohol. All subjects smoked considerably less during the drinking period than during the pre- and postalcohol periods although all described themselves as usually smoking at least a pack each day. It has been reported that alcoholics exceed the general population in terms of proportion of smokers and of heavy (+20/day) smokers and that alcoholics tend to smoke cigarettes exclusively (Dreher and Fraser, 1968). During a 15-day period of unlimited access to alcohol, three subjects were required to continue working for cigarettes. All subjects stopped working for cigarettes after the first 1 or 2 days of drinking and rarely resumed working for cigarettes once their accumulated cigarette supply was exhausted. These data are illustrated in Fig. 5.

None of the 18 subjects studied in the free access paradigm drank all of the alcohol available during the drinking period. Tokens that could have been exchanged for between 60 and 206 oz of alcohol were returned at the end of the drinking period. A rather typical pattern is shown in Fig. 5. Twelve of the 18 subjects did not drink all the alcohol available on the first day of alcohol access (32 oz) and four of these never consumed 32 oz within a single 24-hr period. Thirteen of the other 14 subjects drank 32 oz within a 24-hr period on two or more occasions. The first maximum peak alcohol consumption occurred between days 4 and 7 for 12 subjects and only four drank an amount on the first day equivalent to later peak consumption. These data are contrary to any predictions derived from the questionable concept of craving discussed in a later section.

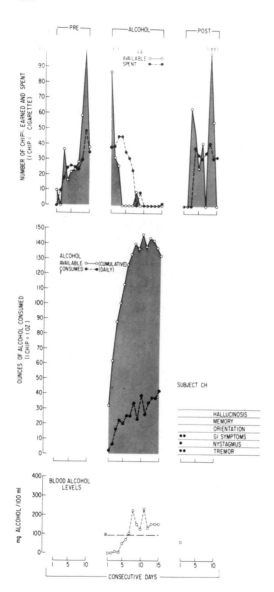

FIGURE 5. The pattern of working and spending for cigarettes during a 10-day baseline, a 15-day drinking and a 10-day withdrawal period by a single subject is shown in the top row. Cigarette chips earned by pressing a portable operant box were paid each morning at 8 a.m. and could be spent at any time during the entire 35-day experimental period.

Thirty-two ounces of alcohol were available daily without performance of an operant task. Thirty-two tokens which could be used to buy alcohol from an automatic dispenser were provided each morning at 8 a.m. and could be used to buy alcohol at any time during the 15-day drinking period. The daily quantity of alcohol purchased and the cumulative amount of alcohol available are shown in the middle row. The type and duration of withdrawal signs and symptoms observed upon cessation of drinking are shown at the right of the middle row. The daily mean blood alcohol levels (based on three daily measurements) are shown in the bottom row. [From Mello and Mendelson (1971a).]

Assessment of deliberate reduction of alcohol intake at the end of a drinking period to attenuate the severity of withdrawal signs and symptoms was complicated by the discordance between volume ingested and blood alcohol levels recorded. Of the 23 subjects studied in the long-term work-contingent drinking and the free alcohol access paradigms, five subjects increased their alcohol intake on the day before withdrawal. The three subjects studied in both paradigms increased their alcohol intake prior to cessation of drinking on both occasions. However, this increase in alcohol consumption increased the blood alcohol level over the previous 24-hr period in only one instance. In three cases, blood alcohol levels actually decreased. Nine subjects decreased their alcohol intake on the day before withdrawal; however, only four of these showed a tendency to taper their drinking over the several preceding days. In six instances, a slight decrease in alcohol intake or maintenance of a steady alcohol intake resulted in an average increase in blood alcohol levels in the 24-hr period immediately prior to cessation of drinking.

The Interaction of Eating, Drinking, and Intoxication. These data amplify our previous observations that fluctuations in blood alcohol levels are often unrelated to changes in the volume of alcohol ingested (Mello and Mendelson, 1970a). Such volume-independent variations in blood alcohol levels may be related both to the subject's degree of metabolic tolerance and to his food intake and gastrointestinal status. We have observed that gastrointestinal symptoms are often accompanied by marked elevations in blood alcohol levels during a period of programmed drinking (Mendelson *et al.*, 1971). One subject reported that he intended to stop eating in order to increase the effect of his alcohol and consequent reduction of food intake did result in a threefold increase in his blood alcohol levels (Mello and Mendelson, 1970a). It is possible that alcoholics learn that eating less food effectively enhances the intoxicating properties of a given dose of alcohol. It has been shown that the rate of ethanol metabolism is reduced in fasted or starved rats (Smith and Newman, 1959; Forsander *et al.*, 1965). Recent studies in our laboratory have shown that reduction of caloric intake in man with controlled maintenance of alcohol dosage is associated with a significant decrease in the rate of alcohol metabolism (see Mendelson, 1970b).

It has long been postulated that the poor dietary intake of the alcoholic during drinking is a reflection of the fact that he requires fewer calories from food because of the high caloric yield from alcohol. We attempted to estimate the total caloric intake of subjects studied in the 62-day work-contingent drinking paradigm. Representative findings for two subjects are shown in Fig. 6. The combined daily caloric intake from food (about 2000 calories) and from alcohol averaged between 4 and 5000 calories over a 2-month period. However, no subject showed a substantial increase in weight and one subject lost weight during this study. These data challenge the notion that calories in alcohol are

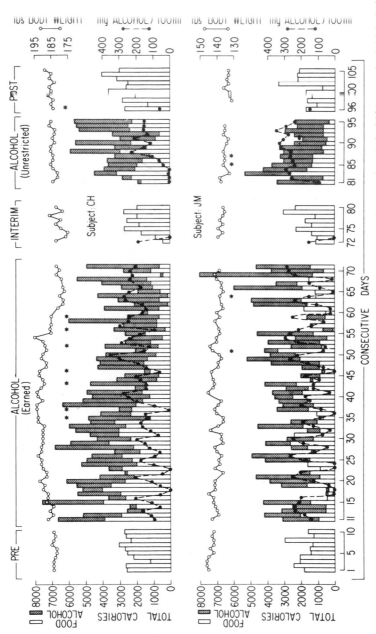

FIGURE 6. Total caloric intake from food and from bourbon are shown for two subjects for a total period of 105 days. An initial 10-day baseline period was followed by two drinking periods of 62 and 15 days, each of which was followed by a 10-day alcohol withdrawal period. Body weight was recorded daily and is shown by the open circles at the top of each row. Calories from food are indicated by the open bars and calories from alcohol by the shaded bars. Blood alcohol levels (mean per day based on three measurement) are shown as closed circles superimposed on the calorie bar graph. Episodes of partial withdrawal signs during drinking are shown as asterisks.

During the 62-day drinking period, subjects obtained their alcohol by working at a simple operant task. During the second unrestricted drinking period, subjects were given tokens to purchase 32 oz of bourbon each morning and these tokens could be spent at any time during the drinking period. (From Mello and Mendelson (1971a).)

equivalent to and are substituted for calories in food. They strengthen the impression that the alcoholic's poor dietary intake may be, in part, a deliberate maneuver to increase his intoxication level with less alcohol. This may be an effective way for him to counteract the effects of tolerance and to intensify and prolong a drinking experience for less money. The role of nutritional deficiencies in exacerbating the many medical complications related to the toxic effects of alcohol consumption and withdrawal have been well documented (Victor and Adams, 1953; Victor, 1966; Collins, 1966).

Delay in Reinforcement

Subjects have consumed a comparable daily total volume of alcohol (four-fifths to one quart of bourbon) in most of the experimental paradigms that we have studied. It has been shown that manipulation of the work requirement to obtain alcohol can decrease alcohol consumption. Immediate and delayed reinforcement paradigms also appear to produce differences in the drinking pattern within a day (Mello et al., 1968; Mello and Mendelson, 1971a). The daily pattern of drinking for an immediate and a delayed reinforcement group is shown in Fig. 7. The frequency with which subjects earned (or purchased) 1–14 oz of bourbon at a time is expressed as a percentage of the total number of purchase events which occurred over the entire drinking period.

The immediate reinforcement condition resulted in spaced and moderate drinking, i.e., men tended to work at a vigilance task for 1 or 2 oz of bourbon and then resume working again after some time had elapsed (Mello et al., 1968). The resultant daily drinking pattern was somewhat comparable to programmed alcohol administration in which a fixed dose of alcohol is administered once every 4 hr.

In a delayed reinforcement paradigm in which tokens earned during one day were available only on the next day, moderate and spaced drinking were seldom observed. There were no constraints as to when subjects could spend their tokens once they received them, or how many tokens they could spend at one time, and subjects tended to mass their drinking. It was not uncommon for a subject to buy 6 oz of alcohol in one 2-hr period, and 4 and then 3 oz in the immediately subsequent 2-hr periods (Mello and Mendelson, 1971a). The frequency distribution of purchase volumes made by 21 subjects given 32 free tokens each morning was most similar to that of the delayed reinforcement group shown in Fig. 7. Two-ounce purchases accounted for 44% of all purchases in this group. Three ounces (22%), 4 oz (15%) and 1 oz (10%) were purchased in descending frequency. None of these subjects purchased more than 10 oz on one occasion; however, 5 and 6 oz purchases both accounted for about 2% of the mean purchase frequency (Mello and Mendelson, 1971b).

Although these subjects could accumulate their tokens and spend them over the entire drinking period, the mean volume per purchase remained very

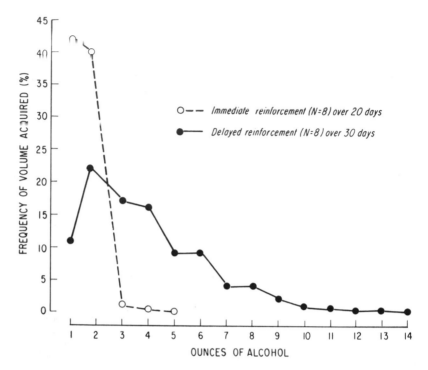

FIGURE 7. The distribution of the frequency with which 1 through 14 oz of alcohol were purchased at a single time during drinking periods in which operant performance for alcohol was followed by an immediate alcohol reinforcement (open circles) and by a delayed alcohol reinforcement (solid circles). These data are expressed as percent frequency of purchase volume episodes (Mello and Mendelson, 1971b).

stable from days 3 through 12 of the drinking period. These subjects tended to purchase less alcohol per occasion during the first 2 days of the drinking period (Mello and Mendelson, 1971b).

Of the many variables assumed to contribute to patterning of alcohol consumption within a drinking episode (e.g., gastrointestinal function; social interaction patterns; research ward milieu; the difficulty and aversiveness of an operant task) delay in alcohol reinforcement has the advantage of being easily specified. The potential efficacy of delay in reinforcement as a tool for the modification of drinking patterns remains to be determined.

Social Interaction

A Simulated "Bottle Gang" (Mendelson *et al.*, 1968). We became interested in trying to identify some interactional factors which might correlate with periodic fluctuations in drinking over a 30-day period. In particular, we wanted to focus upon the role of group interaction patterns in determining an individual's drinking behavior. We anticipated that if the critical variables in the maintenance of addictive drinking are physiological and host-agent specific, then group pressures should have a minimal effect on an individual's drinking pattern. However, if each alcoholic were to show parallel drinking patterns, this would suggest that the presence of alcohol alone is not the only crucial factor contributing to the maintenance of drinking behavior.

The apparatus used in this study is shown in Fig. 8. In order to simulate one essential feature of the Skid Row "bottle gang" who share their alcohol, all alcohol earned by the subjects was dispensed into a common reservoir. Each man had a key which activated the alcohol withdrawal reservoir and allowed him to withdraw as much alcohol as he wished at any time. Each subject also had a key to turn on the driving machine and his task was to steer a model automobile and keep it on the road. Each time the auto touched a metal contact on the road, a point was registered by programming circuitry located in an adjoining room. After 120 points had been earned, 10 ml of bourbon were automatically dispensed into a common alcohol reservoir. The maximum amount of alcohol that could be earned was 300 ml or 10 oz per hour. The total time that each subject worked, the number of alcohol reinforcements that he earned, and the amount of alcohol that he withdrew from the group reservoir were automatically recorded.

Subjects were told that they could work at the machine and drink as much alcohol as they wished for 30 days, provided that they remained in good health and ate their meals.

The group consisted of four subjects who knew one another and drank together in South Boston. One subject was dismissed from the study because he destroyed furniture and physically assaulted other subjects. This subject drank very little and tended to overdramatize his degree of inebriation, apparently to excuse his lack of impulse control and as a means of soliciting hostility and rejection from other subjects and from the staff. His drinking behavior appeared to be motivated by a desire to engage in hostile and provocative interactions in a context where alcohol was being consumed.

The other three subjects evolved a stable pattern of group interaction and maintained their mutually defined roles independent of the quantity of alcohol consumed. However, the behaviors involved in the procurement, the sharing and the group consumption of alcohol were specific to alcohol and did not occur in connection with food or cigarettes. The consistency of the roles assumed, i.e., provider, taker, freeloader, and isolate, suggested that these interaction patterns might be similar to those which occurred in real life. The ostensible group leader consistently earned and drank an average of over a fifth ($\frac{4}{5}$ qt) of bourbon a day for 30 days. He consistently contributed more alcohol to the reservoir than he consumed. This alcohol providing behavior was consistent with his tendency to be supportive to other group members. Another subject consistently

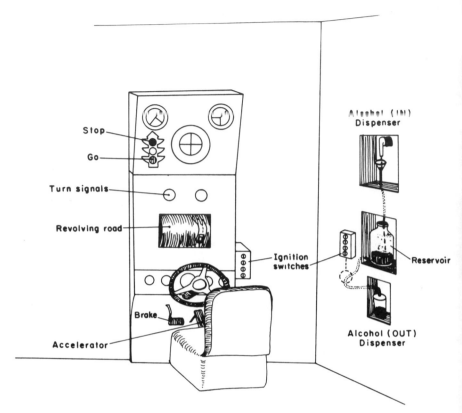

FIGURE 8. Schematic diagram of the operant apparatus. Left: A modified driving machine with a steering wheel, brake, and accelerator which controlled the movement of a model automobile on the revolving road drum. Periodically, signals to stop, go, or turn appeared on the panel above the revolving road. However, points were earned only for keeping the car on the road. Each subject had a key to one of the four ignition switches located to the right of the revolving road. Right: Every 120 points earned for keeping the auto on the road resulted in 10 ml of alcohol being directly dispensed from the alcohol IN dispenser into the group reservoir. Each subject had a key to one of the four ignition switches located to the right of the reservoir. Any subject could withdraw alcohol from the group reservoir by placing his key in the ignition switch. Alcohol was dispensed into a glass underneath the OUT dispenser and would flow for as long as the ignition switch was activated. [From Mendelson *et al.* (1968).]

consumed more alcohol than he contributed to the group reservoir; however, because of his manipulative abilities, this behavior was never challenged by the other group members. By verbal manipulation alone, this subject was able to control behavior of the other two group members without ever assuming the overt role of "leader." The third subject was the least intelligent of the three and showed an insatiable need for companionship and reassurance while drinking.

He was the only subject who contributed an amount of alcohol to the group reservoir equivalent to the amount that he withdrew. Following a period of illness during which this subject was required to stop drinking, he also began withdrawing more from the reservoir than he contributed. This behavior was openly resented by the other two subjects who described him as a "freeloader" and began to isolate and insult him.

One of the primary aims of this experiment was to examine the periodicity and concordance of drinking episodes. The termination of a drinking episode was arbitrarily defined by at least one 16-hr period of abstinence from alcohol as inferred from a blood alcohol level of zero mg/100 ml. According to this criterion, the "provider" initiated and terminated four separate drinking episodes ranging in duration from 3 to 10 days over the 30-day drinking period. His periods of abstinence extended from 16 hr to 3 days. Two of these periods of abstinence did overlap with those of the subject who was the "taker." The "taker" engaged in three separate drinking episodes which ranged from 5 to 16 days in duration; his intervening periods of abstinence never exceeded 24 hr. However, the volume consumed and pattern of drinking within each day showed little concordance between subjects. The third subject, the "isolate" showed only one instance of voluntary abstinence simultaneously with the "provider." After his intercurrent illness, the "isolate" initiated two separate drinking episodes of 6 and 7 days respectively. His single period of abstinence was 16 hr in duration.

In each instance, cessation of drinking was impulsive and abrupt. Moreover, cessation of drinking followed an obvious stress situation in four of the seven instances in which subjects spontaneously terminated a drinking episode. It was somewhat surprising to find that cessation of drinking was correlated with the occurrence of a stress situation. In contrast, there were seldom clearly definable events which accompanied resumption of drinking. On each occasion, subjects appeared less anxious and less depressed when they resumed drinking than when they terminated a drinking episode. These data complement clinical reports that an alcoholic may start drinking with little subjective feeling of tension, stress, or depression after deliberately planning a drinking spree (cf. Merry, 1966; Steinglass et al., 1971).

These subjects were able to continue to work to obtain alcohol despite blood alcohol levels ranging between 200 and 300 mg/100 ml. They also tended to drink intermittently throughout the day and night and to sleep sporadically. However, these subjects showed wide fluctuations in blood alcohol levels. Consequently, their tendency to work increasingly for alcohol at night may have been related to the increased anxiety and agitation that occurred throughout the course of the drinking period. During the intermittent periods of abstinence, each subject slept most of the time. We wondered if prolonged drinking is associated with a degree of sleep deprivation which can be tolerated only for a finite period of time. It was tempting to postulate that as subjects drank longer and became increasingly anxious and insomniac, their subjective discomfort reached a critical level such that an additional discrete stressor prompted a change in behavior, i.e., cessation of drinking.

Our previous observations of wakefulness associated with nocturnal drinking were interpreted as an effort by the subject to titrate his blood alcohol intake to maintain a constant blood alcohol level. Since an alcoholic subject may metabolize his alcohol more rapidly as a function of prolonged drinking (Mendelson et al., 1965), sustained wakefulness could reflect the necessity of ingesting alcohol over progressively shorter time intervals in order to maintain a consistent low blood alcohol level.

In summary, it seemed that part of the reward value of the alcohol lay in its effect as a catalyst to facilitate a complex pattern of social interaction. A detailed analysis of social structure in a "bottle gang" has been provided by Rubington (1968). In the present study, it appeared that these individuals assumed roles in the context of group drinking which may not have been possible in other aspects of their daily life. This was perhaps most clearly shown by the subject who assumed the role of group leader and consistently expressed a caretaking attitude toward the other subjects. It is possible that a "provider" may actively lead others into drinking behavior. A parallel role is acted out by the narcotic addict who is also a "pusher." The use of narcotics may actually be secondary to narcotic procurement and distribution. Another correlate of this phenomenon may occur when the ardent Alcoholics Anonymous member tries to lead the alcoholic away from drinking. It is not at all unusual to observe a strong polarization among individuals who have alcohol-related problems.

The significance of group interaction patterns and/or dyadic relationships in influencing individual drinking patterns is difficult to determine. In this group of men there appeared to be a greater concordance of abstinence than of drinking periodicity within a day. Since abstinence seemed most often to be a response to a stressor which affected the entire group, it is not possible to conclude that within-group interactions outweighed other possible determinants of each individual's drinking pattern. Further examination of role behaviors in a drinking group, using a cooperative structured task involving a "leader" and "follower" role is being studied by Dr. Steinglass in our laboratory. This approach permits examination of structured role behavior and its generalization to interaction patterns in a broader group context.

Familial Interactions During Experimentally Induced Intoxication (Weiner et al., 1971; Steinglass et al., 1971). Recently in our laboratory, Drs. Weiner and Steinglass have attempted to examine the individual dynamics and interactions between an alcoholic father and an alcoholic son and between two pairs of alcoholic brothers observed before, during, and after a period of experimentally induced intoxication. In each of these dyadic relationships, alcohol and drinking were used as a basis for the definition of roles.

In the father-son pair, the father was 51 years old and his son, one of five children, was 26, with a 10-year history of heavy drinking. Both men left school in the seventh grade and worked at a series of sporadic jobs. Asked about their motivation for drinking, the father stated that it was because of a compulsion and to relieve his depression. The son indicated that he drank because he got so lonesome.

During the predrinking period, each man became a member of a different subgroup of the other four patients, and both reacted to each other with separateness, aloofness, and distrust. Both men expressed a preference for individual, rather than joint psychotherapy sessions with the ward psychiatrist. During the joint sessions, the son was usually verbally abusive to his passive father. The son was able to express feelings of ambivalence toward his father characterized by an alternating attraction and repulsion.

The father was able to admit to positive feelings for his son only during the initial part of the drinking period. The son responded by bitter verbal attacks at his father and continuing to describe his own ambivalent feelings toward him. This ambivalence was illustrated by the son's alternation between caretaking and criticism. When the father drank heavily and appeared stuporous, the son became frightened, expressed his concern. Later, he helped his father to shower and shave and was able to show considerable warmth toward him.

The son appeared to be quite ambivalent about his mother and repeatedly pleaded with his father to tell him the truth about her. The father asserted that the mother was a whore and after this painful interchange, he dramatically decreased his alcohol intake. He was not able to remember this conversation on the following day and it appeared to the psychiatrist that he felt guilty for depriving his son of an idealized mother figure. Reduction of drinking following an external stress is concordant with our previous observations of group interaction (Mendelson et al., 1968).

It was of particular interest to observe the alcohol-induced personality changes and concomitant role reversals in these men. In this dyadic relationship, these alterations in role behavior were often accompanied by fluctuations in drinking patterns such that the members of the pair were never simultaneously drunk. This alternation in drinking allowed each man to play a variety of roles, rather than to be rigidly cast in the single role he maintained during sobriety In these particular patients, the most inebriated of the pair would be helpless, dependent and childlike, whereas the person who was relatively sober would assume responsibility for caring for a helpless partner. The alternation of these roles seemed to relieve some pressure and tension. It appeared that there was an enhancement of direct communication and expression of warmth and positive feelings with a concomitant decrease in guilt and hostility as a result of this interaction during drinking. However, upon cessation of drinking, both father and son reverted to their previous mode of interaction. Within the first 24 hr following cessation of drinking, they were each able to reflect on the drinking experience and to synthesize some of their newer insights. However, within 48 hr their interactions were again as they had been prior to the drinking period. An alcoholic's inability to synthesize and recall the changes in his behavior and affect that occur during intoxication, when he becomes sober again is a serious impediment to psychotherapy. The relationship of this alcohol-induced dissociative behavior to the concepts of state-dependent learning will be discussed in the section on memory and dissociative patterns (pp. 266–274).

The two pairs of brothers also showed an alteration in role behavior as a function of drinking. The first pair of brothers studied tended to drink at different times so that the two members of the pair would rarely be drunk simultaneously. They reported that alternate drinking sprees characterized their usual drinking behavior. During sobriety, the "leader" of the pair (age 39) presented a façade of composure and self-assurance. He was frequently critical of his "follower" brother for expressing anxiety and concern over major life stresses, such as deaths in their immediate family. The "follower" brother (age 46) appeared to be warm, friendly, and deferential to his younger brother.

During the early phase of drinking, a central issue in the brothers' interaction seemed to be control over drinking. The "leader" alternately enticed, teased, and encouraged the "follower" to drink, then ridiculed him for his inebriated behavior. By taking the first drink, the "follower" had admitted his own lack of control and weaker position in relation to the "leader." The implicit equation operating appeared to be that intoxication equaled loss of control which equaled weakness which equaled a nonleader role.

However, as the drinking period progressed, the dyadic role relationship was reversed and friction increased between the two brothers. In order to remain in the role of "leader," the "leader" would have to remain sober. He openly resented his brother's pressure on him to remain the leader. The "leader" characteristically responded to drinking by becoming violent and abusive whereas the "follower" remained quite affable and friendly while drinking heavily. However, in contrast to his earlier deferential behavior, the "follower" became assertive and forceful in describing his brother as a "dangerous character" when drinking. In contrast to his earlier listlessness and confusion, the "follower" now appeared alert and purposeful in his behavior while drinking. As drinking progressed, this role reversal became increasingly stable and structured.

In the second pair of brothers during sobriety, the "leader" (age 37) appeared intelligent, talkative, hyperactive, and initially impressive in his command of a situation. The "follower" (age 40) seemed subdued, sullen, often confused and he seemed to have difficulty keeping up with his brother's rapid conversation and tended to agree automatically when he sensed himself getting lost.

The "follower" initiated drinking for the entire group of subjects. In contrast to the other dyadic pairs studied, the "leader" remained totally sober throughout the entire drinking period. He was verbally abusive and critical of his inebriated brother, constantly berating him for drinking behavior which was in no way dissimilar to his own previous drinking behavior. The "leader" accused his brother of being the "lowest of the low" and reacted punitively, no matter what his brother said. Despite these scathing attacks, the "leader" also deliberately perpetuated his brother's drinking and was observed to purchase 4 oz of alcohol for him from the machine and to help him to drink it by holding the cup to his mouth when he stopped. After cessation of drinking, the "leader" once again became friendly and supportive and the "follower" appeared defeated and quiet.

These clinical vignettes illustrate stable dyadic drinking relationships in which drinking and drunkenness formed the basis for role definition, i.e., relative sobriety defined the "leader." In these subjects, alcoholism had become a way of life since adolescence and patterns of behavior that had occurred in previous generations of their nuclear families were repeated. There was a tendency to accept drinking as inevitable and, despite verbal affirmations to the contrary, no serious attempts at abstinence or moderate drinking had been made. The two pairs of brothers maintained a recurrent, programmed pattern of drinking, despite considerable external chaos in their lives. This pattern included predictable sequences of negotiating a time for a drinking spree; assignment of tasks to build up a cash reserve; initial purchase of alcohol and alternate drunkenness, which also served the function of one man protecting his drunken partner from the external world. Despite the similarities in their interaction patterns, these men exhibited very different clinical pictures and appeared to show great differences in individual personality structure. These data are consistent with the many previous observations that testify to the essential heterogencity of personality in alcoholics (McNamee *et al.*, 1968; Rosen, 1966).

The Effect of Social Isolation on Drinking Behavior (Nathan *et al.*, 1970a,b, 1971). The studies described in the preceding section have suggested the importance of social interaction factors in influencing an individual's drinking pattern (Mendelson and Mello, 1966; Mendelson *et al.*, 1968; Weiner *et al.*, 1971, Steinglass *et al.*, 1971).

A series of studies by Nathan and his associates have explored the influence of social isolation on drinking patterns and on the effects of inebriation in alcoholics. Twenty alcoholic subjects were studied under research ward conditions in which a 3-day period of free socialization was alternated with a 3-day period of isolation during a baseline, drinking, and withdrawal period. Drinking periods lasted 6, 12, and 18 days in three respective studies. Each subject had a private bedroom equipped with a TV set, an operant response panel, an alcohol dispenser, counters to indicate accumulated points, and a TV monitor screen

and microphone via which a subject could communicate with another patient
or with staff if he chose to ~~~~~~~~ ~~~~~~~~~~~~~~~ ~~~~~~~~ ~~~~. During isolation
periods, subjects were totally restricted to their bedrooms. During socialization
periods, subjects had access to an adjacent dayroom with TV, ping-pong, and
other recreational facilities.

Subjects earned points for alcohol or socialization by disrupting a photocell
beam. It was necessary to make 3000 responses (which took about 10 min) to
earn 20 ml of bourbon or 15 min out of social isolation. Subjects could earn
about 4 oz of alcohol each hour by working steadily. Points earned during the
baseline period could be accumulated to spend for alcohol or socialization during
the drinking period. The drinking patterns of these alcoholic subjects seemed
relatively unaffected by the condition of isolation. Five subjects drank slightly
less during isolation and the rest drank about the same amount as during
socialization periods. Only two subjects spent points to break isolation on one
occasion. During socialization periods, these subjects seemed to prefer to
remain alone in their rooms drinking, reading, or watching TV to socializing or
watching TV in the adjacent dayroom. The considerable variability in blood
alcohol levels from day to day did not seem to correspond to the conditions of
socialization or isolation in any systematic way. The major effect of isolation in
this series of studies was to increase anxiety and depression as assessed by
self-ratings on a mood adjective checklist. It is of interest that these subjects did
not try to alter their reported mood state by increasing or decreasing their
alcohol consumption.

Nathan and his associates (1971) suggested that perhaps these subjects
did not socialize because their customary focal point of interaction, a bar and
bartender, were not available. Moreover, the lack of effect of isolation may have
reflected the fact that subjects knew how long each isolation period would last.
Consequently, four additional subjects were studied over an 18-day drinking
period in which the duration of the 3-day alternations of socialization and
isolation were not explained. A bar and a bartender to talk, provide free mixers
and ice, and sell snacks were available. These subjects tended to socialize
considerably more at the bar than had previous subjects, but they drank somewhat less. Nathan and his associates suggested that the lower alcohol consumption may have reflected uncertainty about when the alcohol period would be
terminated and a deliberate effort to avoid abrupt withdrawal.

These subjects did spend significantly more points to socialize both during
and after the drinking period than the previous group. Most spending for
socialization occurred during the first isolation period of the drinking phase and
the consequent exhaustion of the accumulated store of points resulted in subjects
having to work for almost every drink during the later phases of the study.
These subjects also earned and spent points for socialization during the postdrinking period. The choice between alcohol and socialization seemed to depend

primarily on the amount of currency available. When a large backlog of points had been accumulated, subjects spent freely for both alcohol and socialization. However, once the supply of points had been exhausted, to the extent that it was necessary to work for each drink, working and spending for alcohol to the exclusion of socialization occurred. These data indicate that alcohol remains a powerful reinforcer, even in the absence of an opportunity to socialize while drinking.

Comparison of Alcohol with Other Reinforcers

The Cost of Alcohol

The ultimate price of alcoholism for the alcoholic is often the loss of society's material and social reinforcers, to say nothing of physical health, self-esteem, and an opportunity to renew any sense of self-worth. The argument that the momentary pleasures of drinking obscure and prevent appreciation of these several aversive consequences has been challenged by mounting evidence that the transient ebullience produced by alcohol is momentary indeed. The chronic alcoholic becomes progressively more anxious, depressed, and self-demeaning during the course of a drinking episode (see pp. 263–266). The alcoholic's apparent inability to recall his alcohol-induced despondency when sober and a tendency to restructure his inebriated experience in terms of a wistful expectancy (McGuire et al., 1966) is one compelling argument for exploration of therapeutic audiovisual techniques that focus on the immediate consequences of alcoholism (Parades and Cornelison, 1968; Parades et al., 1969).

The paradox of sustained drinking behavior, given both immediate and eventual punishing consequences, can be resolved by the behaviorist and the psychoanalyst with equal (ineffectual) facility; i.e., the behavior is maintained by the aversive contingencies rather than "rewards" and/or unconsciously determined masochism. The intriguing data of Morse and Kelleher and their associates (1967) that monkeys maintained on an avoidance schedule will eventually work to produce noxious shock identical to that they previously worked to avoid, lends some credence to this notion. Regardless of one's ideological persuasion, it can be agreed that examination of the nature of the reinforcing properties of alcohol or any other addicting drug for the addict is a question of critical importance for understanding the addictive process (cf. discussion by Woods and Schuster, 1970; Kelleher and Morse, 1968).

Recently, several research groups have attempted to study the reinforcing properties of alcohol by asking: (1) how hard will an alcoholic work for his alcohol, and (2) if given a choice between alcohol and another reinforcer, how consistently will he choose alcohol? Each of these studies has been conducted within an operant conditioning framework, using concepts and methods of data collection and analysis which derive from the innovations of B. F. Skinner (cf.

1959 for collected papers). At the risk of seeming gratuitous, it may be well to remind the reader that the term reinforcement does not have a connotation of "reward" or punishment but rather refers to any consequence of behavior which increases the probability that the behavior will reoccur. A reinforcement schedule sets up a pattern of responding which in turn generates stimuli which affect control of the rate of responding. It is then the "combination of schedule and performance which generates reinforcing contingencies" (Skinner, 1959, p. 136). To extrapolate to drinking behavior, what are the reinforcing consequences of sustained alcohol consumption for the alcoholic?

Table 1 summarizes the relative costs of alcohol in the several studies in which alcoholics have had to work for their alcohol. Most of these studies have been reviewed in preceding sections of this paper.

Two important findings are illustrated by these data:

1. Despite the ready availability of more than 10 oz of alcohol per hour, subjects did not engage in uncontrolled drinking eventuating in stupor.

2. The relative cost of alcohol did influence the amount of alcohol consumed as inferred from blood alcohol levels.

Liebson and co-workers have suggested that the relative cost of alcohol may also influence the stability of drinking patterns. Initially, they were interested in determining if the cost of alcohol, defined in terms of the number of work units required to buy alcohol, affected the amount of alcohol consumed. When a fixed ratio of 50 envelopes stuffed (a task requiring about 20 min) was required to buy 1 oz of alcohol, subjects earned about 20 and about 32 oz per day over periods of 14 and 9 days respectively. When the cost of alcohol was varied between a fixed ratio of 100, 50, 10 and free, alcohol consumption was fairly stable and inversely proportional to the work requirement, thus confirming the observations of Mello et al. (1968) (Liebson et al., 1971).

In the several studies which compare alcohol with an alternative reinforcer, alcohol has consistently proved to be preferred in a forced choice situation. Alcohol was preferred even in a situation where the alternate reinforcer, money, could be used to buy alcohol (Mello et al., 1968).

Alcohol versus Socialization. Nathan and his associates (1971) compared spending for alcohol with spending for socialization in a situation where subjects were kept in isolation for 3-day periods. During the first isolation period, when subjects had accumulated and saved many points from their baseline period, they spent freely for 15-min socialization contacts via a television intercom system. However, once their supply of points was exhausted and they had to work for every drink, there was no further spending for socialization.

Subjects only spent points for socialization in a situation where a bar and a bartender were present. When only the usual dayroom recreational opportunities were available only two subjects spent points for socialization on one occasion.

TABLE 1. A Comparison of the Cost of Alcohol in Several Behavioral Experiments

Reference	Number of subjects	Type of task	Responses/ reinforcement	Volume/ reinforcement	Possible ounces/hr
Liebson et al. (1971)	2	Envelope stuffing	50–100	1 oz	3–1½
Nathan et al. (1970a,b, 1971)	20	Break photocell beam	3000	20.0 ml	4
Mendelson and Mello (1966)	2	Tracking (driving machine)	20	0.75 ml	5
Mello et al. (1968)	14	Vigilance task	16–32	10 ml	6¼–13⅓
Mello and Mendelson (1965)	2	Multiple chain schedule	Variable	10 ml	10
Mendelson et al. (1968)	3	Tracking (driving machine)	120	10 ml	10
Mello and Mendelson (1971a)	8	Portable operant box	1000	1 oz	12

These data suggest that access to alcohol was more important than access to social companionship for these subjects.

Alcohol versus Cigarettes. Comparable results were obtained in a study in which subjects could work for either alcohol or cigarettes but not for both simultaneously. Once their supply of points earned during the baseline period was depleted, their major work output was for alcohol. Working for cigarettes decreased as the drinking period progressed. These data were somewhat surprising since subjects complained bitterly about the lack of cigarettes and competed for any cigarette butts inadvertently left by staff (Mello and Mendelson, 1971a).

The Cost of Moderate Drinking

Liebson *et al.* (1971) attempted to devise an adequate reinforcement of moderate drinking in a subject. Each morning, the subject had to decide whether to drink up to 4 oz or up to 18 oz of alcohol that day. A variety of consequences [including remunerative work, chlordiazepoxide (25 mg Q 2h PRN)] were investigated.

The most effective combination proved to be an opportunity to work (and thereby please the staff) and a bonus of $5.00 for 7 successive days of drinking less than 4 oz. This procedure maintained moderate drinking for 7 days. The duration of efficacy and selective contribution of the several reinforcers of moderate drinking are currently under investigation.

The Cost of Abstinence

An interesting corollary of the question, "how much is an alcoholic willing to work for alcohol" is "how much will it cost to keep an alcoholic from drinking ?" Cohen and her associates have attempted to pose this question to alcoholic volunteers living on a research ward for 50 and 60 days (Cohen *et al.*, 1971).

In the context of a token economy, it was possible to buy abstinence in two alcohol addicts for periods up to 7 days. During the baseline period, a titrating schedule of payments for abstinence was used to determine the abstinence purchase threshold for each subject (i.e., $7.00 and $12.00 respectively). The investigators then attempted to determine if abstinence so established could be disrupted, either by a delay in payment or consumption of a priming dose of alcohol (zero to 10 oz in 3 hr).

These subjects were able to tolerate up to a 1-week delay in payment but abstinence was disrupted by 2 to 3 weeks' delay. Ingestion of over 6 oz of alcohol disrupted abstinence; however, the effects of both types of disruption could be reversed by increasing the amount of the abstinence payments. Some inference can be made about the relative disruptive potency of delay of payment and alcohol by comparing the subsequent cost of abstinence. After a priming dose of alcohol, only $3.00 was required to reestablish abstinence, whereas any delay in payment exceeding 1 week required a $7.00 or $10.00 increase over the baseline payment rate. This would appear to be another datum inconsistent with the concept of craving which has been so uncritically advanced to account for addictive drinking. The extent to which this price differential may have been affected by the sequence of conditions was not discussed by the investigators (Cohen et al., 1971). However, it is encouraging for the token economy approach to rehabilitation to find that abstinence also has its price.

It should be noted that the method used to obtain these data was dia-metrically opposite to the usual approach of reinforcing the desired behavior. In establishing the cost of abstinence, payment was increased if subjects drank and decreased if subjects abstained. In determining the disrupting effect of a delay in payment, if a subject drank, payment was increased and if a subject abstained, the delay in payoff was increased. Consequently, abstinence was achieved in a situation where drinking was consistently followed by an increase in payment. The investigators do not discuss whether this aspect of the contingency situation was apparent to the subject.

Misbehavior: A Possible Reinforcing Consequence of Drinking

A direct comparison of alcohol and other reinforcers suggests something about its relative potency for controlling behavior; however, a study of the effects of alcohol on "misbehavior" and attempts to control that "misbehavior" by punishment, the removal of cigarettes, has suggested in more precise terms the nature of the reinforcer that is alcohol. The operant approach to alcoholism holds that drinking behavior is maintained by its consequences. The problem is to determine the "positive" consequences which maintain excessive drinking despite the many negative consequences. One hypothesis, suggested by both the psychodynamic (Alexander, 1956) and behaviorist (Shoben, 1956) points of view, is that alcohol releases repressed or inhibited behavior. Studies of pro-longed drinking in alcoholics in controlled settings have not reported any consistent pattern of regressive or disruptive behavior related to blood alcohol levels per se. Anecdotal reports concur that the degree of disruptive behavior is least when social constraints on the research ward are greatest.

In our present laboratory, we have observed a relatively high frequency of regressive and hostile acting-out behavior. Dr. Poppen has recently subjected these alcohol-associated misbehaviors to more careful scrutiny in an effort to determine if the opportunity to "let oneself go" is one of the consequences which maintain drinking behavior (Poppen, 1970). It was first necessary to develop a measure of regressive behavior and to determine if such behavior increased with alcohol consumption. The next step was to determine if such behavior could be manipulated apart from changes in alcohol consumption. If regressive behavior could be reduced, would alcohol consumption be reduced concomitantly ? That is, if the presumed reinforcing consequences could be attenuated, would the drinking behavior also decrease ?

A behavior checklist was developed which dealt with cooperation with ward routine, self-care, and acceptable social behavior. Specific items of behavior were listed and the nursing staff checked them as they occurred. The behaviors to be considered were made as explicit as possible to reduce any need for "interpretation" by the staff. It was found that regressive behavior, as measured by the behavior checklist, did increase concurrently with alcohol consumption. The constraints of the experimental program made it impossible to try to manipulate regressive behavior by restricting alcohol. Consequently, the availability of cigarettes was made contingent on not "messing up." Thus, subjects had a choice between (1) drinking and engaging in regressive behavior and not smoking, or (2) drinking and not engaging in regressive behavior and smoking. All subjects characteristically smoked a pack of cigarettes a day.

In the first study, subjects were given 30 cigarettes a day during a 5-day predrinking period and the first 5 days of an alcohol-available period. During the baseline period, a copy of the behavior checklist was posted in the dayroom and subjects were told that their behavior would be recorded daily by the nursing staff. On the sixth day of drinking, subjects were told that five cigarettes would be withheld for each item scored on the checklist on the previous day. These contingencies continued in effect for the remaining 5 days of drinking.

The frequency of regressive behavior was reduced in the three subjects who continued to drink when the cigarette contingencies were placed in effect. Two subjects showed little change in amount of alcohol consumed and one showed a slight decrease for the second 5 days of drinking. Two other subjects did not drink at all and spent a considerable time complaining and arguing. These subjects also showed a decrease in misbehavior during imposition of the cigarette contingency. This procedure was repeated with a second group of four subjects. The base rate of regressive behavior during the first 5 days of free drinking with noncontingent cigarettes was lower than in the previous group and the application of the cigarette contingencies had little effect.

These studies indicate that cigarette contingencies are not a sufficiently powerful way to manipulate regressive behavior. There were wide individual differences in the degree to which cigarettes were important. There is also the management problem of cigarette sharing. Subjects who earn many cigarettes are usually willing to share with those who get few and such sharing is virtually impossible to control. A more compelling paradigm would be to require a subject to choose between drinking and maintaining his decorum or not drinking at all. If subjects had maintained their alcohol consumption under these circumstances, it would have indicated that regressive behavior is not a necessary reinforcing consequence of drinking and that other factors are responsible for maintaining drinking behavior. If subjects alternated between "good" behavior while saving up chips and "binges" during which they spent their savings for alcohol and engaged in regressive behavior, it would have indicated that such behavior is a necessary consequence of drinking and that the subject will choose not to drink unless he can also engage in regressive behavior.

THE EFFECTS OF ALCOHOL ON BEHAVIORAL AND BIOLOGICAL FACTORS

Craving: An Unvalidated Construct

The disease concept of alcoholism has long been encumbered by the notions of "need" and "craving" which are frequently advanced to account for addictive drinking. "Craving" has been defined as a loss of control over drinking and it implies that "every time the subject starts drinking, he is compelled to continue until he reaches a state of severe intoxication" (Mardones, 1963, p. 146). The circularity inherent in this reasoning is evident. The lack of experimental data about drinking patterns has led to an implicit reification of concepts like "need" and "craving" which are defined by the behavior that they are invoked to explain.

The term "craving" is an attempt to account for perpetuation of drinking but not for resumption of drinking after sobriety. This distinction, emphasized by the WHO expert committees on Mental Health and Alcoholism in 1955, has tended to become somewhat blurred in common practice. "Craving" is often used to explain relapse after abstinence as well as drinking to postpone or diminish withdrawal signs and symptoms. Isbell (1955) indicated clearly that resumption of drinking cannot be explained by an acquired physical craving any more than can the initial excessive drinking which must precede the development of physical dependence.

No empirical support has been provided for the notion of "craving" by direct observation of alcoholic subjects in a situation where they can choose to drink alcohol in any volume at any time by working at a simple task. Although most subjects have consistently consumed enough alcohol on the first day of the experiment to raise their blood alcohol levels above 150 mg/100 ml, subsequent drinking patterns have been highly variable.

The following data, collected by a number of investigators, are inconsistent with the notion of "craving":

1. No subject allowed to freely program his drinking has shown a "loss of control" of drinking or a tendency to "drink to oblivion" (Mello and Mendelson, 1965; Mendelson and Mello, 1966; Mendelson et al., 1968; Mello et al., 1968; Mello and Mendelson, 1970a, 1971a; Nathan et al., 1970a,b, 1971).

2. No subject given an opportunity to drink 32 oz of alcohol per day has consumed all the alcohol available, even though drinking did not involve performance of any task (Mello and Mendelson, 1971a).

3. Subjects allowed to drink alcohol continuously over long periods of 30 to 60 days, spontaneously initiate and terminate several drinking episodes. No subject has ever consumed alcohol for more than 20 consecutive days (Mendelson et al., 1968; Mello and Mendelson, 1970a, 1971a; Nathan et al., 1970a,b, 1971).

4. The amount of alcohol consumed has been consistently shown to be a function of the amount of work required to obtain it (Mello et al., 1968; Mello and Mendelson, 1971a; Liebson et al., 1971).

5. It is possible to buy abstinence from alcoholic subjects and a "priming" dose of alcohol (up to 10 oz in 3 hr) disrupts abstinence less than a delay in abstinence payment (Cohen et al., 1971).

6. It has been repeatedly demonstrated that the availability of alcohol alone is not sufficient to maintain long-term drinking. There have been several examples of subjects who voluntarily stop drinking when a partner is no longer available or in response to a stressful event (Mendelson et al., 1968; Mendelson and Mello, 1966; Weiner et al., 1971).

7. The observation that some alcoholics deliberately "taper" their drinking in an effort to avoid severe consequences of abrupt alcohol withdrawal is further evidence of the degree of control that alcoholics are able to exercise over their drinking behavior (Mello et al., 1968; Mello and Mendelson, 1970a, 1971a; Nathan et al., 1970a,b, 1971).

8. Clinical observations indicate that some alcoholics can drink socially and function well for continuous periods of $2\frac{1}{2}$ to 11 years (Davies, 1962; Bailey and Stewart, 1967). A number of investigators have reported better overall adjustment and social functioning in alcoholics who drink moderately than in ex-alcoholic abstainers (cf. Pattison, 1966 for review).

9. No differences in subjective reports of "craving" by nine alcohol addicts were observed on days that they received 4 oz of vodka in an orange-flavored mixture and days when they received the orange-flavored mixture alone. These two mixtures were given after an overnight fast, in alternate 2-day sequences over a period of 18 days (Merry, 1966).

These findings argue strongly against the validity and general applicability of a construct such as "craving" which implies that ingesting some alcohol triggers a sequence of compulsive drinking with an eventual "loss of control." The usual goal of total abstinence for the alcoholic patient has been based on a fatalistic "craving" notion. General awareness of the limitations of this concept may lead to a more rational therapeutic approach to problem drinking which acknowledges individual differences in potential capacity for controlled drinking.

The adequacy of a criterion of abstinence to define successful treatment of alcoholism has been repeatedly challenged by Pattison and his associates

(Pattison, 1966, 1968; Pattison *et al.*, 1968) who suggest that moderate drinking may facilitate adjustment in some patients. Stein *et al.* (1968) have developed a questionnaire to try to distinguish "loss of control" drinkers from controlled drinkers on the basis of empirical item selection. Further studies will be required to determine if this psychometric approach can provide a basis for more effective treatment strategies for alcoholic individuals.

Although we have assembled evidence to show that "craving" is a logically and empirically inadequate explanatory concept to account for addictive drinking, our intention has not been to argue by implication that moderate drinking is the best therapeutic goal for all alcoholics. Rather, these data inconsistent with a craving hypothesis have been presented to reduce the constraining influence of the spector of "craving" in its various forms and to facilitate a reexamination of treatment goals for individual alcoholics.

Another issue that is relevant to social drinking in alcoholics is the question of their potential for readdiction (rapid development of tolerance and subsequent abstinence signs and symptoms upon alcohol withdrawal) as compared with problem drinkers. Unsystematic observations [made prior to the Easter-Driver (1966) and Powell *vs.* Texas (1968) decisions] of alcoholics incarcerated for public drunkenness for 1 to 6 months (cf. Taylor, 1966) testify to the occurrence of severe abstinence signs and symptoms upon abrupt termination of a brief drinking period following prolonged alcohol abstinence. Often, these alcohol addicts had only four or five brief opportunities to drink each year since the remainder of their time was spent in a "correctional" institution. Yet it appeared that these few drinking episodes were sufficient to sustain or to reinduce physical dependence as manifest by withdrawal signs and symptoms. Consequently, the fact that the alcoholic is vulnerable to readdiction upon reexposure to the agent is one constraint on social drinking. However, the expression of withdrawal signs and symptoms must require an as yet undetermined time, dose and pattern of alcohol consumption (cf. Mello and Mendelson, 1970a). Glatt (1967) has suggested that there may be an individual threshold, defined in terms of a critical blood alcohol level beyond which an alcoholic is more likely to resume compulsive drinking. Since the alcoholic apparently maintains some residual tolerance for alcohol after a period of abstinence, he requires progressively more alcohol to produce a change in feeling state. Adequate techniques to assess such residual tolerance have not been developed. As Cochin and Kornetsky (1964) have pointed out, the assessment of the rate of disappearance of tolerance is necessarily confounded since the procedures used to test for tolerance appear to perpetuate the phenomenon.

The extent to which alcohol addiction is biologically and behaviorally comparable to narcotics addiction has been the subject of considerable unresolved speculation. A loss of tolerance following drug withdrawal in narcotic addicts has been well documented and addicts may undergo withdrawal

voluntarily to reduce the amount of drug that they require each day (Goldstein
et al., 1968). However, there are data which attest to the long term (3-6 months)
effects of chronic narcotics addiction (Goldberg and Schuster, 1969;
Himmelsbach, 1942; Fraser and Isbell, 1952; Martin et al., 1963; Sloan and
Eisenman, 1968) and even of acute doses of morphine (Cochin and Kornetsky,
1964; Kornetsky and Bain, 1968). We have suggested in an earlier section (p. 221)
that the persistent effects of addiction may represent a form of "memory." Since
there is no specific pharmacological antagonist for alcohol, comparable to
nalorphene, naloxone, or cyclazocine for narcotics, assessment of physical dependence following various alcohol administration schedules has not been possible.

The implicit assumption that physical dependence is one aspect of an
addict's motivation for the agent is a complex and difficult issue to approach
experimentally (cf. discussions by Wikler, 1967; Jaffee, 1968). Initiation of a
readdictive sequence by a withdrawn addict is probably the complex resultant
of a number of psychogenic and stress response factors. For the ex-morphine
addict, reexposure to morphine is a euphoria-inducing experience, whereas for
the nonaddict, morphine produces dysphoria (Wikler, 1961). The possible
initial euphorogenic effects of alcohol for the alcoholic are currently being
studied by Dr. Davis in our laboratory. However, in contrast to the euphoric
effect that alcohol usually produces in normal drinkers, it produces a progressive
dysphoria in alcoholics (Davis, 1971).

Once the addictive drug consumption pattern has been reestablished, the
role of physical dependence in maintaining the pattern is less clear for the
alcoholic than for the narcotics user. If avoidance of withdrawal signs were the
factor which motivates an alcoholic to continue drinking, then he should consistently taper his drinking when forced to stop by an external constraint.
Moreover, it would be expected that during a drinking spree, he should drink
consistently enough to avoid partial withdrawal signs and symptoms. However,
our observations have shown that alcoholics frequently experience partial withdrawal signs during a drinking episode. Despite the attendant discomfort, the
alcoholic does not invariably respond to incipient withdrawal signs by increasing
his drinking. On occasion, these partial withdrawal signs have persisted for 3 or
4 days, modulated by a minimal intake of alcohol (Mello and Mendelson,
1970a, 1971a). This situation may resemble that of the narcotics addict in which
incipient withdrawal signs may add to both the gratification and perpetuation
of drug use (Wikler, 1961). Although "the intensity of the initial 'euphoria' is
not regained as long as the uninterrupted schedule of drug administration is
maintained . . ." drug use may come to produce another sort of pleasure, ". . .
namely that arising from the relief of such abstinence discomfort as developed
toward the end of intervals between injections" (Wikler, 1961, p. 75).

One promising approach to the question of the role of physical dependence
in maintaining drug administration is to determine the reinforcing properties of

small doses of drugs within an operant conditioning framework. Reviews of experiments on alcohol (Woods *et al.*, 1970) and opiates (Woods and Schuster, 1970) indicate that monkeys will respond to self-administered i.v. doses of these drugs at levels below that required to produce physical dependence. It is well established that physical dependence will maintain responding for narcotics in an addicted monkey, presumably to avoid withdrawal signs (Woods and Schuster, 1970). The extent to which the reinforcing properties of a drug may be enhanced following withdrawal from the drug has not been established.

Affect and Self-Esteem

Descriptions of the effect of alcohol on the affective states have usually been anecdotal and uncritical of the validity of self-report data. Two major problems limit attempts to study this issue systematically. One problem, common to all behavioral science, is the difficulty of developing adequate measures of the variables in question. Despite the plethora of psychometric instruments with demonstrated intertest reliability and content validity, the construct validity of these instruments remains open to question. It can only be inferred that the individual's behavior has some relationship to his performance on the test and in turn to the behavioral variables indicated in the test title. A second problem, specific to the studies of the effects of alcohol on behavior, is the assumption that a drinking experience for an alcoholic is the same as that for a normal drinker. This pervasive and tacit assumption apparently discouraged any laboratory efforts to examine affective behavior in inebriated alcoholics prior to 1964.

In trying to account for the persistence of addictive drinking, it is tempting to extrapolate from one's own alcohol-induced euphoria and to imagine that the immediate pleasure of drinking negates either the awesome prospect or the concurrent awareness of its many aversive consequences. The common assumption that alcohol reduces anxiety and depression in the alcoholic was first challenged by the clinical observations of Mendelson (1964). Ten alcoholic subjects studied in a programmed drinking paradigm became progressively more tense and anxious while drinking. One subject showed severe depression early in the drinking period and as the 24-day drinking period continued, many subjects evidenced depression, hyperaggressiveness and a decrease in general activity. All subjects verbalized considerable ambivalence about their drinking.

We confirmed these basic findings in a second group of 14 subjects allowed to work for their alcohol at an operant vigilance task over a 7-day period (McNamee *et al.*, 1968). Observations made during the predrinking baseline period were compared with those made during the drinking and withdrawal periods. Psychiatric interviews were carried out with each subject once or twice daily. The interview was nondirective and focused upon affect and general behavior, interpersonal relationships, thought content, and expectations.

Interview data were supplemented with information obtained from the nursing staff.

Nine of the 12 subjects showed a marked increase in anxiety and depression during the second or third day of drinking and this dysphoria grew more intense the longer the drinking period continued. In addition, subjects expressed other emotions not previously displayed, e.g., hostility, guilt, resentment. There appeared to be a relationship between the amount of alcohol consumed and the severity of anxiety and depression. However, in no instance was drinking stopped voluntarily as a result of these unpleasant mood changes. During the withdrawal period, subjects were almost completely preoccupied with their symptoms and frequency·of their medication. They were hostile, demanding of attention, irritable, and anxious. Depression was not a prominent symptom during alcohol withdrawal.

Although it is possible that the changes in affect observed during experimentally induced intoxication may be different from those which occur in real life, it seems more probable that the alcoholic reports alcohol-induced changes which fulfill his own expectancies when sober or which are concordant with the expectancies of the interviewer. These subjects verbalized expectancies concerning their drinking behavior and the effects of alcohol did not predict their actual behavior observed during the drinking period (McNamee *et al.*, 1968).

Studies of the effect of acute doses of alcohol on perception of mood have been consistent with these findings concerning the effects of prolonged alcohol ingestion. The available data suggest that there may be a gradient of alcohol efficacy in producing positive mood changes which is inversely related to experience with alcohol. Patient groups can be ordered from least to most favorably affected by alcohol as follows: alcoholics, excessive drinkers, moderate drinkers, depressed patients with no significant drinking history (Mayfield and Allen, 1967; Mayfield, 1968a,b).

Responses on the Clyde Mood Scale prior to and following intravenous infusion of a 5% ethanol solution (equal to $3\frac{1}{3}$ oz of 100-proof alcohol) were compared in alcoholics, normals, and clinically depressed patients. The six mood factors evaluated by the Clyde Mood Scale are friendly, energetic, clear thinking, aggressive, jittery, depression. The alcoholic subjects showed the least change in mood and the depressed patients showed the greatest mood improvement (Mayfield and Allen, 1967).

The scores obtained on the Clyde Mood Scale prior to alcohol infusion were significantly different for the alcoholic and the depressed patients. It is possible that the range of sensitivity of this test is so narrow that significant mood change can only be detected against a baseline of severe depression. It was observed that alcohol improved the mood scores of depressed patients significantly more during a period of depression than during a period of symptom remission (Mayfield, 1968a). However, even when the variable of depression was constant (as assessed by mood scale scores), alcohol produced a significantly greater improvement in mood scores of moderate than of excessive drinkers (Mayfield, 1968a). It appears that these findings cannot be accounted for solely as a function of the alcoholic's relative tolerance for alcohol since neither a low ($3\frac{1}{3}$ oz) nor a high ($6\frac{2}{3}$ oz) dose of alcohol was followed by a significant mood improvement in 24 alcoholic subjects (Mayfield, 1968a) with comparable baseline scores. Mayfield concludes from his studies that the psychopharmacological effects of alcohol are to a large extent a function of the affective state.

Studies of the affective changes in normal drinkers also suggest that depression and anxiety tend to increase at high doses of alcohol (Williams, 1966). Responses to a self-report adjective checklist made by 91 college students before, during, and after an "experimental cocktail party" indicated discernible increases in anxiety and depression following ingestion of 8 or more ounces of alcohol as contrasted with a significant decrease in anxiety and depression at low levels of alcohol consumption. In contrast to observations of affective changes in alcoholics during a prolonged period of drinking (Mendelson, 1964; McNamee et al., 1968), increases in anxiety and depression observed in college students did not exceed their preparty levels, whereas in alcoholics, increases in anxiety and depression considerably exceeded those observed during the predrinking control phase of the study.

The notion that alcoholics drink to improve their self-concept has been studied by Vanderpool (1969) by assessing a group of alcoholic subjects during acute inebriation. Most previous attempts to study the self-concept of alcoholics have involved the administration of a variety of psychometric indices to alcoholic subjects during periods of sobriety (MacAndrew and Garfinkel, 1962; Connor, 1962; White and Porter, 1966; Rosen, 1966). Vanderpool (1969) compared 50 inebriated alcoholics with 50 sober alcoholic and nonalcoholic controls (matched for age, IQ and education) on the Gough adjective checklist and the Tennessee self-concept scale. Tests were administered four times and during the second test, the alcoholic experimental group was allowed to drink the beverage of their choice ad libitum prior to and during the hour of testing. The average blood alcohol levels obtained were 94 mg/100 ml with a range of 44 to 230 mg/100 ml. During the third test, each subject was given one-half of the quantity consumed during the second test and the average blood alcohol levels were 63 mg/100 ml with a range of 29 to 133 mg/100 ml.

Contrary to expectation, the self-concept of the alcoholic subjects was significantly poorer during drinking on the dimensions of self-esteem and self-acceptance, adequacy, estrangement and social worth, and tolerance to stress. There were no changes on those measures presumed to reflect feelings of dependency, immaturity, and insecurity. These data were interpreted to suggest that drinking tends to confirm and aggravate feelings of inadequacy and lack of personal and social worth (Vanderpool, 1969).

Comparisons between the alcoholic and nonalcoholic subjects indicated that the alcoholics had lower self-esteem scores (Vanderpool, 1969). In this connection it is of interest that Williams (1965) found that college students categorized as "problem drinkers" showed a more negative self-evaluation than nonproblem drinkers and were very similar to alcoholic subjects assessed with the same (Gough) adjective checklist (cf. Connor, 1962). Williams (1965) suggests that loss of self-esteem may precede alcoholism rather than following primarily as a consequence of prolonged excessive drinking.

The somewhat paradoxical increase in disturbing affect observed in alcoholics during studies of experimentally induced intoxication is difficult to reconcile with information that most alcoholics provide about their drinking experiences during sobriety in a clinical interview. A partial resolution of this paradox may be that the alcoholic does not recall the seemingly aversive aspects of his drinking experience during a subsequent period of sobriety and consequently these aversive consequences cannot effectively modify his future drinking experience. There are considerable data which converge to suggest that there is a substantial dissociation of experience during drinking and expectancy and recall following drinking (Diethelm and Barr, 1962; McGuire et al., 1966; McNamee et al., 1968; Ryback, 1970a; Tamerin and Mendelson, 1969; Tamerin et al., 1970; Goodwin et al., 1969a,b). A comparable dysphoria during chronic drug use has been observed in morphine addicts (Wikler, 1952). Addicts frequently increase their narcotics intake in an effort to regain an initial euphoria (Martin and Fraser, 1961). Continued drug use appears to be motivated by an effort to avoid abstinence phenomena (cf. Wikler, 1967 for review).

It has also been suggested that the alcoholic may have a different future time perspective than nonalcoholics (Smart, 1968). It has been argued that as the unpleasant consequences of chronic drinking accumulate, "the alcoholic perceives such a bleak future that he refrains from extending it or ordering what little future is perceived" (Smart, 1968, p. 83). Alcoholics did show far less extensive time perspective than social drinkers on an unstructured task with no specific mention of time. No differences were observed between the two groups on structured tasks involving specific mention of time (Smart, 1968).

Memory and Dissociative Phenomena

In 1962, Diethelm and Barr interviewed alcoholic patients under conditions of acute experimentally induced intoxication. It was found that patients talked more freely and expressed emotions, especially hostility and guilt, which had not been displayed when they were sober. Occasionally feelings and thoughts never reported during sobriety were volunteered by these patients when they became intoxicated. Most often the patients forgot both the incident and the content of these reports when they regained sobriety.

The first direct examination of the phenomenon of dissociation between drinking experiences, recall, and expectancy was made by McGuire et al. in our laboratory in 1966. Four chronic alcoholics were compared with four non-alcoholics prior to, during, and after a period of experimentally induced inebriation. Nondirective interviews were conducted daily with each subject to ascertain mood, wishes and expectancies, perception of personal and environmental changes, and introspective concerns. During the baseline period, the alcoholics reported that they expected transformations in their relationships and feelings when they became intoxicated. They believed they would become "masculine," "admired by women," "more sociable," feel less anxious and more integrated as individuals. Similar expectations were not reported by the non-alcoholic subjects. When the alcoholic subjects were drinking, they reported that their predrinking expectancies were fulfilled. They showed a high level of interest in their environment and spoke more about their past experience, which McGuire et al. (1966) have postulated may reflect a form of "ego integration." Observations of these subjects during drinking were not concordant with their fantasy beliefs. The alcoholic subjects became withdrawn, sullen, preoccupied, and depressed as drinking continued. The nonalcoholic group initially became more sociable and jovial but also expressed anger and depression about their plight as convicted sex offenders. These nonaddicted subjects were unable to tolerate alcohol in programmed doses of about 28 oz (4 g/kg) per day and developed gastritis and vomiting.

Recently, Drs. Tamerin and Weiner in our laboratory attempted to examine an alcoholic's expectancies about his affective states and behavior prior to drinking and to compare these with self-reports during drinking and subsequent recall following cessation of drinking using both clinical assessments (Tamerin and Mendelson, 1969) and a self-report Q sort (Tamerin et al., 1970). The investigators devised a series of simple self-report items which they assumed reflected the following categories: aggression (8 items), sexuality and closeness (11 items), heterosexuality (5 items), dysphoria (9 items), responsibility (8 items), activity, passivity (9 items). Items were presented to subjects on cards, which they sorted into one of three categories of self-description; rarely, sometimes, often. Prior to the initiation of drinking, subjects were asked to do a Q-sort of these items to indicate how they perceived themselves at that time and, on a second occasion, how they expected they would be during drinking. During the drinking period, subjects did two self-report sortings; once during the first week of drinking and, on a subsequent occasion, after two or three weeks of drinking. During the week of withdrawal, subjects were asked to sort the same self-report cards to determine if they recalled their behavior and feelings during the drinking experience (Tamerin et al., 1970).

The findings confirmed the previous observations of Mendelson (1964) and McNamee et al. (1968) that alcoholics become more dysphoric as a function of drinking. These data also amplified McGuire's impression of a dissociation between predrinking expectancy and drinking experience (McGuire *et al.*, 1966). Subjects predicted that they would become more aggressive while drinking and, in fact, became more aggressive than they had predicted. Subsequently, they were able to recall their alcohol-related aggression. These subjects predicted less sexuality and closeness during drinking, but reported significantly more of these feelings and behaviors than they had anticipated. An increased awareness of heterosexual interests was poorly recalled following cessation of drinking. These men did not predict an increase in dysphoria, but all reported progressively more dysphoria as the drinking period progressed and some were able to recall this increase in dysphoria. Subjects consistently predicted that they would become more passive during drinking. In fact, they became more active and did not recall this discrepancy. Subjects often predicted that they would become more "irresponsible" during drinking. They did become more "irresponsible" and recalled this well. These data have been interpreted in accordance with the notion that drinking may be a way of facilitating regressive behavior (Tamerin *et al.*, 1970). This notion has been examined by Poppen (1970).

A second type of dissociative reaction commonly reported to occur in alcoholics during periods of inebriation is the "blackout" in which the patient professes total amnesia for a series of events which culminate in "finding himself" in an unexpected or unfamiliar situation. Information concerning this type of dissociative phenomena has been based upon retrospective reports obtained during periods of relative sobriety. Frequently, these dissociative reactions are not accompaniments of unacceptable behavior, although the occurrence of the "blackout" is usually described as a frightening experience for the subject. We have never observed dissociative reactions to innocuous events in our experimental studies of chronic inebriation. In the case of more un-acceptable and threatening situations, it is impossible to adequately differentiate between intentional denial and genuine dissociation in a clinical interview.

Goodwin and his colleagues have attempted to clarify some of the ambiguities surrounding the term "blackout" by synthesizing the self-descriptions of alcohol-associated memory loss by 64 alcoholics into a phenomenological account (1969a). In this sample of subjects, "blackouts" ranged in duration from 1 hr (25%) to 5 days (one subject). Since most "blackouts" end in sleep, estimates of the length of time involved are necessarily imprecise. Most subjects could report when a blackout began. The importance of a distinction between an "enbloc" memory loss (defined as amnesia with a definite onset point, involving memory loss for significant events and ending with a sense of "lost time") and a "fragmentary" memory loss (wherein awareness of forgetting occurs in response to a reminder) emerged from these studies. Several subjects volunteered that drinking seemed to improve their recall for events experienced during a previous drinking episode. Some deliberately drank to facilitate remembrance.

These anecdotal reports illustrate an experimentally demonstrated phenomenon termed "drug dissociation" or "state-dependent learning" in animals (cf. Overton, 1968, 1970a and Chapter 8, this volume for review). Experimental drug dissociation is based on the observations that:

1. A drug can acquire discriminative properties and gain stimulus control over behavior.

2. Performance on a discrimination task may be impaired when there is a change from nondrug to drug state; from drug to nondrug state and from one drug state to another drug state. Drug dissociation can be produced by short-term drug administration during training and testing and is not dependent upon chronic drug use or drug addiction.

The possible commonality between the "blackout" experience reported by alcoholics and "state-dependent learning" was first recognized by Storm and Smart (1965). They pointed out the parallel between state-dependent learning and a stimulus generalization decrement effect, i.e., decreases in the strength of learned responses which occur under stimulus conditions different from those in which they were learned. They suggest that memory for experiences in the intoxicated state also shows a decrement when recall is attempted during sobriety. Although this phenomenon has been repeatedly demonstrated in animals, the data on man are somewhat equivocal. Considerably more research is required to establish the experimental validity of this phenomenon in man and to determine the drugs, doses, and conditions under which it occurs (cf. Overton, 1968). However, if the conditions that determine the occurrence of "drug dissociation" could be defined and manipulated, then clarification of the basic mechanisms involved in dissociative phenomena could proceed more rapidly.

On the basis of their interviews with 100 hospitalized alcoholics, Goodwin et al. (1969b) concluded that blackouts were positively associated with the severity and duration of alcoholism and the amount of drinking. Over one-third of the subjects had never experienced blackouts and those who did experience blackouts reported that this began late in their illness. The authors emphasize that their data are inconsistent with the notion advanced by Jellinek (1952) that blackouts after drinking predict future addiction.

In collecting these data, groups of three to five patients were interviewed by a psychiatrist using a 78-item structured interview (Goodwin et al., 1969b). Subjects were encouraged to raise questions about each item that seemed ambiguous. The psychiatrist was able to clarify difficult points and patients contributed their own experiences and interpretations. The factors that these patients reported as associated with blackouts were: eating poorly (83%); gulping drinks (61%); and fatigue (36%). It was of interest to note that of the 32 subjects in the blackout group with a history of delirium tremens, one-half had experienced delirium tremens prior to or during the same year as their first blackout. Spree drinking or binges also preceded or coincided with the first occurrence of a blackout (Goodwin et al., 1969b).

The clinical observations of Ryback (1970) on seven alcoholic subjects during a 7- to 12-day drinking period on a research ward indicate that "blackout" periods tend to occur after a rapid rise in blood alcohol levels following abstinence. "Blackouts" occurred early in the drinking period in four subjects and did not recur in the same individual. The three subjects that did not have "blackouts" gradually increased their alcohol consumption during the first few days of drinking.

Ryback assessed the occurrence of "blackouts" by asking subjects each morning if anything unusual had happened during the preceding day, and then specifically about particular incidents on the ward. Ryback's observations agreed with those of Goodwin et al. (1969a) that subjects could usually describe precisely when a blackout period began. These subjects tended to black out for a period of time (9 hr to 3 days) rather than for a single event. One subject did not remember trying to hit another subject over the head with a chair within 10 min of the event (Ryback, 1970).

In summary, these clinical data suggest that an alcohol-induced dissociation for negative aspects of a drinking experience may be a frequent occurrence for alcoholics (McNamee et al., 1968; McGuire et al., 1966; Tamerin and Mendelson, 1969; Tamerin et al., 1970) whereas the development of less common severe dissociative reactions, i.e., "blackouts," parallels the severity and duration of alcoholism (Goodwin et al., 1969b). The discrete occurrence of a "blackout" appears to accompany a rapid rise in blood alcohol levels at the beginning of drinking in susceptible individuals (Ryback, 1970; Goodwin, 1970). The determinants of blackout susceptibility are unknown. It is also unclear whether persons prone to "forget" material revealed or experiences during inebriation are more likely to experience "blackouts," or the converse.

West (1967) has proposed that dissociative reactions be conceptualized in an information processing network (input-integration-output). In such a schema, an inaccessibility of affect-associated material during sobriety would reflect an inability to integrate stored information with current reactions. The "blackout" would reflect a dissociation of output insofar as the behavioral response is minimally controlled by and subsequently inaccessible to conscious awareness. Such a formulation has the advantage of emphasizing a difference between the two dissociative reactions without the implication of a gradient of relative severity.

These data raise a series of questions about the specificity of alcohol effects on dissociative phenomena and the effects of alcohol on memory function generally. It is unlikely that alcohol has a unique pharmacological capacity to induce dissociative states in man. Experimental studies have shown that a variety of drugs can produce "state-dependent learning" in animals and more-over, drug dissociation induced by one drug does generalize to other presumably similar drugs, e.g., other CNS depressants (cf. Overton, 1968, 1970, and Chapter 8, this volume). However, clinical observations indicate that dissociative states comparable to those observed in alcoholism are not a prominent feature of chronic morphine and barbiturate intoxication. Amnesia for events occurring during intoxication has been reported for glue sniffing and chronic salicylate (aspirin) intoxication (Ewing, 1967). Moreover, loss of memory for events, pictures, and associated pairs of letters and words learned under thiopental sedation has been reported (Osborn et al., 1967). Recall was not facilitated by reinstatement of sedation, and material learned prior to thiopental administration could be recalled during sedation (Osborn et al., 1967). Whether the dissociative effects of alcohol are specific to the alcoholic or whether the cross-tolerance shown by addicts effectively subserves a "cross-dissociative reaction" as well is unknown. There are data which suggest that alcohol can produce a variant of dissociative reaction in normals (Goodwin et al., 1969c).

Goodwin et al. (1969c) attempted to examine the conditions under which alcohol-dependent dissociative effects occur in man. Forty-eight male medical student volunteers performed four memory tasks either while sober or while inebriated. Blood alcohol values averaged 111 mg/100 ml ($+/-$ 80 to 140 mg/ 100 ml). Within 24 hr of training, subjects were tested either under identical or different drug states. Errors on an avoidance reversal task (assumed to reflect interference from previous training) were less under changed drug states than same state conditions, thus suggesting "state dependence." In tasks measuring recall, state-dependent effects were also apparent since learning transfer was better when the subject was intoxicated during both the training and test session than when he was intoxicated only during the training session. Performance on a task measuring recognition was not significantly affected by a change in drug state. Transfer from sober to drug state was more complete than transfer from drug state to sober state. A comparable asymmetry of transfer has been reported by Overton (1968).

Generalization of the mystical aura which has long overshadowed objective analysis of dissociative reactions to state-dependent learning may be avoided by describing this effect in a very simple way. Responses established under specific conditions are most easily elicited when these conditions are reestablished. How a drug state is able to acquire discriminative control of behavior is not understood. Constraints on existing explanatory models have been fully discussed by Overton (1970a). It should be emphasized that drug dissociation effects cannot be attributed to a drug-specific memory decrement *per se* since training in a drug state results in a poorer performance under nondrug than drug conditions. Nonetheless, the issue of the effect of alcohol on "memory" is a question of considerable interest.

It is well known that drugs can influence the processes involved in the storage and retrieval of information. The establishment of the awesomely complex phenomenon we call "memory" is usually thought to be a sequential process in which at least two consolidation or storage processes follow a stimulus event. These phases of consolidation are differentiated in terms of time of onset as inferred from the relative lability of memory by other stimuli. In a recent incisive analysis of these data and discussion of the mechanisms of memory, John (1967) has suggested the following time estimates (p. 39) for the phases of memory establishment. Representation, involving the transmission of information to a neural population, may require 3 min. The reverberatory activity subserving "representation" may induce two temporary information-holding mechanisms. The first, lasting about 3 hr, appears to mediate recall but is inadequate for consolidation. The second, lasting about 11 hr, is inadequate for recall but sufficient for consolidation. The consolidation process itself requires about 5 hr. These temporal estimates are presented here to aid in interpretation of drug effects on "memory" since there has been a regrettable tendency to neglect operational definition of constructs like "short-term memory" or to discuss "memory" as a unitary, undifferentiated phenomenon.

There is some experimental evidence to suggest that alcohol has a direct effect on memory function in normals (Carpenter and Ross, 1965; Ryback, 1969) and in alcoholics (Tamerin et al., 1971). However, this is a controversial question, since other studies in which memory was required for successful performance have reported no impairment in alcoholics at blood alcohol levels as high as 200 mg/100 ml (Talland et al., 1964; Talland, 1966). Consistency of performance at a variety of tasks involving attention, vigilance, memory, motor skills, and reaction time define behavioral tolerance for alcohol in the alcoholic (cf. Mello, 1968).

Carpenter and Ross (1965) report that blood alcohol levels exceeding 70 mg/100 ml produced deterioration of performance on a task involving continuous attention and memory. Normal subjects were required to perform two tasks simultaneously on each trial. The numbers 1 or 2 appeared on the subject's left and his task was to report whether the number was the same or different from the one immediately preceding it. The symbols + or − appeared on the subject's right and his task was to report whether each symbol was the same or different from the one two symbols back. Each stimulus was visible for 2 sec and the interstimulus interval was $\frac{3}{4}$ sec. The effect of alcohol on errors on this task was related to the subject's initial performance. Subjects with the greatest proficiency showed a linear deterioration with increasing doses of alcohol (24 mg/100 ml) and less absolute performance decrement than the most skillful subjects.

Ryback (1969) asked normal subjects to indicate if one of a pair of objects had been presented previously during the experimental session. Items were presented by a film projector and the smallest separation between test items was 1 min (or 24 items). The other separations between test items were 2 min (or 48 items) and 9 min (or 192 items). Alcohol (1.2 ml/kg) mixed with orange juice was consumed within 20 min by 10 subjects who achieved blood alcohol levels between 70 and 88 mg/100 ml. After 30 min, there was a significant difference in errors between 1-min and 9-min presentation intervals. After 45 min, even 1-min interstimulus intervals showed errors. Ryback described these data as differentiating between immediate (1 min) and short-term (9 min) memory.

Investigators in our laboratory have recently reported that a derangement of "short-term" and 24-hr memory occurs in inebriated alcoholics and that the extent of the derangement is dependent upon the magnitude of blood alcohol levels (Tamerin *et al.*, 1971). Fourteen alcoholics with a history of repeated blackouts were studied prior to, during, and following a 12- to 14-day period of experimentally induced intoxication.

Three tests were constructed to assess memory function: a picture-recall test; a questionnaire which determined adequacy of recall for events of the preceding day; and a hidden object test in which a cigarette was hidden in one of 12 identical drawers in full view of the subject. Subsequently the subject was asked to find the cigarette after fixed intervals of interpolated and distracting tasks. Motivation to perform well on these tasks was facilitated by providing cigarettes for correct responses. All subjects were heavy smokers and there was no other way to obtain cigarettes.

No subject showed evidence of any memory impairment during the baseline period and "performed at almost perfect criterion levels for all 3 tests." During the drinking period, subjects could consume up to 32 oz of 100-proof beverage alcohol on a free choice basis. At moderate blood alcohol levels (150 mg/100 ml) subjects demonstrated a significant time-dependent decrement in memory function.

Picture recall was not significantly impaired at 5 sec, but did show significant impairment at 60 sec and 5 min following stimulus presentation. At high blood alcohol levels (above 150 mg/100 ml) picture recall was also significantly impaired at 5 sec.

Performance on the hidden object task was also significantly impaired at moderate intoxication levels at delays of 60 sec and 5 min. At high blood alcohol levels, performance on the hidden object task was not impaired at 5 sec.

The questionnaire assessment of global recall of ward events during the preceding 24 hr was significantly worse at moderate levels of intoxication and became progressively poorer as intoxication levels increased.

No comparisons of the effects of alcohol on memory function in alcoholics without a history of "blackouts" were made. Therefore no conclusions can be drawn about a continuity between alcohol-induced memory impairment and severe dissociation.

These data are at variance with an earlier sequence of studies conducted in our laboratory by Talland. Nine alcoholic subjects were given a series of tests

10 times over a 5-week period during which they received alcohol in increasing programmed doses (6–40 oz) over a 24-day period. In a running digit span test of attention, 8 randomized strings of digits, 10 to 20 digits in length, were presented at a rate of 1 digit every 2 sec. At the sound of a buzzer, the subject had to reproduce the last five digits in the order in which they occurred. This task required a recall span of at least 8 sec. The subject did not know in advance how long a digit sequence would be and had to continually process this incoming information. Blood alcohol levels as high as 200 mg/100 ml did not significantly affect performance on this test as compared with baseline measures (Talland et al., 1964). In a second test of memory span in which blue, green, red, and yellow slides were shown in randomized sequences for 2 sec each, blood alcohol levels up to 200 mg/100 ml also did not affect ability to report what color occurred five slides back or in some other position varying between one and five steps back (Talland et al., 1964). In a subsequent study on a more complex attention task, alcohol addicts and normal controls were not affected by acute doses of alcohol (0.5–1.0 g). Their task was to identify sequences of three consecutive odd or three consecutive even numbers presented at a rate of one per second. Participation in this experiment was rewarded with ten packs of cigarettes per day (Talland, 1966).

These differences in effects of alcohol on immediate memory span at comparable blood alcohol levels are probably a combination of differences in behavioral technique, motivation, and selection for "blackout" history. Most studies of drug effects on memory have studied immediate pre- or posttrial acute injections of an agent, and generalizations on the effects of chronic alcohol administration are difficult (cf. reviews by Steinberg; Jarvick; McGaugh, 1968). Impairment of learning under near anesthetic levels of thiopental has been reported by Osborn et al. (1967). A tentative generalization has been offered by John (1967) to the effect that anticholinergic substances, barbiturates, or compounds with depressant action tend to impair learning or retention. Further investigation of the effects of alcohol and other CNS depressants on delayed matching to sample performance is currently in progress at the NIMH, National Center for Prevention and Control of Alcoholism.

Sleep Patterns

Despite the wealth of anecdotal material testifying to the sleep-inducing properties of alcohol, there has been little systematic study of the effects of alcohol on sleep patterns of alcohol addicts. The existing EEG data on the influence of prolonged alcohol consumption on sleep in alcoholics (a total N of 7) do not confirm the anecdotal impression that alcohol improves sleep. It has been generally agreed that a relative decrease in stage 4 sleep and any deviation from the normal (20 to 25%) REM states are characteristic of "poor sleep" (*Current*

Research on Sleep and Dreams, 1966). A decrease in REM stage 1 activity follows chronic inebriation in alcoholics (Greenberg and Pearlman, 1967; Gross and Goodenough, 1968). This finding is concordant with the considerable data on the effects of acute doses of alcohol on sleep patterns in alcoholics (Johnson *et al.*, 1970); in normal subjects (Gresham *et al.*, 1963; Yules *et al.*, 1966a, 1967; Knowles *et al.*, 1968) and in cats (Yules *et al.*, 1966b). It has been consistently observed that alcohol (as well as barbiturates, hypnotics, and certain tranquilizers) induces a decrease in REM activity in normal subjects when compared with baseline adaptation levels, and a compensatory increase in REM activity occurs on initial postalcohol nights (Oswald *et al.*, 1963, 1969; Kales *et al.*, 1969). These recent experimental studies are concordant with the early observations of Galen who commented before 200 A.D. that ". . . in drunken people when their head is full of drink; the heaviness leads to a coma and at the same time prevents sleep" (Liebowitz, 1967, p. 84).

A review of the electroencephalographic sleep correlates of alcohol intake appears in Chapter 13 of this volume. A critical review of the status of sleep research in alcoholism appears in Mello and Mendelson (1970b).

The potential importance of a phenomenological study of sleep-wakefulness behavior over 24 hr was suggested to us by our initial observations of subjects allowed to freely determine their pattern of drinking by working at a simple operant task. We found that as the drinking period progressed, subjects tended to work in frequent, short sessions increasingly more at night (Mello and Mendelson, 1965; Mendelson and Mello, 1966). Since there is evidence that alcoholic subjects may metabolize alcohol more rapidly as a function of prolonged drinking (Mendelson *et al.*, 1965), it could be argued that increased wakefulness might reflect a subject's need to ingest alcohol over progressively shorter time intervals in order to maintain a consistent blood alcohol level. The net effect of the increase in nocturnal drinking was to increase the amount of alcohol ingested.

In subsequent studies, 16 subjects showed a similar pattern of increased nocturnal drinking but there was no consistent tendency to maintain a stable blood alcohol level (Mello *et al.*, 1968; Mendelson *et al.*, 1968). Over a long period of drinking (30 days), we observed that subjects initiated several spontaneous periods of abstinence during which they spent their time almost totally in sleep (Mendelson *et al.*, 1968). Since each subject also showed a progressive increase in anxiety during the course of drinking, concomitant with the changes in sleep-wakefulness behavior, we speculated that prolonged drinking might be associated with a degree of sleep deprivation which can be tolerated only for a finite period of time. Since abstinence periods were also prompted by a stress event on the ward, it was tempting to postulate that, as subjects drank longer and became increasingly anxious and insomnic, their subjective discomfort reached a critical level such that an additional discrete stressor prompted a change in behavior, i.e., the cessation of drinking (Mendelson *et al.*, 1968).

As a consequence of these observations, we became interested in examining the possibility that working for alcohol during the night might reflect an alcohol-induced alteration in the normal sleep-wakefulness pattern rather than a change in sleep patterns determined by an effort to maintain a stable blood alcohol level. Twenty-four hour sleep patterns of 50 male alcohol addicts were assessed behaviorally during a 5-day baseline period; a 7–62-day period of spontaneous drinking; and a subsequent alcohol withdrawal phase (Mello and Mendelson, 1970b). Subjects were studied in groups of four to six and each subject had a private bedroom. Subjects had free access to 32 oz of alcohol per day and were able to determine their own pattern of alcohol consumption. The nursing staff observed each subject's sleep status once every hour around the clock and made a judgment as to whether or not a subject was sleeping most of the hour. The beginning of an experimental day was arbitrarily set at 8 a.m. However, if a subject slept until 9 a.m. or later, it was counted as a continuous period of sleep in the calculation of sleep distributions. Sleep distributions were calculated by summing the total hours of sleep during an experimental period (e.g., the entire 5-day baseline period) and determining what percentage of the total sleep time was accounted for by discrete episodes of sleep lasting 1 hr, 2 hr, 3 hr, etc. The daily total sleep duration reflected the hours of sleep that actually occurred within an experimental day, 8 a.m. to the following 8 a.m. It should be noted that the baseline period began at 8 a.m. the day following admission to the research ward and therefore does not include the subject's first night of sleep.

The analysis of distribution of consecutive hours of sleep provided the basis for individual comparisons between the control period and the effects of drinking and withdrawal. Only those subjects showing what was defined as a "normal" sleep pattern were used for the final analysis. In the illustrative sleep distribution data presented in Fig. 9, a normal baseline sleep pattern is illustrated in the left-hand column for each subject. In the "normal" sleep pattern, the highest percentage peak consists of a night's sleep (usually 6–8 hr) and a lower percentage peak of 1–3 hr, indicating a nap. Of the 50 subjects studied, only eight subjects did not show this normal predrinking baseline sleep pattern and consequently were discarded from the analysis. Two subjects elected not to drink during a 10-day drinking period and these data were included as a control for the effects of prolonged residence on the research ward.

Figure 9 presents illustrative data for nine subjects who received no medication during the 3 days of the withdrawal period summarized here. The four subjects in the lower portion of Fig. 9 illustrate one of the major findings concerning the direct effects of alcohol on the distribution of consecutive hours of sleep. These subjects each showed a tendency to sleep in predominantly shorter blocks of time relative to their baseline pattern during drinking. The criterion of fragmentation used was over 50% of the total sleep time in blocks

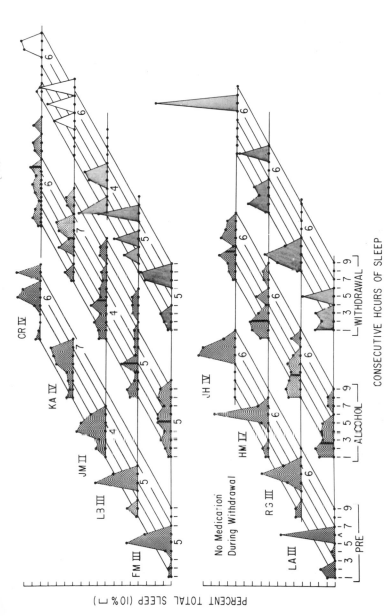

CONSECUTIVE HOURS OF SLEEP

FIGURE 9. Each row presents sleep distribution data for an individual subject for the baseline period (PRE), the spontaneous drinking period (ALCOHOL) and the three days immediately following cessation of drinking (WITHDRAWAL). This graph shows the percent of total sleep time during an experimental period that the subject spent in blocks of sleep of 1 or more consecutive hours. Sleep distributions were calculated by summing the total hours of sleep during an experimental period (e.g., PRE) and determining what percentage of the total sleep time was accounted for by discrete episodes of sleep lasting 1 hr, 2 hr, etc. No medication was given during withdrawal.

of sleep $1\frac{1}{2}$ or more hours shorter than during the predrinking baseline period. The space between 1 hr and the vertical black bar indicates the point at which approximately 50% or more of the total sleep distribution has occurred. A total of 32 of the 40 drinking subjects showed changes in sleep pattern during drinking which involved some sleep fragmentation. In 22 of these subjects the sleep pattern was primarily characterized by sleep fragmentation. In the remaining 10 subjects sleep fragmentation is accompanied by flattening, which is the second predominant pattern of alcohol-induced change in sleep distribution. The distribution of consecutive hours of sleep appeared to be flattened by comparison to the subjects' baseline sleep pattern and there was no dramatic primary peak. Those subjects shown in the upper portion of Fig. 9 display a predominantly flattened sleep distribution.

Similar changes were not shown by the two control subjects who elected not to drink. Their sleep patterns during the period when the other subjects were drinking were strikingly similar to the usual "normal" sleep pattern. The observed changes in sleep patterns appeared to be induced by alcohol *per se* and not by other aspects of the hospital routine or other uncontrolled factors. Since all but two subjects slept more, on the average, during the drinking period as compared to their baseline period, the observed sleep fragmentation cannot be accounted for by an overall decrease in time spent sleeping, but rather reflects an alcohol-induced change in the pattern of sleeping.

Fragmentation of sleep patterns was the most reliable correlate of alcohol ingestion and was a frequent accompaniment of alcohol withdrawal. However, as illustrated in Fig. 9, there were no common sleep distribution patterns during alcohol withdrawal. Neither symptom severity nor type of withdrawal medication used resulted in systematic changes in sleep patterns. Since the maximal expression of the major withdrawal signs and symptoms (tremor, hallucinosis, seizures) usually occurs within 72 hr following cessation of drinking (Victor and Adams, 1953), these data reflect the major period of expression of the abstinence syndrome.

Contrary to the prevailing clinical impression (Victor and Adams, 1953; Victor, 1966), abrupt cessation of drinking did not invariably produce an initial insomnia. Our criterion of "insomnia" was any day on which the total hours of sleep were less than the lower limit of daily hours of sleep observed during the baseline period. According to this criterion, only seven of the 40 subjects were insomnic during the first 24 hr of alcohol withdrawal. A complete absence of insomnia was observed during the first 48 hr of alcohol withdrawal in 30 subjects, 23 of whom showed severe withdrawal signs and symptoms. The infrequent occurrence of insomnia in this large series of alcoholics suggests that the insomnia observed clinically may be a composite effect of the severity of alcohol withdrawal signs and symptoms and a variety of intercurrent illnesses commonly found in a relatively indigent "Skid Row" alcoholic population.

Many investigators have studied the possible relationship between changes in sleep activity during alcohol withdrawal and hallucinations and delusions (Gross et al., 1966; Gross and Goodenough, 1968; Greenberg and Pearlman, 1967; Johnson et al., 1970). Feinberg and Evarts (1969) have reviewed studies relevant to the notion, first advanced by Hughlings Jackson and William James (cf. Evarts, 1962), that dreams are associated with the neurophysiologic processes which are also related to some types of hallucinations occurring in the waking state. Feinberg and Evarts conclude that current research supports the general notion of a neurophysiological continuity between dreaming sleep and waking hallucinatory activity (1969). Of particular interest is the finding that the spontaneous activity of visual cortical neurons during REM is comparable to that during waking vision and about twice as high as during non-REM sleep or in an awake subject without direct visual experience (Feinberg and Evarts, 1969). Hallucinosis is a frequent concomitant of alcohol withdrawal and is sometimes associated with difficulty in discriminating between sleeping and waking states. A temporal association between alcohol withdrawal-induced hallucinosis or delirium tremens and a high percentage of REM sleep has been consistently observed (Johnson et al., 1970; Gross et al., 1966; Gross and Goodenough, 1968).

We observed a consistent dissociation between hallucinosis and insomnia (Mello and Mendelson, 1970b). Of the 15 subjects with hallucinosis, six did not have insomnia, four developed hallucinosis and insomnia simultaneously and four began to hallucinate at least 24 hr before developing insomnia. Interpretation of this finding requires documentation of antecedent sleep conditions since a relative insomnia could have preceded alcohol withdrawal. However, only three of the 10 subjects who began to hallucinate within 24 hr of cessation of drinking had insomnia immediately prior to alcohol withdrawal. We conclude, therefore, that hallucinosis may occur as a concomitant of alcohol withdrawal and independent of a previous or a concurrent insomnia.

The behavioral implications of the fragmentation of sleep patterns observed during drinking remain to be clarified. Previously, we have speculated that the consistent increase in anxiety and depression observed in alcoholic addicts during chronic inebriation may be related to sleep fragmentation and consequent REM deprivation (Mello and Mendelson, 1969b). Dement (1960) reported that REM deprivation does produce an increase in irritability, anxiety, and despondency in normal subjects. These observations have not been consistently replicated (Kales et al., 1964). However, the extent to which sleep fragmentation may be accompanied by a change in REM stage 1 activity is not known. Perhaps the most relevant study of drug effects in an addicted population which provides adequate baseline measures is that of Kay et al. (1969). Eight ex-morphine addicts given a single weekly dose of morphine sulfate (7.5, 15, or 30 mg/kg) showed a significant dose-related decrease in both the number and duration of

REM periods. The relationship of alcohol-induced changes in REM activity to the two predominant patterns of sleep fragmentation and flattening observed in the present study remain to be determined.

SUMMARY AND CONCLUSIONS

The data summarized in this review present a very different picture of the effects of alcohol on the alcoholic than has been derived from anecdotal accounts based on the self-reports of alcoholic subjects during sobriety. The voluminous psychiatric literature on alcoholism has tended to present "the alcoholic" as an impulsive hedonist who drinks to dissolve his anxieties and achieve a diffuse sense of omnipotence. Moreover, the alcoholic has been described as a person possessed by a demonic "craving" for alcohol such that "the first drink" would trigger an uninterrupted sequence of compulsive drinking until he achieved a "state of oblivion" or the alcohol supply was exhausted. Empirical observations have not supported these prevailing notions about alcoholism and thereby re-emphasize the need for systematic investigation of the basic phenomenology of this complex behavior disorder. The following commonalities have emerged from recent studies of alcoholism.

Evidence of Alcohol Addiction

Virtually all of the alcoholic subjects studied in behavioral paradigms in our own and other laboratories have shown tolerance for alcohol and withdrawal signs and symptoms upon cessation of drinking which cannot be explained by associated nutritional deficiency or intercurrent illness. All subsequent data have supported the experimental observations of Mendelson (1964) and Isbell *et al.* (1955) and the clinical impressions of Victor and Adams (1953) that removal of alcohol *per se* eventuates in expression of the abstinence syndrome.

"The Alcoholic (?)"

Beyond the pharmacological commonality of tolerance for and dependence upon alcohol, alcoholic individuals are a heterogeneous group. Clinical assessments have indicated that there is no common constellation of personality or psychodynamic variables which invariably characterize alcoholic individuals (McNamee *et al.*, 1968; Rosen, 1966; Steinglass *et al.*, 1971). Moreover, it appears that alcohol does not necessarily trigger any particular pattern of social interaction; alcohol may accentuate a patient's characteristic mode of coping with his environment and with his peers. Alcohol may permit the alcoholic to engage in a series of dyadic and intergroup roles which are not available to him during periods of sobriety. Alcohol may be used to define relative dominance roles in stable dyadic relationships (Mendelson et al., 1968; Weiner et al., 1971; Steinglass et al., 1971).

Subjects have shown a persistent idiosyncrasy in their drinking patterns both within and between individuals studied over long periods of time. Those biological and biochemical correlates of addiction which are consistently observed have not clarified the contribution of nonbehavioral factors to either the initiation of or the cessation of drinking (cf. reviews by Mendelson, 1970a,b). The factors that most frequently correlate with cessation of drinking appear to be gastritis or intercurrent illness and, on some occasions, the occurrence of a stress or the loss of a drinking companion (Mendelson and Mello, 1966; Mendelson et al., 1968; Mello and Mendelson, 1970a,c, 1971a). The factors that correlate with resumption of a drinking episode are far less clearly defined. Subjects usually are less anxious and depressed at the outset of a drinking episode than at its termination. Many alcoholics report that they plan to initiate a drinking episode.

Control over Drinking

Behavioral experiments in which alcoholics are given an opportunity to work for virtually unlimited amounts of alcohol have consistently shown that the alcoholic is able to exercise considerable control over his drinking and does not usually elect to drink himself into a stupor (Mello and Mendelson, 1965; Mendelson and Mello, 1966; Mello et al., 1968; Mendelson et al., 1968; Mello and Mendelson, 1970a, 1971a; Nathan et al., 1970a,b, 1971,; Liebson et al., 1971). Moreover, the amount of alcohol that an alcoholic drinks can be affected by the amount of work required for him to obtain it (Mello et al., 1968; Liebson et al., 1971). Not only do alcoholics rarely drink to achieve a state of oblivion, they do not even drink continually when given the opportunity (Mendelson and Mello, 1966; Mello and Mendelson, 1970, 1971a; Nathan et al., 1970a,b, 1971). Subjects have consistently initiated spontaneous periods of abstinence when given an opportunity to work for alcohol for prolonged periods of time (Mendelson et al., 1968; Nathan et al., 1970a,b, 1971; Mello and Mendelson, 1971a). No alcoholic subject studied in our laboratory has ever consistently consumed the total volume of bourbon (32 oz per day) that has been freely available during a drinking period (Mello and Mendelson, 1971a).

All of these data are inconsistent with the notion that after an alcoholic subject begins drinking, he is compelled to continue until he reaches a state of severe intoxication. Perhaps the most compelling data which are inconsistent with the notion of "craving" are from the study of Cohen et al. (1971) in which it was shown that abstinence was not significantly disrupted by consumption of as much as 4 oz of alcohol per day. Such a "primary dose" of alcohol was less disruptive than a delay in payment for abstinence.

The implications of these data are encouraging for prospects of rehabilitation of alcoholics based on a controlled drinking program. These experimental findings are compatible with the several clinical studies of alcoholics who are able to drink normally (Davies, 1962; Pattison, 1966, Pattison et al., 1968). The usual therapeutic goal of total abstinence for the alcoholic patient has been based on a fatalistic "craving" notion. General awareness of the limitations of this concept may lead to a more rational therapeutic approach to problem drinking.

Manipulation of Intoxication

Recent research on alcoholism has resulted in a series of unexpected findings concerning eating and drinking. Although alcohol provides a source of calories, it appears that these calories are not used in the same way as calories from food since alcoholic individuals drinking and eating as much as 7000 calories per day do not show any significant weight gain (Mello and Mendelson, 1970c, 1971a). These data challenge the common assumption that the reason that the alcoholic eats poorly while drinking is because the alcohol supplies calories. Our data suggest that rather, the alcoholic reduces his food intake in a deliberate effort to increase his subjective feelings of intoxication (Mello and Mendelson, 1970a,c, 1971a). It has been shown that the reduction of food intake does decrease the rate of alcohol metabolism (Smith and Newman, 1959; Forsander et al., 1965; Mendelson 1970b).

Affect and Memory

Alcoholics most frequently show an increase in anxiety and depression and further impairment of an already fragile self-esteem during the course of a drinking episode (Mendelson, 1964; McNamee et al., 1968; McGuire et al., 1966; Mello and Mendelson, 1965; Mendelson and Mello, 1966; Mendelson et al., 1968; Mello et al., 1968; Nathan et al., 1970a,b, 1971; Tamerin and Mendelson, 1969; Tamerin et al., 1970; Mayfield and Allen, 1967; Mayfield, 1968a,b; Vanderpool, 1969). This increase in disturbing affect observed in alcoholics during studies of experimentally induced intoxication is difficult to reconcile with information that most alcoholics provide about their drinking experiences during sobriety in a clinical interview. The sober alcoholic appears to be unable to remember his despondency and dysphoria during drinking and he cannot predict that such dysphoria and despondency will accompany a subsequent drinking episode. This dissociation between experience and recall during drinking and sobriety provides a partial resolution to the seeming paradox that alcohol induces psychological pain rather than pleasure. Thus, if an alcoholic does not recall the seemingly aversive aspects of his drinking experience during a subsequent period of sobriety, these aversive consequences could not effectively modify his future drinking experience. There are considerable anecdotal and experimental observations which converge to suggest that a substantial dissociation of experience during drinking and expectancy and recall following drinking frequently occurs in the alcohol addict (Diethelm and Barr, 1962; McGuire *et al.*, 1966; McNamee *et al.*, 1968; Ryback, 1970; Tamerin and Mendelson, 1969; Tamerin *et al.*, 1970; Goodwin *et al.*, 1969a,b).

Sleep Patterns

Contrary to the prevailing clinical impression, insomnia does not invariably occur within the first 72 hr of severe alcohol withdrawal. There also appears to be a frequent dissociation between the occurrence of hallucinosis and the occurrence of insomnia during alcohol withdrawal (Mello and Mendelson, 1970b).

Conclusions

The nature of the addictive process, the developmental sequence of events, and the central nervous system alterations which define the condition of alcohol addiction are unknown. Beyond the obvious requirement of ingestion of sufficient quantities of alcohol over a long enough period of time, the determinants of alcohol tolerance and dependence remain a matter of conjecture. The development of approaches to these very basic questions constitutes perhaps the major challenge to the biological scientist concerned with addiction. Studies of the interaction between alcohol and the electroencephalographic and behavioral correlates of sleep constitute another important area requiring investigation. At a behavioral level, the nature of the reinforcing properties of alcohol is only beginning to be analyzed. If alcohol induces dysphoria, what are the immediate consequences of drinking that maintain this behavioral response? Establishing the extent to which an alcoholic can control his drinking and function in a useful social role and determining the environmental contingencies important for maintaining control of drinking are questions of immediate practical concern to the behavioral scientist confronted with a serious public health problem.

Many of the persistent misconceptions about the alcohol addict have arisen from a failure to recognize the differences in the effects of alcohol on the moderate or heavy drinker and the alcoholic. Acceptance of alcoholism as a disease, a form of addiction involving dependence upon and tolerance for alcohol has been an important step toward reducing the confusion surrounding this disorder. Within this framework, investigators from many disciplines can develop approaches which may elucidate not only the nature of alcoholism, but the addictive disorders generally. It is anticipated that within the next 5 years, basic research on alcoholism will have clarified many of the ambiguities and unresolved issues that have been described herein.

ACKNOWLEDGMENT

I am grateful to the many investigators who kindly provided preprints of their current research. I thank my colleagues at the NIMH National Center for Prevention and Control of Alcoholism for their careful reading of this paper and for their many helpful suggestions. I gratefully acknowledge the able assistance of Mrs. Lillian Light and Mrs. Donna Ondrish in the preparation of this manuscript.

REFERENCES

Alexander, F., 1956. Views on the etiology of alcoholism. II. The psychodynamic view, in *Alcoholism as a Medical Problem* (H. D. Kruse, ed.) Hoeber–Harper, New York.

Ayllon, T. and Michael, J., 1959. The psychiatric nurse as a behavioral engineer, *J. Exper. Anal. Behav.* 2: 323.

Bailey, M. B. and Stewart, J., 1967. Normal drinking by persons reporting previous problem drinking, *Quart. J. Stud. Alc.* 28: 305.

Bloomquist, E. R., 1959. Addiction, addicting drugs and the anesthesiologist, *JAMA* 171: 518.

Carpenter, J. A. and Ross, B. M., 1965. Effect of alcohol on short-term memory, *Quart. J. Stud. Alc.* 26: 561.

Cochin, J. and Kornetsky, C., 1964. Development and loss of tolerance to morphine in the rat after single and multiple injections, *J. Pharmacol. Exp. Ther.* 145: 1.

Cohen, M., Liebson, I., Faillace, L., and Speers, W., 1971. Alcoholism: Controlled drinking and incentive for abstinence, *Psychol. Rep.* 28: 575.

Collins, J. R., 1966. Major medical problems in alcoholic patients, in *Alcoholism* (J. H. Mendelson, ed.) Vol. 3, pp. 189–214, International Psychiatry Clinics. Boston, Little, Brown & Co.

Connor, R. G., 1962. The self-concepts of alcoholics, in *Society, Culture and Drinking Patterns* (D. J. Pittman and C. R. Snyder, eds.) pp. 455–467, Wiley, New York.

Davies, D. L., 1962. Normal drinking in recovered alcohol addicts, *Quart. J. Stud. Alc.* 23: 94.

Davis, D., 1971. Mood changes in alcoholic subjects with programmed and free-choice experimental drinking, in *Recent Advances in Studies of Alcoholism* (N. K. Mello and J. H. Mendelson, eds.) U.S. Govt. Printing Office, Washington, D.C., in press.

Dement, W. C., 1960. The effect of dream deprivation, *Science* 131: 1705.

Diethelm, O. and Barr, R. M., 1962. Psychotherapeutic interviews and alcohol intoxication, *Quart. J. Stud. Alc.* 23: 243.

Dreher, K. F. and Fraser, J. G., 1968. Smoking habits of alcoholic out-patients. II. *Internat. J. Addict.* 3: 65.

Evarts, E. V., 1962. A neurophysiologic theory of hallucinations, in *Hallucinations* (L. J. West, ed.) pp. 1–13, Grune & Stratton, New York.

Ewing, J. A., 1967. Addictions. II. Non-narcotic addictive agents, in *Comprehensive Textbook of Psychiatry* (A. M. Freedman and H. I. Kaplan, eds.) pp. 1003–1011, The Williams & Wilkins Co., Baltimore.

Feinberg, I. and Evarts, E. V., 1969. Some implications of sleep research for psychiatry, in *Neurobiological Aspects of Psychopathology*, Proc. of the 58th Annual Meeting of the American Psychopathological Association (J. Zubin and C. Shagass, eds.) pp. 334–393, Grune & Stratton, New York.

Ferster, C. B. and Skinner, B. F., 1957. *Schedules of Reinforcement*, Appleton–Century–Crofts, New York.

Flannigan, B. I., Goldiamond, I., and Azrin, N., 1958. Operant Stuttering: The control of stuttering behavior through response-contingent sequences, *J. Exper. Anal. Behav.* **1**: 173.

Forsander, O. A., Raiha, N., Salaspuro, M., and Maenpaa, P., 1965. Influence of ethanol on the liver metabolism of fed and starved rats, *Biochem. J.* **94**: 259.

Fraser, H. F. and Isbell, H., 1952. Comparative effects of 20 mg of morphine sulfate on non-addicts and former morphine addicts, *J. Pharmacol. Exp. Ther.* **105**: 498.

Glatt, M. M., 1967. The question of moderate drinking despite "loss of control," *Brit. J. Addict.* **62**: 267.

Goldberg, S. R. and Schuster, C. R., 1969. Nalorphine: Increased sensitivity of monkeys formerly dependent on morphine, *Science* **166**: 1548.

Goldstein, A., Aronow, L., and Kalman, S. M., 1969. *Principles of Drug Action*, Harper & Row, New York.

Goodwin, D. W., 1970. Loss of short term memory as a predictor of the alcoholic "blackout," *Nature* **227**: 201.

Goodwin, D. W., Crane, J. B., and Guze, S. B., 1969a. Phenomenological aspects of the alcoholic "blackout," *Brit. J. Psychiat.* **115**: 1033.

Goodwin, D. W., Crane, J. B., and Guze, S. B., 1969b. Alcoholic "blackouts": A review and clinical study of 100 alcoholics, *Amer. J. Psychiat.* **126**: 191.

Goodwin, D. W., Powell, B., Bremer, D., Hoine, H., and Stern, J. 1969c. Alcohol and recall: State-dependent effects in man, *Science* **163**: 1358.

Greenberg, R. and Pearlman, C., 1967. Delirium tremens and dreaming, *Amer. J. Psychiat.* **124**: 133.

Gresham, S. C., Webb, W. B., and Williams, R. L., 1963. Alcohol and caffeine: Effect on inferred visual dreaming, *Science* **140**: 1226.

Gross, M. M. and Goodenough, D. R., 1968. Sleep disturbances in the acute alcoholic psychoses, in *Clinical Research in Alcoholism* (J. O. Cole, ed.) Psychiatric Research Report 24, pp. 132–147, American Psychiatric Association, Washington, D.C.

Gross, M. M., Goodenough, D., Tobin, M., Halpert, E., Lepore, D., Perlstein, A., Serots, M., Debeanco, J., Fuller, R., and Kishner, I., 1966. Sleep disturbance and hallucinations in the acute alcoholic psychoses, *J. Nerv. Ment. Dis.* **142**: 493.

Himmelsbach, C. K., 1942. Clinical studies of drug addiction: Physical dependence, withdrawal and recovery, *Arch. Intern. Med.* **69**: 766.

Isbell, H., 1955. Craving for alcohol, in WHO Report, *Quart. J. Stud. Alc.* **16**: 38.

Isbell, H., Fraser, H., Wikler, A., Belleville, R., and Eisenman, A., 1955. An experimental study of the etiology of "rum fits" and delirium tremens, *Quart. J. Stud. Alc.* **16**: 1.

Jaffe, J. H., 1968, Psychopharmacology and opiate dependence, in *Psychopharmacology. A Review of Progress 1957–1967* (D. H. Efron, ed.) PHS Publ. No. 1836, U.S. Govt. Printing Office, Washington, D.C., pp. 853–864.

Jarvik, M. E., 1968. Consolidation of memory, in *Psychopharmacology. A Review of*

Progress 1957–1967 (D. H. Efron, ed.) PHS Publ. No. 1836, U.S. Govt. Printing Office, Washington, D.C., pp. 885–890.

Jellinek, E. M., 1952. The phases of alcohol addiction, *Quart. J. Stud. Alc.* 13. 673.

John, E. R., 1967. *Mechanisms of Memory*, Academic Press, New York.

Johnson, L. C., Burdick, J. A., and Smith, J., 1970. Sleep during alcohol intake and withdrawal in the chronic alcoholic, *Arch. Gen. Psychiat.* 22: 406.

Kater, R. M. H., Tobon, F., and Iber, F. L., 1969. Increased rate of tolbutamide metabolism in alcoholic patients, *JAMA* 207: 363.

Kater, R. M. H., Zeive, P. D., Tobon, F., Roggin, G. M., and Iber, F. L., 1969. Heavy drinking accelerated drug's breakdown in liver, *JAMA* 206: 1709.

Kales, A., Hoedemaker, F., Jacobson, A., and Lichtenstein, E., 1964. Dream-deprivation: An experimental reappraisal, *Nature* 204: 1337.

Kales, A., Malmstrom, E. J., Scharf, M. D., and Rubin, R. T., 1969. Physiological and biochemical changes following use and withdrawal of hypnotics, in *Sleep: Physiology and Pathology* (A. Kales, ed.) Lippincott & Co., Philadelphia.

Kay, D. C., Eisenstein, R. B., and Jasinski, D. R., 1969. Morphine effects on human REM State, Waking State and NREM Sleep, *Psychopharmacologia* 14: 404.

Kelleher, R. T. and Morse, W. H., 1968. Determinants of the specificity of behavioral effects of drugs, in *Ergebnisse der Physiologie* (Reviews of Physiology, Biochemistry and Experimental Pharmacology) Bd. 60: 1, Springer-Verlag, Berlin.

Knowles, J. B., Laverty, S. G., and Kuechler, H. A., 1968. Effects of alcohol on REM sleep, *Quart. J. Stud. Alc.* 29: 342.

Kornetsky, C. and Bain, G., 1968. Morphine: Single-dose tolerance, *Science* 162: 1011.

Krantz, C. and Carr, T., 1965. *The Pharmacological Principles of Medical Practice*, The Williams & Wilkins Co., Baltimore.

Lee, T. K., Cho, M. H., and Dobkin, A. B., 1964. Effects of alcoholism, morphinism and barbiturate resistance on induction and maintenance of general anesthesia, *Canad. Anaesth. Soc. J.* 11: 354.

Leibowitz, J. O., 1967. Studies in the history of alcoholism. II. Acute alcoholism in ancient Greek and Roman medicine, *Brit. J. Addict.* 62: 83.

Liebson, I. A., Cohen, M., Faillace, L. A., and Ward, R. F., 1971. The token economy as a research method in alcoholism (in preparation).

Lindsley, O. R., 1956. Operant conditioning methods applied to research in chronic schizophrenia, *Psychiat. Res. Report* 5: 118.

Lindsley, O. R., 1960. Characteristics of the behavior of chronic psychotics as revealed by free-operant conditioning methods, *Diseases of the Nervous System*, Monograph Supplement Vol. XXI (No. 2), Feb. 1960.

MacAndrew, C. and Garfinkel, H. A., 1962. A consideration of changes attributed to intoxication as common-sense reasons for getting drunk, *Quart. J. Stud. Alc.* 23: 252.

Mardones, J., 1963. The alcohols, in *Physiological Pharmacology* (W. S. Root and F. G. Hofmann, eds.) Academic Press, New York, pp. 99–183.

Martin, W. R. and Fraser, H. F., 1961. A comparative study of physiological and subjective effects of heroin and morphine administered intravenously in postaddicts, *J. Pharmacol. Exp. Therap.* 133: 388.

Martin, W. R., Wikler, A., Eades, C. G., and Pescor, T. F., 1963. Tolerance to and physical dependence on morphine in rats, *Psychopharmacologia* 4: 247.

Mayfield, D., 1968a. Psychopharmacology of alcohol. I. Affective change with intoxication, drinking behavior and affective state, *J. Nerv. Ment. Dis.* 146: 314.

Mayfield, D., 1968b. Psychopharmacology of alcohol. II. Affective tolerance in alcohol intoxication, *J. Nerv. Ment. Dis.* 146: 322.

Mayfield, D. and Allen, D., 1967. Alcohol and affect: a psychopharmacological study, *Am. J. Psychiat.* **123:** 1346.

McGaugh, J. L., 1968. Drug facilitation of memory and learning, in *Psychopharmacology. A Review of Progress 1957–1967* (D. H. Efron, ed.), PHS Publ. No. 1836, U.S. Govt. Printing Office, Washington, D.C., pp. 891–904.

McGuire, M. T., Mendelson, J. H., and Stein, S., 1966. Comparative psychosocial studies of alcoholic and nonalcoholic subjects undergoing experimentally induced ethanol intoxication, *Psychosom. Med.* **28:** 13.

McNamee, H. B., Mello, N. K., and Mendelson, J. H., 1968. Experimental analysis of drinking patterns of alcoholics: Concurrent psychiatric observations, *Amer. J. Psychiat.* **124:** 1063.

Mello, N. K., 1968. Some aspects of the behavioral pharmacology of alcohol, in *Psychopharmacology. A Review of Progress 1957–1967* (D. H. Efron, ed.) PHS Publ. No. 1836, U.S. Govt. Printing Office, Washington, D.C., pp. 787–809.

Mello, N. K. and Mendelson, J. H., 1965. Operant analysis of drinking patterns of chronic alcoholics, *Nature* **206:** 43.

Mello, N. K. and Mendelson, J. H., 1969. Alterations in states of consciousness associated with chronic ingestion of alcohol, in *Neurobiological Aspects of Psychopathology,* Proc. of the 58th Annual Meeting of the American Psychopathological Association (J. Zubin and C. Shagass, eds.) pp. 183–218, Grune & Stratton, New York.

Mello, N. K. and Mendelson, J. H., 1970a. Experimentally induced intoxication in alcoholics: A comparison between programmed and spontaneous drinking, *J. Pharmacol. Exp. Ther.* **173:** 101.

Mello, N. K. and Mendelson, J. H., 1970b. Behavioral studies of sleep patterns in alcoholics during intoxication and withdrawal, *J. Pharmacol. Exp. Ther.* **175:** 94.

Mello, N. K. and Mendelson, J. H., 1970c. The effects of prolonged alcohol ingestion on the eating, drinking, and smoking patterns of chronic alcoholics, in *Learning Mechanisms in Smoking* (W. A. Hunt, ed.) pp. 207–8, Aldine, Chicago.

Mello, N. K. and Mendelson, J. H., 1971a. Drinking patterns during work-contingent and non-contingent alcohol acquisition, *Psychosom. Med.*, in press.

Mello, N. K., McNamee, H. B., and Mendelson, J. H., 1968. Drinking patterns of chronic alcoholics: Gambling and motivation for alcohol, in *Clinical Research in Alcoholism* (J. O. Cole, ed.) pp. 83–118, Psychiatric Research Report 24, American Psychiatric Association, Washington, D.C.

Mello, N. K. and Mendelson, J. H., 1971b. A quantitative analysis of drinking patterns in alcoholics, *Arch. Gen. Psychiat.*, in press.

Mendelson, J. H. (ed.), 1964. Experimentally induced chronic intoxication and withdrawal in alcoholics, *Quart. J. Stud. Alc.*, Suppl. No. 2.

Mendelson, J. H., 1968. Ethanol-1-C^{14} metabolism in alcoholics and nonalcoholics, *Science* **159:** 319.

Mendelson, J. H., 1970a. Biochemical mechanisms of alcohol addiction, in *The Biology of Alcoholism, Vol. 1: Biochemistry* (H. Begleiter and B. Kissin, eds.) Plenum Press, New York (1971).

Mendelson, J. H., 1970b. Biological concomitants of alcoholism, *New Engl. J. Med.* **283:** 24–32, 71–81.

Mendelson, J. H. and Mello, N. K., 1966. Experimental analysis of drinking behavior of chronic alcoholics, *Ann. N.Y. Acad. Sci.* **133:** 828.

Mendelson, J. H. and Mello, N. K., 1969. A disease as an organizer for biochemical research: Alcoholism, in *Psychochemical Research in Man* (A. J. Mandell and M. P. Mandell, eds.) pp. 379–403, Academic Press, New York.

Mendelson, J. H. and Stein, S., 1966. The definition of alcoholism, in *Alcoholism* (J. H. Mendelson, ed.) Vol. 3, pp. 3–16, International Psychiatry Clinics. Little, Brown, Boston.

Mendelson, J., Wexler, D., Leiderman, P., and Solomon, P., 1957. A study of addiction to nonethyl alcohols and other poisonous compounds, *Quart. J. Stud. Alc.* 18: 561.

Mendelson, J. H., Stein, S., and Mello, N. K., 1965. Effects of experimentally induced intoxication on metabolism of ethanol-1-C^{14} in alcoholic subjects, *Metabolism* 14: 1255.

Mendelson, J. H., Stein, S., and McGuire, M. T., 1966. Comparative psychophysiological studies of alcoholic and nonalcoholic subjects undergoing experimentally induced ethanol intoxication, *Psychosom. Med.* 28: 1.

Mendelson, J. H., Mello, N. K., and Solomon, P., 1968. Small group drinking behavior: An experimental study of chronic alcoholics, in *The Addictive States* (A. Wikler, ed.), Vol. 46, Res. Publ. Ass. Nerv. Ment. Dis., pp. 399–430, The Williams & Wilkins Co., Baltimore.

Mendelson, J. H., Ogata, M., and Mello, N. K., 1971. Adrenal function and alcoholism: I. Serum cortisol, *Psychosom. Med.*, 33: (2) 145.

Merry, J., 1966. The "loss of control" myth, *Lancet* 1: 1257.

Morse, W. H., Mead, R. N., and Kelleher, R. T., 1967. *Science* 157 (3785): 215.

Myerson, D. J., 1957. A three-year study of a group of Skid Row alcoholics, in *Alcoholism* (H. E. Himwich, ed.). Publ. No. 47 of the American Association for the Advancement of Science, Washington, D.C.

Narrol, H. G., 1967. Experimental application of reinforcement principles to the analysis and treatment of hospitalized alcoholics, *Quart. J. Stud. Alc.* 28: 105.

Nathan, P. E., Lowenstein, L. M., Solomon, P., and Rossi, A. M., 1970a. Behavioral analysis of chronic alcoholism. *Arch. Gen. Psychiat.* 22: 419.

Nathan, P. E., Zare, N. C., Ferneau, E. W., Jr., and Lowenstein, L. M., 1970b. Effects of congener differences in alcoholic beverages on the behavior of alcoholics, *Quart. J. Stud. Alc.*, Suppl. No. 5, pp. 87–100.

Nathan, P. E., O'Brien, J. S., and Lowenstein, L. M., 1971. Operant studies of chronic alcoholism: Interaction of alcohol and alcoholics, in *Biological Aspects of Alcohol* (P. J. Creaven and M. K. Roach, eds.). University of Texas Press, Austin, in press.

Nelson, B., 1967. The small beginnings of a significant Federal program, *Science* 158: 475.

Osborn, A. G., Bunker, J. P., Cooper, L. M., Frank, G. S., and Hilgard, E. R., 1967. Effects of thiopental sedation on learning and memory, *Science* 157: 574.

Oswald, I., Berger, R., Jaramillo, R., Keddie, K., Olley, P., and Plunkett, G., 1963. Melancholia and barbiturates: A controlled EEG, body and eye movement study of sleep, *Brit. J. Psychiat.* 109: 66.

Oswald, I., Evans, J. I., and Lewis, S. A., 1969. Addictive drugs cause suppression of paradoxical sleep with withdrawal rebound, in *Scientific Basis of Drug Dependence* (H. Steinberg, ed.) pp. 243–258, J. & A. Churchill Ltd., London.

Overton, D. A., 1968. Dissociated learning in drug states (State dependent learning), in *Psychopharmacology. A Review of Progress 1957–1967* (D. H. Efron, ed.), PHS Publ. No. 1836, U.S. Govt. Printing Office, Washington, D.C., pp. 918–930.

Overton, D. A., 1970. Discriminative control of behavior by drug states, in *Stimulus Functions of Drugs* (G. Heistad, T. Thompson, and R. Pickins, eds.) Appleton–Century–Crofts, New York, in press.

Paredes, A. and Cornelison, F. S., Jr., 1968. Development of an audio–visual technique for the rehabilitation of alcoholics, *Quart. J. Stud. Alc.* 29: 84.

Paredes, A., Ludwig, K. D., Hassenfeld, I. N., and Cornelison, F. S., Jr., 1969. A clinical study of alcoholics using audiovisual self-image feedback, *J. Nerv. Ment. Dis.* 148: 449.

Pattison, E. M., 1966. A critique of alcoholism treatment concepts; with special reference to abstinence, *Quart. J. Stud. Alc.* **27**: 49.

Pattison, E. M., 1968. Abstinence criteria; a critique of abstinence criteria in the treatment of alcoholism, *Int. J. Soc. Psychiat.*, **14**: 268.

Pattison, E. M., Headley, E. B., Gleser, G. C., and Gottschalk, L. A., 1968. Abstinence and normal drinking, *Quart. J. Stud. Alc.* **29**: 610.

Poppen, R., 1970. Misbehavior as a possible reinforcing consequence of alcoholism (in preparation).

Root, W. S. and Hofmann, F. G., 1963. *Physiological Pharmacology*, Academic Press, New York.

Rosen, A. C., 1966. Some differences in self perceptions between alcoholics and non-alcoholics, *Percep. Motor Skills* **23**: 1279.

Rubington, E., 1968. The bottle gang, *Quart. J. Stud. Alc.* **29**: 943.

Ryback, R. S., 1970. Alcohol Amnesia: Observations on seven drinking inpatient alcoholics, *Quart. J. Stud. Alc.* **31**: 616.

Ryback, R. S., 1969. The effects of ethanol on short-term memory, Proceedings of the annual meeting of the AAAS, Pharmaceutical Sciences Section, in Boston, December 1969, in press.

Seevers, M. H. and Deneau, G. A., 1963. Physiological aspects of tolerance and physical dependence, in *Physiological Pharmacology* (W. S. Root and F. G. Hofmann, eds.), pp. 565–640, Academic Press, New York.

Shoben, E. J., Jr., 1956. Views on the etiology of alcoholism. III. *The behavioristic view*, in *Alcoholism as a Medical Problem* (H. D. Kruse, ed.) Hoeber–Harper, New York.

Skinner, B. F., 1953. *Science and Human Behavior*, Macmillan Company, New York.

Skinner, B. F., 1959. *Cumulative Record*, Appleton–Century–Crofts, New York.

Skinner, B. F., Solomon, H. C., and Lindsley, O. R., 1954. A new method for the experimental analysis of the behavior of psychotic patients, *J. Nerv. Ment. Dis.* **120**: 403.

Sloan, J. W. and Eiseman, A. J., 1968. Long persisting changes in catecholamine metabolism following addiction to and withdrawal from morphine, in *The Addictive States* (A. Wikler, ed.), Vol. 46, Res. Publ. Ass. Nerv. Ment. Dis., pp. 96–105, The Williams & Wilkins Co., Baltimore.

Smart, R. G., 1968. Future time perspectives in alcoholics and social drinkers, *J. Abnormal Psychol.* **73**: 81.

Smith, M. E. and Newman, H. W., 1959. The rate of ethanol metabolism in fed and fasting animals, *J. Biol. Chem.* **234**: 1544.

Stein, L. I., Niles, D., and Ludwig, A. M., 1968. The loss of control phenomenon in alcoholics, *Quart. J. Stud. Alc.* **29**: 598.

Steinberg, H. and Tomkiewicz, M., 1968. Drugs and memory, in *Psychopharmacology. A Review of Progress 1957–1967* (D. H. Efron, ed.) PHS Publ. No. 1836, U.S. Govt. Printing Office, Washington, D.C., pp. 879–884.

Steinglass, P., Weiner, S., and Mendelson, J. H., 1971. A systems approach to alcoholism: A model and its clinical application. *Arch. Gen. Psychiat.* **24**: 401.

Storm, T. and Smart, R. G., 1965. Dissociation: A possible explanation of some features of alcoholism, and implication for its treatment, *Quart. J. Stud. Alc.* **26**: 111.

Talland, G. A., Mendelson, J. H., and Ryack, P., 1964. Experimentally induced chronic intoxication and withdrawal in alcoholics, Part 5, Tests of attention, *Quart. J. Stud. Alc.*, Suppl. No. 2, 74–86.

Talland, G. A., 1966. Effects of alcohol on performance in continuous attention tasks, *Psychosom. Med.* **28** (II): 596.

Tamerin, J. S. and Mendelson, J. H., 1969. The psychodynamics of chronic inebriation: Observations of alcoholics during the process of drinking in an experimental group setting, *Amer. J. Psychiat.* 125: 886.

Tamerin, J. S., Weiner, S., and Mendelson, J. H., 1970. Alcoholics' expectancies and recall of experiences during intoxication, *Amer. J. Psychiat.* 126 (12): 1697.

Tamerin, J. S., Weiner, S., Poppen, R., Steinglass, P., and Mendelson, J. H., 1971. Alcohol and memory: Amnesia and short-term function during experimentally induced intoxication, *Amer. J. Psychiat.* 127 (12): 1659.

Taylor, W. J., 1966. Alcoholism: The police aspect, in *Alcoholism* (J. H. Mendelson, ed.) International Psychiatry Clinics, Vol. 3, No. 2, pp. 81–90, Little, Brown and Company, Boston.

Vanderpool, J. A., 1969. Alcoholism and the self-concept, *Quart. J. Stud. Alc.* 30: 59.

Victor, M., 1966. Treatment of alcoholic intoxication and the withdrawal syndrome. A critical analysis of the use of drugs and other forms of therapy, *Psychosom. Med.* 28, No. 3 (II): 636.

Victor, M. and Adams, R. D., 1953. The effect of alcohol on the nervous system, *Res. Publ. Ass. Nerv. Ment. Dis.* 32: 526.

Weiner, H., 1969. Controlling human fixed-interval performance, *J. Exp. Anal. Behav.* 12: 349.

Weiner, S., Tamerin, J. S., Steinglass, P., and Mendelson, J. H., 1971. Familial patterns in chronic alcoholism: A study of a father and son during experimental intoxication. *Amer. J. Psychiat.* 127 (12): 1646.

West, L. J., 1967. Dissociative reaction, in *Comprehensive Textbook of Psychiatry* (A. M. Freedman and H. I. Kaplan, eds.) pp. 885–899, The Williams & Wilkins Co., Baltimore.

Westerfeld, W. W. and Schulman, M. P., 1959. Metabolism and caloric value of alcohol, *JAMA* 170: 197.

White, W. F. and Porter, T. L., 1966. Self concept reports among hospitalized alcoholics during early periods of sobriety, *J. Counsel. Psychol.* 13: 352.

W.H.O. Expert Committee on Mental Health and on Alcohol, 1955. Symposium on "The Craving" for Alcohol, *Quart. J. Stud. Alc.* 16: 34–66.

Wikler, A., 1952. A psychodynamic study of a patient during experimental self-regulated re-addiction to morphine, *Psychiat. Quart.* 26: 270.

Wikler, A., 1961. On the nature of addiction and habituation, *Brit. J. Addict.* 57: 73.

Wikler, A., 1967. Personality disorders. III: Sociopathic type: The Addictions, in *Comprehensive Textbook of Psychiatry* (A. M. Freedman and H. I. Kaplan, eds.) pp. 939–1003, Williams and Wilkins, Baltimore.

Williams, A. F., 1965. Self-concepts of college problem drinkers. I. A comparison with alcoholics, *Quart. J. Stud. Alc.* 26: 586.

Williams, A. F., 1966. Social drinking, anxiety and depression, *J. Personality Soc. Psychol.* 3: 689.

Woods, J. H. and Schuster, C. R., 1970. Opiates as reinforcing stimuli, in *Stimulus Functions of Drugs* (G. Heistad, T. Thompson and R. Pickins, eds.) Appleton–Century–Crofts, New York, in press.

Woods, J. H., Ikomi, F. I., and Winger, G., 1970. The reinforcing properties of ethanol, in *Biological Aspects of Alcohol* (P. J. Creaven and M. K. Roach, eds.) University of Texas Press, Austin, in press.

Yules, R. B., Freedman, D. X., and Chandler, K. A., 1966a. The effect of ethyl alcohol on man's electroencephalograph sleep cycle, *EEG Clin. Neurophysiol.* 20: 109.

Yules, R. B., Ogden, J. A., Gault, F. P., and Freedman, D. X., 1966b. The effect of ethyl alcohol on electroencephalographic sleep cycles in cats, *Psychonom. Sci.* **5:** 97.

Yules, R. B., Lippman, M. E., and Freedman, D. X., 1967. Alcohol administration prior to sleep, the effect on EEG sleep states, *Arch. Gen. Psychiat.* **16:** 94.

CHAPTER 10

The Effects of Alcohol on the Central Nervous System in Humans

Henri Begleiter and Arthur Platz

Department of Psychiatry
State University of New York, Downstate Medical Center
Brooklyn, New York

INTRODUCTION: RESEARCH QUESTIONS AND METHODOLOGICAL PROBLEMS

Although gross changes in personality and behavior are readily apparent during acute alcoholic intoxication, these changes have only become the subject of systematic study within the past 100 years. Miles (1932) has summarized the different stages of clinical intoxication in the form of a scale relating the subjective states and typical behavioral changes seen with increasing blood alcohol levels. The earliest effects, tingling sensations in the mucous membrane of the mouth and throat, may appear with a blood alcohol level as low as 10 mg%. At the upper extreme (300 mg%) the subject passes into a stuporous condition, and at still higher levels (400 mg%) falls into a state of deep anesthesia which may end in death. This description of successive stages in clinical intoxication represents the typical or modal response commonly seen with a given blood alcohol level. The association between blood alcohol concentration and stages of clinical intoxication is not a clear one-to-one relationship. As with other psychotropic drugs, there are large individual differences in response to a given dosage as well as considerable variability in the subject's response at different times or in different settings.

The Miles scale summarizes the changes in subjective states and social behavior induced by drinking. More recently Carpenter (1962) has reviewed the experimental literature dealing with the effects of alcohol on sensory functions and different measures of motor performance. Since the various changes in subjective states, personality characteristics, and changes in sensory and motor functioning are mediated by alterations in the activity of the central nervous system under alcohol, considerable research effort has been devoted to uncovering possible electrophysiological correlates of these psychological changes. An extensive literature has accumulated on the effects of alcohol on the neural functioning in animals using implanted electrodes to study single unit and mass activity in different brain structures. Human studies have been largely limited to scalp-recorded measures of brain activity. The raw electroencephalogram yields a number of frequency and associated amplitude characteristics which may be scored separately, or combined in the form of a spectrum analysis showing percent time or amount of energy plotted as a function of wave frequency. For clinical purposes and for evaluating toxic drug effects, the amount of EEG abnormality is frequently evaluated by means of relatively standard criteria on a 4- or 5-point pathology scale.

The EEG provides an ongoing record of the neuroelectric activity of the brain, either in the resting state or under different activation procedures (hyperventilation, repetitive photic stimulation, drug ingestion, etc.). The neural response to stimulation in different sensory modalities may also be examined by time locking the recording to successive presentations of a repetitive stimulus. Such summated measures of neural activity as the average evoked response and the recovery function show the neural response to specific stimulation which is frequently hard to detect or to analyze in the ongoing EEG record.

Although admittedly the scalp-recorded EEG is a gross measure of brain activity, it provides the best and most direct measure currently available for assessing the functional state of the central nervous system, and detecting abnormal or impaired functioning found in certain pathological states. (The pneumoencephalograph will frequently provide confirmatory evidence when EEG abnormalities are related to structural changes or brain damage.)

The ability to monitor ongoing brain activity makes it possible for researchers to examine the relationship between subjective states, behavioral changes, and the electrophysiological activity of the central nervous system. In the field of alcoholism early interest was focused primarily on investigating whether the ingestion of alcohol affected the EEG and whether chronic alcoholics show increased evidence of EEG abnormalities. Of particular interest is the question whether alcohol-induced changes in the EEG closely parallel the more or less stepwise changes in subjective state and behavior during drinking. Unfortunately a parametric dosage study showing changes in the EEG as a function of increasing blood alcohol level over the full range of values has not yet been systematically done. This is the counterpart of the Miles scale of subjective and behavioral changes commonly found at given concentrations of blood alcohol and is needed to determine the degree of correspondence between psychological changes and changes in the electrophysiological activity of the brain during intoxication.

The second question has a more practical goal. If distinctive EEG signs are characteristic of the chronic alcoholic, these may point to possible neural mechanisms underlying alcohol-related symptomatology and provide some basis for the diagnosis and treatment of the alcoholic during the course of the disease.

As is true in most research areas, what appeared to be easily answered questions—does alcohol affect the EEG and do chronic alcoholics show distinguishing EEG characteristics—turned out to be difficult to investigate. These questions break down into a series of questions requiring investigation, some of which present difficult methodological problems which make clear-cut answers hard to obtain. The review of the literature will be organized around these basic questions:

The Effects of Alcohol on the Electroencephalogram

1. Does alcohol affect the electrical activity of the brain as measured by the EEG?
2. Are alcohol-induced changes in the EEG either quantitatively or qualitatively different in the chronic drinker as compared to the nonalcoholic?
   a. Do alcoholics show EEG differences reflecting tolerance effects due to the prolonged use of alcohol or differences related to impaired efficiency of alcohol metabolism due to liver damage, etc.?
3. Does the EEG change progressively during extended periods of drinking?
   a. Is there evidence for either tolerance or sensitization effects on CNS activity during sustained high blood alcohol levels?
4. Is alcohol a central nervous system depressant, or does it have both a stimulant and depressant action depending upon dose level and time of testing, as some investigators have suggested (see Mello and Mendelson, 1968)?

Comparison of EEG Recordings in Alcoholics *vs.* Nonalcoholics

1. Are the EEG's of chronic alcoholics between drinking bouts different from those of nonalcoholics?

2. Do alcoholics have a higher incidence of abnormal recordings (persistent arrhythmias and dysrhythmias, paroxysmal spiking, etc.) than normal controls ?
    a. To what extent does the impairment in cerebral functioning reflect underlying structural pathology or brain damage ?
3. If EEG abnormalities are more frequent in alcoholics, do these abnormalities appear in the resting EEG or only under activation procedures ?
    a. Is the cerebral dysfunction widespread or predominately localized in specific brain areas ?
4. Do differences in the EEG precede the development of alcoholism or only occur following several years of sustained drinking ?
    a. If such differences exist, are they related to the predisposing causes of alcoholism or primarily the effects of drinking ?
    b. Does the extent of such changes have any diagnostic or prognostic utility in assessing either the severity or the clinical course of the illness, or the nature and extent of underlying brain damage caused by alcohol ?

The Electroencephalogram During Acute Alcoholic Psychosis

1. Are there distinctive EEG signs characteristic of the acute withdrawal syndrome ?
    a. Do these signs change progressively during the course of the illness and subsequent recovery ?
2. Are there distinctive EEG signs differentially associated with the specific symptom patterns seen during alcoholic psychosis: hallucinosis, convulsive seizures, delirium, etc. ?
3. Do changes in the EEG rhythm occur only during the course of the illness, or are there long-lasting changes indicating functional pathology and possible permanent CNS damage ?

Specific methodological questions raised by the studies reviewed will be discussed in the main body of the text. However, since some methodological problems occur so frequently, they will be considered at this point.

Definition of the Chronic Alcoholic and Selection of Study Samples

Since most studies of alcoholism are carried out in a hospital, setting the diagnosis of "chronic alcoholism" is implicitly defined by two criteria: (1) a history of drinking, and (2) the occurrence of alcohol-related symptoms severe enough to require hospitalization. Because of this bias in sampling, if studies of patients report a higher incidence of EEG abnormalities, this should not be interpreted to mean either that the chronic use of alcohol generally produces cerebral dysfunctioning, or that a completely random sample of alcoholics would show a higher incidence of abnormalities. Hospital-based samples include only patients in whom drinking produced severe symptomatology and also necessarily excludes those persons in whom heavy drinking did not produce psychiatric symptoms. These two groups, although similar in their consumption of alcohol, are undoubtedly quite different in other characteristics, possibly including their response to alcohol and their EEG records. An alternative hypothesis which requires testing is that individuals with preexisting abnormalities are also more likely to develop psychiatric symptoms as a result of drinking and consequently be more likely to be hospitalized.

Hospital-based samples are biased in other ways which affect the interpretation placed on the reported frequency of abnormalities found in these groups. Upper middle-class and upper-class patients more frequently enter private hospitals than state hospitals, and if they do enter the latter, are perhaps more often admitted to a general medical rather than a detoxification ward. Patients admitted with alcohol-related physical symptoms (cirrhosis, alcohol-aggravated ulceritis, etc.) rather than psychiatric symptoms are also less likely to be included in studies of chronic alcoholism. Such implicit selection of patients making up the group defined as "chronic alcoholics" necessarily qualifies the interpretation placed on the frequency of EEG abnormalities reported in the literature.

A related problem which helps to account for some of the discrepancies between studies is the wide individual differences in patients who are diagnosed as "chronic alcoholics" (cf. Kaim et al., 1968). The only characteristic which they appear to have in common is hospitalization because of alcohol-related symptoms, while they may differ markedly in the pattern or type of drinking, amount of alcohol consumption, duration of drinking, history of alcohol-related disturbances, and nature of presenting symptoms. And contrary to some psychoanalytic writers, there are little objective data supporting the hypothesis that alcoholics share a common personality pattern (Shagass and Jones, 1957). Some researchers (e.g., Arentsen and Sindrup, 1963; Predescu et al., 1967) have attempted to deal with this problem by breaking their sample down into various psychiatric groups (normal, psychopathic, neurotic, psychotic, etc.). While this procedure is useful for obtaining clinical information about subgroups of alcoholics, it is of doubtful value in assessing the effects of chronic alcoholism *per se* on CNS functioning. Since psychopathic personalities (Knott, 1965; Simon, O'Leary and Ryan, 1946) and neurotics (Wilson and Short, 1965) also show a higher incidence of EEG abnormalities, the role of alcoholism in these groups is difficult to assess.

Generally, the more homogeneous the sample, the greater the reliability of the data, and the more interpretable the findings. Perhaps one way out of the dilemma which has not yet been tried systematically would involve the classification of patients into relatively homogeneous subgroups either in terms of their past medical history or in terms of their current symptomatology. Jellinek's (1946) interview schedule on the phases of the drinking history records the time of the first appearance of the behavioral symptoms defining chronic alcoholism: morning drinking, sleeping difficulties, uncontrollable tremors, first appearance of amnesia or blackouts, hallucinations, delirium, etc. Since these symptoms tend to occur in a natural sequence and generally appear within a fixed number of years of heavy drinking, the questionnaire provides a natural index of the progression and severity of the disease prior to hospitalization. If chronic drinking does result in permanent impairment of CNS functioning, the incidence of EEG abnormalities should show a progressive increase related to the severity of the score on the Jellinek scale.

Differences in the kinds of patients included in the alcoholic samples studied at different hospitals probably account for much of the discrepancy in the reported frequency of EEG abnormalities in alcoholics and for the controversy as to whether this incidence is significantly greater than in normal subjects. Contributing to the problem of comparability of studies is the tendency of individual researchers to use different criteria in subject selection. In the papers to be reviewed, subjects range from nonhospitalized individuals with a history of heavy drinking to patients hospitalized with delirium tremens. Criteria for inclusion in different studies varied from selection on the basis of the occurrence of specific symptoms (e.g., blackouts) in the medical case history, to the presence of specific characteristics in the EEG record (e.g., occurrence of a predominant alpha pattern).

Nature of the Control Group

The logic of the control group requires that it be identical to the experimental group in all characteristics except the variable being investigated. However, in most studies of group differences, the variable defining membership in a clinical group is also associated with a number of other extraneous characteristics which differ from a true random sample (Feldman and Hass, 1970). Where possible, the experimental and control groups are matched on extraneous variables which might be expected to affect the dependent variable being studied.

If matching is not adequately done, the interpretation of group differences becomes quite ambiguous. As an example, alcoholics as a group have a history of more frequent accidents involving head injuries with consequent brain trauma than the normal population. Since such trauma may also affect cerebral activity, the possible finding of a higher incidence of pathological EEG's in alcoholics, while characteristic of alcoholics as a clinical group, could not be interpreted as evidence that alcohol *per se* results in functional brain impairment. Similarly, although Korsakov's psychosis and Wernicke's disease are commonly associated with a history of heavy drinking, the neurological deterioration found in these disorders is attributed to thiamine deficiency and not to alcohol (Victor and Adams, 1953). In Laennec's cirrhosis, the EEG abnormalities are a result of the toxic effect of high blood ammonia levels leading to hepatic coma (Green, 1965). Although these states are typically the result of prolonged heavy drinking, the EEG abnormalities characterizing them cannot be interpreted as evidence of a direct effect of alcohol on CNS functioning.

Sometimes even the most obvious contaminating variables are not controlled by matching. In one study alcoholic patients were classified on the basis of the presence or absence of EEG abnormalities, but age was not controlled. Patients showing EEG abnormalities in general were slightly older than the other group. Since age had the same effect on the dependent variable being investigated (alpha blocking) as the independent variable (EEG), it is difficult to determine how much of the reported difference is actually related to the EEG differences.

Longitudinal *vs.* Cross-Sectional Studies

Since alcoholics only become available for evaluation when they are hospitalized, almost all of the studies reported in the literature are limited to data collected at a single point of time during the life history of the alcoholic. While such cross-sectional studies are useful in establishing that two variables are correlated, the meaning of the association and the direction of the causal relation are frequently difficult to interpret. Two examples from the literature on alcoholism illustrate the difficulty involved. Several investigators (cf. Greenblatt *et al.*, 1944) have reported that the frequency of EEG abnormalities increases in older alcoholics. The usual interpretation is that age is related to the length of drinking and that cerebral dysfunctioning is more frequent since the patient has been exposed to the toxic effects of alcohol for a longer time. However, an alternative interpretation is possible. Several studies on the treatment of outpatient alcoholics indicate that those patients most likely to become abstinent are those showing least pathology on both social and psychological measures of adjustment (Kissin and Platz, 1968). Possibly older alcoholics show greater pathology than younger patients primarily because the more "healthy" alcoholics have become abstinent and consequently dropped out of the sample at each successive age grouping. How much of the increased pathology in the older group is related to age *vs.* selective dropout of the healthier alcoholics can only be adequately determined by a longitudinal study with repeated measurements of the same subjects over time.

A second illustration relates to the interpretation of EEG differences between heavy drinkers and nondrinkers. Although it is questionable whether alcoholics as a group show an increased incidence of EEG abnormalities, there are consistent findings across several studies indicating differences in alpha activity compared to normal controls (Davis *et al.*, 1941; Funkhouser, 1953; Little and McArry, 1952). However, since the findings are based on a single testing of patients with a long history of drinking, the temporal or causal relation between the impoverished alpha and alcoholism is unclear. Two rival interpretations may be suggested: (1) the impoverished alpha pattern precedes heavy drinking and may be related to possible neurological and psychological states which predispose the individual to alcoholism; or (2) the poor alpha is a neurological consequence of prolonged drinking. Again, it is clear that a longitudinal study involving repeated measurements is necessary in order to choose between the rival hypotheses.

Time of Testing and Concurrent Medication

Since most of the generalizations about the electroencephalogram in alcoholism are made on the basis of tests run on patients hospitalized for acute withdrawal effects, it is important to know the clinical state of the patient, the time of testing in relation to the cessation of drinking, and whether the patient was under medication at the time of testing. This information is frequently not reported or the variable adequately controlled.

On the basis of extensive observation of the withdrawal pattern, Victor and Adams (1953) have concluded that the appearance of symptoms falls into three distinct stages: (1) tremulousness and transient hallucinosis; (2) seizures; and (3) motor and autonomic hyperactivity and confusional states, which follow a somewhat different time course. The incidence of tremulousness and hallucinosis peaks during the first 24 hr following cessation of drinking. Seizures peak slightly later, while the incidence of delirium and confusional states is greatest between 72 and 96 hr postdrinking. Not all patients show the same symptoms, and the time of appearance and duration of symptoms varies widely. Approximately 90% of the patients are symptom-free by the fifth day, although in some cases symptoms may persist for as long as 2 weeks.

That the time course of the separate components of the withdrawal syndrome is related to CNS excitability is shown in a subsequent study by Victor and Brausch (1967). Patients during withdrawal were tested at 4- to 8-hr intervals by exposure to fast frequency photic stimulation (4–24 Hz). The incidence of abnormal photic responses (photomyoclonus, photoconvulsions, or paroxysmal discharges on the EEG) showed a close temporal relationship to the time course of spontaneous seizures. Photosensitivity tended to be greatest shortly after the occurrence of a seizure, and lasted from several hours to as long as 4 days. Patients not showing overt seizures showed a similar time course of photosensitivity. Of 84 patients, only one showed an abnormal photic response during the first 12 hr immediately following cessation of drinking, and by 72 hr the frequency had dropped to near zero. Peak frequency occurred between 31 and

48 hr. Lloyd-Smith and Gloor (1961) also report that CNS hyperexcitability characteristic of the withdrawal state is associated with heightened sensitivity to photic flicker which may produce epileptiform disturbances in the EEG.

The Victor and Brausch data indicate that the time of testing should be known in order to evaluate the frequency of abnormalities obtained in alcoholics compared to the observed rate in normals. The frequency of paroxysmal spiking in the photically activated EEG is time related, with the period of photosensitivity transient and generally limited to the five days immediately following alcohol withdrawal. Testing during this period would give a falsely high estimate of EEG abnormalities in alcoholics if the results were generalized to nonhospitalized alcoholics or alcoholics between drinking bouts.

A related problem in drawing conclusions about chronic alcoholics as a group from data based on hospitalized patients is that the latter are frequently under medication at the time of testing. In one study 90% of the patients were tested within 2 weeks of admission (exact time neither specified nor analyzed in relation to incidence of abnormalities) and 60% "were known to be on" some type of medication, generally a phenothiazine or barbiturate. Another study reports approximately 50% of its patients having received Antabuse sometime within the week preceding testing. While the effects of such drugs on the EEG are not precisely known, a recent study by Ulett et al. (1965) should make one extremely cautious in making generalizations about the EEG of alcoholics on the basis of patients who have recently received drug treatment. Ulett et al. studied the effects of eight ataractic drugs, each administered for a period of 3 weeks, on the electroencephalogram of 21 psychiatric patients. Changes in the EEG occurred with all drugs, with the drugs distinguishable on the basis of the effects produced. Although the drugs were distinguishable and there were marked individual differences in response, the usual pattern seen under tranquilization was a slowing in frequency and an increase in dysrhythmias. Some phenothiazines (notably chlorpromazine) induced paroxysmal discharges in some nonepileptic patients, especially at higher dose levels. Especially noteworthy in connection with alcoholism studies were two findings: (1) a majority of the drugs produced a worsening of the dysrhythmia in patients who showed evidence of dysrhythmia prior to medication, and (2) typically, the effects of the drugs were still evident in the EEG as long as 5 or 6 weeks after medication had been discontinued. In one case (chlorpromazine) effects were still present after 10 weeks.

A similar problem arises in investigating whether the EEG shows systematic changes characteristic of the different stages of the withdrawal syndrome. If a treatment drug like paraldehyde is prescribed, its chemical similarity to alcohol may produce some degree of cross tolerance which would attenuate the full-scale development of withdrawal symptoms.

The methodological problems discussed are common to many of the studies in the area and provide the framework for evaluating the reliability and validity of the findings reported in the specific studies reviewed. The review will be divided into four sections and be limited to human studies:

    I. The Electroencephalogram in Chronic Alcoholics

    II. The Effects of Short-Term Alcohol Administration on the Electroencephalogram

    III. The Effects of Long-Term Alcohol Administration on the Electroencephalogram

    IV. The Effects of Alcohol on the Average Evoked Response and Recovery Function

THE ELECTROENCEPHALOGRAM IN CHRONIC ALCOHOLICS

The electroencephalogram provides an index of the ongoing electrophysiological activity of the brain and a basis for assessing the functional and structural changes resulting from brain injuries and various toxic conditions such as acute alcoholic intoxication. In interpreting the EEG in alcoholism studies, several questions must be kept in mind in determining whether the reported findings are characteristic of chronic alcoholics as a group, or whether they are temporary manifestations which reflect either current signs or sequelae of the acute illness for which the patient was hospitalized. Since the acute phase of withdrawal typically lasts from 3 to 7 days, aberrations in the EEG's taken during this period may characterize only the course of the illness. In addition, the report by Ulett et al. (1965) that changes in the EEG induced by 3 weeks' administration of chlorpromazine can still be detected in the recordings up to 10 weeks after cessation of the drug should increase one's caution in generalizing about the EEG pattern based on alcoholics undergoing medical treatment. Although several experimental studies involving sustained alcoholization over a period of weeks have been reported, there is little comparable data on how long EEG changes may persist after the termination of drinking. Mello and Mendelson (1968) emphasize that most patients admitted with withdrawal signs usually have a number of intercurrent illnesses (primarily nutritional deficiencies) which may also contribute to derangements in mental states. Finally, if the patient is tested while still being treated with psychoactive drugs, or even for a period of several weeks after discontinuance of the drug, this may have an undeterminable effect on the EEG, making it impossible to separate changes attributable to alcoholism from those due to other causes. The research literature will be reviewed with these considerations in mind in evaluating the reported findings. In each section one or two studies will be examined in detail in order to focus on the methodological problems common to many studies in the area, and then the findings of the remaining studies will be briefly summarized.

One of the best and most extensive electroencephalographic investigations of chronic alcoholics is a Danish study by Arentsen and Sindrup (1963) based on a mixed sample of 317 hospitalized and outpatient alcoholics. Approximately one-third of the patients had not received any medication for at least 8 days prior to testing; the remaining two-thirds were under a daily regimen of disulfiram. Although not explicitly stated, the manner in which patients were selected suggests that a very large percent had not been drinking heavily for at least a week preceding testing, nor were they acutely ill when the EEG was administered. The incidence of serious medical complications due to alcoholism (delirium tremens, convulsions, etc.) was apparently low, and the patients probably less seriously disturbed than those usually included in American studies.

Twenty-one percent showed either borderline or slightly abnormal EEG's; 11% had moderate to severe abnormalities. Approximately half the abnormalities were exclusively or mainly in the temporal region. Two-thirds of the abnormal records were characterized by diffuse theta activity (4–7 cycles/sec). In comparison, the base rate for EEG abnormalities in "normals" is usually reported to run between 10 to 15%.

The incidence of abnormalities was further studied in more homogeneous subgroups of patients classified by either drinking pattern or psychiatric diagnosis. The simple alcoholic (excessive social drinking) showed a 13% rate of abnormality, which falls within the range reported for normals. Symptomatic alcoholism (dipsomania without loss of control of drinking) and addictive alcoholism (loss of control) had abnormality rates of 39% and 30% respectively. In the "complicated" group (history of delirium tremens, seizures, etc.) six of eight patients showed abnormalities.

The psychiatric classification was also related to the incidence of abnormalities, with the lowest rate in the "normal" group (18%); intermediate in the neurotics (25%) and highest in the psychopaths (42%). Several other writers have reported similar findings, with the percent of patients showing EEG irregularities generally increasing with the severity of the concurrent psychiatric illness (Predescu et al., 1967; Greenblatt et al., 1944). The rate reported for specific diagnostic categories, however, varies widely, presumably because certain psychiatric classifications are difficult to make reliably and because different investigators use somewhat different criteria for rating pathological signs in the electroencephalogram. The findings, although valid from a clinical point of view in describing the electroencephalographic picture of different subgroups of alcoholics, are difficult to interpret. Many of the functional mental disorders are also associated with an increased frequency of EEG abnormalities (Wilson, 1965). Data indicating whether the alcoholic who is also psychotic or psychopathic differs in degree, kind, or frequency of EEG abnormalities from the nonalcoholic psychotic or psychopath are not reported. Consequently, one cannot assess to what degree chronic drinking has contributed to the observed pathology in cerebral functioning.

The occurrence of abnormality was not related to age which, the authors state, distinguishes alcoholism from other psychiatric disorders where there is a tendency toward decreasing abnormalities with increasing age. However, Greenblatt (1944) in a study investigating the relation between EEG abnormalities and age reports a trend toward increasing abnormalities in older psychiatric patients, including neurotics and psychopaths. The relation between age and EEG findings in alcoholics is difficult to interpret with cross-section sampling since the patients hospitalized in their twenties may differ on a number of extraneous variables from patients hospitalized in their fifties. As a single example, the age of Negroes at the time of first hospitalization for alcoholism is several years younger than whites, and the mortality rate higher at any given age level. If this factor alone were operating, it would produce a consistent decrease in the percent of Negroes in each successively older age sample. Only a relatively small percent of patients hospitalized in their twenties for detoxification are hospitalized again for the same reason in their fifties. Since the nature of the patient sample is changing in a number of unknown ways, which may be reflected in the EEG findings, the effect of age *per se* can only be evaluated on the basis of longitudinal studies using repeated tests on the same individuals.

A weakness in the authors' interpretation of their data is illustrative of one of the pitfalls frequent in studies in this area. The authors point out that in the normal group the incidence of abnormalities in "simple alcoholism" is 1 in 23, while in "addictive alcoholism" it is 13 out of 62. They suggest that "addiction" to alcohol causes brain damage which is reflected in the increased percent of EEG irregularities. An analysis of their data ($X^2 = 2.27$, $p < 0.20$) indicates that this difference is not statistically significant; that is, a difference this large could be due to sampling error rather than to the independent variable (type of drinking) being investigated. (Many studies in this area lack adequate statistical analyses, with the result that much time is spent discussing data which are not statistically significant.) Second, the groups based on drinking pattern probably vary systematically on a number of other variables, and since they are based on different "kinds" of people, the possibility exists that the EEG differences antedated and were possibly a causative factor in the development of the drinking pattern rather than a consequence of it. The failure to find an effect related to age, which should be highly correlated with length of drinking, also weakens the argument somewhat. In contrast to these findings, Greenblatt *et al.* (1944) in a study of 157 hospitalized chronic alcoholics reported increased EEG pathology with age, which was especially marked in the over-50 group. The two studies are strikingly discrepant in their under-30 group where Greenblatt *et al.* report a 5% incidence of abnormalities (higher than his "normal" control group) while Arentsen and Sindrup report a 39% incidence (the highest of all their age groups). Greenblatt *et al.* also report that while age is related to EEG abnormalities, duration of chronic drinking in nonpsychotic alcoholics is not associated with increased abnormality. Since one would normally expect age and duration of drinking to correlate highly, this finding would also suggest that the nature of the patient sample has changed systematically over the age groups studied. The use of correlational procedures to measure the degree of association between such variables as age or length of drinking and measure of pathology would help in partialling out the contribution each makes in producing EEG irregularities. Until this is done within a well-designed longitudinal study, it will be difficult to specify the precise role that duration of drinking (with age statistically controlled by partial correlation procedures) or age may play in producing EEG pathology. Similarly, alcoholics subdivided into various psychiatric groupings should be compared to the appropriate group of psychiatric patients rather than to a normal group in order to control for the effect of an extraneous variable (mental illness) on the dependent variable.

The findings of similar studies on the incidence of EEG pathology in chronic alcoholics may be briefly summarized. Dyken *et al.* (1961) report that approximately 10% of their sample of 553 patients admitted to an alcoholic care unit showed minimal to marked abnormalities in the electroencephalogram. However, in 70% of the cases where the abnormality was marked, causes other than alcoholism (severe head trauma, syphilitic damage to the central nervous system, evidence of epilepsy preceding alcoholism, etc.) were also present. Since the incidence of EEG abnormalities in their patient group is comparable to the usual base rate found in normative samples, the authors conservatively conclude that if long-term drinking impairs CNS functioning, this impairment may not necessarily be reflected in the EEG record.

As reported earlier, Greenblatt *et al.* (1944) found only a 5% incidence of EEG abnormalities in their subgroup of alcoholics without psychoses. Arentsen and Sindrup's (1963) "simple" alcoholic group showed a 13% abnormality rate. Funkhouser *et al.* (1953) report that in a group of 81 "uncomplicated" alcoholics (patients who had never shown convulsions or psychotic manifestations) 21% showed either abnormally fast or slow wave activity. Little and McAvoy (1952) report that 80% of their alcoholic group had normal records as compared to 84% of their normal control group. The alcoholics included showed no evidence of mental deterioration or CNS disease, and were not intoxicated or in delirium tremens when tested.

In summary, several studies report that the percent of EEG abnormalities found in chronic alcoholics without complications ranges from approximately 5 to 20%, which is roughly comparable to the 10–15% incidence usually accepted as a normal base rate. As suggested earlier, considerable fluctuation in the incidence of reported abnormalities is to be expected across studies for a number of reasonal differences in the makeup and selection of the patient sample, differences in the length of time between the patient's last intoxication and the electroencephalographic examination, frequent lack of control of concurrent medication, and the less than perfect reliability and the use of somewhat different criteria in the ratings of EEG abnormalities. Interestingly, European investigators tend to report considerably higher percentages of abnormal recordings for alcoholics (Delay et al., 1957; Lafon et al., 1956). Partly this is due to the use of somewhat less severe criteria for judging abnormalities, as suggested by Arentsen and Sindrup, or possibly to differences in the type of liquor, especially wines, consumed. In an American sample Dyken et al. (1961) consider the excessive use of wine to be a sign of the increasing severity of the drinking problem. Murphree, Schultz, and Jusko (1970) have also reported that the congener content of liquor affects the EEG, so possibly differences resulting from the long-term use of different beverages might also reasonably be expected. The effects of absinthe in producing brain damage, which resulted in its prohibition, is perhaps an obvious example.

The American studies generally support the conclusion by Naitoh and Docter (1968) and Green (1965) that chronic alcoholism without complications is not associated with pathological changes in the EEG rhythm in the form of persistent arrhythmias and dysrhythmia or abnormal spikings and paroxysmal high voltage slow waves. This conclusion can only be tentative on the basis of the available research and should be supported by additional studies. A longitudinal study of changes in the same subjects over time is needed so that the incidence of EEG abnormalities may be plotted as a function of duration of drinking. These data would provide a more definitive answer to the question of whether progressive changes occur during long-term excessive drinking. Studies reporting significantly higher rates of abnormality in different subgroups of alcoholics also require replication with appropriate control groups in order to assess the relative contribution of alcoholism vs. psychiatric disorders in EEG abnormalities.

As reported earlier, Arentsen and Sindrup (1963) found impairment in cerebral functioning to increase with severity of the drinking problem ("type of drinking pattern") and with the severity of concurrently present psychiatric symptoms. The classification of drinking pattern is somewhat confusing since it is apparently based on two different variables: degree of control over drinking and the past occurrence of alcohol-related psychiatric disorders. Because of this confusion, and the selective nature of patients included in both classification systems, it is difficult to tell whether the increased EEG pathology is necessarily related to excessive alcoholism or may be primarily accounted for by pre-existing patient characteristics. Greenblatt et al. (1944) report that a ranking of clinical groups of alcoholics in terms of the incidence of EEG abnormalities roughly corresponds to the severity of the clinical picture, chronicity of symptoms, and "probably the severity and extent" of brain damage. Especially high rates of abnormality are associated with "alcoholic deterioration" and Korsakov's psychosis.

Lafon *et al.* (1956) found minimal to severe disturbances in the EEG pattern of 80% of nonselected chronic alcoholics admitted for detoxification or seen during periods of severe agitation. Although some of the cases had severe psychiatric and neurological symptoms, the high rate of abnormality may be attributed primarily to the use of somewhat lenient criteria for judging EEG disturbances and to the testing of patients during the clinical course of the withdrawal syndrome. The most frequent findings were instability or disappearance of the alpha rhythm and the occurrence of low voltage, fast activity, both common characteristics of agitated states. Somewhat more compelling are the pneumoencephalographic findings of some degree of cerebral atrophy in 78% of the cases, the atrophy generally being diffuse in nature and frequently "latent" in its clinical expression. (The base rate using the same criteria on patients in the same age range is not known.) In 58% of the cases there is good correspondence between the electroencephalographic and pneumoencephalographic findings. In long-term alcoholics severe cortical atrophy was associated with marked perturbations of the EEG, while mild EEG disturbances were associated with relatively discrete cerebral atrophy. Although the correspondence is apparently striking in specific cases, the authors do not evaluate whether the overall correspondence between the PEG and EEG was significantly different from chance in terms of the criteria used for evaluating deviations from normal functioning. On a chance basis, if the two measures were not related, one would expect to find a 66% agreement between the presence or absence of irregularities in the EEG pattern and evidence of cerebral atrophy $\overline{(78.80 + 22.20)}$. Whether this actual correspondence is significantly greater than this is not clear from the data.

Predescu *et al.* (1967) also found increasing EEG disturbances paralleling the severity of concomitant psychological disorders. Approximately 22% of their sample showed moderate to severe anomalies, mostly diffuse theta and delta waves and medium voltage spiking in the frontal and temporal regions.

In a series of papers, Bennett and his associates (1956, 1960a, 1960b, 1967) have argued that EEG abnormalities indicate the existence of "alcoholic brain disease" which in the chronic stage (organic dementia, or Korsakov's and Wernicke's disease) is usually characterized by nonreversible brain damage. [However, Victor and Adams (1953) have pointed out that some of the symptoms of Wernicke's disease are partially reversible by thiamine administration.] Eighty percent of 48 patients in the chronic stage showed EEG abnormalities. Of 11 patients given psychological testing, all showed evidence of organic brain damage, and seven of eight patients evaluated by the PEG showed signs of cortical atrophy. In general, the more severe the "alcoholic brain disease," the less reversible the pathology shown in the EEG records. In repeat examinations 87% of the "acute stage" showed decreased abnormality, 34% of the "inter mediate stage," but only 25% of the chronic showed improvement, while 16% actually showed increased abnormality. (The interval between testings is not given, but apparently ranged from several days to over a year. It is not possible to tell from the data whether the interval between tests was approximately the same for the three groups, or to what extent the length of time between testings was related to the probability of improvement.)

Although severe abnormalities in the EEG do not occur with greater frequency than in normal groups except in the case of advanced, deteriorated alcoholics, there is considerable evidence that the percent alpha time and characteristics of the alpha rhythm differ significantly between alcoholics and normals. Davis et al. (1941) were among the first to point out this difference. In a group of hospitalized chronic alcoholics they observed that only two of 15 patients showed a strong alpha pattern, the most common pattern found in relaxed normal subjects, while 13 of their patients showed mixed frequency records. The period of time elapsing between the EEG examination and cessation of drinking was not reported so that one cannot judge whether the poor alpha pattern is characteristic of the chronic alcoholic (either as a result of prolonged drinking or as an antecedent characteristic of CNS functioning which may be a predisposing factor in alcohol addiction), or whether the impoverished alpha is a transient characteristic of the withdrawal syndrome. Patients newly admitted for detoxification are typically in a state of heightened anxiety or agitation which is frequently associated with a poor or unstable alpha pattern and the presence of diffuse, low voltage, fast activity beta waves (Henry, 1965; Wilson and Short, 1965; Lafon et al., 1956; Predescu et al., 1967). Bennett et al. (1956) note that the heightened percentage of fast activity decreases gradually during treatment and that clinical improvement seems to coincide with the restoration of normal alpha activity. Varga and Nagy (1960) noted similar changes in newly admitted patients tested the first day after withdrawal and again at 2 weeks. Using a visual histogram method, they found a relative shift of the frequency band toward the slower frequencies and less dispersion across frequencies. Usually a dominant alpha frequency appeared at 2 weeks or grew stronger if previously present. However, the period required for normalization of the EEG pattern may extend over a period of several days to as long as several weeks in some cases. Kennard et al. (1945) also noted that during symptomatic recovery from delirium tremens there was a parallel decrease in the amount of fast activity and either an initial appearance or increase in slower alpha activity. Corresponding increases in amplitude and regularity in the EEG rhythm occurred during the same period. Patients who showed the most fast activity and lowest amplitude at the onset of delirium generally showed the slowest recovery rate.

In this connection the observation by Engel and Rosenbaum (1945) that a moderate dosage of ethanol (1 g/kg of body weight) resulted in some abnormally fast records becoming more "normal" during intoxication is of interest. It is now generally accepted that withdrawal symptoms are usually precipitated either by abrupt cessation of drinking or by a relative drop in blood alcohol levels (Mello and Mendelson, 1968). To some extent the abstinence syndrome may be temporarily prevented or ameliorated by the readministration of alcohol. Varga and Nagy (1960), for instance, view the faster and more labile frequencies seen during this period as a manifestation of a functional disturbance in cerebral homeostasis "which seems to be temporarily normalized by acute alcohol consumption." The literature on the acute effects of small doses of alcohol suggests that the CNS counterpart of the abeyance of the withdrawal syndrome (e.g., the use of a "morning after" drink to quiet the "shakes") may be a partial "normalization" of the EEG rhythm.

From a somewhat different perspective, the question of whether the addictive drinker derives some immediate short-term physiological "benefits" from alcohol intake has been investigated in a series of studies by Kissin, Schenker, and their co-workers (1959a, 1959b, 1960). Their data indicate that chronic alcoholics show a high frequency of abnormal values on a number of tests of endocrine and autonomic nervous system functions (measures of adreno-cortical responses, regulation of arterial blood pressure, etc.) and that these abnormalities may be primarily constitutional in nature rather than the effects of alcoholism since they were also found in a group of alcoholics who had been abstinent for a period of at least 2 years. The most interesting observation of these studies was the finding that the ingestion of small amounts of alcohol tended to normalize these disturbances in physiological functioning. On the basis of these data, the authors suggest that the underlying functional abnormalities provide a continual source of discomfort which motivates the alcoholic to drink in order to relieve or "normalize" the physiological dysfunctioning producing the discomfort.

Naitoh and Docter (1968) have made a similar argument regarding the possible relationship between quantitative characteristics of the EEG which differentiate chronic alcoholics from nonalcoholics and the motivation to drink. In summarizing the literature they conclude that global ratings of EEG pathology are a poor method of differentiating chronic alcoholics since gross disturbances in the recordings such as spikings and paroxysmal high-voltage diffuse slow waves occur only infrequently, and probably not significantly more often than in normal groups. However, they point out that chronic alcoholics as a group tend to show poor alpha activity. In their study they report that low dosages of alcohol (0.5 mg/kg) in alcoholic subjects had primarily a stimulant-euphoriant effect, with the subjects reporting that they felt more alert, pepped up, and sociable. (Ekman et al., 1963 and 1964, report similar effects in nonalcoholics, with a majority of their normal subjects rating themselves more "elated," "happy, and talkative" and less "tired" after drinking. Peak effects occurred between 30 and 40 min after ingestion, with subjective variables showing greater change than performance variables.) Paralleling the affective changes, the EEG measure of brain activity showed an increase in the amount of alpha activity and a slight slowing of approximately 1 cycle/sec in its frequency. On the basis of these data, Naitoh and Docter suggest the intriguing hypothesis that the alcoholic drinks in order to achieve the psychological state (calm-alert, mildly stimulated) which is associated with an increase and slowing of alpha activity. While carefully disclaiming that persons with alpha-poor records are necessarily inclined to chronic alcoholism, or that they drink specifically to achieve a "good alpha," the suggestion of an underlying CNS state which may be related to the motivation to drink does open up a potentially valuable direction for future research.

Before the testable consequences of the hypothesis can be evaluated, several questions should be explored. The first concerns how close the association is between affective states and specific EEG characteristics such as cycle frequency or percent time of alpha. The subjective reaction to a fixed dosage of alcohol may vary considerably, both in different people and at different times. Are the different effects of alcohol related in any systematic way either to the kind of prealcohol EEG activity, or to the kind and amount of change following alcohol? Engel and Rosenbaum (1945) report that a close correlation exists between the EEG and level of consciousness but not with the "more personal aspects of behavior" during alcoholization. The amount of slowing rather than the attainment of a specific frequency seemed to be the critical variable, with the development of intoxication being accompanied by progressive slowing of the brain waves. Gross intoxication usually was associated with an average change of 2 to 3 cycles/sec.

A second question which requires more extensive investigation concerns how accurately the addictive drinker can titrate or regulate his intake to maintain a consistent subjective state over time. Mello and Mendelson (1968) have reviewed the evidence indicating that alcohol acts as a stimulant only at low doses. At higher doses it exerts an increasingly depressant effect at both the neurophysiological and behavioral level. Casual observation at bars or parties suggests that many drinkers are not too successful in maintaining the "alert-pepped up" state which they supposedly drink to achieve. In addition, the subjective effects of drinking also apparently change during the course of sustained drinking. Nathan (1970) observed that alcoholics who were allowed *ad lib* alcohol in an operant conditioning situation initially showed a reduction in rated anxiety and depression during the first 24–48 hr of drinking. However, after the second or third day anxiety and depression invariably increased, with the increased level being maintained during the remaining course of drinking.

Nevertheless, the Naitoh–Docter hypothesis does suggest several interesting studies:

1. Are individuals with poor alpha activity more likely to become alcoholics?
2. In alcoholics whose drinking pattern is markedly aperiodic, is the occurrence of a drinking bout related to a temporary impoverishment of alpha activity, possibly induced by environmental stress or intercurrent constitutional factors?
3. In long-term *ad lib* alcoholization studies, is the tendency to drink at a given time related to the amount of preceding alpha activity?
4. Are there drugs which produce similar alterations in EEG activity as alcohol and, if so, would the chronic administration of such drugs reduce alcohol intake?

Studies such as these might help delineate the possible relationship between measures of CNS activity and alcohol addiction. Several studies do support the observation of alpha impoverishment in alcoholics as a group, although the interpretation of this relationship is not yet clear. Little and McAvoy (1952) compared the EEG during the resting state and after hyperventilation in 34 alcoholics and 55 controls. The alcoholics had been abstinent from 1 to 21 days and showed no clinical evidence of CNS disease, mental deterioration, or delirium tremens. There was little difference between the two groups in the percentage showing some alpha activity (80% of the controls and 70% of the alcoholics) or in the average amplitude of the alpha rhythm. However, when a 100-sec epoch of the record showing the greatest amount of alpha activity was evaluated, the groups were clearly different. The percent time alpha for the normal controls was 72% compared to only 46% in the alcoholics. A "blind" rating of alpha modulation (degree of differentiation of the alpha activity in the ongoing record) showed "good" modulation in 86% of the controls but in only 50% of the alcoholics.

Many of the alcoholics were tense and restless at the time of examination and showed the suppressed alpha activity during the resting EEG which is also typically seen during anxiety states. For instance, Wilson and Short (1965) report a mean alpha index of 0.55 in a group of chronic alcoholics and a mean alpha of 0.51 in patients diagnosed as "anxiety reaction." The authors argue that their group differences could not be attributed to the effects of anxiety *per se* since few of the alcoholics showed the rapid increase in alpha activity usually seen in anxiety states during hyperventilation. Little and McAvoy also propose a possible CNS state (low alpha activity) which may underlie addictive drinking, although their psychological interpretation of this association is quite different from that of Naitoh and Docter. Poor alpha is assumed to be a possible predisposing factor in the development of anxiety which leads to drinking for its anxiety-relieving effects. Thus, poor alpha activity may reflect a cerebral condition which is a cause rather than a result of alcoholism, although the authors recognize the desirability of testing this hypothesis with a longitudinal study.

Funderburk (1949) divided chronic alcoholics into two groups depending upon whether alcoholism was felt to be the primary difficulty or only secondary. Patients with "secondary" alcoholic symptoms usually showed an alpha type tracing, while the other group showed little alpha activity. Seventy-three percent of the alcoholics showed a fast type record without alpha. This is markedly different from the 23% reported by Little and McAvoy, although the comparability of the patient samples, time of testing, concurrent medication, etc., cannot be evaluated from the written reports. [Medication commonly given to relieve withdrawal symptoms may also affect the prevalence of alpha activity in the EEG record. Fink (1965) for example, found that both acute and chronic administration of imipramine reduced alpha abundance, while chlorpromazine increased alpha in subjects with low predrug alpha index but decreased alpha when the predrug level was high. Ulett *et al.* (1965) found similar effects with a number of phenothiazines, although there were marked individual differences in drug response.]

Funkhouser *et al.* (1953) recorded the EEG in patients grouped according to predominant symptomatology. Approximately 53% of the "uncomplicated" alcoholics and patients with hallucinosis had an alpha pattern rated "poor." This is not appreciably different from the 45% incidence of "mixed" and "rare" alpha reported in a normal sample by Davis and Davis, cited by Funkhouser *et al.*, which they consider comparable to their "poor" rating. This suggests that finer measures of alpha activity such as those used by Little and McAvoy may be necessary to detect possible impairment in alcoholics. Patients tested shortly after delirium tremens or convulsions showed a somewhat higher incidence of poor alpha, 58 and 68% respectively. Over half of the patients showed increased beta activity, probably reflecting the agitation and restlessness typical of the withdrawal syndrome. A final study by Kessler (1949) also reports fast, low amplitude activity in all regions, and the absence of a stable alpha rhythm. The time of testing is not recorded, but her patient sample appears to be more severely organically impaired than those tested in the other studies reviewed.

An interesting variant in the investigation of the alpha pattern is a study by Delamonica *et al.* (1966) on the alpha blocking response in chronic alcoholics. Citing studies indicating that brain-damaged patients show decreased alpha blocking to photic stimulation, the authors felt that the procedure might also provide a possible measure of the degree of impairment of cerebral functioning and/or the amount of brain damage in alcoholic patients. Forty-two hospitalized alcoholics who showed no abnormal neurological signs and had been drug-free for at least 1 week were divided into two groups, one showing normal EEG's and the second showing minimal to severe abnormalities. A Grass stroboscopic unit was triggered to present a 1.5-sec train of flashes during periods of prominent alpha activity for a total of 50 trials. The alcoholics with normal baseline EEG's averaged 37 trials on which blocking occurred as compared to an average of 29 for the patients showing EEG abnormalities. The authors suggest that the reduction in alpha blocking in the second group is due to "probable brain damage," although they later note that there was no relationship between the frequency of alpha blocking and the severity of the EEG abnormality.

Although the authors suggest a response measure which may be quite useful in assessing the CNS effects of chronic alcoholism, their study is difficult to evaluate. The statistical significance of the difference is not reported nor is the possible contaminating factor of age considered. Obrist and Busse (1965) note that with increased age there is both a tendency for less desynchronization of the alpha rhythm to visual stimulation and a faster habituation curve, with the older person adapting sooner and more completely with repeated stimulation. In the study by Delamonica et al., reanalysis of the data from their abnormal EEG group gives a rank order correlation of -0.35 between age and number of alpha blocking responses; i.e., the older patients showed fewer trials on which alpha blocking occurred. Although the mean ages of the groups are not given, the data reported suggest that the group with EEG abnormalities is somewhat older. Since age and brain damage are both related to alpha blocking, the control of the extraneous effect due to age, either by matching subjects or by partialling the effect out statistically, would attenuate the reported differences to some degree. The addition of a nonalcoholic control group in order to evaluate the alpha blocking response in the alcoholic group not showing EEG abnormalities would also strengthen the study. In light of the number of studies reviewed which indicate differences in the alpha activity of alcoholics as a group, this would appear to be a profitable line of investigation to follow. A related study investigating the frequency of alpha blocking and its rate of habituation as a function of blood alcohol level would also be of some interest because of the possible biphasic stimulant-depressant action of alcohol at different dosage levels (cf. Mello and Mendelson, 1968).

EXPERIMENTAL STUDIES OF CNS ACTIVITY DURING ACUTE ADMINISTRATION OF ALCOHOL

In contrast to clinical studies of the EEG in alcoholics where there is still considerable controversy, the experimental studies investigating the effects of alcohol on the EEG are generally quite consistent. Most studies report an increase in percent time alpha and alpha abundance, greater synchronization of the EEG pattern with less dispersion and greater stability of component waveforms, and a slowing in the dominant alpha frequency. Loosely paralleling these changes in CNS activity are corresponding changes in the level of consciousness

and affective state of the subject varying as a function of dosage and change in
blood alcohol level over time.

In one of the earliest investigations Davis *et al.* (1941) studied the effects
of ethanol administered 2 ml/kg body weight to six normal subjects over a 1-hr
period. A spectral analysis of the distribution of energy by wave frequency
showed a moderate shift indicating less energy at the faster frequencies, primarily
between 10 and 13 cycles, and relatively more energy at the slower frequencies,
particularly between 6–8 cycles. Although the peak alpha frequency (about 10
cycles) showed little change, the increase at the slower frequencies would indicate a slower mean alpha frequency. EEG changes appeared soon after alcohol
ingestion when the blood alcohol level was less than 0.35 mg%. During the first
hour the amount of displacement roughly paralleled the increase in blood
alcohol level. However, the peak change in the EEG was not reached until after
the BAL began to decline, and was maintained over a longer time period. At
5 hr the BAL had dropped from its maximum of 120 mg% to approximately
80, while the EEG displacement was still near its maximum value even though
the subjects were judged fairly sober.

The authors conclude that the EEG changes were "surprisingly slight"
given the marked changes in mood and behavior of the subjects. During periods
of lethargy brief episodes of 2 or 3 sec of slow activity (4–8 Hz) frequently
occurred interspersed between the usual alpha pattern. These changes were not
like those seen during light sleep but rather resembled the pattern seen when
breathing a low oxygen mixture. Engel *et al.* (1945) have drawn a similar analogy
between the EEG pattern seen during alcoholic intoxication and anoxia. Prealcoholization irregularities in the EEG were either maintained or somewhat
accentuated during the period of intoxication.

In two studies Engel and Rosenbaum (1945) and Engel *et al.* (1945)
reported a close correspondence between clinical ratings of the degree of intoxication, the extent of disturbances in consciousness and level of awareness,
and the amount of slowing of the brain waves. Gross intoxication was associated
with a decrease in the mean frequency of 2 to 3 cycles/sec. The amount of
slowing in the EEG was not related to the mean frequency before alcoholization,
although the range of initial values was relatively small and mostly within
normal limits. In subjects showing fast normal or even abnormally fast patterns
before drinking, the EEG became more "normal" during intoxication. [Varga
and Nagy (1960) observed a similar "normalization" in fast, low voltage records
taken during withdrawal when alcohol was administered to the patients.] After
intoxication the EEG gradually returned to the predrinking pattern. The
authors argue that changes in the level of consciousness during progressive
intoxication are related to the amount of slowing in the alpha rhythm, regardless
of the initial pattern, and not to the absolute frequency obtained. Subjects
showed similar degrees of intoxication and impaired consciousness when the

change in the mean frequency of the EEG was equivalent even though the spectral frequency distribution of the record was quite dissimilar, both immediately before drinking and throughout the period of intoxication. However, this correlation apparently breaks down during recovery, since patients become sober before the EEG has returned to the prealcohol pattern. This finding is consistent with the Davis study in which a considerable drop in blood alcohol level occurred while the EEG still showed peak changes.

The authors also note that with similar EEG patterns during the development of and the subsequent recovery from intoxication, both subjective and objective measures of the subject's state were consistently better during recovery. Victor and Adams (1953) have pointed out a similar phenomenon with patients showing greater evidence of intoxication at a given blood alcohol level during the ascending than during the descending BAL curve.

Two findings reported by Engel et al. are discrepant from results discussed earlier. The subjects in the Engel and Rosenbaum study showed periods of pronounced somnolence during which the EEG resembled the pattern seen during normal sleep. While the subjects in the study by Davis et al. occasionally fell into "stuporous naps" characterized by very low-voltage, flat periods seen at certain stages of sleep, for the most part the alpha rhythm remained prominent instead of dropping out as in sleep. This difference is possibly related to differences in the alcoholization procedures in the two studies. Although the dosages were roughly comparable, the subjects in the Engel–Rosenbaum study were administered alcohol after an overnight fast and required to drink it more quickly than in the Davis study. This difference in administration and time of day of testing may account for the appearance of typical sleep EEG's in one study but not the other.

Second, Engel and his associates (1944, 1945a, 1945b, 1959) emphasize the relationship between the amount of slowing in wave frequency and both the degree of intoxication and change in level of consciousness, but also point out that the EEG changes were not correlated with "the more personal aspects of behavior," such as the affective changes and mood occurring during intoxication which differed considerably between subjects. This would appear contradictory to the assertion by Naitoh and Docter (1968) that the alcoholic drinks specifically in order to achieve a state of feeling more alert, perked up, and sociable which the authors state accompanies the increase in alpha abundance and slowing of alpha frequency produced by drinking.

A possible limitation of the Naitoh–Docter hypothesis lies in the extreme variability in the subjective response to alcohol by different people, and by the same individual at different times. Partly because of these differences, the association between the specific affective state postulated by Naitoh and Docter and the reported alcohol-induced changes in the alpha rhythm is somewhat tentative. A reanalysis of the EEG data presented in Fig. 4 (in Engel et al., 1945) in conjunction with the authors' discussion of the subjective changes during intoxication in the article by Engel et al. (1915) suggests a possible line of inquiry which might strengthen the Naitoh–Docter hypothesis. Although the N is too small to warrant drawing any conclusions, the graph indicates that all four subjects showed an almost identical slowing of slightly less than 1 cycle/sec in their alpha frequency during the earliest signs of intoxication (approximately 45 min after drinking) However, the two subjects who showed a euphoriant, "happy drunk" response had initial mean frequencies between 10.6 and 10.8 cycles/sec, while the other two subjects who showed only slight behavioral changes had initial levels of 8.8 and 9.2.

The question of whether predrinking characteristics of the EEG pattern partially determine the degree and kind of affective and behavioral changes produced by alcohol, or even whether initial brain state determines whether small amounts of alcohol have primarily a stimulating or depressant effect, would appear to be a fruitful area of investigation. An observation by Doenicke, Kugler, and Laub (1967) that preadministration irregularities in the EEG are sometimes associated with atypical or marked reactions to anesthesia provides some reason for believing that similar factors may account for some of the individual differences in response to alcohol.

Since the recordings of alcoholics typically show poor or impoverished alpha activity, different indices of the alpha rhythm—mean frequency, percent time alpha, alpha abundance, degree of alpha modulation—are logical starting places for investigation. Positive findings would not only help explain individual differences in reaction to alcohol, but would also be useful in predicting which individuals are most likely to become addicted to drinking; or within individuals, at what times they are most likely to drink. The finding of a relation between a specific subjective state and a specific characteristic of the brain rhythm which modulates either the craving for, or the response to alcohol would stimulate the search for drugs capable of inducing the appropriate changes in the brain state controlling addictive drinking.

The slowing in the frequency of the alpha rhythm after drinking has been confirmed in a number of studies using a wide variety of patient and nonpatient samples, including alcoholics during the withdrawal period, hospitalized alcoholics tested after remission of symptoms, alcoholic groups based on the severity of past alcohol-related symptoms, schizophrenics, nonhospitalized chronic drinkers, and normal nonalcoholic control groups (Davis et al., 1941; Docter et al., 1966; Engel and Rosenbaum, 1945; Engel et al., 1945; Holmberg and Martens, 1955; Kotani, 1965; Naitoh and Docter, 1968; Newman, 1959; Varga and Nagy, 1960). Although there were some differences between the groups both in the kind and extent of the EEG changes observed, as well as in the time course, all studies reviewed reported the characteristic slowing in the alpha rhythm. The extent of alpha slowing tended to parallel the BAL curve, especially during the ascending portion of the curve, reaching its maximum at approximately the same time or shortly after the peak blood alcohol level, and declining somewhat more slowly than the alcohol curve (Davis et al., 1941; Holmberg and Martens, 1955; Newman, 1959). These findings are somewhat impressionistic since no one has yet reported any statistical measure (perhaps some form of cross-correlational analysis) of the degree of correspondence between the two curves representing the BAL and changes in the EEG. Ideally, a more complete picture of the changes during alcoholization could be obtained by collecting time course data simultaneously on four major variables: blood alcohol concentration, measures of brain activity (EEG), measures of subjective states, and behavioral measures for a given dose and regimen of alcohol. A statistical analysis of the degree of correspondence between any two curves would answer the question of whether the timing and amount of change during intoxication was parallel for these variables, and also indicate whether some measures showed a continuous change under alcoholization, while others followed a discrete all-or-none pattern. Since the correlation between curves can be run separately for each individual, atypical values, or correlations markedly different from those based on group values, may point to some factor causally related to either the motivation to drink or to the effects of alcohol. For example, Greenblatt et al. (1944) discuss a clinical syndrome which they refer to as "pathologic intoxication" in which small amounts of alcohol produce disproportionate "clouding of consciousness" and "violent, aggressive overactivity." Three of the five patients showed abnormal EEG's after recovery from intoxication but whether small amounts of alcohol also produced atypical blood alcohol curves and concurrent EEG changes consistent with the subjective and behavioral changes in these patients was not determined.

Under some conditions, and for certain types of patients, the usual correlations may be markedly distorted. The extent of the correspondence between the BAL and changes in the EEG is apparently higher during the ascending portion of the BAL curve than during the descending phase (Davis et al., 1941). The correlation between the two curves may also differ between alcoholics and nonalcoholics since Holmberg and Martens (1955) data indicate that the BAL peaked at approximately the same time (about 1 hr past ingestion) for their alcoholic and normal control groups, but the maximum slowing in mean EEG frequencies lagged behind the peak concentration by only 6 min in the alcoholic group but by an average of 45 min in the nonalcoholics.

A number of variables affect the relationship between the amount of alcohol ingested and the appearance of behavioral changes. The phenomenon of tolerance indicates that more alcohol is required to produce either subjective changes or behavioral impairment in the chronic drinker than in the nondrinker. In the Holmberg and Martens study the alcoholic group showed less ataxia and almost none of the nausea and vomiting seen in the control group's reaction to a

standard dose of alcohol, even though their blood alcohol level was moderately
higher throughout the 4½-hr test period (mean peak values of 177 and 150 mg
per 100 ml respectively). (The mean age of the alcoholic sample is 16 years
greater than that of the control group, so that age differences are a possible contributing factor.) Both the rate of intake and changes in the usual amount of
alcohol ingestion may affect the relation between dosage, BAL, and psychological
effects. Subjective and behavioral changes are more marked at comparable levels
during a rapidly rising BAL than in one increasing slowly, even though the peak
BAL is the same under the two conditions. In the classic study by Isbell *et al.*
(1955) on the effects of experimental chronic alcoholization, it was found that
small increases in dosage over the usual daily maintenance intake resulted in
marked increases in blood alcohol level and signs of gross intoxication. However,
if the raised dosage was maintained, the blood alcohol level and degree of
intoxication declined rapidly over a period of days, indicating a fairly rapid
habituation to a repeated level of alcohol intake. Victor and Adams (1953) have
discussed some of the factors which lower the correlation between amount of
alcohol ingested and subjective and behavioral signs of intoxication. Whether
these same factors would attenuate the relation between alcohol intake and
alpha slowing has yet to be investigated. It would be of considerable interest to
know whether the EEG paralleled the psychological states, or if, instead, it
remained consistent to the alcohol dosage.

In summarizing their work on experimentally induced slowing in the EEG
during hypoxia, hypoglycemia, and alcohol intoxication, Engel and Romano
(1959) draw three major conclusions. The first is that drugs or physiological
states which produce a slowing in the EEG also reduce the "level of consciousness and the efficiency of cognitive processes." The psychological changes
"correlating most precisely" with the slowing of EEG frequency have to do
with functions such as awareness, attention, memory, and comprehension.
Although the cognitive changes were similar, changes in behavior and emotional
expression varied considerably between subjects. Second, the degree of impairment in cognitive functioning is related to the amount of slowing rather than to
the absolute frequency of the EEG during the intoxicated state. However, in
hypoxia at least, EEG changes can be detected before any cognitive deficit
occurs. (Whether the same is true following alcohol ingestion, or if changes in
cognitive functioning sometimes precede, or occur without changes in the EEG
frequency, apparently has not been investigated.) Third, the degree of slowing
is not related to either the initial frequency of the EEG or to the postintoxication
frequency. Consequently, an initially fast record may be slowed sufficiently
under the drug condition so that the EEG appears more "normal" according to
the accepted criteria, yet the "normal" EEG may be accompanied by "an
appreciable degree of cerebral insufficiency and reduction in the level of
awareness."

While these general conclusions are probably valid for major changes in the EEG such as might occur during gross intoxication, some qualifications should be made regarding their applicability to the effects of low to moderate dosages of alcohol, and to their usefulness in attempting to predict or account for individual response differences under similar conditions. In regard to the psychological effects of alcohol, the review by Carpenter (1962) supports the conclusion that moderate to heavy drinking generally impairs cognitive functioning and motor performance. However, individual differences in response to a fixed dosage of alcohol are large, and obviously both the occurrence and the extent of impairment are dose and task related. Under some conditions, lower dosages may improve performance. Korman et al. (1960) report that alcoholics did better in solving simple arithmetic problems after drinking than without alcohol. Docter et al. (1966) found that 0.5 mg/kg of ethanol administered to alcoholics improved performance on a 50-min signal detection task, primarily because there was less deterioration in performance over time under the alcohol condition than during the control run. This result is consistent with the authors' argument that low dosages of alcohol act as a stimulant, even though the blood alcohol level of 30 mg% at the start of testing was within the range where Davis et al. reported EEG slowing. However, the apparent failure to find an alcohol-control difference in normal subjects (Naitoh and Docter, 1968) suggests several testable alternative interpretations—perhaps that alcohol has a "normalizing" effect on alcoholics as discussed earlier, or that the alcoholic has learned to habitually compensate for the effects of drinking on his behavior. In any case, it is likely that alcohol produces a different subjective state in the alcoholic than the normal, and that their responses on the alcohol-sensitive items of the Addiction Research Center Inventory for evaluating subjective drug effects would differ significantly from normals (Hill et al., 1963).

The finding by Docter et al. (1966) that alcohol, at a dose level reported to produce slowing in the alpha rhythm in other studies, had an apparent stimulant effect and improved performance on a cognitive task suggests that Engel's assumption of impairment of cognition concomitant with EEG slowing probably only holds true with relatively large changes in EEG frequency. The assumed correlation between BAL, amount of slowing, and degree of cognitive impairment is open to the same criticism. Newman (1959) in a small sample study (seven normals, two alcoholics) concluded that the EEG slowing was roughly proportional to the blood alcohol level, and that subjects with a history of greater use of alcohol showed a high tolerance both clinically, as measured by the ability to balance on one foot, and electroencephalographically. This is inconsistent with the Holmberg–Martens data which showed a partial dissociation between the EEG changes and clinical measures of intoxication in the alcoholic group as compared to the normal controls. Although the degree of slowing in the alpha rhythm was roughly comparable for the two groups (mean value of -1.4 *vs.* -1.5 Hz respectively), the alcoholics showed less ataxia and markedly less evidence of intoxication. A reanalysis of their data presented in Table 1 also indicates that slowing in the EEG record was not related to either the concentration of blood alcohol or the degree of ataxia across subjects administered a standard dose of aquavit equivalent to 1.25 g/kg of ethanol. Rank order correlations indicating the degree of association between the peak values of the three variables are shown in Table 1. (The range and mean values are reproduced from Holmberg and Martens, 1955, p. 414.)

Two findings are apparent from the table. First, there were marked individual differences in response, especially in the control group, on all three variables. Second, none of the correlations between the variables is statistically significant. (Possibly with a larger N the relation between BAL and ataxia would be significant.) The alcohol intake was sufficient to produce intoxication and nausea, marked cognitive and behavioral changes (drowsiness, ataxia), peak blood alcohol levels ranging up to 200 mg/100 ml, and slowing of the EEG by as much as 3 cycles/sec. Yet, across subjects the maximum BAL was not related to the amount of slowing in the EEG, nor was the slowing in the EEG related to the degree of ataxia.

A third observation from the Holmberg–Martens data indicates that the time course for the three variables differs, so that the peak change in ataxia, for instance, occurs over an hour before the peak EEG change in the control group.

TABLE 1. Correlations Between Blood Alcohol Concentration, Slowing in EEG Frequency and Degree of Ataxia[a]

Alcoholic Group ($N = 10$)			
	EEG	*BAL*	*Ataxia*
EEG (1.40, 0.70–1.76)	—	0.04	0.10
BAL (177, 156–196)		—	0.19
Ataxia (3.6, 2.0–5.5)			—
Control Group ($N = 10$)			
	EEG	*BAL*	*Ataxia*
EEG (1.52, 0.81–3.03)	—	0.02	0.01
BAL (150, 108–187)		—	0.38
Ataxia (5.5, 2.5–8.0)			—

[a] Rank order correlations based on data presented by Holmberg and Martens (1955). The EEG measure is maximum slowing in cycles per second; BAL is in milligrams per 100 ml, and ataxia is based on ratings of several behavioral tests. Range and mean values are given in parentheses. None of the correlations is significantly different from chance.

Since the relation between the time curves apparently differs between subjects, and is markedly different between the alcohol and control group, it is possible that the correlation between variables would have been somewhat higher if they had been based on values at the same time period. However, this analysis suggests that in a group study using a fixed dosage, knowing the blood alcohol concentration for a given individual would not make it possible to predict the degree of slowing in his alpha rhythm, nor would knowing the change in alpha frequency allow prediction of the severity of ataxia. The reason that prediction of change in the EEG cannot be made from the blood alcohol concentration, or why the extent of EEG slowing does not predict ataxia can be illustrated by examining the response of individual subjects. Normal control subjects 9 and 10 had almost identical blood alcohol levels (187 vs. 183) yet differed markedly in the extent to which they showed alpha slowing (1.38 vs. 3.03 Hz) or exhibited signs of ataxia (3.0 vs. 8.0). Similarly, subjects 1 and 2 showed identical EEG slowing (1.53 vs. 1.52 Hz), but very different maximum blood alcohol levels (179 vs. 108) and degree of ataxia (8.0 vs. 4.5). Although it has not been investigated, the failure to find a correlation between EEG changes and either BAL or ataxia shown in Table 1 also makes it appear unlikely that variability in an individual's response at different times to identical amounts of alcohol would be highly correlated with the degree of alpha slowing. The correlation between EEG changes and accompanying changes in level of awareness apparently holds true only when the differences between doses are large and extend over a wide range of values.

Engel's third generalization, that the degree of slowing in the alpha rhythm is independent of the initial mean frequency, should be evaluated by a correlation coefficient to determine if they are related. The law of initial values, which holds true for a large number of physiological variables, states that the magnitude of the response change in an ongoing physiological response to a stimulus is dependent upon the initial level of activity; e.g., the amount of change in skin conductance to stimulation varies as a function of the prestimulus conductance level. On this basis one would expect the amount of slowing in the mean EEG frequency under alcoholization to be related to the predrug mean frequency. There is considerable evidence that drug effects on the EEG, most notably on the percent time of activity within a given frequency band, are dependent upon the predrug level, and are an important source of individual differences in the EEG response to drugs (cf. Murphree et al., 1970). As previously discussed, some of the phenothiazines may either increase or decrease percent alpha time, depending upon its rate before drug administration (Fink, 1965; Ulett et al., 1965). The virtual disappearance of the low voltage fast activity beta waves after drinking, with the concomitant appearance of an alpha pattern, has also been commented upon (Engel and Rosenbaum, 1945; Murphree et al., 1970; Varga and Nagy, 1960). At the low end of the spectrum, Murphree et al. (1970) have pointed out that the relaxed subject with a slow alpha pattern is more apt to be made drowsy by alcohol than the tense-alert subject, and consequently shows an opposite effect: a decrease in alpha activity. This point is further shown in the Holmberg–Martens study. Although the degree of slowing in the mean frequency was almost identical for the alcohol and control groups (1.40 vs. 1.52 Hz), the alcoholics had a prealcoholization mean frequency 0.5 cycles lower than the controls (9.5 vs. 10.0). As a consequence, the alcoholics showed a much greater amount of activity within the 4–6 Hz range after alcoholization than did the controls, although neither group showed an appreciable amount of theta activity before drinking. In evaluating drug effects, the predrug EEG, especially when such measures as percent time of a given frequency or wave amplitude are used, is an important determinant of the postdrug pattern. Failure to take into account the effect of different initial patterns may account for some of the discrepancies between different studies of alcohol effects using these measures. Whether there is an initial level effect in the amount of alpha slowing under alcohol has yet to be adequately evaluated. In the Holmberg–Martens study shifts in the mean alpha frequency varied widely in the control group, from 0.81 to 3.03 cycles/sec. Since the amount of slowing was not related to the blood alcohol concentration, it would be worth investigating whether such large individual variations in response may be partially accounted for in terms of the prealcohol level.

Although the slowing of the alpha rhythm after drinking has been consistently reported in a number of studies, Docter et al. (1966), in a well-designed study, have shown that alcohol affects different measures of alpha activity in somewhat different ways. Healthy nonhospitalized male alcoholics were given five administrations of vodka equivalent to 0.3 ml/kg of alcohol at 15-min intervals. Breath sample estimates of mean blood alcohol levels increased linearly from 0.026% to 0.104% at the last administration. Alpha abundance (total alpha activity reflecting both the amplitude and the number of waves occurring during a time sample) increased markedly after the first drink, but then showed a tendency to decrease slightly after the fourth drink and with higher blood alcohol levels. However, the number of seconds of alpha activity tended to increase regularly with the increasing blood alcohol level over successive drinks. The authors point out that the different course of these two measures of alpha activity suggests that the early change in alpha abundance reflects initial amplitude changes which are not maintained over the successive periods of alcoholization. If the amplitude of the alpha waves does show a curvilinear relation to blood alcohol or varies over time, this might partially account for the conflicting reports in the literature on alcohol effects on amplitude measures. Holmberg and Martens, using a single administration of alcohol given orally, reported a 50 to 100% increase in the amplitude of the EEG. However, it is not clear whether the amplitude of individual alpha waves increased, or whether the change is due to an increase in alpha abundance. The authors note that as the amplitude increased, the number of countable waves in the EEG also rose. The latter effect is consistent with the increase in the amount of alpha activity reported by Docter et al. (1966),and Kotani (1965), using a drip infusion procedure extending over 2 hr, reported slower alpha but with lower amplitudes. Murphree et al. (1970) also report a reduction in alpha amplitude.

Regarding specific frequencies, the major findings were substantial reductions in 10 and 11 Hz activity and a concomitant increase in 8 and 9 Hz. An increase in slow wave activity below the alpha range which had been reported in other studies was not seen, probably because of the low blood alcohol levels. The time course of individual frequencies, whether measured in terms of abundance (Docter et al., 1966) or number of waves per interval (Holmberg and Martens, 1955), shows distinctive changes with increasing blood alcohol. Although the rate at which blood alcohol level increases may modify the curves, generally the faster frequency waves, 9–11 Hz, show an initial increase and then begin declining as the BAL increases. With increasing time after alcohol ingestion, progressively slower wave frequencies successively appear and gradually increase in frequency of occurrence. With sufficiently high alcohol levels, bursts of slow wave activity within the theta range (4–7 Hz) may appear, interspersed between the dominant alpha pattern, usually during periods of pronounced drowsiness or alcoholic stupor (Davis et al., 1941; Newman, 1959).

Several investigators have studied the effects of alcohol on the EEG in special subgroups of alcoholics classified on the basis of the presence or absence of specific symptom patterns in the medical history. Kotani (1965) used four patient groups: two groups with endogenous psychoses, "typical schizophrenia" ($N = 15$) and "atypical psychoses" ($N = 20$), and two groups of chronic alcoholics, those with a history of clouding of consciousness and/or hallucinations ("complex form," $N = 9$) and a group who had not shown these symptoms ("simple form," $N = 7$). The resting EEG's of the alcoholics and psychotics were similar on a 3-point rating scale of normality, although both the "complex form" alcoholics and "atypical psychotics" showed a higher frequency of abnormal recordings characterized by either high voltage slow waves or dysrhythmia.

One hundred grams of ethanol in solution were administered by drip infusion, with EEG's taken at regular intervals. The first detectable change to appear was a slowing in the alpha rhythm, followed at a slightly higher dosage by a reduction in amplitude. There was little difference in the EEG response between the alcoholics as a group and the psychotics. However, in both the "complex form" alcoholics and the "atypical psychotics," changes appeared earlier and were generally greater until the final stages of alcoholization. The greater rate in the development of EEG changes in the atypical groups is assumed to reflect a faster rise time in blood alcohol level relative to a given dosage, which is a distinguishing characteristic between normal and pathological drunkenness. In general, a fast increase in BAL produces more severe psychological and somatic changes than a slow increase (see Victor and Adams, 1953). Appearance of theta waves was infrequent in any of the groups.

In regard to psychological changes, initial euphoria followed by sleepiness was more frequently seen in the simple than in the complex alcoholics. The latter, however, showed more subjective changes sometimes associated with abnormal or pathological drunkenness, such as moodiness and restless excitement. A tolerance effect, similar to that reported in other studies, was also found, with the psychotic group showing more frequent and severe somatic symptoms such as nausea, vomiting, and changes in the pulse rate than the alcoholic group. Although the greater frequency of abnormalities in the prealcoholization records of the "atypical" groups (24% vs. 0%) would suggest that the initial brain state is related both to the greater magnitude of the EEG changes under alcohol and to the development of symptoms of pathological drunkenness (dysphoria, agitation), this relationship was not directly tested. Such a finding, however, would be consistent with the observation by Doenicke et al. (1967) that atypical and stronger reactions to anesthesia are frequently associated with mild abnormalities in the predrug EEG.

In two studies, Marinacci (1955, 1963) investigated the alcohol-activated EEG in 402 patients in whom alcohol produced abnormal states of consciousness: confusional episodes, trance-like states, fugues, or convulsions. Prealcohol EEG's showed normal records in 80% of the cases, borderline abnormalities in 16%, and 4% with moderate generalized slowing. These frequencies are within the limits usually found in normal control groups. After drinking (variable dosage and type of liquor) no diagnostic abnormalities were found in 86% of the cases, but 14% showed anterior temporal lobe spikes, generally about $\frac{1}{2}$ hr after the first drink. About a third of these patients showed "definite automatic (psychomotor) episodes" associated with the EEG abnormalities, and another third showed moderate to severe mental confusion. The author concludes that in a select few cases alcohol may lower the convulsive threshold sufficiently to trigger temporal lobe seizures with associated psychomotor epileptic attacks even in the absence of known organic brain pathology. However, many of these patients showed some irregularities in the prealcohol EEG, suggesting a possible predisposition to paroxysmal dysrhythmias. Victor (1968) also reports that alcohol may precipitate seizure discharges in patients with idiopathic epilepsy (with unknown organic basis and with the first appearance of seizures antedating the onset of drinking by several years) and also in patients with definite cerebral trauma. In some of the latter patients, seizures occurred only in connection with drinking, but usually followed the cessation of drinking by several hours. In some, but not all cases, the seizures were associated with focal EEG abnormalities.

Thompson (1963) studied the alcohol-activated EEG in three cases of pathological intoxication; that is, patients who showed either abnormal mental or behavioral responses to relatively small amounts of alcohol, followed by partial or total amnesia. Three types of abnormalities were found: (1) localized spiking, usually in the temporal or frontal lobes, (2) bursts of high voltage slow wave activity, from 2 to 6 Hz, in the same areas, and (3) mixtures of spike and slow wave activity in localized bursts. The author argues that pathological intoxication is usually indicative of lesions in the frontal or temporal lobes, or the connecting subcortical pathways, although one of the cases reported showed a normal prealcohol electroencephalogram.

Two groups of investigators have looked for distinctive EEG characteristics related to the kind of liquor ingested. Murphree et al. (1967) studied the effects of equal amounts of alcohol administered to normal moderate drinkers in three forms: vodka (low congener content), bourbon, and "superbourbon" (artificially increased congener content). All three beverages produced similar effects: a reduction in alpha amplitude and an increase in slow wave activity consistent with behavioral drowsiness. The added congeners in the superbourbon tended to increase both the degree and the duration of the EEG changes, and to heighten the depressant effect of the alcohol, although the blood alcohol concentrations as measured by the Breathalyzer were not significantly different for the three beverages (see also Murphree et al., 1970).

Lolli et al. (1964) studied the effects of low dosages of alcohol (equivalent to 0.40 g/kg of ethanol) administered in the form of either a dry red wine or a dry martini (gin and dry vermouth) to 10 normal males in each group. Within subject comparisons of EEG activity before and after alcohol were made under four conditions: resting with eyes closed, during a reaction time task, arithmetic tests, and photic flicker. Mean blood alcohol values ranged between 0.03 and 0.04% during the alcohol runs. The index of EEG activity used was a combined measure reflecting both the number of occurrences of a wave of a given frequency and their amplitudes.

At these blood alcohol levels most of the tests were not statistically significant. However, it was apparent that wine produced a much greater effect than the martini in enhancing alpha activity (21% of the comparisons showing a significant increase vs. 11%), theta activity (11% vs. 2%), and delta activity (14% vs. 3%). Little significant change under either beverage was seen in beta activity, although slightly more decreases were observed than increases. Equally noteworthy was the variability in the EEG changes. Although only about 2–3% of the tests showed a statistically significant decrease in alpha activity, non-significant decreases ($0.05 < p < 0.25$) occurred in a fairly large percent of the cases, especially in the martini group. Under the latter condition, alpha activity decreased in 30% of the tests; theta in 15%; and delta in 29%. To a lesser extent decreases in the four rhythms also occurred under the wine condition, although the majority of the changes indicated a slowing of the mean EEG frequency. Presumably these contradictory changes are partly due to the low dose of alcohol administered, since larger doses generally produce a more uniform response across subjects and a more consistent shift to slower frequencies. To some extent differences between subjects in the initial EEG pattern may also contribute to the discrepancy. A subject whose initial prealcohol alpha was in the high range, or who showed considerable beta activity, would show an increase in alpha abundance under alcohol-induced slowing; while the subject whose initial mean alpha frequency was in the low range, 8–9 Hz, might show a decrease in alpha abundance because the same amount of slowing would increase the amount of theta activity.

The "magnification" of the alpha rhythm from the pre- to postalcohol condition was greatest on those tests where the external stimulus was highly salient (reaction time, flicker). Since the initial effect of photic stimulation is usually to disrupt the alpha rhythm and initiate a low-voltage, fast activity arousal pattern, the authors argue that the increased alpha abundance suggests a decreased receptivity to external stimuli under alcohol. This interpretation is similar to that offered by Engel to the effect that alcohol reduces the level of awareness, although Engel might also predict an equal impairment in cognitive functioning as reflected in the arithmetic tests. The suggestion of a decrease in stimulus receptivity is supported by a number of studies reporting a reduction in sensory evoked potentials under alcohol to repetitive stimulation, which has been interpreted as indicating an inhibitory or depressant effect of alcohol on the cerebral cortex.

THE EFFECTS OF LONG-TERM ADMINISTRATION ON THE ELECTROENCEPHALOGRAM

Beginning with the classic studies by Isbell *et al.* (1955) and Wikler *et al.* (1956), several studies have investigated EEG changes recorded at regular intervals during experimental chronic alcoholization and the subsequent withdrawal period. Wikler *et al.* (1956) present data on three subjects who were maintained on a variable dosage of 95% ethyl alcohol, averaging between 458 and 489 ml daily. Alcohol was administered regularly throughout the day over a 48–55 day period, followed by abrupt withdrawal. Blood alcohol levels were variable, partly because of the development of tolerance effects during periods of constant daily dosages, but remained over 200 mg% for long periods. Prior to alcoholization, EEG records were within normal limits and subjects showed no signs of CNS pathology.

The initial change in the EEG was one of diffuse slowing which persisted in a milder degree throughout the alcoholization period and which was much like that seen after the ingestion of a single large dose of alcohol. In general, there was a marked increase in the percentage of slow wave activity (4–6 Hz), increase in the occipital alpha percentage and slowing of the mean alpha frequency. (The relation between changes in percent alpha time and the degree of slowing after alcoholization may be either positive or negative, depending upon the amount of slowing—primarily a function of the amount of alcohol ingested—and the initial mean frequency. Diffuse slowing may produce either an increase or decrease in percent alpha time in different subjects.) When the same dosage was maintained over several days, tolerance effects become apparent in the declining BAL, the rapid disappearance of signs of behavioral intoxication, and a partial return of the EEG pattern to that characteristic of the prealcoholization period. A small increase in the alcohol dosage (e.g., a 1-ml change from 19 to 20 ml hourly) reinstated the cycle, producing large increases in the BAL and concomitant behavioral and electroencephalographic changes. The authors note, however, that the correlation between behavioral intoxication and the EEG pattern was sometimes inconsistent since on occasion the subject might appear to be more intoxicated when the degree of slowing in the EEG frequency was slight or, conversely, greater slowing in the EEG pattern would occur with little behavioral indication of intoxication. Even with high daily alcohol intake, lower blood alcohol levels and lesser degrees of intoxication were seen in association with a "normal" EEG pattern. In this connection, the observation by Mello and Mendelson (1968) that the textbook descriptions of the behavioral effects of high blood alcohol levels are probably not accurate for the chronic drinker is of some relevance. In their studies they found no significant decrement in performance on vigilance and reaction time tasks despite blood alcohol levels approaching 200 mg/100 ml, and relatively little disruption of verbal, motor, or social behavior during periods of sustained blood alcohol levels ranging between 150 and 300 mg/100 ml.

After abrupt withdrawal of alcohol, the subjects showed similar EEG changes. At approximately 12 hr, when the BAL had declined from over 200 mg% to between 30 and 40 mg%, the EEG resembled the prealcohol pattern. At 15 to 20 hr, when the blood alcohol level was zero, subjects exhibited marked anxiety and tremulousness and EEG activity characterized by moderate to high voltage, rhythmic slow waves (4–6 Hz) and a consequent marked drop in alpha percent. Random spikes and paroxysmal bursts of slow wave, high voltage activity and transient, mild dysrhythmias appeared at the same time and lasted throughout the second day. Some subjects later showed one or more of the classical signs of the withdrawal syndrome: hallucinosis, autonomic irregularities, convulsive seizures and full-blown delirium tremens. No specific EEG patterns were associated with the specific mental states occurring during the later stages of withdrawal. At 3 months there was no evidence of residual impairment or abnormalities in the EEG record.

These data on the effects of experimental chronic alcoholization appear remarkably consistent with the data reported by Victor (1968) on naturally occurring withdrawal symptoms. Photomyoclonus, usually accompanied by paroxysmal discharges in the EEG to a high intensity flickering light, generally did not appear until some 15 hr after cessation of drinking, and reached its peak frequency from 31 to 48 hr after withdrawal. Abnormal responses to photic stimulation are infrequent after the fifth day, suggesting that the period of CNS hyperexcitability is quite brief, and roughly parallels the time course of the clinical withdrawal syndrome.

Isbell *et al.* and Wikler *et al.*, on the basis of experimental chronic intoxication, and Victor, on the basis of clinical observations of the withdrawal syndrome, agree on three major conclusions:

1. Patients with normal EEG patterns and no evidence of CNS pathology may go into convulsions after prolonged drinking.
2. The seizures and abnormal paroxysmal EEG activity usually occur after withdrawal from alcohol rather than during drinking. However, a sharp drop in blood alcohol from a higher level maintained over several days may also precipitate withdrawal symptoms. In the Victor sample 50% of the patients developing seizures did so within 13–24 hr after the last drink. This roughly corresponds to the time at which EEG spiking and paroxysmal slow wave activity appeared in Wikler's subjects.
3. The EEG abnormalities appearing during withdrawal are short lasting and do not result in any detectable residual impairment. EEG's recorded shortly after seizures or between drinking bouts generally fall within normal limits.

Isbell *et al.* also note that the severity of symptoms in their experimental subjects correlated roughly with the amount of alcohol consumed and the duration of the drinking period. Mello and Mendelson (1968), however, feel that in clinical cases the severity and duration of symptoms "do not appear to be directly related" to either the amount of alcohol consumed or the duration of the drinking bout, and that nutritional deficiencies, concurrent illnesses, and environmental factors play an important role in the development of symptoms after withdrawal.

Weiss *et al.* (1964) studied the effects of 24 days of chronic alcoholization on 10 subjects who had previously experienced withdrawal symptomatology, but with a negative history of convulsive seizures. A fixed incremental dosage schedule was followed, with the subjects receiving between 20 and 30 oz of 86 proof whiskey by the fourteenth day and between 30 and 40 oz on the twenty-fourth day.

The dominant alpha frequency recorded from a monopolar occipital lead slowed significantly from the fourteenth to the twenty-fourth day of alcoholization (10 Hz to 8 Hz) and increased significantly (to 10.5 Hz) by the second day of withdrawal. Hyperventilation produced little effect, but a flickering stimulus produced significantly less photic driving from the fourteenth to twenty-fourth day with a return to normal by the second day of withdrawal. Unlike Wikler *et al.*, no indication of seizure patterns was observed.

The slowing of the alpha rhythm during the period of heaviest alcoholization parallels the findings of Wikler *et al.* The authors suggest that the failure to find EEG seizure activity may be related to the shorter alcoholization period used: 24 days *vs.* 48–55 days in the study by Wikler *et al.* Other differences in the alcohol regimen may also be involved. The BAL's appeared to be generally lower, averaging 100 mg/100 ml during most of the first 2 weeks, and the 4-hr intake *vs.* the hourly intake in the Wikler study may have resulted in a higher and more constant BAL in the latter study.

The finding of significantly reduced photic driving is interpreted to indicate alcohol-induced suppression of the cortical response to photic stimulation. Some support for this interpretation is provided by studies showing a reduction in amplitude of the scalp-recorded sensory-evoked potentials after alcohol. Lolli *et al.* (1964), using a similar flicker procedure, have also interpreted their finding of a relatively greater increase in alpha activity during this task after a single administration of alcohol as indicating a decreased receptivity to external stimulation since flicker usually disrupts alpha activity.

Docter and Bernal (1964) studied pre- to postdrinking changes in the EEG recorded during a sustained period of alcoholization lasting 2 weeks. Two paid male alcoholics received vodka twice a day in an amount equivalent to a daily intake of 1.8 ml/kg of ethanol. Daily Breathalyzer readings ranged from 0.01 to 0.04% during the morning predrink period, and averaged 0.15% and 0.19% for the two subjects 40 min after alcoholization.

The most striking effect was a marked pre- to postdrink increase in seconds of alpha activity recorded from bipolar occipital leads. The amount of change in alpha activity did not appear to vary systematically during the 14-day course of alcoholization. Changes during the course of alcoholization in the daily pre-drink EEG were not reported. Changes in the EEG, in frequency of rapid eye movements, and social behavior were discussed as possible indicators of an "excitatory effect of alcohol."

Newman (1959) investigated the effects of sustained heavy drinking in two chronic alcoholics. A male patient received a daily dose averaging 480 ml of alcohol over a 4-day period. When blood alcohol was maximal, 150 mg%, the EEG's showed a marked increase in slow wave activity in the theta range not seen before alcoholization. Records taken at 1, 2, and 3 days after withdrawal were similar to the predrinking records.

A female who received an average daily dose of 216 ml of alcohol over 5 days showed considerably less slowing in spite of generally higher blood alcohol levels. However, at 48 hr after withdrawal, short bursts of high-voltage

3-4 Hz waves appeared, which were not present before or during the alcoholization period. The patient's history contained several episodes of grand mal type seizures associated with cessation of drinking in the past. Consistent with the discussion by Wikler *et al.*, the paroxysmal slow activity is interpreted as reflecting a hyperexcitable brain state attributable to the withdrawal of alcohol.

In summary, these studies show that a high blood alcohol level sustained over a period of several days to several weeks produces some of the same EEG changes seen after a single large dose of alcohol. a general slowing in the frequency of the predominant wave seen in the EEG and usually an increase in the percent time of alpha activity. Depending upon the alcohol dosage and schedule, tolerance effects may be noted in the EEG records taken during the course of the alcoholization, and paroxysmal slow wave activity typically seen during convulsive seizures may appear from 12 to 48 hr after abrupt termination of drinking.

THE EFFECTS OF ALCOHOL ON BRAIN EVOKED RESPONSES

Technique

The relation between the electrical responses in the human brain and mental processes of integration and association is perhaps the most challenging of all the problems facing psychophysiologists today. Until quite recently, the prospect of unifying physiological and psychological concepts by EEG techniques seemed to be receding because of the baffling complexity of the electrical rhythms, and this difficulty has still not been overcome. The most intriguing, and at the same time most elusive, of the properties of these rhythms is that although often remarkably constant in their variations with respect to time, they fluctuate also, in a much less regular manner, within the three-dimensional space of the brain. The continuous analysis and display of such phenomena presents serious difficulties, and no method has yet given entirely satisfactory results.

However difficult they may be to unravel, the time and space relations of the intrinsic brain rhythms cannot be ignored, if only because so intricate and orderly an arrangement seems unlikely to have survived the struggle for existence with no functional identification. The awkward fact that these rhythms are highly individual—even to the extent of total absence in some people—must be accepted as a fascinating part of the enigma, where personality and disposition are essential features in the architecture of human physiology.

The introduction of more versatile and sophisticated methods for extracting information about transient components of the EEG inevitably diverted interest from the background activity because, by definition, the methods of transient analysis tend to efface or at least diminish those rhythmic features which are most prominent in the conventional EEG record. This unfortunate technical incompatibility has somewhat discouraged correlative studies, but interaction between the multitude of intrinsic rhythms and the response evoked by sensory stimuli seems an indispensable part of the cerebral information flow system. These influences are complex and often reciprocal: intrinsic rhythms of excitability variation can modify the amplitude and latency of evoked potentials, and the arrival of signals in an afferent channel can modulate the amplitude, phase, and frequency of intrinsic rhythms.

By an evoked potential is meant the detectable electrical change of any part of the brain in response to deliberate stimulation of a peripheral sense organ, a sensory nerve, a point on the sensory pathway, or any related structure of the sensory system. This stimulation can be photic in nature, such as a flash of light; auditory, such as a distinct click or tone; electric, such as a pulse of voltage or current; olfactory, such as a distinct odor; or of any other nature that can be sensed by the nervous system. The stimulus must be controlled as to its rate of occurrence, duration, and amplitude, since each factor may affect the shape of the response.

Each of the above-mentioned stimuli has one basic characteristic in common: the occurrence of the stimulus can be controlled from some external source, such as a pulse generator and, hence, a time reference point for each response is established.

If one looks at the time-varying neuroelectric potential waveforms (EEG) immediately after each stimulus (reference point), we will actually see the total random fluctuations, part of which are caused by the stimulus. The other portions of the fluctuations in the total (noise) are not related to the stimulus and, therefore, are not repetitive or at least not locked in time to the reference point.

The basic assumption made in the method of detecting signals in noise concerns the properties of the noise. The noise component of the signal under consideration must be composed of or approximated by stationary Gaussian random processes with zero averages. By stationary we mean that the random process is independent of time and therefore is unaffected by translations of the origin of time. Although it is not strictly imperative that the probability distribution of the noise be Gaussian, we would not know as much statistically about our results if it were not. Another property sometimes mentioned in relation to noise is that of ergodicity. Since we do not operate on a time function of infinite extent but rather with an ensemble of finite pieces of such functions, it is required that averages across the ensemble be equivalent to averages over time along a stationary function of infinite length. Such a property is termed ergodic. The absence of the above properties can be circumvented to a certain extent in some cases when using the average response method.

To obtain an increase in the signal-to-noise ratio of some functions, one must increase the period of time over which the measurement is made. Since we are dealing with integrative processes, our increase in the signal-to-noise ratio will be approximately proportional to the square root of the time over which the measurement is made.

The theory behind the average response technique is a relatively simple concept. Upon the occurrence of the first timing pulse (stimulus), the analogue function is sampled at regular intervals, the samples being stored in the memory of the computer. The rate of sampling and the number of samples made for each response is determined prior to the start of computation and often depends upon the highest frequency component present in the response and the length of time of the response respectively. Upon the occurrence of the second timing pulse, the signal is again sampled and each sample is added to the value stored during the sample number at the previous response. This cycle is repeated until the desired number of responses have been summated. This method achieves a number of results. Those components of the time function which are random and therefore not phase-locked to the time reference (i.e., the noise) will add algebraically and if enough responses are summed, will tend to cancel or average out to zero. The components of the time function locked in phase to the stimulus are additive themselves with each successive summation. The improvement in the signal-to-noise ratio can be shown to be proportional to the square root of the number of responses summed.

The study of evoked potentials in different brain structures is a powerful tool for obtaining increased insight into the functioning and communication of the brain. Evoked potentials spread and travel from one part of the brain to another. By means of simultaneous averaging processes with separate electrodes, the way in which the evoked potential travels can be mapped. This spread and transformation of evoked potentials in brain space constitutes an important measure which can also, under some circumstances, be related to psychological, physiological, and pharmacological variables. Many drugs have been shown to affect the manner of occurrence of evoked potentials in different brain areas.

Drug Effects

In recent years a few investigators have studied the evoked potentials of alcoholics and the effects of alcohol on evoked potentials in man.

Bergamasco and Gandiglio (1965) investigated the somatosensory evoked potentials in chronic alcoholics. Ten chronic alcoholics without signs of peripheral neuropathy were used as subjects. In each subject the ulnar nerve was stimulated at the wrist and at the epitrochleo-oleocranic groove, and the lateral popliteal nerve at the capitulum fibulae and the neck of the foot. The evoked potentials were obtained by means of electrode needles attached to the scalp in a position corresponding to the somatosensory area of the leg and hand. In the same subjects, the motor and sensory conduction velocity of the lateral popliteal nerve was measured.

The latencies of various components of the somatosensory evoked potentials were clearly longer than those obtained in normal subjects. The authors state that the increase in latencies and duration might be an indication of the time dispersion at the cortical level of a signal coming from peripheral stations. In these same subjects Bergamini et al. (1965) studied nerve conduction velocity and found a slowing of the afferent volley. The authors concluded that a sensory fiber lesion and damage of root and posterior medullary columns are two pathological conditions which alter somatosensory potentials evoked by electrical nerve stimulation. A lesion of the afferent peripheral fiber reduces its excitability and elicits a temporal dispersion of the afferent volley. This causes a decrease in the peripheral afferent conduction velocity, which expresses itself in the cortex by an increase in evoked potential latencies. At the same time the evoked response will have a longer duration accompanying the temporal dispersion of the impulses arising from the periphery. In nerve lesions the somatosensory evoked potential is characterized by an increase of the different peak latencies and particularly by an increase of wave duration.

In a recent study Spilker and Callaway (1969) reported that the average evoked response to sine wave light is apparently related to "augmenting/reducing" since augmentors (as defined on a kinesthetic test) have visual evoked responses that increase in amplitude as the depth of modulation is increased. In contrast, "reducers" show a leveling off or an actual decrease in visual evoked responses at high depths of modulation. In an attempt to test the effects of arousal, these investigators studied the effects of various drugs on the amplitude of the visual evoked response. They found that sodium pentobarbital and ethyl alcohol both significantly decreased the slope of the visual evoked response amplitude at the four highest depths of modulation.

The effects of alcohol on the auditory evoked response have been studied in our laboratory and reported by Gross et al. (1966). We found that the amplitudes of the auditory evoked response are significantly reduced after alcohol ingestion, with maximal effects observed at 15–30 min after ingestion.

Salamy et al. (1969) have reported that the late components of the somatosensory evoked response are also quite sensitive to the depressant effects of alcohol. They found the amplitude of this late component to be inversely related to the alcohol level in the blood. In keeping with these results, Lewis et al. (1970) reported that after ingestion of 3 oz of alcohol, the amplitude of a number of late waves of both visual and somatosensory-evoked responses recorded from central areas was significantly decreased.

In conclusion, it may be said that alcohol significantly reduces the late component of the visual, auditory, and somatosensory evoked responses in man.

Recently, Stohr and Goldring (1969) reported that the late components of the somatosensory-evoked response originate in the primary cortical area and Vaughan and Ritter (1970) concluded that the late vertex response to sound originates in the primary auditory cortex of the brain. Consequently, it appears quite likely that the cortex is the primary site of action for alcohol. In a preceding chapter, Himwich and Callison (Chapter 3) reached a similar conclusion based on the effects of alcohol on evoked potentials of various parts of the central nervous system of the cat.

THE EFFECTS OF ALCOHOL ON THE RECOVERY FUNCTION OF EVOKED POTENTIALS

The concept of a cortical excitability cycle rests principally on amplitude measures of cortical potentials evoked by a sensory stimulus or by direct cortical stimulation, although other criteria could be used (rate of neuron firing, thresholds of single neural units, convulsive threshold). Typically, it has been based on the observed phenomena that when a stimulus is presented to the nervous system, the amplitude of its resulting evoked potential varies as a function of the temporal relationship between the stimulus and the spontaneous potentials or previously evoked potentials in the brain.

Recovery time studies using paired stimuli are good indicators of temporal periodicities. The cycle activity of evoked potentials in anesthetized cats elicited by direct cortical stimulation (Chang, 1951) and by afferent stimulation (Chang, 1950) reflected changes in excitability in terms of the amplitude of a second evoked potential elicited by a second stimulus. Such recovery cycles have also been found when nonanesthetized animals were used (Evarts et al., 1960; Palestini et al., 1965).

Changes in cortical excitability cycles have also been studied with various drugs. Schwartz et al. (1962) reported that the recovery cycle of somatosensory-evoked responses was more sensitive to pentobarbital sodium than was the amplitude of single evoked responses. Gartside et al. (1966) studied the effects of lithium carbonate on the somatosensory recovery function of nondepressed volunteers. They were able to produce a decrease in the recovery function comparable to that found in depressive patients. Shagass and Schwartz (1962) found that imipramine and tranylcypromine were able to bring the recovery function of patients with psychotic depression back to a normal level.

Evarts et al. (1961) studied the effects of alcohol on the recovery cycle in cats and reported an increase in excitability. Consequently, we undertook a study (Begleiter et al., in preparation) of the effects of alcohol on the somatosensory recovery function in humans.

The experiment was performed on 16 healthy adult male volunteers. Somatosensory responses were evoked by stimulating the median nerve of the right wrist through electrodes placed on the skin 3 cm apart. The stimulus was a pulse of 1 msec duration at an intensity 3 mA above the subject's thumb twitch.

Recording electrodes were placed in the parasagittal plane 7 cm left of the midline. The posterior lead was 2 cm behind a line from vertex to external auditory meatus and the other was 6 cm anterior to it. The EEG was amplified and fed into a computer using a 512 msec analysis time.

Twelve interstimulus intervals were used for recovery cycle determinations. These were as follows: 2.5, 5, 10, 15, 20, 35, 50, 65, 80, 95, 110 and 130 msec. These intervals were randomized across subjects. Stimulus repetition frequency was variable from 1 to 3 sec. Each stimulus sequence involved alternating presentation of two paired and two unpaired stimuli. Fifty pairs and fifty single stimuli were summated.

Recovery curves were derived only from the initial, or primary, response. The amplitude taken was the deflection from the maximum negative trough to the positive peak.

Since a recovery function determination may last over 2 hr, it became important for us to maintain a fairly constant blood alcohol level during that period of time. In order to accomplish this, we conducted a pilot study using eight subjects. Multiple dose administration with doses spaced to maintain a constant blood alcohol level was followed in accordance with the method developed by Goldberg (1960, 1961).

In the recovery function experiment the subjects received alcohol (80-proof bourbon) on one morning and an equal amount of water on the other morning. These two conditions were counterbalanced for all 16 subjects. Before the electrodes were placed on the scalp, each subject was asked to drink an amount of alcohol in the ratio of 1.5 g of alcohol per kilogram of body weight. The subject was given a period of 5 min to finish his drink. Approximately 60 min after the intake of alcohol, the first blood alcohol level was determined. The second dosage of alcohol given was calculated on the first blood alcohol level. Two hours after alcohol intake another blood alcohol level was obtained which determined the amount to be given in the third dose.

The usual way of illustrating recovery functions has been to plot the ratio of the second to the first response, i.e., the R_2/R_1 ratio. If we display the data in this fashion (Fig. 1) the difference between the alcohol curve and water curve is statistically significant. This would support the findings of Evarts *et al.* (1961) who found greater excitability with alcohol.

Recently Shagass (1968) reported that R_1 and R_2 are significantly correlated, and that the regression of R_2 and R_1 does not pass through the origin. In order to correct R_2, the correlation between R_1 and R_2 was determined for each interstimulus interval, with calculation of the "within-groups" regression equation. The regression equation was then used to adjust the R_2 value for its correlation with R_1. The adjusted R_2 values (Fig. 2) were then compared to determine the significance of treatment differences. The difference between the adjusted R_2 alcohol curve and that for the water curve was not statistically significant.

In recent years, a number of investigators (Isbell *et al.*, 1955; Mendelson *et al.*, 1964) have postulated that alcohol withdrawal represents a process of physiological addiction or physical dependence and that this process is similar to addiction induced by other pharmacological agents. We have postulated that the mechanisms of physical dependence become operative much before total withdrawal from alcohol. It is felt that after a relatively short period of drinking, the cessation of alcohol intake might be accompanied by incipient withdrawal symptoms.

In their studies of critical flicker fusion, Weiss *et al.* (1964) advanced the hypothesis that the effect of alcohol on the nervous system is to suppress both excitatory and inhibitory components, the latter more than the former. This differential suppression becomes greater as the duration and extent of alcohol intake increase. After alcohol withdrawal, the excitatory components recover

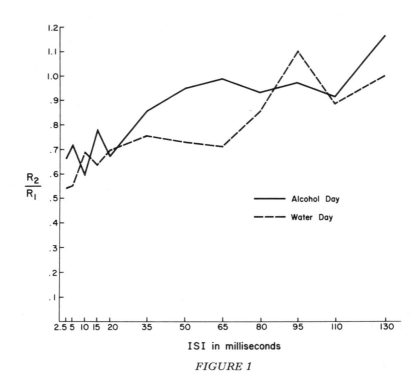

FIGURE 1

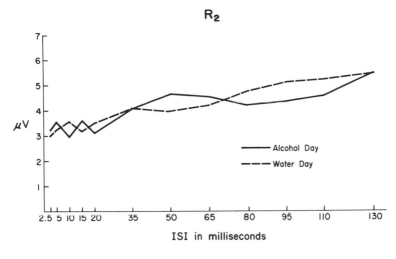

FIGURE 2

more rapidly than the inhibitory components; this inhibition is manifested as a seeming hyperexcitability.

In an attempt to test this hypothesis, we have recently undertaken to study the excitability cycle of the somatosensory recovery function in man, during alcoholization and withdrawal. The four subjects used were all alcoholics who had been sober in the hospital for a period of 6 to 8 weeks. A recovery function determination was always made in the morning during the 2 days of baseline, 4 days of alcoholization, and the 4 days subsequent to alcoholization. The subjects were asked to drink 30 oz of 90-proof whiskey during the 4 days of alcoholization. The alcohol intake was divided in four equal doses and always took place in the afternoon between 1 p.m. and 11 p.m.

Each subject was also tested for a comparable period of days without alcohol. Two subjects received the drug condition first and then the no-drug condition. The other two subjects received the no-drug condition first and then the alcohol condition. The recovery function was always taken at 9 a.m. in the morning after the subject had received his last drink at 11 p.m. the preceding day.

We postulated that after each of the 4 days of alcoholization, the cessation of drinking at night might be accompanied by incipient withdrawal the next morning.

The preliminary results indicate a progressive increase of excitability starting with the alcoholization period and reaching asymptote with the first day of total alcohol withdrawal. During the subsequent days of testing the recovery function decreased, approaching the level obtained during baseline determinations.

The recovery function determinations obtained during the control period for the four subjects showed no significant change over time.

The results we have obtained with the recovery function of somatosensory-evoked potentials during alcoholization and withdrawal appear to be in general agreement with the findings of Isbell *et al.* (1955), Wikler *et al.* (1956), Weiss *et al.* (1964), and Victor (1968).

SUMMARY

It is obvious that many alcoholics with a long history of heavy drinking develop certain brain aberrations. However, electroencephalographers have not enjoyed much success in detecting EEG abnormalities in chronic alcoholics. It appears quite reasonable to suspect that our present methods of EEG recording and analysis are rather insensitive to the damaging effects of chronic alcohol intake.

Acute intoxication produced by increasing concentrations of alcohol in the blood produces impairment of psychological functions such as perception, discrimination, association, and voluntary response. These functions are often attributed to neural activity at the cortical levels of the central nervous system. The study of direct effects of alcohol upon brain processes is rather limited by the close reciprocal influences exerted between cortical and subcortical systems. Consequently, an effect of alcohol upon changes in electrical activity of the cortex may result from either a direct action on cortical neurons or an indirect one exerted via a change in modulatory influences of subcortical neurons.

It is quite possible that instead of a progression of alcohol effects from the cortex downward, there may be a progression of effects at all levels concurrently, with the preponderance of effects being subcortical.

At this point it is clear that alcohol exerts direct and indirect actions at many levels of the nervous system. The possible sites of primary action of alcohol in the brain should be greatly clarified by further single neuron studies in the intact organism.

REFERENCES

Arentsen, K. and Sindrup, E., 1963. Electroencephalographic investigation of alcoholics, *Acta Psychiat. Scand.* **39**: 371.

Begleiter, H., Platz, A., and Porjesz, B. The effects of alcohol on the somatosensory recovery function in man (in preparation).

Bennett, A. E., 1960. Diagnosis of intermediate stage of alcoholic brain disease, *J. Amer. Med. Assoc.* **172**: 1143.

Bennett, A. E., 1967. Treatment of brain damage in alcoholism, *Curr. Psychiatric Therapies* **7**: 142.

Bennett, A. E., Doi, L. T., and Mowery, S. L., 1956. The value of electroencephalography in alcoholism, *J. Nerv. Ment. Dis.* **124**: 27.

Bennett, A. E., Mowery, S. L., and Fort, J. T., 1960. Brain damage from chronic alcoholism: The diagnosis of intermediate stage of alcoholic brain disease, *Amer. J. Psychiat.* **116**: 705.

Bergamasco, B. and Gandiglio, G., 1965. Alterazioni delle risposte corticali a stimoli somatoestesici in soggetti alcoolisti cronici privi di segni clinici di neuropatia periferica, *Riv. Pat. Nerv. Ment.* **86**: 170.

Bergamini, L., Gandiglio, G., Bergamasco, B., Bram, S., and Mombelli, A. M., 1965. Alterazioni della conduzione nervosa e motoria in alcoolisti cronici privi di segni clinici di neuropatia perferica, *Riv. Pat. Nerv. Ment.* **86**: 31.

Carpenter, J. A., 1962. Effects of alcohol on some psychological processes, *Quart. J. Studies Alc.* **23**: 274.

Chang, H. T., 1950. The repetitive discharges of cortico-thalamic reverberation circuit, *J. Neurophysiol.* **13**: 235.

Chang, H. T., 1951. Changes in excitability of cerebral cortex following single electric shock applied to cortical surfaces, *J. Neurophysiol.* **14**: 95.

Davis, P. A., Gibbs, F. A., Davis, H., Jetter, W. W., and Trowbridge, L. S., 1941. The effects of alcohol upon the electroencephalogram (brain waves), *Quart. J. Stud. Alc.* **1**: 626.

Delamonica, E., Marshall, C., and Kurland, A. A., 1966. The alpha blocking response in chronic alcoholics, *Dis. Nerv. Syst.* **27**: 451.

Delay, J., Verdaux, A., and Chanoit, P., 1957. L'éléctroencephalogramme des alcoholiques chroniques. Essai statistique, *Ann. méd.-psychol.* **115**: 427.

Docter, R. F. and Bernal, M. E., 1964. Immediate and prolonged psychophysiological effects of sustained alcohol intake in alcoholics, *Quart. J. Stud. Alc.* **25**: 438.

Docter, R. F., Naitoh, P., and Smith, J. C., 1966. Electroencephalographic changes and vigilance behavior during experimentally induced intoxication with alcoholic subjects, *Psychosom. Med.* **28**: 605.

Doenicke, A., Kugler, J., and Laub, M., 1967. Evaluation of recovery and "street fitness" by E.E.G. and psychodiagnostic tests after anaesthesia, *Canad. Anaesth. Soc. J.* **14**: 567.

Dyken, M., Grant, P., and White, P., 1961. Evaluation of electroencephalographic changes associated with chronic alcoholism, *Dis. Nerv. Syst.* **22**: 284.

Ekman, G., Frankenhaeuser, M., Goldberg, L., Bjerver, K., Jarpe, G., and Myrsten, A. L., 1963. Effects of alcohol intake on subjective and objective variables over a five hour period, *Psychopharmacologia* **4**: 28.

Ekman, G., Frankenhaeuser, M., Goldberg, L., Hagdahl, R., and Myrsten, A. L., 1964. Subjective and objective effects of alcohol as functions of dosage and time, *Psychopharmacologia* **6**: 399.

Engel, G. L. and Romano, J., 1959. Delirium, a syndrome of cerebral insufficiency, *J. Chron. Dis.* **9**: 260.

Engel, G. L. and Rosenbaum, M., 1944. Studies of the electroencephalogram in acute alcoholic intoxication, *Proc. Cent. Soc. Clin. Res.* **17**: 62.

Engel, G. L. and Rosenbaum, M., 1945. Delirium III. Electroencephalographic changes associated with acute alcoholic intoxication, *Arch. Neurol. Psychiat.* **53**: 44.

Engel, G. L., Webb, J. P., and Ferris, E. B., 1945. Quantitative electroencephalographic studies of anoxia in humans; comparison with acute alcoholic intoxication and hypoglycemia, *J. Clin. Investigations* **24**: 691.

Evarts, E. V., Fleming, T. C., Etienne, M., and Posternak, J. M., 1961. Action de quelques anesthésiques sur le cycle d'excitabilité du cortex visuel du chat, *Helv. Physiol. Acta* **19**: 70.

Evarts, E. V., Fleming, T. C., and Huttenlocher, P. R., 1960. Recovery cycle of visual cortex of the awake and sleeping cat, *Am. J. Physiol.* **199**: 373.

Feldman, C. F. and Hass, W. A., 1970. Controls, conceptualization, and the interrelation between experimental and correlational research, *Amer. Psychol.* **25**: 633.

Fink, M., 1965. EEG and human psychopharmacology. Changes in acute and chronic administration of chlorpromazine, imipramine, and placebo (saline), in *Applications of Electroencephalography in Psychiatry* (W. P. Wilson, ed.) pp. 226–240, Duke Univ. Press, Durham, N.C.

Funderburk, W. H., 1949. Electroencephalographic studies in chronic alcoholism, *Electroenceph. Clin. Neurophysiol.* **1**: 369.

Funkhouser, J. B., Nagler, B., and Walke, N. D., 1953. The electroencephalogram of chronic alcoholism, *Southern Med. J.* **46**: 423.

Gartside, I. B., Lippold, O. C., and Meldrum, B. S., 1966. The evoked cortical somato-sensory response in normal man and its modification by oral lithium carbonate, *Electroenceph. Clin. Neurophysiol.* **20**: 382.

Goldberg, L., 1960. Metabolism and action of alcohol, *Proc. 26th Intern. Congr. Alcohol and Alcoholism*, Stockholm.

Goldberg, L., 1961. Alcoholism, tranquilizers, and hangover, *Quart. J. Stud. Alc.* Suppl. No. 1, 37.

Green, R. L., 1965. The electroencephalogram in alcoholism, toxic psychoses, and infection, in *Applications of Electroencephalography in Psychiatry* (W. P. Wilson, ed.) pp. 123–129, Duke Univ. Press, Durham, N.C.

Greenblatt, M., 1944. Age and electroencephalographic abnormality in neuropsychiatric patients, *Amer. J. Psychiat.* **101**: 82.

Greenblatt, M., Levin, S., and di Cori, F., 1944. The electroencephalogram associated with chronic alcoholism, alcoholic psychosis and alcoholic convulsions, *Arch. Neurol. Psychiat.* **52**: 290.

Grenell, R. G., 1959. Alcohols and activity of cerebral neurons, *Quart. J. Stud. Alc.* **20**: 421.

Gross, M. M., Begleiter, H., Tobin, M., and Kissin, B., 1966. Changes in auditory evoked response induced by alcohol, *J. Nerv. Ment. Dis.* **143**: 152.

Henry, C. E., 1965. Electroencephalographic correlates with personality, in *Applications of Electroencephalography in Psychiatry* (W. P. Wilson, ed.) pp. 3–18, Duke Univ. Press, Durham, N.C.

Hill, H. E., Haertzen, C. A., Wolbach Jr., A. B., and Miner, E. J., 1963. The addiction research center inventory: standardization of scales which evaluate subjective effects of morphine, amphetamine, pentobarbital, alcohol, LSD-25, pyrahexyl and chlor-promazine, *Psychopharmacologia* **4**: 167.

Holmberg, G. and Mårtens, S., 1955. Electroencephalographic changes in man correlated with blood alcohol concentration and some other conditions following standardized ingestion of alcohol, *Quart. J. Stud. Alc.* **16**: 411.

Isbell, H., Fraser, H. F., Wikler, A., Belleville, R. E., and Eisenman, A. J., 1955. An experimental study of the etiology of "rum fits" and delirium tremens, *Quart. J. Stud. Alc.* **16**: 1.

Jellinek, E. M., 1946. Phases in the drinking history of alcoholics, *Quart. J. Stud. Alc.* **7**: 1.

Kaim, S. C., Chalmers, T. C., Fox, V., Hartman, C. H., Pittman, D. J., and Reinert, R. E., 1968. Symposium: Treatment Programs in Alcoholism, in *Highlights, XIII Ann. Conf. V.A. Cooperative Studies in Psychiatry*.

Kalant, H., 1962. Some recent physiological and biochemical investigations on alcohol and alcoholism, *Quart. J. Stud. Alc.* **23**: 52.

Kennard, M. A., Bueding, E., and Wortis, S. B., 1945. Some biochemical and electro-encephalographic changes in delirium tremens, *Quart. J. Stud. Alc.* **6**: 4.

Kessler, L. B., 1949. Alcoholism: a psychological and electroencephalographic study, *Amer. Psychol.* **4**: 275.

Kissin, B. and Platz, A., 1968. The use of drugs in the long term rehabilitation of alcoholics, in *Psychopharmacology: A Review of Progress 1957–1967* (D. H. Efron, ed.) pp. 835–851, Washington, D.C.

Kissin, B., Schenker, V., and Schenker, A. C., 1959a. Adrenal cortical function and liver disease in alcoholics, *Amer. J. Med. Sci.* **238**: 344.

Kissin, B., Schenker, V., and Schenker, A., 1959b. The acute effects of ethyl alcohol and chloropromazine on certain physiological functions in alcoholics, *Quart. J. Stud. Alc.* **20**: 480.

Kissin, B., Schenker, V., and Schenker, A. C., 1960. The acute effect of ethanol ingestion on plasman and urinary 17-hydroxycorticoids in alcoholic subjects, *Amer. J. Med. Sci.* **239**: 690.

Knott, J. R., 1965. Electroencephalograms in psychopathic personality and in murderers, in *Applications of Electroencephalography in Psychiatry* (W. P. Wilson, ed.) pp. 19–29, Duke Univ. Press, Durham, N.C.

Korman, M., Knopf, I. J., and Austin, R. B., 1960. Effects of alcohol on serial learning under stress conditions, *Psychol. Rep.* **7**: 217.

Kotani, K., 1965. EEG studies on endogenous psychoses and alcohol intoxication, *Bull. Osaka Med. Sch.*, Suppl. **12**: 11.

Lafon, R., Pages, P., Passouant, P., Labauge, R., Minvielle, J., and Cadilhac, J., 1956. Les donnees de la pneumoencéphalographie et de l'électroencéphalographie au cours de l'alcoolisme chronique, *Rev. Neurologique* **94**: 611.

Lewis, E. G., Dustman, R., and Beck, E. C., 1970. The effects of alcohol on visual and somatosensory evoked responses, *Electroenceph. Clin. Neurophysiol.* **28**: 202.

Little, S. C. and McAvoy, M., 1952. Electroencephalographic studies in alcoholism, *Quart. J. Stud. Alc.* **13**: 9.

Lloyd-Smith, D. C. and Gloor, P., 1961. Abnormal photic sensitivity in alcohol with-drawal syndrome, *Electroenceph. Clin. Neurophysiol.* **13**: 496.

Lolli, G., Nencini, R., and Misiti, R., 1964. Effects of two alcoholic beverages on the electroencephalographic and electromyographic tracings of healthy men, *Quart. J. Stud. Alc.* **25**: 451.

Marinacci, A. A., 1955. The electroencephalogram in forensic alcoholism, *Bull. Los Angeles Neurol. Soc.* **20**: 177.

Marinacci, A. A., 1963. A special type of temporal lobe (psychomotor) seizures following ingestion of alcohol, *Bull. Los Angeles Neurol. Soc.* **28**: 241.

Mello, N. K. and Mendelson, J. H., 1968. Alterations in states of consciousness associated with chronic ingestion of alcohol, in *Neurobiological Aspects of Psychopathology: Proc. 58th Ann. Meeting Amer. Psychopathological Assoc.* (J. Zubin and C. Shagass, eds.) pp. 183–213.

Mendelson, J. (ed.), 1964. Experimentally induced chronic intoxication and withdrawal in alcoholics, *Quart. J. Stud. Alc.* Suppl. No. 2.

Miles, W. R., 1932. Psychological effects of alcohol on man, in *Alcohol and Man*, Macmillan, New York.

Murphree, H. B., Greenberg, L. A., and Carroll, R. B., 1967. Neuropharmacological effects of substances other than ethanol in alcoholic beverages, *Fed. Proc.* **26**: 1468.

Murphree, H. B., Schultz, R. E., and Jusko, A. G., 1970. Effects of high congener intake by human subjects on the EEG, *Quart. J. Stud. Alc.* Suppl. **5**, 50.

Naitoh, P. and Docter, R. F., 1968. Electroencephalographic and behavioral correlates of experimentally induced intoxication with alcoholic subjects, 28th Intern. Congr. Alcohol and Alcoholism, Washington, D.C.

Nathan, P., 1970. Symposium: Learning principles, their clinical application, in *Highlights, XV Ann. Conf. .VA. Cooperative Studies in Psychiatry.*

Newman, H. W., 1959. The effect of alcohol on the electroencephalogram, *Stanford Med. Bull.* **17**: 55.

Obrist, D. and Busse, E. W., 1965. The electroencephalogram in old age, in *Applications of Electroencephalography in Psychiatry* (W. P. Wilson, ed.) p. 185, Duke Univ. Press, Durham, N.C.

Palestini, M., Pisano, M., Rosadini, G., and Rossi, G. F., 1965. Excitability cycles of the visual cortex during sleep and wakefulness, *Electroenceph. Clin. Neurophysiol.* **19**: 276.

Predescu, V., Roman, I., Christian, C., Viani, I., and Terzi, A., 1967. Electro clinical correlations in chronic alcoholism with physical disturbances, *Electroenceph. Clin. Neurophysiol.* **22**: 576.

Salamy, A., Rundell, O. H., and Williams, H. L., 1969. The effects of alcohol on the cortical evoked response. Paper presented at the Ann. Meeting Southwestern Psycholog. Assoc., Austin, Texas.

Schwartz, M. and Shagass, C., 1964. Recovery functions of human somatosensory and visual evoked potentials, *Ann. New York Acad. Sciences* **112**: 510.

Schwartz, M., Shagass, C., Bittle, R., and Flapan, M., 1962. Dose related effects of pentobarbital on somatosensory evoked responses and recovery cycles, *Electroenceph. Clin. Neurophysiol.* **14**: 898.

Shagass, C., 1968. Evoked responses in psychiatry, in *Computers and Electronic Devices in Psychiatry* (N. Kline and E. Laska, eds.) Grune & Stratton, Inc., New York.

Shagass, C. and Jones, A. L., 1957. A neurophysiological study of psychiatric patients with alcoholism, *Quart. J. Stud. Alc.* **18**: 171.

Shagass, C. and Schwartz, M., 1962. Cerebral cortical reactivity in psychotic depressions, *A.M.A. Arch. Gen. Psychiat.* **6**: 235.

Simon, B., O'Leary, J. L., and Ryan, J. J., 1946. Cerebral dysrhythmia and psychopathic personalities, *Arch. Neurol. Psychiat.* **56**: 677.

Spolker, B. and Calloway, E., 1969. Effects of drugs on "augmenting/reducing" in averaged visual evoked responses in man, *Psychopharmacologia* **15**: 116.

Stern, J. A., 1965. Relationships between the EEG and other physiological measures in man, in *Applications of Electroencephalography in Psychiatry* (W. P. Wilson, ed.) pp. 206–225, Duke Univ. Press, Durham, N.C.

Stohr, P. E. and Goldring, S., 1969. Origins of somatosensory evoked scalp responses in man, *J. Neurosurg.* **431** (2): 117.

Thompson, G. N., 1963. The electroencephalogram in acute pathological alcoholic intoxication, *Bull. Los Angeles Neurological Soc.* **28**: 217.

Ulett, G. A., Heusler, A. F., and Wood, T. J., 1965. The effect of psychotropic drugs on the EEG of the chronic psychotic patient, in *Applications of Electroencephalography in Psychiatry* (W. P. Wilson, ed.) pp. 241–257, Duke Univ. Press, Durham, N.C.

Varga, B. and Nagy, T., 1960. Analysis of α rhythm in the electroencephalogram of alcoholics, *Electroenceph. Clin. Neurophysiol.* **12**: 933.

Vaughan, H. G. and Ritter, W., 1970. The sources of auditory evoked responses recorded from the human scalp, *Electroenceph. Clin. Neurophysiol.* **28**: 360.

Victor, M., 1968. The pathophysiology of alcoholic epilepsy, *The Addictive States: Assoc. Res. Nerv. Ment. Dis.* **46**: 431.

Victor, M. and Adams, R. D., 1953. The effect of alcohol on the nervous system, *Res. Publ.: Assoc. Res. Nerv. Ment. Dis.* **32**: 526.

Victor, M. and Brausch, J., 1967. The role of abstinence in the genesis of alcoholic epilepsy, *Epilepsia* **8**: 1.

Weiss, A. D., Victor, M., Mendelson, J. H., and La Dou, J., 1964. Experimentally induced chronic intoxication and withdrawal in alcoholics, *Quart. J. Stud. Alc.* Suppl. No. 2, 96.

Wikler, A., Pescor, F. T., Fraser, H. F., and Isbell, H., 1956. Electroencephalographic changes associated with chronic alcoholic intoxication and the alcohol abstinence syndrome, *Amer. J. Psychiat.* **113**: 106.

Wilson, W. P. (ed.) 1965. *Applications of Electroencephalography in Psychiatry*, Duke Univ. Press, Durham, N.C.

Wilson, W. P. and Short, M. J., 1965. The neuroses and EEG, in *Applications of Electroencephalography in Psychiatry* (W. P. Wilson, ed.) pp. 140–145, Duke Univ. Press, Durham, N.C.

CHAPTER 11

Changes in Cardiovascular Activity as a Function of Alcohol Intake

David H. Knott

Alcoholism Treatment Center
Tennessee Psychiatric Hospital and Institute
Department of Physiology and Biophysics
Department of Psychiatry
University of Tennessee College of Medicine
Memphis, Tennessee

and
James D. Beard

Alcohol Research Center
Tennessee Psychiatric Hospital and Institute
Department of Physiology and Biophysics
University of Tennessee College of Basic Medical Sciences
Memphis, Tennessee

MYTHOLOGY OF ALCOHOL AND THE CARDIOVASCULAR SYSTEM

If one would truly appreciate the classic description of alcohol as "man's psychological blessing and physiological curse" then much of the scientific mysticism surrounding this drug could be removed. The deleterious effects of alcohol on the heart and blood vessels have long been recognized, yet recent and current medical literature tends to promote the "discretionary" use of ethanol in the treatment of various cardiovascular disorders such as angina pectoris, hypertensive cardiovascular disease, and obliterative vascular disease.

Early laboratory studies, especially by Sulzer (1924), which demonstrated that alcohol exerted a dose-dependent depressant effect on the heart and depressed cardiovascular reserve have, until recently, been largely disregarded.

Unfortunately the use and abuse of beverage alcohol is so plagued by emotionalism and personal prejudice that investigative and clinical judgments have been compromised. Importantly, the effect of alcohol on cardiovascular function is being well delineated by recent basic and clinical research efforts and, hopefully, comprehension of this area will be accomplished when the research data from sophisticated studies corroborate many of the observations made by astute clinicians years ago.

The endorsement in the eighteenth century of alcohol in the treatment of angina pectoris by Heberden (1786), and in the twentieth century by Russek et al. (1950) received better acceptance than simultaneous reports dealing with many of the cardiovascular sequelae of alcohol ingestion, some of which have been termed "Munchner Bierherz," (Bollinger, 1884), "alcoholic myocarditis," (Aufrecht, 1895), "myocardie of alcoholics," (Laubry, 1936). Although the concept of alcohol's being a "cardiovascular stimulant" and a "coronary vaso-dilator" is being seriously questioned by medical scientists, it is widely accepted by the lay public.

The use of alcohol in the management of hypertensive vascular disease is based on reports of its hypotensive effects and vasodilatory effects (Lintz, 1934). However, the effect of increasing and decreasing blood alcohol levels on catecholamine release and the dual vasodilating and vasoconstricting properties of alcohol and its metabolites cause one to scrutinize the use of this drug in hypertensive vascular disease.

Advocating ethanol in the treatment of arteriosclerosis with thrombotic complications was originally based on its basic dilatory and analgesic properties (Cook and Brown, 1932).

The literature is abundant with reports extolling the salutary effects of alcohol on the heart and blood vessels; many reports also exist outlining the cardiotoxicity of the drug and condemning its clinical use—and in some instances its social use. Confusion has been the natural consequence. As the reader interprets much of the biochemical, physiological, psychological, and pathological information concerning alcohol use and abuse, the following points must be remembered:

1. Different species of laboratory animals have different sensitivities to ethanol; comparison of the data between species and extrapolation of the data to the human situation must be done with great caution.

2. Too often abnormalities associated with acute alcohol poisoning are used to explain those found with chronic alcohol ingestion. Care must be exercised in this regard, since there are many differences in the physiological and biochemical sequelae of acute versus chronic alcohol ingestion.

3. Often the physiologic benefit assigned to the use of alcohol has been primarily a psychologic benefit. The thymoleptic, analgesic, and sedative effects of ethanol do not necessarily make this drug physiologically profitable.

4. Clinical observations and studies involving the "alcoholic patient" must be scrutinized in terms of the diagnostic criteria for alcoholism. Unfortunately, too often "the alcoholic" is considered to be the malnourished, vomitus and feces covered, wine-drinking, jobless, homeless, totally despairing person found on Skid Row. This attitude, for many years, fostered the idea that the primary form of heart disease associated with alcohol ingestion was beriberi heart disease. This concept is as absurd as the postulate of cirrhosis being the most common form of liver disease resulting from the excessive consumption of alcohol. In these instances, nutritional deficiencies were prominent etiologically, and appreciation of the pathophysiologic effects *per se* of ethyl alcohol were obscured.

As the disease concept of excessive alcohol ingestion is accepted and modified, it is essential that emphasis also be directed toward the "alcoholic population" as a whole, since only 8–10% of this group classically fits into the Skid Row category. Important to the physician is the distinct possibility that alcoholism can be a medical disease without necessarily having the usually associated sociological or psychological stigmata. As knowledge of the normal and abnormal dynamics of the cardiovascular system progresses, it behooves the interested scientific experimenter and practitioner to consider objectively the effects of the ubiquitous and misunderstood drug, ethyl alcohol, on the structure and function of the heart and blood vessels. Thereby, this subject will be demythologized.

ALCOHOL AND THE CENTRAL CIRCULATION

Alcohol and Cardiac Metabolism

Earlier reports elucidating ethanol-induced functional impairment of the myocardium have stimulated investigators, especially within the past 5 years, to explain this impairment on a metabolic basis. To date, the significant work has involved primarily dogs and humans as experimental subjects. While an occasional attempt has been made to study the effect of alcohol in the chronic experimental situation, most of the information gained thus far has been derived from measurements made during and after acute alcohol administration.

In experimental animals, e.g., rats and dogs, and in chronic alcoholic patients given ethanol on an acute basis, the metabolic pattern of cardiac muscle undergoes similar changes. Principally the triglyceride content of myocardial tissue increases significantly. Regan *et al.* (1966) after infusing intravenously 0.1 mg/kg/min of 15% ethyl alcohol to dogs, observed an immediate increase in glyceride content of cardiac tissue, apparently on the basis of an augmented triglyceride uptake by the heart without triglyceridemia. Concomitant with this was a decrease in free fatty acid uptake by the myocardium. Beard and Knott found a marked elevation of left ventricular triglyceride after administering 3 g/kg ethanol (33% v/v solution) daily for 2 weeks via gastric tube to mongrel dogs compared to pair-fed controls given an isocaloric, isovolumetric amount of glucose daily. No differences were noted, however, in cardiac tissue phospholipids and cholesterol between the control and experimental groups. Marciniak *et al.* (1968) examined the influence of chronic experimental alcoholism in dogs which consumed a daily average of 400–600 ml of 20% ethanol for 10 weeks. At the end of the experiment cardiac triglyceride content was increased 182% in the dogs drinking alcohol compared to pair-fed controls. Using chronic alcoholic patients, Wendt *et al.* (1966) investigated the acute effects of alcohol ingestion on metabolic pathways of the human myocardium and reported an increment in cardiac triglyceride without an increase in triglyceride uptake. This was accompanied by a decrease in free fatty acid uptake. While previous studies in dogs suggested accumulation of myocardial glyceride on the basis of increased uptake, these authors postulate an enhanced triglyceride production by cardiac tissue, utilizing as a substrate increased available amounts of ethanol and acetate consequent to alcohol metabolism.

The increased ratio of NADH/NAD resultant from the intra- and extra-myocardial metabolism of alcohol to acetaldehyde could stimulate the incorporation of acetate into an enhanced fatty acid synthesis. Interestingly, the changes observed in cardiac lipid metabolism due to the acute effects of ethanol are similar to those noted with the acute effects of catecholamine infusion (Maling *et al.*, 1960).

While there is general agreement concerning the nature of—if not the exact mechanism of—altered fat metabolism in the heart, the influence of alcohol on carbohydrate metabolism is somewhat more enigmatic. Regan *et al.* (1965) and Wendt *et al.* (1966) noted a shift toward predominately carbohydrate metabolism in the heart following the administration of alcohol to experimental animals and chronic alcoholics. In both studies, immediately following alcohol infusion or ingestion, cardiac uptake of glucose and lactate increased while that of pyruvate decreased; the respiratory quotient also changed in the direction suggestive of an augmented utilization of carbohydrate. However, these changes were not consistent, as noted by Wendt *et al.* (1966) who calculated the extra-mitochondrial oxidation-reduction potential difference across the heart and found it to be negative in some patients (indicating some degree of glycolysis) and positive in others, especially those patients in whom lactate was liberated by the myocardium following alcohol ingestion. However, the intramitochondrial oxidation-reduction potential as calculated from the ratios of acetoacetate to betahydroxybutyrate in coronary vein and arterial blood increased in the majority of patients, indicating the absence of glycolysis. In chronic study with dogs, Marciniak *et al.* (1968) found no change in the activity of glycolytic enzymes in the myocardial tissue of dogs after the ingestion of 400–600 ml of 20% ethanol daily for 10 weeks, while the activity of these enzymes was increased significantly in brain and liver tissue. This suggests an acute but not chronic effect of alcohol on carbohydrate metabolism of the heart. In the acute studies, Regan *et al.* (1966) reported a reversion of the respiratory quotient to control values within $2\frac{1}{2}$ hr after the infusion of ethanol in dogs. Thus the acute effect of alcohol appears to be an increased cardiac uptake of glucose, lactate, and acetate, the latter two of which also increase in arterial blood primarily due to the metabolism of ethanol *per se*. Metabolism of these substrates temporarily decreased the primary utilization of lipids for energy; however, the effects are short lived, and data thus far do not indicate a permanent effect on enzyme activity specifically concerned with glycolysis.

Little information exists concerning the chronic effect of ethanol on cardiac electrolyte metabolism, and the few studies dealing with the acute effect of ethanol in this regard need further extension. Hypomagnesemia has long been associated with acute and chronic alcoholism presumably due to increased urinary excretion rate of magnesium. This hypomagnesemia has been speculatively associated with arrhythmias frequently seen in the alcoholic patient. Wendt *et al.* (1966) measured blood levels of and myocardial extraction of magnesium 30 min after the ingestion of 6 oz of vodka (84% alcohol by weight) in 11 chronic alcoholic patients and observed no change in either of these parameters. Even though these negative data are based on an acute study, valid evidence does exist of depleted total body magnesium stores resultant from ethanol ingestion (Flink *et al.*, 1954). The impact of this depletion on cardiac magnesium stores demands further investigation.

Regan *et al.* (1966) observed a release of potassium and phosphate ions from the myocardium of dogs infused with alcohol, and this ion egress was sustained for 2 hr after the infusion of ethanol was stopped. The authors linked the electrolyte loss to that seen in ischemic necrosis, except the defect produced by ethanol was of shorter duration and appeared to be reversible. Beard (1963) reported a significant increase in intracellular sodium concentration and a significant decrease in intracellular potassium of skeletal muscle of dogs receiving via gastric tube 3 g/kg 33% ethanol (v/v) daily for 8 weeks. Although the same trend was noted in cardiac tissue, the changes were not of statistical significance when compared with those of pair-fed control animals. There is evidence, however, that ethanol may inhibit the active transport of sodium from within the cell, thus lowering the transcellular membrane potential and possibly increasing the sensitivity of affected tissue to various stimuli (Israel-Jacard and Kulant, 1965) Such an effect awaits investigation in regard to the myocardium.

Improvement of the laboratory methodology in measuring biogenic amines, in addition to appreciation of the profound effect of ethanol on biogenic amine metabolism, has directed attention to the clinical implications of this effect on cardiovascular dynamics. James and Bear (1967) concentrating on the cardiac effects of both ethanol and acetaldehyde on the heart, studied the physiologic response of the sinus node of dogs to these compounds. Interestingly, ethanol exerted only a depressant effect (negative chronotropism) on sinus node activity while acetaldehyde effected a positive chronotropic and inotropic effect. The mechanism is apparently a release of myocardial norepinephrine caused by acetaldehyde, and this direct cardiac effect is enhanced by increased release of extracardiac catecholamines (primarily from adrenal medulla) also caused by acetaldehyde. Further, acetaldehyde can stimulate release of serotonin which can cause paradoxically, both a depressing and stimulating effect on the myocardium, depending on the circumstances. Although this information is based on acute studies, if further research should substantiate a progressive and sustained depletion of myocardial norepinephrine due to chronic exposure to alcohol, this deficiency may be involved in the genesis of alcohol-induced cardiac disease. The complicating influence of decreased myocardial norepinephrine reserves during congestive heart failure of many causes is already recognized (Chidsey and Braunwald, 1966).

Recent evidence defining the effect of alcohol on serotonin and catecholamine metabolism allows speculation that chronic ethanol insult could result in a cardiac tissue buildup of hydroxylated analogues of these amines with a consequent detriment to both structure and function.

Basic experimental and clinical observations of the cardiac sequelae of trace metal deficiencies, particularly zinc and copper (Shields, 1962), and the recent implication of cobalt toxicity in cardiovascular disease of beer drinkers has aroused scientific suspicion of the role which ethanol-induced abnormalities in trace metal metabolism may play in various forms of alcoholic cardiomyopathies. Wendt et al. (1966) reported that zinc was liberated from the myocardial cell in 6 of 10 patients at 3 hr after the ingestion of 6 oz of vodka (84% alcohol by weight). Of these 6 patients, 2 showed an increase in alcohol dehydrogenase activity in coronary venous blood 30 min after alcohol ingestion. These authors postulated a positive correlation between the increase in serum zinc concentration and release of alcohol dehydrogenase, which occurs chiefly from extramyocardial sources (e.g., liver). In the same study no significant changes occurred in serum copper levels. On the other hand, Gudbjarnason and Prasad (1969) noted a significant decrease in serum zinc accompanied by an increase in urinary excretion of zinc at 1–3 hr after ingestion of 6 oz of vodka (42% ethanol) in alcoholic patients. A significant increase in serum copper was also observed simultaneously. The authors postulate that these changes could be due to an altered cellular permeability (cardiac and extracardiac tissue) with a consequent leakage of these trace metals into the circulation. The role of the trace metal, cobalt, in alcohol-induced cardiac impairment appears to be one of toxicity of excess combined with malnutrition (Kesteloot *et al.*, 1968). Obviously this is an area in which the concepts are fragmentary and future research should delineate the etiologic aspect and the diagnostic and prognostic value of ascertaining alterations in trace metabolism due to ethanol, not only in regard to cardiac dysfunction, but also to the entire spectrum of pathophysiology.

Alcohol and Cardiac Mechanical Performance

The primary focus of investigative attention in regard to hemodynamic effects of ethanol has been the central circulation—i.e., the myocardium. Although some of the data are conflicting, owing primarily to differences in experimental subjects and methodology, there is general agreement that alcohol, as a drug *per se*, can exert a cardiotoxic effect resulting in impairment of mechanical performance.

Webb and associates (1967), employing an open chest heart-lung preparation in which aortic pressure, stroke volume, heart rate, pH, p_{CO_2}, HCO_3 and temperature were all experimentally manipulated to remain within a normal range, observed that extremely high blood levels of ethanol (900 mg/100 ml) did not produce any impairment of myocardial contractility. Schmitthenner *et al.* (1958) effected a blood alcohol concentration of 70–120 mg/100 ml in anesthetized, open chest dogs and consequently noted an increased cardiac output and left ventricular work without a concomitant increment in coronary blood flow.

In vitro experiments have strongly suggested a direct depressive effect of alcohol on cardiac contractility. Using the isolated rat atrium, Gimeno *et al.* (1962) reported an ethanol-induced decrease in contractility which was dose-dependent. A concentration of greater than 40 mg/100 ml in perfusing fluid effected progressive cardiac dilatation and a decreased myocardial contractility of the isolated turtle heart according to Wakim (1946). It is difficult, however, to interpret data derived from isolated heart-lung and open-chest preparations or *in vitro* experiments in which important variables influencing cardiac function are artificially controlled or removed.

As early as 1924, Sulzer, working with the intact dog and measuring the volume of the heart as well as pressures found a progressive dilatation of the heart which appeared to be ethanol dose-dependent. Sulzer concluded that "the power of the heart to adapt itself to more work suffers under the influence of alcohol."

Cardiac output, peripheral resistance, coronary flow, coronary resistance, stroke work, arterial blood pressure, and myocardial functional capacity were evaluated in intact anesthetized dogs before and after the infusion of ethanol (0.5 g/kg body weight) to a calculated blood alcohol level of 70–100 mg/100 ml by Degerli and Webb (1963). Coronary blood flow decreased with a concomitant elevation of coronary resistance, while the work load of the heart increased. The function curves showed marked cardiac deterioration 1 hr after ethanol infusion. In another acute study, Regan et al. (1966) ascertained myocardial contractility by simultaneously measuring left ventricular end diastolic pressure and stroke volume in dogs infused intravenously with 15% ethanol (0.1 mg/min) for 2 hr to an average total dose of 36 g ethanol. Alcohol produced evidence of depressed left ventricular contractility within 15 min after beginning the infusion; however, no concomitant changes in heart rate or systemic arterial pressure were noted. The impaired contractility persisted with only partial recovery at 5 hr (3 hr after infusion of ethanol). Coronary blood flow did not decrease until 30 min after beginning the infusion and the data suggest that the reduction in coronary blood flow was secondary to impaired ventricular function. In addition to the decreased coronary flow, O_2 extraction by the left ventricle was also reduced. As noted previously, these changes in mechanical performance were accompanied by increases in potassium, phosphate, and transaminase concentrations in coronary sinus blood.

Only a few attempts have been made thus far to study the central hemodynamic effects of chronic experimental alcoholism. In a pilot study recently completed, Knott and Beard administered ethanol (33% v/v, 1.65 g/kg body weight) via gastric tube daily for 6 months to six apparently healthy, well-nourished mongrel dogs and measured cardiac output, arterial pressure, circulation time, stroke volume and heart rate in the unanesthetized, nonintoxicated state on a weekly basis and found no significant change in any of these parameters when compared to average preethanol values. However, in another chronic study Maines and Aldinger (1967) administered orally 35% ethyl alcohol daily for 7 months to rats. After 4 months, a consistent and significant decrease in ventricular isometric systolic tension, blood pressure, and heart rate was noted in thoracotomized, anesthetized rats as compared to similarly prepared, pair-fed controls. Careful attention was afforded the nutritional status of the alcohol-fed rats and the authors were satisfied that the functional impairment evident in the experimental group was due to the ethanol itself rather than to nutritional or vitamin deficiencies. The current paucity of and conflicting nature of data obtained from chronic studies need further elucidation.

A number of clinical reports dealing with the compromise of cardiovascular function in patients apparently suffering from "alcoholic cardiomyopathy" provides a wealth of retrospective information concerning the influence of chronic ethanol ingestion in the human. These reports have prompted a number of studies dealing with the acute effects of ethanol on cardiac performance in both alcoholic and nonalcoholic patients.

In the previously cited study, Wendt *et al.* (1966) administered 6 oz of vodka to 11 hospitalized chronic alcoholic patients and although at 30 min after ingestion, demonstrable metabolic abnormalities had occurred, no concomitant change was noted in heart rate, mean arterial pressure, cardiac output, stroke volume, and peripheral vascular resistance. In an experiment of somewhat longer duration, Regan *et al.* (1965) investigated the central hemodynamic response in eight, apparently well-nourished alcoholic patients with no evidence of heart disease who ingested 110 g alcohol for 2 hr. Left ventricular function was then measured for the subsequent 4 hr. There was a progressive decrease in stroke output attended by significant elevation of left ventricular end diastolic pressure after the first hour of alcohol ingestion before the blood alcohol level had reached 150 mg/100 ml, which incidentally is still the "legal limit" for public intoxication in many states. Thus, while the exact mechanism is still enigmatic, it is becoming increasingly obvious that the acute effects of ethyl alcohol involve a depression of the mechanical performance of cardiac muscle.

A somewhat more subtle but extremely important aspect to this problem is the possible effect of acute and chronic alcohol ingestion on the functional reserve of the heart and cardiovascular system—i.e., the capacity of the heart to respond to a superimposed stress. The occurrence of, but not the prevalence of, clinically ostentatious cardiovascular dysfunction in "heavy drinkers" is related not only to difference in individual susceptibility but also the nature and duration of any superimposed stress on the heart and blood vessels.

Left ventricular function was evaluated in chronic alcoholic patients without evident heart disease by progressively elevating aortic pressure with infusions of angiotensin and observing the relation of ventricular filling pressure to stroke output and work of the left ventricle (Regan *et al*, 1965). In each case, the alcoholic subject exhibited a greater rise in end-diastolic pressure and a concomitantly smaller increment in stroke work than that observed in controls.

A common and often dread phenomenon in both civilian and military medicine is the acutely or chronically alcohol-intoxicated patient who suffers trauma (e.g., hemorrhage, burns, muscle crushing). Using an acute, sublethal, standardized hemorrhage technique, Knott *et al.* (1963) and Knott and Beard (1967) studied the response in terms of survival and cardiovascular function of dogs subjected to acute or chronic alcohol administration. There was no difference in the cardiovascular response and survival in hemorrhaged dogs after one episode of acute intoxication. However, when the hemorrhagic stress was repeated weekly for 6 weeks, during which time alcohol (3 g/kg body weight, 33% v/v solution) was given via gastric tube daily, a significant difference was noted between the pair-fed controls and experimental animals. The latter group, in addition to having a higher mortality rate, also exhibited signs of cardiovascular deterioration post hemorrhage—such as more severe and prolonged hypotension, frequent arrhythmias, a more seriously depressed cardiac output and stroke volume. As the influence of alcohol plus other stress factors is being studied, it is becoming increasingly obvious that the functional capacity of the cardiovascular system (and other physiologic systems) is impaired by alcohol.

Alcohol and Cardiac Morphology

At necropsy, early observers described the alcohol-damaged heart as being dilated, flabby, with gross and microscopic evidence of fibrosis of ventricular muscle. The present ability of experimental medicine to anatomically and chemically dissect the cell and its subcellular elements has offered exciting new evidence of the cardiotoxicity of ethanol. Ferrans *et al.* (1965) histochemically and electron microscopically examined autopsy material from chronic alcoholic patients in whom the clinical diagnosis of alcoholic cardiomyopathy had been made. Seven of the eight patients died in congestive heart failure, and it is important to note that malnutrition was a complicating factor in most of these patients. Structurally, hypertrophy and degeneration of cardiac muscle fibers, varying degrees of myocardial fibrosis, and endocardial fibroelastosis were noted. Myofibers were characterized as exhibiting hyalinization, edema, vacuolization, and increased granularity. Histochemical analysis of cardiac tissue revealed no accumulation of carbohydrate, a marked accumulation of lipid material, increased lipofucsin possibly suggestive of increased lysosomal activity, and a decrease in staining reaction for several mitochondrial oxidative enzymes which indicated mitochondrial damage. These authors were quick to emphasize, however, that many of the changes observed could be attributed to hypoxia, congestive heart failure, increased levels of catecholamines, and postmortem changes. Their data provide a comparative basis to delineate structural changes in the progress of alcoholic cardiomyopathy at a time earlier than necropsy.

In this regard Alexander (1966) attempted to correlate the electron microscopic picture of myocardial needle biopsy material from patients with a history of alcoholism and suffering heart failure from obscure causes. A destruction of the contractile elements, megamitochondria, and a dilated sarcoplasmic reticulum were found in those patients with a history of excessive alcohol ingestion. Alexander noted that these findings were similar to those observed in experimental potassium and magnesium deficiency. There is no information thus far that defines a morphological lesion specific to alcohol-induced cardiac disease; however, these data are invaluable in the ultimate attempt to delineate the biochemical and physiologic mechanism(s) involved.

Alcohol and the Electrophysiology of the Heart

Simultaneous with the use of electrocardiography as a diagnostic tool was the recognition that heart disease associated with excessive alcohol ingestion was characterized by aberrant cardiac electrical activity. Practically every clinical and experimental report dealing with alcohol and the heart describes electrocardiographic abnormalities; among those most frequently mentioned are conduction defects consisting of increased P-R intervals, decreased P-R intervals, right or left bundle branch block or both, tall peaked T waves, low slurred T waves, prominent U waves, and alterations of rhythm described as atrial fibrillation, atrial and ventricular premature beats, ventricular prefibrillatory tachycardia, and ventricular fibrillation (Alexander, 1968; Evans, 1964; Burch et al., 1966). Obviously, the particular abnormal pattern is dependent on the status of the patient, his blood alcohol level, nutritional status, fluid and electrolyte balance, etc. In addition to the cardiotoxicity of alcohol, a number of concomitant disorders have been implicated in the genesis of the EKG alterations—hypokalcemia, hypomagnesemia, acid-base shifts associated with hyperventilation, hypocalcemia, etc.

Evans (1964) has attempted to define an EKG pattern pathognomonic for alcoholic cardiomyopathy. He describes specific changes in the following areas: (a) T-wave changes: a spinous, tall T-wave seen best in the precordial leads; a cloven, low T-wave seen best in leads I and II; a dimpled T-wave seen best in lead I. For the most part, abstinence from alcohol is followed by return to normal of the T-wave pattern, (b) arrhythmias—extrasystoles arising from multiple and diverse foci usually accompanied by tachycardia or atrial fibrillation and (c) conduction defects consisting of transient bundle branch blocks.

The zeal of Evans to use the EKG diagnostically for alcoholism is not shared by other clinicians. His description of the EKG associated with alcoholism is quite valid; however, most persons agree that, while EKG abnormalities are frequently associated with heavy drinking, diagnostic specificity of these abnormalities for alcoholism or alcohol-induced heart disease is lacking (Alexander, 1968; Burch et al., 1966).

Interest in the influence of alcohol on the excitability of neuromuscular tissue is one of long standing. In 1797 von Humboldt observed an initial increase in excitability followed by a decrease ultimately resulting in complete block, when he applied ethanol to frog nerve-muscle preparations. Only recently has attention been focused on the mechanism involved in changes in excitability. Using intracellular microelectrodes, Knutsson (1961) measured the effects of varying concentrations of ethanol on the membrane potential and membrane resistance of sartorius muscle fibers of the frog. An increase in membrane conductance, lowering of membrane resistance, and a decrease in resting membrane potential were noted and appeared to be somewhat dose-dependent. These changes were reversed after the ethanol was washed out of the muscle bath. Knutsson speculated that alcohol altered membrane permeability to sodium or potassium or both. Subsequent research data suggest that ethanol affects many tissues accordingly, i.e., by changing membrane permeability to sodium and allowing intracellular sodium to accumulate (Beard, 1963). This initially lowers resting membrane potential and the tissue becomes hyper-excitable. Theoretically, if enough sodium accumulates within the cell, excita-bility will essentially be abolished. An alternative or perhaps additional theory, postulated on the work of Israel-Jacard and Kalant (1965), is that alcohol impairs the active removal of sodium which inherently leaks into the cell, the end result being the same as described above. Thus, one aspect of the mechanism of alcohol-induced altered electrical activity of tissues is an increment in intra-cellular sodium concentration with its consequent effect on membrane potential and excitability. Although there are yet no specific data relating to cardiac muscle *per se* in this regard, the generalized status of the patient as described previously probably accounts for the electrophysiologic abnormalities associated with acute and chronic alcoholism. However, the effect of alcohol on calcium and magnesium availability and binding at the cell membrane needs to be elucidated, in addition to more extensive investigation of sodium-potassium transport across cell membranes.

Although there is still some confusion concerning the exact influence of ethanol on the heart and some conflict does exist in the data, there is general agreement that ethanol is cardiotoxic, directly or indirectly, or both. Mechanisms to explain the biochemical and physiologic basis for this toxicity are currently largely speculative in nature and demand further investigation. However, in these authors' experience and in a selected review of the literature, the following areas represent the most salient opportunities for basic and clinical research and thought:

1. The increased osmolality of the serum and extracellular fluid caused by alcohol is certainly of physiologic significance. Although alcohol will eventually equilibriate in the total body water, this process is not immediate and the ethanol molecule *per se* will increase osmolality of the serum and extracellular fluid. An increased osmolar gradient is known to depress myocardial contrac-tility and to effect a loss of potassium, phosphate, and transaminase from cardiac muscle cells (Regan *et al.*, 1964). The deleterious effects of a rapid increase in serum osmolality can be partially abrogated by sympathectomy. Osmolality changes may account for some of the acute effects of alcohol; however, the reported delay in transcapillary distribution of ethanol needs to be further delineated and corroborated. It is interesting to speculate that the deleterious effects of increased serum osmolality due to acute alcohol intoxication on cardiac muscle and function may be a factor with other tissues—such as the central nervous system.

2. Many of the biochemical and physiologic sequelae in the heart of acute alcohol administration are similar to the effects of a sudden increase in catechol-amines. The increase in cardiac triglyceride uptake and increased cardiac work

are examples of this. However, the increased work of the heart caused by catecholamines is usually accompanied by an increased O_2 consumption; conversely O_2 consumption generally decreases with the increased work load caused by alcohol. Certainly alcohol and its metabolites can cause augmented release of catecholamines; investigation of the influence of alcohol on the sensitivity of tissues to catecholamines should prove interesting.

3. While an increase in catecholamines may be associated with acute alcoholism, theoretically, continued alcohol ingestion or repeated acute episodes could deplete the stores of these amines. This is suggested by the depletion of myocardial norepinephrine by acetaldehyde. The ultimate effect of this depletion on cardiac reserve and its relationship to other stresses (e.g., infection, trauma, exercise) awaits further clarification. Certainly research concerning the acute and chronic effects of ethanol on biogenic amine metabolism in regard to all physiologic systems is an exciting area.

4. The metabolic consequences of acute and chronic alcohol administration including primarily the decreased utilization of normal energy substrates with an accumulation of cardiac triglycerides, an increased NADH/NAD ratio with its complications, a secondary reduction in coronary blood flow, the release of, and altered activities of extra- and intramitochondrial enzymes, and electrolyte and trace metal abnormalities must play a major role in the various types of cardiac dysfunction observed. The exact mechanism and specificity of effect of alcohol on these aspects of metabolism are still somewhat obscure. Although overt malnutrition is an exacerbating factor, there is consensus that alcohol can impair cardiac function in the apparently well-nourished organism. Further explanation, however, should be afforded functional versus absolute deficiency states in this regard. The direct and indirect effect of alcohol and its metabolites on cardiac function is indeed a complex phenomenon. Future examination of some of the areas outlined above should be of great diagnostic, therapeutic, and prognostic benefit. The obvious intent is medical management based on scientific fact rather than mythology.

ALCOHOL AND THE PERIPHERAL CIRCULATION

The basic and clinical descriptions of the result of alcohol administration on the dynamics of the peripheral circulation (pressure-volume-flow relationships) indicate no effect, a hyperdynamic effect, and a hypodynamic effect (Fewings et al., 1966). The conflicting data are caused primarily by differences in investigative methodology, doses of alcohol, choice of experimental subjects, presence or absence of anesthesia, presence or absence of coexisting cardiovascular disease, etc. There is a paucity of information concerning the effect of ethanol on the peripheral vasculature; it appears that any drastic change in peripheral hemodynamics caused by alcohol is largely a reflection of the action this drug exerts on the central circulation.

There is one effect which has been attributed to alcohol for many years—i.e., that it exerts a vasodilatory action on blood vessels. Early and recent reports indicate a dilation of cutaneous arterioles of the extremities with a concomitant reduction in blood flow to the corresponding musculature of that extremity (Cook and Brown, 1932; Fewings et al., 1966). Recently, however, investigators have observed a distinct difference in the changes in regional blood flow depending on whether or not alcohol was ingested orally or infused intravascularly directly into the region (usually an extremity) being studied. Effecting forearm arterial blood concentrations of alcohol ranging from 34 mg/100 ml to 1875 mg/100 ml, Fewings et al. (1966) noted constriction of the arterioles of both the skin and musculature. Since neither sympathectomy nor previous treatment with phenoxybenzamine abolished this vasoconstriction, vasoconstrictive nerve stimulation or the constricting action of catecholamines did not appear to be involved. Rather, the data suggested that ethyl alcohol *per se* exerted a direct vasoconstrictive action on arteriolar smooth muscle of both the cutaneous and muscle vasculature. Conversely, when alcohol was given orally to human subjects, vasodilation of arterioles supplying the skin of the upper extremities was observed, while vasoconstriction of vessels supplying the corresponding muscle mass occurred simultaneously. The authors further postulated that the dilatory action of alcohol is a central reflex phenomenon involving neural vasomotor regulatory centers while the vasoconstricting action is a direct effect on arterioles. An additional theory states that ethyl alcohol is totally vasoconstrictive in its effect and that the metabolite acetaldehyde is the compound responsible for vasodilation occurring after alcohol ingestion.

No matter which mechanism(s) is involved, current data make it mandatory that the old myth of alcohol's being a peripheral (and coronary) vasodilator be reevaluated. The direct vasoconstrictive effect and the unpredictable central vasomotor effect of ethanol suggests that the use of this drug in the treatment of obliterative peripheral vascular disease and its use associated with small artery surgery (Arrants et al., 1967) may actually be detrimental.

There is little information concerning morphologic changes in the peripheral vasculature following acute or chronic alcohol administration. Appreciation of many factors which affect the central circulation, such as osmolality increases, intracellular metabolic abnormalities, solute retention, transcellular electrolyte shifts, and catecholamine release and depletion should stimulate electron microscopic and histochemical study of peripheral vascular tissue in an effort to correlate local hemodynamic effects of ethanol with structural changes.

The time-honored and clinically promoted concept of alcohol as a vasodilator is obviously open to serious scrutiny. This epitomizes the embryonic nature of present knowledge concerning alcohol and the peripheral vascular system. As further research and clinical observation are correlated concerning the central and peripheral cardiovascular action of ethanol and its metabolites, then attention can be properly directed to the functioning of this entire physiologic system, including central and peripheral reflexes, functional capacity, etc.

ALCOHOL AND SPECIFIC CARDIOVASCULAR DISORDERS

Cardiovascular Abnormalities Associated with the Acute Withdrawal Syndrome

Prominent cardiovascular manifestations of acute withdrawal include sinus tachycardia, frequent arrhythmias, (primarily consisting of ventricular premature contractions—although atrial premature beats are not uncommon) and systolic and diastolic hypertension. Unless dehydration (which occurs infrequently) is a concomitant, blood volume is normal or often elevated (Beard and Knott, 1968). The physiologic basis for these phenomena include not only the cardiotoxicity of ethanol but also increased release of catecholamines associated with withdrawal. If the total medical management of the patient is skillful and well informed, the signs and symptoms mentioned above are readily reversible—usually within a few hours. Important points to consider in treatment are:

1. Unless the tachycardia and extrasystoles are obviously hemodynamically detrimental, no specific antiarrhythmic measures are necessary.

2. Care should be taken in the use of intravenous fluids in the acutely withdrawing patient. Although this has been frequently employed, recent evidence indicates that many acute alcoholics are actually overhydrated (Knott and Beard, 1969). Since the cardiac reserve in these patients may be decreased, a further increase in vascular volume could seriously compromise cardiovascular function.

3. Unless the blood pressure is extremely high, specific antihypertensive measures are not needed. Also, care must be taken with the use of some psychopharmacologic agents, such as the phenothiazines, which can produce rapid and severe hypotensive episodes.

If cardiovascular abnormalities persist after the withdrawal syndrome has been successfully treated, then more severe pathophysiology must be suspected and diagnosed.

Alcoholic Myocardiopathy

Myocardial disease which cannot properly be attributed to congenital, hypertensive, or arteriosclerotic causes is becoming increasingly subject to etiologic, diagnostic, therapeutic, and prognostic consideration. The association between alcohol and primary cardiac disease has been recognized for over a hundred years; medical appreciation of this association, however, is more recent. For many years, clinical consideration centered around malnutrition's being the primary factor involved and seldom was alcohol endorsed as an important etiologic agent in the heart disease of chronic alcoholics, most of whom were malnourished. Realization of cardiac dysfunction due to alcohol without apparent nutritional deficiencies has added a new dimension to the diagnosis and treatment of heart disease. Although a number of reports and review articles exist concerning alcoholic myocardiopathy, those by Evans (1964), Burch et al. (1966), and Alexander (1968) are particularly pertinent and useful.

The disorder known as alcoholic myocardiopathy covers a broad spectrum of signs and symptoms and exists to different degrees of severity; prognosis is directly dependent on early diagnosis and treatment. Early diagnosis is a direct reflection of the physician's willingness to deal with alcohol-related problems in patients other than those of the Skid Row variety. The following may be helpful in the diagnostic approach to alcoholic myocardiopathy:

1. Consumption of large quantities of beer has been frequently associated with this disorder; however, it appears that any type of alcoholic beverage can be involved.

2. The patient is often obese and will complain of shortness of breath, palpitations, decreased exercise tolerance, intermittent paroxysmal nocturnal dyspnea, persistent tachycardia; chest pain is rare except in advanced stages; sweating is common, paresthesia of hands and feet and nocturnal cramping of muscles of the lower extremities occur frequently; premature arcus senilis is a frequent finding. Too often these signs and symptoms are attributed to obesity—by both the patient and the physician.

3. The electrocardiogram, which may be of special value, especially in early forms of myocardiopathy, often shows cloven, blunted, or dimpled T-waves; sinus tachycardia with frequent extrasystoles from multiple foci; and a T-P phenomenon described by Alexander (1968) as a prolongation of the S-T segment so that the P-wave is inscribed before the T-wave returns to the isoelectric line.

4. Additional laboratory tests, especially of liver function, are generally abnormal. The hepatic dysfunction may be clinically asymptomatic. Electrolyte concentrations are usually normal; hyperventilation can effect respiratory alkalosis which may be superimposed on a frequent tendency toward metabolic (lactic) acidosis.

5. Radiologic findings depend on the stage of the disease process. Early findings may include only prominent hilar vascular shadows with little or no congestion in the peripheral lung fields. The hilar vessels return to normal size after diuresis.

The above points apply primarily to earlier forms of alcoholic myocardiopathy; more advanced forms present with overt congestive heart failure often characterized by atrial fibrillation, marked congestion of peripheral lung fields, S-T segment depression and frequent bundle branch blocks, generalized cardiac enlargement, prominent venous distention and pulse in the neck, gallop rhythm, systolic murmur of either mitral or tricuspid insufficiency; hepatomegaly with markedly elevated enzymes, hypesthesia and paresthesia in the lower extremities, occasionally signs of pericardial effusion, electrolyte abnormalities with equivocal changes in p_{CO_2} and HCO_3.

The aggressiveness of the treatment obviously depends on the severity of the pathophysiology. Early cases respond well to diuresis. If congestive signs persist, digitalization is helpful—although care must be taken to ensure against hypokalemia and hypomagnesemia, both of which adversely affect the action of the cardiac glycosides. Proper use of safe psychopharmacologic agents is a useful adjunct in controlling anxiety, depression, etc. Advanced forms often demand a vigorous antiarrhythmia regimen (any arrhythmia is poorly tolerated), correction of any thromboembolic tendency which can occur, and immediate correction of any concomitant disorder (e.g., infection, electrolyte depletion, etc.). Prognosis is poor with advanced stages; early diagnosis is extremely important. Tantamount to recovery are psychotherapeutic measures which will encourage total abstinence from alcohol. The willingness of the practicing physician to involve himself—not only with the medical management of the heart disease, but also with the psychosocial rehabilitation of the patient, is often a critical factor in the patient's ultimate recovery or demise.

Beriberi Heart Disease

Thiamine is essential for normal carbohydrate metabolism, being directly involved in the conversion of pyruvic to lactic acid. Thiamine deficiency leads to the condition of beriberi. The thiamine deficiency can occur owing to a diet deficient in thiamine or the metabolism of excessive amounts of carbohydrate, or both. Chronic alcoholism, with associated malnutrition, is definitely related etiologically to some cases of beriberi heart disease (Evans, 1964), although this disorder occurs comparatively less frequently than alcoholic myocardiopathy. Diagnosis depends on a suggestive dietary history, a hyperkinetic circulation (e.g., increased cardiac output and decreased circulation time; in most cases of alcoholic myocardiopathy there is a hypokinetic dynamic pattern with decreased cardiac output). The physiologic basis for circulatory dysfunction in beriberi is a marked reduction in peripheral vascular resistance with a reflex tachycardia and compensatory increase in cardiac output. Conversely, failure of the central circulation (heart) is the primary process in alcoholic myocardiopathy. Generalized cardiac enlargement with pulmonary artery dilatation, peripheral neuritis, elevated blood concentration of pyruvic acid, and decreased blood thiamine levels also are common findings. Treatment consists of aggressive thiamine replacement and supportive care. Psychotherapeutic recalcitrance in this group is more common than with those suffering alcoholic myocardiopathy since beriberi heart disease caused by alcoholism is observed chiefly in the chronic court, recidivistic type of inebriate.

Alcoholic Perimyocardiopathy ("Beer Drinker's Cobalt Myocardosis")

As diagnostic sophistication was afforded alcohol-induced cardiovascular disease, a number of reports began to appear (Kesteloot et al., 1968) describing a clinical syndrome in beer drinkers with similar and distinctive features. In the differentiation between this and alcoholic myocardiopathy, these features include pericardial effusion, polycythemia, EKG change consisting of decreased QRS voltage, S-T segment depression, and T-wave inversion primarily in the left precordial leads, increased circulation time; usually signs of congestive failure are not as prominent. Although this clinical picture has been described in patients drinking beer which apparently did not contain cobalt, this trace metal was not measured. It appears that alcoholic perimyocardiopathy of the beer drinker is a result of two factors—cobalt toxicity (large doses of cobalt experimentally can cause the cardiovascular changes noted above) and malnutrition—specifically a protein deficiency. Treatment is directed toward correcting the immediate circulatory embarrassment (pericardial effusion and increased blood viscosity) and prognosis depends on the stage of the disorder and the ability of the patient to remain abstinent—especially from beer.

Hypertensive-Cardiovascular Disease

There are conflicting impressions concerning the incidence of hypertensive vascular disease in an alcoholic population. Retrospective analysis of data derived from the chronic, indigent alcoholic population reveals no increase in occurrence of hypertensive vascular disease (Sullivan and Hatch, 1964); however, if one is willing to extend the diagnosis of "alcoholism" to those residing outside the social and emotional ambient of Skid Row, then a somewhat different situation obtains. D'Alonzo and Pell (1968) report that hypertension was 2.3 times greater in problem drinkers than in nondrinking controls. The primary criterion for "hypertension" used was elevated diastolic and systolic blood pressure.

Hypertensive vascular disease has a complex etiology. Too often the diagnosis of hypertensive disease is made in the alcoholic (or "heavy drinker") on the basis of frequently elevated blood pressures, when indeed the hypertension is based on emotional lability, or possibly related to acute or subacute withdrawal from alcohol. Certainly the pathophysiology associated with alcohol ingestion (e.g., sodium retention, tissue inflammation, necrosis) could contribute to the genesis of hypertensive vascular disease. But in these authors' experience, hypertensive vascular disease is no more common in the alcoholic patient (not Skid Row) than in the general population. The lability of the blood pressure, however, is more pronounced; thus care must be exercised in diagnosing hypertensive vascular disease (not hypertension) in the patient suffering from alcoholism.

Fortunately, the medical consequences of ethanol ingestion are being recognized, investigated, diagnosed, and treated. Credibility is thus being afforded the "disease concept" of alcoholism and the medical profession is necessarily becoming more involved diagnostically and therapeutically. Notwithstanding its relevance to the "alcoholic," appreciation of the toxicity of the drug, alcohol, will augment the general health of the population—approximately 70-75% of which consume beverage alcohol.

Medicine is faced with the responsibility of demythologizing ethanol as a "prescription" drug and of improving physiologic rehabilitative measures. An exciting area in this regard is the cardiovascular impairment resultant from the effect of alcohol. The thorough investigation of this subject is exemplary of the increasing effort to strip the quasimoralistic pseudoreligious veneer from the use and abuse of ethyl alcohol, and to define objectively and pragmatically "man's psychological blessing and physiological curse."

ACKNOWLEDGMENT

The authors' work has been supported in part by PHS Research Grant HE-11355 from the National Institute of Health, and by a continuing grant from the State of Tennessee Department of Mental Health, Division on Alcoholism.

REFERENCES

Alexander, C. S., 1966. Idiopathic heart disease. II. An electron microscopic examination of myocardial biopsy specimens in alcoholic heart disease, *Amer. Heart J.* **41:** 229.
Alexander, C. S , 1968. The concept of alcoholic myocardiopathy, *Med. Clin. North Amer.* **52:** 1183.
Arrants, J. E., Clontz, F. D., and Jurkiewicz, M. J., 1967. Intravenous ethyl alcohol in small artery surgery, *Amer. Surgeon* **33:** 457.
Aufrecht, G., 1895. Die Alkoholische myocarditis mit nachfolgender leberer Krankung und Zeitweiliger albuminurie, *Dtsch. Arch. Klin. Med.* **54:** 615.

Beard, J. D., 1963. Some Influences of Chronic Ethanol Administration in the Dog, Ph.D. Thesis, University of Tennessee, (I.C. Card No. Mic 64-7849) 144p. Univ. Microfilms. Ann Arbor, Michigan

Beard, J. D. and Knott, D. H., 1968. Fluid and electrolyte balance during acute withdrawal in chronic alcoholic patients, *J. Amer. Med. Assoc.*

Bollinger, O., 1884. Veber die haufigkeit und ursachen der idiopathischen herzhypertrophie in Munchen, *Dtsch. Med. Wschr.* **10**: 180.

Burch, G. E., Phillips, Jr., J. H., and Ferrans, V. J., 1966. Alcoholic cardiomyopathy, *Amer. J. Med. Sci. 1921 69.*

Chidsey, C. A. and Braunwald, E., 1966. Sympathetic activity and neurotransmitter depletion in congestive heart failure, *Pharmacol. Rev.* **18**: 685.

Cook, E. N. and Brown, G. E., 1932. The vasodilating effects of ethyl alcohol on the peripheral arteries, *Proc. Mayo Clinic* **7**: 449.

D'Alonzo, C. A. and Pell, S., 1968. Cardiovascular disease among problem drinkers, *J. Occup. Med.* **10**: 344.

Degerli, I. V. and Webb, W. R., 1963. Alcohol, cardiac function and coronary flow, *Surg. Forum* **14**: 252.

Evans, W., 1964. Alcohol and the heart, *The Practitioner* **196**: 238.

Ferrans, V. J., Hibbs, R. G., Weibaecher, D. G., Black, W. C., Walsh, J. J., and Burch, G. E., 1965. Alcoholic cardiomyopathy, a histochemical study, *Amer. Heart J.* **69**: 748.

Fewings, J. D., Hanna, M. J. D., Walsh, J. A., and Whelan, R. F., 1966. The effects of ethyl alcohol on the blood vessels of the hand and forearm in man, *Brit. J. Pharmac. Chemother.* **27**: 93.

Flink, E. B., Stutzman, F. L., Anderson, A. R., Konig, T., and Fraser, R., 1954. Magnesium deficiency after prolonged parenteral fluid administration and after chronic alcoholism complicated by delirium tremens, *J. Lab. Clin. Med.* **43**: 169.

Gimeno, A. L., Gimeno, M. F., and Webb, J. L., 1962. Effects of ethanol on cellular membrane potential and contractility of isolated rat atrium, *Amer J. Physiol.* **203**: 194.

Gudbjarnason, S. and Prasad, A. S., 1969. Cardiac metabolism in experimental alcoholism, in *Biochemical and Clinical Aspects of Alcohol Metabolism* (V. M. Sardesai, ed.) pp. 266–272, Charles C. Thomas, Springfield, Ill.

Heberden, W., 1786. Some account of a disorder of the breast, *M. Tr. Roy. Coll. Physicians*, London, **2**: 59.

Humboldt, F. A., von, 1797. Versuche uber die gereizte muskel-und nervenfaser. Band II, Decker und compagnie, Heinrich August Rottmann, Berlin.

Israel-Jacard, Y. and Kalant, H., 1965. Effect of ethanol on electrolyte transport and electrogenesis in animal tissues, *J. Cell. Physiol.* **65**: 127.

James, T. N. and Bear, E. S., 1967. Effects of ethanol and acetaldehyde on the heart, *Amer. Heart J.* **74**: 243.

Kesteloot, H., Roelandt, J., Willems, J., Claes, J. H., and Joossins, J. V., 1968. An inquiry into the role of cobalt in the heart disease of chronic beer drinkers, *Circulation* **37**: 854.

Knott, D. H. and Beard, J. D., 1967. The effect of chronic ethanol administration on the response of the dog to repeated acute hemorrhages, *Amer. J. Med. Sci.* **254**: 172.

Knott, D. H. and Beard, J. D., 1969. A diuretic approach to acute withdrawal from alcohol, *Southern Med. J.* **62**: 485.

Knott, D. H., Barlow, G., and Beard, J. D., 1963. Effects of alcohol ingestion on the production of and response to experimental hemorrhagic stress, *New Eng. J. Med.* **369**: 292.

Knutsson, E., 1961. Effects of ethanol on membrane potential and membrane resistance of frog muscle fibers, *Acta. Physiol. Scand.* **52**: 242.

Laubry, C., 1930. Les myocardie, in *Noveau Traite de Pathologie Interne*, pp. 530–552, Doin, Paris.

Lintz, W., 1934. Practical consideration of essential hypertension, *Clin. Med.* **41**: 412.

Maines, J. E. and Aldinger, E. E., 1967. Myocardial depression accompanying chronic consumption of alcohol, *Amer. Heart J.* **73**: 55.

Maling, H. M., Highman, B., and Thompson, E. C., 1960. Some similar effects after large doses of catechol amines and myocardial infarction in dogs, *Amer. J. Cardiol.* **5**: 628.

Marciniak, M., Gudbjarnason, S., and Bruce, J. A., 1968. The effect of chronic alcohol administration on enzyme profile and glyceride content of heart muscle, brain and liver, *Proc. Soc. Exptl. Biol. Med.* **128**: 1021.

Regan, T. J., Weisse, A. B., Oldewurtel, H. A., and Hellems, H. K., 1964. The hyperosmotic effects of ethanol and sucrose on the left ventricle, *J. Clin. Invest.* **43**: 1289.

Regan, T. J., Weisse, A. B., Moschos, C. B., Lesnick, L. J., Nadami, M., and Hellems, II. K., 1965. The myocardial effects of acute and chronic usage of ethanol in man, *Trans. Assoc. Am. Physns.* **78**: 282.

Regan, T. J., Koroxendis, G., Moschos, C. B., Oldewurtel, H. A., Lehan, P. A., and Hellems, H. K., 1966. The acute metabolic and hemodynamic responses of the left ventricle to ethanol, *J. Clin. Invest.* **45**: 270.

Russek, H. I., Naegele, C. F., and Regan, F. D., 1950. Alcohol in treatment of angina pectoris, *J. Amer. Med. Assoc.* **144**: 355.

Schmitthenner, J. E., Hafkenschiel, I. F., Williams, J., and Riegels, C., 1958. Does alcohol increase coronary blood flow and cardiac work? *Circulation* **18**: 778.

Shields, G. S., 1962. Studies on copper metabolism, XXXII, cardiovascular lesions in copper deficient swine, *Amer. J. Path.* **41**: 603.

Sullivan, J. F. and Hatch, L. K., 1964. Alcoholism and vascular disease, *Geriatrics* **19**: 442.

Sulzer, R., 1924. The influence of alcohol on the isolated mammalian heart, *Heart* **11**: 141.

Wakim, K. G., 1946. The effects of ethyl alcohol in the isolated heart, *Fed. Proc.* **5**: 109.

Webb, W. R., Gupta, D. N., Cook, W. A., Sugg, W. L., Bashour, F. A., and Unal, M. O., 1967. Effects of alcohol on myocardial contractility, *Dis. of the Chest* **52**: 602.

Wendt, V. E., Ajluni, R., Bruce, T. A., Prasad, A. S., and Bing, R. J., 1966. Acute effects of alcohol on the human myocardium, *Amer. J. Cardiol.* **17**: 804.

CHAPTER 12

The Effect of Alcohol on the Autonomic Nervous System of Humans: Psychophysiological Approach*

Paul Naitoh

Navy Medical Neuropsychiatric Research Unit
San Diego, California

ELLIE.   What do you run away for ? To sleep ?
CAPTAIN SHOTOVER.   No. To get a glass of rum.
ELLIE (frightfully disillusioned)   Is that it ? How disgusting! Do you like being drunk ?
CAPTAIN SHOTOVER.   No: I dread being drunk more than anything in the world.
—I drink now to keep sober—rum is not what it was: I have had ten glasses since you
came; and it might be so much water . . .

Heartbreak House, by G. Bernard Shaw
(vol. 1, pp. 567–568, Dodd, Mead, & Co., New York, 1963)

INTRODUCTION

This chapter presents the modern psychophysiological approach to alcoholism
to assist those who are actively engaged in this area and searching for new ways
to hasten solutions of such medicosocial problems. Since the problems of

---

*List of Abbreviations can be found on p. 424.

alcoholism have been investigated under various scientific disciplines, it is not too presumptuous to assume that the scientific background of research workers on alcoholism is necessarily heterogeneous, covering a wide spectrum of disciplines.

This chapter is written for three classes of potential readers. First, those who are primarily trained in neuroanatomy and neurophysiology but relatively unaware of recent progress in the psychophysiology of alcoholism should read the first, third, and fourth section of this chapter. A cursory reading of the section on the autonomic nervous system will suffice, as it contains no new information. Second, those who are well acquainted with psychophysiological work but relatively unfamiliar with recent advances on alcoholism research and who also require a quick overview of neuroanatomical and neurophysiological facts and theories will find the first, second, and fourth sections useful. They do not need to read the section on psychophysiological concepts. Finally, beginning students and clinicians of alcoholism who are willing to explore all the materials necessary for undertaking the psychophysiological approach to alcoholism will find that the chapter provides sufficient details on all relevant topics.

Although neurophysiologists and psychophysiologists can skim over the materials presented in the second and third sections without impairing comprehension of the remaining materials in the chapter, all readers will benefit by at least one careful reading of all sections, as they contain concrete examples related to important concepts in research on alcoholism.

In reviewing the current state of knowledge in a medical area, the writer is faced usually with the task of choosing only a few of many research findings because of their sheer bulk. The situation appears to be quite different in the psychophysiological literature on alcoholism. Although psychophysiological interests in alcoholism are old and extensive, as evidenced in many clinical observations, the number of papers which satisfy modern methodological rigor has remained small. Unlike the usual review, then, this chapter includes details on the manner in which the experiments have been conducted as well as the experimental results. Instead of brief and somewhat cryptic descriptions of many studies, a few studies will be examined in depth to provide the reader with a real appreciation of how a psychophysiological study on alcoholism is carried out.

A rough organization of the chapter is as follows: First, an anatomical description of the autonomic nervous system (ANS) will be given. Then, two ANS systems, cardiovascular and electrodermal, are singled out of many others for relatively detailed descriptions. [The author is indebted to Rickles (in press) for the organization of the neuroanatomical data included in this review.] This basic anatomical review is followed by some examples of psychophysiological studies and psychophysiological concepts. Finally, alcohol effects on cardiovascular and electrodermal systems are discussed in some detail. A close examination of these sections will show some differences and similarities between the psychophysiological approaches and physiological or physiopathological research strategies.

Psychophysiology is an interdisciplinary science, as much as biochemistry and biomedical engineering have been. Mastery of its principles requires mature understandings in both psychology and physiology of the ANS and behaviors. Such a mastery is very hard to achieve, and the only justification for such an interdisciplinary approach is in the new information it has been able to discover. The reader is entrusted with the task of evaluating these studies of alcoholism to see how they can increase the effectiveness of therapeutic processes and drug education, and how they can improve the chances of rehabilitating the chronic alcoholic.

Alcoholics and Nonalcoholics

In biomedical researches involving human patients, selection of experimental subjects with pathognomonic symptoms has been as crucial as the choice of adequate methods of research. However, in some instances, reliable discrimination of those patients with the disease of interest was very difficult because of ill-defined disease characterization and inaccuracy in diagnosis. Psychophysiological studies of alcoholism have been hampered by ambiguity and lack of consensus on what patients would be regarded as alcoholics.

Jellinek's definition (1960) of five species of alcoholism—alpha (problem drinkers), beta, gamma, delta, and epsilon (periodic drinkers)—is often cited, and sometimes used in alcoholism research. Gamma alcoholism is distinguished by an increased tissue tolerance to alcohol, the presence of withdrawal symptoms, cravings for alcohol, loss of control over drinking, yet an intact ability to "go on a water wagon." The gamma alcoholics have poor health and impaired interpersonal relations. They constitute the predominant type of alcoholism in the United States and Canada. Delta alcoholism is characterized by control over drinking, but an inability to abstain from drinking. In agreement with Jellinek, Keller (1960) regards "loss of control" over drinking distinctly characteristic of alcoholism. Mardones (1963) considers the incapacity to control drinking as a sign of "functional alteration of the central nervous system appearing through prolonged use of liquors" (p. 146).

Is a loss of control over drinking the pathognomonic symptom of alcoholism? Recent studies on drinking behaviors of the alcoholics conducted by Mendelson and his associates and summarized by Mello (1968) suggest strongly that a loss of control over drinking may remain an "unvalidated construct."

"Alcoholismic" drinking by alcoholics could be defined mostly on the social and interpersonal frame of reference, skirting around the use of unvalidated constructs, such as loss of control over drinking and an inability to abstain. Such social and interpersonal definitions of alcoholism stress a noticeable decline in annual income, deteriorated interpersonal relations, and a lack of smooth social and economic gains. However, such behavioral characterizations fail to encompass a group of the alcoholics who are not jailed for drunkenness, and are not on Skid Row. The non-Skid Row alcoholics who are among the financially successful are said, according to *Manual on Alcoholism* (1968, p. 7), to be "one of the most sizeable, and certainly one of the most seriously neglected, groups" of alcoholics.

Despite a lack of a universal and explicit definition of alcoholism and alcoholics, most alcoholism researches do require, one way or another, a provisional but sufficiently detailed definition of the alcoholics. This is because alcoholics, through their prolonged use of alcohol, are quite different quantitatively as well as qualitatively in their reactions to alcoholic beverages in comparison with the nondrinkers and nonalcoholics. Without a carefully screened group of alcoholics as the experimental subjects, any researches could easily be sidetracked to pharmacological studies of alcohol effects, rather than the primary objective of studying alcoholism. Whatever definitions are used, it is always feasible for the investigators to clarify disposition of the alcoholics in explicit terms. The validity of such definition of a group of alcoholics could be examined later in a separate epidemiologic and behavioral study. For example, alcoholics could be defined as those who abuse alcoholic beverages, crave more alcohol after consumption of a certain amount, show tremor, anxiety, tension, insomnia, anorexia, and other withdrawal symptoms; need "the morning drink" (Holmberg and Marten, 1955). The jailed alcoholics offer unique opportunity to the researchers as they are completely dry for a known period of time. Thus, Mendelson and his colleagues (1964) selected alcoholics from approximately 800 inmates in a correction institution, on the basis of histories of alcoholism of 6–22 years, as well as experiences of withdrawal symptoms of tremulousness, hallucinosis, and delirium tremens.

Another way of choosing alcoholics is the procedure utilized by Docter and his associates (1964, 1966). They hired a group of casual laborers through a local employment service. First the vocational placement office judged some casual laborers as "alcoholics" mainly through knowledge about their histories of employment. Then, an interview was conducted to establish four points: (1) at least 10 years of heavy drinking with or without blackouts, delirium tremens, tremulousness, or hallucinosis; (2) a progressively decreasing employability or an inability to sustain constant employment at the given occupational level (hence, showing a decreasing amount of annual income), (3) whether they acknowledge that drinking had been a significant daily problem, and (4) at least one arrest due to drunkenness (including drunken driving, disorderly conduct, criminal conduct associated with intoxication or with a need for additional drink). After the referrals answered "yes" to the above four questions, they were regarded as alcoholics: then they were subjected to a physical examination and a further medical interview to screen out those with cirrhosis of the liver, recent ulceration of the gastrointestinal tract, hyperacidity, and gross neurological disorders. The mean profile of such chosen 25 "non-Skid Row alcoholics" (Docter *et al.*, 1966) was age 45; weight, 166 lb; 11 years of school; median annual income of $6000; arrested three or four times; and roughly 26 years of heavy drinking.

Obviously, the outcome of research depends on the rigor exercised in selecting the experimental subjects. This is particularly true in alcoholism studies; efforts are made in this chapter to describe the kinds of subjects utilized in experiments under discussion.

Autonomic Nervous System (ANS)

The nervous system consists of somatic and autonomic components, although anatomically and physiologically neither nervous system component could claim complete independence from the other (Mitchell, 1953). The somatic nervous system includes the motor and sensory neurons and their nerve fibers innervating the skin, the skeletal muscles, the joints, and those nervous structures involved in audition, vision, pain, touch, proprioception, and olfaction. The autonomic nervous system (ANS) includes all neurons and their fibers which sense and regulate the visceral organs and the glands.

In psychophysiological studies of alcoholism, as much importance should be attached to the understanding of functional roles of the ANS as to the selection of subjects. This is because the psychophysiological disciplines are based heavily on the findings of physiology and anatomy of the ANS.

The term autonomic was suggested by John N. Langley in 1898 to reflect his contemporary thinking that the ANS activities are largely independent of conscious and volitional control.

Current conceptualization of the anatomical organization of the ANS has undergone some changes since Langley. The ANS can no longer include only the peripherally situated collections of the ganglia, the plexuses, and the nerves entirely out of the central cerebrospinal axis. In this chapter, the ANS is discussed as a neural structure found not only in cerebral cortex, limbic system, hypothalamus, medulla and midbrain, and spinal cord, but also in the neural structures outside of the cerebrospinal axis.

Another recent reformulation in understanding the ANS reflects a partial dissolution of the dichotomy between the somatic and autonomic nervous system, and a stress placed on the somatovisceral integrations (Gellhorn, 1967; Germana, 1969; Ingram, 1960). A recent modification of the traditional concept that the ANS function could not come under voluntary control has been one of many challenges exercised to break down a dichotomy of the somatic *vs.* autonomic activities.

Within the ANS, a functional antagonism has been described by Gaskell in 1885 as the anabolic or catabolic type of the autonomic nerves, but it is Langley who conceptualized a division of the sympathetic and parasympathetic nervous systems (SNS and PNS). The great sympathetic nerve was conceived by J. B. Winslow in 1772, because the sympathetic ganglia are in frequent communication (in sympathy) with almost all the other principal nerves of the body. As a general rule, most vital organs are innervated by both the SNS and PSN. Both nervous system components are in antagonistic relations; blockade of the PNS often resembles a stimulation and an excitation of the SNS. Hence, measurements of the visceral organs may not permit a sure estimation of the SNS or the PNS influence alone. Various autonomic functioning tests indicate the balance of two antagonistic divisions of the ANS. Only when one nervous system has been placed under pharmacologic or physiological inhibitions, e.g., atropine to block the parasympathetic mechanism, can one obtain relatively sure information about the other nervous system. Table 1 shows an expected pattern of autonomically regulated visceral organs under four possible combinations of (1) SNS excitation and PNS inhibition S^+P^-, (2) SNS inhibition and PNS excitation S^-P^+, (3) SNS and PNS in excitation S^+P^+, and (4) SNS and PNS in inhibition S^-P^-.

ANS, Psychophysiology, and Alcoholism

In psychophysiological studies, the experimental arrangements are made to induce a certain discriminable psychological state in the subjects, then attempts are made by the experimenters to determine the effects of the induced psychological state on the functions of autonomic variables. In some psychophysiological studies, however, a preexisting psychological state such as that of schizophrenia is examined, instead of an artificially induced psychological state. In other psychophysiological experiments, a psychological task is given to the subjects to create certain task-oriented psychological states, such as vigilance and focused attention. The induced psychological state could be fear, anger, euphoria (Ax, 1964; J. Schachter, 1957; Schachter and Singer, 1962), or anxiety (Goldstein et al., 1965, 1966; Kelly, 1966).

A variety of methods can be used to establish a desired psychological state, and the induction of some psychological states would require a subtler technique than others. An elaborately constructed instruction to the experimental subjects (see "explicit sets" of Sternbach, 1966), deception of the subjects (Ax, 1953; Schachter and Singer, 1962; Schachter, 1966), presentation of a movie (Sternbach, 1962; Goldstein et al., 1965, 1966; Speisman, 1965), a manipulation of ingrained attitudinal and learned sets (see Sternbach, 1966), hypnosis (Abrams, 1964; Blum and Blum, 1967; Lazarus, 1965), conditioning (Finkelstein et al., 1945; Franks, 1963; Gantt, 1957; Hobson, 1966; McGonnell and Beach, 1968) and

TABLE 1. Model of Autonomic Response Patterns[a]

	Apparent sympathetic dominance (S^+P^-)[b]	Apparent parasympathetic dominance (S^-P^+)	ANS Hyperactivity (S^+P^+)	ANS Hypoactivity (S^-P^-)
Salivary output	low	high	high	low
Heart period	short	long	?	?
Systolic blood pressure	high	low	?	?
Palmar skin conductance	high	low	high	low
Finger temperature	low	high	low	high
Pupillary diameter	large	small	small	large

[a] Taken from Wenger (1957) with modification.
[b] S = Sympathetic; P = Parasympathetic; + = Excitation; − = Inhibition.

drugs (e.g., F. G. Johnson, 1969, Kissin, Schenker, and Schenker, 1959) have been used in establishing certain psychological states as a preliminary step to be taken before psychophysiological studies are conducted.

In a narrow sense, the discipline of psychophysiology is represented by the scientific efforts to find ANS and, on occasions, electromyogram (EMG) and electroencephalogram (EEG) correlates of artificially induced or naturally occurring psychological states within the individual subjects. The independent variables are the psychological states, and the dependent variables are autonomic, EMG, and EEG functionings. The basic premises of psychophysiology would be: (1) participation of the visceral and muscular responses are *sine qua non* for successful induction of each psychological state, and also for the existence of distinct psychological states, and (2) each different psychological state involves different bodily processes. A formal definition of the discipline of psychophysiology is proposed by Stern (1964), and is discussed fully by Sternbach (1966).

Although whether there is a unique physiological pattern for each psychologically discriminable state remains unresolved (S. Schachter, 1966; Plutchik and Ax, 1967; L. C. Johnson, 1969), the psychophysiological approach can pose and answer a number of very important questions, for example, the effects of sustained pathologic psychological states on the internal organs as exemplified in psychosomatic medicine.

The utility of such psychophysiological approaches to the problems of alcoholism unfortunately has not been explored fully, and psychophysiology has contributed much less than it could to clarify alcoholism. Among the few psychophysiological studies conducted in the past, an evaluation of the ANS function during alcohol intoxication has yielded measures which assisted not only a medico-legal determination of drunkenness, but also helped establish a concept of tissue tolerance to alcohol and in developing a concept of equally effective dose (EED) of alcohol for both alcoholics and nonalcoholics (Goldberg, 1966; Mizoi et al., 1963, 1967, 1969; Morikawa et al., 1968). Similar studies involving ANS and EEG activities during a period of sustained experimentally induced intoxication have revealed, at least partially, the nature of the psychological state which alcoholics had been seeking to attain by their drinking (Bernal and Docter, 1962; Docter et al., 1964, 1966; Mendelson, 1964; Mello, 1968). The traditional pharmacologic emphasis of alcohol being a sedative, hypnotic, or tranquilizer is beginning to be replaced by more psychophysiologically adequate conceptualization of alcohol as a drug that has both stimulant and sedative properties, depending on dose level and the individual subjects.

After an adequate and fully documented selection of the experimental subjects with sufficient grasp of the ANS in the role of genesis of adaptive behaviors, the psychophysiological studies start with earnest intent to unravel genesis and sustenance of alcoholism in man.

AUTONOMIC NERVOUS SYSTEM

Anotomical Overview

Details of the ANS organization have been given in many monographs (Gillilan, 1954; Kuntz, 1953; Mitchell, 1953; Monnier, 1968). The somatic and autonomic nervous systems can be distinguished in the CNS.

The somatic nervous system provides man with control of locomotion, and with muscular, sensory, and intellectual capacities to manipulate his external environments. The ANS sustains, through its autonomous and involuntary controls over the vital organs, the optimal conditions for the circulatory, respiratory, alimentary, and genitourinary functions. The ANS keeps man's thermal and metabolic conditions in his body within certain limits of tolerance. This active tendency of the human organism to maintain the "inner" environment stable within set limits, despite fluctuating external environments, was called by Claude Bernard "constance du milieu intérieur" in 1858. Walter Cannon named this function of the body "homeostasis." In general, it is agreed that the most important function of the ANS is imposing homeostatic restraints so as to limit physiological and biochemical variations inside the human body within certain tolerable limits.

The ANS has a complex hierarchical organization. This refers not only to the peripherally situated collections of ganglia, plexuses, and visceral nerves which innervate effector organs, but also to the central mechanism located within the cerebrospinal axis (Ingram, 1960). Mitchell (1953) defines the ANS as synonymous with a visceral, vegetative, or involuntary nervous system consisting of central and peripheral parts. The central elements are intrinsic parts of the central nervous system. They are located in the cerebrum, cerebellum, brainstem, and cord. Two paravertebral ganglionated trunks, and various prevertebral, visceral, and vascular nerve plexuses and their branches form the peripheral part.

That the ANS peripheral component can be safely dispensed with in laboratory animals was recognized early in studies of autonomic regulations (Moore, 1930). The autonomically innervated organs will not atrophy in an absence of ANS nerves. Recent development of "immunosympathectomy" which enables a destruction of more than 90% of the sympathetic branch of the ANS in animals (Zamis, 1964) shows again the dispensability of the peripheral ANS for survival.

However, a recognition of the psychophysiologically important somatovisceral integrations was delayed, and only now has it begun to receive adequate attention (Gellhorn, 1967; Ingram, 1960; Germana, 1969). That the ANS-regulated visceral activities cannot be subjugated to voluntary controls has been challenged by the establishment of instrumental (voluntary) conditionings of

autonomically regulated functions (Miller, 1969; see also Katkin and Murray,
1969). Thus, recent advance in our understanding of the ANS modus operandi
tend to dull a once very sharp demarcation line between the somatic and autonomic nervous systems.

The preganglionic neurons in the brainstem and spinal cord are under a
continuous and fluctuating influence through numerous inputs. Some of the
influences are segmental, or suprasegmental; others are supraspinal In contrast
to clearly worked-out anatomical details of the peripheral ANS, the exact
pathways describing the supraspinal influences on the preganglionic neurons
are not available due to their fibers being diffusely scattered, particularly in the
brainstem (Gillilan, 1954).

According to the schema of Monnier (1968), the functions of the peripheral
and central ANS are briefly: (1) the autonomic peripheral organization, consisting of smooth muscle effector organs, glands, autonomic ganglia, and plexuses
ensures proper autonomy of the visceral functions, (2) the lowest central ANS
organization at the spino-rhombo-mesencephalic level ensures homeostatic
restraints on the circulatory, respiratory, alimentary, and other functions
through a variety of vegetative reflexes, (3) the diencephalic organization level
couples neural and hormonal regulation through hypothalamic-hypophyseal
integration, and achieves synergistic interaction of the visceral and somatic
activities of, for instance, defecation and micturition, attack or flight, and a
quest for food, (4) the archicortical and paleocortical level offers the purposeful
viscerosomatic and somatovisceral couplings, and (5) finally the neocortical level
provides man with viscerosomatic integrations of such complexities as regulation
of blood flow of the fingers during fine skilled movements, and adjustment of
breathing during speech; and an increase of blood flow to the muscles in preparation for exercise and in anticipation of flight or fight. At the neocortical level of
somatovisceral integrations, the visceral functions are often subjugated to somatic
functions. Indeed, it has become more and more "justifiable to admit a participation of the hypothalamocortical connections in the regulation of visceral,
motor and affective behavior" (Monnier, 1968, p. 292).

Within the ANS, a psychophysiologically significant functional antagonism
exists between the SNS and PNS. The SNS is known also as the thoracolumbar
division, and the sympathicoadrenal system, whereas the PNS is called also as
the craniosacral division, and the vagoinsulin system.

Anatomically, the SNS consists of (1) the visceral afferents whose cell
bodies are located at the dorsal ganglia of the spinal cord, (2) the neurons which
are situated in the lateral horns of the gray substance at the intermediolateral cell
columns, extending from the first thoracic segment to the second lumbar segment,
and (3) the neurons in the sympathetic trunk ganglion chains. The neurons in
the lateral horns of the spinal cord synapse with autonomic afferents, and in turn
send their myelinated preganglionic fibers as a part of the spinal nerves and

later as the white rami communicantes to enter the paravertebral ganglionated chains. In the sympathetic trunk ganglion chains, the axons of the neurons in the intermediolateral cell column synapse with the neurons in this sympathetic ganglion chain which consists of 22 ganglia (3 cervical, 11 thoracic, 4 lumbar, and 4 sacral ganglia). The neurons in the lateral horns are called the preganglionic neurons, and those neurons in the paravertebral ganglionated trunk are called postganglionic neurons. One preganglionic neuron has been observed to synapse with ten or more postganglionic neurons in the cat. The postganglionic neurons send their unmyelinated axons out of the sympathetic ganglion chains as the gray rami communicantes, and reenter the spinal nerves to reach the effector organs. Some postganglionic fibers leave the sympathetic ganglion trunks sooner and form the sympathetic nerves to reach the effector organs.

The parasympathetic neurons which synapse with the visceral afferents are distinctly grouped in the cranial and sacral portions of the spinal cord. The groups of the preganglionic neurons of visceral roots of the oculomotor, facial, glossopharyngeal, vagus, and accessory cranial nerves send their long parasympathetic preganglionic fibers to the specific target organs in the head and the neck. They terminate at the ganglion situated adjacent to the target organ or within the target organ, and synapse with very few postganglionic neurons. Owing to this anatomical arrangement, the effects of PNS stimulation are sharply circumscribed, and confined to the single organ or even to part of the organ. The sacral parasympathetic component has its preganglionic neurons in the lateral portions of the gray substance of the spinal cord at the level of the third and fourth sacral segments.

As a general rule, the vital visceral organs are usually innervated by both the SNS and the PNS. There are a few exceptions to this principle of double innervation: (1) the sweat gland is innervated only by sympathetic cholinergic postganglionic fibers; (2) the adrenal medulla receives only the preganglionic sympathetic fiber; and (3) most superficial blood vessels are innervated only by the SNS fibers which are both vasodilators and vasoconstrictors.

One additional difference between the SNS and the PNS is found in the fact that different chemical transmitters are involved at the sites of the neuroeffector junction. All preganglionic fibers, both sympathetic or parasympathetic, are cholinergic. In contrast, postganglionic sympathetic fibers are "adrenergic" in that their chemical transmitter at the neuroeffector junctions is norepinephrine and epinephrine.

Table 2 shows the SNS and PNS innervations of the vital organs.

ANS Integration

The ANS regulates many organ systems, and a dominance of SNS over the PNS, or vice versa, can be indirectly shown in many bodily functionings: thus,

TABLE 2. Influences of Sympathetic and Parasympathetic Efferents on Some Visceral Organs[a]

Sympathetic branch				Parasympathetic branch		
Pregang. neurons	Postgang. neurons	Effects of stimulation	Organs	Pregang. neurons	Postgang. neurons	Effects of stimulation
T_{1-2}	Sympathetic trunk	Sweat secretion	Sweat glands	—	—	—
T_{1-2}	Superior cervical ganglia	Pupil dilation	Pupil	Edinger–Westphal components of oculomotor nuclei	Ciliary ganglia	Pupil constriction
T_{1-2}	Superior cervical ganglia	Vasoconstriction and secretion	Parotid salivary glands	Inferior salivary nuclei	Otic ganglia	Secretion of saliva; vasodilation
T_{1-2}	Superior cervical ganglia	Vasoconstriction and secretion	Submandibular and sublingual salivary glands	Superior salivary nuclei	Submandibular ganglia	Secretion of saliva; vasodilation
$T_{1-4(5)}$	All cervical and upper thoracic ganglia	Increase in heart rate; dilation of coronary vessels	Heart	Groups of cells near nuclei ambigui and dorsal vagal nuclei	Intrinsic cardiac ganglia	Cardiac slowing; constriction of coronary arteries
$T_{10}-L_1$	Chromaffin cells	Secretion of epinephrine and norepinephrine	Adrenal medulla	—	—	—

[a] See Mitchell (1953, Tables I and II, pp. 120–123) for details.

increased parasympathetic dominance is suspected when the pupil constricts (miosis), the secretions of the submaxillary and sublingual glands increase, the heart rate slows, the coronary arteries constrict, the bronchial musculatures contract, peristalsis of digestive tract and secretion of hydrochloric acid in the stomach increase, and the anal and vesical sphincter muscles are inhibited.

Psychophysiology has been principally concerned with two ANS integrations of the cardiovascular and electrodermal systems although there have been strong indications that psychophysiology will broaden its scope by exploring many other autonomic functions (Brown, 1967; Venables and Martin, 1967).

Cardiovascular System

The neuroanatomical and physiological bases of the cardiovascular system arc very complicated (Bard, 1960; Berger, 1964; Hillarp, 1960; Hilton, 1966; Ingram, 1960; Lacey, 1967; Mitchell, 1953; Monnier, 1968; Rasmussen, 1957; Timberline Conference, 1956). Many pressor and depressor representations are found on the cerebral cortex; i.e., the motor and premotor areas and the frontal cortex. There are several grounds on which to base an argument that the cerebral cortex participates in the controls of the cardiovascular system. First, anticipation of physical exercise, eating, or emotional situations causes cardiovascular changes. Second, the observed cardiovascular response to physical exercise is too quick to be triggered by the results of peripherally initiated changes. Third, human patients with cortical lesions show an acute vasodilation of the contralateral extremities.

The limbic structures have two separate cardiovascular representations: (1) the posterior-orbital-insular system, and (2) the temporal-cingulate system. In lightly anesthetized cats, a stimulation of the cingulate in the region of the genu of the corpus callosum results in a host of cardiovascular changes through the sympathico-inhibitory system; there is a generalized inhibition of spontaneous movements and respiratory inhibition. The amygdala appears not to be involved in maintaining the cardiovascular tone, but participates mainly in phasic cardiovascular adjustments necessary for emotional behaviors.

Electrical stimulation of the hypothalamus—the integration center for the ANS activities—produces various cardiovascular responses. Anterior hypothalamic excitation produces hypertension and EKG alterations. Supraoptic stimulation brings about a 50–200% increase in the venous outflow of the skeletal muscles without a change in arterial blood pressures. Gellhorn (1943, 1963, 1967) has contributed a great deal in organizing the data to suggest that the hypothalamus can be divided into the parasympathetic division (the anterior hypothalamus, including preopticus, supraopticus, suprachiasmaticus, and hypothalamicus anterior nuclei) and the sympathetic division (the posterior hypothalamus, including mamillaris, ventrolateralis, lateralis, and posterius nuclei). These divisions are based on the heart rate and the blood pressure response after electrical stimulation. Gellhorn also espouses a concept of "tuning" in which a given nervous system reacts more toward sympathetic or parasympathetic dominance. Thus, a "sympathetic tuning" is created by an injection of a hypotensive drug, increasing the reactivity of the posterior hypo-thalamus. However, Bard (1960) has criticized Gellhorn's division of the hypothalamus to SNS and PNS components, and has maintained that the only established parasympathetic pathways are the vagal outflow to heart, the sacral vasodilator fibres to the external genitalia, and secretory fibers to the salivary glands. Bard concluded that there is no validity in attributing a reflex fall in arterial pressure to "any parasympathetic activity other than vagal cardiac inhibition" (Bard, 1960, Suppl. No. 4, p. 19).

Two major working hypotheses have been proposed for the ANS cardio-vascular controls which could become critical in furthering the psychophysio-logical understanding of the cardiovascular regulations.

1. Ordinarily the blood flow through most tissues and organs is controlled by adrenergic sympathetic vasoconstrictor nerve fibers, and the vessels are under tonic vasoconstriction through these fibers. These nerve fibers are a part of a homeostatic loop of vasomotor controls, and the vasomotor status of given vessels is fed back as information assisting the vasomotor center to stabilize the vasomotor tones. However, there are cholinergic sympathetic vasodilator fibers in the skeletal muscles, which play no part in the maintenance of the vasomotor tone—have nothing to do with homeostasis—but which are activated, as shown by Blair *et al.* (1959), by emotional stress and anxiety. These cholinergic *sympathetic* vasodilator fibers originate in the motor cortex, relay at the hypothalamus and tectum, bypass the medullary vasomotor center, and pass into the lateral fasciculus of the spinal cord. Hilton (1966) localized the hypothalamic relay station of this fiber group at the tuber and its neighboring area. Electrical stimulation there elicited not only muscular vasodilation, but also vasoconstric-tion of skin and intestines, tachycardia, pupil dilation, and other autonomic features of the "defense reaction." During the elicitation of this defense reaction, the homeostatic vasomotor reflexes are inhibited. Although the above autonomic response pattern is observed in the cat, Hilton has suggested that the vascular components of preparatory response in man appear quite similar to the "defense response" observed in the cats.

2. Past studies show that an increase of cardiovascular afferent impulses along the glossopharyngeal and the vagus (to the ascending bulbar inhibitory mechanism at the head of the nucleus of the tractus solitarius) result in "a prompter termination of an episode of central, motor and other autonomic activation" (Lacey, 1967, p. 28). That this autonomic feedback deactivates the CNS is experimentally confirmed by a decorticate preparation whose sham rage has been under a tonic inhibitory influence from the carotic pressor receptors; a

transient interruption of impulses from the baroreceptors (i.e., ostensibly a removal of a tonic inhibition) has been immediately and predictably followed by an outburst of sham rage.

The presence of the cholinergic sympathetic vasodilators of the skeletal muscles and also the fact that autonomic negative feedback deactivates the ANS and CNS has left an impact on psychophysiology, and psychophysiological studies of alcoholism. The former observations have been applied in measuring the forearm blood flow rate for an assessment of "anxiety" (Kelly *et al.*, 1966; Rosenberg and Butterworth, 1969), and the latter construct has led to Lacey's (1963, 1967) directional fractionation of the autonomic responses to be explained in the third section.

Electrodermal System

In January of 1888, Féré reported that electrostatic charge on the surface of the body was influenced not only by weather and state of nutrition of skin, but also by various psychological events, such as sensorial stimulation, emotional experiences, and moral emotions. Independently of Féré, Tarchanoff (1890) reported an electrical potential generated by skin when the body was connected directly with a sensitive galvanometer. In 1904, E. K. Müller rediscovered the Féré phenomenon and brought it to the attention of Veraguth, who later published a book on the "psychogalvanic reflex." The acceptance of Féré and Tarchanoff phenomena is spurred by Wechsler's (1925) offering of evidence that the skin responses are specific to emotion and can be used as a measure of emotion.

The skin resistance level (SRL) and skin resistance response (SRR, Féré's exosomatic method) are obtained from an electrical potential applied between two electrodes placed on the palmar or planter surfaces, or fingertips [see Brown (1967) or Venables and Martin (1967) for details]. The SRL and SRR are largely determined by the activities of the sweat glands—their presecretory activities, their number per unit area, a relative rate of the sweat duct filling, and also by certain epidermal factors representing electrochemical properties of the epidermis. The roles of sweat glands on the SRL, and SRR (known also as psychogalvanic response, and galvanic skin response, GSR) were examined by administering atropine to the skin with a process of iontophoresis, blocking cholinergic neuroeffector transmission of sympathetic fibers to the sweat glands. Such atropinization of the skin (i.e., cutting off the sweat glands) results in an increased SRL and an elimination of SRR. However, the SRL and SRR are influenced by the factors other than the sweat gland activity, as shown in the case of an intense vasoconstriction that depresses large SRR's while potentiating the smaller SRR's. Also, by raising the skin temperature, a large increase in the small SRR is observed, leaving the large SRR intact.

Skin potential level (SPL) and skin potential response (SPR, Tarchanoff's phenomenon method) are obtained by placing an electrode on the palm and another reference electrode on an inactivated (i.e., skin-drilled, or a preparation of the skin of which the "horny" layer and the barrier layer are stripped to expose a wet mucous layer) site, and then connecting these two nonpolarizing electrodes to a high input impedance voltmeter. With these electrodes, an endogenous potential difference of -5 to -50 mV can be recorded on the active skin site in reference to the inactivated skin site. This negative standing potential is the SPL. As in the SRR which is superimposed on slowly changing SRL, the SPR occurs on a background of a slowly fluctuating SPL. The SPR is usually a biphasic response—an initial negative wave (alpha wave), followed by a larger positive wave (beta wave). A large negative overshoot after the beta wave is called the gamma wave. The role of the sweat glands in generating negative and positive waves of the SPR remains controversial. Both negative and positive waves of the SPR are eliminated after iontophoresis of atropine to the skin, indicating participation of the sweat glands. The SRR and the negative wave of the SPR have a high correlation, indicating perhaps that these electrodermal responses share the sweat gland activities in common.

At best, the psychological significance of the SPR waves is obscure. However, the SPR has great promise as shown by Fowles and Venables (1969). They have suggested the significance of a large potential across the wall of the sweat glands. They have noted that SPL variations reflect sodium concentration in the sweat gland duct filled with sweat. Solid constituents of sweat are sodium, potassium, chloride, urea, and lactic acid. Sweat is hypotonic in terms of chloride, sodium, and hypertonic in terms of potassium, urea, and lactic acid, when it is compared with plasma. Fowles and Venables have postulated an active sodium pump across the walls of sweat ducts to move sodium out of the sweat in the sweat gland duct into the interstitial tissues. They have proposed further that adrenal cortical secretion of aldosterone, which regulates sodium reabsorption in the kidneys, might be serving a similar function over the 1–4 million sweat glands of man, reducing salt loss by 95%. They cited clinical examples to support their view: a low adrenal activity seen in Addison's disease produces high sweat sodium concentration, and low sodium content in sweat of the patients with excessive adrenal cortical activity of Cushing's disease. Particularly interesting to the psychophysiologist is an observation that sodium reabsorption at the sweat glands increases during stress as a result of overall activation of the hypothalamico-pituitary-adrenal axis, with a consequent rise of aldosterone level and less sodium concentration in sweat, making the SPL more negative than otherwise.

Neuroanatomical and neurophysiological bases of the electrodermal responses are relatively well established. At the cortical level, the premotor area 6 and posterolateral somatic area 2 are known to be involved in both the SPR and the SRR. Area 6 has a strong inhibitory effect on the SPL and SPR. The ablation of the area 6 eliminates, however, the SRR. A frontal cortical lesion eliminates or reduces the SRR. The corticifugal pathways for the SRR involve the pyramidal tracts, frontopontine and temporopontine tracts, vestibular nuclei, nuclei gracilis and cuneatus, corticospinal tracts and finally the posterior and dorsal columns at the cervical cord. Stimulation of the anterior lobe of the cerebellum inhibits the SRR. At the limbic system, a stimulation of the anterior cingulate cortex produces the SRR. A time-locked sustained SRR is observed in synchrony with the amygdaloid discharges. Stimulation of the baso-orbital cortex produces the SPR. Similar stimulation of the tuber region of the hypothalamus results in the SPR and its facilitation. At the midbrain and medulla level of electrodermal response organization, the mesencephalic reticular formation is found mainly facilitatory on the SPR, but the ventromedial pontine and medullary reticular formation are principally and powerfully inhibitory on the SPR. At the level of the spinal cord, ganglia, and nerves, a disappearance of both alpha and beta waves of the SPR is observed after the severance of peripheral nerves, the lumbar and thoracic sympathetics, and the cervical and thoracic cord.

The electrodermal responses of the SRL, SRR, SPL, and SPR are usually taken to be good measures of "anxiety," tension, and an overall high "activation." Darrow (1943) considers that the sweat glands could be the indicator of the intact sympathetic system, but he points out also that it would be questionable to regard the electrodermal responses of the SRL, SRR, or SPR as uncomplicated measures of sympathetic activity, because the sweat gland effector fibers are cholinergic and are under higher influences than the segmental level.

PSYCHOPHYSIOLOGICAL STUDIES OF HUMAN ANS

Some Psychophysiological Experiments

Some psychophysiological experiments are inspired by a scientific desire to describe and confirm the existence of certain psychological states such as sleep, hypnosis, psychotic delusions, instrumentally controlled autonomic functions, chronic stress accompanying chronic diseases (Mahl, 1953), and many other psychological states (L. C. Johnson, 1969). Some psychophysiological studies are initiated by scientific curiosity to look into the bases of "commonsense" knowledge, myths, and traditional views on the interrelations between the psychological processes and physiology.

In the psychophysiology of alcoholism, researchers are spurred by their desire to pin down the validity of commonsense and clinical observations made on alcoholism, and of a myth about the effects of alcohol—its miraculous potency in reducing anxiety, tension, grief, anger, stress, and pains (see Gantt, 1957).

For example, previously a reference was made to Jellinek's five species of alcoholism: alpha, beta, gamma, delta, and epsilon. Some of the discriminators for these species as proposed by Jellinek (1960) appear to lack precise behavioral foundations. Under the conditions of an experimentally regulated "spree" of 30 days in which free as well as operantly determined access to alcoholic beverages was permitted, the chronic alcoholics did not drink themselves into a stupor. They stopped and restarted spontaneously several drinking periods. Their alcohol consumption was under the external control of a reinforcement contingency (Mello, McNamee, and Mendelson, 1968). Mello and her associates have shown that "a loss of control over drinking" could be an "unvalidated construct," a myth of alcoholismic drinking. However, Jellinek's definition of alcoholism species using the constructs of "loss of control" and of "inability to abstain" has remained very influential in research thinking about alcoholism. A psychophysiological study of a "craving for alcohol" appears an eminently appropriate topic, but such a study to find autonomic and EEG correlates of a psychological state of "craving for alcohol" would have a strong possibility, judging from the studies by Mello and her colleagues, of treading into dangerous terrain of scientific facts intricately entangled with the myth of alcoholismic drinking. A difficulty of psychophysiological studies is, then, in establishing unequivocally, and defining operationally, the psychological state before attempts are made to discover its autonomic and EEG correlates. The explicit and operational definition of a given psychological state implies immediately the necessity of extended behavioral studies, or even of longitudinal studies.

Although Jellinek's characterization of the species of alcoholism on the basis of "a loss of control over drinking" is in doubt, his use of an acquired increased tissue tolerance to alcohol (Jellinek, 1960, p. 36) as a definition of alcoholism has been found to have a solid psychophysiological foundation. Habitual and excessive use of alcohol results in increased tolerance to alcohol, and the blood alcohol level becomes less reliable in indicating behavioral as well as physiological impairment.

A task of psychophysiology would be to develop the most reliable measure of the extent of psychologically and subjectively agreed-on "drunkenness," or of the extent to which an individual feels "drunk," regardless of blood alcohol level. Thus, some people feel drunk with a small dose of alcohol, while others require a heavy dose to feel drunk and to show signs of sensorimotor impairment. Another complication of the use of blood alcohol level for expressing the extent of intoxication is the individual difference in response to alcohol. The same blood alcohol level represents psychologically and physiologically quite different levels of intoxication, when a comparison is made between the rising alcohol level of a rapid absorptive phase of drinking and the phase of a declining blood alcohol level. Rosenbaum (1943) has reported an experiment which shows chronic alcoholics becoming clinically intoxicated at the beginning of drinking with 192 mg/100 ml, and becoming sober 5 hr later with a blood alcohol level of 273 mg/100 ml. One subject who became intoxicated at first with 219 mg/100 ml, sobered up 8 hr later with 282 mg/100 ml. Another drink was given at this point, resulting in a second episode of intoxication with a level of 304 mg/100 ml. The subject sobered up 3 hr later at 324 mg/100 ml. Abstinence signs were observed by Isbell and his colleagues (1955) and Mendelson (1968) in experimental subjects who had a blood alcohol level of 100 mg/100 ml. Clearly, there is a state of "drunkenness," operationally defined, which correlates very highly with the blood alcohol level (Mendelson and La Dou, 1964; Goldberg, 1966), but sometimes drunkenness does not correlate with a blood alcohol level.

Psychophysiological Measures of Intoxication

Can the psychophysiological method come up with a measure of alcohol intoxication which is better than the blood alcohol level? An objective measure of alcohol intoxication other than a blood alcohol level would enable individuals to find the amount of alcohol they can drink without incurring gross intoxication. For researchers who wish to compare the alcoholics and the nonalcoholics, a measure which shows the amount of alcohol required to produce a known amount of intoxication for the alcoholics and for the nonalcoholics (that is, an "equally effective alcohol dose"—EED) would be highly desirable.

In psychophysiological experiments, the desired objective measures of alcohol intoxication have been developed by comparing subjectively felt "drunkenness" with blood alcohol level, degree of slurring in speech, degree of face flushing, changes in pupil size, deterioration in balance, positional alcohol nystagmus (PAN), flicker fusion frequency, finger-finger position test, and many others. Recent attempts to establish objective measures of alcohol intoxication have been published by Mizoi and his associates (1963, 1967, 1969).

Electromyogram and Equally Effective Dose

First, Mizoi and his associates (1963) utilized an observation that EMG spikes from the temporal muscle of man disappear in mild alcoholic intoxication. Can the EMG spike be employed as an objective index of alcohol intoxication? At the very outset of the experiment, the individual subjects were interviewed to determine how much they drank daily, and they were grouped into three classes: (1) "virtual" nondrinkers, (2) moderate drinkers, and (3) heavy drinkers. To complement these interview-derived classifications, the subjects were also tested by the ingestion of a quantity of alcohol larger than they usually took, and the experimenters noted episodes of drowsiness, feelings of lethargy, paling of the face, and nausea. On the day of the main experiment, the subjects were asked to sit down on a chair, and needle EMG electrodes were inserted to register the neuromotor unit activities in the temporal muscle. Alcoholic beverage was given to the subjects. For the 12 virtual nondrinkers, an ingestion of 200 ml of Japanese rice wine was sufficient to produce "drunkenness" with respect to flushed face, profuse sweating, hyperactivity, and talkativeness; coincidentally with the subjective feeling of drunkenness, the EMG spikes from the temporal muscles disappeared. Their blood alcohol level was up to 82 mg/100 ml. Among the moderate drinkers, the same extent of a subjective feeling of "drunkenness" coincided again with the disappearance of the temporal muscle EMG spikes, but with a higher blood alcohol dose of 72–120 mg/100 ml. Finally, for three heavy drinkers, a blood alcohol level of 131–139 mg/100 ml (i.e., roughly 600 ml of Japanese rice wine) was needed to induce disappearance of the temporal muscle spikes and the same degree of drunkenness as observed in the virtual nondrinkers and the moderate drinkers. This study has shown, then, that disappearance of the temporal muscle spikes can be used to indicate how much the individuals must drink to achieve an operationally defined "drunkenness." This sort of a psychophysiological study appears to be caught in a circular definition of "drunkenness": drunkenness coincided with the temporal muscle spikes' disappearance, and then the disappearance of the EMG spikes was used to define "drunkenness"—apparently a tautology. However, the information that the temporal muscle EMG spikes disappeared with drunkenness was cross-validated with a new group of experimental subjects, resulting in the data that the heavy drinkers require roughly 130 mg/100 ml of blood alcohol in comparison to roughly 60 mg/100 ml in the virtual nondrinkers, for the same subjectively felt drunkenness. In other words, a dose of 130 mg/100 ml of blood alcohol for the heavy drinkers corresponds to an "equally effective alcohol dose" (EED) of 60 mg/100 ml for the virtual nondrinkers. A later study by Mizoi and his associates (personal communication) utilized simple self-rating scales to derive an index of general "alcohol intoxication." Also used were a host of performance tests such as letter-cancellation, manual dexterity, and others, so as to evaluate the relations among the blood alcohol level, general "alcohol intoxication index" and the temporal muscle spikes, and these confirmed the relation between drunkenness and the temporal muscle spike disappearance. The method of the temporal muscle spike is, however, rather difficult to administer, because it is affected by how tightly or loosely the jaw has been closed, and by the head position. Hence, it requires time-consuming preparations of the experimental subjects.

Nystagmus aud Equally Effective Dose

To obviate prolonged and sensitive adjustments of the subject in measuring temporal EMG spikings, Mizoi and his colleagues developed the optokinetic test which can estimate very efficiently the individually tailored equally effective alcohol dose (Mizoi et al., 1969). Nystagmus was produced by a variety of stimuli: position lateral gaze, rotations, and caloric stimulation. The studies by Aschan and his associates (1956), Fregly and his colleagues (1967), and Goldberg (1966) are but a few examples of the research on nystagmus and alcoholism. Goldberg and his associates at the Karolinska Institute identified and utilized three different kinds of alcohol nystagmus: (1) the first and second phases of positional nystagmus (PAN I and PAN II), (2) an alcohol gaze nystagmus (AGN), and (3) roving ocular movements (ROM). PAN I is a horizontal positional nystagmus which is occasioned by lateral positioning of the head when the subject is supine. It starts $\frac{1}{2}$ hr after a single dose of alcohol and lasts 3–4 hr. With the head in the right lateral position, the fast component of the nystagmus beats to the right, PAN II is the same positional nystagmus, but occurs in the opposite pattern of PAN I, appearing 5–6 hr after alcohol ingestion, and lasting up to 10 hr—many hours after alcohol leaves the blood. Higher intensities of PAN I and PAN II are accompanied by headache, vertigo, dizziness, nausea, and diplopia. Alcohol gaze nystagmus (AGN) is again a horizontal nystagmus which is elicited upon maintaining a lateral gaze, i.e., a fixation of the eyes on an object of 30- to 40-degree lateral deviation. AGN is in the direction of the gaze, and its appearance is dependent on a certain amount of alcohol. AGN intensity reflects alcohol dose. Higher intensities of the AGN are associated with dizziness and vertigo as well. The ROM are spontaneous sinusoidal eye movements behind the closed eyelids when the subjects are supine, tired, and sleepy. There is an antagonism between the ROM and the PAN in that the increase of ROM signifies a decrease in PAN intensity and vice versa. Most of the CNS-depressant drugs in combination with alcohol increase the ROM and decrease the PAN. The PAN and AGN can be used as a psychophysiological assessment of drunkenness.

Mizoi and his colleagues have used an "optokinetic stimulator" (Mizoi, 1967; Mizoi et al., 1969). Optokinetic nystagmus is induced by an undirectionally moving object which appears in the subject's visual field. Mizoi and his colleagues use a 3-cm-wide black vertical strip which is moved to the right or left. The speed of the moving black vertical strip is adjustable up to 125°/sec with a rate of speed change set at 1°/sec/sec. In this optokinetic test, the slow phase of nystagmus constitutes eye movement in the same direction as the moving black strip (i.e., foveal nystagmus), while the rapid phase consists of eye movements in the opposite direction of the moving strip. By the optokinetic method, Mizoi and his associates have been able to estimate the EED in any subject, regardless of the increased acquired tissue tolerance to alcohol, constitutional differences of the individuals to alcohol, and behavioral adaptation to alcohol effects. This test requires the subject's willingness to attend to the moving black strip in the visual field, and the test results show a small practice effect. On the other hand, this optokinetic test is superior to many tests in the past in that it does not require verbal reports of the subjects, does not demand an elaborate preparation of the subject or a variety of physical restraints, is reliable within the subject, and finally, it takes 2 min to allow the angular velocity to reach the maximum of 125°/sec. Thus, once the electrodes are attached to the lateral canthi of the eyes, the optokinetic test can be given to the subjects repeatedly in a short period of time. The data of the optokinetic nystagmus are analyzed by measuring the eye speed during the slow phase of the nystagmus in degrees/sec. Such eye speed measurements are accomplished either by manual measurements or by automatic tachometer arrangements. Four phases are distinguished in describing the relation between the speed of slow eye movements, and the speed of moving black strips. In phase 1, the black strip moves slowly enough so that eye movement is able to keep pace. In phases 2 and 3, the eye movements are able, to a lesser extent, to follow the increasingly faster movement of the black strip, and eye movements tend to become slower. In phase 4, the slow eye movement of the nystagmus completely fails to follow the target, and the speed of eye movements is irregular and slower (the optokinetic fusion limit, and the retinal nystagmus). With alcohol ingestion, Mizoi and his associates have observed that phases 2, 3, and 4 start at a slower speed of the black strip; the method has been reliable in detecting a blood alcohol dose as low as 50 mg/100 ml.

Establishment of the equally effective alcohol dose is very desirable in conducting drug experiments where tissue tolerance and addiction develop, and the psychophysiological approach succeeds in just giving such estimates. However, psychophysiological contributions to alcoholism research also cover the much wider issues of the etiology and therapy of alcoholism. Examples of these contributions will be detailed as we examine basic psychophysiological concepts.

Psychophysiological Concepts and Alcoholism

Activation

The concept of activation places human behaviors along a continuum whose one pole is death, coma, apathy, or stupor and the other, intense emotional excitement. Along the activation continuum the behaviors have only intensity; the qualitative and directional differences of the behaviors are not considered, "the directions" of behavior being, for example, approach or withdrawal—a selection of behavior based on the goals. In an activated state, the autonomic and EEG measures are said to vary in such a way that they reflect usually the Cannon-like sympathetic massive discharges. HR, blood pressure, palmar conductance, respiration rate, and the EMG tonus become higher and/or faster. Pinneo (1961) has shown that a generalized activation, induced by squeezing a dynamometer during an auditory tracking task, results in an overall increased level of activity in measures of palmar conductance, HR, and respiration rate in the same direction, i.e., an increase from the basal level. Such a generalized activation in Pinneo's study is made possible through the proprioceptive feedback from the induced muscular tension. In Schnore's study (1959), the subjects engaged in a visual pursuit tracking task and an arithmetic multiplication task, under high and low arousing conditions. High arousal level was created by intense auditory distraction and a threat of shock for a lack of improvement. Recorded autonomic and EMG variables were the forearm and neck EMG's, HR, systolic BP, respiration rate, palmar conductance, and wrist skin temperature. As predicted by the activation theory, some autonomic and EMG activities have discriminated the high arousal from the low arousal by showing faster HR, higher systolic BP, faster respiration rate, and higher right forearm muscle tension under the high arousal condition. Schnore also found reliable individual differences with respect to favored autonomic responses to activation, i.e., a subject was not equally aroused across all autonomic and EMG variables, but tended to show more intense responding in some of the physiological variables than others. With the judicious use of the autonomic and EMG measures, Schnore was able to differentiate correctly 86% of the low and high arousal conditions. From this observation, Schnore concluded that the notion of "a general arousal state" may be supported. However, Schnore pointed out that any given level of arousal is reflected differently in different individuals, and that the individual differences in autonomic and EMG responses could not be explained simply by means of a broad dichotomy, such as autonomic vs. somatic, or sympathetic vs. parasympathetic.

A contention of activation theory is, then, that each activation level can be measured by a set of autonomic and other variables whose intensities of response will reflect the level of arousal. However, even granted that there would be a measurable continuum of activation, the activation theorists are faced with some methodological problems. First, there appears to be no universal measure of activation. Sternbach (1960) showed that a high autonomic activation was not necessarily accompanied by a highly activated EEG. The other difficulties of the activation theory are (1) construction of an activation continuum to cover all psychological states of differing activation value, from coma, sleep, to panic, using the autonomic measures, (2) an inverted U relation between activation on the one hand, and performance or autonomic responses on the other hand, and (3) unexpected direction of some of the autonomic measures under high arousal condition, e.g., an increased HR with a decreased palmar skin conductance. Let us detail them item by item.

1. The activation theorists envision an activation continuum which discriminates and arranges the entire spectrum of our behaviors from the depth of coma to panic state, according to the monotonically increasing activities of autonomic, EMG, and EEG variables. However, recent studies show that such a continuum construction from the currently employed variables is impossible, because the similar autonomic response patterns can be observed under divergent

conditions of arousal. One such example is the spontaneous electrodermal activity which occurs during episodes of emotional turmoil as well as during sleep stages 3 and 4. Data from numerous sleep studies indicate clearly that sleep cannot simply be placed below the waking state along the activation continuum, because some autonomic variables have shown a larger degree of "activation" during sleep than in waking (L. C. Johnson, 1969).

? There has been a general agreement that the optimal behavior performance would be expected when the individuals have been at the less than maximal activation. Within a narrow state of "waking," an increasing activation would bring forth an increasing behavioral efficiency to a certain optimal point, beyond which additional increase in activation results in the decline of behavioral efficiency—the inverted U relation. McDonnell and Carpenter (1959) describe, for example, an inverted U relation between anxiety and skin conductance levels (SCL). Due to this curvilinear relation between SCL and anxiety, a decreased SCL for the low anxiety group means a reduced tension, but in the high anxiety group a similar SCL could mean increased tension, hence, requiring "prudence in assigning a general psychological significance to increase or decrease in skin conduction level" (McDonnell and Carpenter, 1959, p. 49).

3. Degree of activation can be varied by changing the task difficulties, and kinds of stimuli and tasks used. The harder task would be more arousing than the easy one, and the noxious stimuli would be more arousing than the nonnoxious. However, when Lacey and his associates (1963) used eight task or stimulus situations (i.e., the make-up sentences task, mental arithmetic, and others), the pattern of activation indicated by HRR and SCR was quite unlike the one expected under the activation theory, or the Cannon-like view of massive sympathetic discharges in response to the activating stimuli. Instead of expected increases in HR and SC, subjects showed a decreased HR, and an increased palmar conductance level, depending on the nature of the activating stimulus or task situations. Activation theory cannot explain such contingencies.

Despite the above difficulties, activation theory has nevertheless retained its usefulness in psychophysiological researches, particularly when the researchers have made sure to obtain data on subjective state of the individuals in the experiment—how they have felt during the experiment—simultaneously with collection of autonomic, EMG, and EEG data. Within a very limited range of psychological state, i.e., the awake state, we can still discuss the degree of "arousal."

The utility of the activation theory for alcoholism research is limited to an exploration of folklore about alcoholismic drinking, specifically, that alcohol reduces a high degree of activation of anxiety and tension. Scientific attempts to clarify the myth of alcohol-induced tension reduction will be discussed later.

Finally, with respect to the activation theory, a critical note should be added that "in such continuum there is no qualitative difference between emotions, nor can emotion be distinguished from effort" (Arnold, 1960, Vol. 2, p. 143).

Autonomic Balance

Autonomic balance between the two opposing forces of the SNS and PNS has been very intensively studied by Wenger and his colleagues (1948, 1957, 1966, 1960) by an estimate of the autonomic factor ($\bar{A}$), or "scores of autonomic balance."

A computation of $\bar{A}$ for any individual is a relatively easy matter, because the procedures of collecting the autonomic data, the process of converting the raw score to a standard score, and then inserting the Z-transformed autonomic data into one of the available equations—all these necessary steps in the computation of $\bar{A}$ have been explicitly and clearly described. Table 3 shows a data collection protocol for $\bar{A}$ computation. As shown in Table 3, the $\bar{A}$ score represents the resting level of the individual subjects except for the palmar skin conductance readings which are taken during strain.

TABLE 3. Experimental Protocol for Autonomic Data to Be Used in $\bar{A}$

---

1. Record room temperature and time of day.
2. Subject sits down; holds and covers a thermometer bulb between the thumb and tips of the first two fingers of his nonpreferred hand for 3 min (first finger temperature).
3. Simultaneously with first finger temperature measurement, measure sublingual temperature for 3 min. While measuring the finger and sublingual temperatures, the experimenter applies the electrodes for skin conductance measures.
4. Measure the pupil size with the pupilometer card.
5. Measure the salivary output, timing for 3 min.
6. If the electrodes are on the skin for more than 5 min by this time, ask the subject to stand up, his hands naturally relaxed, facing toward blank wall, and think nothing, but relax. Measure the skin resistance at the end of 1 min and at the end of 2 min.
7. Ask the subject to sit well balanced on an edge of a chair with the arm extended without extending fingers, and then raise legs as high as possible, stiff at the joint, without leaning back on the chair.
8. Ask the subject to lie on his side on the bed. Measure dermographic persistence.
9. Three minutes later, obtain four readings of palmar resistance approximately at 3-min intervals.
10. Record the forearm resistance of the skin at least four times approximately at 3-min intervals.
11. Measure the systolic blood pressure at least four times at 3-min intervals.
12. Measure similarly the diastolic blood pressure.
13. Measure heart period.
14. Repeat finger temperature (second measurement).

What does $\bar{A}$ represent once the computation has been completed? In brief, $\bar{A}$ represents the adult individual's relative standing of his "autonomic balance," in reference to the group of 460 young Army Air Force (AAF) male personnel tested at the Santa Ana Army Air Base in 1944, or a group of 201 operational fatigue patients at the above air base in 1944. Thus, the $\bar{A}$ score remains relative to the reference group. The mean $\bar{A}$ of the 460 AAF reference group was 69.89, with a standard deviation of 7.36; the $\bar{A}$ score is constructed so that scores lower than the mean represent relative SNS dominance, those higher than the mean, the PNS dominance. The individual with an $\bar{A}$ score of 62.53 is one standard deviation below the mean of the normal reference group, i.e., 460 AAF personnel, and shows relative SNS dominance—a statistical allocation of this subject.

Wenger (1948) has examined seven chronic alcoholics. The $\bar{A}$ of this small alcoholic group which is computed from the published data by the author of this chapter, was 66.32, a figure very close to the norm of 69.89, indicating no gross autonomic imbalance in this group of the alcoholics. (Table 4 lists additional variables not used in the computation of $\bar{A}$. The equation utilized for computing the estimate of autonomic factor is also shown in Table 4, using beta weights appropriate for the occasion when the normative male group of 460 AAF is used as the reference group.) However, this finding is only suggestive: (1) the sample size is too small to afford any definitive conclusion on the alcoholics, and (2) the detailed diagnostic criteria for the alcoholics are not available in the published materials. With respect to the individual autonomic responses shown in Table 4, it is of considerable interest to note that some autonomic variables deviate from the norm more than 1 S.D. Resting salivary output is low in the alcoholics, and this fact has been confirmed later by an independent study of Stern and his associates (1968). Resting diastolic blood pressure of the alcoholics is relatively higher, while systolic blood pressure remains unchanged (see Cutshall, 1965). In the alcoholics, respiration rate is faster, the pupil is dilated, and salivary pH is low.

Later, Wenger (1957) attempted a pattern analysis of 14 autonomic measures. The pattern analysis results in a few psychophysiological profiles: S (a relative sympathetic dominance), P (a relative parasympathetic dominance), M (mean pattern; autonomic balance), B (a beta pattern; mixed, or a modal pattern for the psychosomatics), TB (a tuberculous patient pattern, mixed, or a modal pattern), and A (an asthmatic patient pattern, mixed, or a modal pattern).

Table 5 shows the psychophysiological profile prepared by the present author, of the seven alcoholic subjects originally reported by Wenger (1948). The mean psychophysiological profile $\bar{A}$ of the alcoholics is again not impressively different from the norm, but some measures deviate from the AAF norm of resting autonomic levels.

TABLE 4. Autonomic Variables and Ā in a Group of Seven Chronic Alcoholics[a]

Variables (unit of measurement)	Alcoholics[b] Raw scores	Alcoholics[b] Standard scores	Normative mean ± S.D.	Beta weights
Salivary output, SO (ml)	2.5	40	4.2±1.7	0.14
Sublingual temperature, ST (°F)	98.8	55*	99.0±0.4	0.30
Palmar conductance, PC (micromhos)	14.1	54*	16.8±7.1	0.09
Volar conductance, VC (micromhos)	6.1	55*	7.3±2.2	0.09
Log conductance change, LCC (log units)	26.0	47	30.1±13.7	0.17
Diastolic blood pressure, DBP (mm Hg)	76.0	42*	70.0±7.4	0.18
Heart period, HP (millimin)	149.9	46	160.4±23.5	0.41
Dermographia persistence (min)	15.3	48	16.8±9.2	—
Systolic blood pressure (mm Hg)	115.7	55	111.1±9.0	—
Pulse pressure (mm Hg)	39.7	49	41.1±10.0	—
Finger temperature (1st) (°C)	33.1	40	34.9±1.9	—
Finger temperature (2nd) (°C)	36.0	54	35.4±1.4	—
Respiratory period (sec)	3.5	39	5.1±1.4	—
Pupillary diameter (mm)	3.9	36	5.25±0.093	—
Salivary pH	6.4	30	7.2±0.4	—
Dermographia latency (sec)	12.3	48	13.3±4.5	—
Sinus arrhythmia (0–5 rating unit)	0.0	44	0.7±1.1	—
Tidal air mean (mm)	17.6	44	21.8±7.0	—
Tidal air sigma (mm)	5.5	54	4.5±2.8	—
Oxygen consumption (cal-hr/m²)	51.6	51	50.4±8.3	—

[a] Rearranged and modified from Wenger (1948, p. 40).
[b] The variables with asterisked standard scores are reflected so as to receive low values with sympatheticlike response, and high values with parasympatheticlike responses. Normative mean and standard deviation (S.D.) are based on the 460 Army Air Force cadets reported by Wenger (1948). $A = 0.14(SO) + 0.30(ST^*) + 0.09(PC^*) + 0.09(FC^*) + 0.17(LCC) + 0.18(DEP^*) + 0.41(HP)$, which is in the alcoholic data, $0.14 \times 40 + 0.30 \times 55 + 0.09 \times 54 + 0.09 \times 55 + 0.17 \times 47 + 0.18 \times 42 + 0.41 \times 46 = 66.32$. For the normative AAF group, the mean A was 69.89.

TABLE 5. Psychophysiological Profile

Group: Seven Alcoholics (Wenger, 1948)

Test	S	−3σ 20	−2σ 30	−1σ 40	M 50	1σ 60	2σ 70	3σ 80		M	σ (No. N 488)
Salivary output	low			X[40]					high	4.2	1.7
Dermographia persistence	short				X[48]				long	16.8	9.2
Palmar conductance	high					X[54]			low	16.8	7.1
Log conductance change	low				X[47]				high	30.1	3.7
Volar conductance	high					X[55]			low	7.3	2.2
Systolic blood pressure	high					X[55]			low	111.1	9.0
Diastolic blood pressure	high			X[42]					low	70.0	7.4
Pulse pressure	low				X[49]				high	41.1	10.0
Heart period	short				X[46]				long	160.4	23.5
Sublingual temperature	high					X[55]			low	99.0	0.4
Finger temperature (*1st*)	low			X[40]					high	34.9	1.9
Finger temperature (*2nd*)	low					X[54]			high	35.4	1.4
Respiration period	short			X[39]					long	5.1	1.4
Pupillary diameter	large			X[36]					small	5.3	0.9

Although the Ā score has been primarily looked upon as the index of resting or basal autonomic balance representing the permanent disposition of the individual's ANS, a study by Smith and Wenger (1965) showed that the Ā score could be used to detect phasic anxiety. In their study, phasic anxiety experienced shortly before a preliminary oral examination of doctoral candidates brought down the Ā score as much as 26.7 points (on the average, −12.3), i.e., a sympathetic dominance due to stress of a preliminary oral examination. One of the interesting findings was that both palmar skin conductance and forearm skin conductance measures failed to contribute to overall assessment of autonomic functions, particularly in contrast to the significant contribution of systolic BP, diastolic BP, salivary output, sublingual temperature, heart period, and palmar SRR in showing the stress experience.

Response Specificities

In some experiments, as in the studies by Wenger and his colleagues, many autonomic, EMG, and EEG variables are recorded simultaneously from a group of subjects under a variety of stimulus and task conditions. For example: in an experiment conducted by Engel and Bickford (1961), subjects were exposed to (1) honking of an automobile horn, (2) mental arithmetic, (3) recognition of scrambled proverbs, (4) lifting of the extended left leg, and (5) immersion of the extremities in ice water, while the subjects' autonomic measures of systolic BP, diastolic BP, palmar skin resistance, finger, toe, and face temperatures, heart rate and respiration rate were recorded simultaneously. Or, in an experiment of Johnson, Hord, and Lubin (1963), subjects were exposed to flickering lights, tone, buzzer, and engaged with tasks of multiplication and spelling, while their palmar skin resistance, HR, respiration rate, and finger temperature were simultaneously recorded.

When activation theory is applied to the data of these experiments, the activation theorists anticipate that a change of one autonomic variable toward an apparent sympathetic dominance would be accompanied by a similar trend in all other remaining autonomic variables. However, not all autonomic variables are activated or deactivated to the same extent. Rather, a given individual might respond to one kind of stimulus situation consistently with only one of the autonomic variables. For example, a subject may show maximal increase in his HR when he is exposed to automobile horns, whereas some other subjects may respond to the horn consistently by the maximal response in SR. Individual response specificity (IRS) is the concept that some individuals are "heart responders," "skin responders," "stomach responders," or "blood pressure responders." The IRS can be defined in three progressively restrictive manners (Engel, 1960): (1) Among a set of autonomically mediated functions, maximal change occurs in the same function within each subject to a set of stimuli (broad IRS). (2) Consistent rank orders of responses occur within the same subject to a set of stimulus situations (e.g., an individual shows the highest response magnitude in HR, the second highest in BP, etc. a more restricted definition of the IRS, involving a set of autonomic responses); this is equivalent to Engel's total pattern IRS, "response stereotypy" of Johnson and his associates (1963), and Lacey's IRS (1967). (3) Consistent interresponse correlations occur within the same subject to a set of stimulus situations.

The kinds of stimulus and task situations influence the response pattern, i.e., autonomic response pattern may covary with the nature of stimulus situations. For example, an "anger"-inducing situation creates a particular response pattern across the subjects, in comparison with a "fear"-inducing situation (Ax, 1953). This is stimulus response specificity (SRS). Engel (1960) defines the SRS in three progressively restrictive manners: (1) maximal change occurs in the same autonomic function to a given stimulus in a group of subjects, or (2) consistent rank orders of response to a given stimulus occur in a group of subjects (stimulus stereotypy), or (3) consistent interresponse correlations to a given stimulus occur in a group of subjects.

The IRS and SRS are basically statistical concepts, and the details of how to evaluate the extent of IRS and SRS in a given group under multiple stimulus and task situations are given by Johnson and his associates (1963), Engel and Bickford (1961), and Engel (1960).

The tendency of individuals to respond to various stimuli with an idiosyncratic autonomic response pattern helps to reveal a dynamic individual difference in autonomic reactivity, much as the $\bar{A}$ score discovers static (resting) individual differences in the autonomic makeup. The IRS encompasses a much wider spectrum of autonomic functioning than an $\bar{A}$ score usually would, as the IRS reflects widely differing active as well as passive autonomic responses. The importance of the IRS was recognized early in 1960 by F. Alexander in his *Psychosomatic Medicine*, by Malmo, Shagass, and Davis (1950), and Lacey and his associates (1953). The IRS appears to be very powerful in revealing an idiosyncrasy of the autonomic reactivity of a well-circumscribed disease (see Sternbach, 1966).

Modern studies of the stimulus or situational stereotypy of response have been conducted by Davis (1957), Ax (1953), J. Schachter (1957), and Engel and Bickford (1961). These studies confirm feasibility of identifying autonomic, EMG, and EEG identity for each psychological state induced by stimulus situations. However, as Ax (1964) has pointed out, any stimulus situation can be subjected to motivation, attitude, and personality of the subjects who perceive and appraise the stimulus situations, that is, the stimulus situation cannot be fully specified by objective and physical parameters. This is a phenomenon of motivational response specificity (MRS). Averill and Opton (1966) have cited an experiment of Zimney and Miller (1966) in which the arms of the subjects were exposed to hot or cold stimuli. Usually, the physical objective nature of cold or hot stimuli should cause a local thermoregulatory effect of vasoconstriction or vasodilation, respectively. However, the initial presentations of the hot stimulus were found to be vasoconstrictive. This vasoconstriction to the hot stimulus continued until orienting response (i.e., MRS) habituated out. Only then, did a vasodilation follow a stimulation by heat.

A major development in the SRS was anticipated by Davis (1957). Davis found four autonomic response patterns on the basis of eight autonomic variables and one EMG measure. One pattern observed in male subjects who looked at 12 pictures consisted of increased muscular tension, palmar sweating increase, peripheral vasoconstriction, but slower and larger pulse and inhibition of respiration. This P (picture) pattern of autonomic responses shows what Lacey has named "directional fractionation." Instead of exhibiting a consistent pattern of autonomic activation, (i.e., increased palmar sweating, increased muscle tension, and increased pulse rate) the autonomic pattern of the subjects looking at, for example, a picture of a nude female, has been an increase in some variables, and a decrease in other variables. Later Lacey identified this directionally fractionated autonomic response pattern as reflecting a psychological process where "cardiac deceleration accompanied and perhaps facilitated ease of environmental intake" (Lacey, 1963, p. 165).

Although the concepts of the IRS, SRS, and MRS have been very fruitful in psychophysiological researches in general, efforts to find unique SRS to subtle sentiments and emotions created, for example, by watching a movie, *Bambi*, have been unsuccessful (Sternbach, 1962). Perhaps such failure derives not from conceptual difficulties, but rather from restricted kinds of autonomic data we can obtain from the human subjects. No studies were published to determine the IRS, SRS, or MRS in the alcoholics, although highly interesting data were collected from such a group (Docter, personal communication).

Law of Initial Value (LIV)

The earliest definition of the law of initial value (LIV) was formulated in the 1930's by Wilder (who studied the pulse and systolic blood pressure of healthy individuals and "vegetative neurotics" after injections of atropine, epinephrine, or pilocarpine), and was recently given in his book, *Stimulus and Response: The Law of Initial Value* (1967): "the factor which in the first place determines intensity, direction, and form of a pulse or blood pressure curve is the level of pulse or blood pressure prior to the injection. The higher this initial value, the more pronounced is the tendency to a drop, the smaller, the tendency to a rise of the curve" (p. 4). A later definition of the LLV is: "given a standard dose of stimulus and standard period of measurement, the response, that is, the change from the initial (pre-stimulus) level, will tend to be smaller when the initial value (IV) is higher; this applies to function-raising stimuli. For function depressing or function-inhibiting stimuli this negative correlation becomes positive" (Wilder, 1962). The LIV shows a dependence of the autonomic response on the preexisting state of the individual subjects. The higher the prestimulus level of the autonomic variable is, the smaller the response to the stimulus, and on occasions the response may become even "paradoxical" (Lacey, 1956) when the initial level is too high. The LIV can be established only for the response of a subject to one and the same intensity of one and the same stimulus, because a different intensity and different kind of stimulus would have different effects quantitatively and qualitatively on the LIV. Wilder has not regarded the LIV as a theory, but as a physiological and statistical law amenable to a mathematical formulation (Wilder, 1967).

As pointed out by Averill and Opton (1968), mathematical details involved in the LIV are somewhat formidable. However, a simple understanding of the LIV is quite possible. For example, if there is a significant negative correlation between the prestimulus level and the magnitude of response, then Wilder's LIV holds. More precisely speaking, assume that two prestimulus values X_1 and X_2 have been measured over many trials, along with the poststimulus value, Y, and that the response to the stimulus has been defined as $D = Y - X_1$. Then, taking a Pearson product moment correlation between the prestimulus (basal) value X_2 and D (difference, i.e., a response magnitude), the obtained $r_{X_2 D}$ is defined by

$$ r_{X_2 D} = \frac{r_{X_2 Y} S_Y - r_{X_2 X_1} S_1}{S_Y^2 + S_{X_1}^2 - 2r_{X_1 Y} S_{X_1} S_Y}, \tag{1} $$

where S_Y is a standard deviation of Y, and S_{X_1} is a standard deviation of X_1; $r_{X_2 Y}$, $r_{X_2 X_1}$, and $r_{X_1 Y}$ are each Pearson product moment correlation coefficient between X_2 and Y, X_2 and X_1, and X_1 and Y respectively. The $r_{X_2 D}$ can be computed either for a group, or for an individual under a condition where he will not habituate to a given stimulus.

When $r_{X_2 D}$ is negative, the LIV holds. Now, the numerator of $r_{X_2 D}$ reflects a very critical quantity, $b_{Y X_2} - b_{X_1 X_2}$, the difference between the regression slope when a stimulus is given and the regression slope measured in the absence of stimulus (Johnson and Lubin, in press).

The LIV implies a presence of the optimal level of autonomic functions; i.e., that the poststimulus level, Y, tends to be constant regardless of the prestimulus level. Beyond a certain prestimulus level, additional stimulation produces not a pure form of excitation, but more and more inhibitory influence, so as to bring back the autonomic responses to a preestablished constancy—a concept of homeostasis. Wilder (1967) notes that the concept of homeostasis by Cannon was published almost simultaneously but independently of Wilder's LIV. The difference between the LIV and homeostasis is that the LIV is less concerned in the homeostatic middle line which the organism is trying to maintain than in the limits of variability, "homeo*kinesis*."

In an evaluation of "true" response scores of the autonomic variables, it is desirable to isolate the LIV effect, or partial out the LIV effect on the evoked response to the stimulus or task situations. The simplest way to partial out the LIV effects would be to subtract prestimulus value X from the observed post-stimulus response value Y, i.e., to obtain a difference score $D = Y - X$. Lacey (1956) has proposed an autonomic lability score (ALS) which uses linear regression to subtract out the effect of the prestimulus level. ALS is:

$$\text{ALS} = 50 + 10 \frac{Y - a_{YX} - b_{YX}X}{s_Y\sqrt{1 - r^2_{XY}}}, \tag{2}$$

where

$Y = $ poststimulus response value
$a_{YX} = $ the Y intercept
$b_{YX} = $ the slope of regression line of Y on X
$s_Y = $ standard deviation of Y

The quantity $s_Y\sqrt{1 - r^2_{XY}}$ is standard deviation of the Y residuals, the quantity $\tilde{Y} - a_{YX} + b_{YX}X$ is the expected value of Y on the basis of linear regression on X, and the quantity $Y - a_{YX} - b_{YX}X$ represents the residual between the observed poststimulus value and the predicted value of Y from X. Lubin, Hord, and Johnson (1964) showed that the ALS would have greater validity (and possibly reliability) than the D score when the LIV holds. But, the D score has greater validity when the LIV does not hold.

To illustrate the use of ALS, let us say that a subject has a prestimulus HR of 60 beats per minute (bpm) and 71 bpm after a stimulation. He is one of 50 subjects who participate in an experiment. In the group, prestimulus HR has a mean of 50 bpm with the standard deviation of 10 bpm; the group mean HR response, poststimulus level, is 60 bpm with a standard deviation of 10 bpm. The observed correlation between the prestimulus and poststimulus HR in this group is 0.8. In order to compute the ALS score of this particular subject, substitute the values into the formula:

$$\text{ALS} = 50 + 10 \left[\frac{71 - 20 - 0.8 \times 60}{10\sqrt{1 - 0.8^2}} \right] = 55,$$

with a resulting linear regression equation of $\tilde{Y}$ (bpm) $= 20 + 0.8X$. The coefficient b_{YX} can be calculated from

$$b_{YX} = r_{XY}\left(\frac{sY}{sX}\right);$$

the Y intercept by [mean $Y - b$ (mean X)].

The LIV is operative when the slope, b_{YX}, is greater than zero, but less than unity. The closer the regression slope is to zero, the stronger is the LIV, representing heavier homeostatic restraints on the poststimulus level.

The ALS can be computed for the resting condition. ALS can be computed similarly for each subject under a stimulus or task situation. By replacing the group of 50 subjects given previously as illustration, with a group of responses to a stimulus or task situation given repeatedly for 50 times within each subject, and also by replacing the group mean with trial means, the ALS can be computed for each trial within the subject (Lacey, 1956; Docter and Perkins, 1961). ALS scores are, however, not "inherently fairer" than other types of scores, such as the D score, percent change score, difference between standardized scores (Johnson and Lubin, in press). The interpretation of b_{YX} by itself as an index of homeostatic restraints is questioned by Surwillo and Arenberg (1964). Because of error of measurement, b_{YX} will almost always be less than unity. Therefore, a regression coefficient b_{YX} after stimulation (a situation where presumably a homeostatic mechanism would be operative) is usually significantly less than the b_{YX} computed when no stimulation was given (a situation where presumably stimulus-initiated homeostatic restraints were not in operation).

The ALS were computed in a study by Docter and Perkins (1961) to measure the reactivities of autonomic and EMG variables to the cold pressor test and venipuncture stress in nonalcoholic subjects before and after an alcohol dose of 0.5 ml/kg of body weight, and blood alcohol level ranging from 11 mg/100 ml to 67 mg/100 ml. With this small dose of alcohol, no changes in autonomic reactivities were observed. Wilder applied the LIV concept to appraise alcohol effects (1967). He noted that alcohol has a stimulosedative nature. He states: "small doses of alcohol may excite us; large doses make us drowsy and sleep. On the other hand, we can easily observe changes of reaction to the identical dose in one individual . . ." (Wilder, 1967, p. 245). He maintains that he can tell an individual's initial values—autonomic, psychological, etc.—if he can observe the subjects' reaction to wine, i.e., *in vino veritas*! He maintains that alcohol effects are such that they will pick you up if you are tired, and that they will calm you down when you are upset. Alcohol is regarded as a great restorer of normalcy.

According to Wilder, a study of the relation between alcohol effects and initial values would yield practical results in explicating mechanisms of alcoholismic drinking, and even aid drug education by showing how to drink alcohol without introducing undesirable "paradoxical effects."

Cognitive and Social Determinants of Emotions

On occasions, some visceral activities, such as palpitation, rapid respiration, peripheral temperature tone (e.g., cold feet, flushed face), and salivation can be perceived. The roles of perceived autonomic activities have been discussed extensively in the context of emotions (Arnold, 1960; Ax, 1953; Averill, 1969; Cannon, 1929; Gellhorn and Loofbourrow, 1963; J. Schachter, 1957; S. Schachter, 1966; Schachter and Singer, 1962; Wenger et al., 1960). Cannon criticized the theory of William James who has concluded that emotions are only perceptions of changes in the body (Cannon, 1929; see S. Schachter, 1966). A persisting difficulty in finding distinct and replicable autonomic, EMG and EEG patterns for each subjectively discriminable emotional state (that is, as autonomic pattern unique to fear, anger, etc.) has created a challenge to any one-to-one isomorphism between the psychological states and the physiologically defined states. One of the most challenging formulations of emotions has come from a social psychologist, S. Schachter (1966).

A subcutaneous epinephrine injection for activation of the peripheral SNS induces no emotions at all in a group of young healthy human subjects, or only "as if" emotions, although such injection is observed to cause real emotions of nervousness, and even anger in a group of hospitalized cancer patients (Wenger et al., 1960). Indeed, the observation that human subjects can perceive all of the autonomic changes without subjectively experiencing real emotions is one of the many grounds on which Cannon criticized James' theory of emotions.

S. Schachter (1966) reports a study by Hohmann on human paraplegics with spinal cord lesion at various levels, who are deprived of most of their peripheral sympathetic functions. In the absence of "physiological activation" mediated by the ANS, these patients have reported only weaker, superficial, and cold emotions. A paraplegic patient has stated: ". . . it's (emotions induced by epinephrine) sort of cold anger. Sometimes I act angry when I see some injustice. I yell and cuss and raise hell, because if you don't do it sometimes, I've learned people will take advantage of you, but it just doesn't have the heat to it that it used to. It's a mental kind of anger" (Schachter, 1966, pp. 74–75).

The absence of real emotions in the cases of epinephrine-induced physiological activation alone without any psychological and cognitive context must be contrasted to the similar absence of real subjectively felt emotions when the individuals are aware of social and cognitive environment and contexts which must lead to genuine emotions, but cannot feel emotions owing to lack of the ANS-mediated physiological activation. To S. Schachter, true emotions are made possible only when a proper physiological activation (PA) has occurred in a proper socially defined context which the subjects have understood and labeled.

In S. Schachter's theory of emotions, a physiological activation remains the sine qua non of the emotional experiences. A relation of the social psychological theory to alcoholism is indirectly found in S. Schachter's discussion of smoking marihuana. Physiological activations perceived after marihuana smokings are tremor, ataxia, vertigo, and increased heart rate, not quite unlike the effects of drinking alcohol. Schachter states that once the user has learned the techniques of smoking marihuana, he learns to label his physiological symptoms as being "high." That is there appear to be a great number of social learnings which are involved in interpreting autonomic and other changes to be desirable and rewarding, although they might be neutral by themselves. In this context, the early process of addiction might involve social and cognitive attempts to associate the physiological activation with certain psychologically desirable states. Unfortunately, there are no systematic studies (but many anecdotal data) conducted to demonstrate what sorts of physiological changes have been selected by the alcoholics to be associated with the psychological state of "pleasantly drunk." Warm hands, slightly increased muscular tensions, quickened heart rate, and pleasingly moist palms could be used, together with signs of gross CNS impairments of ataxia, dizziness, and slurred speech, as the measures of "being drunk."

The theory of S. Schachter, which stresses the role of cognitive and social aspects of emotional experiences contributes to the psychophysiology of alcoholism in two ways: (1) it has emphasized the importance of "atmosphere" and also cultural and ethnic background where the drinking takes place, because they are going to provide the "labels" to alcohol-induced physiological changes (i.e., in experimental intoxication studies, it would be crucial to have a well-structured environment in which the subjects drink alcohol), (2) it might help bring out the psychological interpretation of the autonomic changes due to alcohol drinking. Is a slight palpitation pleasant at the beginning of drinking? Is a palpitation a part of the bodily feeling sought after by the alcoholic? The answers to these questions would undoubtedly advance drug education.

PSYCHOPHYSIOLOGICAL STUDIES OF ALCOHOL EFFECT ON THE HUMAN ANS

Once we decide on the kinds of concepts to be explored, many adequate psychophysiological techniques (see Table 6) can be found for such examination. There is no shortage of etiological, diagnostic, and prognostic concepts with respect to alcoholism, since a multitude of such theories have been published and summarized (Jellinek, 1942, 1960; *Manual of Alcoholism*, 1968).

Recently, an acute awareness of a need to reexamine the concepts of what alcohol does for the alcoholics has been felt through the works of Mendelson and his colleagues (1964), Goldberg (1966), Docter and his associates (1966), and Mayfield (1968). The traditional view of what alcohol drinking does for (not what alcohol drinking does to) the individuals is expressed eloquently by Masserman and Yum (1946). They noted in cats that alcohol lessens efficiency in some task performances, but simultaneously makes the cats more adaptive by resolving complex neurotic processes. Conger (1951) agreed with Masserman and Yum, and maintained that one of the effects of alcohol is to reduce the

TABLE 6.   Some Tests for Describing Autonomic Functions[a]

Name of test	Description
Cold pressor test	A procedure developed by Hines and Brown (see Darrow, 1943) to immerse one hand or one foot in ice water for 2 min. A rise in blood pressure of 20 mm Hg or more represents a general hyperexcitability of the sympathetico-adrenal system (Monnier, 1968; Docter and Perkins, 1961).
Mecholyl test	Developed by Funkenstein. Induce a pharmacologic stress by injecting mecholyl intramuscularly, 10 mg/subject. Measure the systolic blood pressure after injection. Blood pressure response (3 types) presumably reflects the central sympathetic reactivity. Mecholyl itself lowers the systolic blood pressure as in acetylcholine (Gellhorn and Loofbourrow, 1963; Kissin and Platz, 1968).
Epinephrine/norepinephrine injection	Intramuscular or intravenous injections. Normally, the blood pressure rises with tachycardia, hyperglycemia, leukocytosis, and hyperthermia, with epinephrine injection. The pulse rate is down, and blood pressure up, with norepinephrine injection (Wenger *et al.*, 1960; S. Schachter, 1966).
Optokinetic test	Developed by Mizoi and his associates (1969). Unlike Goldberg's positional alcohol nystagmus, this test uses a moving target strip to cause the foveal and retinal nystagmus. Unlike Goldberg's PAN II, the optokinetic nystagmus is not yet used to gauge a degree of need for alcoholic drink during a hangover. The optokinetic nystagmus measures alcohol intoxication.
Bicycle ergonometer	Application of a work load, such as 1500 kg-m/min, on the cardiovascular and respiratory systems (Karvinen *et al.*, 1962).

[a] See Monnier (1968, pp. 638-642) for other tests, such as "the orthostatic adaptation" test and "cold-rewarming test."

strength of fear and anxiety. A similar recurring theme that alcohol is tranquilizing and sedative is echoed in the studies by Fleetwood and Diethelm (1951), and Fleetwood (1955) in which alcohol ingestion has abolished a tension or resentment chemical "factor" in the blood. However, recent studies have suggested a complex "rewarding" nature of alcohol to the alcoholics. Mendelson and his colleagues (1964) have observed a progressive increase in anxiety for alcoholics during a 24-day drinking spree experiment with alcohol doses of up to 7 g/kg of body weight/day. Goldberg notes that the nonalcoholic subjects have shown, in response to alcohol doses as low as 35 mg/100 ml, a heterogeneous change in mood. These subjects after alcohol were absent-minded, irritated, sleepy and tired, calm and content. Recently, Mayfield (1968) showed that the mood of the alcoholics did not improve much with doses of alcohol averaging 132.4 mg/100 ml (ranging from 80 to 189 mg/100 ml), unless the alcoholics were depressed. The mood improvement reported by the alcoholics is derived not from the actually occurring subjective change in the mood, but from "more myth than reality, based perhaps on commonly held notions about the effects of drinking" (p. 326). Docter and his associates (1960, 1964, 1966) concluded that a stimulatory phase of alcohol intoxication, during which the alcoholics have shown autonomic, EMG, and EEG signs of excitation, is what alcohol does for the alcoholics. Thus, there remains, all told, a research need to clarify what alcohol does for the alcoholics, and then how alcohol does this.

One must resort to the time-consuming method of prospective study, a developmental psychophysiology, when the research objective is related to etiological aspects of alcoholism. In a developmental psychophysiology, individuals will be followed from their early adolescence to middle and old age and examined periodically with respect to their histories of drinking behaviors. McCord, McCord, and Gudeman (1959) have already shown the effectiveness of developmental and longitudinal studies in resolving some etiological problems. First, their study raises doubts that a nutritional deficiency and metabolic dysfunction or endocrine abnormalities are causes of the alcoholism by showing that children suffering from such deficiency and dysfunction have not shown a greater than normal percent of adult alcoholics. Second, they have posed a serious criticism for the etiological theory that emphasizes hereditary factors. Third, they have not been able to confirm a theory which relates self-destructiveness, oral tendencies, or latent homosexuality to the etiology of alcoholism; the majority of their alcoholics have not manifested any such tendencies before the onset of alcoholism. Another theory which McCord and his associates have failed to confirm involves overmaternal pamperings and overprotection as the root of alcoholism. Finally, they are able to support an etiological theory involving a sociological approach; the highest incidence of alcoholism can be found in an ethnic-cultural group where the tension has been high and drinking habits are not subjected to consistent social control. Native Americans, Irish, and other Europeans produce significantly higher numbers of alcoholics than do other ethnic-cultural groups. Although developmental and longitudinal studies are costly and slow in completing the data collection, they are the only way to settle certain classes of alcoholism-related problems, such as whether or not certain predispositions or personality traits or autonomic patterns exist prior to the onset of alcoholism.

In the literature of psychophysiology of alcoholism, many methods have been used with a varying success, some of which are listed below:

1. The measurements of resting "baseline" records of the autonomic and other variables (Wenger, 1948; Holmberg and Martens, 1955; Aschan *et al.*,

1956; Bernal and Docter, 1962; Sutherland *et al.*, 1962; Mizoi *et al.*, 1963; Franks, 1963; Docter and Bernal, 1964; Wendt *et al.*, 1965; Docter *et al.*, 1966; Fewings *et al.*, 1966; Mizoi, 1967; Fregly *et al.*, 1967; Gillespie, 1967; Stern *et al.*, 1968; Carson *et al.*, 1969; Mizoi *et al.*, 1969).

2. Induction of an affective state by stimulating the subjects (Lineret and Traxel, 1959; Coopersmith, 1964).

3. Use of a mild to strong stressor (Carpenter, 1957; Goddard, 1958; McDonnell and Carpenter, 1959; Docter and Perkins, 1960; Graf and Strom, 1960; Garlind *et al.*, 1960; Karvinen *et al.*, 1962; Hebbelinck, 1962; Lolli *et al.*, 1964; Boutin, 1967; Wilkinson and Colquhoun, 1968; Rosenberg and Butterworth, 1969; Wilkinson, 1969).

4. Classical or instrumental conditioning (Finkelstein *et al.*, 1945; Gantt, 1957; Vogel, 1960, 1961; Franks, 1963; Hobson, 1966; Mendelson and Mello, 1966; McGonnell and Beach, 1968; Mello, 1968).

5. Desensitization or aversive conditioning under hypnosis (Abrams, 1964; Lazrus, 1965; see also Blum and Blum, 1967, pp. 113–119).

6. Drugs (Finkelstein *et al.*, 1945; Roth and Sheard, 1947; Fazekas *et al.*, 1955, Kissin and Hankoff, 1959; Kissin, Schenker, 1959; F. G. Johnson, 1969).

7. Simulation of an alcoholic spree by chronic experimentally induced intoxication (Bernal and Docter, 1962; Docter and Bernal, 1964; Mendelson, 1964, 1968; Mendelson and Mello, 1966).

Questions of Experimental Design

A few words on the design of the psychophysiological experiments may be in order. Among many publications related to statistics and experimental design in psychophysiology, the works of Johnson and Lubin (in press), Edwards (1954), and Mefferd (1966) are helpful. First of all, it should be clear that in any experiments except those involving the developmental and longitudinal studies as previously mentioned, results cannot determine any etiologically contributing factors to alcoholism, because whatever may be found among the alcoholics to be deviant in comparison with the nonalcoholic might be a result of the longstanding addictions to alcohol instead of a cause. Lester (1966) points out that findings which show alcoholics to be significantly afflicted by respiratory and gastrointestinal complaints and skin allergies are more likely the results of chronic ingestion of alcohol, than the causes of alcoholism. Lester similarly indicates a fallacy in interpretation of data when hypothyroidism is offered as the cause of alcoholism. In short, research findings of consistently observable deviations for the alcoholic group must be interpreted carefully so as not to go beyond the data.

Another point of interest in designing experiments in alcoholism research has been raised by Carpenter (1967). First, he cites four types of experiments which can be conducted in the context of alcoholism: (1) experiments which compare the nonalcoholic normal subjects under no-alcohol and alcohol conditions (i.e., "alcoholization" study—the most frequently used type of experiment), valid for determining the pharmacologic effects of alcohol, and possibly of a great utility when this is coupled with a long-term follow-up study from preadolescence to the late middle age, (2) experiments in which alcoholics are compared with nonalcoholics under the no-alcohol condition [when the two groups are ideally matched—see Edwards (1954), MacMahon, Pugh, and Ipsen (1960, pp. 235–247) on "comparison groups"—then the difference between the two groups would tell the results of prolonged immoderate use of alcohol, and/or the predisposing factors for alcoholism], (3) alcoholics are compared under no-alcohol and alcohol conditions (any observed difference may not be unique to alcoholics, because the observed difference may be derived from a factor which has nothing to do with alcoholism, but is unique to task situations, (see Vogel, 1960, 1961) and (4) experiments which compare normal and alcoholic subjects before and after both have had alcohol, where the observed difference would be due definitely to alcoholism. Carpenter states in his 1967 paper that "without a control group, an experiment provides useful information, but considerably less than its potential" (p. 17).

Considering the above four experimental types, a simple 2×2 design (i.e., the alcoholics and the nonalcoholics; no-alcohol and alcohol conditions) or the three-phase design of Johnson and Lubin (in press) would be ideal. In designs involving nonalcoholics and alcoholics, two aspects of the experiment must be carefully executed; the experiment is of the *ex post facto* type, needing very careful matching of the nonalcoholic subjects with the alcoholic subjects, and alcohol dose must cover a sufficient range for the alcoholics and for the nonalcoholics requiring the experimenter to know the equally effective dose (EED) of alcohol for these two groups.

1. The *ex post facto* design (see Edwards, 1954). In the McGonnell and Beach study (1968), differences of the SRR in adaptation, acquisition, and extinction phases between the alcoholics and nonalcoholics were tested for significance. There would be no statistical difficulties in testing the differences. However, the allocation of the individual subjects to the categories of alcoholics and nonalcoholics was not random, but performed in *ex post facto* fashion. This nonrandom allocation of "treatment" brings up a conceptual difficulty in interpreting the observed significant differences. The observed differences cannot unambiguously be attributed to alcoholism. The minimum requirement is a thoroughly explicit and detailed matching of the nonalcoholics. In MacMahon, Pugh, and Ipsen's terminology (1960, pp. 235–247), the nonalcoholic group is a "comparison group," and "the comparison group should not differ from the affected group in any respect (other than not being affected) which might be likely to influence the frequency of the variable or variables suspected of being

casually connected" (p. 235). Wexberg (1950) realized a need for the matched group in alcoholism studies when he deplored the lack of identical twin studies where one twin is an alcoholic and the other not. Edwards (1954) exemplified the difficulty in achieving a satisfactory degree of matching in an example where only 23 successful matches were obtained out of an initial 1130 members, taking only six factors into consideration.

2. Equally effective alcohol dose for alcoholics and nonalcoholics. Owing to an acquired increased tissue tolerance to alcohol in the alcoholics, alcohol dose must necessarily be larger for them to produce the same sort of change as experienced by the nonalcoholics. Goldberg (1943) found it impossible to give the same alcohol dose to abstainers, moderate drinkers, and habitual drinkers. In this regard, the previously mentioned studies by Mizoi and his associates (1969) are very promising in estimating the "equally effective alcohol dose."

3. Hypothesis testing approach—some examples. One of the most profitable ways of conducting psychophysiological experiments on alcoholism would be the approach of "hypothesis testing" (Lester, 1966). In this approach, the experiment starts with a working hypothesis; then data are collected to see how well the predictions from the working hypothesis match with the data. As examples, the work of Docter and his associates (1961, 1964, 1966) may be given in detail.

The basic working hypothesis of Docter and his associates is that a dose of alcohol does something desirable for the alcoholics; autonomic, EMG, and EEG measures will be able to describe the alcohol-induced state after which the alcoholics seek. That is, their studies are scientific efforts to determine what alcohol does for the alcoholics, and also for the nondrinkers. How have they arranged the experiment to define such positive psychological and physiological states after alcohol? In the 1961 study, Docter and Perkins assigned nonalcoholic subjects to either an alcohol group (receiving 0.5 ml/kg, and blood level ranging from 11 mg/100 ml to 67 mg/100 ml), or to a control group. Physiological variables measured were SRR, FP, HR, respiration, and right forearm flexor EMG. With the alcohol dose used, there were no major changes in autonomic variables, except that resting forearm EMG level of the alcohol group remained high in contrast to a progressive relaxation of EMG in the control subjects. In addition to the basal recordings, all subjects were exposed to two stimulus situations: (1) the cold pressor test, and (2) a venipuncture of right arm. The autonomic lability scores (LAS) were computed for each variable and for each subject which showed no change in autonomic reactivities to these stimulating situations. A detailed analysis of averaged evoked HR change to cold pressor and anticipation of venipuncture (Fig. 1) shows an absence of profound cardiac deceleration after the initial cardiac acceleration with alcohol ingestion. Figures 2 and 3 show the finger pulse volume and right forearm flexor EMG during the course of the experiment. The increased EMG tension of the forearm

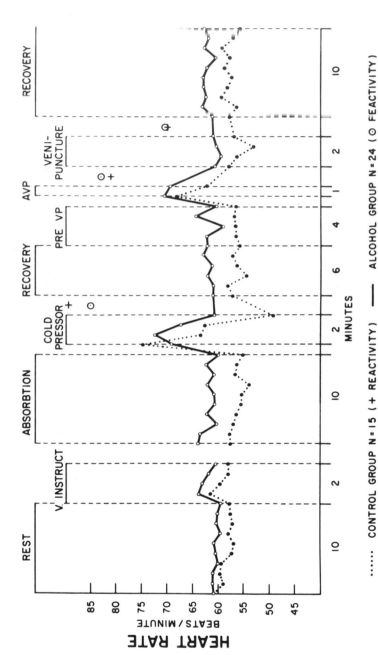

FIGURE 1. Heart rate (beats/min) averaged over 1-min period, from the start of the experimental session to the end. Rest = V. Instruct (verbal instructions given and drinking initiates); absorption (postabsorptive period); cold pressor task; recovery; Pre VP (prevenipuncture baseline period); venipuncture; recovery. AVP represents a period anticipating the venipuncture. "Reactivity" indicates the greatest change following cold pressor task, and AVP and venipuncture itself. Nonalcoholics at a dose of 0.5 ml/kg. [Taken from Docter and Perkins (1961).]

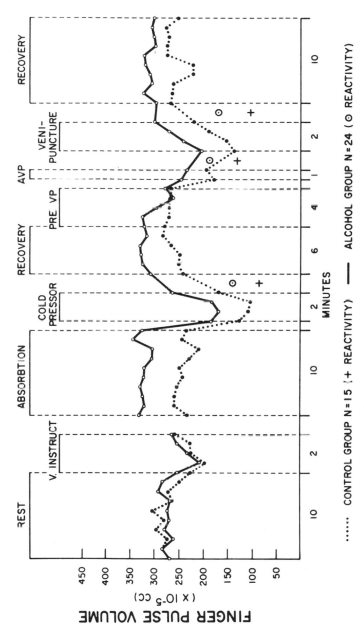

FIGURE 2. Finger pulse volume ($\times 10^{-5}$ cc) averaged over 1-min period, from the start of the experiment to the end. See Fig. 1 for definitions of terms and symbols. [Taken from Docter and Perkins (1961).]

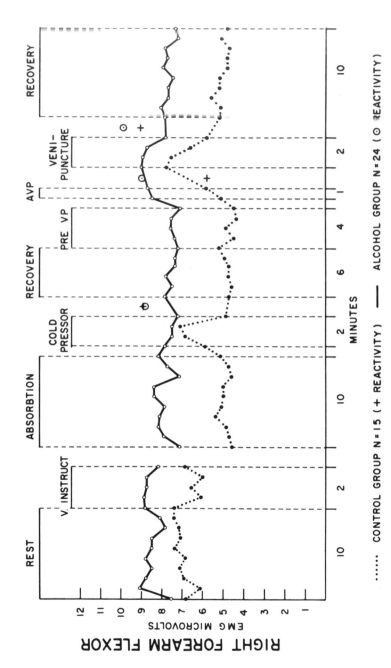

FIGURE 3. Right forearm flexor muscle tonus (EMG microvolts) obtained with surface electrodes, averaged over 1-m_n period. See Fig. 1 for definitions of terms and symbols. [From Docter and Perkins (1961).]

is taken to represent alcohol's stimulating property, and also it is interpreted to reflect a positive effect of alcohol for this group of subjects, i.e., a feeling of excitement. Increased basal HR after alcohol also supported the hypothetical stimulating property of alcohol. In a 1964 study, Docter and Bernal pursued a similar course in testing their working hypothesis in studying two alcoholic subjects on a 14-day experimental binge. Their experimental design utilized the three-phase scheme: a 7-day period of the initial control (baseline) period, a 14-day period of experimental drinking spree, and finally a 7-day final control (recovery) period. The alcoholic subjects were under 24-hr surveillance throughout the 4-week experimental session. Vodka was given to the subjects two times a day during the binge period at a dose of 1.8 ml/kg of body weight, equal to roughly a "fifth" a day. Blood alcohol levels varied considerably: in the morning before drink, blood alcohol level was as low as 10–40 mg/100 ml; a high of 190 mg/100 ml was observed in the postabsorption period. During the postabsorptive period, the subjects were very talkative, more demanding and assertive, in contrast to silent and uncommunicative behaviors when sober. The most remarkable autonomic change was a sustained increase in HR (Fig. 4), and this increased HR persisted 6 days following the last alcohol drink. Most interestingly, both subjects showed a significantly larger number of spontaneous rapid eye movements in the postabsorptive period (Fig. 5). The experiment of Docter and Bernal (1964) studied one additional factor, i.e., the effect of

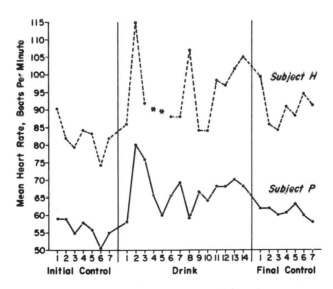

FIGURE 4. Effects of a 14-day experimental "spree" on average heart rate of two alcoholic experimental subjects. The asterisks indicate missing data. [From Docter and Bernal (1964).]

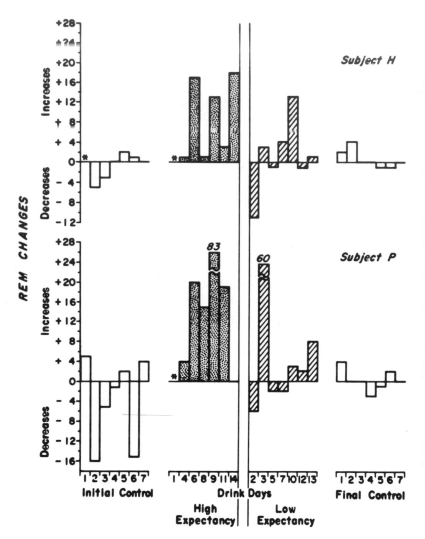

FIGURE 5. Effects of a 14-day experimental "spree" on rapid eye movements of two alcoholic subjects. [From Docter and Bernal (1964).]

"expecting" an alcohol drink only 4 hr later (low expectancy *vs.* high expectancy condition in which the subjects received the alcohol drink without delay). Figure 5 shows that episodes of rapid eye movements are largely determined by ingestion of alcohol. By combining all of these changes in the autonomic and EEG variables, Docter and Bernal concluded that alcohol drinking has some excitatory effects. However, the persistent HR increase after the last drink could have reflected a hangover.

In a 1966 study of Docter and his colleagues, the excitatory properties of alcohol drinking in the alcoholic subjects were reconfirmed on the basis of vigilance task performance, EEG, and autonomic measures. A crucial question remaining for the working hypothesis of Docter and his associates is whether the excitatory properties of alcohol are the effects which all types of alcoholics would be seeking after with drinking alcohol. Are the alcoholics really conscious of slightly increased HR, warm hands and fingers, slightly increased muscular tension of the extremities, increased visual scannings, and other events as part of being pleasantly "drunk"? There are many other questions to be asked and explored, but at least Docter and his associates have shown that such a hypothesis testing approach is productive.

Cardiovascular System and Alcohol

Ritchie (1965) in his review of the literature concluded that alcohol does not exert significant effects on the cardiovascular system, except in acute alcoholic intoxication where cardiovascular and respiratory depressions are observed. As described by Ritchie, the effect of a moderate dose of alcohol on the peripheral circulation is vasodilation, resulting in warming and a flushed skin and larger finger pulse volume. Docter and Perkins (1961) and Docter and Bernal (1964) have found a vasodilation of finger pulse after ingestion of alcohol, both in nonalcoholics and alcoholics. In the Docter and Perkins study (1961), a greater variability in finger pulse is observed during the postabsorptive period. Roth and Sheard (1947) have measured vasoconstriction and vasodilation of fingers and toes indirectly by recording skin temperature. The subjects were 65 normal nonalcoholic males and females, aged 19 to 59. Many of them were physicians and all of them were habitual smokers. Roth and Sheard observed the usual vasodilation of fingers and toes following 30 ml of 95% alcohol. The alcohol-induced vasodilation had a certain response latency, requiring 50 to 60 min to reach the maximal dilation, and persisting for 1 to $1\frac{1}{2}$ hr. A primary object of Roth and Sheard's research was to determine the effects of cigarette smoking on the cardiovascular system and their modification by alcohol, or a substantial meal. Alcohol prevented, in some subjects, the occurrence of smoking-induced vasoconstriction, but, in 72% of the subjects, vasoconstriction of the toes after smoking was not prevented by alcohol ingestion. The authors concluded that the vasoconstriction from smoking was not prevented by alcohol- or food-induced vasodilation. It is noteworthy that one out of 65 subjects showed a complete inhibition of effects of smoking on the vessels by alcohol ingestion; in others only finger vasoconstrictions were prevented by alcohol.

From this study alone the belief that drinking a cocktail will necessarily nullify the effect of smoking was not confirmed, but it was very suggestive in raising questions about what happens when drinking and smoking occurred together. Would alcohol-induced peripheral vasodilation be subjectively felt as a part of being drunk? Would smoking-induced peripheral vasoconstriction be subjectively felt as rewarding? Or, are these autonomic responses a source of annoyance, or simply epiphenomena of no reinforcing significance? Would a combined use of alcohol drinking and smoking be more rewarding? These questions of autonomic feedbacks to the individuals' awareness (Mandler, Mandler, and Uviller, 1958; Mason, 1961) and discriminative interpretation of these autonomic changes remain unanswered.

A recent study by Morikawa and his colleagues (1968) answered partly a remark made by Docter and Bernal (1964) about the need for a careful study of the latency, duration, and individual differences in vascular changes following alcohol ingestion. In the study by Morikawa and his colleagues, the purpose of the research was to determine whether the extent of alcohol effects on the CNS could be measured. They chose peripheral vasodilation as an index of the CNS effect of alcohol, because alcohol at the specified dose is known not to act upon the blood vessels directly to cause dilation, but rather on the vasomotor center (Ritchie, 1965). Morikawa and his associates studied 157 nonalcoholics before and after ingestion of 120–240 ml of 14% alcohol-containing beer. The finger pulse volume was evaluated by first measuring the maximal finger dilation, and again the finger volume at the dichrotic notch. Then, the finger volume at the dichrotic notch was divided by the maximal finger volume to yield the dichrotic index (DI). Alcohol ingestion reduced the pulse volume at the dichrotic notch; hence, reduced the DI. The DI has been found to be very sensitive, so that the DI can detect drunkenness. An advantage to using a photoelectric reflectance finger pulse volume and its DI is the relatively easy manner of recording such autonomic data with an A-C method. However, Morikawa and his associates reported that 14% of the subjects failed to develop a lower DI after ingestion of alcohol. It should be noted that in any of the studies using FP variables, a DC recording of the FP has not yet been performed to examine alcohol effects on blood content in the fingers.

The heart rate increase due to alcohol has been found to be very reliable and replicable from one study to another. Without any exception, HR has increased with ingestion of alcohol. In the Docter, Naitoh, and Smith study (1966), using 1.5 ml/kg in 12 alcoholic subjects, HR increased linearly with an increase of blood alcohol level (ranging from 20 mg/100 ml to 100 mg/100 ml). The computed rank order correlation between HR and blood alcohol was 1.00, and a curve-fitting technique showed that 99% of the total variance can be explained by a linear term.

Using 10 hospitalized male alcoholics and 10 male hospital attendants, Holmberg and Martens (1958) observed HR change in response to 1.25 g of absolute alcohol per kilogram of body weight, and a blood alcohol level of roughly 110 mg/100 ml. They found that the HR increase after alcohol was significantly greater among nonalcoholics than in alcoholics. For all the non-alcoholic group, the initial HR increase was followed by a HR decrease below the prealcohol baseline value after 15–30 min in the postabsorptive period, whereas only 6 out of 10 alcoholics showed a similar overcompensation. The further course of HR recovery also differed between alcoholics and nonalcoholics. The most interesting finding of this study concerned a feeling tone associated with each phase of HR change. At the initial HR increase, a feeling of "excitation" was reported and the subsequent HR decrease was accompanied by a feeling tone of "narcosis." In nonalcoholic subjects, the second sharp increase in HR was often accompanied by nausea. In some nonalcoholics, the feeling tone of "drowsiness" was accompanied by an HR decrease. In terms of HR change, the two groups showed no overlap on the average HR response in the entire $4\frac{1}{2}$ hr postabsorptive period. The finding of these authors indicates that HR response can be used to estimate the equally effective dose of alcohol.

Mendelson and La Dou (1964) studied an experimental spree of 10 chronic alcoholics who drank an 86-proof bourbon whiskey-alcohol mixture every 4 hr. The alcoholic subjects were maintained on a total dose of 30 oz every day for 14 consecutive days, and 40 oz for 6 consecutive days. All the subjects developed an increased HR during the alcohol drinking phase, and, judging from the published graphs, the alcoholics maintained a high HR during the withdrawal phase in agreement with the findings by Isbell and his associates (1955) and Docter and Bernal (1964).

Hebbelinck (1962) studied HR response of 10 nonalcoholic males during rest, during a 5-min work load of 1000 kg/min on a bicycle ergometer, and again during a 3-min rest period, with or without alcohol ingestion. The alcohol dose was 0.6 ml/kg of body weight, resulting in a blood alcohol level of 30 mg/100 ml, 30–60 min after drinking. Alcohol increased the resting HR, and an additional marked increase of HR was observed during ergometer work after alcohol. Karvinen and his colleagues (1962) observed a high HR during the resting hangover phase and a greater HR increase during the work performed in a hangover period. Finally, Cutshall (1965) indicated that, in 205 cases of delirium tremens, 61% showed tachycardia. Of this group 35% had HR's of 120 beats per min or more, and the highest body temperature was less than 100°F. HR was, however, of no prognostic significance.

A few studies of blood pressure changes due to alcohol are available (Cutshall, 1965; Schnall and Wiener, 1958; Wenger, 1948), but the psychophysiological significance of blood pressure changes among the alcoholics remains uncertain. Schnall found that alcoholics were less hypertensive and less hypotensive than the matched general population. The studies by Kissen and Hankoff (1959), Kissen, Schenker, and Schenker (1959), and Kissen and Platz (1968) are of particular interest with respect to blood pressure responses. They applied the Funkenstein mecholyl test (see Gellhorn and Loofbourrow, 1963, pp. 117–127) to alcoholics. Their studies suggested a hypothesis that "alcoholics, like other psychiatric patients, suffer from anxiety and autonomic imbalance, and alcohol, like other sedatives, reduces the tension and autonomic imbalance" (Kissin and Platz, 1968, pp. 836–837). In their studies, mecholylchloride (acetyl-β-methylcholine) was injected into the muscle of the arm (10 mg per patient), and it usually caused a sharp drop in the systolic blood pressure, and then a recovery.

Gellhorn and Loofbourrow (1963) used mecholyl to measure what they have called the central sympathetic reactivity (CSR). Statistically, there are three types of CSR. Type I, the hyperactive CSR, is a large hypertensive response to a mecholyl-induced initial drop of the systolic blood pressure. Type III has a hyporeactive CSR, a large hypotension response after mecholyl. Type II are those responses which show the systolic blood pressure fall of 15–25 mm Hg initially to the injection of mecholyl and a return to the baseline after 5–8 min. Type II represents the normal central sympathetic reaction to mecholyl. Kissin and Hankoff injected mecholyl in a group of 19 male alcoholics, aged 24 to 56 (mean age of 38.5 years), before and after alcohol ingestion at 1 g/kg of body weight dose. Eleven out of 19 alcoholic subjects did not change their CSR type to mecholyl under alcohol (among the 11 subjects, one alcoholic subject belonged to type I, eight to type II, and two subjects to type III). In eight subjects who changed their response pattern to mecholyl under alcohol, six subjects became type II, the intermediate or normal CSR, from either type I or type III. From this finding, it was concluded that alcohol did not create a uniformly CSR depressing or a CSR stimulating effect. Rather, alcohol appears to have reduced the extreme autonomic blood pressure responses to mecholyl. In other words, alcohol effects on the CSR would be depressing when the subjects had initially a high CSR, but alcohol would be actually stimulating in the alcoholics who had originally a low CSR. This, then, is direct evidence for the idea expressed by Wilder (1962) about LIV and drug effects, and supports the hypothesis of Docter and his colleagues (1966) concerning what alcohol does for alcoholics.

A recent promising development in the cardiovascular psychophysiology of alcoholism is an application of Kelly's forearm blood flow plethysmography (1966) to the measurement of anxiety in alcoholics (Rosenberg and Buttsworth, 1969). By using an intermittent venous occlusion without interfering with arterial flow to the forearm, the blood flow rate can be measured by sealing the forearm in a cylinder which is kept airtight. The forearm volume is largely determined by the blood flow to forearm muscles, and the vessels are innervated by cholinergic sympathetic vasodilator fibers, forming an integral part of the "defense reaction." Kelly has established the relationship between the increase in forearm blood flow and a variety of stressors. Rosenberg and Buttsworth (1969) used 35 hospitalized alcoholics, and have tested forearm blood flow before and after the stress of mental arithmetic problems conducted under continuous criticism and harassment. The results were compared with those of 30 control nonalcoholic subjects drawn from the hospital staff. Results indicated that the resting forearm blood flow of the alcoholics is quite similar to those of the controls, but during the arithmetic stress, the alcoholics showed a significantly lower forearm blood flow of 5.65 ml/100 ml/min, compared with 10.68 ml/100 ml/min of the control subjects, reflecting "a poor motivation and a tendency to discharge defensively from the task rather than attempt to cope with it" among alcoholics. The finding of no difference in the resting forearm blood flow in alcoholics without alcohol (i.e., the alcoholics are no more or no less anxious than the nonalcoholic) may have a considerable significance in future experiments.

Gillespie (1967) measured the blood flow of the feet, calves, forearms, and wrists of healthy adult subjects, and of patients with occlusive arterial disease affecting legs, using a venous occlusion plethysmography. All subjects first received an alcohol dose of 2 ml/kg per body weight to evaluate alcohol effects on the blood flow into the healthy or occluded leg. Blood alcohol level ranged from 46 mg/100 ml to 224 mg/100 ml (an average of 92 mg/100 ml). He confirmed that alcohol is a potent cutaneous vasodilator in normal subjects. Alcohol increased the blood flow of 7 out of 11 limbs with blocked arteries, although the increase of pedal blood flow was not as high as in the healthy limbs. With an alcohol dose of 1 ml/kg of body weight, the increase in pedal blood flow was not remarkable. Most important of all, alcohol had little or no effect on the muscle blood flow, the vasodilation being exclusively cutaneous. Alcohol increased blood flow at the wrist (where the total flow is mainly in skin), but did not change the blood flow in the forearm where the total blood flow is largely determined by blood flow into the muscles.

Electrodermal System and Alcohol

There are some studies of SRL and SRR and alcoholism (Wenger, 1948; Carpenter, 1957; Greenberg and Carpenter, 1957; Lineret and Traxel, 1959; McDonnell and Carpenter, 1959; Vogel, 1960, 1961; Coopersmith, 1964; Docter and Bernal, 1964; Coopersmith and Woodrow, 1967; McGonnell and Beach, 1968), and none on SPL and SPR.

Some of these studies are based on an assumption that SRL and SRR can be a good measure of anxiety, tension, and a generally high degree of activation. McGonnell and Beach (1968) postulated that alcoholism is a result of learning to use alcohol for a reduction of anxiety and tension, and used an aversive classical conditioning of SRR (or GSR conditioning) as the measure of anxiety. They chose a group of 32 nonalcoholic subjects and tested them under four experimental conditions: alcohol aversive conditioning, alcohol pseudoconditioning,

placebo conditioning, and placebo pseudoconditioning. Aversive conditioning consisted of the conditional stimulus (CS) of tone, and uncondi-
tional stimulus (UCS) of 0.2-sec, 50 V electrical shock given during the CS with
the UCS during its 4.5–5.0-sec period. The hypothesis under test was that
alcohol inhibits the acquisition and maintenance of a conditional SRR, possibly
through the route of anxiety reduction, assuming that stable SRR conditioning
is possible to start with in the subjects. The experimental results appear to have
confirmed the hypothesis, when an alcohol dose of 0.34 ml of 95% alcohol per
pound of body weight was given orally to the group of nonalcoholics. Vogel
(1960, 1961) used male alcoholics and nonalcoholics in his studies of conditioning
SRR. In his studies, the SRR conditioning used a CS of presenting a nonsense
syllable and a UCS of an unpleasantly loud doorbell buzzer. In these studies,
personality factors of extraversion (E score) and neuroticism (N score) were also
obtained with the Maudsley Personality Inventory. Only alcoholic subjects
were used in his 1960 study, in which there was an equal number of introverts
and extroverts. Among the alcoholics, the introverted alcoholics showed a
quicker acquisition of the conditional SRR and higher resistance to extinction.
Vogel also found that an increasing degree of extraversion was associated with a
need for more acquisition trials and faster extinction. The implication of this
study is similarity of conditional SRR to the conditioning of nausea as an
aversive therapeutic method in alcoholism. The introverted alcoholics will be
more amenable to aversive conditioning therapy. No relation was observed
between the neuroticism score and SRR conditionability, or its retention in the
alcoholics. Since this 1960 study of Vogel used only alcoholic subjects, one
cannot be sure whether the better conditionability which was observed in the
introverted alcoholics was due to the introversion or alcoholism, or both. In his
1961 study, Vogel employed both alcoholics and nonalcoholics to show that
alcoholism *per se* did not affect the conditionability, because both introversive
alcoholics and introversive nonalcoholics showed a conditional SRR more
quickly and were more resistant to extinction than those extraversive alcoholics
and nonalcoholics. Although alcoholics had a high average neuroticism score, it
did not affect conditionability. Those alcoholics who failed to be conditioned
had extremely high extraversion scores. A lack of relation between the neuroticism and a conditional SRR casts some doubt on the hypothesis that an SRR
conditioning revealed anxiety, a part of neuroticism measures.

Lienert and Traxel (1959) used the SRR as the measure of affective reactivity, as modified by different medications in orangeade: 800 mg of meprobamate, 20 ml of 98% ethanol, or a placebo. The objective of this study was to
discover the psychotropic effect of meprobamate against that of "the oldest
known tranquilizer," alcohol. The experimental subjects were clinically normal
nonalcoholic male students. Emotional stimuli were given: a word association
test, and an association test involving emotionally loaded statements. Results

showed that emotional reactivity as measured by the SRR was significantly decreased by alcohol and meprobamate.

Carpenter and his associates also studied the effects of alcohol on SRL and SRR. Carpenter (1957) examined the hypothesis that ANS activities might be decreased by alcohol as a result of a change in an overall activation level. Both skin conductance level (SCL) and skin conductance response (SCR) were measured, using eight moderate social drinkers. The task of filing name cards alphabetically was imposed on the subjects to establish a constant activity level, before and after the ingestions of alcoholic beverages: two doses (50 ml and 350 ml) of wine, or two doses (50 ml and 350 ml) of 12% alcohol in water were used. The SCR was induced by suddenly sounding an electrical horn at 97 db for 10 sec, approximately 35 min and again 47 min after the end of drinking. Results showed no significant SCL change due to alcohol in the early postdrink period. In the late postdrink period, the interaction between the kinds of alcoholic beverages and doses became statistically significant. At 50 ml, alcohol was more effective in lowering the SCL than wine, whereas wine was more effective in lowering SCL at the 350-ml dose. With respect to the SCR evoked to a horn stimulation, 50 ml of either beverages had little effect on the response magnitude, i.e., only 8% (for wine) and 5% (for alcohol) reduction. With the 350-ml dose, SCR was reduced by 53% with wine drinking, and 49% by alcohol-in-water drinking. Carpenter's conclusion about alcohol and skin conductance was clear: alcohol reduced the magnitude of the SCR. In contrast, the skin conductance level was affected in a complex manner: the SCL was influenced by the kind of alcoholic beverage, the amount of alcohol ingested, and the elapsed time after the end of the drinking period. With a moderately high dose, the SCL level fell.

In the Greenberg and Carpenter study (1957), the SCR data of Carpenter's 1957 study was reinterpreted. Two points in Carpenter's 1957 study were emphasized: (1) in the previous study, alcohol reduced the SCL while wine did not, when alcohol dose was 50 ml, and (2) with 350 ml of 12% alcohol strength, however, wine was much more potent in reducing the SCL than drinking alcohol in water. Greenberg and Carpenter's reinterpretations were that the difference in potency in reduction of "emotional level" (as reflected in high SCL) at a low dose of 50 ml of 12% alcohol strength may be due to a rapid absorption and a quick buildup of the blood alcohol level after alcohol ingestion in comparison with wine, and that an unpleasant taste and disagreeable gastric action associated with drinking a large (i.e., 350 ml) quantity of alcohol in water in comparison to the pleasant taste of wine became a stress, and raised the SCL, or at least counteracted the reduction of the SCL. To examine the tension-arousing effects of drinking strong alcoholic beverages, an experiment with a different dose of whiskey was performed to confirm that each alcoholic beverage exercised its own degree of stress with respect to palatability and gastric activities.

Greenberg and Carpenter concluded that the alcoholic beverages at less than intoxicating doses can reduce tonic emotional tension, and also diminish phasic emotional responses to sudden onset of weak, or of intense stimulation.

In 1959, McDonnell and Carpenter cautioned, however, that the general psychological significance of emotional tone and other psychological dispositions must be used carefully in interpreting either the increase or decrease of the SCL. They emphasized the need for a questionnaire method to ascertain the individual's subjective evaluation of tension or anxiety, when the SCL or SCR were measured. In this study, they used nonalcoholic graduate students. The skin conductance measures were obtained simultaneously from two groups of four subjects each, playing cards on two separate tables. In one session, the subjects drank two 12-oz bottles of near beer (0.5% alcohol), and on another occasion, they drank fortified near beer (4.8% alcohol). The results showed that drinking in group increased the SCL from the start to the end of the session. The SCL of the subjects, and this subjectively related anxiety as measured by the Mandler–Sarasen anxiety scale showed a curvilinear relationship, with a significant correlation ratio of 0.722. Hence, the SCL reduction may not necessarily mean a reduction in anxiety, if the tonic anxiety happens to be very high. Does a high anxiety group differ from a low anxiety group in the response to alcohol ingestion ? Before drinking, the two groups exhibited significantly different SCL's but after alcohol ingestion, the difference disappeared. The study of McDonnell and Carpenter established two important observations: (1) the SCL and the general anxiety level had a curvilinear or an inverted U relation, and (2) alcohol drinking in a group was different from solitary drinking in terms of SCL. Their conclusion was singularly important for a psychophysiology of alcoholism: "the effects of small amounts of alcohol on the autonomic nervous system will depend on the circumstances under which drinking takes place" (1959, p. 51).

Coopersmith and Woodrow (1967) measured the SCL's of eight alcoholics and also those of healthy nonalcoholic subjects from the upper middle class. The subjects were seated in a darkened room, and SCL was measured from the electrodes on the plantar surface of the feet. Mean SCL's between alcoholics and nonalcoholics prior to drinking were the same. The SCL's of nonalcoholics were again measured 30 min after 0.86 ml of 86-proof whiskey/kg per body weight. Alcohol reduced the SCL and possibly reduced the level of arousal. They concluded that alcohol seems to relieve the early vague distress experience with attendant rewarding experience. Another Coopersmith study (1964) showed that normal adult male subjects responded more to affective stimuli after a moderate dose of 0.86 ml of 86-proof whiskey/kg of body weight, but their subjectively felt distress to affective stimuli was lessened. That is, alcohol ingestion made the subjects focus better on the work at hand, their behaviors becoming more realistic and appropriate to situational and task demands. Thus, alcohol reduced task-associated distress and helped the subjects pay more attention to the demands of the task.

Docter and Bernal (1964) studied the SRL of two alcoholics examined during a 2-week period of experimental binge. They observed that one of the subjects showed a large drop in the SRL during this period of drinking, along with slurred speech, slight ataxia, and increased verbalization.

Salivation, Eye Movements, Respiration, Digestive System, EMG, and Alcohol

There are but few experiments on alcohol effects on salivation in human subjects (Beazell and Ivy, 1940; Wenger, 1948; Kissin et al., 1959; Sutherland et al., 1962; Stern et al., 1968). Beazell and Ivy (1940) noted an immediate increase in salivation followed by a decrease after alcohol. Wenger found a low salivary output in alcoholics. Kissin and his colleagues (1959) found that salivary output and saliva sodium show a sharp drop after alcohol in active alcoholics— a drop of 50% both in saliva sodium, and interpreted these changes as due to parasympathicolytic effects of alcohol, and also to its dehydration effects. Saliva sodium in active and abstaining alcoholics was higher than in controls. The saliva potassium was higher in active and abstaining alcoholics. Alcohol ingestion increased saliva potassium further in alcoholics. Sutherland and his associates (1962) found only two out of 26 male hospitalized alcoholics to have a normal salivary secretion under a classical salivary conditioning paradigm (the CS of a brief auditory stimulation reinforced by the UCS of sweetened synthetic lemon juice). Stern and his associates (1964) examined, using a dental-roll technique, 40 male hospitalized alcoholics with respect to resting state salivation, and in response to instruction and lemon juice. Resting salivary output was smaller than the quantities of the salivary outputs of depressed patients. Salivation volume, and particularly a chemical analysis of saliva, may yield additional valuable data on the ANS functions.

Other psychophysiological variables of promise would be (1) "eye movement" as defined by Docter and his associates (REM; the lateral movements of eyes), or ROM of Goldberg (1966) in addition to the others mentioned previously; (2) various aspects of respiration (Shenker et al., 1962); (3) gastric and other digestive tract data (e.g., Engeset et al., 1963; Woodward et al., 1957); and (4) EMG (Carlson et al., 1969; Hed, 1962).

SUMMARY

Alcoholism has been studied psychophysiologically to discover its etiology and to develop new diagnostic and therapeutic approaches. Most current psychophysiological research has studied the effects of alcohol on only one autonomic variable. In some psychophysiological experiments, psychological data were simultaneously obtained to aid interpretation of the altered autonomic activities due to alcohol ingestion. Some psychophysiological experiments are based on the relatively naive hypothesis that an increase or decrease of one autonomic activity will directly and unambiguously reflect a certain psychological or physiological state. Modern developments in psychophysiology have, however, shown that a problem as complex as alcoholism should not be handled by a one-variable study; the activity level and the direction of activity of a single autonomic measure will not by itself be sufficient to warrant a uniform psychological interpretation, such as an increase or a decrease of the level of anxiety.

In the most unfavorable light, contemporary psychophysiological studies on alcoholism have failed so far to produce a breakthrough in understanding of the mechanisms underlying the long process of becoming addicted to alcohol, and of maintaining alcohol abuse in face of great personal loss. Contemporary psychophysiological studies on alcoholism have also failed to provide advances in the clinical aspects of alcoholism—prevention, therapy, and prognosis.

However, there are notable exceptions. First, psychophysiology has succeeded in communicating the importance of what alcohol does for the individual drinkers over the usual emphasis on what alcohol drinking does to them. In this new emphasis, psychophysiological studies have destroyed some of the myth surrounding alcoholism and alcoholismic drinking; alcoholismic drinking may not be regarded simply as "an escape from stress, anxiety, high tension," nor may it be regarded as an act of fulfilling a self-destructive wish. Alcoholismic drinking is the result of a complex failure to discriminate and cope with data coming from social as well as "internal" (i.e., coming from the inside of the body) environments. Psychophysiological studies have shown clearly that alcohol drinking has quite different effects on alcoholics, as compared with nonalcoholics. All of these findings eventually will help us understand how alcoholics maintain their drinking.

Second, psychophysiological studies have found many autonomic measures which help diagnose alcoholism in terms of a learned increased tissue tolerance to alcohol. Thus, some autonomic measures can be used as a biological ruler better than the blood alcohol level in expressing the level of alcohol intoxication. Such autonomic measures result in a crucial concept of "equally effective dose of alcohol," permitting the comparison of alcoholics and nonalcoholics: e.g., the PAN (Goldberg, 1943, 1966), temporal muscle spikes (Mizoi and his associates, 1963), optokinetic nystagmus (Mizoi and his associates, 1967, 1969), and the dichrotic index (Morikawa and his colleagues, 1968).

Psychophysiology has found also that alcohol effects depend on many factors: physical condition; the affective, cognitive and perceptual characteristics of the drinker; and the physical, social, and ethnic environment in which alcohol drinking takes place.

The slow progress of the psychophysiology of alcoholism in contributing to management of alcoholics may be accelerated by a careful scrutiny of its past approaches.

How can such acceleration in progress of psychophysiology of alcoholism be achieved ?

The use of autonomic variables other than the conventional ones of the cardiovascular and electrodermal systems would be desirable, to cover a wider spectrum of the ANS activities. One such example is the use of salivation.

In parallel with the efforts to describe the autonomic effects of alcohol by means of recording many new and old psychophysiological variables simultaneously, a psychophysiological exploration of some therapies for alcoholics would accelerate our understanding. LSD therapy (see negative results of LSD therapy, F. G. Johnson, 1969), and a combination of classical or operant aversive conditioning techniques with hypnosis in counteracting alcoholismic drinking (Abrams, 1969; Lazarus, 1965; see Blum and Blum, 1967, pp. 112–116) would offer a good starting point for the psychophysiological studies. Such studies can show how some therapeutic methods work and some do not. Also, it would be worthwhile to explore whether the alcoholics can become aware of and perceive some ANS signs of alcohol effects, and even to control such ASN activities voluntarily through operant conditioning methods (Katkin and Murray, 1968; see also Miller, 1969). An increased awareness of the ANS activities might be helpful for some alcoholics to discriminate the stress-associated ANS changes which lead to drinking from the need for alcoholic drink associated with the ANS changes of hunger, thirst, and others.

There has been wide recognition of a need for research in which both chronic alcoholics and nonalcoholics are compared with each other. Similarly, a need for a long-term experimentally controlled spree has been recognized. Due largely to enormous expense and a slow rate of data collection coupled with uncertain outcome, some types of psychophysiological experiments have not been attempted, although a large potential contribution of such research efforts is recognized. First, there have been only few longitudinal or developmental psychophysiological studies in the context of alcoholism. This sort of research requires the examination of a large sample of young persons, followed for years, using certain psychophysiological methods. The purpose of these longitudinal studies would be to detect emerging alcoholism in certain individuals and to find the etiology and predisposing characteristics by reexamination of earlier records. Second, there has been no epidemiologic approach in which a cross section of the entire population has been studied psychophysiologically. An example of a research plan which combines psychophysiology with epidemiology would be to measure the acquired increased tissue tolerance to alcohol (with the method of, say, a nystagmus, or a HR increase) of a large group of subjects in a variety of epidemiological categories, age, sex, occupation, religious, socioeconomic class, ethnic-cultural group, and many others. A particular interest would be to find the relation between the increased tissue alcohol tolerance and age. Or, the course of the tissue alcohol tolerance can be followed over years for each individual of a "cohort." If one particular individual's tissue alcohol tolerance goes up precipitously, then a close examination of such an individual will be of utmost urgency. With the use of digital computers and a recent automatic device to measure satisfactorily an acquired increased tissue tolerance to alcohol (such as the optokinetic device of Mizoi *et al.*, 1969) such a study has become feasible.

These studies would be desirable not only for an understanding of the process of addiction, but also for achieving the ultimate goal of psychophysiological studies: the prevention of alcoholism. Future psychophysiological studies, together with those of many other disciplines, would certainly play a part in achieving that goal.

ACKNOWLEDGMENTS

This report is supported by the Bureau of Medicine and Surgery, Department of the Navy, under Research Task MF. 12.524.004-9008D. The opinions expressed in this chapter are those of the author and are not to be construed as necessarily reflecting the view or endorsement of the Department of the Navy. The author wishes to express his appreciation to L. C. Johnson, A. Lubin, and W. L. Wilkins for their editorial assistance, to R. A. Sternbach for his critical comments and suggestions, and to M. A. Wenger who indicated to the author the source of the Ā study on the alcoholics. The author gratefully acknowledges the permission from R. F. Docter and the *Quarterly Journal of Studies of Alcohol* to reproduce four figures used in the chapter.

LIST OF ABBREVIATIONS

Ā	Autonomic Balance	EED	Equally Effective Dose
AAF	Army Air Force	EEG	Electroencephalogram
AGN	Alcohol Gaze Nystagmus	EMG	Electromyogram
ALS	Autonomic Lability Score	EOG	Electrooculogram
ANS	Autonomic Nervous System	FP	Finger Pulse
BP	Blood Pressure	FPR	Finger Pulse Response
CNS	Central Nervous System	HR	Heart Rate
CS	Conditional Stimulus	HRR	Heart Rate Response
CSR	Central Sympathetic Reactivity	IRS	Individual Response Specificity
D (Score)	Difference Score	LIV	Law of Initial Value

MRS	Motivational Response Specificity	SPL	Skin Potential Level
		SPR	Skin Potential Response
PA	Physiological Activation	SRL	Skin Resistance Level
PAN-I-II	Positional Alcohol Systagmus I and II		(Basal Skin Resistance)
		SRR	Skin Resistance Response
PNS	Parasympathetic Nervous System		(Galvanic Skin Response)
		SRS	Stimulus Response Specificity
ROM	Roving Ocular Movements		
SCL	Skin Conductance Level	UCS	Unconditional Stimulus
SCR	Skin Conductance Response	X_1; X_2	Prestimulus Levels
SNS	Sympathetic Nervous System	Y	Poststimulus Level

REFERENCES

Abrams, S., 1964. An evaluation of hypnosis in the treatment of alcoholics, *Amer. J. Psychiat.* **120:** 1160.

Arnold, M. B., 1960. *Emotion and Personality: Vol. 1. Psychological Aspects; Vol. 2, Neurophysiological and Physiological Aspects*, Columbia Univ. Press, New York.

Aschan, G., Bergstedt, M., Goldberg, L., and Laurell, L., 1956. Positional nystagmus in man during and after alcohol intoxication, *Quart. J. Stud. Alc.* **17:** 381.

Ax, A. F., 1953. Physiological differentiation between fear and anger in humans, *Psychosom. Med.* **15:** 433.

Ax, A. F., 1964. Goals and methods of psychophysiology, *Psychophysiology* **1:** 8.

Averill, J. R., 1969. Emotion and visceral activity: A case study in psychophysiological symbolism. Paper presented at the Ninth Annual Meeting of the Society for Psychophysiological Research, October, Monterey, Calif.

Averill, J. R. and Opton, E. M., Jr., 1968. *Psychophysiology*, assessment: Rationale and problems, in *Advances in Psychological Assessment* (P. McReynolds, ed.), Science and Behavior Books, pp. 265–288, Palo Alto, Calif.

Bard, P., 1960. Anatomical organization of the cerebral nervous system in relation to control of the heart and blood vessels, *Physiol. Rev.* **4** (Suppl. 4): 3.

Beazell, J. M. and Ivy, A. C., 1940. The influence of alcohol on the digestive tract, A review. *Quart. J. Stud. Alc.* **1:** 45.

Benjamin, L. S., 1963. Statistical treatment of the law of initial values (LIV) in autonomic research: A review and recommendation, *Psychosom. Med.* **25:** 556.

Benjamin, L. S., 1967. Facts and artifacts in using analysis of covariance to "undo" the law of initial values, *Psychophysiology* **4:** 187.

Berger, L., 1964. Interrelationship between blood pressure responses to Mecholyl and personality variables, *Psychophysiology* **1:** 115.

Bernal, M. E. and Docter, R. F. 1962. Autonomic studies of sustained alcohol intake, *Psychophysiology Newsletter* **8** (4): 32.

Blair, D. A., Glover, W. E., Greenfield, A. D. M., and Roddie, I. C., 1959. Excitation of cholinergic vasodilator nerves to human skeletal muscles during emotional stress, *J. Physiol.* **148:** 633.

Blum, E. M. and Blum, R. H., 1967. *Alcoholism: Modern Psychological Approaches to Treatment*, Jossey-Bass, Inc., San Francisco.

Boutin, L. D., Pain Tolerance of Essential and Reactive Alcoholics, Unpublished doctoral dissertation, Univ. Utah, 1967.

Brown, C. C. (ed.), 1967. *Methods in Psychophysiology*, Williams and Wilkins, Baltimore, Md.

Cannon, W. B., 1929. *Bodily Changes in Pain, Hunger, Fear and Rage*, Appleton–Century, New York. (Torchbook Edition, 1963, Harper & Row).

Cannon, W. B., 1930. The sympathetic division of the autonomic system in relation to homeostasis, in *The Vegetative Nervous System* (W. Timme, T. K. Davis, and H. A. Riley, eds.), The Proceedings of A.R.N.M.D., Vol. 9, pp. 181–198, Williams and Wilkins, Baltimore.

Carlsson, C., Denckers, S. J., Grimby, G., and Tichy, J., 1969. Muscle weakness and neurological disorders in alcoholics, *Quart. J. Stud. Alc.* **30**: 585.

Carpenter, J. A., 1957. The effects of alcoholic beverages on skin conductance. An exploratory study, *Quart. J. Stud. Alc.* **18**: 1.

Carpenter, J. A., 1967. Issues in research on alcohol, in *Alcoholism: Behavioral Researches, Therapeutic Approaches* (R. Fox, ed.), pp. 16–23, Springer, New York.

Conger, J. J., 1951. The effect of alcohol on conflict behavior in the albino rat, *Quart. J. Stud. Alc.* **12**: 1.

Coopersmith, S., 1964. Adaptive reactions of alcoholics and nonalcoholics, *Quart. J. Stud. Alc.* **25**: 262.

Coopersmith, S., 1964. The effects of alcohol on reactions to affective stimuli, *Quart. J. Stud. Alc.* **25**: 459.

Coopersmith, S. and Woodrow, K., 1967. Basal conductance levels of normals and alcoholics, *Quart. J. Stud. Alc.* **28**: 27.

Cutshall, B. J., 1965. The Saunders–Sutton syndrome: An analysis of delirium tremens, *Quart. J. Stud. Alc.* **26**: 423.

Darrow, C. W., 1943. Physiological and clinical tests of autonomic function and autonomic balance, *Physiol. Rev.* **28**: 1.

Davis, R. C., 1957. Response patterns, *Trans. N.Y. Acad. Sci.*, **19**: 731.

Docter, R. F. and Bernal, M. E., 1964. Immediate and prolonged psychophysiological effects of sustained alcohol intake in alcoholics, *Quart. J. Stud. Alc.* **25**: 438.

Docter, R. F. and Perkins, R. B., 1960. The effects of ethyl alcohol on autonomic and muscular responses in humans, *Quart. J. Stud. Alc.* **22**: 374.

Docter, R. F., Naitoh, P., and Smith, J. C., 1966. Electroencephalographic changes and vigilance behavior during experimentally induced intoxication with alcoholic subjects, *Psychosom. Med.* **28**: 605.

Edwards, A. L., 1954. Experiments: Their planning and execution, in *Handbook of Social Psychology* Vol. 1 (G. Linzey, ed.), pp. 259–288, Addison Wesley, Cambridge, Mass.

Ekbom, K., Hed, R., Kirstein, L., and Astrom, K. E., 1964. Muscular affectations in chronic alcoholism, *Arch. Neurol.* **10**: 449.

Engel, B. T., 1960. Stimulus–response and individual–response specificity, *Arch. Gen. Psychiat.* **2**: 305.

Engel, B. T. and Bickford, A. F., 1961. Response specificity, *Arch. Gen. Psychiat.* **5**: 478.

Fazekas, H., Albert, S. N., and Alman, R. W., 1955. Influence of chlorpromazine and alcohol on cerebral hemodynamics and metabolism, *Amer. J. Med. Sci.* **230**: 128.

Fewings, J. D., Hanna, M. J. D., Walsh, J. A., and Whelan, R. F., 1966. The effects of ethyl alcohol on the blood vessels of the hand and forearm in man, *Brit. J. Pharmacol.* **27**: 93.

Finkelstein, N., Alpern, E. B., and Gantt, W. H., 1945. Amphetamine (benzedrin) sulfate upon higher nervous activity compared to alcohol. II. Human experiments, *Johns Hopkins Hosp. Bull.* **76**: 61.

Fleetwood, M. F. and Diethelm, O., 1951. Emotions and biochemical findings in alcoholism, *Amer. J. Psychiat.* **108**: 433.

Fleetwood, M. F., 1955. Biochemical experimental investigations of emotions and chronic alcoholism, in *Etiology of Chronic Alcoholism* (O. Diethelm, ed.), pp. 43–109, Charles C. Thomas, Springfield, Ill.

Fowles, D. C. and Venables, P. H., 1969. The production of palmar skin potential by a sodium pump, Paper presented at the Ninth Annual Meeting of the Society of Psychophysiological Research, October, Monterey, Calif.

Franks, C. M., 1963. The apparent failure of ethyl alcohol to inhibit the formation of conditioned eyeblink responses in man, *Psychopharmacologia* **4**: 433.

Franks, C. M., 1964. The effects of alcohol upon fluctuation in perspective, blink rate and eye movements, *Quart. J. Stud. Alc.* **25**: 56.

Fregly, A. R., Bergstedt, M., and Graybiel, A., 1967. Relationships between blood alcohol, positional alcohol nystagmus and postural equilibrium, *Quart. J. Stud. Alc.* **28**: 11.

Gantt, W. H., 1957. Acute effect of alcohol on autonomic (sexual, secretory, cardiac) and somatic responses, in *Alcoholism: Basic Aspects and Treatment* (H. E. Himwich, ed.) pp. 73–89, Amer. Assoc. Adv. Sci., Washington, D.C.

Garlind, T., Goldberg, L., Graf, K., Perman, E. S., Strandell, T., and Strom, G., 1960. Effect of ethanol on circulatory, metabolic, and neurohormonal function during muscular work in men, *Acta Pharm. Tox. Kbh.* **17**: 106.

Gellhorn, E., 1943. *Autonomic Regulations. Their Significance for Physiology, Psychology and Neuropsychiatry*, Interscience Publishers, New York.

Gellhorn, E., 1967. *Principles of Autonomic-Somatic Integration*, Univ. of Minnesota, Minneapolis, Minn.

Gellhorn, E. and Loofbourrow, G. N., 1963. *Emotions and Emotional Disorders*, Univ. of Minnesota, Minneapolis, Minn.

Germana, J., 1969. Central efferent processes and autonomic-behavioral integration, *Psychophysiology* **6**: 78.

Gillespie, J. A., 1967. Vasodilator properties of alcohol, *Brit. Med. J.* **2**: 274.

Gillilan, L. A., 1954. *Clinical Aspects of the Autonomic Nervous System*, Little, Brown and Co., Boston.

Goddard, P. J., 1958. Effect of alcohol on excretion of catechol amines in conditions giving rise to anxiety, *J. Appl. Physiol.* **13**: 118.

Goldberg, L., 1943. Quantitative studies on alcohol tolerance in man. The influence of ethyl alcohol on sensory, motor and psychological functions referred to blood alcohol in normal and habituated individuals, *Acta Physiol. Scand.* **5** (Suppl. 16): 1–128.

Goldberg, L., 1966. Behavioral and physiological effects of alcohol on man, *Psychosom. Med.* **38**: 570.

Goldstein, J. J., Acker, C. W., Crockett, J. T., and Riddle, J. J., 1966. Psychophysiological reactions to films by chronic schizophrenics: I. Effects of drug status, *J. Abnorm. Psychol.* **71**: 335.

Goldstein, M. J., Jones, R. B., Clemens, T. L., Flagg, G. W., and Alexander, F. G., 1965. Coping style as a factor in psychophysiological response to a tensions-arousing IIIII, J. Pers. Soc. Psychol. 1. 290.

Graf, K. and Strom, G., 1960. Effect of ethanol on arm blood flow in healthy and young men at rest and during leg work, *Acta Pharm. Tox. Kbh.* **17L**: 115.

Greenberg, L. A. and Carpenter, J. A., 1957. The effects of alcoholic beverages on skin conductance and emotional tension. I. Wine, whisky and alcohol, *Quart. J. Stud. Alc.* **18**: 190.

Hebbelinck, M., 1960. The effects of a small dose of ethyl alcohol on certain basis com ponents of human physical performance. I. The effect on cardiac rate during muscular work, *Arch. Int. Pharmacodyn.* **140**: 61.

Hed, C., Lundmark, C., Fahlgren, H., and Orell, S., 1962. Acute muscular syndrome in chronic alcoholism, *Acta Med. Scand.* **171**: 585.

Hillarp, N.-A., 1960. Peripheral autonomic mechanisms, in *Handbook of Physiology, Vol. II, Neurophysiology*, Sec. 1 (J. Field, H. W. Magoun, and V. E. Hall, eds.), American Physiological Society, Washington, D.C.

Hilton, S. M., 1966. Hypothalamic regulation of the cardio-vascular system, *Brit. Med. Bull.* **22**: 243.

Hobson, G. N., 1966. Ethanol and conditioning, *Quart. J. Stud. Alc.* **27**: 612.

Holmberg, G. and Martens, S., 1955. Electroencephalographic changes in man correlated with blood alcohol concentration and some other conditions following standardized ingestion of alcohol, *Quart. J. Stud. Alc.* **16**: 411.

Ingram, W. R., 1960. Central autonomic mechanisms, in *Handbook of Physiology: Vol. II, Neurophysiology*, Sec. 1 (J. Field, H. W. Magoun, and V. E. Hall, eds.) pp. 951–978, American Physiological Society, Washington, D.C.

Isbell, H., Fraser, H., Wikler, A., Belleville, R., and Eisenman, A., 1955. An experimental study of etiology of "rum fits" and delirium tremens, *Quart. J. Stud. Alc.* **16**: 1.

Jellinek, E. M., 1942. *Alcohol, Addiction and Chronic Alcoholism*, Yale Univ. Press, New Haven.

Jellinek, E. M., 1960. *The Disease Concept of Alcoholism*, Hillhouse Press, Highland Park, N.J.

Johnson, F. G., 1969. LSD in the treatment of alcoholism, *Amer. J. Psychiat.* **126**: 481.

Johnson, L. C., 1969. A psychophysiology for all states, Paper presented at the Ninth Annual Meeting of the Society for Psychophysiological Research, October, Monterey, Calif.

Johnson, L. C., Hord, D. J., and Lubin, A., 1963. Response specificity for difference scores and autonomic liability scores, U.S. Navy Medical Neuropsychiatric Research Unit Rep. No. 63–12, pp. 17.

Johnson, L. C. and Lubin, A. On planning psychophysiological experiments: Design, measurement and analysis, in *Handbook of Psychophysiology* (N. S. Greenfield and R. A. Sternbach, eds.), Holt, Rinehart & Winston, New York, in press.

Kalant, H., 1961. The pharmacology of alcohol intoxication, *Quart. J. Stud. Alc.* Suppl. No. 1:1.

Kalant, H., 1962. Some recent physiological and biochemical investigations on alcohol and alcoholism, *Quart. J. Stud. Alc.* **23**: 52.

Karvinen, E., Miettinen, M., and Ahlman, K., 1962. Physical performance during hangover, *Quart. J. Stud. Alc.* **23**: 208.

Katkin, E. S. and Murray, E. N., 1968. Instrumental conditioning of autonomically mediated behavior: Theoretical and methodological issues, *Psychol. Bull.* **70**: 52.

Keller, M., 1960. Definition of alcoholism, *Quart. J. Stud. Alc.* **21**: 125.

Kelly, D. H. W., 1966. Measurement of anxiety by forearm blood flow, *Brit. J. Psychiat.* **112**: 789.

Kissin, B. and Hankoff, L., 1959. The acute effects of ethyl alcohol on the Funkenstein Mecholyl response in male alcoholics, *Quart. J. Stud. Alc.* **20**: 696.

Kissin, B. and Platz, A., 1968. The use of drugs in the long term rehabilitation of chronic alcoholics, in *Psychopharmacology: A Review of Progress 1957–1967* (D. H. Efron, ed.) pp. 835–851, Public Health Service Publication No. 1836, Washington, D.C.

Kissin, B., Schenker, V., and Schenker, A., 1959. The acute effects of ethyl alcohol and chlorpromazine on certain physiological functions in alcoholics, *Quart. J. Stud. Alc.* **20**: 480.

Kissin, B., Schenker, V., and Schenker, A. C., 1960. The acute effect of ethanol ingestion on plasma and urinary 17-hydroxycorticoids in alcoholic subjects, *Amer. J. Med. Sci.* **239**: 690.

Kuntz, A., 1953. *The Autonomic Nervous System*, Lea & Febiger, Philadelphia.

Lacey, J. I., 1956. The evaluation of autonomic responses: Toward a general solution, *Ann. N.Y. Acad. Sci.* **67**: 123.

Lacey, J. I., 1959. Psychophysiological approaches to the evaluation of psychotherapeutic process and outcome, in *Research in Psychotherapy* (E. A. Rubinstein and M. B. Parloff, eds.) pp. 160–208, American Psychological Assoc., Washington, D.C.

Lacey, J. I., 1967. Somatic response patterning and stress: Some revisions of activation theory, in *Psychological Stress* (M. H. Appley and R. Trumbull, eds.) pp. 14–42, Appleton–Century–Crofts, New York.

Lacey, J. I., Bateman, D. E., and Van Lehn, R., 1953. Autonomic response specificity, an experimental study, *Psychosom. Med.* **15**: 8.

Lacey, J. I., Kagan, J., Lacey, B. C., and Moss, H. A., 1963. The visceral level: Situational determinants and behavioral correlates of autonomic response patterns, in *Expression of the Emotions in Man* (P. Knapp, ed.) pp. 161–196, International Universities Press, New York.

Lacey, J. I. and Lacey, B. C., 1962. The law of initial value in the longitudinal study of autonomic constitution: Reproducibility of autonomic responses and response patterns over a four-year interval, *Ann. N.Y. Acad. Sci.* **98**: 1257.

Lazarus, A. A., 1965. Towards the understanding and effective treatment of alcoholism, *S. A. Med. J.* **39**: 736.

Lester, D., 1966. Self-selection of alcohol by animals, human varieties, and the etiology of alcoholism, A critical review, *Quart. J. Stud. Alc.* **27**: 395.

Lieber, C. S., 1967. Metabolic derangement induced by alcohol, *Ann. Rev. Med.* **18**: 35.

Lienert, G. A. and Traxel, W., 1959. The effects of meprobamate and alcohol on galvanic skin response, *J. Psychol.* **48**: 329.

Lolli, G., Nencini, R., and Misiti, R., 1964. Effects of two alcoholic beverages on the electroencephalographic and electromyographic tracings of healthy men, *Quart. J. Stud. Alc.* **25**: 451.

Lubin, A., Hord, D., and Johnson, L. C., 1964. On the validity and reliability of the autonomic lability score, U.S. Navy Medical Neuropsychiatric Research Unit, Report No. 64–20.

MacMahon, B., Pugh, T. F., and Ipsen, J., Jr., 1960. *Epidemiologic Methods*, Little, Brown, Boston.

Mahl, G. F. 1953. Physiological changes during chronic fear, Ann. N. Y. Acad. Sci. 66: 210.

Malmo, R. B., Shagass, C., and Davis, F., 1950. Symptom specificity and bodily reactions during psychiatric interview, *Psychosom. Med.* 12: 362.

Mandler, G., Mandler, J. M., and Uviller, E. T., 1958. Autonomic feedback: The perception of autonomic activity, *J. Abnorm. Soc. Psychol.* 56: 367.

Mandler, G., Mandler, J. M., and Uviller, E. T., 1968. *Manual on Alcoholism*, American Medical Assoc.

Mardones, J., 1963. The alcohols, in *Physiological Pharmacology* (W. S. Root and F. G. Hofmann, eds.) pp. 99–183, Academic Press, New York.

Martin, I. and Venables, P. H., 1966. Mechanisms of palmar skin resistance and skin potential, *Psychol. Bull.* 65: 347.

Mason, R. E., 1961. *Internal Perceptions and Bodily Functioning*. International Universities Press, New York.

Masserman, J. H. and Yum, K. S., 1946. An analysis of the influence of alcohol on experimental neuroses in cats, *Psychosom. Med.* 8: 36.

Mayfield, D. G., 1968. Psychopharmacology of alcohol. I. Affective change with intoxication, drinking behavior and affective state, *J. Nerv. Ment. Dis.* 164: 314.

Mayfield, D. G., 1968. Psychopharmacology of alcohol. II. Affective tolerance in alcohol intoxication, *J. Nerv. Ment. Dis.* 146: 322.

McCord, W., McCord, J., and Gudeman, J., 1959. Some current theories of alcoholism: A longitudinal evaluation, *Quart. J. Stud. Alc.* 20: 727.

McDonnell, G. J. and Carpenter, J. A., 1959. Anxiety, skin conductance and alcohol. A study of the relation between anxiety and skin conductance and the effect of alcohol on the conductance of subjects in a group, *Quart. J. Stud. Alc.* 20: 38.

McGonnell, P. C. and Beach, H. D., 1968. The effects of ethanol on the acquisition of conditioned GSR, *Quart. J. Stud. Alc.* 29: 845.

McGuire, M. T., Stein, R., and Mendelson, J. H., 1966. Comparative psychosocial studies of alcoholic and nonalcoholic subjects undergoing experimentally induced ethanol intoxication, *Psychosom. Med.* 28: 213.

Mefferd, R. B., 1966. Structuring physiological correlates of mental processes and states: The study of biological correlates of mental processes, in *Handbook of Multivariate Experimental Psychology* (R. B. Cattell, ed.) pp. 684–710, Rand McNally, Chicago.

Mendelson, J. H., 1964. Experimentally induced chronic intoxication and withdrawal in alcoholics. Part 10. Conclusions and Implications, *Quart. J. Stud. Alc.* Suppl. No. 2: 117.

Mendelson, J. H., 1968. Biochemical pharmacology of alcohol, in *Psychopharmacology: A Review of Progress 1957–1967* (D. H. Efron, ed.), Public Health Service Publication No. 1836, Washington, D.C.

Mendelson, J. H. and La Dou, J., 1964. Experimentally induced chronic intoxication and withdrawal in alcoholics. Part 1. Background and experimental design, *Quart. J. Stud. Alc.* Suppl. No. 2: 1.

Mendelson, J. H., La Dou, J., and Solomon, P., 1964. Experimentally induced chronic intoxication and withdrawal in alcoholics. Part 2. Psychiatric findings, *Quart. J. Stud. Alc.* Suppl. No. 2: 40.

Mendelson, J. H. and Mello, N. K., 1966. Experimental analysis of drinking behavior of chronic alcoholics, in *Alcohol and Food in Health and Disease* (E. M. Weyer, ed.) Vol. 133, pp. 828–845, *Ann. N.Y. Acad. Sci.* New York.

Mendelson, J. H., Stein, S., and McGuire, M. T., 1966. Comparative psychophysiological studies of alcoholic and nonalcoholic subjects undergoing experimentally induced ethanol intoxication, *Psychosom. Med.* **28**: 1.

Mello, N. K., McNamee, H. B., and Mendelson, J. H., 1968. Drinking patterns of chronic alcoholics: Gambling and motivation for alcohol, *Psychiat. Res. Rep.*, Rep. No. 24: 83.

Mello, N. K., 1968. Some aspects of the behavioral pharmacology of alcohol, in *Psychopharmacology: A Review of Progress 1957–1967* (D. H. Efron, ed.) Public Health Service Publication No. 1836, Washington, D.C.

Miller, N. E., 1969. Learning of visceral and glandular responses, *Science* **163**: 434.

Mitchell, G. A. C., 1953. *Anatomy of the Autonomic Nervous System*, E. & S. Livingstone, Edinburgh and London.

Mizoi, Y., 1967. Experimental studies on optokinetic test under the influence of alcohol, *Jap. J. Stud. Alc.* **17**: 1.

Mizoi, Y., Hishida, S., and Macba, Y., 1969. Diagnosis of alcohol intoxication by the optokinetic test, *Quart. J. Stud. Alc.* **30**: 1.

Mizoi, Y., Kimura, A., Ohga, N., and Isido, T., 1963. Electromyographical studies for diagnosis of mild drunkness, *Jap. J. Leg. Med.* **17**: 1.

Monier, M., 1968. *Functions of the Nervous System: Vol. 1, General Physiology/Autonomic Functions*, Elsevier, Amsterdam.

Moore, R. M., 1930. The dispensability of the sympathetic nervous system, in *The Vegetative Nervous System* (W. Timme, T. K. Davis, and H. A. Riley, eds.) Proceedings of A.R.N.M.D. Vol. 9, pp. 385–393, Williams and Wilkins, Baltimore.

Morikawa, Y., Matsuzaka, J., Kuratsune, M., Tsukamotor, S., and Makisumi, S., 1968. Plethysmographic study of effects of alcohol, *Nature* **220**: 186.

Pinneo, L. R., 1961. The effects of induced muscle tension during tracking on level of activation and on performance, *J. Exp. Psychol.* **62**: 523.

Plutchik, R. and Ax, A. F., 1967. A critique of *Determinants of Emotional State* by Schachter and Singer (1962), *Psychophysiology* **4**: 79.

Rasmussen, A. T., 1957. *The Principal Nervous Pathways*, Macmillan, New York.

Rickles, W. H. Some nervous substrates of psychophysiological variables, in *Handbook of Psychophysiology* (N. S. Greenfield and R. A. Sternbach, eds.), Holt, Rinehart & Winston, New York, in press.

Ritchie, J. M., 1965. The aliphatic alcohols, in *The Pharmacological Basis of Therapeutics* (L. S. Goodman and A. Gilman, eds.) pp. 143–158, Macmillan, New York.

Rosenbaum, M., 1942. Adaptation of the central nervous system to varying concentrations of alcohol in the blood, *Arch. Neurol. Psychiat.* **48**: 1010.

Rosenberg, C. M. and Buttsworth, F. J., 1969. Anxiety in alcoholics, *Quart. J. Stud. Alc.* **30**: 729.

Roth, G. M. and Sheard, C., 1947. Effect of smoking on the vasodilation produced by the oral administration of 95 per cent ethyl alcohol or a substantial meal, *Amer. Heart J.* **33**: 654.

Schachter, J., 1957. Pain, fear, and anger in hypertensives and normotensives, A psychophysiological study, *Psychosom. Med.* **19**: 17.

Schachter, S., 1966. The interaction of cognitive and physiological determinants of emotional state, in *Advances in Experimental Social Physiology* (L. Berkowitz, ed.) Vol. 1, pp. 49–80, Academic Press, New York.

Schachter, S. and Singer, J. E., 1962. Cognitive, social and physiological determinants of emotional state, *Psychol. Rev.* **69**: 379.

Schenker, A. C., Schenker, V. J., and Kissin, B., 1962. Abberations in the pulmonary respiratory pattern in alcoholics and the acute effects of ethyl alcohol and chlorpromazine upon such patterns, in *Proc. of Third World Congress of Psychiatry* (R. A. Cleghorn, A. D. Moll, and C. A. Roberts, eds.) pp. 389–396, Univ. of Toronto Press and McGill University Press, Toronto/Montreal.

Schnall, C. and Wiener, J. S., 1958. Clinical evaluation of blood pressure in alcoholics, *Quart. J. Stud. Alc.* **19**: 432.

Schnore, M. M., 1959. Individual patterns of physiological activity as a function of task differences and degree of arousal, *J. Exp. Psychol.* **58**: 117.

Smith, D. B. D. and Wenger, M. A., 1965. Changes in autonomic balance during phasic anxiety, *Psychophysiology* **1**: 267.

Speisman, J., 1965. Autonomic monitoring of ego defense process, in *Psychoanalysis and Current Biological Thought* (N. S. Greenfield and W. C. Lewis, eds.) Univ. Wisconsin Press, Madison, Wis.

Stern, J. A., 1964. Toward a definition of psychophysiology, *Psychophysiology* **1**: 90.

Stern, J. A., Schwarz, L., and Gospodinoff, M. L., 1968. Salivary output of the alcoholic: effect of treatment with Amitriptyline, *Conditional Reflex* **3**: 254.

Sternbach, R. A., 1960. Two independent indices of activation, *Electroenceph. Clin. Neurophysiol.* **12**: 609.

Sternbach, R. A., 1962. Assessing differential autonomic patterns in emotions, *J. Psychosom. Res.* **6**: 87.

Sternbach, R. A., 1966. *Principles of Psychophysiology*. Academic Press, New York.

Surwillo, W. W. and Arenberg, D. L., 1964. Communications on the law of initial value and the measurement of change, *Psychophysiology* **1**: 368.

Sutherland, G. F., Katz, R. A., and Kurland, A. A., 1962. Salivary flow patterns in alcoholics, *Psychophysiology Newsletter* **8**(4): 43.

Thompson, G. N. (ed.), 1956. *Alcoholism*. Charles C. Thomas, Springfield, Ill; Timberline Conference on Psychophysiological Aspects of Cardiovascular Disease, 1964, *Psychosom. Med.* **26**: 405.

Venables, P. H. and Martin, I., 1967. *A Manual of Psychophysiological Methods*. Wiley, New York.

Vogel, M. D., 1960. The relation of personality factors of GSR conditioning of alcoholics: an exploratory study, *Canad. J. Psychol.* **14**: 275.

Vogel, M. D., 1961. GSR conditioning and personality factors in alcoholics and normals, *J. Abnorm. Soc. Psychol.* **63**: 417.

Wendt, V. E., Wu, C., Balcon, R., Doty, G., and Bing, R. J., 1965. Hemodynamic and metabolic effects of alcoholism in man, *Amer. J. Cardiol.* **15**: 175.

Wenger, M. A., 1948. Studies of autonomic balance in Army Air Forces personnel, *Comp. Psychol. Monogr.* **19** (4) (Serial No. 101).

Wenger, M. A., 1957. Pattern analyses of autonomic variables during rest, *Psychosom. Med.* **19**: 240.

Wenger, M. A., 1966. Studies of autonomic balance: A summary, *Psychophysiology* **2**: 173.

Wenger, M. A., Engel, B. T., and Clemens, T. L., 1957. Studies of autonomic response patterns: rationale and methods, *Behav. Sci.* **2**: 216.

Wenger, M. A., Clemens, T. L., Darsie, M. L., Engel, B. T., Estess, F. M., and Sonnenschein, R. R., 1960. Autonomic response patterns during intravenous infusion of epinephrine and norepinephrine, *Psychosom. Med.* **22**: 294.

Wexberg, L. E., 1950. A critique of physiopathological theories of the etiology of alcoholism, *Quart. J. Stud. Alc.* **11**: 113.

Wilder, J., 1962. Basimetric approach (law of initial value) to biological rhythms, *Ann. N.Y. Acad. Sci.* **98**: 1211.

Wilder, J., 1967. *Stimulus and Response: The Law of Initial Value*, John Wright & Sons, Bristol.

Wilkinson, R. T., 1969. Some factors influencing the effect of environmental stressors upon performance, *Psychol. Bull.* **72**: 260.

Wilkinson, R. T. and Colquhoun, W. P., 1968. Interaction of alcohol with incentive and with sleep deprivation, *J. Exp. Psychol.* **76**: 623.

Woodward, E. R., Robertson, C., Ruttenberg, H. D., and Shapiro, H., 1957. Alcohol as a gastric secretory stimulant, *Gastroenterology* **32**: 727.

Zaimis, E., 1964. Pharmacology of the autonomic nervous system, *Ann. Rev. Pharmacol.* **4**: 365.

Zimney, G. H. and Miller, F. L., 1966. Orienting and adaptive cardiovascular responses to heat and cold, *Psychophysiology* **3**: 81.

CHAPTER 13

Alcohol and Sleep

H. L. Williams and A. Salamy

Department of Psychiatry and Behavioral Sciences
University of Oklahoma Medical Center
Oklahoma City, Oklahoma

Systematic analysis of sleep as a fundamental biological process is a new scientific enterprise. Yet, since the mid-1950's, the rate of scientific publication on its neural and behavioral correlates, its alteration by drugs, and the effects of its deprivation has risen from a few articles a year to something like sixty articles a month, and there is no hint that we are approaching asymptote. Several factors are responsible for the astounding growth of this field of study. Along with advances in electrophysiological, pharmacological, and behavioral technology which occurred during the past two decades, there emerged a conviction that sleep was not simply a passive, resting state, somewhere near the lower pole of a continuum of vigilance. Instead, sleep was seen as a complex, constantly changing but cyclic succession of active psychophysiological phenomena, qualitatively, not quantitatively, different from those of waking. Furthermore, it was realized that the phenomenology and perhaps the neural mechanisms of sleep were similar if not identical among humans, the other mammals, and birds. Neurobiologists were challenged by the remarkably long-term processes implicated by research on its deprivation or its alteration by drugs, and behavioral scientists were challenged by the realization that the transition from waking to sleep was not a natural boundary for behavioral investigation, that sleep was not an empty state, psychologically. The demonstration by Aserinsky and Kleitman (1955) that the periodic occurrence of vigorous ocular activity in the presence of EEG desynchrony was associated with vivid visual dreams, and the confirmation by Dement (1958) of similar periodic bioelectric patterns in the cat stimulated the interest of investigators from nearly every discipline of the behavioral and biological sciences.

Despite the extraordinary growth of research on sleep, its phenomenology, its mechanisms, and its response to drugs, there have been remarkably few systematic studies of the acute or chronic effects of alcohol on this complex state, either in humans or animals. It has been known for centuries that ingestion and withdrawal of alcohol could alter sleep patterns, but the first experimental analysis of these effects was undertaken only a few years ago. For the most part, such investigations have been empirical rather than conceptual in their orientation. Consequently, although the results found in different laboratories have an encouraging consistency, we are a long way from understanding the fundamental neural and biochemical mechanisms by which alcohol alters sleep processes. Undoubtedly, this state of ignorance results partly from the fact that viable concepts about the neurobiological mechanisms of sleep are just now emerging, and partly from the fact that the neural sites of action, the biochemical targets and the effects of alcohol on functions of the brain are not yet clarified.

After a brief description of the phenomena of sleep and some effects of sleep deprivation, followed by a review of the known effects of acute and chronic ingestion of alcohol on the complex states of sleep, this chapter summarizes part of the work which led to current notions about neural and biochemical mechanisms of sleep and about the effects of alcohol on the brain. Since recent investigations of the effects of alcohol on the central nervous system (CNS) have implicated the same biochemical substrates thought to be involved in sleep processes, examination of findings from both fields of study may suggest concepts for interpreting the alterations in sleep which are induced by alcohol.

PHENOMENA OF HUMAN SLEEP

Electroencephalographic (EEG) Patterns

In 1937, Loomis, Harvey, and Hobart found that sleep in humans is associated with a series of EEG states which they labeled A through E for their order of occurrence after sleep onset. Twenty years later, Dement and Kleitman (1957) proposed a similar but somewhat simplified classification into stages 1–4, and their system is now in general use. [See Rechtschaffen and Kales' (1968) manual.] Visual analysis of the EEG usually begins with identification of the awake state for which the most ubiquitous sign in the record of the young adult is the 8–12 cycles/sec alpha rhythm, found most prominently in the occipital region of the scalp. During the period of drowsiness just prior to sleep, the alpha rhythm intermittently appears and disappears for a few seconds or minutes, then gradually fades from the record to be replaced by lower voltage, variable frequency activity in which 4–6 cycles/sec (theta) waves can usually be seen (stage 1). Stage 1 may persist for several minutes during which the EEG rhythms gradually slow in frequency and increase in amplitude, and then the first 12–15 cycles/sec (sigma) spindle appears (stage 2). A number of investigators consider this latter event a signal for the true onset of sleep, the initial stage 1 being regarded as a state of deep drowsiness. Superimposed on the relatively low-voltage background of stage 2, there appear transient, apparently spontaneous, high voltage patterns called K-complexes. These striking episodic events can also be evoked by stimulation of any sensory modality and are believed by many investigators to represent momentary periods of arousal (e.g., Johnson and Karpin, 1968). After several minutes of stage 2, higher voltage, randomly occurring delta waves (1–4 cycles/sec) appear (stage 3) and eventually the record of the young adult is dominated by high-voltage (up to 200–300 μV) delta activity (stage 4). The normal subject moves rapidly through this succession of stages, remaining in stage 4 about half an hour. Stage 4 then gives way to 3 or 2, after which the low-voltage irregular pattern of stage 1 emerges, accompanied by bursts of rapid conjugate eye movements (stage REM). If awakened from the latter stage, subjects are likely to report vivid, visual, hallucinatory dreams. Figure 1 shows EEG samples representing waking, stages 1–4, and REM.

During a normal night of sleep, the cycle described above is repeated every 90–100 min, but with decreasing amounts of stage 4 and increasing amounts of REM. Typically, REM and slow-wave (SW) sleep (stages 3 and 4 summed) each occupy about 20% of the total night's sleep. Figure 2 represents schematically a typical night of sleep for a normal young adult. The discovery by Aserinsky and Kleitman (1953) of this recurrent cyclic pattern of sleep stages, and of the relation of the REM state to dreaming, laid the foundation for a new field of research on the biology of sleep and dreaming.

An important reason for using the EEG as a fundamental measure of sleep processes is that it correlates reasonably well with behavioral criteria of waking and sleep. It is a particularly sensitive indicator of the onset of sleep, and in general, as Loomis et al. (1937) showed, thresholds for behavioral arousal and the likelihood of organized behavioral patterns are decreasing functions of the amplitude and period of background EEG rhythms. There has been controversy, however, concerning classification of the REM state. In this phase, thresholds for awakening are higher than for stage 1 at the onset of sleep (Dement and

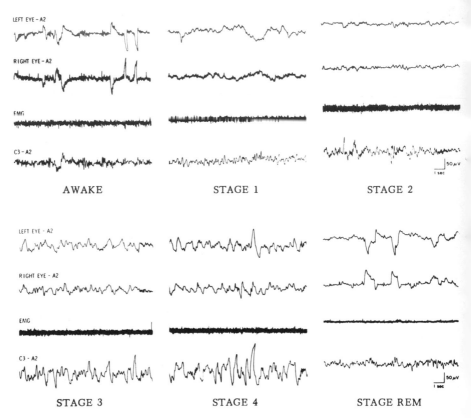

FIGURE 1.   Samples of EEG, submental EMG, and ocular activity in waking and the five stages of sleep taken from one subject in a single session.

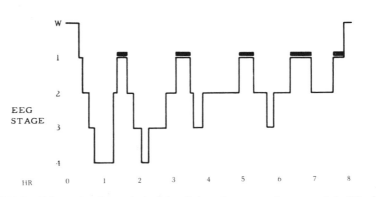

FIGURE 2.   Schematic of a typical night of sleep in a normal young adult. The heavy lines indicate periods of stage REM. [Slightly modified from Hartmann (1967, p. 6).]

Kleitman, 1957; Williams *et al.*, 1964) and though there are signs of cortical and autonomic activation in REM sleep, there is extreme tonic loss of postural tone. More than for the other stages of sleep, response thresholds in stage REM appear to be a function of the meaning of the stimuli presented to the subject (Williams *et al.*, 1966). It should be emphasized that whereas there is reliable evidence that the REM state is controlled by brain mechanisms different from those responsible for non-REM sleep (e.g., Jouvet, 1969), it is not known whether the several sleep stages recognized in the non-REM phase are actually controlled by qualitatively different brain processes. For that reason, most investigators who use animal subjects distinguish only two sleep states, REM and non-REM, and a few (e.g., Rosadini and Rossi, 1969, pp. 106–110) have recommended a similar dichotomous classification for man.

Autonomic Patterns

Alterations of peripheral autonomic patterns during sleep have been recognized since Aristotle, who noted slowing of respiration in sleeping humans, and have been examined in detail in recent years by Aserinsky and Kleitman (1955), Aserinsky (1965), Snyder and his colleagues (1963, 1964) and several others. Mean blood pressure gradually declines after sleep begins, reaching a low and relatively stable level about 1.5 to 2.5 hr after sleep onset, then rises gradually over the rest of the night to presleep levels. Heart and respiration rates usually show a progressive decline through the night, but in some subjects, lowest levels may be found during the early hours of sleep (Schaff *et al.*, 1962; Snyder *et al.*, 1964). In humans, mean levels for these cardiorespiratory variables tend to increase during stage REM, but far more diagnostic of the REM phase is the extreme increase in their moment-to-moment variability (Snyder *et al.*, 1963; Snyder *et al.*, 1964). Apparently, these variations are specifically associated with bursts of rapid eye movements (Aserinsky, 1965). In cats, cardiorespiratory activity also shows increased variability during stage REM, but mean levels of heart rate and blood pressure are reduced (Candia *et al.*, 1962; Jouvet *et al.*, 1960; Kanzow *et al.*, 1962).

The pupil is constricted during sleep in humans and animals and tends to remain in extreme tonic myosis during stage REM (Jouvet, 1962a). However, Berlucchi *et al.* (1964) demonstrated slow tonic variations in pupillary diameter during REM sleep with abrupt dilation during bursts of eye movements. They found that these phasic changes were not eliminated by preganglionic cervical sympathectomy and concluded that they were probably due to phasic inhibition of parasympathetic systems.

Basal skin resistance is increased during sleep (e.g., Kamiya, 1961), but probably does not change systematically with the stages of the EEG cycle.

However, spontaneous, brief changes in skin resistance and skin potential (GSRs and SPRs) are found to be very frequent during non-REM sleep and virtually absent during stage REM in both humans (e.g., Asahina, 1962) and cats (Tokizane, 1965). The dissociation between autonomic variables implied by this surprising finding challenges psychophysiological theories which postulate a system of arousal represented by general autonomic activation with slow-wave sleep near its lower pole.

In 1944, Ohlmeyer *et al.* reported that penile erection, averaging about 25 min in duration occurred about every 85 min during sleep. Several recent studies confirmed this observation and showed that the erection cycle is concordant with the REM-sleep cycle (Oswald, 1962; Fisher *et al.*, 1965; Karacan *et al.*, 1966). F. Snyder* has found a similar relationship in the rhesus monkey.

It was hoped that systematic studies of cardiorespiratory activity during dreaming would demonstrate specific correlations between autonomic changes and dream content. In general the results of such investigation have been disappointing although Hobson *et al.* (1965) did show, with awakenings from both REM and non-REM sleep, that the likelihood of dream recall was a function of the rate and variability of respiration just prior to awakening. In general, in awakenings which followed high frequency, variable respiratory rhythms, dream reports were judged to be most vivid, emotional and active. Similar relationships have been reported between eye-movement density and intensity of dream content (Berger and Oswald, 1962a; Dement and Wolpert, 1958).

In summary, like the somatic nervous system, the autonomic system generally exhibits a pattern of activation during stage REM which is similar to that found during active waking, whereas during non-REM states, autonomic variables show reduced and relatively stable rates or levels. However, the depression of nonspecific electrodermal activity found during stage REM and its vigorous occurrence during SW sleep as well as the tonic disappearance of postural tone during REM indicate that such notions as "activated" or "depressed" are probably not viable concepts for interpreting the phenomena of sleep.

THE NEED FOR SLEEP

Apparently there is a biological need for both REM and SW sleep. When a human or animal subject is selectively and chronically deprived of stage REM there is a systematic tendency for this state to appear at shorter and shorter intervals, and when, subsequently, undisturbed sleep is allowed, a specific

---

*Personal communication.

rebound effect is found, where the amount of REM considerably exceeds baseline levels (Dement, 1960).

The normal occurrence of stages 3 and 4 at the beginning of the sleep cycle suggests that SW sleep may have important biological priority, and studies of total sleep deprivation support this notion. During recovery from moderate sleep loss, human subjects first show excess SW sleep, whereas REM compensation is usually delayed until the second recovery night (Berger and Oswald, 1962b; Williams *et al.*, 1964).

These data support the view that the two kinds of sleep are organized by different neurological systems and indeed, this inference is sustained by the fact that with various drugs, specific brain lesions, aging, pregnancy, and certain psychiatric disorders, either stage of sleep can be suppressed without altering the other.

Among the better documented phenomena in clinical psychiatry is the observation that most forms of mental illness, especially in acute phases, are associated with disturbed sleep. Could sleep deprivation have causal significance in the etiology of psychotic states? Several experimental studies have demonstrated that total sleep deprivation over 4 or 5 days can cause psychoticlike manifestations (West *et al.*, 1962; West, 1967). However, this consequence is apparently not inevitable (Ross, 1965; Brodan *et al.*, 1969, pp. 175–181) but may depend on individual predisposition. In susceptible subjects, the syndrome develops progressively from a prodrome of drowsiness, lassitude, lapses of awareness, visual illusions and dreamy states (Morris *et al.*, 1960) to a delirioid psychotic state with vivid visual hallucinations, paranoid thinking, overt confusion, and disorientation for time, place, and person. The delirium varies in intensity with time of day. "By night the symptoms resemble those of a toxic delirium, with lucid intervals growing fewer and shorter. By day the picture resembles that of a reactive schizophrenic illness, usually paranoid in type; the subject may be guarded, withdrawn, suspicious, or expansive; emotionally flat, labile or inappropriate with delusions of reference, grandeur or persecution" (West, 1967, p. 539). West *et al.* (1962) stated that "the total impression is of a progressive disorganization of ego structure, modified by the influence of a 24-hour cycle and, also, by other, briefer periodic influences, perhaps in the range of 90 to 120 minutes. This is particularly noticeable at night, when a series of gross psychotic episodes may be seen to occur, for all the world like dream episodes during sleep, and very likely reflecting the same neurobiological periodicity or rhythm that underlies dreaming" (p. 69).

As early as 1886, Robert wrote, "A human being deprived of the possibility of dreaming would have to become mentally disturbed after some time . . ." (W. Robert, 1886), and the observations cited above encouraged the guess that REM deprivation alone could induce a psychotic state. The results of Dement's classic experiment (1960) to some extent sustained this view. With REM deprivation for five consecutive nights, his subjects showed a progressive increase in attempts to enter stage REM, marked REM rebound on recovery nights, and increased irritability and tension, several investigations have corroborated Dement's finding of increased REM pressure in humans (Kales et al., 1964; Sampson, 1965; Snyder, 1963) and in animals (e.g., Dement et al., 1967; Hartmann and Freedman, 1966; Khazan and Sawyer, 1963). However, with human subjects the psychological findings in followup studies have been rather disappointing. For example, Kales et al. (1964) detected no psychological effects at all in REM-deprived humans. These negative findings could be due partly to the fact that with manual techniques of waking the subject, it is almost impossible to eliminate stage REM altogether, and partly to the fact that dreaming is not absolutely concordant with stage REM, there being some types of mental activity throughout the night. In a more recent study, Dement (1964), using premedication with d-amphetamine (a REM suppressor), succeeded in depriving humans of stage REM for about 15 nights. Two of three subjects did show notable psychological changes, one of them developing paranoid ideation. Prolonged REM deprivation in cats (Dement, 1965) causes marked alterations in behavior which include bizarre sexual activity, reduced inhibitory controls, and lowered seizure thresholds.

It does seem possible that chronic total or partial sleep deprivation may have etiological significance in some of the psychiatric conditions, and possibly in the delirioid states which sometimes occur during alcohol withdrawal. However, the specific psychological effects of sleep loss in humans apparently depend upon the age, psychological health, personality structure, and motivation of the subject. In this regard, two studies in which psychopathological groups were deprived of sleep for several nights are of interest. Koranyi and Lehman (1960) reported that chronic schizophrenic patients were apparently more sensitive to sleep deprivation than normal subjects. One hundred hours of sleep loss reinstated, in each patient, florid psychotic symptoms which had not occurred for months or years. Vojtechovsky et al. (1969) found that healthy young volunteers tolerated 127 hr of total sleep deprivation better than a group of chronic alcoholics. However, no psychotic manifestations appeared in the normal group, and only two of the 20 alcoholics showed severe psychological disturbance. One of these patients developed a full-blown delirium after the third night of the vigil. As a group, the alcoholics showed more transient perceptual distortions, time disorientation, and impairment of short-term memory than controls, and performance was generally more impaired in middle-aged (mean age 44) than in younger (mean age 26) alcoholics. The symptoms observed in the alcoholic group, particularly for the two who developed delirioid states, resembled Korsakoff's syndrome rather than a hallucinosis. The authors concluded that sleep deprivation could be a precipitating factor in the withdrawal psychoses for predisposed alcoholic subjects.

EFFECTS OF ALCOHOL ON SLEEP

Acute Studies (Normal Subjects)

Experiments concerned with the manner in which single or repeated doses of alcohol influence the normal sleep cycle are remarkably uniform in their findings. These investigations generally rely on a common research strategy. After two or three nights of adaptation to the laboratory, several nights of base-line data are collected, following which alcohol is administered either in single or repeated doses. On subsequent sessions, the time course of recovery from the drug is examined.

Apparently the first experimental analysis of the effects of a single dose of alcohol on sleep phenomena was conducted in 1933 by Mullin *et al.* who administered 300–375 ml of 19% alcohol (the equivalent of about a quart of light wine) to four young adults 45 min before retiring, and measured body movements and rectal temperature throughout the night. Alcohol caused a distinct reduction in both motility and body temperature during the first half of the night, and an increase in both measures over control levels in the second half. As will be seen, this transient effect of alcohol, with a tendency toward rebound in the last half of the night, has since been found with other physiological measures.

Thirty years after the experiment by Mullin *et al.*, Gresham *et al.* (1963) investigated the effect of a single dose of alcohol on stage REM. Pointing out that CNS depressants were known to decrease the frequency and increase the amplitude of EEG waves, and that CNS stimulants had the opposite effect, they predicted that alcohol would increase the depth of sleep, diminish light sleep and thereby reduce the amount of stage REM, whereas stimulants like caffeine would increase REM time. Their subjects, seven young adult volunteers, were studied for 5 nights, on two of which they received either 1 g of alcohol per kilogram body weight (equivalent to about 6 oz of 100-proof liquor for a 150 lb man) or 0.005 g/kg of caffeine, each in 400 ml of orange juice, orange juice alone being drunk on control nights. Alcohol caused a significant decrease in the amount of stage REM, whereas caffeine had no systematic effect on the REM state. Data from other sleep states were not presented. It should be stressed that despite confirmation of the predicted reduction of REM sleep by alcohol, the experimental hypothesis was probably wrong. As was pointed out earlier in this chapter, the concept of "depth" of sleep has doubtful validity, and furthermore it is now known that most drugs, including CNS stimulants like amphetamine, cause transient impairment of REM sleep. (See, for example, Hartmann, 1967, Chapter 7; or Kales, 1969, Sec. III.)

Yules and his colleagues (Yules *et al.*, 1966, 1967) conducted two studies of the effects of repeated doses of alcohol (1 g/kg) on the sleep of normal young men. For the first experiment, three subjects were studied for four baseline, five successive alcohol, and four recovery nights. On the control and postalcohol nights, 45 min before retiring, they received 200 ml of orange juice. On alcohol ~~nnnninni 1 n nf nlonhol nar lilonnrom hndn noinht nno nddnd tn thn innin n dnnn~~ expected to produce peak blood alcohol concentrations (BAC) of 85–105 mg%. On the first alcohol night, stage REM showed a systematic decrease, but on subsequent alcohol nights it gradually increased to and then exceeded control levels. For one subject, by the fifth alcohol session, stage REM had risen from a baseline average of 31% to 50%, a level considerably beyond the normal range. Stage REM percents remained high during the recovery sessions but stabilized around control levels on the fourth recovery night. The transient decrease in REM sleep found in the first alcohol session occurred primarily during the first half of the night, and the increases found on subsequent alcohol nights occurred primarily in the second half. The alcohol-induced changes in stage REM were accounted for by inverse alterations in stage 2, not in stages 3 or 4. The latter stages varied unsystematically around baseline averages, as did latency of the first epoch of stage REM, frequency of shifts from stage to stage, number of body movements and amount of waking. Yules and his colleagues emphasized that only the length of the REM episodes and not their number was influenced by alcohol, and concluded that alcohol alters the mechanisms which regulate the duration of sleep stages rather than the number of stage shifts.

The alterations of sleep caused by alcohol in the first half of the night are probably associated with the highest BAC's, but as Yules *et al.* pointed out, if alcohol metabolism curves of awake man are applied to sleeping man, BAC levels would have decreased on the average to about 50 mg% at the half-way point in the session. It has been shown by Mirsky *et al.* (1941) that when this level is reached from higher BAC's, no signs of inebriation can be demonstrated. Thus, the sleep changes observed in the second half of the alcohol nights were probably not directly related to blood alcohol levels.

The second study by Yules and his co-workers was intended to test the notion that sleep changes in the first half of the night were directly related to high BAC's. After a series of baseline nights, four young men received alcohol (1 g per kg) 4 hr before retiring. The effects of alcohol on stage REM were similar to but of lesser magnitude than those observed in the earlier study, and failed to occur at all in one subject. In this experiment, shifts in REM time were mirrored by reciprocal changes in stages 2, 3, and 4. Since the alterations in the sleep profile for this study were qualitatively about the same as those found in the first experiment, these authors concluded that ". . . it is the immediate and perhaps direct effect of alcohol itself on central nervous system centers that initiates the changes in sleep stages noted on alcohol nights" (p. 97).

The results of an investigation by Knowles *et al.* (1968) support this conclusion. A single subject, studied over 27 virtually consecutive nights, was given approximately 3.5 or 6.0 oz of alcohol on experimental nights, doses which produced peak BAC's of about 80 and 150 mg%. With the low dose, mean percent REM was reduced to zero during the first half of the night. During the second half of the night, however, there was a rebound of stage REM sleep such that the total percent of this stage for the entire night did not differ from control levels. After 6.0 oz of alcohol, percent REM sleep diminished during both halves of the night, whereas average total sleep time was not altered. This study indicates that with larger doses of alcohol than those used in earlier investigations, REM sleep can be impaired throughout the night, presumably because BAC remains high for a larger proportion of the night.

During four of their experimental nights, Knowles *et al.* awakened the subject "at frequent intervals" in order to examine changes in BAC. The BAC curves shown in their Fig. 1 (p. 345) indicate that after peak BAC's for both doses were reached, alcohol disappeared from blood in approximately linear fashion at a rate of about 10 to 20 mg% per hour. This rate is within the normal range for awake subjects, but we decided to examine this question in our own laboratories,* prior to undertaking a series of single- and repeated-dose studies with normal young volunteers. If the rate of elimination of alcohol from blood is about the same during sleep as during waking, one would not expect to find systematic effects of alcohol on sleep much beyond the first 4 hr of bedtime.

Ten previously adapted college student volunteers who had fasted for 4 hr and who described themselves as moderate drinkers reported to the laboratory for two sessions a week apart. On each session, the subject was given three divided drinks of 190-proof ethanol mixed with 750 ml ginger ale, the total dose of alcohol being 0.5 ml per pound body weight. On one of the two sessions, the subject was allowed to go to sleep 30 min after the drinks were consumed. In the other condition he was kept awake. For both treatments, BAC's were assayed with a Breathalyzer at 30 min after the third drink was consumed and then every hour and a half until a reading of zero mg% was obtained, the sleeping subject being awakened briefly for this procedure.

Figure 3 shows the linear regressions of blood alcohol on time for the asleep and awake conditions, beginning with peak BAC's of 79 and 74 mg%, respectively. The slopes of the two regression lines are nearly the same (not significantly different) and correspond to disappearance rates of 0.124 mg/ml/hr for the awake and 0.109 mg/ml/hr for the asleep condition. Thus, with a moderate dose, the rate of disappearance of alcohol from blood is about the same during either waking or sleep and about 50% of the peak BAC is metabolized in approximately 3.6 hr.

Two unpublished studies (a single- and a repeated-dose experiment) conducted in the Oklahoma laboratory essentially confirm previous findings. Each subject was studied for two baseline, one or three alcohol sessions, two recovery

---

*The unpublished studies summarized here were conducted by O. H. Rundell, B. K. Lester, and H. L. Williams.

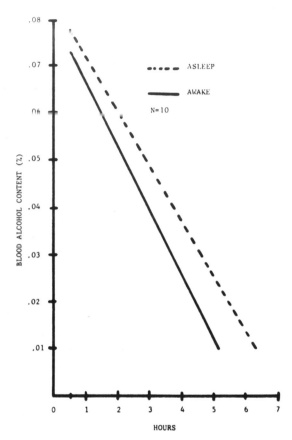

FIGURE 3. Linear regression of blood alcohol on time for asleep and awake conditions. The slopes of the two regression lines correspond to disappearance rates of 0.124 mg/ml/hr and 0.109 mg/ml/hr for awake and asleep conditions, respectively.

and a final baseline session a week later. In the single-dose study on ten fasted subjects with 0.5 ml alcohol per pound body weight, mixed with 750 ml ginger ale, the principal effects of alcohol occurred during the first 4 hr of sleep (Table 1), where percent stage REM was significantly reduced and percent SW sleep increased. As Yules et al. (1967) and Knowles et al. (1968) had found, there was a significant rebound of stage REM during the last half of the night. This latter change was associated with a corresponding inhibition of stage 2, but not SW sleep. Along with these effects, the latency of onset of sleep (stage 2) was shorter with alcohol and the duration of the first epoch of stage REM was decreased. There were no changes in the length of the REM-to-REM cycle or in the frequency of such phasic events as brief arousals, rapid eye movements in stage

TABLE 1.   Effect of a Single Dose of Alcohol on Sleep[a]
(Mean Percents)

| | Session | | | | | |
| | First half of night | | | Second half of night | | |
Stage	B[b]	A	R	B	A	R
Awake	7.7	5.5	10.1	4.3	4.6	2.0
1	4.0	3.3	4.3	3.4	4.0	2.6
2	49.0	51.3	49.6	56.5	46.8	57.8
SW	27.7	31.0	23.7	6.7	7.5	2.6
R	11.8	9.1	12.2	29.2	37.0	34.0

[a] 0.5 ml/lb body weight.
[b] Average of three baseline sessions; A = Alcohol; R = Postmedication recovery session.
Note: Alcohol caused a small but systematic loss of REM sleep in the first half and rebound of the REM state in the second half of the night. SW sleep (stages 3 and 4 summed) was potentiated during the first half of the alcohol session. There were no significant rebound effects in session R.

REM, sigma spindles or K-complexes in stage 2, but alcohol did cause a reduction in nonspecific GSR activity (normally found in SW sleep) which was accompanied by increased cardiac and respiration rates. The latter cardiorespiratory effect had been reported in 1964 by Marbach and Schwertz. In our study, sleep measures taken on the recovery night following alcohol ingestion were not different from baseline. Thus, with this small dose, rebound effects did not persist beyond the night of alcohol ingestion.

In general, the effects of this single dose of alcohol were similar to but not as pronounced as those of secobarbital (Lester et al., 1968). The latter compound also inhibited stage REM and potentiated SW sleep in the first half of the night, while reducing GSR frequency and increasing cardiorespiratory rates. However, secobarbital also reduced eye-movement density, the rate per minute of sigma spindles, and the amount of cardiorespiratory variability, effects which occurred only as nonsignificant trends in the alcohol experiment.

Procedures for the repeated-dose study were the same as in the single-dose experiment except that during the alcohol phase, six subjects received three (0.5 ml per pound body weight) doses of alcohol on three successive evenings, which were followed by two consecutive recovery sessions. Again, the only significant findings were those related to the first 4 hr of sleep (Table 2). As in the studies of Yules and his co-workers (1966, 1967), percent stage REM in the first half of the first alcohol session declined significantly, then recovered to and slightly exceeded baseline levels by the third alcohol session. For our subjects, however, stage REM returned to baseline levels on the first night of recovery sleep. With successive doses of alcohol, the trend for percent SW sleep during

TABLE 2. Effect of Repeated Doses of Alcohol on Sleep[a]
(Mean Percents)

			Session			
Stage	B	A_1	A_2	A_3	R_1	R_2
First half of night						
Awake	4.8	4.5	3.8	3.2	9.0	6.9
1	5.3	4.1	3.4	3.0	6.4	4.1
2	45.4	50.0	41.2	44.8	45.8	43.2
SW	28.6	32.0	36.3	31.4	24.4	29.6
R	16.1	9.4	15.3	17.7	14.4	16.2
Second half of night						
Awake	0.8	2.4	1.8	4.0	1.8	2.4
1	4.9	7.0	4.9	9.0	5.9	6.8
2	51.0	58.3	51.7	52.6	55.2	52.1
SW	10.6	6.0	7.4	4.9	4.8	8.5
R	32.8	26.2	34.2	29.6	32.3	30.1

[a] Significant alcohol effects were found only for the first alcohol session, where REM sleep was depressed and SW sleep potentiated during the first half of the night, with rebound of stage REM in the second half. No rebound effects occurred on recovery sessions.

the first half of the night was the inverse of that for the REM pattern, but the effect was not quite statistically significant. The latency of sleep onset was again reduced during the alcohol sessions but there were no other significant effects on the sleep cycle. At this writing, the effects of repeated doses of alcohol on the other physiological measures are still being analyzed.

As Yules and his colleagues (1966, 1967) concluded, the transient alterations of sleep found in these studies are apparently due to the direct effects of alcohol on central nervous system structures which regulate the duration of sleep stages rather than their periodicity. However, as they also point out, there are compensation effects for REM sleep which extend beyond the effective period of blood alcohol concentration. These findings suggest that alcohol (like many other drugs) produces a "self-sustaining disregulation" (Yules et al., 1967, p. 97) of the brain mechanisms responsible for sleep processes. Since mechanisms for the induction of both REM and SW sleep have been found in lower regions of the brainstem reticular formation (see, for example, Jouvet, 1969), we might expect to find evidence in the pharmacological literature that pontomedullary areas are preferred targets for alcohol. As will be seen, however, this issue has not yet been clarified.

We were able to locate only two studies of the acute effects of alcohol on sleep in animals. The first, by Yules *et al.* (1966), examined the effect of 1 g of alcohol per kilogram body weight, administered 15 min prior to sleep in cats. With four consecutive alcohol nights, stage REM decreased below control levels on the first two nights, then returned progressively to control levels on the third and fourth alcohol sessions. As in the human studies, the alteration of REM sleep was more prominent during the first half of the night, the change being reflected in the duration of REM episodes, not their number. The second animal experiment, performed on the rat by Branchey *et al.* (1970), confirmed and extended the findings of Yules *et al.* by showing that the suppression of stage REM was dose related, and that alcohol also had sedative effects in rats in that it potentiated non-REM sleep. No rebound effects were observed during a 24-hr period following the administration of alcohol.

As has been mentioned, the effects of alcohol on sleep in both humans and animals are similar to those found with the barbiturates (e.g., Lester *et al.*, 1968; Kales *et al.*, 1969). Although the barbiturates are general depressants, affecting all levels of the central nervous system, the reticular formation is exquisitely sensitive to their depressant action. Experiments by Magni *et al.* (1959) suggest that during the induction stage of anesthesia, the primary site of action of the barbiturates may be the medullary inhibitory structures of the reticular formation. Whether alcohol also has somewhat specific, early effects on deep brain structures is not yet entirely certain.

Chronic Effects (Alcoholic Patients)

Extreme disturbances of sleep in the chronic alcoholic patient, especially during acute alcoholic psychoses, were recognized many years ago, but Gross and his colleagues (Gross *et al.*, 1966; Gross and Goodenough, 1968) beginning in 1959 were apparently the first to undertake systematic studies of sleep in these patients. Describing the clinical histories of a group of patients who suffered acute alcoholic psychoses, they wrote (Gross *et al.*, 1966, pp. 493–494):

> In reconstructing the clinical histories of our patients, there is often an initial insomnia associated with the onset of the drinking episode. In fact, some of the patients describe this as the apparent precipitating factor in that only after consuming large quantities of alcohol can they sleep. This is usually followed by a variable period of heavy drinking which at first is not manifestly associated with sleep disturbances other than the need for alcohol in order to sleep. . . . Gradually nightmares develop. At first they do not interrupt sleep but with time they cause increasing disturbance and disruption. . . . After a transitional phase, which many report, in which the patient is uncertain as to whether he is asleep and having a nightmare, or awake and hallucinating, the patient enters a predominantly sleepless state associated with hallucinations.

Baseline sleep studies in sober alcoholics, of various ages, with various drinking histories and not in acute withdrawal states, have not been done, although such investigation is very much needed. Mello (1968) commented on the fragmentation of sleep in the chronic alcoholic. Johnson *et al.* (1970) confirmed this observation, and found almost no SW sleep in a group of alcoholic patients withdrawn from alcohol for several days (aged 33–45) who averaged 17 years of excessive drinking. The fragmentation of sleep was manifested by frequent awakenings, frequent changes of EEG stage, and frequent body movements, and was most pronounced during stage REM, in the last third of the night. For the last few nights of a 10-day period of hospitalization and withdrawal from alcohol, total stage REM reached normal levels (21–22%) but frequent arousals from REM sleep persisted. The increase in stage REM found during the withdrawal nights was not due to an increase in length of REM episodes, but to a decrease in time to the first epoch of REM, and in the time between REM periods, which resulted in increasing frequency of REM episodes. In fact, in the latter third of the withdrawal nights, the median REM-to-REM interval (computed by us from Johnson *et al.*'s Fig. 2) was about 29 min, considerably less than the 90 to 100 min cycle found in normal young adults. The alcoholic seemed unable to sustain the REM state. "With increasing frequency as the night progressed, the patients would enter stage REM only to have it quickly interrupted. Forty-six percent of these interruptions were by waking or by gross movements followed by waking" (Johnson *et al.*, 1970, p. 410).

Although stage 3 increased somewhat during the 10-day withdrawal period, stage 4 remained totally absent in nine of the 14 patients.

Analysis of phasic events in the withdrawal records of Johnson *et al.* revealed that the frequency of sigma spindles was somewhat below, and the frequency of well-formed K-complexes considerably below that found in normal subjects. Spontaneous skin potential responses were apparently inhibited in the early stages of withdrawal, but approached normal levels by the tenth night.

In general, the sleep patterns of Johnson *et al.*'s alcoholic patients resembled those of elderly subjects (e.g., Feinberg and Carlson, 1968; Kahn and Fisher, 1969) more than those of normals in their age range (Webb and Agnew, 1968).

These data indicate that chronic excessive use of alcohol is associated with qualitative changes in sleep patterns which are different from those found in acute studies. As will be discussed later, the loss of SW sleep, the fragmentation of the REM state, the probable acceleration of the REM cycle (rather than shortening of the length of its episodes) and the suppression of phasic events such as K-complexes may have special significance for interpreting the long-range effects of alcohol on sleep mechanisms in the brain.

In studies of patients with delirium tremens and alcoholic hallucinosis, both Greenberg and Pearlman (1967) and Gross and his colleagues (1966, 1968) reported fragmentation of sleep and absence of slow-wave sleep, although the latter investigators observed at least two such patients who had exceptionally high amounts of SW sleep.

Alcohol intake in these patients (and in Johnson *et al.*'s chronic alcoholics) caused some suppression of REM sleep, increased latency to REM onset and further suppression of SW sleep. However, the most remarkable finding in the deliria and hallucinoses was the astounding increase in percent REM sleep associated with withdrawal. In some of Gross' patients, stage REM occupied 100% of total sleep time. Such patients often had violent nightmares which tended to merge into frightening waking hallucinations. To account for this aberrant sleep pattern, Gross *et al.* (1966) proposed that while alcohol consumption is still heavy, the drug acts to "intensify the propensity for REM" yet at the same time it "inhibits REM discharge." Thus, upon withdrawal, an explosive release of REM takes place, spilling over, as it were, into the waking state in the form of vivid visual hallucinations.

Johnson *et al.* proposed an alternative to this "hydraulic" theory of increasing REM pressure. They point out that transient suppression of the REM state is a common accompaniment of drug intake, stress and illness, whereas chronic conditions are associated with suppression of SW sleep (e.g., Kales *et al.*, 1969; Caldwell and Domino, 1967; Zung *et al.*, 1964; Mendels and Hawkins, 1967). They propose that these acute and chronic effects arise as sequelae to biochemical dispositions, particularly altered metabolism of the biogenic amines. As will be discussed later in this chapter, the biogenic amines apparently have fundamental roles in the control of sleep states, and their metabolism is affected by alcohol. However, before we begin addressing these problems, it will be useful to review briefly some of the neural systems responsible for sleep, and the effects of alcohol on these systems.

NEURAL MECHANISMS OF SLEEP

Slow-Wave Sleep

In 1924, and again in 1925, Hess argued that sleep is not a passive state of the brain, but a positive vegetative function to be classed with such related activities as respiration, circulation, temperature regulation and digestion, the common function of which is regulation of the internal milieu. This idea received support with Hess' (1933, 1944) finding that sleep can be induced by electrical stimulation of certain structures in the brain. He showed that low frequency (about 4 per second) pulses delivered through medial thalamic placements in the nonanesthetized cat induced a typical sequence of presleep behaviors culminating in a sound, long-lasting sleep. Stimulus trains delivered through electrodes located lateral to the medial thalamus caused some but not all of the symptoms of natural sleep. Hess' observations have since been confirmed by several investigators (e.g., Akert *et al.*, 1952; Hess *et al.*, 1950). One important aspect of these findings is that they implicate the medial thalamus as a hypnogenic area. Possibly, as Koella (1967) has suggested, the thalamus is the "head ganglion" for the organization of sleep. Despite the well-established role of nonspecific thalamic structures in the modulation of sleep spindles and recruiting responses, Koella's proposal has not been popular. The search for neural mechanisms of sleep has been focused primarily on brainstem and limbic structures.

Hess' report that sleep could be induced by electrical stimulation of the brain had little impact on theorists who viewed sleep as a passive state. One reason for this was the finding that sleep, or at least some of its symptoms, could be induced by electrical or chemical stimulation of the cortex, thalamus, sub-thalamus, hypothalamus, mesencephalon, pons, cerebellum, medulla, and even spinal cord and sensory nerves. Furthermore, since the undisturbed cat sleeps about two-thirds of the time anyway, it was alleged that Hess' conclusions were not valid. Kleitman (1939, p. 502) wrote "there is not a single fact about sleep that cannot be equally well interpreted as a let-down of waking activity," and Bremer and Terzuolo (1954) doubted the existence of subcortical inhibitory mechanisms acting upon the cortex. However, in light of modern neuro-physiological studies in which no significant degree of cortical inhibition has been found during sleep, and in which plausible neural systems for the active induction of sleep have been identified, the pioneering work of Hess is being reevaluated.

The identification of regions in the brain initiating the state of sleep was advanced by Bremer's (1935) first studies of the EEG of the brains of cats after midcollicular decerebration. This *cerveau isolé* preparation showed an EEG pattern of slow delta activity typical of SW sleep. Furthermore, the pupils were constricted and the nictitating membranes covered the eye as in normal sleep of the cat. In this preparation, only the first three cranial nerves (olfactory, optic, and oculomotor) remain connected with the brain. Bremer found that strong olfactory stimulation would cause EEG arousal, and concluded that the brain was asleep rather than comatose. When a transection was made through the caudal medulla (encephale isolé) a more or less normal wake–sleep pattern was seen. Bremer concluded that the greater number of sensory inputs to the brain-stem of the latter preparation accounted for the difference in wake–sleep patterns and that sleep was a passive state resulting from reduced sensory input, a kind of deafferentiation of the brain.

In 1949, Moruzzi and Magoun showed that repetitive electrical stimulation of the midbrain reticular formation was effective in transforming a slow-wave sleep pattern to a low-amplitude fast wave pattern typical of the waking state.

The period of EEG activation so obtained usually outlasted the period of stimulation, and the EEG desynchrony was usually accompanied by behavioral arousal.

Damage to the midbrain reticular formation causes prolonged sleep. Such lesions occur in encephalitis lethargica, often in the central gray of the midbrain. Lindsley *et al.* (1949) showed that experimental lesions in the midbrain reticular formation caused a prolonged state of somnolence, whereas lesions in the specific sensory pathways adjacent to the reticular formation did not cause EEG sleep. Thus the integrity of the reticular formation is required for EEG and behavioral wakefulness.

In their original study, Moruzzi and Magoun suggested that the ascending influence from the reticular formation acted on the nonspecific thalamic nuclei to interfere with this pacemaker activity. This was shown by the fact that recruiting waves excited from the thalamus could be blocked by stimulation of the reticular formation. It is also possible that the reticular system exerts direct inhibitory influence on the cortex, and finally, in addition to ascending reticulo-cortical influences, corticofugal actions on the reticular formation are now well established.

Reduction of activity in a tonic activating system is certainly one way that sleep can come about, and in this sense, passive theories of sleep induction are sustained. But it appears that sleep and waking are also influenced by active sleep-producing mechanisms. The soporific effect found by Hess of electrical stimulation of the medial thalamus and other parts of the diencephalon could result from active inhibition of the reticular system of the midbrain, and furthermore, the presence of the reticulo–cortico–reticular loop permits inhibition of the reticular activating system by feedback from the cortex. In addition, active suppression of the reticular activating system can arise from the lower brainstem. Lesions in the mid pons cause an EEG arousal pattern, while lesions a few millimeters higher at the rostropontine level result in EEG sleep (Batini *et al.*, 1958, 1959). This implies that a mechanism present in the caudal regions of the reticular system can induce sleep by inhibiting its rostral portions. Magnes, Moruzzi, and Pompeiano (1961a,b) elicited widespread bilateral synchronization of the cortical EEG by slow stimulation of the region of the nucleus of the solitary tract, whereas high frequency stimulation of the same brainstem site caused desynchronization of the EEG, again suggesting that structures in the caudal brainstem participate in the active induction of sleep.

Thus it is now evident that there are structures in the lower pons and medulla that are capable of synchronizing cortical rhythms, thereby inducing and possibly sustaining behavioral sleep, their presence having been demonstrated both by ablation and stimulation. Apparently, these systems act by damping or modulating more rostral regions of the midbrain reticular formation.

REM Sleep

The experiments mentioned above and many others convinced most neurophysiologists that there are brain mechanisms capable of the active induction of sleep. This view was further encouraged by the discovery of stage REM. Animal experiments with depth recording have revealed that the cortical desynchrony of REM sleep is associated with characteristic electrical patterns in other parts of the brain. For example, a synchronized 4–6 cycles/sec theta rhythm is found in the hippocampus of the cat (Cadilhac et al., 1961) and a 6–8 cycles/sec rhythm is reported for the pontine reticular formation (Koella, 1967, p. 18). A remarkable series of studies by Michel Jouvet and his colleagues made use of these deep brain rhythms and other caudally controlled phenomena in their search for systems responsible for REM sleep (e.g., Jouvet et al., 1964; Jouvet, 1961, 1962a,b). They found that with a transection through the rostral border of the midbrain, more caudal indicators of SW sleep disappeared, but REM sleep, identified by the periodic occurrence of atonia associated with bursts of rapid eye movements was preserved. Thus, it appeared that an intact cerebrum was necessary for the EEG manifestations of SW sleep, but that control systems for REM sleep were situated behind the midbrain. More caudally placed transections failed to eliminate the observable symptoms of REM sleep until the brainstem was transected at the lower border of the pons. The implied localization of a REM trigger in the pons was confirmed by a series of coagulation studies in which complete destruction of the nucleus reticularis pontis caudalis eliminated REM sleep. The otherwise intact cat continued to have SW sleep with normal periodicity. It is not yet certain whether it is possible to trigger the REM state by stimulation of this pontine center. Several investigators have reported that they could induce REM sleep by stimulating this or nearby areas (Jouvet and Michel, 1960; Faure et al., 1962; Favale et al., 1961; Parmeggiani and Zanocco, 1961). However, Kripke, Weitzman, and Pollack (1966) were not able to confirm this effect in the monkey.

Most investigators agree that the center for the initiation of REM sleep is in the pons, but the route by which the cortex is desynchronized is not certain. Jouvet's group first thought that limbic pathways were involved (Jouvet, 1962a), but lesions and transections of suspected limbic structures and pathways have failed to eliminate cortical desynchrony during REM (Carli et al., 1965; Hobson, 1965). Thus the mechanism may be diffuse and nonspecific, or it may be humoral rather than neural.

The phasic and tonic features of REM sleep appear to be organized in separate structures. Jouvet found that bilateral destruction of the locus coeruleus of the pons would abolish the tonic atonia of the REM state (Jouvet, 1967a), but the neural basis of the phasic components probably includes the lateral vestibular nuclei (Pompeiano and Morrison, 1965), and oculomotor control regions as well as pontine centers.

SITES OF ACTION OF ALCOHOL IN THE CNS

Although Jouvet and his co-workers, and Kogan (1969, pp. 141–148) have shown that an intact cerebral cortex is necessary for the EEG manifestations of SW sleep to occur, it is probable that this state actually results from passive and active inhibition of the midbrain reticular formation, and that the REM state is triggered and sustained by active mechanisms in the pons. The first effect of a single dose of alcohol administered to humans or animals is sedative. Onset of sleep is brisk, body movements are reduced, and the SW sleep states are potentiated while the first epoch of stage REM is delayed or shortened. These findings suggest that both the rostral and caudal portions of the brainstem reticular formation are prime targets for the inhibitory effects of alcohol. However, as will be seen, the results of neuropharmacological studies have not generated a decisive answer to this question. Some evidence in favor of the proposition is the following:

Alcohol loading in the normal waking subject produces fairly reliable effects on spontaneous electrical activity of the cortex. Spectrum analysis of the EEG of alcoholized human subjects (e.g., Davis et al., 1940) revealed a sharp energy drop on the fast side of the frequency spectrum (10–13 cycles/sec) while the reverse was true for the slow side (6 cycles/sec). Even at relatively low BAC's (35 mg%) this trend was quite pronounced, and as alcohol concentration approached 120 mg%, rhythmic 4–8 cycles/sec bursts appeared, accompanied by increasing energy in the corresponding frequency band.

In more conventional terms, the EEG under moderate doses of alcohol was characterized by gradual slowing of the dominant frequency, with a concomitant increase in EEG amplitude. As BAC reached 100–120 mg%, episodes of 4–8 cycles/sec theta waves predominated in the bioelectric pattern. Coincident with the occurrence of theta activity were typical behavioral signs of intoxication (Davis et al., 1940; Newman, 1959). When BAC's were elevated further, high voltage delta rhythms appeared with subsequent loss of consciousness (Holmberg and Martens, 1955; Gibbs et al., 1937). Potentials recorded from the cerebral cortex, intralaminar thalamic nuclei, and caudate nucleus of the cat are similarly affected at comparable BAC's (Horsey and Akert, 1953).

There is also evidence that at relatively low BAC's, prior to the onset of cortical synchrony, a transient period of electrocortical activation occurs. This effect was first reported by Gibbs et al. (1937) and has since been noted by others (Holmberg and Martens, 1955; Horsey and Akert, 1953; Hadji-Dimo et al., 1968) in both animals and humans with BAC's below 55 mg%. Temporary potentiation of the auditory evoked response and of direct cortical responses have also been demonstrated in the cat with infusion of small amounts of ethanol (Grenell, 1957), larger doses leading to the usual neural depression.

Note that the effects of alcohol on the waking EEG are similar to but not entirely the same as those found with the barbiturates. It is well known that those compounds potentiate fast beta activity in the EEG (Brazier and Finesinger, 1945), a tendency which persists throughout a night of sleep following a single clinical dose (Lester et al., 1968). As was mentioned earlier in this chapter, experiments by Magni et al. suggest that this effect results from specific inhibition of medullary inhibitory structures of the reticular formation, causing release of the midbrain activating system from feedback inhibitory control, and resulting in desynchrony and fast activity in the EEG. With increasing dosage of the barbiturates, however, EEG rhythms become slow and synchronous. The EEG data reviewed here suggest that alcohol also acts first to block medullary synchronizing structures, but that its suppressing influence reaches the level of the mesencephalic tegmentum faster and at relatively lower doses than for the barbiturates.

Attempts to localize the pharmacological action of alcohol deep in the brain have relied on the evoked potential technique. Several studies by Himwich and his colleagues have found evidence which, although indirect, favors the notion of a "functional lesion" of the rostral reticular formation as the mechanism for alcohol-induced slow waves (Himwich et al., 1966; Diperri et al., 1968; Schweigerdt et al., 1965; Dravid et al., 1963). By implanting electrodes at successive locations along the somatosensory pathway in the cat, they were able to demonstrate a differential susceptibility to alcohol at various recording stations. Evoked potentials recorded from the midbrain reticular formation to radial or sciatic nerve stimulation were markedly depressed by an alcohol dose of 1 g/kg, while the primary cortical receiving area and the specific thalamic relay nucleus were barely affected. However, in terms of relative amplitude loss, the somatosensory association area showed the most profound effect.

Because those structures with the greatest polysynaptic development were affected to the greatest extent, the synapse was assumed to be the most vulnerable nervous structure to the narcotic action of alcohol. This interpretation agrees with the findings of French et al. (1953), and Arduini and Arduini (1954) in which potentials initiated by peripheral nerve stimulation under barbiturate or ether anesthesia were found to be suppressed along multineural pathways, but not along classical (paucisynaptic) paths. Evoked potential changes in humans given barbiturates suggest a similar interpretation (Allison et al., 1963; Abrahamian et al., 1963). That is, a striking reduction in amplitude of the late components of the cortical (scalp)-evoked response is observed after infusion of a barbiturate. These late-occurring slow components are believed by many investigators to represent a composite of extralemniscal activity projected via nonspecific thalamic and reticular networks (e.g., Goff et al., 1962; Allison, 1962). In contrast, early components of the evoked potential thought to represent pre- and postsynaptic radiations are unaltered or may even be enhanced (French et al., 1953) with deepening anesthesia, implying release of these systems from tonic reticular inhibition.

Our own studies on humans (Salamy *et al.*, 1969) indicate that the large late occurring components of the somatosensory-evoked response, best recorded from nonspecific frontal regions of the scalp, are also highly sensitive to the depressant effects of alcohol. The amplitude of this long latency response was found to be inversely related to the BAC, the correlation with subjects averaging better than −0.90 (Fig. 4). As alcohol was dissipated from the blood, the late components of the evoked response gradually recovered to control levels. On the other hand, the so-called primary waves, easily visualized with postrolandic parasagittal leads, were resistant to alcohol, showing decrement only at relatively high BAC's (100–120 mg%). Similar results were reported by Gross *et al.* (1966) and Lewis *et al.* (1969).

The notion that polysynaptic brain systems are especially vulnerable to the narcotic actions of both alcohol and the barbiturates receives support from these studies, but it should be recalled that this interpretation relies on the unproved assumption that different generator sources can be ascribed to the various deflections of the scalp-evoked response. Evidence that this assumption may not be valid comes from a recent study by Stohr and Goldring (1969) who found evidence in surgically treated seizure patients that all components of the somatosensory-evoked response originate in the primary cortical receiving area, and in studies by Vaughn and Ritter (1970) who concluded that the late occurring

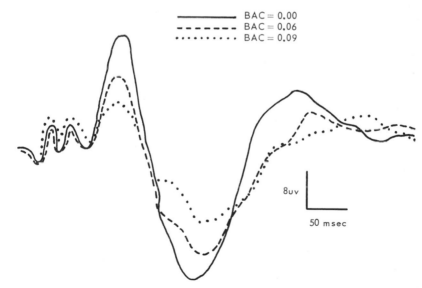

FIGURE 4. The effect of alcohol on the human vertex response to electrical stimulation of the median nerve.

vertex response to acoustic stimulation arose in the primary or nearby auditory cortex of the brain.

Another approach to the question of the central effects of alcohol was taken by Sauerland *et al.* (1967). They had found that the masseteric and soleus reflexes normally elicited by electrical stimulation of the trigeminal nucleus are completely inhibited by a train of impulses applied to the orbital cortex of the cat. Since the projection fibers from the orbital gyri descend without synaptic transfer to the medullary inhibitory centers in the reticular formation, their finding that small quantities of alcohol (480–590 mg/kg) interfered with this inhibitory process led to the conclusion that the bulbar reticular formation was the likely site of alcohol suppression.

Taken together, the human and animal studies cited above do encourage the view that alcohol first suppresses brainstem functions. But many of these results could just as well represent cortical depression, and there is positive evidence which has persuaded several investigators that the cortex *is* the primary target of alcohol. For example, Himwich's group (Dravid *et al.*, 1963; Diperri *et al.*, 1968) found greater suppression of evoked activity from association cortex than from mesencephalic reticular formation in alcoholized cats, an effect which could have originated either in cortical or subcortical sites. Furthermore, Nakai and Domino (1969) found evidence in cats suggesting the relative integrity of the reticular formation under alcohol. The visual evoked potential to a single optic tract volley is normally enhanced following a conditioning train delivered to the midbrain reticular formation. Both pentobarbital and alcohol suppressed the postsynaptic components of the test response, and pentobarbital also damped reticular facilitation of the cortical potential. In contrast, alcohol did not impair the effectiveness of reticular facilitation.

To summarize, research has not yet provided a decisive answer concerning the CNS targets of single doses of alcohol. The preponderance of evidence from neuropharmacological studies, and from sleep research as well, implicates the brainstem as the most vulnerable site of action, but there are other indications that the cortex is also involved early in the course of alcohol effects.

The alterations in sleep found in chronic alcoholics are qualitatively different from those observed with single doses of alcohol given either to normal adults or animals. Specifically, the relative absence of delta activity (and K-complexes) and the extreme exacerbation of REM sleep in alcoholic delirium and hallucinosis could not be predicted from acute studies. It seems likely in these cases that the cortex is damaged. Although the pacemakers for the various cortical rhythms are probably located in subcortical structures, their generators appear to be in the cortex itself. Investigations by Jouvet and his co-workers showed that an intact cerebral cortex was necessary for more caudal manifestations of SW sleep to occur, and Kogan (1969, pp. 141–148) found evidence in cats that the initiation of slow-wave activity is an excitatory process which originates in deep layers of the frontal cortex and propagates first to superficial cortical layers, and other regions of the cortex, then to subcortical structures. The results of under-cutting and cross-cutting operations showed, however, that following this early phase of cortical control, more sustained slow-wave activity is organized by systems ascending from deeper brain structures. Nevertheless, diffuse cortical damage, particularly in frontal regions, might impair the ability of the brain to initiate delta activity (and K-complexes), and consequently, EEG signs of slow-wave sleep. On the other hand, there is no evidence that cortical damage alone should impair stage REM, and it will be recalled that in nondelirious sober chronic alcoholics, Johnson *et al.* (1970) found no impairment of the REM state. Feinberg and co-workers (1967) reported a considerable deficit in stage 4, as well as a marked increase in wakefulness in elderly patients with chronic brain syndromes. Stage REM was also reduced in these patients, perhaps because of diffuse impairment of their brain processes.

Prolonged drinking does seem to be associated with permanent brain damage. Courville (1955) found deterioration in autopsied chronic alcoholics to be maximal in the dorsolateral aspects of the frontal lobe, although posterior portions of the cortex were also affected. Haug (1968) recently reported that chronic alcoholics have decidedly enlarged ventricles and demonstrated a relationship between amount of alcohol ingested over years and degree of ventricular enlargement. Bennet *et al.* (1960) identified an "intermediate" syndrome of alcoholic brain disease in which 79% of their subjects had abnormal EEG records. Hiddema (1965) and Hudolin and Gubarev (1967) reported that EEG abnormalities, when found, were diffuse in nature and sometimes involved paroxysmal discharges. Generally speaking, however, the waking EEG of the chronic alcoholic is said to be of low amplitude, often displaying sigma sleep spindles (Hiddema *et al.*, 1965), and delta activity can be found only at very high BAC's (Newman, 1959; Homberg and Martens, 1955). The alpha rhythm in the chronic alcoholic is said to be slowed, reduced in voltage, unstable and not susceptible to the normal inhibitory effect of opening the eyes (Hudolin and Gubarev, 1967; Little and McAvoy, 1952).

The presence of transient sleep spindles in the waking EEG of the chronic alcoholic as well as the reduced voltage and instability of the alpha rhythm could be due to functional disturbance of the brainstem (Hiddema, 1965) or thalamus, but since the neural generators for these rhythms are believed to be situated in the cortex (Andersen and Andersson, 1968) the findings are also consonant with the view that the cortex is damaged in many chronic alcoholics (Hudolin and Gubarev, 1967; Delay *et al.*, 1957).

SLEEP AND THE BIOGENIC AMINES

The long time course of sleep phenomena and their slow recovery after chemical, physiological, or psychological challenge imply that humoral factors other than those responsible for short term neural functions are involved in their modulation. Recent studies suggest that the induction and maintenance of the stages of sleep (and waking) are controlled in part by biogenic amines, specifically serotonin and norepinephrine. However, there are contradictory data and conflicting opinions concerning which of these neurohumors is associated with what stage of sleep. Serotonin (5-HT), which occurs naturally in the brain (Amin *et al.*, 1954) and may be involved as a transmitter substance in the CNS organization of trophotropic functions (Brodie and Shore, 1957a, 1957b), is a strong candidate as a hypnogen. For example, in 1965 and 1966, Koella and co-workers (Koella, 1966; Koella *et al.*, 1965) found that 5-HT injected by intracarotid route in the cat induced a biphasic change of the EEG consisting of an initial arousal pattern lasting from $\frac{1}{2}$ min to 2 min, followed by prolonged hypersynchrony. This sequence was accompanied first by a decrease, and then a prolonged increase in thalamic recruiting responses, and by pupillary dilation followed by constriction. Other studies by Koella's group implicated the area postrema of the fourth ventricle in this serotonergic effect. Surgical destruction of this extra-blood–brain barrier region prevented the 5-HT effect, and local application of 5-HT on the area postrema induced cortical hypersynchrony. Koella suggested that 5-HT acted upon receptor sites in the area postrema, and that this stimulating effect was transmitted by dendrites to neurons in the nucleus of the solitary tract. As was mentioned earlier in this review, the hypersynchronizing properties of the solitary tract nucleus were demonstrated by Moruzzi (1960). Several investigators have found that i.v. or i.p. injection of the precursor of serotonin, 5-hydroxytryptophan (5-HTP), which crosses the blood–brain barrier, could induce a state closely resembling SW sleep (e.g., Monnier and Tissot, 1958) while Jouvet (1967a) reported that large doses of 5-HTP in cats caused suppression of REM sleep for 5 or 6 hr. In 1964, Matsumoto and Jouvet found that high doses of reserpine (0.5 mg/kg) caused prolonged insomnia in cats, with SW sleep absent for about 2 days, and REM sleep eliminated for 2–4 days or more. When reserpine was followed by an injection of 5-HTP, SW sleep reappeared immediately, but recovery of stage REM was apparently not observed. In contrast, when reserpine was followed by dihydroxyphenylalanine (DOPA), a precursor of norepinephrine (NE), both SW sleep and stage REM were restored. These findings constituted evidence that serotonin is involved in the control of SW sleep, whereas the catecholamines are necessary for REM sleep.

The substance *p*-chlorophenylalanine (*p*CPA) depletes animal tissues, more or less selectively, of 5-HT, apparently by inhibition of the enzyme, tryptophan hydroxylase, thus blocking synthesis of 5-HT at the rate-limiting step. Jouvet (1969) found that a single injection of *p*CPA (400 mg/kg) in the cat had no notable effect for 24 hr, but following this there was a sudden decrease in both states of sleep and a period of insomnia which persisted for the next 36 hr, after which there was gradual recovery of both sleep stages. The decrease and recovery of SW sleep paralleled the decrease and recovery of 5-HT in cerebral tissue. Weitzman and his colleagues (1968) partially confirmed these results in monkeys. Total sleep was reduced subsequent to pCPA administration, but this was due principally to inhibition of SW sleep, the absolute reduction in REM sleep being small. Clara Torda (1969) found that repeated doses of pCPA selectively depleted 5-HT from the brain of the rat, leaving NE levels unaffected, and that both stages of sleep were suppressed following pCPA. She also confirmed and extended Jouvet's results by showing that EEG indicators of SW sleep could be reinstated immediately after small amounts of serotonin were injected into either the third or lateral ventricle.

Another line of investigation employs the fluorescent technique developed by Falck and his co workers (1962, 1964), with which it is possible to map serotonergic and noradrenergic terminals throughout the brainstem. Serotonergic neurons, with their yellow fluorescence, are found in high density in the raphé region of the medulla, pons, and mesencephalon (Dahlstrom and Fuxe, 1964, 1965). Jouvet (1967b) showed that after destruction of the nuclei of raphé (a lesion which caused depletion of brain 5-HT), the cat was awake constantly for 2 or 3 days. Very scanty anatomical evidence suggests that the raphé system may be acting directly on diencephalic or telencephalic structures rather than on the mesencephalic reticular formation.

As was mentioned, Jouvet believes that NE is necessary for REM sleep to occur. His finding with reserpine and DOPA in cats would seem to support such a view, and he has other evidence to bolster this notion. For example, he found that cauterization of the locus coeruleus of the pons, a region rich in NE-containing neurons, eliminated the tonic manifestations of stage REM. The lesion did not, however, affect the phasic components (eye movements and ponto-geniculo-occipital spike discharges) of REM sleep. However, there are several difficulties with the NE concept. Among them is the finding that precursors of NE (or NE itself) injected into the nondrugged brain cause EEG arousal and behavioral activation rather than REM sleep (e.g., Torda, 1969). Norepinephrine can be selectively depleted from body and brain with α-methyl-p-tyrosine which blocks the synthesis of DOPA from tyrosine. Using this chemical, Marantz and Rechtschaffen (1967) depleted cerebral NE in rats to about half the normal value, but found no effect on either stage of sleep. Torda (1969) with repeated doses of α-methyl-p-tyrosine, succeeded in reducing NE levels in the rat brain to about 1% of normal levels. Sleep EEG measures indicated increased SW sleep and decreased REM. However, the presence of some REM sleep (inferred from cortical desynchrony combined with hippocampal theta activity) in the NE-depleted brain implied that NE alone was not required for the occurrence of the REM state. In the same series of studies,

Torda depleted rat brains of both 5-HT and NE, after which she was able to induce either EEG state of sleep with various combinations of the two mono-amines. These experiments and others convinced Torda that "the various phases of the sleep-wakefulness cycle depend on the relative concentrations of serotonin and norepinephrine (and/or related substances) released at their pertinent intracerebral sites of action" (p. 807).

Tryptophan and Phenylalanine

Several investigators working primarily with humans, who agree that serotonin probably has something to do with the control of SW sleep believe that it also modulates REM sleep. Oswald *et al.* (1966) found that five of sixteen normal adults given 5–10 g of L-tryptophan (amino acid precursor of 5-HT) orally at bedtime tended to enter stage REM abnormally soon after sleep onset, while lactose, L-tyrosine or DL-methionine did not cause this effect. In two of the REM responders, studied over many trials, L-tryptophan invariably shortened REM-onset latency except when methysergide, an effective central and peripheral 5-HT blocking agent, was used. The effect of 5-HTP was not as consistent as that of L-tryptophan but at times produced the same early onset of stage REM.

Tryptophan is rapidly absorbed from the gut (Oswald *et al.*, 1966, p. 392) and like 5-HTP, it quickly reaches the brain, causing a rapid rise in the 5-HT content of brain regions in which it is normally present (Costa and Rinaldi, 1958; Bogdanski *et al.*, 1957; and Hess and Doepfner, 1961). Thus it could be expected to have fairly rapid central effects. Hartmann (1966a) gave oral doses (6–10 g) of L-tryptophan to normal adults and found a small but significant increase in REM sleep. He did not, however, find the early onset of stage REM which Oswald had reported. Mandell *et al.* (1964) found a large increase in REM sleep after i.v. injection of 5-HTP.

It has been observed that patients with idiopathic narcolepsy frequently move directly from waking to REM sleep, a phenomenon which does not occur in normal animals or humans (Rechtschaffen and Dement, 1967). Evans and Oswald (1966) administered 5 g of L-tryptophan orally to several narcoleptic patients 15 min before bedtime. The average duration of their initial REM period was doubled from about 14 to about 30 min.

In a series of rat studies, Hartmann (1967) also found a tryptophan effect, not on REM sleep itself, but on the normally stable REM-to-REM cycle. A tryptophan loaded diet increased the frequency of REM epochs, whereas a diet free of tryptophan lengthened the period of the REM cycle, and decreased REM frequency. As will be seen, similar effects are found in man. It will be recalled that Johnson *et al.*'s data suggest the same acceleration of the REM cycle in chronic alcoholics.

Since none of the investigators of amino acid effects had examined the entire sleep profile, we undertook a replication and extension of the Oswald and Hartmann studies in human subjects (Williams *et al.*, 1969). After three baseline nights, two doses (7.5 g), of either L-tryptophan or L-phenylalanine (amino acid precursor of NE) were administered in applesauce to 11 normal young men at intervals of 1 week, with baseline sessions scheduled in the middle and following the end of each series. Although on the average this dose of tryptophan had no effect on the total amount of REM sleep, or the latency of its onset, it did (as in Hartmann's rats) cause a small but systematic shortening of the REM-to-REM cycle from a baseline average of 97 min to 91 min after tryptophan. Two of our 11 subjects also showed increases in percent stage REM as well as decreases in latency of the first REM epoch on each night of tryptophan load. One of these REM responders submitted to four more tryptophan and four more baseline nights over a period of 3 months. For this subject, tryptophan load was consistently associated with early onset of REM sleep, but total amount of stage REM varied unsystematically around baseline levels.

Both amino acids tended to increase the percent of SW sleep, but this trend was significant only for L-tryptophan. Percent time awake declined with tryptophan as did time to sleep onset and the frequency of brief arousals. Phenylalanine load had no significant effects on any of the sleep variables studied.

L-Tryptophan had other interesting effects on human behavior. Less than 20 min after its ingestion, our subjects began to complain of drowsiness. In fact, several of them went to sleep as electrodes were being applied. They noticed mild feelings of disorientation and drunkenness, and some of them reported that the state resembled a psychedelic trip. Oswald and co-workers (1966) observed these same phenomena both with L-tryptophan and with 5-HTP.

Our results encouraged the tentative conclusion that tryptophan, and perhaps serotonin, are involved in the mechanisms controlling SW sleep. When there were effects on REM sleep they seemed to be on the ultradian cycle, the biological clock which organizes REM periodicity, rather than on the REM state itself.

Since doses of L-tryptophan between 5 and 10 g had revealed two of ten subjects who appeared to be REM responders, we decided to repeat the study with tryptophan load increased to 12 g. In this unpublished study* on eight subjects, sedation effects in the first half hour were more intense, and feelings of euphoria, drunkenness, and disorientation were greater than for the smaller tryptophan load. The effects on sleep were qualitatively different with the high dose. Although there was a trend toward increased SW sleep, particularly on the first dose session, it was not statistically significant. There was, however, a reliable increase in SW sleep on the postmedication (P-M) recovery night. With

---

*Conducted by William Griffiths, B. K. Lester and H. L. Williams.

the larger dose of tryptophan each subject showed a dramatic increase in the amount of REM sleep. On the average, this stage increased from 96 min on baseline-placebo nights to 125 on tryptophan nights, and reverted to 88 min on the post-tryptophan recovery night. Under high tryptophan load the latency of onset of REM sleep was variable between subjects, but two subjects had zero latencies, and two more entered REM sleep after 2–5 min of stage 2. These figures are far below the cutoff for normal subjects, estimated by Oswald to be about 45 min. The reduction in the REM-to-REM cycle which had been found in the lower-dose study was no longer a systematic effect. Instead, within tryptophan sessions the period of the REM cycle became highly variable. Furthermore, the marked increase in total REM sleep was due primarily to increased duration of each REM episode.

These results indicate that in humans, alterations in sleep caused by tryptophan (and probably serotonin) are dependent on dose. Moderate loads of the amino acid cause a reliable increase in SW sleep, shortening of the period of the REM cycle, and sedation. Larger loads also cause early sedation, but the increase in SW sleep is delayed until the postmedication recovery night. The amount of REM sleep is greatly increased under high tryptophan load, an effect which results partly from reduced latency of REM onset but mostly from lengthening of the REM episodes. Thus it is reasonable to speculate that in man, at least, serotonin is involved in the mechanisms controlling both REM and non-REM sleep.

Reserpine

The effect of reserpine on sleep is interesting from a biochemical perspective because it interferes with storage of the biogenic amines, thereby depleting the brain and other tissues of both serotonin (Brodie *et al.*, 1955; Shore *et al.*, 1957) and the catecholamines (Holzbauer and Vogt, 1956; Bertler *et al.*, 1956). As was mentioned earlier, Jouvet found that a large dose of reserpine caused prolonged insomnia in cats, but that SW sleep could be restored in the reserpinized cat with 5-HTP, and that REM sleep recovered with DOPA. Hoffman and Domino (1969) in a carefully controlled dose-response study, confirmed the activating effect of reserpine in the cat and showed that the decrease in both states of sleep was a function of dose.

In rabbits (Khazan and Sawyer, 1964), monkeys (Reite *et al.*, 1969), and man (Tissot, 1965; Hartmann, 1966b; Hoffman and Domino, 1969) moderate to large doses of reserpine caused increases in the amount of REM sleep. In humans given oral reserpine at bedtime, this effect was dose related and especially great on the postmedication night (Hoffman and Domino, 1969). These different dose-response effects of reserpine in cats and other animals may result from species differences in metabolism of the monoamines. For example, Pscheidt *et al.* (1964) reported that in primates, drugs which inhibit monoamine oxidase (MAO) potentiate both brain 5-HT and NE, whereas in cats the MAO inhibitors enhance only serotonin.

Our studies (Williams *et al.*, 1969; Coulter *et al.*, in press) examined the effects of single and repeated oral doses of reserpine (1 mg a half hour before retiring) on the amount and distribution of the EEG stages of sleep in ten young adult males. The drug caused no systematic changes in EEG sleep profiles on the night the dose was given. However, on the postmedication recovery night there was for nine of the ten subjects a marked increase in stage REM. Along with this change, there was a decrease in time to onset of the first REM epoch, and in the average period of the REM cycle. There was no change in the average duration of REM episodes. The increase in total minutes of REM was due precisely to reduced latency of the first REM epoch, and acceleration of the REM cycle, resulting in an increase in the number of REM epochs. These alterations in the REM cycle were mirrored by a corresponding decrease in the amount of SW sleep.

In the repeated-dose experiment, ten young males were given 1 mg of reserpine on three successive evenings, the fourth being a postmedication recovery session. As in the single dose study, there were no systematic changes in sleep scores on the first night of medication, but beginning on the second drug night, the percent stage REM rose and continued to rise through the third drug night, then reversed toward, but did not reach control levels on the P-M night. By the third drug night the average gain in REM was 30 min, the REM level remaining 18 min above baseline on the P-M session. Reserpine again shortened the time to onset of the first epoch of stage REM, and reduced intervals between successive REM episodes, effects which increased through the medication nights and remained above control levels during the P-M session. The average duration of REM epochs was not altered by reserpine. Thus the systematic increase in stage REM could again be accounted for entirely by reduced latency of the first REM epoch and a decrease in the period of the REM cycle, which resulted in increasing frequency of REM epochs. The latter score rose from 3.6 during baseline to 5.2 on the third drug night, remaining at 5.0 on the P-M session. Changes in SW sleep were the inverse of those found for stage REM. The amounts of stages 3 and 4 decreased systematically after the first drug night, and remained below baseline levels on the P-M night.

It appears from the studies just reviewed that the effects of tryptophan and reserpine on REM sleep are rather similar while their effects on SW sleep are opposite. The suppression of SW sleep by reserpine and its potentiation by moderate loads of L-tryptophan may be related to their differential effects on 5-HT stores, since reserpine depletes while tryptophan enhances brain levels of this amine. On the other hand, the reduced latency of onset of stage REM and the acceleration of the REM-to-REM cycle which can occur with both substances would suggest some common effect on 5-HT which is not directly related to the amount of this compound in the brain. This ability of reserpine and tryptophan to cause comparable changes in the REM cycle might be accounted for by their similar effect on the synthesis and turnover of 5-HT. L-Tryptophan as a 5-HT precursor easily passes the blood–brain barrier, enhances serotonin pools (Hess and Doepfner, 1961), and potentiates its turnover (Ashcroft et al., 1965; Moir and Eccleston, 1968). Similarly, when reserpine depletes the monoamine pools, steady-state feedback control mechanisms apparently invoke increased synthesis and turnover of 5-HT (Tozer et al., 1966; Neff and Tozer, 1968). Jouvet (1969) has outlined a mechanism by which enhanced turnover of serotonin might accelerate the REM-to-REM cycle. He found that the more potent MAO inhibitors caused rapid and complete inhibition of REM sleep in cats while SW sleep was unaffected or enhanced. Since in cats, MAO inhibitors apparently block the deamination of 5-HT but not the catabolism of NE, he proposed that the action of some deaminated catabolite of 5-HT might be involved in the triggering of REM sleep. Our interpretation of the apparently similar effects of tryptophan and reserpine on the REM cycle is consistent with Jouvet's suggestion.

ALCOHOL AND THE BIOGENIC AMINES

The transient increase in SW sleep and decrease in stage REM which are caused by a single dose of alcohol are similar to the alterations of sleep found with the barbiturates, and at least reminiscent of the much more dramatic changes which occur with a potent monoamine oxidase inhibitor. Jouvet's hypothesis as well as a considerable amount of data from human and animal subjects suggest that such a modification of the sleep profile could be based on a transient increase in levels of free serotonin in the brainstem, a situation which could temporarily enhance the priority of SW sleep and inhibit or delay stage REM. Do alcohol and the barbiturates, like the MAO inhibitors, block metabolism of the monoamines, causing increases in their CNS levels? Possibly. It is known that the effects of various types of narcotics, including the barbiturates and alcohol, are potentiated by increased levels of either serotonin or 5-hydroxy-tryptophan, its precursor (Garattini and Valzelli, 1965, p. 209).

On the other hand, the long-range effects of chronic excessive ingestion of alcohol, with almost complete loss of SW sleep, extreme disruption of sleep patterns and, during withdrawal, the remarkable increase in stage REM are more reminiscent of the effects of reserpine found in our repeated-dose study. Possibly alcohol also causes release and eventual depletion of the monoamines from their storage sites in brain and body tissues.

Both the MAO inhibitor model and the reserpine model have been recommended as explanations for the effects of alcohol on brain functioning, but recent studies suggest that neither model is adequate to the task.

The MAO Inhibition Model

As is well known, the MAO inhibitors compete with the enzyme, monoamine oxidase, thereby preventing deamination of serotonin and norepinephrine in brain and other tissues. Consequently, in most animals including man, MAO inhibition raises endogenous levels of the monoamines (e.g., Pletscher, 1967). If alcohol functions like a MAO inhibitor, then at least two phenomena should be demonstrated in the alcoholized subject: an increase in brain and body levels of the monoamines and a decrease in levels of their major deaminated catabolites.

Using a bioassay technique, Paasonen and Giarman (1958) examined the effect of high doses of ethanol on 5-HT levels in rat brains. Evidence for a small but nonsignificant increase in 5-HT was found approximately 4 hr after subcutaneous administration of the drug. Bonnycastle et al. (1962) performed similar bioassays for rat brain 5-HT, approximately 1 hr after i.p. infusion of ethanol (4.5 g/kg) and found substantial elevations in serotonin levels. Thus, time of sampling could be an important consideration. In a study of acute experimental intoxication using human subjects, Rosenfeld (1960) had observed a pronounced decrease in urinary excretion of 5-hydroxyindoleacetic acid (5-HIAA) during a 5-hr collection period following ingestion of 100 g of alcohol. Since 5-HIAA is the major deaminated end product of 5-HT metabolism, it appeared possible that alcohol caused temporary inhibition of the oxidative conversion of endogenous serotonin. The Rosenfeld experiment involved parenteral administration of 5-HT to mice, pretreated with alcohol (4.5 g/kg) and subsequent colorimetric analysis of total body 5-HT, 5-HIAA, and other indole compounds. His finding of reduction in the amount of 5-HIAA, with a concomitant increase in total unmetabolized 5-HT recovered from animals pretreated with alcohol, suggested an early (within an hour of infusion) inhibitory effect of alcohol on serotonin metabolism. More recently, alcohol (or its major metabolite, acetaldehyde) has been shown to impair the conversion of exogenously administered serotonin-^{14}C to 5-HIAA in man (Davis et al., 1967a; Feldstein et al., 1964; Feldstein et al., 1967).

The results of these studies are consonant with the notion that alcohol (or possibly acetaldehyde) behaves like a MAO inhibitor, blocking oxidative conversion of 5-HT, and perhaps other monoamines as well. However, it should be emphasized that since exogenous serotonin does not pass the blood–brain barrier, none of the the experiments of Rosenfeld, Davis et al., or Feldstein et al. necessarily implicate processes in the brain. Furthermore, as these investigators made clear, the apparent block in formation of 5-HIAA could result from other alterations in the amine degradation pathways. One such mechanism could be interference at the aldehyde dehydrogenase (Ald-DH) step in both alcohol and monoamine metabolism. Figure 5 shows the normal metabolic pathways for 5-HT and alcohol. Serotonin and alcohol are first converted to their intermediate aldehydes, serotonaldehyde and acetaldehyde, each of which requires Ald-DH for oxidation to its catabolic end product. According to Truitt and Walsh (1968), acetaldehyde is the preferred substrate of Ald-DH and has greater affinity for this oxidating enzyme than the aldehyde intermediates of the monoamines. Competition for Ald-DH could cause shunting of serotonin metabolism from the oxidative to the reductive pathway, terminating in 5-hydroxytryptophol. A second alternative involves the nicotinamide adenine dinucleotide (NAD) linkage with Ald-DH. Because the oxidation of the mono-amines, alcohol and acetaldehyde, all require this coenzyme as a cofactor, alcohol ingestion might exhaust vital supplies of NAD, an event which would result in reduced output of 5-HIAA.

In the studies by Davis *et al.* (1967a) and Feldstein *et al.* (1967), human subjects ingested alcohol 30 min to an hour before receiving serotonin-[14]C. This treatment resulted in a striking decrease in the excretion of 5-HIAA, but the diminution in the oxidative route of serotonin metabolism was completely accounted for by an increase in the reductive pathway to 5-hydroxytryptophol. A second study by Davis *et al.* (1967b) demonstrated a similar modification of the metabolism of norepinephrine. Normally, 3-methoxy-4-hydroxymandelic

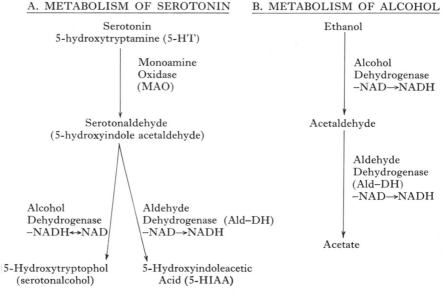

FIGURE 5.   The normal metabolism of serotonin and alcohol.

acid is the primary excretory product of NE metabolism. Under alcohol, NE was preferentially converted to 3-methoxy-5-hydroxyphenylglycol. Davis and her colleagues concluded that alcohol-induced reduction in levels of the major catabolites of the monoamines did not result from decreased monoamine oxidation but from diversion of the intermediate biogenic aldehydes from acid to alcohol end products. Feldstein *et al.* (1967), however, felt that the possibility of weak MAO inhibition by acetaldehyde, derived from alcohol, should still be considered.

Thus, the MAO inhibitor model which was first invoked to explain alcohol-induced changes in monoamine metabolism has not received strong or consistent support. On the other hand, it has not been entirely discredited. The argument of Davis and co-workers may be flawed by the fact that exogenously administered monoamines do not penetrate the blood–brain barrier. Their conclusions rely on the risky assumption that CNS metabolism, if examined, would follow the same course as that found for the rest of the body. Furthermore, Rosenfeld's finding of an increase in unmetabolized 5-HT in his alcoholized mice is difficult to reconcile with the metabolic shunt hypothesis. The hypothesis of MAO inhibition deserves further study.

The Reserpine Model

Reserpine impairs storage sites of the monoamines, releases them for degradation, and blocks their further uptake from interneuronal pools. It is possible that alcohol, like reserpine, causes release of the monoamines from storage sites. If so, one could expect to find a decline in monoamine levels persisting for some time after alcohol ingestion. Gursey *et al.* (1959) and Gursey and Olson (1960) using spectrofluorimetric techniques reported a rapid decline of both 5-HT and NE in rabbit brainstem following a single dose (2 g/kg) of alcohol. Chronic administration of alcohol resulted in faster depletion of the monoamines, and these effects persisted for as long as 6 days, resembling the time course and slow recovery found with reserpine. Moreover, reserpine combined with alcohol enhanced this long-term depletion effect. If replicated, these findings would have given strong support to the reserpine model. Unfortunately, Pscheidt *et al.* (1961), Efron and Gessa (1961, 1963), and Haggendal and Lindquist (1961) failed to confirm the Gursey *et al.* report. No alteration or only small decreases in brain serotonin and catecholamines were found in brainstems of rabbit, rat, and mouse. Pscheidt *et al.* did find a 19% decrease of 5-HT in rabbit brainstem after five daily injections of ethanol (3 g/kg) and a 20% depression of NE following a single large dose of alcohol. In contrast, reserpine (0.2 mg/kg) induced about 50% depletion of both amines within an hour after injection. The generally negative results of these replication studies imply that alcohol and reserpine must operate by different mechanisms.

The issue is not quite settled, however; Corrodi et al. (1966), after finding that alcohol caused no apparent changes in brain levels of NE or dopamine, examined the possibility that the physiological activity of catecholamine neurons might nevertheless be increased by alcohol. Rats were given alcohol (2 g/kg i.p.) followed by injection of DL-α methyl-tyrosine-methylester (MTM) which blocks NE and dopamine synthesis, resulting in eventual depletion of the catecholamines from adrenergic nerve terminals. Using the histochemical fluorescence technique, they found that alcohol and MTM combined sharply reduced brain levels of NE below those reached with MTM alone. The combined treatment had no greater effect on dopamine levels than MTM alone. With a second dose of alcohol, depletion of NE from the brain was further accelerated. Alcohol alone had no systematic effect on dopamine or NE levels. These results imply that alcohol could induce release, turnover, and eventual depletion of NE, and suggest that the absence of depletion effects in studies using alcohol alone might be due to steady-state feedback mechanisms which operate to correct depletion of the monoamines by triggering increased synthesis. We were unable to locate a comparable study where serotonin synthesis was blocked prior to infusion of alcohol, but it is reasonable to anticipate a similar outcome.

In summary, the results of recent studies of the effects of alcohol in the brain provide little sustenance for the hypothesis that this drug directly inhibits monoamine oxidase. Instead, alcohol's major metabolite acetaldehyde is probably responsible for switching metabolism of the monoamines from the normal oxidative to a reductive pathway. Investigation of effects on sleep of the reductive end product for 5-HT, 5-hydroxytryptophol (and its analogues) is already under way. Feldstein et al. (1970), using loss and recovery of the righting reflex in mice as their sleep criterion, found a systematic dose-response effect with i.p. injection of 5-hydroxytryptophol, tryptophol, and 5-methoxytryptophol. The average latencies of sleep onset ranged from 1.2 to 2.8 min for the latter two compounds, whereas 5-hydroxytryptophol induced long episodes of sleep (up to 93 min) but with considerable delay. Pointing out that both 5-hydroxytryptophol and 5-methoxytryptophol are found in the pineal gland, Feldstein and his co-workers concluded that the tryptophols or their metabolites, the indoleacetaldehydes, might regulate sleep by acting on nonspecific receptor sites in the sleep circuits of the brain. Ethanol, which has structural similarities to the tryptophols, might also induce sleep by acting on the same receptor sites.

Davis and Walsh (1970) formulated a second hypothesis, also derived from the finding that alcohol ingestion alters metabolism of the monoamines. Their in vitro studies of rat brainstem and liver showed that alcohol-evoked modification in the metabolic disposition of dopamine (catecholamine precursor of NE) can result in the formation of morphinelike alkaloids, especially in brain. Their finding suggests new approaches to the study of alcohol and sleep as well as a biochemical hypothesis for the role of catecholamines in the genesis of alcohol dependence.

The notion that alcohol causes release of the monoamines from their storage sites by activating monoaminergic neurons (a version of the reserpine model) may have weathered the investigative storm. Single high or repeated moderate doses of alcohol do cause modest depletion of brain levels of the monoamines, and for NE, apparently, this effect is potentiated when catecholamine synthesis is blocked at the rate-limiting step. Because of the similarities between the NE and 5-HT systems in their biosynthesis, their metabolism and their response to drugs, it is reasonable to guess that this effect will also be found for serotonin. A somewhat modified reserpine model remains a useful working hypothesis for the researcher concerned with the effects of alcohol on sleep. In Johnson *et al.*'s studies, for example, the alterations in sleep found after 17 years of excessive drinking might indeed be due to depletion of 5-HT from serotonergic sites in the brain.

SUMMARY AND CONCLUSIONS

Despite the extraordinary research effort expended on sleep in the past 15 years, we still know only a little about this extremely complex state. For example, we do not know why the brain and body require sleep. Studies of the effects of sleep deprivation have not revealed systematic alterations in any biological mechanism from which a functional theory of sleep could be constructed. We are, however, learning something about its neural and biochemical substrates. Most neural scientists would now agree that there are active CNS mechanisms for the induction and maintenance of sleep, which include, among others, pontobulbar, cortical, and perhaps thalamic systems capable of actively inhibiting the mesencephalic reticular activating system. Koella, and other students of Hess, however, would emphasize that the syndrome of sleep involves the entire brain, organized hierarchically, in a way which differs qualitatively, not quantitatively, from the organization of waking. Hess and Koella would locate the direction of this symphony in the head ganglion, the thalamus. Perhaps few neuroscientists would agree, but it is true that most investigators have neglected the thalamus in favor of brainstem systems in their search for the neural substrates of sleep.

The long-term temporal features of the states of sleep, of their regular, almost imperturbable ultradian cycle, and of their response to pharmacological, neurological, or psychological perturbation recommends neurobiochemistry as the basic science of sleep, but examination of the biochemical substrates of sleep has only begun. Nevertheless, there is already a rather impressive body of evidence, generated in large measure by Jouvet and his colleagues, that serotonin or one of its major metabolites is a basic hypnogenic substance. Data from chicks, rabbits, rats, cats, monkeys, and humans indicate that its depletion is correlated with insomnia and its potentiation with sedation and slow-wave sleep. Furthermore, serotonin or its metabolic by-products may be involved in the triggering and maintenance of REM sleep. Jouvet's studies of cats, Torda's studies of rats and our (as well as Hartmann's, Oswald's, Mandell's and Domino's) studies of humans permit two guesses. First, that a critical level of free serotonin in serotonergic brainstem tissue is necessary for SW sleep, and that within limits SW sleep will increase as a function of those levels. Second, that the rate of turnover of serotonin or some catabolic by-product of the amine controls the periodic occurrence, and perhaps the duration of each episode of REM sleep.

The importance of the catecholamines, and specifically norepinephrine, in the control of REM sleep is not so certain. Precursors of NE induce arousal and waking rather than stage REM. Specific depletion of NE from brain and body tissues reduces but does not totally eliminate REM sleep. Surgical destruction of the NE-rich locus coeruleus in the pons eliminates tonic but not phasic components of REM. As Jouvet suggests, the REM sleep mechanism must require more than one biochemical key in order to operate.

Despite its brevity, the research literature concerned with the acute and chronic effects of alcohol on the states of sleep shows a gratifying consistency. Moderate single or repeated doses of alcohol administered to young adult humans or to animals cause early onset of sleep, small increases in cardio-respiratory rates accompanied by decreased motility, and transient potentiation of SW sleep with delay or inhibition of stage REM. These alterations of waking and sleep increase as a function of alcohol dose and are concordant with the curve of blood alcohol concentration. The latter function is apparently the same for sleeping and waking, and is not differentially affected by the EEG stages of sleep. Thus, the initial alterations of sleep caused by alcohol are probably due to its direct effects on brain systems which are responsible for the states of sleep, mechanisms which control the duration rather than periodicity of sleep stages. However, moderate inebriation is associated with other sleep effects which outlast the period of significant blood alcohol concentration. As Yules et al. (1967) put it, this drug, like many others, produces a "self-sustaining disregulation" of sleep. In their investigation, rebound effects, positive for stage REM and negative for SW sleep, persisted for several days beyond a series of 5 days of alcohol ingestion. It should be emphasized that neither we, in single- and repeated-dose trials (three successive days) with human subjects, nor Branchey et al. (1970) using single doses in rats, observed prolonged rebound effects for the stages of sleep. As the latter investigators pointed out, the failure to observe sustained compensatory effects with one or a few doses of alcohol suggests that the rebound of stage REM associated with withdrawal from chronic ingestion of alcohol is not due to simple compensation for the loss of REM sleep. Instead it may be an indication of the physical dependence induced by prolonged administration of the drug. Several investigators, including Oswald and Kales, have concluded that drugs with addictive potential are characterized not only by their inhibitory effect on REM sleep but also by the intense and sustained rebound effects which accompany their withdrawal. Following the recent studies of Davis and Walsh, it is now possible to suggest that physical dependence on alcohol is based on the fact that acetaldehyde, its major metabolite, by modifying the metabolic disposition of dopamine, can cause the formation of morphinelike alkaloids in the brain.

The transient acute effects of alcohol on sleep are similar to those caused by barbiturates, and to some extent by the monoamine oxidase inhibitors. Considered with the biphasic alterations of EEG and sensory-evoked potentials sometimes found with low blood alcohol concentrations, these changes in sleep suggest that alcohol, like the barbiturates, acts first on the medullary inhibitory regions of the brainstem, and soon after on the mesencephalic reticular formation. Although the results of a number of neuropharmacological studies favor this view, there are others which implicate the cortex as the preferred target of alcohol. New methods of analysis based on new concepts of brain functioning may be required to settle this issue.

The long-range effects of chronic ingestion of alcohol are qualitatively different from its acute effects. Sober chronic alcoholic patients who are not delirious or hallucinating have normal amounts of stage REM, but with few exceptions, almost no slow-wave sleep. With nocturnal EEG profiles characterized by extreme disruption of sleep and gross alterations of the normally stable REM-to-REM cycle, many of these patients may lack the capacity to generate high-voltage K-complexes and delta waves. There is reason to suppose that the generators for such EEG phenomena are located in the frontal cortex, and furthermore, there is evidence that many alcoholic patients have suffered diffuse damage to these brain regions. Thus, diffuse cortical damage may impair the ability of the brain to generate the high-voltage activity of SW sleep, whereas the REM state, triggered and probably sustained by subcortical structures remains intact. The reasons for the astounding increase in REM sleep which can occur during withdrawal from chronic intake of alcohol, and for that matter, from amphetamine, barbiturates, or morphine, remain obscure.

Among sleep researchers, serotonin enjoys considerable popularity as *the* candidate for a hypnogenic substance. Realizing that a single dose of alcohol causes sedation and transient potentiation of SW sleep, and that years of excessive drinking are accompanied by loss of that state, they might guess that the acute effects of alcohol are like those of the monoamine oxidase inhibitors, whereas its chronic effects are like those of reserpine. That is, biochemical analysis in brain would be expected to show increased 5-HT after acute, and depletion of 5-HT after chronic ingestion of alcohol. Results of the first studies of alcohol's effects on biogenic amine metabolism showed that either the MAO inhibition hypothesis or the monoamine depletion hypothesis, or both, were useful working models, but recent investigations indicate that neither of these models can encompass the complex effects of alcohol on biogenic amines. The MAO inhibitor concept may not be valid at all. The reserpine concept still has some life in it, but recent studies by Davis and her colleagues, and by Feldstein, showing the manifold consequences of alcohol's alterations of biogenic amine metabolism have become the basis for new and more sophisticated hypotheses which undoubtedly will serve as guides for future experimental analyses of the states of sleep, and their modification by drugs.

REFERENCES

Abrahamian, H. A., Allison, T., Goff, W. R., and Rosner, B. S., 1963. Effects of thiopental on human cerebral evoked responses, *Anesthesiology* **24**: 650.

Akert, K., Koella, W. P., and Hess, R., Jr., 1952. Sleep produced by electrical stimulation of the thalamus, *Amer. J. Physiol.* **168**: 260.

Allison, T., 1962. Recovery functions of somato-sensory evoked responses in man, *EEG Clin. Neurophysiol.* **14**: 331.

Allison, T., Goff, W. R., Abrahamian, H. A., and Rosner, B. S., 1963. The effects of barbiturate anesthesia upon human somatosensory evoked responses, in *Physiological Basis of Mental Activity* (R. Hernandez-Peon, ed.) Elsevier, Amsterdam.

Amin, A. H., Crawford, T. B. N., and Gaddum, J. H., 1954. The distribution of substance P and 5-hydroxytryptamine in the central nervous system of the dog, *J. Physiol.* **126**: 596.

Andersen, P. and Andersson, S. A., 1968. *The Physiological Basis of the Alpha Rhythm.* Appleton–Century–Crofts, New York.

Arduini, A. and Arduini, M. G., 1954. Effect of drugs and metabolic alterations on brain stem arousal mechanisms, *J. Pharm. Exp. Therap.* **110**: 76.

Asahina, K., 1962. Paradoxical phase and reverse paradoxical phase in human sleep, *J. Physiol. Soc. J.* **24**: 443.

Aserinsky, E., 1965. Periodic respiratory pattern occurring in conjunction with eye movements during sleep, *Science* **150**: 763.

Aserinksy, E. and Kleitman, N., 1953. Regularly occurring periods of eye motility and concomitant phenomena during sleep, *Science* **118**: 273.

Aserinsky, E. and Kleitman, N., 1955. Two types of ocular motility occurring in sleep, *J. Appl. Physiol.* **8**: 1.

Ashcroft, G. W., Eccleston, D., and Crawford, T. B. B., 1965. 5-hydroxyindole metabolism in rat brain, (Methods) *J. Neurochem.* **12**: 483.

Batini, C., Moruzzi, G., Palestini, M., Rossi, G. F., and Zanchetti, A., 1958. Persistent patterns of wakefulness in the pretrigeminal midpontine preparation, *Science* **128**: 30.

Batini, C., Magni, F., Palestini, M., Rossi, G. F., and Zanchetti, A., 1959. Neural mechanisms underlying the enduring EEG and behavioral activation in the mid-pontine pretrigeminal cat, *Arch. Ital. Biol.* **97**: 13.

Bennett, A. E., Mowery, G. L., and Fort, J. T., 1960. Brain damage from chronic alcoholism: The diagnosis of intermediate stage of alcoholic brain damage, *Amer. J. Psychiat.* **116**: 705.

Berger, R. and Oswald, I., 1962a. Eye movements during active and passive dreams, *Science* **137**: 601.

Berger, R. and Oswald, I., 1962b. Effects of sleep deprivation on behavior, subsequent sleep, and dreaming, *J. Ment. Sci.* **108**: 457.

Berlucchi, G., Moruzzi, G., Salvi, G., and Strata, P., 1964. Pupil behavior and ocular movements during synchronized and desynchronized sleep, *Arch. Ital. Biol.* **102**: 230.

Bertler, A., Carlsson, A., and Rosengren, E., 1956. Release by reserpine of catecholamines from rabbits' hearts, *Naturwissenschaften* **43**: 521.

Bogdanski, D. F., Weissbach, H., and Udenfriend, S., 1957. The distribution of serotonin, 5-hydroxytryptophan decarboxylase and monoamine oxidase in brain, *J. Neurochem.* **1**: 272.

Bonnycastle, D. D., Bonnycastle, M. F., and Anderson, E. G., 1962. The effect of a number of central depressant drugs upon brain 5-hydroxytryptamine levels in the rat, *J. Pharmacol.* **135**: 17.

Branchev, M. H., Begleiter, H., and Kissin, B., 1970. The effects of various doses of alcohol on sleep in the rat, *Communications in Behav. Biol.*, in press.

Brazier, M. A. B. and Finesinger, J. E., 1945. Action of barbiturates on the cerebral cortex: Electroencephalographic studies, *Arch. Neurol. Psychiat.* **53**: 51.

Bremer, F., 1935. Cerveau "isolé" et physiologie du sommeil, *C. R. Soc. Biol.* **118**: 1235.

Bremer, F. and Terzuolo, C., 1954. Contribution à l'étude des mécanismes physiologiques du maintien de l'activité vigile du cerveau, *Arch. Int. Physiol.* **60**: 157.

Brodan, V., Vojtěchovský, M., Kuhn, E., and Čepelák, J., 1969. Changes of mental and physical performance in sleep deprivated healthy volunteers, *Activitas Nervosa Superior* **11**: 175.

Brodie, B. B. and Shore, P. A., 1957a. A concept for a role of serotonin and norepinephrine as chemical mediators in the brain, *Ann. N.Y. Acad. Sci.* **66**: 631.

Brodie, B. B. and Shore, P. A., 1957b. On a role for serotonin and norepinephrine as chemical mediators in the central autonomic nervous system, in *Hormones, Brain Function and Behavior* (H. Hoagland, ed.) pp. 161–180, Academic Press, New York.

Brodie, B. B., Pletscher, A., and Shore, P. A., 1955. Evidence that serotonin has a role in brain function, *Science* **122**: 968.

Brodie, B. B., Comer, M. S., Costa, E., and Dlabac, A., 1966. The role of brain serotonin in the mechanism of the central action of reserpine, *J. Pharmacol. Exp. Ther.* **152**: 340.

Cadilhac, J., Passouant-Fontaine, T., and Passouant, P., 1961. Modifications de l'activité de l'hippocampe suivant les divers stades du sommeil spontane chez le chat, *Rev. Neurol (Paris)* **105**: 171.

Caldwell, D. and Domino, E. G., 1967. Electroencephalographic and eye movement patterns during sleep in chronic schizophrenic patients, *Electroenceph. Clin. Neurophysiol.* **22**: 414.

Candia, O., Favale, E., Guissani, A., and Rossi, G. F., 1962. Blood pressure during natural sleep and during sleep induced by electrical stimulation of the brain stem reticular formation, *Arch. Ital. Biol.* **100**: 216.

Carli, G., Armergal, V., and Zanchetti, A., 1965. Brain stem—limbic connections, and the electrographic aspects of deep sleep in the cat, *Arch. Ital. Biol.* **103**: 751.

Carlsson, A., Lindquist, M., and Magnusson, T., 1957. 3,4-dihydroxyphenylalanine and 5-hydroxytryptophan as reserpine antagonists, *Nature* **180**: 1200.

Corrodi, H., Fuxe, K., and Hokfelt, T., 1966. The effect of ethanol on the activity of central catecholamine neurons in rat brain, *J. Pharm. Pharmac.* **18**: 821.

Costa, E. and Rinaldi, R., 1958. Biochemical and electroencephalographic changes in the brain of rabbits injected with 5-hydroxytryptophan (influence of chlorpromazine ꞏ ꞏ ꞏ ꞏ ꞏ ꞏ), ꞏ ꞏ ꞏ ꞏ ꞏ ꞏ ꞏ ꞏ ꞏ ꞏ ꞏ 101, 211.

Coulter, J. D., Lester, B. K., and Williams, H. L., 1971. Reserpine and sleep, *Psychopharmacologia*, **19**: 134.

Courville, C. B., 1955. *Effects of Alcohol on the Nervous System of Man*. San Lucas Press, Los Angeles.

Dahlstrom, A. and Fuxe, K., 1964. Evidence for the existence of monoamine containing neurons in the central nervous system, *Acta Physiol. Scand.* **62**: 232 (Suppl.).

Dahlstrom, A. and Fuxe, K., 1965. Evidence for the existence of monoamine neurons in the central nervous system. II. Experimentally induced changes in the intraneuronal amine levels of bulbospinal neuron systems, *Acta Physiol. Scand.* **64**: 247 (Suppl).

Davis, P. A., Gibbs, F. A., Davis, H., Jetter, W. W., and Trowbridge, L. S., 1940. The effects of alcohol upon the electroencephalogram (brain waves), *Quart. J. Stud. Alc.* **1**: 626.

Davis, Virginia E. and Walsh, M. J., 1970. A possible biochemical basis for alcohol addiction, *Science* **167**: 1005.

Davis, Virginia E., Brown, H., Huff, J. A., and Cashaw, J. C., 1967a. The alteration of serotonin metabolism to 5-hydroxytryptophol by ethanol ingestion in man, *J. Lab. Clin. Med.* **69** (1): 132.

Davis, Virginia E., Brown, H., Huff, J. A., and Cashaw, J. L., 1967b. Ethanol-induced alterations of norepinephrine metabolism in man, *J. Lab. Clin. Med.* **69** (5): 787.

Delay, J., Verdaux, J., and Chanoit, P., 1957. L'electroencephalogramme des alcoholiques chroniques, *Essai statistique*, *Ann. Medpsychol.* **115**: 427.

Dement, W., 1958. Occurrence of low voltage fast electroencephalogram patterns during behavioral sleep in cat, *Electroenceph. Clin. Neurophysiol.* **10**: 291.

Dement, W., 1960. Effect of dream deprivation, *Science* **131**: 1705.

Dement, W., 1964. Experimental dream studies, in *Science and Psychoanalysis: Scientific Proceedings of the Academy of Psychoanalysis* (J. Masserman, ed.) Vol. 7, pp. 129–162, Grune & Stratton, New York.

Dement, W., 1965. Recent studies on the biological role of rapid eye movement sleep, *Amer. J. Psychiat.* **122**: 404.

Dement, W. C. and Kleitman, N., 1957. Cyclic variations in EEG during sleep and their relation to eye movements, body motility, and dreaming, *Electroenceph. Clin. Neurophysiol.* **9**: 673.

Dement, W. and Wolpert, E., 1958. Relation of eye movements, body motility, and external stimuli to dream content, *J. Exp. Psychol.* **55**: 543.

Dement, W., Henry, P., Cohen, H., and Ferguson, J., 1967. Studies on the effect of REM deprivation in humans and in animals, in *Sleep and Altered States of Consciousness* (S. S. Kety, E. V. Evarts, and H. L. Williams, eds.) Vol. XLV, pp. 456–468, Williams and Wilkins, Baltimore.

Diperri, R., Dravid, A., Schweigerdt, A., and Himwich, H. E., 1968. Effects of alcohol on evoked potentials of various parts of the central nervous system of the cat, *Quart. J. Stud. Alc.* **29**: 20.

Dravid, A. R., Diperri, R., Morillo, A., and Himwich, H. E., 1963. Alcohol and evoked potentials in the cat, *Nature* **200** (4913): 1328.

Efron, D. H. and Gessa, G. L., 1961. Failure of ethanol and barbiturates to alter the content of brain 5ht and Ne, *Biochem. Pharm.* **8**: 172.

Efron, D. H. and Gessa, G. L., 1963. Failure of ethanol and barbiturates to alter brain monoamine content, *Arch. Int. Pharmacodyn*, **142** (1–2): 111.

Evans, J. I. and Oswald, I., 1966. Some experiments in the chemistry of narcoleptic sleep, *Brit. J. Psychiat.* **112**: 401.

Falck, B., 1964. Cellular localization of monoamines, in *Biogenic Amines—Progress in Brain Research* (H. E. Himwich and W. A. Himwich, eds.) Vol. 8, Elsevier, Amsterdam.

Falck, B., Hillarp, N. A., Thieme, G., and Thorp, A., 1962. Fluorescence of catecholamines and related compounds condensed with formaldehyde, *J. Histochem. Cytochem.* **10**: 348.

Faure, J., Bensch, C., and Vincent, D., 1962. Rôle d'un système mésencéphalolimbique dans la "phase paradoxale" du sommeil chez le lapin, *C. R. Soc. Biol. (Paris)* **156**: 70.

Favale, E., Guissani, A., and Rossi, G., 1961. Induziono del sonno profondo nel gatto mediate stimolazione elettrica della sostanza reticolare del tronco encefalico, *Ital. Biol. Sper.* **37**: 265.

Feinberg, I. and Carlson, V. R., 1968. Sleep variables as a function of age in man, *Arch. Gen. Psychiat.* **18**: 239.

Feinberg, I., Koresko, R. L., and Heller, N., 1967. EEG sleep patterns as a function of normal and pathological aging in man, *J. Psychiat. Res.* **5**: 107.

Feldstein, A., Hoagland, H, Wong, K., and Freeman, H., 1964. Biogenic amines, biogenic aldehydes, and alcohol, *Quart. J. Stud. Alc.* **25**: 218.

Feldstein, A., Hoagland, H., Freeman, H., and Williamson, O., 1967. The effect of ethanol ingestion on serotonin-C¹⁴ metabolism in man, *Life Sci.* **6**: 53.

Feldstein, A., Chang, F. H., and Kucharski, J. M., 1970. Tryptophol, 5-hydroxytryptophol and 5-methoxytryptophol induced sleep in mice, *Life Sci.* **9**: 323.

Fisher, C., Gross, J., and Zuch, J., 1965. Cycle of penile erection synchronous with dreaming (REM) sleep: Preliminary report, *Arch. Gen. Psychiat.* **12**: 29.

French, J. D., Verzeano, M., and Magoun, H. W., 1953. A neural basis of the anesthetic state, *Arch. Neurol. Psychiat.* **9**: 519.

Garattini, S. and Valzelli, L., 1965. *Serotonin*. Elsevier, Amsterdam.

Giarman, N. J., Freeman, D. X., and Schanberg, S. M., 1964. Drug-induced changes in the subcellular distribution of serotonin in rat brain with special reference to the action of reserpine, in *Biogenic Amines—Progress in Brain Research* (H. E. Himwich and W. A. Himwich, eds.) Vol. 8, Elsevier, Amsterdam.

Gibbs, F. A., Gibbs, E. L., and Lennox, W. G., 1937. Effect on the electroencephalogram of certain drugs which influence nervous activity, *Arch. Int. Med.* **60**: 154.

Goff, W. R., Rosner, B. S., and Allison, T., 1962. Distribution of cerebral somatosensory evoked responses in normal man, *Electroenceph. Clin. Neurophysiol.* **14**: 697.

Greenberg, R. and Pearlman, C., 1967. Delirium tremens and dreaming, *Amer. J. Psychiat.* **124**: 37.

Grenell, R. G., 1957. Some effects of alcohols on the central nervous system, in *A Symposium of the American Association for the Advancement of Science* (Publication no. 47), pp. 7–18, Washington, D.C.

Gresham, S. C., Webb, W. B., and Williams, R. L., 1963. Alcohol and caffeine: Effect on inferred visual dreaming, *Science* **140**: 1266.

Gross, M. M. and Goodenough, D. R., 1968. Sleep disturbances in the acute alcoholic psychoses, Psychiatric Research Report 24, American Psychiatric Association.

Gross, M. M., Begleiter, H., Tobin, M., and Kissin, B., 1966. Changes in auditory evoked response induced by alcohol, *J. Nerv. Ment. Dis.* **143** (2): 152.

Gross, M. M., Goodenough, D. R., Tobin, M., Halpert, E., Lepore, D., Perlstein, A., Sirota, M., Dibianco, J., Fuller, R., and Kishner, I., 1966. Sleep disturbances and hallucinations in the acute alcoholic psychoses, *J. Nerv. Ment. Dis.* **142** (6): 493.

Gursey, D. and Olson, R. E., 1960. Depression of serotonin and norepinephrine levels in brain stem of rabbit by ethanol, *Proc. Soc. Exp Biol. Med.* **104**: 280.

Gursey, D., Vester, J. W., and Olson, R. L., 1959. Effect of ethanol administration on serotonin and norepinephrine levels in rabbit brain, *J. Clin. Invest.* **38**: 1008.

Hadji-Dimo, A. A., Ekberg, R., and Ingvar, D. H., 1968. Effects of ethanol on EEG and cortical blood flow in the cat, *Quart. J. Stud. Alc.* **29**: 828.

Haggendal, J. and Lindquist, M., 1961. Ineffectiveness of ethanol on noradrenaline, dopamine, or 5-hydroxytryptamine levels in brain, *Acta Pharmacol. Toxicol.* **18**: 278.

Hartmann, E., 1966a. The effect of tryptophan on the sleep-dream cycle in man, Report to the Association for the Psychophysiological Study of Sleep.

Hartmann, E., 1966b. Reserpine: Its effect on the sleep-dream cycle in man, *Psychopharmacologia* **9**: 242.

Hartmann, E., 1967. *The Biology of Dreaming.* Charles C. Thomas, Springfield, Ill.

Hartmann, E. and Freedman, D., 1966. The effect of "dream deprivation" on brain serotonin and norepinephrine levels in the rat, Report to the Association for the Psychophysiological Study of Sleep.

Haug, J. O., 1968. Pneumoencephalographic evidence of brain damage in chronic alcoholics, *Acta. Psychiat. Scand.* **203**: 135.

Hess, R., Jr., Akert, K., and Koella, W., 1950. Les potentials bioélectriques du cortex et du thalamus et leur altération par stimulation du centre hypnique chez le chat, *Rev. Neurol.* **83**: 537.

Hess, S. M. and Doepfner, W., 1961. Behavioral effects and brain amine content in rats, *Arch. Int. Pharmacodyn.* **134**: 89.

Hess, W. R., 1924. Über die wechselbeziehungen zwischen psychischen und vegetativen funktionen, *Arch. Neurol. Psychiat.* **15**: 260.

Hess, W. R., 1925. Über die wechselbezienhungen zwischen psychischen und vegetativen funktionen, *Arch. Neurol. Psychiat.* **16**: 36, 285.

Hess, W. R., 1933. Der schlaf, *Klin. Wschr.* **12**: 129.

Hess, W. R., 1944. Das schlafsyndrom als folge dienzephaler reizung, *Helv. Physiol. Acta* **2**: 305.

Hiddema, F., 1965. Electroencephalographic findings in alcoholics, *Psychiat. Neurol. Neurochir.* **68**: 355.

Himwich, H. E., Diperri, R., Dravid, A., and Schweigerdt, A., 1966. Comparative susceptibility to alcohol of cortical area and midbrain reticular formation of the cat, *Psychosom. Med.* **28** (4): 458.

Hobson, J., 1965. The effects of chronic brain stem lesions on cortical and muscular activity during sleep and waking in the cat, *Electroenceph. Clin. Neurophysiol.* **19**: 41.

Hobson, J. A., Goldfrank, R., and Snyder, F., 1965. Respiration and mental activity in sleep, *J. Psychiat. Res.* **3**: 79.

Hoffman, J. S. and Domino, E., 1969. Comparative effects of reserpine on the sleep cycle of man and cat, *J. Pharmacol. Exp. Ther.* **170**: 190.

Holmberg, G. and Martens, S., 1955. Electroencephalographic changes in man correlated with blood alcohol concentration and some other conditions following standardized ingestion of alcohol, *Quart. J. Stud. Alc.* **16**: 411.

Holzbauer, M. and Vogt, M., 1956. Depression by reserpine of the noradrenaline concentration in the hypothalamus of the cat, *J. Neurochem.* **1**: 8.

Horita, A., 1961. The route of administration of some hydrazine compounds as a determinant of brain and liver monoamine oxidase inhibition, *Toxicol. Appl. Pharmacol.* **3**: 474.

Horsey, W. J. and Akert, K., 1953. The influence of ethyl alcohol on the spontaneous electrical activity of the cerebral cortex and subcortical structures of the cat, *Quart. J. Stud. Alc.* **14:** 363.

Hudolin, V. I. and Gubarev, N., 1967. The characteristics of the alpha rhythm in chronic alcoholics, *Brit. J. Addict.* **62:** 55.

Johnson, L. C. and Karpan, W. E., 1968. Autonomic correlates of the spontaneous K-complex, *Psychophysiology* **4:** 444.

Johnson, L. C., Burdick, J., and Smith, J., 1970. Sleep during alcohol intake and withdrawal in the chronic alcoholic, *Arch. Gen. Psychiat.* **22:** 406.

Jouvet, M., 1961. Telencephalic and rhombencephalic sleep in the cat, in *Ciba Foundation Symposium on the Nature of Sleep* (G. E. W. Wolstenholme and M. O'Connor, eds.) Little, Brown, Boston.

Jouvet, M., 1962a. Recherches sur les structures nerveuses et les mécanismes responsables des différentes phases du sommeil physiologique, *Arch. Ital. Biol.* **100:** 125.

Jouvet, M., 1962b. Sur l'existence d'un système hypnotique ponto-limbique: Ses rapports avec l'activité onirique, in *Physiologie de L'hippocampe* (Colloques Intern. du C.N.R.S. No. 107) (P. Passouant, ed.) pp. 297–330, C.N.R.S., Paris.

Jouvet, M., 1967a. Mechanisms of the states of sleep, in *Sleep and Altered States of Consciousness* (S. S. Kety, E. V. Evarts, and H. L. Williams, eds.) Williams and Wilkins, Baltimore.

Jouvet, M., 1967b. Neurophysiology of the states of sleep, in *The Neurosciences: A Study Program* (G. C. Quarton, T. Melnechuk, and F. O. Schmitt, eds.) The Rockefeller University Press, New York.

Jouvet, M., 1969. Biogenic amines and the states of sleep, *Science* **163:** 32.

Jouvet, M. and Michel, F., 1960. Déclenchement de la "phase paradoxale" du sommeil par stimulation du tronc cérébrale chez le chat interact et mésencéphalique chronique, *C. R. Soc. Biol. (Paris)* **154:** 636.

Jouvet, M., Michel, F., and Mounier, D., 1960. Analyse electroencephalographique comparée du sommeil physiologique chez le chat et chez l'homme, *Rev. Neurol.* **103:** 189.

Jouvet, D., Vimont, P., Delorme, F., and Jouvet, M., 1964. Étude de la privation sélective de la phase paradoxale du sommeil chez le chat, *C. R. Soc. Biol. (Paris)* **158:** 756.

Kahn, E. and Fisher, C. F., 1969. The sleep characteristics of the normal aged male, *J. Nerv. Ment. Dis.* **148:** 477.

Kales, A., 1969. *Sleep: Physiology and Pathology.* J. B. Lippincott Co., Philadelphia.

Kales, A., Hoedemaker, F., Jacobson, A., and Lichtenstein, E., 1964. Dream deprivation: An experimental reappraisal, *Nature* **204:** 1337.

Kales, A., Malmstrom, E. J., Scharf, M. B., and Rubin, R. T., 1969. Psychophysiological and biochemical changes following use and withdrawal of hypnotics, in *Sleep: Physiology and Pathology* (A. Kales, ed.) pp. 331–343, J. B. Lippincott Co., Philadelphia.

Kamiya, J., 1961. Behavioral, subjective and physiological aspects of sleep and drowsiness, in *Functions of Varied Experience* (D. W. Fiske and S. R. Maddi, eds.) Dorsey Press, Homewood, Ill.

Kanzow, E., Krause, D., and Kuhnel, H., 1962. Die vasomotorik der hirnrinde in den phasen desynchronisierter EEG-aktivitat im naturlichen schlaf der katze, *Arch. Gen. Physiol.* **274:** 593.

Karacan, I., Goodenough, D. R., Shapiro, A., and Starker, S., 1966. Erection cycle during sleep in relation to dream anxiety, *Arch. Gen. Psychiat.* **15:** 183.

Khazan, N. and Sawyer, C., 1963. Rebound recovery from deprivation of paradoxical sleep in the rabbit, *Proc. Soc. Exp. Biol. Med.* **114:** 536.

Khazan, N. and Sawyer, C., 1964. Mechanisms of paradoxical sleep as revealed by neurophysiologic and pharmacologic approaches in the rabbit, *Psychopharmacologia,* **5:** 457.

Kleitman, N., 1939. *Sleep and Wakefulness.* U. Chicago Press, Chicago.

Knowles, J. B., Laverty, S. G., and Kuechler, H. A., 1968. Effects of alcohol on REM sleep, *Quart. J. Stud. Alc.* **29:** 342.

Koella, W. P., 1966. The mode and locus of action of serotonin in its effects on the recruiting responses and the EEG of cats, *Amer. J. Physiol.* **211:** 926.

Koella, W. P., 1967. *Sleep: Its Nature and Physiological Organization.* Charles C. Thomas, Springfield, Ill.

Koella, W. P., Trunca, C. M., and Czicman, J. S., 1965. Serotonin: Effect on recruiting responses of the cat, *Life Sci.* **4:** 173.

Kogan, A. B., 1969. On physiological mechanisms of sleep inhibition irradiation over the cerebral cortex, *Activitas Nervosa Superior* **11** (2): 141.

Koranyi, E. and Lehman, H., 1960. Experimental sleep deprivation in schizophrenic patients, *Arch. Gen. Psychiat.* **2:** 543.

Kripke, D., Weitzman, E., and Pollak, C., 1966. Attempts to induce the rapid eye movement stage of sleep in *Macaca mulatta* by brain stem stimulation, *Psychophysiology* **2:** 132.

Lester, B. K., Coulter, J. D., Cowden, L. C., and Williams, H. L., 1968. Secobarbital and nocturnal physiological patterns, *Psychopharmacologia (Berl.)* **13:** 275.

Lewis, E. G., Dustman, R. E., and Beck, E. C., 1969. The effects of alcohol on sensory phenomena and cognitive and motor tasks, *Quart. J. Stud. Alc.* **30** (3): 618.

Lindsley, D. B., Bowden, J., and Magoun, H. W., 1949. Effect upon the EEG of acute injury to the brainstem activating system, *Electroenceph. Clin. Neurophysiol.* **1:** 475.

Little, S. C. and McAvoy, M., 1952. Electroencephalographic studies in alcoholism, *Quart. J. Stud. Alc.* **13:** 9.

Loomis, A. L., Harvey, E. N., and Hobart, G. A., 1937. Cerebral states during sleep, as studied by human brain potentials, *J. Exp. Psychol.* **21:** 127.

Magni, R., Moruzzi, G., Rossi, G. F., and Zanchetti, A., 1959. EEG arousal following inactivation of the lower brain stem by selective ingestion of barbiturate into the vertebral circulation, *Arch. Ital. Biol.* **97:** 33.

Magnes, J., Moruzzi, G., and Pompeiano, O., 1961a. EEG synchronization from medullary structures, *Fed. Proc.* **20:** 336.

Magnes, J., Moruzzi, G., and Pompeiano, O., 1961b. Synchronization of the EEG produced by low-frequency electrical stimulation of the region of the solitary tract, *Arch. Ital. Biol.* **99:** 33.

Mandell, M. P., Mandell, A. J., and Jacobson, A., 1964. Biochemical and neurophysiological studies of paradoxical sleep, *Rec. Advan. Biol. Psychiat.* **7:** 115.

Marantz, R. and Rechtschaffen, A., 1967. Effect of alpha methyltyrosine on sleep in the rat, *Percept. Mot. Skills* **25:** 805.

Marbach, G. and Schwertz, M. T., 1964. Effets physiologiques de l'alcohol et de la caféine au cours du sommeil chez l'homme, *Arch. Sci. Physiol.* **18:** 163.

Matsumoto, J. and Jouvet, M., 1964. Effets de reserpine, DOPA et 5-HTP sur les deux etats de sommeil, *C. R. Soc. Biol.* **158:** 2137.

Mello, N. K., 1968. Some aspects of the behavioral pharmacology of alcohol, in *Psychopharmacology: A Review of Progress, 1957–1967* (D. H. Efron, ed.) Public Health Service Publication No. 1836.

Mendels, J. and Hawkins, D. R., 1967. Sleep and depression, *Arch. Gen. Psychiat.* **16:** 344.

Mirsky, I. A., Piker, P., Rosenbaum, M., and Lederer, H., 1941. Adaptation of central nervous system, *Quart. J. Stud. Alc.* **2:** 35.

Moir, A. T. B. and Eccleston, D., 1968. The effects of precursor loading in the cerebral metabolism of 5-hydroxyindoles, *J. Neurochem.* **15:** 1093.

Monnier, M. and Tissot, R., 1958. Action de la reserpine et de ses mediaterus (5-HTP, serotonine et DOPA-noradrenalinc) sur le comportement et le cerveau de lapin, *Helv. Physiol. Acta* **16:** 255.

Morris, G. O., Williams, H. L., and Lubin, A., 1960. Misperception and disorientation during sleep deprivation, *A.M.A. Arch. Gen. Psychiat.* **2:** 247.

Moruzzi, G., 1960. Synchronizing influences of the brain stem and the inhibitory mechanisms underlying the production of sleep by sensory stimulation, *Electroenceph. Clin. Neurophysiol.* **13:** 231 (Suppl.).

Moruzzi, G. and Magoun, H. W., 1949. Brain stem reticular formation and activation of the EEG, *Electroenceph. Clin. Neurophysiol.* **1:** 455.

Mullin, F. J., Kleitman, N., and Cooperman, N. R., 1933. The effect of alcohol and caffein on motility and body temperature during sleep, *Amer. J. Physiol.* **106:** 478.

Nakai, Y. and Domino, E. F., 1969. Differential effects of pentobarbital, ethyl alcohol and chlorpromazine in modifying reticular facilitation of visually evoked responses in the cat, *Internat. J. Neuropharm.* **8:** 61.

Neff, N. H. and Tozer, T. N., 1968. *In vivo* measurement of brain serotonin turnover, in *Advances in Pharmacology, Biological Role of Indolealkylamine Derivatives* (S. Garattini and P. A. Shore, eds., E. Costa and M. Sandler, assoc. eds.) Vol. 6, Part A, pp. 97–109, Academic Press, New York.

Newman, H. W., 1959. The effect of alcohol on the electroencephalogram, *Stanford Med. Bull.* **17** (2): 55.

Ohlmeyer, P., Brilmayer, H., and Hüllstrung, H., 1944. Periodische vorgänge im schlaf, *Pfluegers Arch.* **248:** 559.

Oswald, I., 1962. *Sleeping and Waking: Physiology and Psychology.* Elsevier, New York.

Oswald, I., Ashcroft, G. W., Berger, R. J., Eccleston, C., Evans, J. I., and Thacore, V. R., 1966. Some experiments in the chemistry of normal sleep, *Brit. J. Psychiat.* **112:** 391.

Paasonen, M. K. and Giarman, N. J., 1958. Brain levels of 5-hydroxytryptamine after various agents, *Arch. Int. Pharmacodyn.* **114** (2): 189.

Parmeggiani, P. and Zanocco, G., 1961. Cortical and subcortical recordings during low voltage fast EEG phase of sleep in the cat, *Helv. Physiol. Pharmacol. Acta* **19:** C97.

Pletscher, A., 1967. Monoamine oxidase inhibitors: Effects related to psychostimulation, in *Psychopharmacology: A Review of Progress 1957–1967* (D. G. Efron, ed.) Proc. Sixth Annual Meeting of American College of Neuropsychopharmacology.

Pompeiano, O. and Morrison, A., 1965. Vestibular influences during sleep: I. Abolition of the rapid eye movements of desynchronized sleep following vestibular lesions, *Arch. Ital. Biol.* **103:** 569.

Pscheidt, G. R., Issekutz, B., and Himwich, H. E., 1961. Failure of ethanol to lower brain stem concentration of biogenic amines, *Quart. J. Stud. Alc.* **22:** 550.

Pscheidt, G. R., Morpurgo, C., and Himwich, H., 1964. Studies on norepinephrine and 5-hydroxytryptamine in various species, in *Comparative Neurochemistry* (D. Richter, ed.) pp. 401–412, Pergamon Press, New York.

Rechtschaffen, A. and Dement, W., 1967. Studies on the relation of narcolepsy, cataplexy and sleep with low voltage fast EEG activity, in *Sleep and Altered States of Con-*

sciousness (S. S. Kety, E. V. Evarts, and H. L. Williams, eds.) Williams and Wilkins, Baltimore.

Rechtschaffen, A. and Kales, A., 1968. *A Manual of Standardized Terminology: Techniques and Scoring System for Sleep Stages of Human Subjects*, N.I.H. Publication No. 204, Bethesda, Maryland.

Reite, M., Pegram, G. V., Stephens, L. M., Bixler, E. C., and Lewis, O. L., 1969. The effect of reserpine and monoamine oxidase inhibitors on paradoxical sleep in the monkey, *Psychopharmacologia* **14**: 12.

Robert, W., 1886. *Der Traum als Naturnotwendigkeit Erklärt*. Ocippel, Hamburg.

Rosadini, G. and Rossi, G. F., 1969. Spectral power analysis of the electroencephalogram during physiological sleep in man, *Activitas Nervosa Superior* **11**: 188.

Rosenfeld, G., 1960. Inhibitory influence of ethanol on serotonin metabolism, *Proc. Soc. Exp. Biol. Med.* **103**: 144.

Ross, J. J., 1965. Neurological findings after prolonged sleep deprivation, *Arch. Neurol.* **12**: 399.

Salamy, A., Rundell, O. H., and Williams, H. L., 1969. The effects of alcohol on the cortical evoked response, Paper presented at the annual meeting of the Southwestern Psychological Association, Austin, Texas.

Sampson, H., 1965. Deprivation of dreaming sleep by two methods: I. Compensatory REM time, *Arch. Gen. Psychiat.* **13**: 79.

Sauerland, E. K., Knauss, T., and Clemente, C. D., 1967. Effect of ethyl alcohol on orbital-cortically induced reflex inhibition in the cat, *Brain Res.* **7**: 181.

Schaff, G., Marbach, G., and Vogt, J. J., 1962. Concomitant variations of the spontaneous motility, the cardiac frequency and respiratory frequency in the course of sleep under the influence of various states of fatigue, *C. R. Soc. Biol.* **156**: 1517.

Schweigerdt, A. K., Dravid, A. R., Stewart, A. H., and Himwich, H. E., 1965. Alcohol and evoked potentials in the cat, *Nature* **208** (5011): 688.

Shore, P. A., Pletscher, A., Tomich, E. G., Carlsson, A., Kuntzman, R., and Brodie, B. B., 1957. Role of brain 5-HT in reserpine action, *Ann. N.Y. Acad. Sci.* **66**: 609.

Snyder, F., 1963. New biology of dreaming, *Arch. Gen. Psychiat.* **8**: 381.

Snyder, F., Hobson, J., and Goldfrank, F., 1963. Blood pressure changes during human sleep, *Science* **142**: 1313.

Snyder, F., Hobson, J., Morrison, D., and Goldfrank, F., 1964. Changes in respiration, heart rate and systolic blood pressure in relation to electroencephalographic patterns of human sleep, *J. Appl. Physiol.* **19**: 417.

Stohr, P. E. and Goldring, S., 1969. Origins of somatosensory evoked scalp responses in man, *J. Neurosurg.* **431** (2): 117.

Tissot, R., 1965. The effects of certain drugs on the sleep cycle in man, in *Progress in Brain Research* (K. Akert, C. Bally, and J. P. Shade, eds.) Vol. 18, pp. 175–177, Elsevier, New York.

Tokizane, T., 1965. Sleep mechanism: Hypothalamic control of cortical activity, in *Aspects Anatomofonctionnels de la Physiologie du Sommeil* (M. Jouvet, ed.) Centre National de la Recherche Scientifique, Lyon, France.

Torda, Clara, 1969. Biochemical and bioelectric processes related to sleep, paradoxical sleep and arousal, *Psychol. Rep.* **24**: 807.

Tozer, T. N., Neff, N. H., and Brodie, B. B., 1966. Application of steady state kinetics to the synthesis rate and turnover time of serotonin in the brain of normal and reserpine-treated rats, *J. Pharmacol. Exp. Ther.* **153**: 177.

Truitt, E. B., Jr. and Walsh, M. J., 1968. The biochemical pharmacology of alcoholism, *Battelle Tech. Rev.* **17**: 3.

Vaughn, H. G. and Ritter, W., 1970. The sources of auditory evoked responses recorded from the human scalp, *Electroenceph. Clin. Neurophysiol.* **28:** 360.

Vojtěchovský, M., Hort, V., Simáné, Z., Brězinová, V., Krus, D., and Skála, J., 1969. The influence of centrophenoxine (lucidril[R]) on the course of sleep deprivation in alcoholics, *Activitas Nervosa Superior* **11:** 193.

Webb, W. B. and Agnew, H. W., Jr., 1968. Measurement and characteristics of nocturnal sleep, in *Progress in Clinical Psychology* (L. E. Abt, and B. F. Reiss, eds.) Vol. 8, pp. 2–27, Grune and Stratton, New York.

Weitzman, E. D., Rapport, M. M., McGregor, P., and Jacoby, J., 1968. Sleep patterns of the monkey and brain serotonin concentration: Effect of P. chlorophenylalanine, *Science* **160:** 1361.

West, L. J., 1967. Psychopathology produced by sleep deprivation, in *Sleep and Altered States of Consciousness* (S. S. Kety, E. V. Evarts, and H. L. Williams, eds.) Vol. XLV, pp. 535–558, Williams & Wilkins Co., Baltimore.

West, L. J., Janszen, H. H., Lester, B. K., and Cornelison, F. S., Jr., 1962. The psychosis of sleep deprivation, *Ann. N.Y. Acad. Sci.* **96:** 66.

Williams, H. L., Hammack, J. R., Daly, R. L., Dement, W. C., and Lubin, A., 1964. Responses to auditory stimulation, sleep loss and the EEG stages of sleep, *Electroenceph. Clin. Neurophysiol.* **16:** 269.

Williams, H. L., Morlock, H. C., Jr., and Morlock, Jean V., 1966. Instrumental behavior during sleep, *Psychophysiology* **2:** 208.

Williams, H. L., Lester, B. K., and Coulter, J. D., 1969. Monoamines and the EEG stages of sleep, *Activitas Nervosa Superior* **11:** 188.

Yules, R. B., Freedman, D. X., and Chandler, K. A., 1966. The effect of ethyl alcohol on man's electroencephalographic sleep cycle, *Electroenceph. Clin. Neurophysiol.* **20:** 109.

Yules, R. B., Ogden, J. A., Gault, F. P., and Freedman, D. X., 1966. The effect of ethyl alcohol on electroencephalographic sleep cycles in cats, *Psychonom. Sci.* **5:** 97.

Yules, R. B., Lippman, M. E., and Freedman, D. X., 1967. Alcohol administration prior to sleep: The effect on EEG sleep stages, *Arch. Gen. Psychiat.* **16:** 94.

Zung, W. W. K., Wilson, W. P., and Didson, W. E., 1964. Effect of depressive disorders on sleep EEG responses, *Arch. Gen. Psychiat.* **10:** 439.

CHAPTER 14

Alcoholism and Learning

M. Vogel-Sprott

University of Waterloo
Waterloo, Ontario, Canada

INTRODUCTION

When man attempts to understand and solve a problem, some explanations or solutions always seem more probable or promising than others. Such is the case when the riddle of alcoholism is considered. Our understanding here is at a stage where many disciplines suggest different explanations with varying degrees of appeal. The purpose of this chapter is to illustrate the potential explanation of alcoholism obtained when this phenomenon is analyzed in terms of psychological principles of learning.

This approach has at least two rather unique aspects. First, it is a behavioral analysis which focuses exclusively on the one distinctive response which defines alcoholism in a given society. This is the alcohol drinking response ". . . which in its extent goes beyond the traditional customary 'dietary' use, or ordinary compliance with the social drinking customs of the whole community concerned . . ." (World Health Organization, 1952, p. 15). The second and equally important aspect of this approach is its assumption that this deviant drinking habit is an instrumental response which is subject to the same learning variables that control instrumental behavior in general.

The chapter begins with some relatively formal definitions of basic concepts and principles of learning. Their explanatory potential then is illustrated by dealing in turn with the development of excessive drinking, factors contributing to its maintenance, and procedures to control this response after it has been acquired. This analysis together with supporting research evidence provides the basis for evaluating the explanation of alcoholism as learned behavior.

LEARNING TERMS AND PRINCIPLES

Reinforcement

In the psychology of learning, reinforcing means presenting some particular stimulus event which will increase the occurrence of a response. Reinforcers customarily are defined empirically. If the presentation or termination of some event (e.g., administration of food or offset of punishment) is shown to increase the probability of occurrence of a response, then this manipulation of the stimulus is said to be reinforcing. The empirical test of the reinforcing ability of a stimulus is relatively straightforward and uncontroversial compared to the difficulty in providing an acceptable theoretical explanation for the mechanism of reinforcement. Some of the theoretical explanations of reinforcement, and their potential relevance to an understanding of excessive drinking may be summarized.

Drive Reduction

Hull (1943) was one of the chief spokesmen for the view that a stimulus event operates as a reinforcer because it reduces some basic need in the organism (e.g., reduction of hunger or pain). The underlying mechanism of reinforcement then is attributed to the alleviation or reduction of some primary physiological need.

If a stimulus which is not directly drive-reducing (e.g., tone) is observed to have reinforcing properties, it may be explained by the organism's prior learning experience where this stimulus has been associated with the drive-reducing stimulus. Pairing the occurrence of tone with food for example, allows the reinforcing properties of food to become conditioned to tone. Tone then is termed a secondary reinforcer, distinct but somewhat similar to the primary reinforcer, food, which actually reduces the basic drive. Thus any stimulus may function as a secondary reinforcer, so long as it has previously been associated with primary need reduction. The ability of such stimuli as money, social approval, or attention to strengthen a response may be attributed to their secondary reinforcing properties. Since deprivation of basic needs is relatively rare in the everyday experience of humans, their behavior would more commonly be under the control of secondary reinforcers.

Although the concept of secondary reinforcement provides a potential explanation for the development of all human behavior on the basis of physiological need reduction, it is now generally recognized that emotions also may function like tissue needs. The reduction of an aversive emotional state thus may be termed drive-reducing and may reinforce a response.

Relatively early in the twentieth century, psychiatry (e.g., Freud, 1920; Horney, 1937) began stressing the important role of anxieties and fears in maladaptive or "neurotic" behavior. With the formal conception of anxiety and fear reduction as reinforcers of behavior (Mowrer, 1947), learning theory held the obvious promise of specifying the mechanism and principles governing the development of many types of maladaptive responses.

Timing and Scheduling

The ability of a given reinforcer to strengthen a habit depends on the temporal relation between response and reinforcement and on the consistency with which the reinforcer is administered for the act (Kimble, 1961, pp. 137–144). Immediate and consistent reward will increase the rate at which the new response is acquired. Intermittency and delay in reward result in slower learning. These principles can be useful in predicting which responses a given individual will acquire more quickly, and in understanding some individual differences in learning a given response.

Extinction

The tendency for a learned response to decline in frequency when reinforcement is withdrawn is termed extinction. An explanation of this phenomenon also relates to the timing and scheduling factors which influence response acquisition. A well-established principle, first called a "paradox" (Humphreys, 1939), is that if a response is acquired under intermittent or delayed reinforcement, it is more resistant to the weakening effect of extinction than if it had been trained with consistent or immediate reinforcement. The seemingly paradoxical quality of this finding is that reinforcement conditions least adequate for rapid response acquisition are best for generating hardier response tendencies which are more resistant to extinction.

A number of different theories have been advanced to account for the superior resistance to extinction generated by intermittent reinforcement (e.g., Amsel, 1962; Festinger, 1961; Mowrer, 1960; Mowrer and Jones, 1945). None is completely adequate, but a few which are pertinent to the interests of this chapter may be considered.

Discrimination Hypothesis

This explanation (Mowrer and Jones, 1945) argues that irregular reinforcement during acquisition is more similar to extinction than is consistent reinforcement. Thus under intermittent reward conditions, it is more difficult to discriminate the onset of extinction when reward is completely withdrawn. This inability to discriminate is assumed to be responsible for enhancing persistence during extinction. Although a failure to discriminate may be a contributing factor in response persistence, such persistence is obtained even when this factor is ruled out (cf. Theios, 1962; Vogel-Sprott, 1967a).

Frustration Tolerance

Other theorists (Amsel, 1962; Mowrer, 1960) point out that under consistent reward training the response always occurs in the presence of reward. In contrast, a response trained under intermittent reinforcement will occur with reward on some trials and with nonreward on others. Reward is assumed to evoke a pleasurable emotion (i.e., incentive, hope) whereas nonreward is assumed to be aversive (i.e., frustrating, disappointing). Thus under intermittent reward training, the response tendency can become classically conditioned to both types of emotion-provoking stimuli (Amsel, 1962). As a result, the experience of hope or frustration may evoke this response. Under this training, the individual learns to tolerate some disappointment and frustration (Mowrer, 1960, p. 470). With the onset of extinction, nonreward stimuli have acquired the ability to evoke responding, and this is reflected in superior persistance during extinction.

Punishment

A punisher is a noxious event which an organism will ordinarily attempt to escape or avoid. The consequences of punishment are extremely varied (Church, 1963). A punished response may be suppressed (e.g., Karsh, 1962), or facilitated as "vicious circle" behavior (Gwinn, 1949; Hurwitz, 1956). It also may lead to the learning and maintenance of a new habit which completely avoids the punishment (Solomon and Wynne, 1953; Solomon et al., 1953). In addition, these various consequences are observed sometimes to be relatively permanent and sometimes to be temporary and transient (cf. Boe and Church, 1967; Estes, 1944; Vogel-Sprott and Racinskas, 1969).

Humans are typically exposed to punishment in one form or another at all stages of their lives. Thus the learning principles known to determine the various consequences of punishment have considerable practical import both for restraining unacceptable behavior and for understanding conditions prompting persistence of an unwanted response in spite of punishment.

Learning theory assumes that fear or anxiety is evoked by a noxious stimulus. Since a reduction in this aversive emotional state may serve as a reinforcer, any response initially associated with fear reduction should tend to recur the next time a similar situation is encountered. These principles apply to all types of punishment situations and the behavioral consequences of punishment vary as a function of certain environmental factors.

Active Avoidance

Consider the situation where a noxious stimulus (e.g., a beating, or electric shock) is directly applied to an individual. Withdrawal or escape behavior is normally observed. Since withdrawal from the punisher will terminate or diminish its intensity, escape is accompanied by fear reduction and its tendency to recur is readily understood. The particular mode of escape (e.g., button-press, running, finger withdrawal) will be determined by the type of environmental punisher applied and the responses available to the individual.

A physical punisher often is consistently preceded by some other stimulus event (e.g., raising the hand to strike, click of a shock generator). These environmental stimuli are not themselves harmful, but the consistent pairing of these cues with punishment allows an individual to anticipate the aversive stimulus and some of the emotion-provoking properties of the punisher become conditioned to these stimuli. Thus escape or withdrawal from these conditioned punishment cues should occur since their termination would be anxiety-reducing.

A response which allows an individual to withdraw from a conditioned punishment stimulus typically also will permit him to avoid the punisher. This response is termed an "active avoidance response" (Mowrer, 1960) and when it is acquired, the subject displays a persistent withdrawal from a stimulus which is actually physically harmless. Since the physical punisher now is never present, this consistent withdrawal behavior may appear to be irrational and might be termed a "phobia." Such behavior however could be explained by the anxiety reduction achieved from terminating the conditioned punishment signal. The occurrence of punishment actually is required only initially, in order to develop the conditioned punishing properties of the cues. Once this conditioning has been achieved, withdrawal from the punishment signal and avoidance of punishment begins to occur, and this behavior may increase even though punishment is not ever again administered.

There are obvious adaptive features in this self-perpetuating quality of active avoidance. Society certainly places great reliance on the potency of conditioned punishment cues in the social and physical environment to generate avoidance of harmful events. Unfortunately, some avoidance responses which develop are judged to be maladaptive. What techniques do learning principles suggest for the elimination of this behavior? Since avoidance responses are triggered by conditioned cues in the environment, removal of these stimuli clearly should terminate the avoidance response. If their removal is not practical, an alternative technique consists of presenting these cues without punishment, in a situation where the learned avoidance response is not physically possible.

With repeated exposure to danger signals which are no longer confirmed by punishment, the anxiety-provoking properties of the cues may weaken and extinguish.

Since punishment of a response often will curtail this behavior, it might seem reasonable to suggest that active avoidance behavior could be suppressed by punishment. It is important here to note that learning principles predict that such a treatment would fail to reduce avoidance behavior and may actually increase its occurrence. Punishment of an avoidance response may increase anxiety and thus raise the need for anxiety reduction. Since the avoidance response in this situation has already been developed as the dominant anxiety-reducing habit, its frequency and vigor increases (e.g., Gwinn, 1949). Thus we see "vicious circle" or "masochistic" behavior (Mowrer, 1960, p. 436, 487), in which punishing an active avoidance response increases it, and this in turn leads to more punishment and more responding.

Passive Avoidance

In contrast to active avoidance behavior which depends upon the presence of punishment cues in the environment, response inhibition or "passive avoidance" (Mowrer, 1960) occurs when there are no discriminable external signals for punishment. Although environmental cues may be absent, there are still many internal stimulus events which could reliably precede a punished response (e.g., symbolic rehearsal of the taboo act, or physical preparatory sensations leading up to the completion of the response). These stimuli also may become conditioned to evoke some of the anxiety-provoking properties of punishment. The termination of these stimuli is obtained by suppressing the response, and this "not-responding" behavior is reinforced by anxiety reduction. Thus an individual inhibits the response and possibly even "forgets" about the taboo act so that the cognitive anxiety-producing stimuli also are terminated.

Although punishment would be required to initiate response suppression, it is not necessary to maintain it because the anxiety reduction obtained by passive avoidance comes from the termination of internalized punishment cues. If a person develops inhibitions which are judged to be maladaptive, what learning procedures could be employed to eliminate passive avoidance ? Since the cues which prompt inhibition are within the individual, it is extremely difficult to remove these stimuli. The individual, however, may be induced to think about and perform the response in a punishment-free situation. Repeated practice under such conditions would weaken or extinguish the conditioned anxiety-provoking properties of the internal cues which accompany the response. A supplementary or alternative procedure would be to induce relaxation by tranquilizing drugs or other treatment. Under these conditions the internalized punishment cues may not evoke as much anxiety, and inhibitions may be lessened because the tension-reducing reinforcement for withholding the response is reduced.

LEARNING PRINCIPLES AND RESEARCH RELEVANT TO ALCOHOLISM

An explanation of excessive drinking in terms of learning principles has been advocated by many writers (Conger, 1956; Kepner, 1964; Kingham, 1956; Shoben, 1956; Vogel-Sprott, 1967b). This section presents a learning analysis of the development, maintenance, and control of excessive drinking, accompanied by supporting research evidence.

Reinforcing Properties of Alcohol

The depressant action of alcohol on the central nervous system (Goodman and Gilman, 1965) is assumed to have tension-reducing effects which serve to reinforce alcohol drinking behavior. Early support (Masserman and Yum, 1946) for this notion was obtained with cats who were trained to perform a complex response for food. After learning this adaptive behavior to reduce hunger, the animals were subjected to a strong painful electric shock at the food box. Approaching the goal box thus acquired two contradictory valences. It was both a highly desirable source of relief from hunger and a locus of traumatic danger and threat. Under this conflict condition, the hungry cats inhibited the response necessary to obtain the food in the goal box. This response, however, was readily reinstated when the animals were mildly intoxicated. Under the influence of alcohol the animals appeared to recover their adjustive behavior, with approach and consumption of food no longer disturbed by the shock.

Masserman and Yum considered the cats' consistent refusal to seek food when frightened as analogous to a neurotic type of emotional conflict. They argued that alcohol reduced fear and thereby weakened the avoidance and inhibitory behavior evoked by fear. With anxiety reduced, responses appropriate to the hunger drive could occur without disturbance. Alcohol here thus appeared to play a therapeutic role, reestablishing adaptive behavior. It is important to note that this evidence alone does not necessarily demonstrate that mild intoxication reduced fear. For example, if alcohol operated to enhance hunger and its associated approach responses, the same observations actually could have been obtained.

A specific test of the hypothesis that alcohol reduces fear was conducted by Conger (1951). After substantially confirming the results of Masserman and Yum, Conger began training a new group of animals to approach the lighted end of an alley for food. A different group was similarly trained to avoid the same end to escape strong shock. Now which group would alter its behavior under

alcohol ? If a moderate dose of alcohol only reduces fear, then avoidance behavior in the second group should be diminished and the approach tendencies
in the first group should not be altered appreciably. The strength of this behavior
was measured by the extent to which animals pulled to approach or avoid the
end of the alley. Half of the animals in each group were tested sober, half when
mildly intoxicated. His observations clearly demonstrated that alcohol has little
effect on approach tendencies but it considerably weakens avoidance responses
evoked by fear. The generality of the effect of alcohol on conflict behavior has
been extended by recent studies manipulating drug dose, punishment intensity,
and length of exposure to conflict (Freed, 1967). Alcohol was found to reinstate
approach behavior both after brief or prolonged conflict training, and when
punishment was mild or intense. The most important determinant of the
alcohol effect appeared to be drug dosage. A moderate dose of alcohol reduced
avoidance tendencies more effectively than either high or low doses of the drug.

These studies have shown that alcohol reliably reduces avoidance behavior
of animals in a conflict situation. Since similar effects of alcohol on conflict
behavior of humans also have been demonstrated (Vogel-Sprott, 1967c), experimental evidence is in accord with the popular notion that "anxiety is soluble in
alcohol." The drinking of alcohol is reinforced by anxiety reduction.

Development of Excessive Drinking

Environmental Stress

Studies examining the contribution of environmental stress to the development of alcohol consumption have typically introduced the organism into a
threatening, dangerous, or painful situation where both alcohol and water are
available to the subject. If stress prompts alcohol drinking, then alcohol consumption should increase during stress periods. Such evidence has been obtained
with monkeys who were found to increase alcohol intake during shock-avoidance
conditioning (Clark and Polish, 1960; Mello and Mendelson, 1966). Casey
(1960) also reported that rats consumed increased amounts of alcohol during
the presentation of unsignaled shocks. Such studies are in accord with the view
that environmental stress facilitates the development of alcohol drinking.

Support for this notion also is suggested by some cross-cultural studies.
Horton (1943), surveying 56 primitive societies, reported strong correlations
between the amount of alcohol consumed and the degree of subsistence hazard
in the societies. The difficulties experienced in maintaining adequate living
conditions would presumably evoke more anxiety, and more hazard was related
to higher alcohol intake. Other supporting observations may be found in
statistical surveys of military personnel which suggest that alcohol consumption
increases after exposure to combat stress (Henderson and Moore, 1944).

All in all, observations from a number of quarters appear to implicate environmental stress in the development of alcohol drinking behavior. Variations among individuals in the amount consumed may in part depend on the amount of environmental stress to which they are exposed, and the availability of alcohol in the culture (Horton, 1943). In many instances however, vast differences in alcohol consumption still are observed when these factors appear to be held fairly constant. Learning principles which may account for individual differences in drinking under relatively constant environmental conditions will be considered in the next section.

Individual Differences

While environmental stress may set the stage for alcohol drinking, some additional characteristics of the individual also must influence the ease of acquiring this response. Mello and Mendelson (1966) for example, report that environmental stress will increase alcohol consumption only in animals which freely select some alcohol in a nonstress condition. Some preliminary investigations* indicate that younger monkeys may consume alcohol more willingly than older animals. These observations might be considered to implicate taste sensitivity or developmental factors as important determinants of differences in drinking. These observations also admit a number of other interpretations. One explanation, pertinent to the purposes of this chapter, is that such variations in the strength of the drinking response are greatly determined by individual differences in the conditionability of emotions.

The ease with which anxiety-reducing responses are acquired is known to vary among humans. These differences have been linked to differences in chronic anxiety drive level as measured by questionnaires (e.g., Taylor, 1953). These differences might reflect the characteristic responsiveness of an individual's autonomic system (Sternbach, 1966) and/or the conditionability of his autonomic responses [e.g., galvanic skin response (GSR), heart rate]. Even if genetic or constitutional factors determine an individual's autonomic responsiveness or conditionability, learning factors may interact with this predisposition to determine autonomic activity. For example, Vogel (1960, 1961a) found that normal and alcoholic males obtaining more "introversive" scores on the Maudsley Personality Inventory (Eysenck, 1957) more quickly acquired a conditioned GSR and more slowly extinguished this response than did subjects with "extraversive" scores. This evidence might be taken to imply that under a given environmental condition, the more introversive persons develop more enduring conditioned emotional responses to more danger signals. This conditioning may be reflected by a higher general level of tension, or by more frequently evoked emotional responses. In either case, such learning could provide more motivation

---

*Personal communication, T. Caddell, University of Waterloo, July 4, 1969.

to acquire a tension-reducing response and this response should yield greater reward. One implication of this view is that introversive alcoholism should more likely display a regular, stable, or steady drinking pattern. Some supporting evidence on alcoholics has already been reported (Vogel, 1961b) but perhaps a better controlled test of this notion could be made by comparing the free choice of alcohol in two groups of animals judged to be high or low in emotionality. Where stress and other environmental conditions are held constant, the highly emotional organisms should willingly consume more alcohol.

In summary, a learning view of alcoholism emphasizes anxiety reduction as the common reward which operates to facilitate alcohol drinking. Individual differences in the strength of this response are linked to the amount of danger or threat an individual perceives. This perception is considered to depend on the amount of exposure to environmental stress, and the emotional liability and conditionability of the individual. The more anxiety or tension developed by these factors, the higher motivation and reward obtained for the tension-reducing response of drinking. These conditions would be expected to encourage the response and to increase its strength at least until some counteracting factor is introduced.

Maintenance of Excessive Drinking

When alcohol drinking is judged by society to exceed acceptable bounds, it usually encounters rather drastic punishment (e.g., loss of job, funds, family ties). The persistence of excessive drinking under these conditions thus may appear to be irrational and somewhat compulsive.

The maintenance of excessive drinking might readily be understood if prolonged ingestion of large amounts of alcohol developed physiological dependence such that withdrawal of the drug endangered life. While some interesting observations on vision suggest that hangover may be a withdrawal symptom (Aschan *et al.*, 1956; Goldberg, 1961), animal studies attempting to develop physiological withdrawal symptoms with alcohol have not been successful (e.g., Mello and Mendelson, 1966) and the question remains controversial (Essig and Lam, 1968). It seems fair to say that the physiological addictive properties are unlikely to provide the complete explanation for the persistence of alcoholic drinking. An application of learning principles here directs the search for an explanation to reinforcement schedules and delays which are known to determine response persistence under punishment.

Reinforcement Schedules and Delays

Although tension reduction has been emphasized as a prime factor facilitating development of alcohol drinking, it has been argued (Vogel-Sprott, 1967b) that when this response becomes excessive, it also accumulates some other rewards and punishments. The aversive consequences (e.g., hangover, social disapproval, economic ruin) have perhaps attracted more attention than the rewards, or "secondary gains" which follow excessive drinking and are derived from such sources as the additional care and attention from others, or increased peer-group status. These sorts of social and environmental rewards and punishments differ on a number of counts from the tension-reducing effect of the drug. They occur irregularly rather than consistently for drinking, and when they do occur, they are more delayed in time from the excessive drinking. Social and environmental rewards and punishments also are more easily withheld and manipulated than are the tension-reducing rewards of the drug. This latter distinction becomes particularly important when treatment strategies are considered in a later section.

Whenever excessive drinking occurs, the tension-reducing drug effect will fairly automatically follow. In addition to the tension-reducing reinforcement for alcohol drinking, the intermittent rewards which later accrue also may operate to strengthen excessive drinking. The intermittency of these rewards is particularly important for it may operate to make the behavior even more resistant to the weakening effect of punishment and extinction. This notion is suggested by research indicating that intermittent reward develops a response persistence to extinction and to punishment which is superior to that obtained from consistent reward (Brown and Wagner, 1964; Vogel-Sprott, 1967a).

The important influence of unpredictable rewards on drinking behavior itself requires more attention. In the ordinary life experience of humans, the environment does not reward "good" responses each time they occur. Rewards come intermittently and somewhat unreliably. Lester (1961) allowed rats free access to alcohol and water while they were being trained to bar-press for food which came unreliably. As training proceeded, the animals drank larger amounts of alcohol more often, until their drinking actually interfered with obtaining food. Many aspects of the situation necessary for developing "compulsive" self-maintained intoxication in the rat appear similar to those existing in human society where alcohol is available in the environment while individuals are striving for rewards which are not predictably obtained.

As well as intermittent reward which may increase the resistance of excessive drinking to punishment, the schedule and delay of punishment itself must be considered. Evidence on passive avoidance learning indicates that intermittent punishment of the response achieves slower suppression than consistent punishment (Vogel-Sprott, 1966). In addition, the longer punishment is delayed from an immediately rewarded response, the less suppression it obtains (Banks and Vogel-Sprott, 1965). It is important to note that these studies examine the inhibiting effect of punishment on a response trained for reward (e.g., money). As a result, the suppressing advantage of introducing immediate, consistent punishment may not necessarily be observed if such treatment is applied to a response, like excessive drinking, which is presumably reinforced by anxiety reduction. Indeed, the learning principles previously described indicate that punishment of a tension-reducing response may have a "paradoxical" facilitating effect on this behavior. The interesting possibility that excessive drinking actually may be increased by punishment pertains to the notion of vicious circle behavior and requires special discussion.

Vicious Circle Behavior

Analysis of the punishment conditions for excessive drinking indicates that whenever punishment occurs, it is considerably delayed from this response. Before punishment is actually received, it is usually preceded by a number of warning cues (e.g., verbal rebuke, threat). These cues, repeatedly associated with punishment, come to evoke some of the anxiety-provoking properties of punishment. Since punishment administration is so delayed from drinking, many of these danger signals which precede punishment actually will follow drinking. They come too late to usefully inhibit the behavior, and the apprehension or anxiety they generate might be termed "guilt" or "remorse." Since excessive drinking is the alcoholic's one dominant tension-reducing response, the increased anxiety evoked by guilt, threats, and punishment would increase the need for tension reduction and may thus prompt more excessive drinking. The individual thus "loses control" of his drinking, and becomes locked into a vicious circle where more guilt and punishment increase his anxiety which can only be reduced by excessive drinking which only yields more guilt and punishment.

Control of Excessive Drinking

The learning analysis of excessive drinking clearly implies that withholding all rewards and punishments for excessive drinking would most likely best reduce this behavior. Unfortunately, the difficulties in achieving total control and removal of all environmental and physiological reinforcers make such a treatment strategy impractical, if not impossible. Many therapies, however, have attempted to control environmental and social reinforcers for excessive drinking. The adequacy of some of these learning-based treatments can be examined in relation to our foregoing analysis of excessive drinking.

Conditioned Aversion

This treatment consists of pairing a painful stimulus with the taking of alcohol. It is one of the oldest treatments (Rush, 1814). The most common method of producing conditioned aversion to alcohol has been the administration of a nausea-inducing drug which takes effect as the patient is tasting alcohol (Skipetrov, 1953; Voegtlin and Lemere, 1940, 1950). The crucial aspect for the development of conditioned aversion here is assumed to be the temporal co-incidence of nausea and the first taste of alcohol. Unfortunately, the variable and fluctuating individual differences in response to emetic drugs virtually prohibit the precise temporal control required for successful application of the conditioning paradigm. As a consequence of this difficulty, current aversion therapies favor the use of aversive stimuli (e.g., electric shock) which can be reliably controlled (Rachman and Teasdale, 1969).

The one promising feature of conditioned aversion would seem to be the introduction of consistent, immediate punishment for drinking which should presumably generate more inhibition than the administration of delayed and inconsistent punishment. The learning analysis, however, has already suggested that additional punishment of a tension-reducing response may increase this habit. Thus it appears that the possible advantage of immediate punishment might better be assured if it were coupled with training designed to hold anxiety within manageable bounds. Blake's (1965) technique is interesting in this regard. His conditioned aversion therapy is conducted in conjunction with relaxation therapy which helps the patient to reduce his anxiety to a tolerable level. Blake's work is particularly noteworthy, for his aversion treatment is designed so that a painful stimulus (electric shock) is not merely associated with the alcohol, but escape from this punishment is only obtained by spitting out the drug. Thus his technique develops both an aversion to alcohol, and an active rejection of the drug.

Blake's procedure would appear to hold more promise than most aversion therapies because he manipulates more learning variables accompanying the drinking of alcohol. Under his treatment the suppressing advantage of immediate punishment for drinking is coupled with training in relaxation to reduce anxiety and with the development of a new response of rejecting alcohol. All three components should operate in concert to weaken the tendency to drink excessively.

Learning principles of stimulus and response generalization suggest that the newly created conditioned aversion of alcohol would be strongest in the laboratory training situation. Aversion could be expected to diminish when the environment changes from the treatment to the social conditions prevailing when the patient typically drinks excessively. Since social influence from peers appears to be an important factor in relapse (Segal, 1967), the efficacy of conditioned aversion treatment may be curtailed by the neglect of social stimuli which play an integral part in the excessive drinking situation. In view of these considerations, it seems advantageous to consider an alternative or supplementary treatment which trains the patient in acceptable behavior under social and environmental conditions more similar to those existing when excessive drinking occurred. One treatment which institutes some considerable control of the patient's social environment and reinforcement for his day-to-day behavior is the behavior modification technique. This treatment is rooted in learning principles and appears to offer a means of training in a social situation new responses to compete with excessive drinking.

Behavior Modification

The particular aspect of this treatment which is pertinent to our discussion is the "token economy" (Ayllon and Azrin, 1968), where patients live in a residence or ward community. They have few comforts or privileges freely supplied, but may "earn" these by engaging in acceptable, constructive activity. This behavior is "paid" for by reward tokens which are accumulated and exchanged for the comforts or privileges which the patient desires. This therapy thus exerts considerable long-term continuous control over social and environmental rewards for normal daily activities. It provides an opportunity to shape up and firmly establish new responses to social situations similar to those which previously prompted excessive drinking.

Such a technique controls the sorts of social and environmental rewards which many writers have identified as important determinants of excessive drinking. For example, Barry (1968) has provided interesting cross-cultural observations to support his argument that stress in the culture only provides motivation to drink alcohol; the occurrence of excessive drinking actually depends on the cultural and social forces which dispense approval and permission for this behavior. Some follow up studies of alcoholic patients also suggest the importance of social factors in maintaining excessive drinking. Segal (1967) investigated neurotic and social characteristics of 544 alcoholic patients. He found little correlation between neuroticism and the patients' ability to restrain excessive drinking after therapy but a strong relation between the social stimulus of friends and successful treatment. He reported that the patients' companions generally considered the consumption of large amounts of alcohol as a prestigious indication of manliness. Sixty-eight percent of the patients who benefited from treatment had broken these friendship ties while only 10% of the patients who relapsed had dropped their old friends.

Since the interest in using token economies with alcoholics is relatively recent, the ability of this treatment to achieve a long-term reduction of excessive drinking cannot yet be fairly evaluated. The dramatic development of constructive behavior by alcoholics during therapy, however, is extremely encouraging. Naroll's (1967) observations here serve to illustrate this point. Patients' training began in a closed ward without comforts or freedom. If they desired, they could work on the hospital labor force for reward tokens which were used to make compulsory purchases of room and board, and ground privileges, plus a number of voluntary purchases (canteen supplies, AA or group therapy, leaves, etc.). Fourteen of the 17 patients voluntarily remained under this regime for more than 2 months and their constructive work output increased to average 8 hr per day as compared to the 4-hr daily average obtained under control ward conditions. Clearly these simulated economies can control the behavior of alcoholics, developing new adaptive behavior patterns which dominate their waking hours to a degree equivalent with normally productive individuals in society. The number of dropouts from this treatment also seems less, or at least no greater than that occurring under other kinds of therapy.

As constructive behavior patterns increase, these token economies provide the individual with more freedom in determining his leisure time activities and opportunities to develop new socially approved recreations. Observation of a particular patient's difficulty in acquiring these adaptive responses also may serve a diagnostic function in treatment. These findings may identify some specific types of social and interpersonal situations for which the alcoholic has no skills other than excessive drinking. The patient then may be gradually exposed to these types of situations under the controlled conditions of the token economy. New social skills (e.g., assertiveness) or responses actually incompatible with drinking (e.g., sports) thus may be developed under the relatively "safe" conditions where failures are not punished and successes are rewarded. In the token economy environment, the patient's therapy thus consists in training him to gradually assume self-control and responsibility for his actions. When treatment terminates, the environmental conditions prevailing thus bear a strong similarity to those existing in society, and considerable transfer or generalization of behavior acquired under token economies might be expected.

EVALUATION

This chapter illustrates the degree to which learning principles may account for the development, maintenance, and control of excessive drinking. It is time now to take stock of this approach and assess its merits and weaknesses.

Conceptualizing Alcoholism as a Learned Behavior

The learning explanation provides a relatively consistent set of assumptions about alcoholism which permit the deduction of a number of specific testable hypotheses. This scientific precision, however, is obtained by a rather artificial simplification of the problem. The possible contribution of genetic, pharmacological, or sociological factors is not fully considered and the explanation has been narrowly focused on the response of excessive drinking. On this basis alone, learning principles appear unlikely to provide a complete explanation for the etiology of alcoholism.

Another logical consideration of an explanation of alcoholism as learned behavior requires special discussion. At the present time there is a phenomenal interest and enthusiasm for learning-based treatment of many maladaptive responses, alcoholism included. Many of these therapies appear to have considerable success. Perhaps because of this, advocates of this therapy sometimes appear to assume that the learning variables effective in changing and controlling the maladaptive response are necessarily the factors which determine the development of this behavior. Davison (1967) has already commented on the prevalence of this questionable assumption among behavior therapists. Even the demonstration that principles of instrumental learning may effectively develop a psychoticlike maladaptive response does not necessarily imply that no other factor or factors could cause such behavior. Thus the observation (Ayllon *et al.*, 1965) that instrumental conditioning can develop an apparently compulsive broom-holding response in a psychiatric patient is merely suggestive evidence for the possible role of learning principles in the etiology of maladaptive behavior patterns. Such a finding, however, is not sufficient to support the claim, "The etiology of many so-called psychotic symptoms exhibited by hospitalized patients or those in need of hospitalization does not have to be sought in the obscure dynamics of a psychiatric disturbance" (Ayllon *et al.*, 1965, p. 51). Identifying the causative factors in the development of a maladaptive response such as excessive drinking is obviously exceedingly difficult and the development of some experimental analogues of such behavior on the basis of learning principles does not automatically make other contributing factors irrelevant or fictional.

The answers to the question of etiology also are not necessarily provided by answers to the question of treatment. Knowledge about how to change behavior is not necessarily tantamount to knowing how the response originated. Considerable evidence on the efficacy of learning principles in changing an unwanted response is accumulating and no doubt further research in this area will indicate the particular variables responsible for this change. However, even if all of the influential treatment factors are found to depend on learning principles, this does not necessarily imply that these learning factors are exclusively responsible for the development of the maladaptive response. Such an assumption would be equivalent to concluding that because penicillin eliminated a fever, the fever was caused by the lack of penicillin. The logical problems involved in inferring etiological causes on the basis of an analogous behavioral model or of treatment efficacy is not peculiar to the learning approach. This difficulty also exists to some extent in other theoretical explanations of alcoholism.

The advantage of adopting some viewpoint about alcoholism comes from the broad logical framework which it provides and which serves much like a road map. The merit of the learning view is the explicit testable predictions it makes about routes and terrain in certain areas, particularly those concerned with treatment and control of excessive drinking. Experiments which attempt to follow the map in this area will allow fairly clear identification of errors and corrections of misconceptions.

Stimulation of Research

Although an understanding of the etiology of alcoholism is urgently required, a more immediate pressing practical question concerns the control of excessive drinking once it has developed. Learning theory makes a valuable contribution here by providing some explicit testable suggestions. An illustration of its role in guiding hypotheses and research can be provided by considering the question, "Can alcoholics learn moderate social drinking?" Davies (1962) presented one report of controlled social drinking among recovered alcoholics and challenged the accepted view that no alcohol addict can ever drink normally again. This is an extremely contentious issue which has evoked a storm of controversy (cf. Block, 1963; Esser, 1963; Lolli, 1963; Pattison, 1966; Selzer, 1963; Tiebout, 1963; Williams, 1963).

Learning principles are based on the assumption that behavior is malleable, and can be controlled. Consistent with this assumption is the hypothesis that the response of excessive drinking may be altered by learning variables. Certain conditions may increase drinking; others may diminish it. It should be possible to train moderate drinking in naive individuals, or to retrain excessive drinkers to display moderate drinking. This retraining may be accomplished by allowing alcoholics to practice moderate drinking under specific reinforcement conditions, different from those maintaining excessive alcohol consumption.

The token economy of behavior therapy would seem to be an appropriate setting for such retraining (Narroll, 1967). Here the relatively tight control of social and environmental rewards and punishments would permit patients to practice self-control of their alcohol intake. For example, patients who have completed a full day's work may be privileged by receiving wine with meals. Such drinking may initially be rigidly controlled so that a sip is contingent upon eating certain portions of the meal. In this case, eating a full meal (something seldom done by alcoholics) is rewarded by a drink of alcohol. Such training allows the alcoholic to practice drinking moderate amounts of alcohol in a socially acceptable fashion. The token economy situation has the advantage of being able to control social and environmental stress. Moderate drinking can be immediately rewarded. Excessive drinking can be immediately punished and any rewards which might accrue from this taboo behavior can be withheld. Under these conditions moderate drinking would yield more rewards than excessive drinking, and the tendency for moderate drinking should strengthen.

The practice of controlled exposure to the dangerous drinking situation might even carry some valuable anxiety-reducing side effects by demonstrating to the alcoholic that he can regain control of his drinking behavior. He is not helpless. The importance of an individual's belief that he is personally responsible for changes in his behavior has already been suggested by some research (Davison, 1966; Davison and Valins, 1968; Nesbett and Schachter,

1966; Valins and Ray, 1967). In the research of Davison and Valins, a pain-killing drug was administered to all subjects who were allowed to adjust electric shock to the maximum tolerable level. Half of these subjects were then misled into believing that the drug which they had received was only a placebo. When the subjects were subsequently retested drug-free, those falsely believing that their first test was conducted under placebo selected a similar high level of shock, whereas those who rightly attributed their previous level of pain tolerance to the influence of the drug chose much lower levels.

Another interesting and important aspect of training moderate drinking is that it allows the individual to experience and possibly come to recognize the more subtle but distinctive social and physiological stimuli which indicate that his drinking behavior has reached the limit of social acceptability. These cues provide the person with immediate warning signals predicting the disastrous consequences of additional alcohol consumption. Some recent learning theory and research (Renner, 1967; Vogel-Sprott, 1969; Vogel-Sprott and Burrows, 1969) suggest that such feedback may greatly assist an individual in choosing the appropriate response. The importance of such cues is implied in Chafetz's (1965) popular argument that people drink excessively because they have not had adequate opportunity to learn moderate drinking. Another observation in line with this notion is the low incidence of alcoholism in the Jewish culture where its young members learn moderate drinking in distinctive situations according to specific social rules and regulations (Snyder, 1962).

It is important to stress that considerable learning research is required before the training of moderate drinking could be advocated as a therapy. The procedures suggested by our analysis call attention to the need for testing the hypothesis that organisms trained to develop self-maintained intoxication can subsequently learn to control alcohol intake at a moderate level. Our analysis also suggests specific reinforcement conditions which may determine the learning of moderate drinking. One now can only speculate about the outcomes of such research, but the findings certainly could contribute invaluable assistance in the practical control of excessive drinking and in further understanding the factors influencing this behavior. Some speculations may be provided to illustrate this point.

Suppose research indicates that retraining moderate drinking can be accomplished after the excessive drinking response has been acquired, but this moderate drinking is developed more efficiently under reinforcement conditions somewhat different from those our analysis suggests. Such information could have fairly direct practical application to the control of excessive drinking, and could also assist in improving and correcting our present understanding of factors controlling excessive drinking.

The practical interest in retraining alcoholics to drink moderately appears to be based on the implicit assumption that this may train the individual to somehow monitor his alcohol intake and resist the development of uncontrollable excessive drinking. Such an assumption suggests some interesting hypotheses. For example, suppose two groups of animals are exposed equally to alcohol, but one group is systematically trained to drink moderately, thus avoiding intoxication. If these two groups subsequently are introduced to a new stress situation where excessive drinking may occur, the moderate drinking group may show more resistance to developing excessive drinking. Investigations of these types of hypotheses should be conducted, for their results may hold some interesting prophylactic implications.

Some hint that retraining alcoholics' drinking may be a promising therapy is suggested indirectly by drug studies which examine the transfer of a learned response from drug to no-drug states and vice-versa. Many depressant drugs, including alcohol, have been investigated (Overton, 1964, 1966). These studies indicate that a response trained when the organism is under drug may fail to occur when the animal is subsequently tested drug-free. This lack of transfer to the no-drug test state does not represent a drug effect *per se*, because the failure to transfer is also obtained when training and test states are reversed. These findings thus might be considered to imply that if new substitute responses for excessive drinking are acquired outside a drinking situation and solely while drug-free, they are less likely to transfer to situations where alcohol is being consumed. Such training does not seem to provide the conditions which would best maximize the transfer of new acceptable responses to the one place they are most vitally required—a drinking situation. In contrast, practicing moderate drinking and other socially acceptable behavior in a drinking situation involves both the drug state and the social and environmental stimuli which are very similar to those which patients encounter after treatment. The training of moderate drinking would therefore seem to maximize the potential transfer of this socially acceptable behavior to drinking situations.

SUMMARY

This chapter reviewed some learning mechanisms which were applied to explain alcoholism as it is reflected in excessive drinking.

Analysis of the development of alcohol drinking emphasized the importance of the anxiety-reducing properties of alcohol. Variations in the ease with which individuals acquire the drinking response were related to differences in emotional conditionability and to environmental conditions which provide stress and training to develop conditioned fear responses.

The learning explanation for the persistence of excessive drinking which consistently violates social standards was related to the timing and scheduling of rewards and punishments for this behavior. The response was considered to receive immediate consistent reward (tension reduction) plus a delayed net of other rewards and punishments occurring intermittently. Although the inability of punishment to inhibit this response was considered to stem partly from the fact that it was delayed rather than immediate, learning principles also suggested that punishment of a tension-reducing response may actually serve to increase this response.

Some practical treatments for alcoholism were evaluated on the degree to which they changed the learning conditions which presumably control excessive drinking. One promising procedure appeared to be administering conditioned aversion treatment where the possible suppressing effect of immediate punishment could be coupled with training in relaxation and with the development of a new response of rejecting alcohol. In order to maximize the transfer from treatment to life situations, a supplementary treatment of behavior modification in a token economy was judged to hold considerable promise.

The advantage of viewing alcoholism as learned behavior was considered to stem from the testable hypotheses and direction it provided in guiding research on this problem. This was illustrated by considering the implications learning principles hold in providing some answers to the clinical controversy over controlled social drinking among recovered alcoholics.

While the learning analysis of alcoholism was seen to be limited by its restricted focus on excessive drinking, it had the advantage of generating questions which could be tested so misconceptions could be corrected and promising leads could be identified. Since the explanation of alcoholism is far from complete at present, any discipline providing such knowledge and guidance can make a valuable contribution to the search for understanding.

REFERENCES

Amsel, A., 1962. Frustrative nonreward in partial reinforcement and discrimination learning: some recent history and a theoretical extension, *Psych. Rev.* **69**: 306–328.

Aschan, G., Bergstedt, M., Goldberg, L., and Laurel, L., 1956. Positional nystagmus in man during and after alcohol intoxication, *Quart. J. Stud. Alc.* **17**: 381–405.

Ayllon, T. and Azrin, N., 1968. *The Token Economy. A Motivational System for Therapy and Rehabilitation.* Appleton–Century–Crofts, New York.

Ayllon, T., Haughton, E., and Hughes, H. B., 1965. Interpretation of symptoms: fact or fiction, *Behav. Res. Therap.* **3**: 1–8.

Banks, R. K. and Vogel-Sprott, M., 1965. The effect of delayed punishment on an immediately rewarded response in humans, *J. Exper. Psych.* **70**: 357–359.

Barry, H., 1968. Sociocultural aspects of alcohol addiction, in *The Addictive States. Research in Nervous and Mental Disease*, Vol. 46, pp. 455–471, Williams and Wilkins, Baltimore.

Blake, B. G., 1965. Application of behaviour therapy to the treatment of alcoholism, *Behav. Res. Therap.* **3**: 75–86.

Block, M., 1963. Comment on the article by D. L. Davies, *Quart. J. Stud. Alc.* **24**: 114–117.

Boe, E. and Church, R. M., 1967. Permanent effects of punishment during extinction, *J. Comp. Physiol. Psych.* **63**: 486–492.

Brown, R. T. and Wagner, A. R., 1964. Resistance to punishment and extinction following training with shock or nonreinforcement, *J. Exper. Psych.* **68**: 503–507.

Casey, A., 1960. The effect of stress on the consumption of alcohol and reserpine, *Quart. J. Stud. Alc.* **21**: 208–216.

Chafetz, M., 1965. *Liquor, the Servant of Man*. Little, Brown and Co., Boston.

Church, R. M., 1963. The varied effects of punishment on behavior, *Psych. Rev.* **70**: 369–402.

Clark, R. and Polish, E., 1960. Avoidance conditioning and alcohol consumption in rhesus monkeys, *Science* **132**: 223–224.

Conger, J. J., 1951. The effects of alcohol on conflict behavior in the albino rat, *Quart. J. Stud. Alc.* **12**: 1–29.

Conger, J. J., 1956. Reinforcement theory and the dynamics of alcoholism, *Quart. J. Stud. Alc.* **17**: 296–305.

Davies, D. L., 1962. Normal drinking in recovered addicts, *Quart. J. Stud. Alc.* **23**: 94–104.

Davison, G., 1966. Anxiety under total curarization: implications for the role of muscular relaxation in the desensitization of neurotic fears, *J. Nerv. Ment. Dis.* **143**: 443–448.

Davison, G. C., 1967. Some problems of logic and conceptualization in behavior therapy research and theory. Mimeographed paper presented at the Association for Advancement of Behavioral Therapies Meeting, Washington.

Davison, G. and Valins, S., 1968. Drugs, cognition and behavior therapy. Mimeographed paper presented at American Psychological Convention, San Francisco.

Esser, P. H., 1963. Comment on the article by D. L. Davies, *Quart. J. Stud. Alc.* **24**: 119–121.

Essig, C. and Lam, R., 1968. Convulsions and hallucinatory behavior following alcohol withdrawal in the dog, *Arch. Neurol.* **18**: 626–632.

Estes, W. K., 1944. An experimental study of punishment, *Psych. Monographs* **57**: No. 3 (Whole No. 263).

Eysenck, H. J., 1957. *Dynamics of Anxiety and Hysteria*. Routledge and Kegan Paul, London.

Festinger, L., 1961. The psychological effect of insufficient rewards, *Amer. Psych.* **16**: 1–11.

Freed, E., 1967. The effect of alcohol upon approach-avoidance conflict in the white rat, *Quart. J. Stud. Alc.* **28**: 236–254.

Freud, S., 1920. *A General Introduction to Psychoanalysis*. Boni and Liveright, New York.

Goldberg, L., 1961. Alcohol, tranquillizers and hangover, *Quart. J. Stud. Alc.*, Supplement No. 1: 37–56.

Goodman, L. and Gilman, A., 1965. *The Pharmacological Basis of Therapeutics*. 3rd ed., pp. 143–153, Macmillan Co., New York.

Gwinn, G. T., 1949. The effects of punishment on acts motivated by fear, *J. Exper. Psych.* **39**: 260–269.

Henderson, J. L. and Moore, M., 1944. The psychoneuroses of war, *New Eng. J. Med.* **230**: 273–278.

Horney, K., 1937. *The Neurotic Personality of our Time*. Norton, New York.

Horton, D., 1943. The functions of alcohol in primitive societies: a cross-cultural study, *Quart. J. Stud. Alc.* **4**: 199–320.

Hull, C. L., 1943. *The Principles of Behavior*. Appleton–Century–Crofts, New York.

Humphreys, L. G., 1939. The effect of random alternation of reinforcement on the acquisition and extinction of conditioned eyelid reactions. *J. Exper. Psych.* **25**: 141–158.

Hurwitz, H. M., 1956. Vicious circle behaviour under two shock intensities, Mimeographed paper, Birkbeck College, London.

Karsh, E., 1962. Effects of number of rewarded trials and intensity of punishment on running speed, *J. Comp. Physiol. Psych.* **55**: 44–51.

Kepner, E., 1964. Application of learning theory to the etiology and treatment of alcoholism, *Quart. J. Stud. Alc.* **25**: 279–291.

Kimble, G. A., 1961. *Hilgard and Marquis' Conditioning and Learning.* Appleton–Century–Crofts, New York.

Kingham, R., 1956. Alcoholism and the reinforcement theory of learning, *Quart. J. Stud. Alc.* **19**: 320–330.

Lester, D., 1961. Self-maintenance of intoxication in the rat, *Quart. J. Stud. Alc.* **22**: 223–231.

Lolli, G., 1963. Comment on the article by D. L. Davies, *Quart. J. Stud. Alc.* **24**: 326–330.

Masserman, J. H. and Yum, K. S., 1946. An analysis of the influence of alcohol on experimental neurosis in cats, *Psychosom. Med.* **8**: 36–52.

Mello, N. and Mendelson, J., 1966. Factors affecting alcohol consumption in primates, *Psychosom. Med.* **28**: 529–549.

Mowrer, O. H., 1947. On the dual nature of learning: a reinterpretation of "conditioning" and "problem solving", *Harvard Educ. Rev.* **17**: 102–148.

Mowrer, O. H., 1960. *Learning Theory and Behavior.* Wiley and Sons, Inc., New York.

Mowrer, O. H. and Jones H. M., 1945. Habit strength as a function of pattern of reinforcement, *J. Exper. Psych.* **35**: 293–311.

Naroll, H. G., 1967. Experimental application of reinforcement principles to the analysis and treatment of hospitalized alcoholics, *Quart. J. Stud. Alc.* **28**: 105–115.

Nesbett, R. and Schachter, S., 1966. Cognitive manipulation of pain, *J. Exper. Social Psych.* **2**: 227–236.

Overton, D. A., 1964. State-dependent or "dissociated" learning produced with pentobarbital, *J. Comp. Physiol. Psych.* **57**: 3–12.

Overton, D. A., 1966. State-dependent learning produced by depressant and atropine-like drugs, *Psychopharmacologia* **10**: 6–31.

Pattison, E. M., 1966. A critique of alcoholism treatment concepts with special reference to abstinence, *Quart. J. Stud. Alc.* **27**: 49–71.

Rachman, S. and Teasdale, J. D., 1969. Aversion therapy, in *Behavior Therapies: Assessment and Appraisal* (C. M. Franks, ed.), McGraw-Hill, New York.

Renner, K. E., 1967. An incentive approach to conflict resolution, in *Progress in Experimental Personality Research* (B. Maher, ed.) Vol. 4, pp. 127–178, Academic Press, New York.

Rush, G., 1814. *An Inquiry into the Effects of Ardent Spirits upon the Body and Mind, with an Account of the Means of Preventing and of the Remedies for Curing Them.* 8th edition, Meriam, Brookfield.

Segal, B. M., 1967. The role of neuroses in the genesis of alcoholism: analysis of psychodynamic conceptions, *Zh. Nervopat.* **67**: 246–253 (Abstract in *Quart. J. Stud. Alc.* **28**: 572–573).

Selzer, M., 1963. Comment on the article by D. L. Davies, *Quart. J. Stud. Alc.* **24**: 113–114.

Shoben. E. J., 1956. Views on the etiology of alcoholism, in *Alcoholism as a Medical Problem* (H. D. Kruse, ed.) pp. 47–55, Hoeber-Harper, New York.

Skipetrov, A. L., 1953. Treatment of chronic alcoholism with apomorphine, *Zh. Nervopat.* **53:** 395–396 (Abstract No. 7718, *Archives of Alcohol Literature*).

Snyder, C. R., 1962. Culture and Jewish sobriety: the ingroup–outgroup factor, in *Society, Culture and Drinking Patterns* (D. Piltman and C. Snyder, eds.) pp. 188–225, John Wiley and Sons Inc., New York.

Solomon, R. L. and Wynne, L. C., 1953. Traumatic avoidance learning: acquisition in normal dogs, *Psych. Monographs* **67:** 1–19.

Solomon, R. L., Kamin, L. J., and Wynne, L. C., 1953. Traumatic avoidance learning: the outcomes of several extinction procedures with dogs, *J. Abnormal Soc. Psych.* **48:** 291–302.

Sternbach, R. A., 1966, *Principles of Psychophysiology*. Academic Press, New York, pp. 95–110.

Taylor, J. A., 1953. A personality scale of manifest anxiety, *J. Abnormal Soc. Psych.* **48:** 285–290.

Theios, J., 1962. The partial reinforcement effect sustained through blocks of continuous reinforcement, *J. Exper. Psych.* **64:** 1–8.

Tiebout, H., 1963. Comment on the article by D. L. Davies, *Quart. J. Stud. Alc.* **24:** 109–111.

Valins, S. and Ray, A., 1967. Effects of cognitive desensitization on avoidance behavior, *J. Personal. Soc. Psych.* **7:** 345–350.

Voegtlin, W. L. and Lemere, F., 1940. The treatment of alcoholism by establishing a conditioned reflex, *Amer. J. Med. Sci.* **199:** 802–809.

Voegtlin, W. L. and Lemere, F., 1950. Evaluation of the aversion treatment of alcoholism, *Quart. J. Stud. Alc.* **11:** 199–204.

Vogel. M., 1960. The relation of personality factors to GSR conditioning of alcoholics: an exploratory study, *Canad. J. Psych.* **14:** 275–280.

Vogel, M., 1961a. GSR conditioning and personality factors in alcoholics and normals, *J. Abnormal Soc. Psych.* **63:** 417–421.

Vogel, M., 1961b. The relationship of personality factors to drinking patterns of alcoholics, *Quart. J. Stud. Alc.* **22:** 394–400.

Vogel-Sprott, M., 1966. Suppression of a rewarded response by punishment as a function of reinforcement schedules, *Psychonomic Sci.* **5:** 395–396.

Vogel-Sprott, M., 1967a. Partial reward training for resistance to punishment and to subsequent extinction, *J. Exper. Psych.* **75:** 138–140.

Vogel-Sprott, M., 1967b. Alcoholism as learned behavior: some hypotheses and research, in *Alcoholism—Behavioral Research, Therapeutic Approaches* (R. Fox, ed.) pp. 46–54, Springer, New York.

Vogel-Sprott, M., 1967c. Alcohol effects on human behavior under reward and punishment, *Psychopharmacologia* **11:** 337–344.

Vogel-Sprott, M., 1969. Aftereffects of punishment on human behavior, *Brit. J. Psych.* **60:** 85–90.

Vogel-Sprott, M. and Burrows, V., 1969. Response suppression in humans as a function of contingent and noncontingent punishment: signal properties of stimuli, *Canad. J. Psych.* **23:** 66–74.

Vogel-Sprott, M. and Racinskas, J., 1969. Suppression and recovery of a response in humans as a function of reward and punishment, *Behav. Res. Therap.* **7:** 223–231.

Williams, L., 1963. Comment on the article by D. L. Davies, *Quart. J. Stud. Alc.* **24:** 111–113.

World Health Organization, 1952, Technical report, series 48, Geneva.

CHAPTER 15

Some Effects of Ethanol on Human Sexual and Aggressive Behavior

John A. Carpenter and Nicholas P. Armenti

The Center of Alcohol Studies and Department of Psychology
Rutgers University, The State University of New Jersey
New Brunswick, New Jersey

INTRODUCTION

The effects of alcohol on behavior are discussed in many reviews, but most do not discuss either sexual or aggressive behavior in any detail, if at all. On the other hand, more extensive sources, such as general textbooks, pharmacology textbooks, and books on abnormal psychology frequently devote space to the effects of alcohol on sexual behavior, usually adding that alcohol increases aggression. As this chapter will show, the amount of experimental evidence for opinions about the actions of ethyl alcohol on either sexual behavior or aggression is extremely small.

Indeed, the cumulative effect of the following studies is that they serve not only as a starting point for additional research, but more importantly, the small number of such studies indicates how little modern society knows of the relationships of three of its more significant aspects—alcohol, sexual behavior, and aggression.

SEXUAL BEHAVIOR AND ALCOHOL

Gantt (1952) summarized the scientific knowledge about sexual behavior and alcohol when he stated, "Shakespeare is still the chief authority for the effect of alcohol on sexual activity." He was referring to the conversation between MacDuff and the porter in Macbeth. According to that source, alcohol increases sexual desire, but reduces ability to perform.* An examination of pharmacology textbooks [see, for example, Krantz and Carr (1965); Gaddum (1959); Grollman (1965); Salter (1952); Goodman and Gilman (1966)] shows that a large proportion refers to Shakespeare, as does almost everyone else [see Murphree (1965); Hart (1968); Masters and Johnson—in Hall (1969)] who writes on the topic. Shakespeare's words have the quality of expressing both lay and scientific opinions, not too difficult to do in the absence of objective information. Very little has been done. Or, in Gantt's words, ". . . there is an amazing vacuity of objective data regarding the influence of this universal beverage and drug on sexual behavior" (1952, p. 124). Ritchie (1966, p. 148) concurs, ". . . much of little worth has been written."

Animal Experiments

The work of Gantt (1940, 1952), Teitelbaum and Gantt (1958), Rasmussen† (1943, 1954), Dewsbury (1967), and Hart (1968) constitutes the total experimental literature on alcohol and the direct observation of sexual behavior that we have been able to find. In Gantt's, Teitelbaum's, and one of Hart's experiments, dogs were used, and sexual stimulation was obtained by manipulations of the penis. Gantt measured latency of erection, duration of erection, and latency of ejaculation. Teitelbaum and Gantt observed latency and degree of bulbar enlargement. Details of stimulation and recording are not available from Gantt's or Teitelbaum and Gantt's papers, but it may be assumed that visual identification of the crucial events was used. Hart and Kitchell (1966) made anatomical studies of dogs, and developed apparatus for the study of the sexual reflexes. The criterion response was the rhythmic contractions of the bulbocavernosus muscle automatically recorded. Latency to the first contraction and duration of the rhythmic contractions during ejaculation were measured. Hart then used these procedures in the study of the effects of alcohol on sexual behavior.

Table 1 presents a summary of three of the experiments on dogs which made use of mechanical penile stimulation. The contents of the table have been adapted from the original papers. All measures of time have been rounded to the

*With equal perspicacity, Nash has said, "Candy is dandy but liquor is quicker."
†We were unable to obtain a translation of any of Rasmussen's numerous works, which were published in Norwegian. There is every evidence that they are important papers, but we were unwilling to accept secondary sources.

TABLE 1. Changes in Sexual Reflexes in Dogs as a Function of Dose of Alcohol

	Dose (ml/kg)	Failures of erection	Latency (sec) of erection		Duration (min) of erection		Failure of ejaculation	Onset (sec) of ejaculation	
			Mean	Range	Mean	Range		Mean	Range
Gantt (1952) Intact dogs	C	0/71	37	(25–57)	7	(3–12)	7/71	21	(9–50)
	0.5	0/16	41	(30–55)	5	(2–9)	3/16	20	(12–27)
	1.0	4/19	46	(43–49)	4	(4–5)	4/19	23	(15–32)
	2.0	16/29ᵃ	40	(29–51)	3	(0–3)ᵃ	17–29	11	(11–)
Teitelbaum and Gantt (1958) Intact dogs	C	1/15	20	(10–30)	4	(1–10)	2/15		
	1.0	1/5	26	(15–40)	5	(1–12)	1/5		
	1.5	3/5	23	(20–25)	4	(1–10)	1/5		
	2.0	5/5	23	(20–25)	2	(1–6)	3/5		
	2.5	5/5	25	(20–30)	1	(1–3)	3/5		
	3.0	4/4	30	—	1	—	2/4		
	C	0/5	18	(10–25)	4	(2–9)	0/5		

	Dose	Failures of erection	Latency of first penile contraction (sec)	Duration of ejaculation (sec)
Hart (1968) Spinal dogs	0.5	0/16	9	35
	2.0	4/16	16	28
	4.0	10/12	No time	No time

ᵃDuration of erection was reported as zero, but onset of erection reported also.

nearest second or minute. The fractions in columns 3 and 6 represent the numb of failures over the number of opportunities for erection or ejaculation. Hart's (1968) measures are not exactly the same as those used by Gantt (1952) or Teitelbaum and Gantt (1958). "Complete erection usually cannot be elicited in the dog without evoking ejaculation" (Hart, p. 841). Recording the contractions of the bulbocavernous muscles yielded measures of the onset and duration of ejaculation, and presumably overlapped with erection. Duration of ejaculation is not given by Gantt (1952) or Teitelbaum and Gantt (1958). Partial or slight erections are included as failures; hence, for the 1.5 ml/kg dose of Teitelbaum and Gantt (1958) there are more failures of erection than of ejaculation.

All three experiments show an increase in failure of erections as dose increases. For the one dose used by all three experiments (1.0 ml/kg), Hart's dogs show only a 25% failure as compared to 55–60% for the other two experiments. This may be a result of the homogeneity and youth of Hart's dogs and the fact that they were spinal preparations. In discussing bulbar enlargement (erection), Teitelbaum and Gantt (1958) comment, ". . . that there is no direct relationship between amount of alcohol administered and degree of inhibition of bulbar enlargement" (p. 396). Duration of erection shows a steady decline as dose increases. Table 1 hides the individual differences that are prominent in both Gantt's (1952) and Teitelbaum and Gantt's (1958) animals. The three dogs that had long duration of erection without alcohol maintained relatively longer durations through the 1.0 ml/kg dose, and two others did so with the 2.0 ml/kg dose. At 3.0 ml/kg, all animals of Teitelbaum and Gantt showed only token duration of erections, and Gantt's (1952) dogs showed the same phenomenon or worse at 2.0 ml/kg.

As already mentioned, there were differences between the subjects used in Gantt's and Hart's experiments. Gantt's dogs had been used in other experiments, tended to be older (3–12 years), and were quite varied as to temperament and kinds of mongrels. Hart's dogs were young (2–3 years), purebred beagles, and seem not to have been used in other experiments. The most important fact is that Hart's dogs were spinal preparations (transection at T_6–T_8); thus, the influence of higher neural structures on the sexual reflexes was eliminated. The dogs were castrates maintained on testosterone proprionate (5 mg/kg every 2 days), a procedure that offsets the effect of spinal transection on male hormone production. Hart's experiments represent a definite methodological advance over the earlier experiments. However, the variation of the ages and temperament of Gantt's dogs and his long association with them provides him material with which to speculate about the individual variations in response to alcohol.

In the course of his experiments, Gantt observed an interesting phenomenon. In two of his dogs, one described as a "stable old dog," the other as a "neurotic dog," on the day after experimental days (2 ml/kg of alcohol), when no alcohol was given, sexual reflexes (duration of erection) were elevated above control levels obtained at the beginning of the experiment. This was particularly true of the neurotic dog in which duration of erection was longer than any other animal. After 9 months without alcohol, control levels were again low, but when alcohol was administered (1 ml/kg), the duration of sexual reflexes increased on both control and alcohol days. Rebound effects were similarly reported by Teitelbaum and Gantt for the latency of bulbar enlargement in at least one dog. One animal described as "catatonic" had no erection on the control dose, but at about 2 ml/kg the dog had an erection for 38 min.

In another experiment, Hart (1968) tested animals without transected spinal cords at the same doses on mating behavior with receptive females. In order to make these dogs comparable to the spinal animals, they were also castrated and maintained on testosterone propionate. Mating behavior is quite different from spinal reflexes, since it contains elements of motivation indicated by interest in the female and mounting. In other words, mating is not passive. Interest in the female and mounting were not eliminated at any dose. At 4.0 ml/kg, no dog completed copulation, but four of six dogs copulated at the intermediate dose, and normal behavior was observed at the lowest dose. One point is worth mentioning here: Hart does not report whether his intact dogs had erections. Although this does not seem likely, failure to complete copulation could have been caused by the clumsiness of the intoxicated dogs. As Hart points out, comparison with the spinal animals is not the parallel it seems to be because the intact dogs had the incentive of receptive females, while in the spinal animals, erection depended solely on mechanical stimulation of the penis. Hart and Kitchell (1966) report that the reliability of response patterns of the penile muscles was greater in the spinal animals than in the intact animals. This was attributed to suprasegmental inhibition of the reflexes in normal dogs. By the same reasoning, suprasegmental stimulation caused by the presence of a receptive female might facilitate the initiation and maintenance of erections in the normal dogs. Nevertheless, sexual motivation remained, but potency or capacity, for whatever reason, was diminished.

Dewsbury's experiment (1967) used the classical techniques of Beach for studying copulation in rats. In this experiment, male rats were allowed to copulate with females brought into estrus by hormone injection. The number of mounts and intromissions up to the first intromission following ejaculation were observed. The test was continued for 20 min if an intromission did not occur. Various time relations between introduction of the female rat, mounting, intromission, and ejaculation were calculated. Each male was tested twice on alcohol and twice on water. The 10% alcohol solution, sweetened by saccharin, was drunk by the rats an hour before testing. The alcohol consumed was reported to be equal to 2.9–3.5 ml of absolute alcohol/kg. The blood alcohol for these doses would be about 0.29–0.35%, assuming that all of the alcohol consumed was absorbed.

TABLE 2.   Result Obtained by Dewsbury (1967)

	Median value	
	Water	Alcohol
Mount frequency[a]	2.0	4,5
Intromission frequency	10.3	8.0
Mount latency	8.5 sec	13.0 sec
Intromission latency	12.5 sec	18.5 sec
Ejaculation latency	324.0 sec	526.0 sec
Mean interintromission interval	36.6 sec	56.1 sec
Postejaculatory interval	314.5 sec	383.0 sec

[a] Definitions: mount frequency, the number of mounts without intromission between introduction of the female and ejaculation; intromission frequency, the number of intromissions between introduction of the female and ejaculation; mount latency, interval between introduction of the female and first mount; intromission latency, interval between introduction of the female and first intromission; ejaculation latency, interval between first intromission and ejaculation; mean interintromission latency, the mean interval between successive intromissions; and postejaculatory interval, the interval between ejaculation and the next intromission.

In general, Dewsbury takes the position that the results are evidence of alcohol's "retardation" effect on copulatory behavior. Intromission frequency was decreased; all intervals between significant events were increased; mount frequency was increased (see Table 2, adapted from Dewsbury, p. 279). Ejaculation latency was lengthened by a factor of 1.6. A calculation based on Table 1 (p. 125) of Beach and Jordan (1956) shows that the time to ejaculation divided by the number of intromissions for successive ejaculation on rats tested to exhaustion remains constant at an average value of 37.7 sec. The same value for rats on water obtained from Dewsbury's data is 30.9 sec. For the alcohol condition, this value is 65.8 sec.* In other words, unlike exhaustion, where the time per intromission remained constant in spite of the increasing number of ejaculations, alcohol more than doubled the time per intromission. This is true even after correcting for the inter-intromission latency (28.3 sec for water; 58.7 sec for alcohol).

Of the 82 ejaculations in 84 tests, two failures occurred during the alcohol tests. "The fact that the only failures to copulate took place after ingestion of alcohol is in itself some indication of the depressant effect of alcohol on sexual behavior" (Dewsbury, p. 278). We disagree with this statement. The exact probability is 0.247 (Fisher's Exact Test), which says that these two failures with alcohol could be expected to occur 25% of the time when in fact no differences existed between alcohol and control groups.

Dewsbury elaborates on two observations. One is the decrease in the number of intromissions necessary to achieve ejaculation, and the other is the

---

*Dewsbury's mean of 30.9 sec for water is 1.5 S.D. from Beach and Jordan's mean of 37.7 sec; for alcohol, 65.8 sec is 6.2 S.D. from Beach and Jordan's mean.

increase in the frequency of mounts without intromission when the animals had alcohol.

When the interintromission interval is artificially increased in rats without alcohol, the number of intromissions necessary to produce ejaculation is reduced. This is thought to be the result of an accumulation of excitations in an hypothetical copulatory mechanism (Beach and Jordan, 1956), which is ordinarily prevented by the normal intromission interval. Dewsbury argues that since alcohol increased the interintromission interval, an indirect mechanism for increasing excitation is a possibility. However, the decreased sensitivity of the penis by local application of anesthetics has been shown to reduce the number of intromissions without affecting the frequency of mounting (Adler and Berment, 1966). Thus, the increase in frequency of mounts without intromission is thought by Dewsbury to reflect a similar reduction in sensitivity of the penis due to alcohol.

These results imply a contradiction to the stereotype for the action of alcohol that is accepted by most scientists; i.e., reduced sensitivity of the penis supports the opinion that alcohol produces deterioration, but the increase in excitation leading to a reduction in the number of intromissions (necessary to obtain ejaculation) runs counter to the stereotype. The contradiction is even more interesting if one considers that desensitization of the penis and increased excitability of the copulatory mechanism are opposite central effects of alcohol which occur concurrently. However, there is no reason why different actions should not occur simultaneously.

These experiments do not constitute a sufficient base for reaching conclusions concerning the relation between alcohol and human sexual behavior. The reasons seem obvious: (1) The experiments were carried out on animals, not on human subjects. (2) The experiments bear only on the behavior of the male; nothing is known from them about the female, that great invisible half of the animal kingdom, to judge by experiments on alcohol. (3) Most of the doses used bear an unrealistic relation to human social use of alcohol. Only in rare and special situations could doses of 2.0 ml/kg or greater be expected. (4) There is more to sexual behavior, even in the male, than is covered by these experiments. (5) Few of the experiments relate enough to mechanisms to tell how alcohol produces the observed results or suggests other results that may be possible.

Human Experiments

In addition to these studies dealing with actual sexual behavior in animals, there are four papers dealing with alcohol and a more remote expression of sex in human beings. All of these used the TAT, the protocols of which were scored for sexual content.

Clark's experiments A and C (1952) are relevant for this discussion. In experiment A, Clark showed slides of attractive nude females to college students, after which the TAT was administered. The control group saw slides of landscapes, architecture, etc., followed by the TAT. The experiment took place in a classroom and no alcohol was administered. Experiment C was carried out at a fraternity beer party during which beer was consumed for about 1¼ hr. The experimental group saw the slides of the nude females and then were tested on the TAT. The control group took the TAT without exposure to any slides. Neither the amount of beer consumed nor BAC's are reported.

The results of Clark's experiments are clear: (1) In the experiment without alcohol, the group exposed to nude slides produced significantly less manifest sex imagery than the group exposed to neutral slides. (2) In the experiment with alcohol, the group exposed to nude slides produced significantly more sex imagery than the group not exposed to these slides. (3) There was no difference between the groups not exposed to nude slides of either experiment. (4) Of those who viewed nude slides, the alcohol group produced more sex imagery than the nonalcohol group. (5) The TAT's were also scored for sex guilt. Those groups that displayed more sex imagery also showed more guilt.

Because of the confounding of conditions in Clark's experiments, it is essential that the control groups of the nonalcohol and alcohol experiments do not differ in sexual responses to the TAT (point 3, above) before the results under alcohol can be taken seriously. This was, in fact, so. Furthermore, these results (point 2, above) indicate that alcohol alone will not produce sexual responses on the TAT unless specific sexual stimulation is used. Of those groups which viewed nude slides, point 4 above suggests that the difference between the nonalcohol and alcohol groups was due to the reduction of sexual responses in the nonalcohol group. This may have contributed, but still the alcohol group with nude slides produced more sexual responses than the nonalcohol group with neutral slides. This supports Clark's conclusion that alcohol increases sexual imagery on the TAT.

Clark's explanation of these results is quite complicated. He assumes two kinds of guilt: stimulus-produced guilt—that produced by the slides and the TAT cards, and response-produced guilt—that produced by writing stories with sexual content. Stimulus-produced guilt leads to a reduction of sexual expression. Alcohol reduces the stimulus-produced guilt, leading to an increased expression of sexual imagery, which, in turn, leads to response-produced guilt. Hence, the alcohol groups produce more sexual imagery and more guilt expression. The nudes in the nonalcohol experiment produced enough guilt to cause suppression of sexual expression as compared to no nudes in the same experiment. The explanation is placed in the context of Miller's (1948) approach-avoidance conflict theory.

There are a great many assumptions involved in Clark's analysis: (1) Guilt reduces sexual expression. (2) "Alcohol reduces guilt, fear or anxiety" (p. 392). (3) There are two kinds of guilt. (4) Alcohol affects each kind of guilt differently. This means that several assumptions are used in testing the effect of alcohol on sexual expression. The use of more than one assumption leaves room for flexibility in explaining the results, but little certainty as to what is going on (Carpenter, 1968). The confounding of the alcohol variable with party and classroom settings makes it even more difficult to decide the reasons for the increases in sexual content.

In Clark's experiment without alcohol, the group exposed to slides of nudes showed less sexual imagery and less guilt. This could be explained on the grounds that the formality of the classroom operates against the expression of sex, even with the pressure of sexual stimuli. On the other hand, perhaps Clark's cover story, which was designed to be plausible, was completely accepted by the subjects. In other words, the procedure reduced the sexual stimulation of the nude slides, or altered the kinds of response the experimenter was calling for. In contrast, the beer party setting was less formal, and sexuality and guilt more acceptable if expressed there.

In another paper, Clark and Sensibar (1955) reexamined Clark's original (1952) experiment for the relation between symbolic and manifest sexuality in the TAT stories. It was found that in the experiment without alcohol the group exposed to the nude slides showed fewer manifest expressions of sex and more symbolic expressions of sex than did the group without exposure to the nude slides. In the experiment with alcohol, both groups expressed large amounts of manifest sex, but very little symbolic sex. The discussion of this interesting finding is beyond the scope of this paper and the reader is referred to Clark and Sensibar's original work.

Kalin, McClelland, and Kahn (1965) and Kalin (1964) performed experiments similar to Clark's (1952), except that more natural settings for drinking were used. This procedure was used to get away from the laboratory and the "pure" or pharmacological action of alcohol in order to study behavior in the context of drinking as a social activity. TAT's were again used, and sex, as well as sex restraints, were scored.

Kalin et al. (1965) performed two experiments. In experiment 1, graduate students attended discussions at an apartment during cocktail time. One of the groups was served alcoholic beverages; the other, nonalcoholic. TAT stories were obtained before drinking, after 25 min of drinking, and again after another 25 min of drinking. The 25-min periods were used to discuss questions and attitudes about the subjects' special interest in graduate business school. Alcohol was served as naturally as possible in the form of cocktails, etc. In experiment II, undergraduates attended parties at fraternity houses. Again, one group was served alcoholic, the other, nonalcoholic beverages. Food and music helped create a natural atmosphere. Experiment II was similar to experiment I, except that no informal discussions with the help of the experimentr ｉｎ ｗｈｉｃｈ Physical sex, nonphysical ｓｅｘ, ａｎｄ ｓｅｘ ｒｅｓｔｒａｉｎｔｓ were scored in the TAT stories. In experiment I, expressions of physical sex or sex restraints were not affected by alcohol. The average amounts consumed were estimated at 1.6 oz and 4.1 oz, respectively, of 86-proof alcohol during the first and second discussion periods in experiment I. In experiment II there was a significant increase in physical sex both for the nonalcohol group and the alcohol group, although in the latter group it was greater. The nonalcohol group started at a much higher level of physical sex, possibly due to their anger at not being served alcohol (p. 446). The authors conclude, on the basis of additional analysis within the alcohol group, that as more alcohol was consumed, more physical sex was obtained. Sex restraints did not change. The amount of alcohol consumed in experiment II was 4.5 and 3.4 times as much as that estimated for similar periods in experiment I.

A third experiment was conducted using male undergraduates, smaller-sized groups (8–17 subjects), cocktail party but with no faculty member present, more definite announcement that alcohol was the subject of study, some new TAT pictures, and control over the amounts of alcohol consumed, so they would be near the mean of experiments I and II. Marked increase in reference to physical sex was obtained. Reference to nonphysical sex was not increased in any of the three experiments.

We find it difficult to reconcile Clark's (1952) and Kalin et al.'s (1965) results. Kalin et al. did not use a stimulus to arouse their subjects, but Clark did. Kalin et al.'s experiments were conducted in a party setting, as were Clark's alcohol groups. The increase in sexual content for the two experiments suggests that it is the party setting and not the nude slides·used by Clark that produced the increase in sexual responses. Clark found an increase in guilt; Kalin et al. found no increase in sexual restraints. Both sets of experiments used the TAT.

The purpose of Kalin's (1964) study was to examine the effects of alcohol on memory, but it contains evidence of the effect of alcohol on recall of physical sex material. This study is similar to experiment II of Kalin et al. (1965). The same kind of fraternity parties was used: one a nonalcoholic, and the other an alcoholic party. Choice of kind of drink was left to the subject. Again, TAT's were administered before drinking, after 25 min of drinking, and again after 25 min more of drinking.

The following day, subjects were asked to describe the pictures they had seen on the previous day, and to rewrite the stories they had written then. The following conclusions were reached: (1) Stories containing sex content are better remembered than stories without sex content if they are written before alcohol. (2) Sex content is less well remembered than nonsex content after consuming alcohol. (3) Less sex content is remembered after alcohol than sex content before alcohol. (4) Stories containing sex content are progressively less well remembered as more alcohol is consumed. This is true for moderate amounts of alcohol; the relation disappears or becomes curvilinear for large amounts of alcohol. (5) In the drinking group, 55% of the pictures which contained sex content were forgotten, as compared to 18% of those which contained nonsex content in the first 25-min period. Although this paper is related to sexuality and alcohol, it says nothing about changes in the production of sexual material under alcohol.

The comment at the end of the section on animal experimentation could apply here: Whatever the findings of these experiments, they could not become an adequate base for understanding the effects of alcohol on human sexual behavior; they were carried out on human subjects, but again, on only the male. The meaning of sexual content on the TAT is not clear. However, the amounts of alcohol used by Kalin et al. (1965) and Kalin (1964) are more realistic in terms of human social usage as compared to the very high doses used in the animal experiments. The attempt to use environments more like those commonly found in natural drinking situations is important.

Discussion

Table 3 shows the doses as reported in the different experiments. These have been converted to grams of alcohol per kilo and to BAC. For the animal experiments, the translation to BAC involves assuming that testing was approximately 1 hr after the dose was administered to the dogs, or consumed by the rats. The rate of metabolism of alcohol is higher for dogs than man, and probably even higher for rats. However, the correction used is one appropriate in determining for human BAC. The estimated BAC's are probably higher by a very small amount than they should be. In the human experiments, the BAC is estimated at $\frac{1}{2}$ hr and 1 hr after beginning of drinking. This again means that the BAC's are probably overestimates, but not by too much.

One point stands out: the maximum BAC's for the animals seem very high. The only criterion we know for choosing appropriate amounts of alcohol for any species is what we think human subjects, excluding alcoholics, would use in social circumstances. If we adopt the social criterion, the maximum BAC estimated for Teitelbaum and Gantt, Hart, and Dewsbury are extremely high. We could speculate that the ability of Hart's intact dogs to stand at 0.45% BAC can only be the result of having four legs. That sexual capacity at these levels should be reduced should surprise no one.

Examination of the human data reveals a similar point. Most social drinkers, we have assumed, rarely obtain BAC's of 0.15%. Nevertheless, in six out of eight instances, the BAC's for the human subjects are estimated at close to this level, or almost twice as high as we would expect in social drinking situations.

TABLE 3. A Summary of Dose and Blood Alcohol Concentrations

Author	Reported dose	Grams per kilo	Estimated BAC (%)	Subjects
Gantt (1940, 1952)	0.5 ml/kg	0.4	0.04	Dogs
	1.0	0.8	0.10	
	2.0	1.6	0.21	
Teitelbaum and Gantt	1.0 ml/kg (95% alc.)	0.84	0.10	Dogs
	1.5	1.26	0.16	
	2.0	1.68	0.22	
	2.5	2.11	0.28	
	3.0	2.53	0.35	
Hart	0.5 ml/kg	0.4	0.04	Dogs
	2.0	1.6	0.21	
	4.0	3.2	0.44	
Dewsbury	2.9–3.5 ml/kg	2.3–2.8	0.29–0.35	Rats
Kalin				
TAT 2	7.2 oz	1.06	0.14	Human
TAT 3	13.8 oz (86 proof)	2.04	0.28	
Kalin *et al.*				
Exp. I, TAT 2	1.6 oz (86 proof)	0.24	0.02	Human
TAT 3	4.1 oz	0.60	0.07	
Exp. II, TAT 2	7.2 oz (86 proof)	1.06	0.14	Human
TAT 3	14.1 oz	2.08	0.28	
Exp. III, TAT 2	7.2 oz (86 proof)	1.06	0.14	Human
TAT 3	13.8 oz	2.04	0.28	
Clark	Not reported			
Clark and Sensibar	Not reported			

Even though these BAC's are only estimates, they suggest that we need to know more accurately just what BAC's are likely to occur in social drinking situations.* This seems to us to be a research problem of paramount importance.

Variability in performance at less than the maximum levels was stressed by Gantt and Teitelbaum and Gantt. These authors use a clinical approach that is often related to the "personality" of their dogs. Teitelbaum and Gantt point out that at moderate and low doses it is not possible to make a uniform statement about alcohol's effect on some of the behaviors they observed. This agrees with crude observation of human subjects for a variety of behaviors.

One difficulty with the group of human experiments is that it is not clear what sexual content on the TAT means. Does it predict sexual behavior ? When ? Does it mean a preoccupation with sex ? Does it mean a permanent heightened

*Only one of forty subjects at similar parties was found by the authors to have a BAC ≥ 0.15.

degree of sexual arousal or sensitization to sexual stimuli ? Suppose the sexual content on the TAT only reflected a response to a sexual stimulus; i.e., if you ask someone to talk about sex, he will, and the TAT may only be a way of asking the question. If this is so, then what is the significance of an increase in sexual content as a result of a drug ? It could mean a sharpening of perception, a channeling of attention, a reduction in distractibility, a clearer understanding of the question, and so on. Because the use of the TAT with alcohol involves a question of what the TAT means, we cannot be sure of what alcohol does. And the reverse is just as true: because we do not know what alcohol does, we cannot use it to say what the TAT response means.

In the section on aggression, the same problem is raised, but we have some help from the theoretical development of aggression. There it is possible to hypothesize that a TAT response refers to hostility as distinguished from aggression. Such a distinction may depend on whose theory one works with, but the reduction in ambiguity about where the TAT fits is intellectually satisfying. The nearest we are able to come to a sexual analogue for the TAT expression of hostility which does not connote pathology is "horny." According to Webster (1964), horny means "easily excited sexually," which differs from our understanding, i.e., a temporary state of sexual excitement. Similar difficulties are found in the sexual content of other projective tests.

A question of considerable interest ought to be the effect of alcohol on female sexual behavior. Most experts comment on human sexual behavior and alcohol as though only males drink and have sexual interests. One can begin speculation by a line of questions such as: How would alcohol affect the receptive female animal brought to estrus by hormones ? Would the "receptivity" of the female be altered by alcohol, for example ? How would a "receptive" female that has been given alcohol change the behavior of a nonalcohol-treated male animal ? Could the female be turned into a receptive female by alcohol without the use of hormones ? No one has really focused attention on a study of the separation of capacity and motivation as a result of the use of alcohol. In summary, the research has only begun.

It is evident from most articles, including some experimental reports, that the authors have preconceived notions about the effects of alcohol. Many nonexperimental papers are frankly moralizing statements—a peculiar position for scientists to take.

It does not seem logical that alcohol or any chemical agent should have a linear dose-response function over the complete range of doses that is used by society for every kind of behavior (Carpenter, 1968). Thus, the study of barely sublethal or subanesthetic doses of alcohol is an exercise in missing the point. Because of this dominant attitude, many papers find retardation and deterioration of behavior that appears contrary to a reasonable social criterion. For example: it is our opinion that most women would consider an increase in the ejaculation latency of a male partner desirable, and not evidence of retardation. People engage in sexual activity for "fun," not to exercise a physiological activity. If something makes that pleasure possible or increases it, that agent will not be considered retarding or deteriorating by the users. For a scientist to find a change evidence of retardation means that he has a criterion for deciding what is good, normal, etc. The scientific criteria are seldom expressed; nevertheless, they have the odd characteristic of being peaked, so that to move in any direction away from the peak is to move downward. This is equivalent to saying that a change upward in an IQ is the same as a change downward, and both are retardation.

In examining alcohol and sex, it is necessary to discuss the nature of sexual behavior. The reason is that the literature treats sex as a very simple process, simply affected by alcohol. Any behavior whose neural substrate is more than a single process has the possibility of being affected by the amount of drug acting in some nonlinear and very complex manner. Sexual behavior and its neurological and humoral mechanisms (e.g., Bors and Comarr, 1960), on examination, turns out to be very complicated.

The neural base of sexual behavior varies from species to species, and between the sexes. In crude outline (for details, see especially Grossman, 1967; Sawyer, 1960), at the spinal level, reflexes for erection and ejaculation exist, and this includes man. Reflexes also exist in the female at the spinal level. "No level of integration below the hypothalamus can maintain more than a partial pattern of sexual behavior in either sex" (Sawyer, p. 1238). The cortex and rhinencephalon appear to be essential in initiating mating behavior in males, but not in females. Hormone activity is importantly related to sexual activity at the level of the hypothalamus, especially in female mating behavior. Damage at most of these levels usually results in some reduction in mating behavior. However, lesions involving the temporal lobes, amygdala, etc., have resulted in hypersexuality, especially in males (including man). The neural substrate of sexual behavior is so intricate and spread throughout all levels of the CNS that it offers a splendid target for the action of alcohol and other drugs. It is apparent that a wide range of changes is possible, from increased activity to the elimination of sexual behavior. A consideration of the interaction of alcohol and hormones, which themselves have a complex relation with the CNS, leaves room for speculation in all directions.

Masters and Johnson (1966), to whom we owe credit for most of our detailed information about the human sexual response, divided the cycle of response into four arbitrary phases (excitement, plateau, orgasmic, resolution), which are accompanied by anatomical and physiological reactions throughout the body as well as in the sex organs. During each phase, different subjective experiences occur. A range of possible actions for alcohol is provided by these phases. For example, in the male, Masters and Johnson describe a "refractory period" which follows orgasm at the beginning of the resolution phase. The existence of the refractory period means that the frequency of orgasm during a single coital act is severely limited to a single orgasm for most men, while multiple orgasms have been observed in more than 50% of the women in Masters and Johnson's sample. If a drug such as alcohol delays the male orgasm without affecting erection, an opportunity for multiple orgasms is provided for the female. Hence, one might reason, greater sexual satisfaction for the female. Since coitus is a social activity, one could speculate that sexual gratification would be enhanced for the male partner in these circumstances also. But the number of female orgasms may not be a measure of satisfaction for either partner.

Masters and Johnson (pp. 267–268) also report that too much alcohol, the "syndrome of overindulgence," reduces the ability to develop and maintain an erection, which in turn has additional consequences: failure to perform due to alcohol can lead to failure in the absence of alcohol. The exact meaning of the "syndrome of overindulgence" is not clear. If Masters and Johnson mean alcoholism, the problem is quite different from those occasions in which inebriation occurred. Probably they have not yet experimentally studied the relation between amount of alcohol and sexual performance.

Gebhard (1965, p. 485) suggests that "Small to moderate amounts of alcohol or some other drugs may promote sexual activity by lowering inhibitions, causing euphoria and greasing the wheels of social interaction, but large amounts of the same substances may decrease sexuality." In principle, Gebhard's observation that small amounts of alcohol may promote sexual activity may be valid, but his reasons should be viewed with caution. The presence of a receptive female in itself is an occasion for euphoria that does not require alcohol. The presence of both a receptive female and alcohol is a simple confound as far as tracing the source of the euphoria. A receptive female, *per se*, may alter inhibitions, but we do not know of any studies on this.

Masters and Johnson (1966) cite an often-reported clinical observation that alcoholics are devoid of sexual tension. Whether the alcoholic's time and attention are so completely concerned with his addiction as to cause a loss of interest in sex, or whether he cannot be aroused even if he were distracted from the addiction is not known. Furthermore, reduction of sexual capacity in alcoholics may be another symptom of physical deterioration. This and many other issues concerning alcohol and sex can be decided by the techniques of Masters and Johnson.

About 70% of Masters and Johnson's book is concerned with the female. The reasons seem to be that females were easier to obtain and they were easier to use as subjects than males. Conversely, studies on alcohol and alcoholism show an overwhelming proportion of experimental work done on the male of all species used, and even the female alcoholic is infrequently studied. When we speculate about alcohol and sex, we combine information from different sources, males and females.

Differences in anatomy and physiology of the male and of the female suggest that alcohol could have very different effects in the two sexes. For example, the first visible sign of the excitement phase in the male is erection of the penis; in the female, it is lubrication of the vagina. In both sexes excitement can develop as a result of physical or psychic stimulation, but Beach (1965, p. 540) points out that ". . . readiness and capability for copulation are more rigidly controlled by gonadal hormones in female mammals than in male; and . . . that susceptibility to sexual arousal may be more dependent upon the cerebral cortex in males than it is in females." Whether or not this applies to human beings is not certain, although Masters and Johnson seem to think it does. What it suggests, of course, is that a drug will act differentially on males and females, depending on its site of action.

Sexual desire may or may not be increased by alcohol. At present there is no real evidence for or against such an idea. One of the problems is the concurrence of alcohol use with ambient sexual stimulation and opportunity. Whether alcohol pharmacologically increases desire or is only coincident with sexual opportunity and provocation is an important question. If alcohol does increase sexual desire, it means that drinkers are subject to more sexual tension than abstainers are, and possibly that drinkers indulge in a greater frequency of attempts to reduce the tension by sexual activity. This, of course, could be tested.

There is a problem of deciding on the meaning of desire. In Hart's (1968) study, it could be defined by the male dogs' interest in the females, and mounting behavior (see also Bors and Comarr, p. 199). In humans, recourse to that kind of simple operationalism is not possible: the human male may fail to copulate when he says he wants to, whereas the human female may copulate when she says she has no sexual reason for doing so (Masters and Johnson, 1966, p. 267; Gebhard, 1965, p. 485). In human behavior, the verbal report of the individual must serve as the data, even though ". . . such reliance on generalizations from introspectional analyses has disappeared completely from other areas of experimental and physiological psychology and are intolerable when applied to sexual behavior" (Grossman, 1967, p. 453). Verbal report is a respectable index of human sexual desire, in our opinion, but some physiological components may be better, though not always usable.

Beach (1965) has a good deal to say about the meaning of the term sexual behavior (p. 535f). For our purposes, and with the help of Beach, we might say that sexual behavior ranges from copulation to mating and to courtship, to which can be added "dating." Dating, courtship, and mating are complex social activities whose goal may be copulation or some other kind of consummatory sexual response. Similarly, the use of alcohol, specifically "drinking" (Bacon, 1958), is a socially defined activity.

Research on alcohol and sexual behavior, the little that has been done, has emphasized copulation or elements of it, and science seems to have selected this aspect of sexual behavior as the significant one. This parallels other areas of scientific study and interests connected with alcohol, for example, alcoholism. In studying alcoholism, a good deal of effort goes into medical, biochemical, physiological, and genetic research in the hope that once the magic balm is found and applied, the alcoholic will become immune to the pressure of any environment, social or otherwise, in which he exists. We are reminded at this point of the baboon: The male baboon is capable of sexual intercourse at the age of five, but he is rarely successful until he is ten or eleven; until ". . . he has achieved sufficient dominance within the troop. . . ." (Beach, 1965, p. 550), which means that physiology alone does not decide events. This has its parallel in human society. In urban centers one frequently sees successful older men with quite young women, not all of whom are their daughters. As with the baboon, this cannot be wholly explained in terms of biology.

What is the role of alcohol in the dating-courtship-mating pattern ? When two activities (drinking, dating-courtship-mating) occur in a large portion of society, the chances are that some individuals engage in both, possibly at the same time. Research which focuses just on physiological and biochemical aspects of drinking and its effects on the ability to copulate will not adequately describe the relationship between two complex, socially defined activities.

ALCOHOL AND AGGRESSION

The effect of alcohol on aggression is supposedly well known (for example, Hoff and Kryspin-Exner, 1962; Markham, 1966; Lemert, 1967). In most discussions, aggression is assumed to be under inhibitory control and alcohol is assumed to be a disinhibitor. The result of inhibited aggression in combination with alcohol consumption is a display of aggression.

Several questions are basic to this problem: (1) Is aggression a pharmacological consequence of alcohol ? (2) When aggression is produced by other means, e.g., central nervous system (CNS) stimulation, does alcohol modify it ? (3) What is the effect of alcohol on aggression that occurs in social contexts ?

To answer these questions, we will use the definition of aggression given by Buss (1961):* Aggression is "a response that delivers noxious stimuli to another organism" (p. 2). Accordingly, the delivery of noxious stimuli and an interpersonal context are necessary elements of aggression. This definition separates aggression (an instrumental response), hostility (an attitudinal response), and anger (a response with autonomic components).

---

*Other models of aggression might serve as well, but we are most familiar with that of Buss.

Buss developed the following experimental paradigm to study human physical aggression in the laboratory: One person delivers noxious stimuli to another person in such a manner that the strength of the stimuli can be scaled for intensity. The person receiving the stimuli, the victim, is an accomplice. The subject believes that his function is to teach the accomplice a discrimination learning task. When the accomplice, by prearrangement, makes an incorrect response, the subject is free to deliver one of ten intensities of shock to the accomplice. The data of the experiment are the levels of shock used by the subject in punishing the accomplice. Alterations in shock level mean changes in aggression.

Two alcohol experiments were carried out using this paradigm. One used male subjects (Bennett, Buss, and Carpenter, 1969); the other, female (Buss *et al.*, 1970). Four doses of alcohol were administered (0, 0.33, 0.67, 1.0 ml/kg), yielding mean BAC's up to 0.09% for the men, and 0.08% for the women. Breath samples were obtained from both subject and accomplice in order to support the belief by the subject that the accomplice had also been given an alcoholic beverage. A base level of shock between 3 and 4, described by Buss (1961, p. 49) as being painful, was present without alcohol. The results in each experiment were the same: alcohol did not affect the level of shock which the subjects delivered to the victims. In the absence of any other factor, an increase in aggression would have meant that the drug alone was responsible. It was concluded that aggression was not a consequence of the pharmacological action of alcohol.

A promising line of experiments are those of MacDonnell and his co-workers (MacDonnell and Flynn, 1966, 1968; MacDonnell and Ehmer, 1969). These experiments concern attack behavior in cats. It is interesting that Buss (1961, p. 1) uses the term attack as a synonym for aggression. MacDonnell's attack behavior is very similar to Buss' aggression. For MacDonnell, attack means approach to an animate object—a human being, another cat, a rat, a dead rat—followed by vicious biting behavior.

Attack patterns are obtained in the awake, unrestrained cat by electrical stimulation of the CNS, using stereotaxically located electrodes. Application of drugs to this phenomenon is an attempt to answer the second question: If aggression is going to occur as a result of another operation, how does alcohol change it ?

Patterns of attack vary in cats according to electrode location and stimulus intensity. The pattern chosen for study with alcohol by MacDonnell and Ehmer (1969) is referred to as a "quiet biting attack," which is described as ". . . a precisely coordinated, direct, deliberate, savage assault with little waste motion and a minimum of sympathetic display (e.g., no hissing). The duration of the attack is tightly determined by the duration of brain stimulation, and its intensity and vigor are easily controlled by manipulating stimulus intensity" (p. 313).

The quiet biting attack is obtained from the hypothalamus and is divided into four phases: (1) behavioral arousal—the cat begins to move; (2) target selection and approach to target; (3) orientation of the head to target; (4) seizure of target. Control of these events involves vision, tactile stimulation of the forepaw, lips, and mouth. The complexity of the behavioral events and the underlying nervous system suggests that a wide range of response changes could occur when different drugs in various amounts are administered. Another dimension of complexity is added by noting that MacDonnell and Flynn (1968) describe five CNS locations, including the hypothalamus, for the production of attack patterns.

Alcohol was infused via jugular catheter at three dose levels, 0.37, 0.75, 1.5 g/kg (MacDonnell and Ehmer, 1969). Two measures of response were used: time from beginning of stimulation of the hypothalamus to a specified translocational movement (a measure of arousal) and time from stimulation to the first bite on the target, an anesthetized rat. As alcohol increased, it took longer for the cats to be aroused by the stimulus and longer to complete the attack pattern. In addition, it was found that the force of biting was increased by alcohol. This observation depends primarily on qualitative description, but is supported by direct measurement in one cat.

Let us summarize to this point. Buss, working with human subjects, and MacDonnell, working with cats, have similar definitions of aggression: the application of a noxious stimulus to another organism. For Buss, aggression results from the failure of an accomplice to learn, thus providing the subject with an opportunity to aggress. MacDonnell's aggression was obtained by electrical stimulation of the hypothalamus in the cat. Buss et al. and Bennett et al. used doses of alcohol up to 0.8 g/kg, whereas MacDonnell's top dose was approximately twice that: 1.5 g/kg. Buss et al. and Bennett et al. found no change in aggression; MacDonnell found that aggression took longer to be aroused at every dose of alcohol used, but had a more savage result.

These experiments attempted to determine the pharmacological effects of alcohol in sterile environments which were designed to contribute as little as possible to the production or modification of aggression. In the experiments that follow, subjects were observed in group behavior, drinking under only mild restraints to control quantity or type of beverage. These experiments bear on the third question, the effect of alcohol on aggression in social context.

Takala, Pihkanen, and Markkanen (1957) performed a rather large experiment from which we have selected for discussion the behavior of the subjects in group interaction. Groups of four to six subjects were studied by the Bales method (see Riley, 1963, p. 98f) while performing as a group and drinking. The beverages, brandy and beer, were consumed at rates expected to produce equivalent BAC's. BAC's of 0.094% and 0.091% were observed for brandy and beer groups, respectively, from blood samples taken between 90–120 min;

0.146% and 0.144% BAC's were found for brandy and beer groups, respectively, from samples obtained at 180, 210 min. Comparisons were made among brandy, beer, and control conditions.

The subjects engaged in two types of group activities. One was a discussion of themes; such as "the right of the police to use arms." The other was a co-operative task such as designing a vacation island, etc. Discussions occurred at about 60 min after starting to drink, and again at 210 min. The other project fell between the two discussion groups during a session. Verbal responses of each subject were categorized according to Bales' 12-category classification scheme. The results are presented as a proportion of all responses falling in each category, and represent an "interaction profile." Two of Bales' categories, 10 and 12, fit Buss' definition of aggression, although some responses are included that might not be considered aggressive. Category 10 seems to be passive aggression; 12 is active aggression, and both are verbal aggression. Bales defines category 10 as "Disagrees, shows passive rejection, formality, withholds help," and category 12 as "Shows antagonism, deflates others' status, defends or asserts self."* It can be seen that the different experimenters (Bennett et al., 1969; Buss et al., 1970; and Takala et al., 1957) are talking about the same thing, and the differences in results cannot be due to differences in definition.

Takala's control group shows almost zero proportion of responses in categories 10 and 12. After both brandy and beer, categories 10 and 12 take on a greater proportion of all responses.

For all three activities, the early discussion, the cooperative project, and the late discussion, the control levels of category 10, passive aggression, were very low: 2%–7% of the total responses. After brandy, there was an increase of 12%–13% in this category. After beer, the increase was 6%–8%. In the two discussion groups, the increase due to brandy significantly exceeded that produced by beer.

The control levels of category 12, active aggression, were virtually zero. After brandy, the proportion of responses rose 6%, 9%, 8% for the three different activities. After beer, the proportion increased 6%, 2%, 2%. The increase in category 12 for the brandy was greater than that for beer during the cooperative project and during the second discussion topic.

Takala et al. attributed the higher proportion of negative responses to brandy, as compared to those of beer, to physiological factors associated with each. Similar, almost identical BAC's were observed for the two beverages.

Bruun takes the position that differences in response among the individuals in groups at the same blood alcohol levels may be due to the "structural

---

*Buss defines verbal aggression as a ". . . vocal response that delivers noxious stimuli to another organism." Noxious stimuli, in this case, means rejection and threat (Buss, p. 6). Passive aggression depends on the failure to act, thereby blocking a goal response or rescuing the victim from harm.

characteristics of groups and the role differentiation within groups" (Bruun, 1962, p. 295). Bruun (1959, 1962) reconvened Takala's subjects and divided them into two groups, one showing a large increase and one showing a small increase or none in negative reactions with brandy as compared to beer. Negative reactions refer to Bale's categories 10 and 12, which we have called passive aggression and active aggression, respectively. Bruun asked them three questions: "Which member of your group would you prefer to drink with, work with, be your foreman?" Central members and isolated members of each group were determined for each of these questions. Central figures were those chosen more than once; isolates were those not chosen at all by the members of the group.

When central figures were specified by the first question—that is, they were preferred as drinking companions—they were found to have an increase in negative reactions. The isolates specified by the same question showed little or no increase in negative reactions. On the other hand, when the central persons were chosen as co-workers or foreman, the results were in the opposite direction. Central figures were those with little or no increase in negative reactions, and isolates tended to have a high increase.

Bruun (1959, 1962) speculates about these results in the following way: Small groups contain two kinds of leaders, instrumental and expressive. Instrumental leaders function in goal attainment; expressive, in social-emotional problems (see Riley, 1963, p. 244). Because alcohol functions to increase emotionality (Bruun, 1962, p. 299, uses Takala et al., 1957 as his authority for this statement), those functioning as instrumental central people will show fewer negative reactions under alcohol. They tend to hold the same position in the groups when drinking as they did when not drinking, because they have more emotional control. Expressive central people will be "those who are able to meet the expectations of the group in this particular situation" (Bruun, 1962, p. 299). Their ordinary function is to express emotion. Those subjects who were chosen in response to the question, "Who would you prefer to drink with?" were designated by an expressive criterion; those chosen by the other two questions were designated by an instrumental criterion. The isolates behave opposite to the central figures for each criterion, which suggests that the isolates for the instrumental criterion are the central figures for the expressive criterion. Bruun also found that subjects who had a permissive attitude about the expression of aggression during intoxication showed a greater tendency to increase these reactions when drinking.

Bruun's results were not significant by ordinary statistical standards, but the number of subjects was small (40). The experiment was not originally designed for the purpose to which he put it, and the interviews were conducted 3 years after the experiment. We do not see how his analysis disproves Takala's opinion that the greater increase in aggressive response with brandy as compared to beer is the result of a different physiological response to the two beverages.

He has shown that the role of the subject leads to different responses. For example, those who increased in aggression, the expressive central people, did so more in response to brandy than to beer. The question remains a matter of physiology or expectation.

Takala *et al.* and Bruun have shown the power of small group research. A reading of Riley (1963, p. 98f) shows that they have made only a beginning, and a great many questions of interest to alcohol research, including those concerning aggression, could be investigated (Bruun, 1959, p. 62).

Hartocollis (1962) administered alcohol intravenously in amounts designed to produce 0.10% BAC. Some of his subjects were tested alone; some in groups of three. Two or three experimenters were present for both individuals and groups, so that a social atmosphere of sorts existed. Although systematic observations of emotion, speech, and action were made using rating scales, other behavior, more casually observed, seemed to be the most pronounced. Aggression was observed in subjects tested singly; those tested in groups were found to be more aggressive. This finding supports those of Takala *et al.*

A number of other experiments investigate the effect of alcohol on "aggression" as measured by less direct means than those discussed up to now. If we accept the notion that aggression is an instrumental response involving the application of a noxious stimulus to another person, none of the following experiments deals with aggression, although they all make that claim. Rather, we are tempted to say that these experiments may be concerned with hostility, defined as an enduring negative attitude leading to verbal expression (Buss, 1961, p. 12). If projective techniques or similar procedures uncover enduring subject characteristics, they may indeed be indicating hostility. The studies of Kalin, McClelland, and Kahn (1965) and that of Clark and Sensibar (1955) are group experiments. Clark and Sensibar scored only their control conditions for aggression. The craftsmanship and the clarity of their presentation is to be commended, and it is unfortunate that their alcohol results on aggression were not presented.

Kalin *et al.* (1965), whose experiment has been described in the section on sex, scored their TAT protocols for physical and nonphysical aggression and aggression restraints. There was no change in either kind of aggression in the relaxed discussion group (experiment I) as a result of alcohol. However, an increase in physical aggression in TAT stories was found for the fraternity party (experiment II). The increase occurred between the first and second TAT. The control group had a significantly higher score for physical aggression than the alcohol group on the first TAT—before any drinking had occurred. Although the control group's aggression score declined after the first TAT, it remained at about the same level as the alcohol group on the two later measures. This was attributed to the anger of the control subjects when they discovered they were not to receive alcoholic beverages. There was no significant change in nonphysical aggression. There was a significant decrease in aggression restraints in the alcohol group of experiment II, but not for experiment I.

Experiment III of Kalin et al. (1965) was described earlier. It differed from experiment II chiefly in that the groups were smaller, and there was greater control over the beverages consumed, an amount between that of experiments I and II. Physical aggression was not affected by the alcohol, but aggression restraints declined.

Kalin et al. (1965) reexamined their data in order to relate them closer to the amount of alcohol consumed. This involved some manipulation of the data not originally contemplated. The results are interesting. In broad outline, the physical aggression scores for the alcohol group of experiment II and experiment III (no control group was used in experiment III) were plotted as a function of the amount of beverage consumed irrespective of the second or third TAT. The curves for the two experiments have exactly the same nonmonotonic shape. Peaks of physical aggression occurred at approximately 5 oz and again at 12 oz or more. Minima occurred in the neighborhood of 3 oz and 9 oz. Most of the effects are exaggerated in the larger cocktail parties as compared to the smaller. No effects on aggression plotted this way occurred for experiment I (discussion groups), and the alcohol consumed did not exceed 9 oz for this group.

Thus it appears that "aggression," whether direct, as in the case of Takala et al. (1957), or indirect, as in the case of Kalin et al. (1965), increases with alcohol in social interaction. This probably needs to be modified to say that social situations must be those with a minimum of organization forced on them (Kalin et al., experiment I).

The experiment of Hetherington and Wray (1964) is different from the others reported up to now in that it makes use of an indirect measure of aggression with subjects who, though they were tested together, do not communicate with each other. The subjects were thus functionally isolated.

In this experiment subjects were selected on two personality dimensions, and their preferences for two kinds of cartoons were evaluated. Male subjects were selected for extremes of need for social approval (NSA, Marlowe and Crowne Social Desirability Scale) and for extremes of need for aggression (NA, Edwards Personality Preference Schedule). Four groups were formed from the combination of high and low need for social approval and need for aggression, with 48 subjects in each group. Half of the subjects received alcohol; half did not. "The quantity of distilled ethyl alcohol (in cubic centimeters per drink) was about 35% of the subject's weight" (p. 686), which we calculate to be about 0.6 g/kg, assuming that weight was measured in pounds and that they mean absolute alcohol. Subjects rated 15 aggressive cartoons and 15 nonsense cartoons on a five-point scale ranging from "extremely unfunny" to "extremely funny."

The entries in Table 4 were obtained from Hetherington and Wray's Table 3 (p. 687) by subtracting the nonalcohol results from the corresponding

TABLE 4. The Difference Between the Alcohol and Nonalcohol Condition for Mean Humor Rating of Cartoons

Subjects	Aggressive cartoons	Nonsense cartoons
High NA		
High NSA	11.7	4.1
Low NSA	0.3	0.1
Low NA		
High NSA	−0.3	1.9
Low NSA	−0.4	−0.8

alcohol results. A positive entry means an increase in humor rating in the alcohol condition over that in the nonalcohol condition.

It can be seen that alcohol was accompanied by a significant increase in humor ratings for aggressive cartoons by those subjects who were high on the need for aggression and need for social approval. The nonsense cartoons were also rated higher after alcohol for this category of subject. However, we are unable to discover from the paper if this difference is significant.

These two results are crucial for an understanding of alcohol's effect. The nonsense cartoons are a baseline condition against which the increase in judged humor due to alcohol for the aggressive cartoons can be interpreted. With this in mind, the rise in high need for aggression-high need for social approval groups for nonsense cartoons after alcohol is disturbing, because it suggests that humor in general increased for these subjects, although the increase for nonsense is a good deal less than that observed for aggressive cartoons. The net effect, however, appears to be that alcohol releases subjects who are high in need for aggression from their high need for social approval.

If all people could be classified in the four categories used by Hetherington and Wray, and assuming a valid relation exists between response to cartoons and significant other forms of behavior, these results point to an important conclusion about alcohol: Alcohol is specific in that it affects only one of the four kinds of people, and the degree of effect depends on how pointed the stimuli are to the relevant personality characteristics. This conclusion is diluted by reality; the subjects represent combinations of the upper and lower quartiles of the need for social approval and need for aggression scales, a single mild dose of alcohol is used, and only men are represented. The generalization that alcohol increases aggression is tenuous.

Discussion

The relation between alcohol and aggression has not been defined, and

TABLE 5.   Classification of Aggression Experiments by Kind of Behavioral Expression and Experimental Context

Context	Behavior	
	Direct	Indirect
Individual	Bennett *et al.* Buss *et al.* MacDonnell and Ehmer	Hetherington and Wray
Group	Takala *et al.* Hartocollis	Kalin *et al.*

there are as many qualifications as there are experiments. Let us begin by examining a classification of the experiments cited in this paper.

Two contexts were used. The individual context has the following characteristics: (1) The attention of the experimenter is directed at the aggressive behavior of a single individual, although another person may be present. (2) The communication between the individuals is severely restricted, but it occurs discontinuously at specific times. (3) The target of aggression is clearly specified by the experiment, and there is no choice. (4) The object of the experiment is to strip away all but a minimum of influences on an individual's behavior. The subjects are functionally alone. The group context is different at each of these points: (1) The attention of the experimenter is directed at the activity of two or more people present at the same time, each of whom has the opportunity to aggress. The group involves a continuing interaction among its members. (2) Communication among individuals is relatively unrestricted. (3) The target of aggression is not specified by the experimenter, and may be the group or any individual. (4) The object of the group context is to allow the "naturally" occurring influences to operate.

Aggression was measured either by direct observations of behavior, or indirectly by responses to projective or similar tests. Aggression directly observed has three characteristics: (1) An interpersonal or interorganismic context; another animal must be present. (2) A noxious stimulus, pain, physical harm, verbal assault, etc., is applied to another organism. It is a physically identifiable response on the part of the aggressive subject. (3) The response is often an instrumental act. Aggression indirectly observed differs from directly observed aggression in that: (1) It is not interpersonal or interorganismic, no other animal is present. (2) The subject does not apply a noxious stimulus to another person. (3) There is no instrumental act. Aggression indirectly observed is supposed to imply that direct aggression would occur if circumstances allowed it, but only indicants of that possibility are observed. However, there is some doubt as to whether this is true. (See Buss, 1961, pp. 127-159.)

Direct Observation of Aggression

Experiments which use the direct observation of aggression are easier to interpret than are those which use indirect observation because no inferences about the meaning of the observed behavior are necessary.

Individual Context

In the MacDonnell and Ehmer (1969) experiment, the only one using animals, aggression was made to occur by an extrinsic manipulation, i.e., stimulation of the hypothalamus. The object of experiments of this type must be to examine any modification of aggression that might result from the drug. MacDonnell and Ehmer found that the time required for all of the events in the attack sequence increased as the dose of alcohol increased. The final event in the sequence, the bite, occurred with greater force for the single dose of alcohol at which a direct test was made.

The object of experiments with individual subjects that do not include extrinsic control over the occurrence of aggression is to see if aggression results from the administration of alcohol. If this should happen, alcohol is analogous to extrinsic manipulation; it is an operation that produced aggression. (See Bennett, 1968 for another discussion of this point.) In Bennett et al. (1969) and Buss et al. (1970), subjects used painful levels of shock even without alcohol. Alcohol did not increase these levels, and, therefore, does not function as a pharmacologic extrinsic stimulus for aggression. The parallel with extrinsic manipulation by hypothalamic stimulation would be clearer if aggression had been absent at the control dose of the drug, because there would be no implication that aggression was only modified by the drug.

Alcohol experiments in human subjects which produce aggression by extrinsic manipulation have not been done. It may be necessary to provoke aggression in the experimental situation by movies, harassment, personal insult, etc., before alcohol has any effect on human subjects studied in the almost isolated conditions of the individual context.

Group Context

Takala et al. (1957) and Kalin et al. (1965) emphasize the importance of the conditions under which people normally drink and the manner of consumption of the beverages. Bacon (1958) points out that alcohol is "administered" or "ingested" in laboratory experiments, and that people "drink" alcoholic beverages in social situations. Thus, "drinking" is an activity that is part of the group activity. This position is strengthened by the fact of the time and quantity limitations on the consumption of alcohol that occur in most laboratory experiments on individual subjects, e.g., 0.8 g/kg consumed in 15 min. Hartocollis (1962) "administered" alcohol intravenously, and in spite of subjects having been observed in groups with free verbal access to other people, it does not really qualify as a social experiment from the point of view of the use of alcohol. Bennett *et al.* (1969) and Buss *et al.* (1970) "administered" alcohol to their subjects, as did MacDonnell and Ehmer (1969).

The importance of a group is that it modifies the behavior of individuals by the presence and actions of other individuals, and for all we know, this may apply to animals. Ordinarily, the group supplies the elements from which aggression and other behaviors can develop. Alcohol intervenes in a background of continuing activity that is quite different from that of a subject in isolation, and possibly different for each member of a group. It is quite possible that alcohol will have different effects for a given individual, depending on his role in the group.

Hartocollis (1962) observed that aggression increased as a result of alcohol. It should be pointed out that this is the only experiment in which the subjects were not informed that alcohol was the drug. Takala *et al.* (1957) found that alcohol increased verbal aggression in the group situation, that the form of beverage, brandy or beer, made a difference in the amount of aggression produced, and that there was not much difference in the aggression produced by different BAC's (about 0.09% and 0.15%).

In summary, the findings of the experiments on direct aggression indicate that: (1) When there was no social contact, alcohol did not produce aggression. (2) Alcohol modified the aggressive act in animal subjects in which aggression was produced by extrinsic stimulation. (3) When subjects interacted in a group context, aggression appeared or increased after alcohol was consumed. The three questions posed at the beginning of this section have been answered, each differently from the other. It appears that what alcohol does with respect to direct aggression depends on which question is asked.

Indirect Observation of Aggression

Hetherington and Wray (1964) and Kalin *et al.* (1965) used projective techniques to evaluate aggression. This means that aggression was not observed directly, but it was indicated. Two questions are involved: (1) Is aggression the response to these projective tests? If we use Buss' criteria, the response is not aggression; the behavior was not interpersonal, noxious stimuli were not applied to anyone or anything, and there was no instrumental act. (2) Is the behavior in response to the projective tests an indication of aggression? Possibly, because according to Buss (1961, pp. 127–159), with college students as subjects there is a correlation between scores on projective tests and physical aggression in the laboratory.

Another question is: Does the increase in "aggressive" behavior, as measured by Hetherington and Wray (1964) and Kalin *et al.* (1965) after alcohol, indicate an increase in the possibility of direct aggression ? In order to answer this question, the *change in directly observed* aggression due to the drug must be related to the *change in indirectly observed aggression due to the* drug. This has not been done. However, Takala *et al.* (1964) and Kalin *et al.* (1965), representing directly and indirectly observed aggression in the social context, can be compared. Both experiments produced increases in their respective measures, which suggests that the change in indirectly observed aggression on the TAT would, indeed, be positively related to the change in Bales' categories 10 and 12. When the same comparison is made for the individual context by comparing Bennett *et al.* (1969) and Buss *et al.* (1970) with Hetherington and Wray (1964), the results do not suggest that a correlation between directly and indirectly observed aggression would exist. Bennett *et al.* and Buss *et al.* did not find an increase in aggression as a result of alcohol; Hetherington and Wray did. It should be noted again that Hetherington and Wray found a rise in aggression in only a quarter of their specially selected subjects. These comparisons only refer the question to the need for a direct test of the relation between the two kinds of measures in both contexts when alcohol is used.

In passing, it should be pointed out that Takala *et al.* (1957) found small, negative, or nonsignificant correlations between aggression on the TAT, Rorschach, and a personality inventory in the nonalcohol condition and in Bales' categories 10 and 12 during intoxication.

In summary, in experiments using indirect aggression, it was found that: (1) Subjects who participated in group experiments showed a rise in indirect aggression after drinking. (2) Some subjects measured in social isolation showed a rise in indirect aggression, depending on a combination of personality characteristics. (3) The relationship between direct and indirect aggression is confused, and the validity of indirect measures as indicants of aggression during a drug condition needs examination.

Alcohol as a Disinhibitor of Aggression

In view of the small number of alcohol experiments on aggression, the differences among the questions they attempt to answer, and the differences in their conclusions, the problem is almost beside the point. But the question is such a recurring one that some attention to disinhibition is required. One of us has discussed disinhibition elsewhere (Carpenter, 1968), and the position was taken that disinhibition is often unnecessary and inappropriate as an explanatory device.

To test the hypothesis that alcohol is a disinhibitor, a behavior *known* to be under inhibitory control must be examined. If it is *assumed* that the behavior is under inhibitory control and alcohol increases that behavior, the conclusion that alcohol has disinhibited it is true only if the assumption is true. A direct test of the assumption becomes necessary. The behavior could have increased because of some other action, such as changing the balance of antagonistic processes, none of which can rightfully be defined as an inhibitory process. Actions which result from a number of events related to each other by "braiding" rather than "chaining" provide many points at which a drug could function, and a change need not be the result of release action. A manifestation of this could be a nonmonotonic dose-response function, in which case it might be straining the disinhibition hypothesis to apply it to only one section of the curve. Recruitment is another possible mechanism. Recruitment requires time, and the process may be slowed or speeded by the drug.

The disinhibition by the action-of-alcohol hypothesis rarely gets tested, although it is frequently used as an explanation. The one experiment of this group that suggests disinhibition is that of Hetherington and Wray (1964).* To test the hypothesis, subjects classified as high need for aggression—low need for social approval must show greater appreciation for aggressive cartoons than those subjects classified as high need for aggression—high need for social approval in the nonalcohol condition. This was true. It means that appreciation for aggressive cartoons is suppressed in the high need for social approval group, but allowed to be expressed in the low need for social approval group. After alcohol, there was no change in the low need for social approval subjects, but the high need for social approval subjects showed a significant increase in appreciation for the cartoons. It may be concluded that alcohol reduced the suppression by high need for social approval of the high need for aggression. The conclusion is supported by the fact that the two low need for aggression groups remained unchanged by alcohol. This position would have been strengthened by measuring a concurrent change in the need for aggression and the need for social approval as a result of the action of alcohol. Also, the effect of alcohol on the rating of nonsense cartoons suggests that more than aggression was inhibited by a high need for social approval.

Kalin *et al.* (1965) did consider concurrent changes in the "inhibitor," aggression restraints, and aggression on their TAT protocols as a result of alcohol. In the discussion groups (experiment I), there was no change in aggression or in aggression restraints; in the large fraternity parties (experiment II), physical aggression increased, aggression restraints decreased; in the small

---

*Hetherington and Wray did not set out to test the disinhibiting action of alcohol. They assumed it was a disinhibitor, based on the authoritative statement of White (1956), whose opinion is not documented. In defense of White, it should be pointed out that he is only making a common assumption.

fraternity parties (experiment III), physical aggression was not affected but aggression restraints declined. Thus, a change in the inhibitor can occur without a change in the inhibited factor, which casts doubt on the way the concept is expressed, if not the concept itself. Concepts die hard, because we can always find another way of expressing them. Given the variations in procedure, situations, and alcohol consumed in the experiment of Kalin *et al.*, the best that can be said is that aggression and its "inhibitor," aggression restraint, are delicately balanced.

MacDonnell and Ehmer (1969) found that alcohol increased the latency of the events in the attack pattern and increased the force of biting. If we assume that alcohol is a disinhibitor, these two facts contradict each other; one not supporting, and one supporting, the assumption. If we modify the concept by assuming that it applies only to intensity and frequency of aggressive events and not to their latency, disinhibition is supported. Then we have two assumptions instead of one. Furthermore, we cannot specify what inhibited biting and was modified by alcohol. If we believe in inhibition, we ought to search for the inhibitor.

By switching from a behavioral to a neurological frame of reference, we can quote MacDonnell and Ehmer: "Our results indicate that all phases of the attack pattern so far identified are affected by the given doses of alcohol, suggesting functional alterations among hypothalamus, cerebral cortex, and brain stem" (p. 318). Whether or not this implies disinhibition is a point we leave to the neurologist, while remembering Dews' statement (1962): "The considerable number of terms used both by psychologists and physiologists almost never have the same meaning in the two universes of discourse" (p. 441).

No change in direct aggression as a result of alcohol was found by Bennett *et al.* (1969) and Buss *et al.* (1970); therefore, there was no evidence for or against the disinhibition hypothesis. Takala *et al.* found an increase in aggression, but no direct evidence for disinhibition. No corresponding response category exists in the Bales system. However, category 2 "shows tension release" etc., and category 11 "shows tension" etc., are suggestive, but were not affected by alcohol.

In the Hartocollis (1962) experiment, aggression increased, but he does not specifically relate this to disinhibition. On the contrary, because the subjects did not know what drug they were being given intravenously, and were forced to remain inactive, Hartocollis believes that anxiety may have increased and led the subjects to attempts to cope with their strange situation. The manifestation of this was aggression and other phenomena. If Hartocollis is right, then anxiety, usually thought to be decreased by alcohol, can increase concurrently with the behavior it is supposed to inhibit.

For alcohol to appear to be a disinhibitor of aggression, an increase in aggression must occur. A conservative count of the opportunities for aggression to be measured in the experiments reported here is eleven.* In these eleven opportunities there were six instances of aggression. Of the six instances one case suggests disinhibition as a reasonable conclusion (Hetherington and Wray, 1964); one case was contrary to disinhibition (Hartocollis, 1962); two cases showed no evidence (Takala *et al.*, 1957); one case was marginal (Kalin *et al.*, 1965); and one case indicated conflicting evidence within the same experiment (MacDonnell and Ehmer, 1969).

Other Sources of Information About Alcohol and Aggression

Psychologists are not alone in exploring the relationship between alcohol and aggressive behavior. Opinions among nonpsychologists about the effects of alcohol on aggression do not seem to be as uniform as among psychologists. For example, Straus and Bacon (1953, pp. 186–195) found that male college students believed that alcohol leads to violence in men, but to sexual behavior in women. Female students expressed the belief that alcohol leads to sexual behavior in both men and women. The possible explanation offered for these differences was that college women drink only in mixed company, and that college men, when they drink with other men, drink more. The clear implication of this is that alcohol may lead to aggression in men depending on whom they drink with, but does not lead to aggression in women. Maddox and McCall (1964) also expressed a belief in a relation between alcohol and aggression, but they suggest that it may not be universal (p. 96). Chafetz and Demone (1962) point out that in the Mojave society drinking rarely leads to aggression (pp. 67–69). The comment of Maddox and McCall is worth mentioning here: "The effects of alcohol on human behavior are, to an important degree, culturally determined" (p. 94) In line with this view, both Bennett *et al.* (1969) and Buss *et al.* (1970) stress the idea that physical aggression is a class-related phenomenon: middle class people indoctrinate their children against an expression of physical aggression (verbal aggression is more gentlemanly anyway and more effective).

COMMENT

In discussing the papers cited in this review, we have often found it necessary to ignore the statistical operations of their authors. Not all of the studies used statistics in evaluating their results, and we prefer this approach when a particular result has been observed for each subject, or when a result has been observed repeatedly on different occasions. However, some authors do

---

*Bennett *et al.* and Buss *et al.*, Hartocollis, and Hetherington and Wray each had one opportunity to show an increase in aggression. MacDonnell and Ehmer, and Takala *et al.* had two. Kalin *et al.* had three.

not distinguish between planned and unplanned comparisons, and they apply the
t test indiscriminately as a *post hoc* test. The Pearson correlation coefficient
suffers from similar indiscriminate use and misapplication. Almost no reliance
can be placed on the probability statements based on statistics used in this
fashion. (See, for example, Barber and Silver, 1968.)

CONCLUSION

In this paper we have treated sexual and aggressive behavior separately.
However, they are often discussed, if not together, as though there were a
connection between them. Agreements can be offered on either side. The
Kalin (1964) and Kalin *et al.* (1965) papers imply a connection. Clark and
Sensibar (1955) found evidence for a connection, but were unable to determine
the nature of the linkage. On the other hand, Buss (1961) does not discuss the
relationship at all, giving the impression that they are quite separate processes.
Because sex can be used aggressively, in the same way that "kindness" can be
used to hurt others, it does not mean that there is a functional link. It is obvious
that the relationship between sex and aggression has not been clearly established.

The chief difficulty in deciding the effect of alcohol is the variation in
response that accompanies its use. Likely contributors to this variation are the
mood of the occasion [e.g., Sicé (1962)], personality of the subject, whether the
subject is alone or with others, sex of the subject as well as the sex of others
present, and so forth. "In stimulating surroundings, the drinker may become
expansive, over confident and excited, or noisy and aggressive. But in other
surroundings, especially when alone, the drinker may become morose, dull, and
sleepy" [Bauman, Rand, and West (1968) p. 584]. It appears that the circumstances of drinking produce greater changes in behavior than the alcohol does.
If this is true, then alcohol does not lead to sexual or aggressive behavior. What
is more likely to be true is that alcohol modifies the expression of sexual or
aggressive behavior if either or both are appropriate to a particular set of stimulating conditions.

According to Schachter (1964), people have to learn to label their own
behavior in order to know how they feel. In this paper we have frequently drawn
conclusions that are different from those of the authors whose work we examined.
By analogy with Schachter, not all scientists have learned to label alcohol's
effects the same way.

REFERENCES

Adler, N. and Bermant, G., 1966. Sexual behavior of male rats: Effects of reduced
     sensory feedback, *J. Comp. Physiol. Psychol.* **61**: 240–243.
Bacon, S. D., 1958. Alcoholics do not drink, *Ann. Amer. Acad. Pol. Soc. Sci.* **315**: 55–64.

Barber, T. X. and Silver, M. J., 1968. Pitfalls in data analysis and interpretation: A reply to Rosenthal, *Psychol. Bull.* (monogr.) **70** (6, part 2): 48–62.

Beach, F. A., 1965. Retrospect and prospect, in *Sex and Behavior* (F. A. Beach, ed.) Chap. 22, pp. 535–569, John Wiley & Sons, Inc., New York.

Beach, F. A. and Jordan, L., 1956. Sexual exhaustion and recovery in the male rate, *Quart. J. Exp. Psychol.* **8**: 121–133.

Bennett, R. M., 1968. The effect of ethyl alcohol on aggression, Unpublished Master's Thesis, Rutgers University, New Brunswick, N.J.

Bennett, R. M., Buss, A. H., and Carpenter, J. A., 1969. Alcohol and human physical aggression, *Quart. J. Stud. Alc.* **30**: 870–876.

Bors, E. and Comarr, A. E., 1960. Neurological disturbances of sexual function with special reference to 529 patients with spinal cord injury, *Urol. Survey* **10**: 191–222.

Bowman, W. C., Rand, M. J., and West, G. B. (1968). *Textbook of Pharmacology*, Blackwell Scientific Publications, Oxford.

Bruun, K., 1959. Significance of role and norms in the small group for individual behavioral changes while drinking, *Quart. J. Stud. Alc.* **20**: 53–64.

Bruun, K., 1962. The significance of roles and norms in the small group for individual behavioral changes while drinking, in *Society, Culture, and Drinking Patterns* (D. J. Pittman and C. R. Snyder, eds.) Chap. 16, pp. 293–303, John Wiley & Sons, Inc., New York.

Buss, A. H., 1961. *The Psychology of Aggression*. John Wiley & Sons, Inc., New York.

Buss, A. H., Carpenter, J. A., Bennett, R. M., and Buss, E. H., 1969. Alcohol and aggression in women, Unpublished.

Carpenter, J. A., 1968. Contributions from psychology to the study of drinking and driving, *Quart. J. Stud. Alc.* Suppl. No. 4, pp. 234–251.

Chafetz, M. E. and Demone, H. W., Jr., 1962. *Alcoholism and Society.* Oxford Univ. Press, New York.

Clark, R. A., 1952. The projective measurement of experimentally induced levels of sexual motivation, *J. Exp. Psychol.* **44**: 391–399.

Clark, R. A. and Sensibar, M. R., 1955. The relationship between symbolic and manifest projections of sexuality with some incidental correlates, *J. Abnorm. Soc. Psychol.* **50**: 327–331.

Dews, P. B., 1962. Psychopharmacology, in *Experimental Foundations of Clinical Psychology* (A. J. Bachrach, ed.) Chap. 12, pp. 423–441, Basic Books, Inc., New York.

Dewsbury, D. A., 1967. Effects of alcohol ingestion on copulatory behavior of male rats, *Psychopharmacologia (Berl.)* **11**: 276–281.

Gaddum, J. H., 1959. *Pharmacology*. Oxford Univ. Press, New York.

Gantt, H. W., 1940. Effect of alcohol on sexual reflexes in dogs, *Amer. J. Physiol.* **129**: 360.

Gantt, H. W., 1952. Effects of alcohol on the sexual reflexes of normal and neurotic male dogs, *Psychosom. Med.* **14**: 174–181.

Gebhard, P. H., 1965. Situational factors affecting human sexual behavior, in *Sex and Behavior* (F. A. Beach, ed.) Chap. 19, pp. 483–495, John Wiley & Sons, Inc., New York.

Goodman, L. S. and Gilman, A. (eds.), 1966. *The Pharmacological Basis of Therapeutics.* The Macmillan Company, New York.

Grollman, A., 1965. *Pharmacology and Therapeutics*. Lea and Febiger, Philadelphia.

Grossman, S. P., 1967. *A Textbook of Physiological Psychology*. John Wiley & Sons, Inc. New York.

Hall, M. H., 1969. A conversation with Masters and Johnson, *Psychol. Today* **3**: 50–60.

Hart, B. L., 1968. Effects of alcohol on sexual reflexes and mating behavior in the male dog, *Quart. J. Stud. Alc.* **29**: 839–844.

Hart, B. L. and Ilitchen, R. L., 1966. Penile erection and contraction of penile muscles in the spinal and intact dog, *Amer. J. Physiol.* **210**: 257–262.

Hartocollis, P., 1962. Drunkenness and suggestion: An experiment with intravenous alcohol, *Quart. J. Stud. Alc.* **23**: 376–389.

Hetherington, E. M. and Wray, N. P., 1964. Aggression, need for social approval, and humor preferences, *J. Abnorm. Soc. Psychol.* **68**: 685–689.

Hoff, H. and Krivpin Rm., 1961. Persönlichkeit und verhalten des alcoholisierten verkehrsteilnehmers. (Personality and behavior of the alcoholized participant in traffic.) *Blutalkohol* **1**: 323–336.

Kalin, R., 1964. Effects of alcohol on memory, *J. Abnorm. Soc. Psychol.* **69**: 635–641.

Kalin, R., McClelland, D. C., and Kahn, M., 1965. The effects of male social drinking on fantasy, *J. Person. Soc. Psychol.* **1**: 441–452.

Krantz, J. C. and Carr, C. J., 1965. *Pharmacologic Principles of Medical Practice.* Williams and Wilkins, Baltimore.

Lemert, E. M., 1967. Secular use of kava in Tonga, *Quart. J. Stud. Alc.* **28**: 328–341.

MacDonnell, M. F. and Ehmer, M., 1969. Some effects of ethanol on aggressive behavior in cats, *Quart. J. Stud. Alc.* **30**: 312–319.

MacDonnell, M. and Flynn, J. P., 1966. Sensory control of hypothalamic attack, *Anim. Behav.* **14**: 399–405.

Maddox, G. L. and McCall, B. C., 1964. *Drinking Among Teen-Agers*, Monograph No. 4 of the Rutgers Center of Alcohol Studies, New Brunswick, N.J.

Markham, J. E., 1966. Alcohol and food in health and disease: Sociological aspects of alcohol and food deviations, *Ann. N.Y. Acad. Sci.* **133**: 814–819.

Masters, W. H. and Johnson, V., 1966. *Human Sexual Response.* Little, Brown, Boston.

Miller, N. E., 1948. Theory and experiment relating psychoanalytic displacement to stimulus-response generalization, *J. Abnorm. Soc. Psychol.* **43**: 155–178.

Murphree, H. B., 1965. Addiction and sexual behavior, in *Sexual Behavior and the Law* (R. Slovenko, ed.) pp. 591–606, Charles C. Thomas, Springfield, Ill.

Rasmussen, E. W., 1943. Alkoholens innflytelse på den seksuelle energi hos albino rotter (Alcohol's influence on sexual energy in the white rat), *Brosjyne Utgitt Av Landsrådet far Edruelinghetsundervisning*, Oslo.

Rasmussen, E. W., 1954. Alkoholens virkning på den seksuelle adferd hos albino rotter (Alcohol's effect on sexual behavior in the white rat), *Norsk Tedskrift Om Alkohol-sporsmalet* **6**: 167–181.

Riley, M. W. (ed.), 1963. *Sociological Research*, Vol. 1, Harcourt Brace and World, New York.

Ritchie, J. M., 1966. The aliphatic alcohols, in *The Pharmacological Basis of Therapeutics* (L. S. Goodman and A. Gilman, eds.) Chap. 11, pp. 143–158, The Macmillan Company, New York.

Salter, W. T., 1952. *A Textbook of Pharmacology.* W. B. Saunders, Philadelphia.

Sawyer, C. H., 1960. Reproductive behavior, in *Handbook of Physiology* (J. Fields, H. W. Magovan, and V. E. Hall, eds.) Vol. II, pp. 1225–1240.

Schachter, S. (1964). The interaction of cognitive and physiological determinants of emotional state, in *Advances in Experimental Social Psychology, Vol. I* (L. Berkawitz, ed.) pp. 49–81, Academic Press, New York.

Sicé, J. (1962). *General Pharmacology*, W. B. Saunders, Philadelphia.

Straus, R. and Bacon, S. D., 1953. *Drinking in College.* Yale Univ. Press, New Haven.

Takala, M., Pihkanen, J. A., and Markanen, T., 1957. The effects of distilled and brewed beverages. A physiological, neurological and psychological study, The Finnish Foundation for Alcohol Studies, Helsinki.

Teitelbaum, H. A. and Gantt, W. H., 1958. The effect of alcohol on sexual reflexes and sperm count in the dog, *Quart. J. Stud. Alc.* **19**: 394–398.

Webster's Third New International Dictionary of the English Language, Unabridged, 1964, G. and C. Merriam Company, Springfield, Mass.

White, R. W., 1956. *The Abnormal Personality*. The Ronald Press, New York.

Index